Treaty

...sumed ...
...ew month...
...ene Road. There we...
...commodation + ...
... finel... tho our s...
... + our foo... was com...
...as elected t... Exce...
... at once (I had ...
...that time) I was...
... O Brien + C O Shann...
... but as that m...
...ol do this as ...
...he foremost mem...
... Later I acted a...
... ...E + men...

HANNA SHEEHY SKEFFINGTON

HANNA SHEEHY SKEFFINGTON

SUFFRAGETTE AND SINN FÉINER
HER MEMOIRS AND POLITICAL WRITINGS

edited by
MARGARET WARD

with a foreword by
MICHELINE SHEEHY SKEFFINGTON

UNIVERSITY COLLEGE DUBLIN PRESS
PREAS CHOLÁISTE OLLSCOILE BHAILE ÁTHA CLIATH
2017

First published 2017
by University College Dublin Press
UCD Humanities Institute, Room H103
Belfield,
Dublin 4
Ireland
www.ucdpress.ie

ISBN 978-1-910820-14-8 hb

CIP data available from the British Library

*The right of Margaret Ward to be identified as the
author of this work has been asserted by her*

Typeset in Scotland in Adobe Caslon and
Bodoni Oldstyle by Ryan Shiels
Text Design by Lyn Davies
Printed in England on acid-free paper by
CPI Antony Rowe, Chippenham, Wilts.

This publication is kindly supported by the
Department of Culture, Heritage and the Gaeltacht

An Roinn
Cultúir, Oidhreachta agus Gaeltachta

Department of
Culture, Heritage and the Gaeltacht

Contents

In memory of Fintan Ward Hillyard 1985–2014

*

Acknowledgements

I am most grateful to the staff in the National Library of Ireland; National Archives, Dublin; Queen's University Belfast; Central Library in Belfast; US National Archives, Washington DC; and to Lord Aberdeen and the Haddo House Estate for permission to reproduce the letter from Hanna to Lady Aberdeen, 1913. Carol Leadenham of the Hoover Institution Archives was most helpful in supplying material by Hanna from the Alice Park Collection.

I owe a huge debt of gratitude to Micheline Sheehy Skeffington, not only for her wonderful foreword, but for her unfailing enthusiasm for everything connected with her grandparents, and, above else, for her continuation of the Sheehy Skeffington tradition of fighting for social justice and gender equality. To her brothers, Francis and Alan, thanks are also due.

Dominic Bryan and Yvonne Galligan of the School of History, Anthropology, Philosophy and Politics have been most helpful in continuing to support my Queen's University Visiting Fellowship. My thanks to Mary McAuliffe and Sonja Tiernan for their enthusiastic endorsement of my proposal to UCD Press. Catriona Beaumont, Marie Coleman and Catherine Morris kindly sent me essential material by Hanna. John Borgonovo encouraged further archival research on Hanna's contacts with Tom Mooney.

Vilma Bisson heroically typed masses of material and I appreciate her patience and interest in what Hanna had to say. Lynn Carvill, a friend and former colleague, has been a great support throughout the process of turning newsprint into a book.

To my colleagues in manelwatch (@manelwatchIre) and all the wonderful researchers in Irish women's history it has been my pleasure to meet during this period of centennial celebrations/reassessment, I hope this collection will be both useful and enjoyable to read.

The support of friends has been a lifeline in what has been a tough few years. Maggie Feeley and Ann Hegarty have shared every moment, good and bad, as has Margy Washbrook. Michael and Orla Farrell are greatly appreciated for their continued maintenance of communications within a far-flung family. The Book Club gals – Marie Abbott, Kathy Colgan, Ann Dullaghan, Roisin McDonough and Marie-Thérèse McGivern – are a very special group. Brenda Collins, Myrtle Hill, Ann Hope, Joanna McMinn and Lynda Walker have shared the journey in ways that they know.

Noelle Moran and Damien Lynam of UCD Press have been a delight to work with, in their understanding of the significance of Hanna and in their exemplary attention to detail.

Above all else, my love to my family, Paddy Hillyard, Medbh Hillyard Nicholl, Rachael Dickson Hillyard and Gavin Nicholl, for total support in sad and happy times. And for the newest member, who lights up all our lives, Rory Fintan.

List of Illustrations

13   Hanna with her sisters after the murder of Frank, May 1916. Image
      courtesy of Library of Congress, Prints & Photographs Division (LC-
      B2-3962-9).

14   Hanna and Joseph Kirwan Bridgeman BL going to the court martial of
      Captain Bowen-Colthurst, 1916. Image courtesy of the NLI.

15   Press clipping from 8 June 1916, showing Captain Bowen-Colthurst
      and Hanna among figures from the court martial. Image courtesy of the
      National Museum of Ireland.

Plates Section II

16   Hanna and her son Owen after their arrival in the USA, December
      1916. Image courtesy of Library of Congress, Prints & Photographs
      Division (LC-B2-4085-15).

17   An announcement for Hanna's lecture tour of the USA in the *Gaelic
      American*, 10 March 1917. Image courtesy of Digital Library@Villanova
      University.

18   The cover of Hanna's pamphlet *British Imperialism in Ireland* (1936).
      Image courtesy of the NLI.

19   A studio portrait of Hanna at the time of her American tour. Image
      courtesy of the NLI.

20   Hanna and the National Woman's Party, Washington DC, *c.* 1917.
      Image courtesy of the NLI.

21   Hanna seated with a large costumed group in America, *c.* 1917. Image
      courtesy of the NLI.

22   Hanna and Mrs Pearse, *c.* 1921, possibly during the Treaty debates.
      Image courtesy of the NLI.

23   'Irish Women's Mission' to America, 1922. Front row, left to right,
      Linda Kearns, Hanna, and Kathleen Boland. Image courtesy of the
      NLI.

24   The Sinn Féin executive 1922. Hanna on extreme right, front row.
      Also in front row, Kathleen Clarke and Dr Kathleen Lynn. Mary
      MacSwiney is in the second row. Image courtesy of the NLI.

25   Mary Thygeson, Alice Park, and Hanna, outside Hôtel de Nice, Paris,
      June 1926. Image courtesy of the NLI.

List of Abbreviations

AOH	Ancient Order of Hibernians
BA	Bachelor of Arts
CC	Catholic Curate
CID	Criminal Investigation Department
DMP	Dublin Metropolitan Police
DORA	Defence of the Realm Act
FOSR	Friends of Soviet Russia
FS	Free State
GAA	Gaelic Athletic Association
GPO	General Post Office
ICA	Irish Citizen Army
ILPI	Independent Labour Party of Ireland
IRA	Irish Republican Army
IRB	Irish Republican Brotherhood
IRL	Irish Women's Reform League
IWFL	Irish Women's Franchise League
IWSLGA	Irish Women's Suffrage and Local Government Association
IWSS	Irish Women's Suffrage Society
IWWU	Irish Women Workers' Union
MA	Master of Arts
MP	Member of Parliament
NLI	National Library of Ireland
NUWSS	National Union of Women Suffrage Societies
NY	New York
PC	Peace Commissioner
PP	Parish Priest
PR	Proportional Representation
QUB	Queen's University Belfast
RIC	Royal Irish Constabulary
RM	Resident Magistrate
RTÉ	Raidió Teilifís Éireann
RUC	Royal Ulster Constabulary
RUI	Royal University of Ireland
SCR	South Circular Road

SF	Sinn Féin
SPI	Socialist Party of Ireland
SU	Soviet Union
TB	Tuberculosis
TCD	Trinity College Dublin
TD	Teachta Dála
UCD	University College Dublin
UIL	United Ireland League
USA	Unites States of America
WFL	Women's Franchise League
WIL	Women's International League
WSPU	Women's Social and Political Union
YIB	Young Ireland Branch
YWCA	Young Women's Christian Association

Foreword

BY MICHELINE SHEEHY SKEFFINGTON

I never knew my grandmother Hanna Sheehy Skeffington; she died in 1946, before I was born. At an early age, I learnt that she, like me, was left-handed and was proud of the fact that, when smashing windows in Dublin Castle (then the seat of British power), the police immobilised her right arm – and she managed to have another go at the windows with her left hand, before being dragged away. As a child, of course I thought this was quite a normal thing one's grandmother might do. But as I grew up, I became increasingly aware that both my grandparents, Hanna and Francis Sheehy Skeffington, were powerful, formidable people and it was somewhat intimidating to learn that I had inherited this legacy.

In 1976, my mother, Andrée, and Rosemary Cullen Owens put on a terrific exhibition about the Irish suffrage movement, where 'household items' I had grown up with became key exhibits. The Irish Women's Franchise League banner, the 'Votes for Women' platform and copies of the *Irish Citizen* were prominently displayed. I learned just how important Hanna's – and indeed Frank's – role had been in the fight for women's votes, which was the core feminist activity of their time.

After my mother died in 1998, I started on my idea to turn our home into a centre for women's studies, a haven (for it was that, in its secluded garden) for women to work and be creative in.[1] Taking unpaid leave, I read the several family biographies, including my mother's biography of my father (*Skeff*) – and I became enthralled by my grandmother's life, as described especially by Margaret Ward in such detail. It occurred to me that it would be fun to follow in Hanna's footsteps and tour the US (as she did from December 1916 to June 1918), giving talks about her and Frank's lives. I was living in our home in Dublin, clearing and sorting the rest of the family papers to give to the National Library of Ireland. The material already archived had many interesting family photos and leaflets and the NLI staff very kindly made slides of them to illustrate my talks. I had met and was in touch with Margaret Ward and she put me in touch with Joanne Mooney Eichacker, who was writing a book on Irish women touring the US from 1916–25. Joanne very kindly sent me a list of all the cities, dates and venues where Hanna spoke. So I was able to locate if not the venues (though I did slip into Carnegie Hall to imagine her addressing a packed audience there in January 1917), then at least the press coverage of her visits and speeches. I saw for myself just what a sensation she had been – the San Francisco papers printed her entire speech on the front page whenever she addressed its citizens.

By giving talks and learning more about Hanna, I was at last honouring her life in my own way. Last year I was delighted so much was done to remember Frank, whose tragic murder during the Easter Rising was 100 years ago last April 2016. But both my grandparents deserve remembering, as they had a different voice to that so often quoted in reference to the 1916 events.

But of course I did not have time to view all the documents in the National Library, especially after resuming my lecturing post in NUI Galway. I realised I had not really heard Hanna's voice, except when reading key pamphlets she published during her US tour. So it was with great delight that I learned that Margaret Ward was undertaking this project – and no better woman, knowing as she does Hanna's life and its historic context.

It is a very opportune time – almost 100 years since Hanna's first US tour – for a fresh, contemporary take on Ireland, its issues and politics before and after the 1916 Rising, itself such a tragedy for Hanna and her son, Owen. Margaret groups Hanna's writings into sections, each with a preamble setting them in their historical context.

One of the issues that exercises many historians is the perceived dichotomy between the feminist/suffrage movement and the nationalists. Hanna, while not detracting from her nationalist sentiments – and credentials – never wavered from the steadfast objective of achieving full participation by women in Irish society. She also gives amusing anecdotal evidence of historical facts, such as how she and her young female colleagues stormed the Young Ireland Branch of the United Irish League, taking the men by surprise.

There is nothing tentative about Hanna's writing. It is bold, sometimes scathing (she abhorred inefficiency and bigoted views) and direct. She assumes that women have equal rights in all domains of Irish life and sets about putting this in place. If only it were no longer an issue! The tales of suffrage activity are amusing, but also give great insight into the women's methods and experiences. Thus the description of the visit to Boyle and Carrick-on-Shannon is eye-opening and that of the deputation to see Prime Minister Asquith and John Redmond in London provides priceless pen-pictures of MPs' and fellow petitioners' views and attitudes. The description of a suffrage fundraiser dance gives insight into the gaiety and fun that accompanied the hard struggle: 'At supper an ex-prisoner was recounting the fact, as the clock struck twelve, that she was in Mountjoy on that day twelve months ago. The table rose and toasted her "Many Happy Returns!"' This last account is signed 'Joan' – my middle name – as Joan Sheehy was sometimes Hanna's *nom de plume* (she admired Joan of Arc and preferred the name to her full name of Johanna).

On war, Hanna was as outspoken as her pacifist husband, Frank. She abhorred the bloodshed and saw no reason to fight on Britain's behalf. In the face of 'the "insensate devilry" of war, [w]hen the Churches of the Peacemaker were silent, womanhood, standing for civilisation and progress, lifted a voice of unanimous protest. But her appeal was as usual disregarded by male states-men, eager to let loose the yelping dogs of war at one another's throats.' She was clear that, voteless across Europe, women had no part in the declaration of this war and she hated the entreaties that subservient womanhood should 'knit "soft woollen comforters" for the departing soldiers'. Unlike the Women's Social and Political Union in Britain, she refused to park the suffrage battle while this war raged across Europe. Subjected to the coercion of Britain, Irish women 'realise that the safety of the subject nation comes not from armaments, but from peace; not from the arbitration of the sword . . . but from the arbitra-tion of the plebiscite'. Her stance, and that of the Irish Women's Franchise League, was strongly anti-war. However, in a private letter to pacifist Louie Bennett, she gave her personal view that were Ireland to have an opportunity to 'be freed for ever from British rule by a swift uprising', the use of arms would be justified, yet 'I should still be radically opposed to War and Militarism'. Although these writings are of course only those of Hanna, it is clear that she played a prominent role in the feminist and nationalist circles of the time, explaining the viewpoint of the IWFL, calling for protest meetings, taking on the naysayers in public debate.

The two pamphlets from her 1916–18 tour of the US are here published together in full, along with a fascinating letter by Major Sir Francis Vane who supported Hanna in her fight for justice after Frank's murder. Hanna was a real sensation in the US and was the only such activist to meet with President Woodrow Wilson. It is interesting also to read her comments on a long interview with Henry Ford.

I often wonder how it was that, after such a successful tour of the US, she was not recognised as a key player in the emerging state and never was offered a winnable seat in the Dáil. In a letter to Alice Park (in the US), Hanna expresses her strong dislike of the Treaty – but gives one explanation as to why women became marginalised after independence: they were dangerous and more radical than most of the men! In this context, her protest to the League of Nations in Geneva makes for telling reading.

Hanna's life was very full after her return from the US in 1918 until her death in 1946. Much of her contemporary views are published here from the New York-based *Irish World* and give great insights into the not-always happy emer-gence of the new Free State and its government's views, especially on women.

It is terrific to have all these writings in one book and many of them are all too relevant to our struggles of today. It is also very timely, as this year sees preparations to celebrate, in 2018, the centenary of women obtaining the vote in Ireland (as in Britain). So much of what was done to obtain this vote and Hanna's views on what women should do with that vote are embodied in this scholarly, interesting – and entertaining book.

I very much look forward to fully reading it and learning still more about my feminist, nationalist and socialist grandmother.

GALWAY
August 2017

Chronology of Hanna Sheehy Skeffington's Life and Times

1877
Born in Kanturk, County Cork, 24 May, to David and Bessie (née McCoy) Sheehy.

1880
Ladies' Land League formed in New York by Fanny Parnell.

1881
Ladies' Land League launched in Ireland with Anna Parnell as organising secretary. Land League proclaimed an illegal organisation; prisoners include David and Eugene Sheehy.

1884
Nine women become the first to receive degrees from the Royal University of Ireland.

1893
Gaelic League formed to promote Irish language and culture.

1896
Hanna enrols as a first-year student of languages at St Mary's College, part of the Royal University. Women Poor Law Guardians (Ireland) Act passed.

1898
Local Government (Ireland) Act allows women to become rural district and urban district councillors.

1899
Hanna Sheehy receives a BA in Modern Languages. Spends time in Paris as an au pair and travels also in Germany.

1900
Inghinidhe na hÉireann formed as first woman-only nationalist organisation.

1902

Hanna Sheehy receives MA with first-class honours. Petition for women's suffrage organised by Esther Roper and signed by women graduates, including Hanna, presented to House of Commons in May. Women Graduates' and Candidates' Association formed. Becomes member of the Women's Suffrage and Local Government Association. Hanna publishes 'Women and the university question'. Starts work as part-time language teacher with Dominican Order.

1903

Hanna Sheehy marries Francis Skeffington on 27 June. In Manchester the Pankhursts form the Women's Social and Political Union with the slogan 'Deeds Not Words'.

1904

Women admitted to Trinity College Dublin. Frank Sheehy Skeffington resigns as registrar of University College Dublin as protest against unequal status of women.

1905

Hanna joins the Young Ireland Branch of the Irish Parliamentary Party. First convention of Sinn Féin held.

1908

Irish Women's Franchise League formed in Dublin by Hanna and Frank Sheehy Skeffington and Margaret and James Cousins to campaign for 'Suffrage First – Before All Else'. Inghinidhe na hÉireann launch their journal *Bean na hÉireann*. The Universities Act grants equality to women in Irish universities. Hanna and Mary Hayden publish 'Women in universities: a reply'.

1909

Owen Sheehy Skeffington born on 19 May, son to Hanna and Frank. *Irish Nation* prints 'Women and the national movement' in three issues in March. 'Sinn Féin and Irishwomen' published in November edition of *Bean na hÉireann*. Hanna is part of IWFL delegation in unsatisfactory meeting with John Redmond, Irish Party leader.

1910

In June Hanna is part of Irish delegation to London when Conciliation Bill is before House of Commons. In July she is one of the speakers on Irish Platform at Hyde Park suffrage demonstration and part of deputation to see Redmond. In October Hanna heckles chief secretary at meeting in Greystones. In

December Hanna and others in IWFL heckle Carson at Rathmines meeting. Mrs Pankhurst tours Ireland in the autumn. Six IWFL members in Holloway Jail after taking part in 'Black Friday' petition to House of Commons.

1911

Hanna first sees Constance Markievicz, acting in *Eleanor's Enterprise* at Gaiety Theatre. Local Government (Ireland) Act enables Irish women to become county councillors. Suffragists evade 'census night' in April.

1912

Irish Party votes kill another Conciliation Bill, 28 March. IWFL members attacked by AOH on 'Home Rule Day'. Hanna resigns from Young Ireland Branch. First edition of *Irish Citizen* published 25 May. On 1 June mass meeting of women calls for Home Rule for Irishwomen. 13 June first act of militancy by eight members of IWFL; Hanna imprisoned for window smashing, hunger strikes and is dismissed from teaching at Rathmines College of Commerce. WSPU travels to Ireland in pursuit of Prime Minister Asquith and three members imprisoned for militancy. Hanna's article 'Irish secondary teachers' published in the *Irish Review* in October. IWFL and Inghinidhe na hÉireann collaborate on School Meals campaign until School Meals (Ireland) Act passed in 1914. In November Snowden amendment to Home Rule Bill to include women defeated by vote of Irish Party.

1913

In January three IWFL members sent to Tullamore Prison for one month and hunger strike. In May three IWFL prisoners given six-month sentences and sent to Tullamore, released under 'Cat and Mouse Act' but not re-arrested. Margaret and James Cousins leave Ireland. Hanna and Frank speak in Ormeau Park, Belfast for Irish Women's Suffrage Society and are heckled. In autumn Dublin Lock Out begins; soup kitchen organised in Liberty Hall supported by suffragists. Hanna arrested and receives seven-day prison sentence in Mountjoy Jail for leafleting Bonar Law and Sir Edward Carson. Released after hunger strike. Irish Volunteers formed in response to Ulster Volunteer Force.

1914

In March Hanna and Meg Connery tour Longford, Leitrim and Roscommon. Daffodil fête in April includes 'Great Women of the Past' tableaux, with Constance Markievicz as Joan of Arc and staging of Frank's suffrage play *The Prodigal Daughter*. 2 April Cumann na mBan formed as women's auxiliary to Irish Volunteers. WSPU militancy begins in north, as war declared on Ulster unionists with Ulster Centre of WSPU established in Belfast. Kathleen

Houston last IWFL prisoner, with six-week sentence. WSPU prisoners in Crumlin Road Jail and Tullamore. Joint Irish suffrage delegation to Westminster in June includes Hanna. First World War begins in August and IWFL ends militancy.

1915

Women's International Peace Congress held in The Hague in May and Women's International League for Peace formed; Hanna one of the Irish delegates refused passport to travel. IWFL organise protest meeting in Dublin, with support from Patrick Pearse and Thomas MacDonagh of Irish Volunteers. In June Frank is given prison sentence for his anti-recruitment speeches and released under 'Cat and Mouse Act' after hunger and thirst strike. Goes to America until December. Hanna takes over editorship of *Irish Citizen*.

1916

15 February Frank debates with Constance Markievicz 'Do We Want Peace Now?' Easter Rising takes place 24–29 April. Frank murdered on 26 April on order of Captain Bowen-Colthurst who is found guilty but insane at court martial. Hanna meets Prime Minister Asquith on 19 July and urges full inquiry into death. Royal Commission conducted by Sir John Simon in August. Brother-in-law Tom Kettle killed at Somme in September. Hanna leaves for America in December.

1917

6 January, Hanna's first public meeting is held in Carnegie Hall, New York. She travels across the country, speaking at 250 meetings before her return to Ireland. Her pamphlet on Frank's murder, *British Militarism As I Have Known It*, is published. In July, death of her uncle, Father Eugene Sheehy.

1918

Hanna meets President Wilson on 11 January and presents him with a Cumann na mBan Memorial on Irish Freedom. Death of her mother, Bessie Sheehy, in January. 6 February, Hanna tells of British attempts to kidnap her. 24 April Hanna arrested in San Francisco, with case dismissed following day. Last speech in America at 'Irish Peace Convention', Madison Square Garden on 4 May. Leaves America with her son on 27 June. Detained in Liverpool on arrival and refused permission to travel to Ireland. In August smuggles herself back to Dublin, is arrested and sent to Holloway Jail and released after hunger strike. 14 September IWFL host welcome home reception. Applies for membership of Sinn Féin and is elected onto executive. November moves into new home on Belgrave Road. 11 November, Armistice Day and end of war. Campaigns for still-imprisoned Countess Markievicz in general election, with vote granted to women over 30. Markievicz is first woman elected. Winifred Carney in Belfast, only other female candidate, is defeated.

1919
Dáil Éireann meets on 21 January. Refused passport to attend Congress of Women's International League for Peace in Zurich, which is attended by Louie Bennett. Speaks at meetings throughout Ireland and in Scotland and England. Co-edits *Irish Citizen* with Louie Bennett. Dáil Éireann declared illegal in September and ministers, including Countess Markievicz, go on the run. Hanna clubbed by police at meeting in Kilbeggan, suffers head injury.

1920
In January, Hanna one of five women elected to Dublin Corporation in local government election. Director of organisation for Sinn Féin. In October, house raided by military and police. Hanna publicises atrocities suffered by women from crown forces. Last issue of *Irish Citizen* appears in September before raid by Black and Tans smashes typeface. Government of Ireland Act partitions Ireland, setting up six-county parliament in the north.

1921
Funds received from American Committee for Relief in Ireland results in establishment of the White Cross. Hanna is appointed to its executive. Sinn Féin members elected to Second Dáil Éireann include six women. In July a truce between British and Sinn Féin called. Prisoners released. Negotiations with British government begin and in December Dáil Éireann begins to debate the Articles of Agreement.

1922
In January Dáil Éireann votes in favour of the Treaty by 64 votes to 57. Éamon de Valera resigns as president. Cumann na mBan vote against Treaty in February. On 2 March Kate O'Callaghan introduces unsuccessful motion for women over 21 to have franchise before Treaty voted upon. Hanna part of delegation of suffragists to leaflet Dáil. Shelling of Four Courts on 28 June signals start of Civil War. Hanna amongst group of women who meet, unsuccessfully, on 2 July to speak to leaders on both sides to hold fire and let new Dáil meet. Maud Gonne MacBride forms Women's Prisoners' Defence League. On 22 October Hanna arrives in New York, sent by de Valera as part of 'Irish Women's Mission' with Kathleen Boland and Linda Kearns to raise funds for prisoners and their families; travels to 25 states.

1923

Civil War ends in May. Hanna leaves America. She is given a contract by the American paper, the *Irish World*, as 'special correspondent'. In June dismissed from post of examiner for Intermediate Board because of political views and opposition to Oath of Allegiance. In November sent by de Valera to Paris to counteract Irish Free State application to League of Nations but is unsuccessful.

1924

Speaks for Sinn Féin around countryside; campaigns against Free State candidate in Limerick by-election; all prisoners released in July; 1924 Juries Act starts process of removing women from Juries, completed by Kevin O'Higgins with 1927 act. National Council of Women in Ireland formed.

1925

Elected to Dublin County Council. Protests against Seán O'Casey's *The Plough and the Stars*. *An Phoblacht* begins publication as organ for republicans. Civil Service Regulation Act gives government power to exclude women from civil service exams. Matrimonial Act outlaws divorce.

1926

Sinn Féin splits over question of abstention from Free State institutions. Fianna Fáil formed and Hanna appointed to its executive. She attends International Women's Suffrage Congress in Paris. In July Women's International League for Peace and Freedom has congress in Dublin with 120 delegates. Hanna gives report on situation in Ireland. Hanna is served with order barring her from entering Northern Ireland.

1927

Fianna Fáil poll three seats less than Cumann na nGaedheal in June election. Kevin O'Higgins assassinated. Constance Markievicz dies. Fianna Fáil enters Dáil and Hanna resigns from the executive and from the party.

1928

Hanna campaigns against the prospect of a censorship act being introduced. Act abolishes the right to referendum under the Free State Constitution.

1929

Censorship of Publications Act passed in July. Hanna stops writing for the *Irish World* and starts to write for *An Phoblacht*. Juries Protection Act passed. Hanna and Rosamond Jacob attend Sixth Congress of Women's International League for Peace and Freedom, held in Prague in July. In September speaks in Dresden on theme of 'A World Without War'. Becomes Secretary of Friends of Soviet Russia.

1930
In August travels to Russia as part of Irish delegation of FOSR. In November gives several speeches on Russia to groups in Dublin. Speaks in Dublin on International Women's Day, 8 March.

1931
Hanna speaks in Paris and London for St Patrick's Day celebrations. Martial law in existence with Public Safety Act. Hanna working with Women's Prisoners' Defence Committee to support prisoners and to challenge Free State. *An Phoblacht* suppressed and Frank Ryan, editor, arrested. Hanna is editor of new paper, *Republican File*. National Aid Association formed to support republicans forced out of employment. Maud Gonne MacBride is chair and Hanna and Charlotte Despard made treasurers.

1932
Funding from America via the *Irish World* for Association reaches $1,563.92 by February. Fianna Fáil wins general election and in March de Valera forms first Fianna Fáil government. Political prisoners released, military tribunals suspended. Oath of Allegiance removed. In April, death of Mrs Pearse. Hanna challenges de Valera's portrayal of Markievicz as a philanthropist rather than revolutionary. December, death of her father, David Sheehy.

1933
In January Hanna travels to Newry to speak on behalf of imprisoned Cumann na mBan members and is arrested for defying Banning Order. After 15 days' detention she is sentenced to one month in Armagh Jail, returning to civic receptions in Drogheda and Dundalk and public meeting in Dublin. IWFL hold supper party on her behalf. In April Hanna resigns from *An Phoblacht*.

1934
In June she wins libel action against *Irish Catholic Herald* who had stated she received a pension from the British government. Travels to America and Canada for lecture tour, returning January 1935. Criminal Law Amendment Act bans importation of contraceptives.

1935
Wedding of son Owen and Andrée Denis in France in March. Hanna speaks at meeting at Minerva Club while in London. Conditions of Employment

Bill passed, restricting women in industrial employment. Joint Committee of Women's Societies and Social Workers formed (chaired by Hanna's sister, Mary Kettle). Hanna speaks at protest meeting in Mansion House.

1936
Spanish Civil War begins. Irish Friends of the Spanish Republic formed; Hanna chairs Women's Aid Committee. Fourth reprint of *British Militarism As I Have Known It*. Writes article 'Women in the Free State: a stocktaking'. De Valera abolishes Irish senate. Joint Committee of Women's Societies begin to lobby de Valera.

1937
De Valera meets Joint Committee on 29 January but no outcome. Hanna gives talk on Irish Women Writers at Minerva Club, London. De Valera publishes draft constitution and all women's organisations lobby against. Passed by Dáil and by referendum. Women's Social and Progressive League formed in November, committee members include Mary Hayden, Mary Kettle and Hanna.

1938
Owen Sheehy Skeffington treated for TB in Switzerland; Hanna goes to America and Canada for last lecture tour. Women's Social and Progressive League circulate 'Open Letter to Women Voters' for 1938 general election. Three women returned to Dáil, none of them feminists.

1939
Hanna returns in May from Canada; Owen, cured, returns to Ireland in August. Hanna on Dublin Anti-War Committee; resumes part-time teaching in technical colleges. In June Kathleen Clarke elected first female mayor of Dublin. Second World War begins; de Valera announces 'Éire' would be neutral.

1942
Irish Housewives Association formed, founded by Hilda Webb and Andrée Sheehy Skeffington.

1943
Hanna stands in general election, one of four women standing as independents, but receives only 917 votes.

1944

Writes eulogy for Dorothy Evans, former WSPU organiser in Belfast.

1945

In April attends fourth 1916–21 Annual Commemoration Dinner with many other republican women. Confined to bed for four months with heart problems. First grand-child born in May, named Francis after his grandfather. Is interviewed about her life for RTÉ in November. Writes for *Workers' Review* on British women MPs in post-war Labour government.

1946

Writes article for first issue of the *Irish Housewife*; writes letter to *Irish Times* in support of national school teachers' pay strike. Hanna dies on 20 April and is buried in Glasnevin Cemetery with her husband.

UNPUBLISHED MEMOIRS

INTRODUCTION

In the last year of her life Hanna began the task of writing her memoirs. She intended to write 14 chapters, of 7,000 words each, but only the first chapter, dealing with her family background and early childhood, can be considered complete in the manner she intended. A third of the chapters were written, ending with the establishment of Dáil Éireann and her work for Sinn Féin. In a letter dated 28 January 1946 Hanna thanked her typist, 'Nora', for the work she had done. However, not all of the chapters were typed up, and the last two, dealing with 1918 onwards, are in handwritten form only, with bracketed notes for further information, which she was unable to complete. They are transcribed as written, retaining her abbreviations and notes.

The Land War of the 1880s was a defining moment for the young Hanna and she describes in detail the involvement of her father and uncle and the impact that the fight between landlord and tenant had on the young Sheehys. Her Fenian ancestry was a source of pride, one which she had referred to frequently in her political career, in speeches and writings.

The most important events in her life – the suffrage campaign and the murder of her husband Frank – are barely alluded to in these memories of the past. The explanation must be that she had already written extensively about both and what she was trying to do, knowing the time she had left was limited, was to record those areas in her life that were less well known. She provides vivid snapshots of the turmoil experienced by Dublin residents during the Rising and devotes much of her memoir to recollections of her return from America and her difficulties in returning to Ireland, experiencing war-time officialdom, several arrests and the novelty of a crossing on a coal boat, disguised as a crew member.

The person of Michael Collins is singled out in her description of republican resistance to British rule and we are provided with an acutely perceptive few lines about a man whose intelligence, bravery and industriousness she admired, but whose political views she disliked, even before the Treaty divisions crystallised people's views. Her account of Sinn Féin courts and the support republicans had from ordinary civilians may now appear rose-tinted, but it was how she remembered those times. Her view of the formation of Dáil Éireann retains the scathing dismissal she had at the time, when she condemned the slavish following of archaic British ritual.

The memoirs end before she deals with the debate over the Treaty and subsequent events. However, we have her journalism and her speeches from her long political career to fill in those gaps.

MEMOIRS[1]

Foreword by Hanna Sheehy Skeffington
The idea of writing as a personal record of my life and experiences has been nagging at my conscience for many years, but always other things that seemed at the time important and urgent kept me from it – mass meetings, protests (how hoarse and weary we are of protests in Ireland!), executions, censorship, prisoners and their dependants, struggling causes; in short life's swift current – seemed to tug at me and pull me off. P. O'Donnell[2] once said: 'You don't care enough just or you would do it and let everything else go by.' Perhaps he's right I am more keen on doing things than writing about them. Then there was the eternal job, the daily bread that doesn't just come by praying for it; and the job – part-timing, free lancing, correcting and setting papers – just absorbed my energy. Now a 'tired heart' has called a halt, and I have to face those memoirs now or never; to clear the decks – and what decks! Dusty, overcrowded with the junk of the years; the minutes of committee work; the diaries, yellow and almost indecipherable; the gaps that the raids (Military – British and our two home governments) have made. I cannot see the Wood for the Trees. 'I have lived too long,' I said to myself as I stirred up the dust: 'It is later than I thought.' Many of my comrades have gone, some have fallen out, much of the toil and passion of the years will never be told, or will be lost in old newspaper files or dusty museums; and, worse nightmare of all, the successful politicians at home or the patronising visitors from abroad will write us up, distort the facts. (It has already been done). Not that I am without prejudice . . . on the contrary. But at least it's up to me to leave a personal record of a life that has been chequered, but which has had moments. Dedicated:[3]

Chapter I
I heard my father say that there were three Sheehy (then MacSheehy) brothers in Limerick after the Siege (1690). One went with Sarsfield and the

Wild Geese and was not heard of after. His descendent may have been the MacSheehy, the friend of Tone. A second brother went 'on the run' in the Tipperary mountains – on his keeping, as it was then called. He was the ancestor of Father Nicholas Sheehy, hanged in Clonmel in March, 1766. Father Nicholas' story is fully told in Madden's 'United Irishmen' and after in Postgate's Life of Emmet. The evidence against him was 'most tainted', because the then government wanted to hush up the peasant risings with a 'popish' plot. There is still a flourishing bunch of the name in Tipperary and Waterford. And there is said to float a cloud over Clonmel ever since the day of the priest's hanging on a 'framed-up' charge. The third Sheehy brother, my ancestor, elected to stay in Limerick; to this day there are many of the name (otherwise not a common one) in West Limerick. In penal days the Mac and O according to the old rhyme – 'You know – An Irishman, they say' were dropped as a protection, as Jews for the same reason assumed Christian or fancy names. Thus many Irish names are corrupted in process of time. The name was in Gaelic Eoghaigh – meaning Peace-maker – and was said to be so called because a certain Eoghaigh of the O'Donnell clan made peace between rival factions. This Eoghaigh was also a noted chess player, chess being a favourite game with Irish clansmen and chieftains, one of the many links between ancient Ireland and the East. My father also favoured the game, but the peaceful proclivities of our far-off ancestor do not appear to have been handed down to any of his later kin. The name is akin to Siochana (the new name in Irish for the police, 'guards of peace'). But I do not like 'peelers' any better on that account.

Other ancestral and family memories come from a paternal great-great-grandmother (whose maiden name was Fitzmorris) from the Kerry border. She remembered young Lord Edward Fitzgerald, who used to visit her father's home, and hunt and fish with her brothers when they were boys. That must have been about 1790, for he was born about 1776. She used to call Lord Edward 'the boyo' because of his high spirits and love of boyish pranks. I remember this great-great-grandmother. I saw her when I was about four, about a year before she died. She lived to be 106. She was tall and spare and wore a stiff white cap with strings, and had a stick, though her hair was still reddish. My grand-father's earliest memory was the news of Waterloo: he was born in 1812. He lived to well over ninety, and my father, who died in 1932, to ninety. A long-lived race on the paternal side. On the maternal my grandmother, Margaret McCoy née Mulcahy, recalled Dan O'Connell; he used to stay in her father's hotel (Mulcahy's) in Rathkeale. The children liked him; he was boisterous in manner, with a breezy, open handed hail-fellow sort of a way. Both my grandparents, paternal and maternal, were hero-worshippers at his shrine while their children openly despised him and scoffed at his time-serving and his failure to call out the masses at Clontarf. We of the next generation naturally sided with the generation nearest to our own; when one is young one is impatient of compromise and some remain always so. Young Ireland appealed to us. A memory of my mother in Fenian days stands out. Bessie McCoy had the fighter in her too. When her two brothers, Pat and Dan, were arrested as Fenians (Kilmallock was a hot centre and County Limerick generally) and lodged in Mountjoy in a general round-up, the people of Ballyhahill were sympathetic, but the old parish priest was bitterly hostile. In response to a request from the parishioners to have the Rosary said at evening devotion in the church he indignantly refused and left the church hurriedly after Mass. As the congregation was dispersing a young girl, Bessie McCoy, stood up and announced that the Rosary would be said that evening at six o'clock. How she managed to get the keys I never learned, but enter she did, and said the Rosary to a packed congregation. Never was such fervour shown in 'storming heaven' as then. It was a gesture none of the men would dare to make, and it worried her mother and the parish priest, but they were wisely silent, and many a time she was chaffed with 'standing with her back to the altar' afterwards. Pity Fenianism was so thwarted and mismanaged – it had the promise of great things.

Thus on my father's and my mother's side Fenianism was strong.

The old house in Curraghmore had, when first I saw it, in kidney stones at the front door the date 1840 and the initials R. and M. Mc. – the date of the marriage of my maternal grandparents – it is still there. Mother recalled stories (folk tales they would be called now) of the famous Limerick witch, Biddy Early, and her marvels, and she recalled being put three times under an ass's belly to cure 'chin-cough.'

My father's earliest memories (they went back to the forties; he was born in 1840) were of the 'levellers'. I have heard him tell how, when he was a young lad of seven or eight, he heard a shout from the village street in Drumcollagher, Co. Limerick, where he lived: 'The levellers – the levellers are here!' and a tumult outside of many voices. He dashed upstairs to see what was going on, and beheld the levellers at work. They were Whiteboy agrarians, so called because they tumbled down fences erected round commonages by grasping landlords who thus scruplessly annexed the common land of the people. 'This form of legal theft of land (says Davitt in his *Fall of Feudalism*) was well known in England and in Ireland, with the difference that the English peasantry never made the same spirited resistance to this despoiling, so that hundreds of acres of land in both countries were thus stolen from the community.' 'Whiteboyism,' says Davitt, 'was the illegitimate child of social oppression.' Limerick suffered her share. The land there is rich and suitable for grazing and for demesnes. Its wide parks and lovely woods and gardens were laid at the expense of the dispossessed Irish peasants.

Another memory passed on from the old people was that of the famine. To my maternal grandmother's house in Curraghmore, Co. Limerick, starving families used to come from Kerry begging for meal or potatoes. Margaret McCoy (née Mulcahy) was married at eighteen, and she used to tell how she was forbidden by her stern father-in-law to give the starving people more lest their own stock be drained, but on the sly at the back door she used to fill her arms with potatoes and give it to them. In those days eagles used to have their eyries in Glen-na-Coppal, a wild Limerick gorge about which a grim legend was current. It was said to be haunted by a woman on whom a curse was put. In the houses more crafts were used – spinning and carding and combing, from the farmers' own wool. An itinerant tailor came round to the houses. Cheese was made, cider brewed, and tallow candles were dipped. It was a more self-contained Ireland. Tea was a guinea per pound in the forties, and my grandmother, who came from the town of Rathkeale to a farm in remote West Limerick, used to have to hide in her bedroom from a strict father-in-law, old Thady McCoy, to sip the clandestine brew on the sly. And such a child was she that she used to have to call in the old servant woman to help to button her dress at the back. It was a patriarchal household, (There are still a few left), and old Thady was head of the clan. They used no titles but had the more respect.

[page missing]

My earliest memories are of an old mill in County Tipperary between Templemore and Thurles. My father owned it, having spent a lot in installing machinery. We had a bakery also and shops in Templemore and Thurles. There was always the smell of newly baked bread and the delight of the old mill race by the Suir where we used to bathe; of the orchard where black cherries grew; of the grove behind the mill, of the doves that came after the grain. There were columbines and white violets wild in the ditches – garden escapes perhaps – and the largest primroses I ever saw, a profusion of lilies, and a huge white rose-tree that used to tap against the panes as we sat in the lamplight on a summer evening. The old people around knew some Irish, but already the generation there that spoke it from the cradle was dying out. My grandfather Sheehy knew finest Irish; he spoke it as a boy, and when he went to the National schools (they were founded about '34) and he was born in 1812 or thereabouts. In the National schools Irish was taboo, and a tally was kept by the teachers of every word of Irish used by the scholars – there must have been many at first – and they received at the end of each day a cut from the rod on the palm of their hands for every Irish word they had spoken.

I owe my life indirectly to my father's objection to taking an oath of allegiance. He desired to become a priest, both he and his elder brother Eugene having at an early age chosen the priesthood as their profession. In those days – the early '60's – an oath of allegiance to the British monarchy was compulsory for all clerical students at Maynooth, which had been endowed by the British government with a substantial grant. Irish clerical aspirants who objected to such oath accordingly had to get their education and training outside Ireland just as in penal days. There were (and still are) colleges in Paris in the Rue des Irlandais, in Spain and in Rome, and to Paris Eugene and David Sheehy went in the early sixties. An epidemic of cholera broke out in Paris about 1865, and my father, who feared the epidemic would spread to new pupils, was sent home by the authorities. He joined the Fenians some time after and never returned to his Paris seminary. His elder brother Eugene was duly ordained later. He, too, remained a rebel, and was one of the few Irish priests active on the side of the people in the Land War. In 1881 he was arrested and taken to Naas jail, where he sent me a box of sugared almonds given him by an admirer: my first introduction to the sweetmeat, henceforward to be linked in my mind with Naas prison. Later Eugene Sheehy was one of the Kilmainham suspects interned by Buckshot Forster with Parnell, Sexton, Wm. O'Brien and many others: some hundreds in all. Father Eugene, then CC in Kilmallock, was one of the founders of the GAA, a personal friend of Parnell, who coined the famous phrase later used by the Chief and immortalised on his statue: 'No man can set bounds to the onward march of a nation.' The phrase is reminiscent of Burke, and Parnell used it in one of his famous speeches.

My first visit to Kilmainham occurred in the eighties when I stayed with my aunt, Mrs Kate Barry, on whom the task of catering for the three hundred odd suspects in the jail fell. She, with her assistants – the task was in the hands of the Ladies' Land League – came with their provisions three times daily. There were wicker baskets in which each separate meal was packed. The dinners were carved on a big counter that ran across the big reception hall, a glass-covered space with galleries and tiers of cells, in which prisoners used to walk around and chat on wet days. The prisoners were allowed political treatment by Forster: they played chess and handball and read the papers. They wrote and worked in their cells. They belonged to every class – were lawyers, doctors, journalists and farmers, and men of that respectable class, the men of no property. My uncle was permitted to say Mass, but the privilege was taken away when he made an announcement one day, at the usual pause for such which the authorities deemed political and therefore dangerous. I came in therefore one day with the rest, and suddenly beheld my uncle (he was my best beloved among all my relatives) walking about beyond the barrier with a tall dark man, John Dillon, as it happened. I darted under the counter flap and dashed to him with a joyful cry, rushing impetuously between him and his companion, who seemed rather startled at the sudden onslaught. My uncle received me joyously and chatted with me until a warder rushed up presently to remove me. Visitors were not allowed – above all, not in that manner. Mr Dillon marked the occasion by the gift of a section of honey. He used to receive all sorts of dainties from his admirers, and being on a strict diet, and a man of austere personal habits, he rejected them all, to the discomfiture of his devoted friends, insisting on a grilled chop for his lunch, without sweet or other varieties.

Such was my first visit to a jail: it was to be only one of many others. A word further about my uncle. On his release, at the time of the famous Kilmainham Treaty (in which Parnell gave away too much, in the opinion of the left-wing supporters, entering into regrettable negotiations with British politicians): he went on a lecture tour with Mr T. M. Healy to the United States. Healy was then young, ambitious, and a rebel. He was also anti-clerical, though later he became a strong bulwark of the church and of the Tories. I recall my uncle stating that Healy disliked the priests, describing theirs as 'peasant intelligence mottled with Latin'. At that time the ecclesiastics almost to a man were upholders of the landlords and of Dublin Castle, hence the rebels' bitterness. A sample of his speeches is given in A. M. Sullivan's Penny Readers. It is called 'An Address to the Men of '48', and is a good sample of the fiery oratory of the day. The style is rhetorical and ornate, the sentences long, with rounded periods and balanced measure, showing a marked preference for antithesis and alliterative effects. In fact, the influence of Burke and Macauley is marked. Here is his tribute to Davis: 'From wherever on this wide earth liberty had a throne, a prison or a grave, there was Thomas Davis. Bigotry was to him the reddest of crimson crimes, blaspheming heaven above while it blasted and burned the earth beneath. The spirit of Davis lives, his principles survive; every breath that liberty breathes in your land will whisper his name in a litany of glory.' Another sample is given from the enemy side in a book called *Ireland under the Land League* by Clifford Lloyd, published in 1892, the author a resident magistrate in Ireland. Kilmallock, my uncle's curacy was then a storm centre, where yet the revolutionary fires of Fenianism blazed. Here the No Rent and Boycott campaign were going strong (launched in June 1881). Father Sheehy was the head of the local Land League Committee, and the author's first task as RM was to order his arrest, which he promptly did so that 'order' be restored. For Law and Order go hand in hand, and Britain's chief task is restoring or maintaining them, the polite fiction being that the population are pining for both and are only cowed by agitators from maintaining them inviolate. The author states that the curate was adored by 'the roughs' for his violent and rebellious views. With a detachment of troop concentration at 5 am from opposite areas in Kilmallock he was taken to Naas. 'Poor Mr Burke', the Under Secretary, besought the author to spare no precautions – as his parcels used to appear an array of deathsheads and crossbones. A guard slept at his door even in the barracks, a sentry was posted under his windows day and night, and ten men with levelled rifles followed him when he went abroad. If he drove, a mounted escort was beside his car.

My earliest recollection by way of political events is the Phoenix Park assassinations in May 1881,[4] when Burke, Under Secretary, and Lord Frederick Cavendish were set upon by a body of men, members of the Invincibles, and despatched in sight of the Viceregal Lodge, where Spencer actually looked out upon the tumult, not knowing that his guest was one of the victims. A cross cut in the turf still marks the spot. Such was the excitement following upon the assassinations that it stands out as one of my first milestones. Lord Frederick was not intended for attack, being the victim of an unhappy accident; he was indeed visiting Ireland in a sympathetic spirit, but he suffered for his companionship with a man who was marked. Five men were hanged – one, at least, innocent of the charge against him – mainly on the evidence of informers, notably that of their comrade, James Carey, who turned Queen's evidence.

Parnell, Davitt and the United Irish Party were shocked by the deaths, and repudiated the slayers in unmeasured terms, conscious of the harm that this assassination did to their constitutional movement, to which it was a bad set-back. But popular sympathy, as ever in Ireland, was on the side of the man in the dock; Joe Brady and Curly, in particular. Ballads were sung in the streets about them, and young Tim, the lad of nineteen, about whose fate a jury three times disagreed, refusing to bring in the verdict of guilty, became a popular hero. The men, even their enemies testified, died bravely, and the man, James Carey, who informed on them (he in his turn betrayed by third degree methods into a 'confession') had to be smuggled out of Ireland secretly, but did not escape his fate, being shot on the high seas on his way to Africa by O'Donnell, who in turn incurred the capital penalty, and became a hero in the eyes of his country men. Of the details, of course, I knew little, but I recall the general atmosphere vividly. About this time, that is on my first visit to Dublin, occurred an incident that indicated a certain vein of bigotry in my disposition which I have never quite freed myself from. I was on a visit to my aunt above mentioned, and we halted one morning at O'Connell Bridge (then called Carlisle Bridge as Sackville was then named instead of O'Connell Street). She turned to show me the view of the Liffey flanked by the Custom House on one side and the Four Courts on the other, with O'Connell on guard between. 'Isn't it lovely!' she asked looking down at me. I really thought it was, but, suspecting a trap, with the craft of the country-bred on guard against town folk and grown-ups, I asked in turn 'Is it Ireland?' I thought somehow that being a city I might have gone outside my own country to the land of the Sassenach. 'Oh, yes, of course it is,' she answered, laughing. Relieved, I echoed, awe-struck: 'Yes, it is lovely,' and took Dublin and its vista to my heart. Later I was to be disappointed to find that other lands were green. I thought that England was surely red, and other places a mottled brown – else why call Ireland the Emerald Isle, Green Erin, and the rest? Children are ever literal minded.

Returning home – in fact I twice ran away from Dublin, disliking in country bred fashion being cooped up so much – my next recollection was the welcome we staged to Archbishop Croke. He had been sent for by Leo XIII to Rome to explain or justify his attitude to the evicted tenants and his Land War activities. It was about then that a papal nuncio had been sent over to inquire into us; British influence being as ever strong at the Vatican and seeking to dip the scales on the side of the vested interests, the landed gentry. As Shaw says in *John Bull's Other Island*: John Bull in Ireland is the Pope's policeman. Dr Croke was sturdy and defended his position. 'I hear you are a sort of Garibaldi,' His Holiness is reported to have said, with an upward glance at that towering figure. There was a pause, and Dr Croke replied: 'I don't know much about Garibaldi, Your Holiness, but if his case is as strong as that of the Irish against the landlords, than I am not surprised that your Holiness is a prisoner at the Vatican.' Leo XIII may have admired the blunt retort: he did not silence or attempt to restrain Archbishop Croke, who returned home having had his say. On his arrival he uttered the memorable words, when asked how he then stood, 'I am unchanged and unchangeable.' He was received as a king in Tipperary. I still did not know much about the rights of the case, but we did know that Dr Croke had stood up for Ireland to the Pope of Rome, so we got together and strung an ivy-bound laurel-decked arch across his path as he entered the village passing the mill at the Suir Bridge. On it was inscribed on one side the words: Unchanged and Unchangeable; on the other: Welcome, in orange upon green canvass. But the handyman who did it was not strong on spelling, and he made it 'Wealcome', to our discomfiture when the scoffing elders saw the work.

As will be guessed, I was brought up in a political household; in our youth we played at Evictions and Emergency Men. It was hard to cast any one for the part of bailiff or peeler; all wanted to be the evicted family guarding the home (it was an outhouse in the mill) against the crowbar, and fortified with water, hayforks and other means of defence. In our school (the National) there were children of a local 'grabber' and these poor things came in for a hard time at our hands, for youth is cruel and given to baiting. I recall that same grabber standing outside the church and being hooted by the people around. I can still see his down-hanging head and sheepish look. The priest, in the interest of peace and harmony, advised him not to come to Mass again. After, he gave up the farm he had taken, so strong was the use of the Boycott in the land, a weapon and a word then coming into use for the first time, one for the oppressed against their oppressors, and one destined to spread all over the world for the use of the under dog.

In those days we heard much of evictions, grabbers, boycotts, mass demonstrations, the Land League. We children learned the Land League Alphabet and sang 'The Peeler and the Goat'. My father in 1886 received a telegram one summer evening from Parnell asking him to stand for South Galway. He had hoped for his native Limerick, as a constituency, but Parnell's word was enough. He accepted, and remained for many stormy years the Member for Galway with constituents in the far-off Aran Islands, the nearest parish to America, as it used to be called. Later he was member for Louth-Meath, which he held till the fateful election of 1918, when Sinn Féin, a young giant, took the field against the Irish Party. David Sheehy did not stand and the seat was won by Eamon Duggan, afterwards one of the signatories to the Treaty. Such are Time's revenge!

I recall my father's first letter from London. He had sold his mill to strangers and transferred his family of six to Dublin to be nearer the seat of things and where he could come over now and then during recess. In that letter he promised us Home Rule before the next Christmas turkey – a Home Rule that got as far as the Statute Book in 1914 to be shelved for the duration of the war.

We learned Thomas Davis, Mangan, the Poets of the Nation, Moore's Melodies, Emmet's Speech from the Dock; we read Mitchell's *Jail Journal*, the *Story of Ireland* by A. M. Sullivan, Mrs Sadler's *Confederate Chieftains*, William O'Brien's *When We Were Boys* (Ron Rohan, the young miller from Mallow was a composite picture drawn from the author's brother and David Sheehy, his boyhood chum). From being a Fenian – after '67 he got away a wanted man to America – he joined the Irish Party, adopting the old militant methods to the new constitutionalism. He remained a bonny fighter, one of those Irish obstructors who helped Parnell and Biggar and the rest to hold up the House of Commons of that day until the guillotine and the *[illegible word]* came to the rescue. Once wanted for a seditious speech he was pursued from Ireland by an over zealous policeman who, ignorant of Parliamentary privilege and procedure, served on the MP for Galway his warrant within the sacred precincts of the House. The arrested man at once called a policeman and had the captor lodged within the Tower while an indignant Speaker delivered a lecture upon decorum and members' privileges, to the delight of the Irish members. Poor officious RIC man, acting in accordance with his idea of police duty – how strange and baffling must he have found it all! For in Ireland the RIC were all-powerful, and they could arrest when and where and whom they pleased.

My father had an excellent speaking voice and good elocutionary powers. He was always interested in dramatics and had a little troupe of amateur actors and actresses in Mallow (of which O'Brien's brother was one). They built the stage, painted the scenery, and produced plays in a converted barn. Reading aloud is now a lost art. My father practised it and used to read aloud to the family while mother sewed and his sister and grandmother knitted. Those were the days before sewing machines and both were glad to be good crafts-women. My first recollection of Shakespeare was father's reading of *King Lear*. We youngsters missed much, of course, but the sonorous periods remained and rang in our ears:

To have a thankless child.

And of Macbeth my one memory was:

Lead on, MacDuff.

Which we used to declaim among ourselves. Another book was a serial then running in the *Catholic Fireside*, called 'Thy Name is Truth'. It thrilled us then, but only the title now clings to my memory. My father used to declaim long patriotic poems: Fontenoy; The Muster of the North; Emmet's Speech from the Dock. Davis was our fare, and we loved the poems; they became part of the very fabric of my mind. It was our way of learning history, for Irish history was not taught in the National schools of that period. I think schools influence children very little; they react to their companions and contemporaries. A loved teacher no doubt can influence and direct, and a hated one can work on the mind by the rule of contraries. (I conceived a hatred of Jane Austen thus, which it took years to overcome). The home atmosphere counts a lot, and those old school men were wise in their generation who said: 'Give me a child till he is seven, and I care not who has him afterwards.' We had a Loyalist textbook in our National school, and I recall a story about a pearl and an oyster (a snobbish one, at that) which afterwards (Oh, glory of glories!) became a jewel in the Queen's (Victoria) crown. I still remember the scorn with which we read that moral tale. It certainly failed to impress Imperialism on our plastic minds. It is wonderful how much one can escape and throw off of the school curricula.

The first ten years of my life were country-spent; my memories centre round the mill, its grove and kitchen garden, its periodic floods that came into the kitchen; the bread maker, the haybarns where I used to read *Jane Eyre* on the sly (my first novel), and the country background.

Part II
[Sketchy, handwritten notes of school and university not included.]

Part III
Here a great revolution came to pass – not without sacrifice from its pioneers.

When the late Czar's rescript for World Peace (headquarters at The Hague before the days of the League of Nations) was published by Stead[5] in his *Review of Reviews* a student pacifist went round seeking signatures thereto: the signers were to pledge themselves that under no circumstances would they engage in arms. Few signatures were forthcoming. Tom Kettle voiced the popular objection to World Peace by saying that he must hold himself free if called upon one day to strike a blow for Ireland. The young pacifist was Francis Skeffington. Joyce, in his *Portrait of an Artist*, covers that period of storm and stress – the Dublin of the early 1900's.

Conventions were changing in the Dublin of the early 20th century. For one thing the bicycle had come in. The first (those contraptions with one large wheel and one small) were called velocipedes. I remember a maid telling my mother, that a gentleman had called during her absence 'riding on a philosopher'. Then came Dunlop and his pneumatic tyres. At first the cycle was strictly for males. When a woman ventured forth along the Quays one evening she was set upon by the mob and narrowly escaped ducking in the Liffey by the shocked male hooligans of the day. But the cycle – and the popular tandem of Daisy Bell fame – had come to stay and it helped more than any single factor to emancipate the 20th century girl. In those days a girl found smoking a cigarette was expelled from a convent school: no girl went alone to the theatre or concert, nor might she dance (it was the day of the chaperone) more than twice with the same young man without censorious comment and reprimand from her elders. And fathers were stern fathers too against whose fist there was no appeal.

The Suffrage (or Votes for Women) struggle spread to Ireland. About 1908 when women had already won the right to free[6] university training and opportunely when women doctors had become general, though the Bar still excluded them from practising or pleading – they began to be politically minded and when the militant suffragists (christened by the English Press in derision suffragettes) began to adopt drastic methods Irishwomen debarred under the Home Rule Bill from the right of voting founded the Irish Women's Franchise League. They enlisted the sympathy of many male intellectuals. James Connolly, then leader of the Irish Socialist Party, was one of their first and warmest advocates. The IWFL and the SPI in fact used the rooms in the Antient Concert Buildings alternately for their meetings. The *Irish Citizen*, the weekly organ of the movement appeared and Irishwomen began to agitate and to go to jail for the movement. The volunteers were also being formed and the Cumann na mBan and all those movements tended to strike in one form or other at the base of the then entrenched authority. So fused were they that when in 1916 Pearse and Connolly proclaimed the Irish Republic the seven signatories to that historic document declared also for the rights of citizenship for Irishwomen.

1912 saw Irishwomen in prison in Mountjoy for breaking windows in Dublin Castle and other government buildings as a protest against exclusion from voting rights in the recently introduced Home Rule Bill. It is hard now to visualise the storm of protest this called forth in the press, pulpit and public. Women were mobbed, their meetings forcibly broken up and their persons assaulted: the rooms in which their offices were set upon by rioting students and wrecked. They were here as in England excluded from political meetings and yet they waylaid Cabinet Ministers, Home Secretaries and leaders of parties and drove these furious by the persistence of their demands. Riots took place in Dublin when Prime Minister Asquith came over in 1912 and when a Suffragette from England, Mary Leigh, threw a blunt hatchet at the carriage in which he and Mr John Redmond sat, popular fury knew no bounds. Six of us, in jail for the previous offence, in Mountjoy, noticed one Sunday morning a number of new-comers, young girls mostly, who wore their own clothes in prison and were exercising in the same yard as ourselves. Thinking they might be new recruits, fired up with our own zeal, I went up to one and asked her what she was in prison for? 'Murdering them suffragettes!' was her unexpected and startling answer. I did not pursue my queries further: ('Murder' in Dublin vernacular means mauling or knocking about, not man-slaughter).

When I was released from prison I found that I was dismissed from my post as teacher of German under the Rathmines Technical School Committee. When I inquired into the Committee's reasons I was informed by a lady member, franker than the rest that I had lost caste by going to prison and that therefore it would be impossible for me to maintain discipline in my classes.

Again time's revenge – in a few years the majority of that Com. being Sinn Féin had themselves served jail terms and the then head of the government had himself been condemned to death.

The next chapter of memories brings the War and 1916. Then truly the face of Dublin was changed – O'Connell Street bombarded, burnt, rebuilt and in 1922 reburnt and again rebuilt. Old landmarks gone or changed beyond recognition and for those who survived the face of life forever altered. In Dublin in Easter Week comic and tragic scenes jostled as in nightmare: certain things stand out – the Tricolour floating free on the College of Surgeons' sandbagged front, the machine guns opposite posted on the Shelbourne Hotel, the first casualties, the Citizens Army, Youth lying cold and stiff, face down-wards on Stephen's Green pathway for days, the civilian with brains oozing out lying on the kerb at Eden Quay, the horses of the British Lancer Regiment that made a gallant silly charge at the GPO only to be cut down with their riders. The ragged smoke-grimed urchin in Grafton Street hugging a huge pineapple to his tattered breast – looted from Knowles' show window – his first and probably last chance of getting his young teeth into that tropic fruit – preserve of the rich, the fight on the Quays beyond the Metal Bridge over a red plush armchair for which two sections of a looting crowd contended fiercely, ending in the chair being flung over the parapet into the Liffey because neither faction was strong enough to maintain possession, yet would not yield it to the other.

Returning homewards from a weary trek all day in the city on Easter Tuesday night I am stopped by an English sentry. To help to smooth suspicion I asked in genteel accents – 'Is all quiet in Rathmines?' He answered fervidly in Cockney tones 'Ah Miss, when you're in Wrawthmines, you're in 'eaven!'

So the dark, yet glory-lit days sped – and tragedy after tragedy followed as Dublin burned and the eternal bombardment went on followed now and then by the sharp reposte of the lone and desperate sniper on the roofs . . . till one by one the lights went out.

One little story of the GPO may be worth recording. Leaving my husband who was engaged in a vain attempt to stop the organised looting I went to the GPO to ask Connolly if there was anything I could do. His face was radiant and he was in the midst of Military activity and preparations. On another floor I met suddenly my uncle (Father Eugene Sheehy of Kilmainham memory). He ejaculated in amazement on seeing me – 'What are you doing here,' I explained that I was bringing a cup of Bovril upstairs to Tom Clarke and then in turn I asked 'And you? What are you doing?' Ah he replied with a smile, I am bringing spiritual comfort to the boys! The old Fenian in him was roused: he stayed in the GPO till its garrison left, burnt out.

1916 makes a fitting break in these reminiscences. It closes a chapter. And it writes *Finis* for many of the dramatic personae of life's stage.

Dublin Memories IV
Continuing these memories of Dublin from 1916 the curtain fell upon Easter Week, with its turmoil, its tragedy and its glory, we who lived in the suburbs, over the Canal Bridge, were completely cut off from the city from about Wednesday (26th) until April 30th. Sentries and a military post were put upon the bridges, illustrating how easily Dublin may be cut off, or held. The entire civilian life of Dublin was, of course, suspended: it presented the atmosphere of a siege, or of a general strike and there was also the excitement and tremor

of a war that was not quite a war. The police were entirely withdrawn after the first day, the 'G' or detective division also (these did not emerge again till April 28th). There were no trams, no transport of any kind: you had to walk everywhere; shops were closed and those that had accessible windows were rapidly cleared. In O'Connell Street, Lawrence's toy shop was ablaze from stray sparks and the looters (there was no Fire Brigade) snatched toys from the embers as in a mad nightmare, dolls, teddy bears, mechanical toys, passing from hand to hand. There was great excitement as rockets and fireworks were brought out by a band of boys and let off.

The Volunteers from the GPO fired shots to disperse the crowd, but this only led to a scattering, as of crows from a ploughed field, only to settle down again. Tyler's boot-shop and Noblett's sweet-shop (at the corner of O'Connell and Earl streets) were the first to be gutted of their contents. Jeweller's shops were also emptied. There was a story of a woman who took a supply of alarm clocks and went to a church the better to hide them temporarily. Imagine her consternation when the clocks suddenly went off in the middle of the devotions.

There was a criminal element behind the looters, but also a childish one and one saw the most unlikely and absurd things being pilfered. It was Dublin's slum on holiday, indifferent to what was happening as between the 'rebels' and their enemies and keen to seize the passing chance. While I was musing sadly on Connolly's sacrifice for the citizens of Dublin, and wondering were they worth it, I heard a man mutter – 'Foolish of them looters to be takin' things. Sure they know they'll be caught when the police comes out again!' He was willing enough to join the band, only timid of consequences when Law and Order resumed their reign.

It was remarkable too, how indifferent the crowd seemed to the shooting and bombardment. They swarmed in the streets and dashed indoors or round corners at each volley, only to emerge again.

After Tuesday night I did not get in to the city till the surrender week-end was over. On Tuesday in O'Connell Street, we heard the pounding of the *Helga* battering at Liberty Hall from the river – the headquarters of Labour and of Connolly's Citizen Army was of course, empty but the enemy regarded it as a fortress and bombarded it with other adjacent buildings impartially.

In the suburbs across the bridges in Rathmines the strange mixture that is Dublin was evident. In some houses tea and sandwiches were being served to the soldiers – along the coastal roads as they came from Kingstown (as it was then) they were met by the inhabitants as saviours and treated accordingly. Yet even there they could never be quite sure for there were rebel sympathisers in unexpected places. The soldiers themselves were sorely puzzled, for they had been shipped off for an unknown destination thinking their goal was

France – and lo! they found themselves in an English-speaking city. One officer with maps frantically asked to be directed to 'Bray' he pronounced it 'Bry' and was sent off on a wild goose chase in an opposite direction. Another asked how he would know Sinn Fyners – were they white? He was told they all wore soft hats!

One of the Munsters happened to be detailed to help to shoot up a street but, coming upon a lone rebel at the corner, he shouted in a stage whisper – 'Tell the boys to clear out! we're going to shell this street!' There were Irish on both sides, fighting. In a house that was being raided, just after the surrender, when the relatives of leaders were being harried, a soldier with a strong Belfast accent turning to the woman of the house (her husband had just been shot) said with an oath, 'My God, I didn't enlist for this!' She said 'What did you enlist for?' And he replied: 'I enlisted to protect Belgium, and for the freedom of small nations. That's what they told me the war was for!' Dublin during that week was a city of rumours, people clustered on their door-steps talking in whispers and the wildest tales circulated and grew from mouth to mouth. At night the city flamed in the distance and lone snipers kept up firing from hidden vantages. One heard the answering rat-tat of machine guns and had the impression that the firing was so close that it would shiver the panes. The Germans were coming! The whole country was up in arms. Cork was in the hands of the rebels! Galway was up! Military coming from the Curragh had been cut down. Dublin was being shelled from the sea by the Navy and would shortly be razed to the ground. The rebels held the town and there was a general massacre – each tale was coloured by the political faith of the circulator

Supplies such as bread and milk were short and neighbours borrowed groceries or hoarded according to temperament. Some of the men folk availed of the fine weather and their unexpected leisure to dig their gardens. The wives of the leaders (Mrs Ceannt, Mrs McDonagh, Mrs Pearse, lived near) were suffering cruel suspense. I saw one (Mrs T. McDonagh – tragically drowned in Skerries a few months after her young husband's execution) – wheeling her baby in a pram along Palmerston Road because her house had been raided and ransacked and she was thrown out. Constance Markievicz's home in Leinster Road (Surrey House), was sacked and pillaged by soldiers from Portobello, left derelict with the hall-door swinging open. So the mob finished what the military left. The soldiers found a MS dealing with Catherine de Medici and inquired was she not a Sinn Féiner too – and what was her present address!

After the dazed first days we heard of the surrender (on Saturday 29th) and a notice was posted up on the police stations giving data . . . the situation was well in hand. Sir Francis Vane in his book on 1916, *Agin' the Government* tells how the first news of the murders at Portobello came to him when an old woman stopped him with the cry of 'Murderer!' Then came day after day the news of the executions.

That turned the tide in favour of the rebels. The sustained horror spreading from May 3rd to May 12th when Connolly and McDermott went proved too much for Dublin's nerves. Instead of terrorising the population the military reprisals of Gen. Maxwell rallied support unexpectedly. Round-ups all over the country, men crowded into Richmond, Kilmainham and other barracks and jails, women taken . . . shipped later to prisons and concentration camps in England . . . sad lines along the quays, weeping women, haggard men bound to unknown destinations.

Requiem masses were the first gatherings . . . at Church Street, at the Carmelites, Whitefriars Street. One saw the widows of 1916 and their children. These Masses were watched by military, and once, I remember, a volley was fired along the street as the congregation came out. I heard a little boy whose father had been shot say to his mother – 'I suppose you don't mind, mammy, since they killed dada if they kill you. But I want to die by myself!' (meaning that he wanted to die in the fullness of time and not by a stray bullet, I expect!)

The first poems we had were 'Who Fears to Speak of Easter Week?' It appeared anonymously and caught on like wild fire, striking a spark from the past with its reminiscence of '98 in the air. As a ballad it had no pretensions, but it struck a chord that vibrated.

The next was the ballad (by the daughter of T. M. Healy, though it too, appeared anonymously) – The Schoolmaster (i.e. Pearse) beginning Schoolmaster of all Ireland. It was inspired by a jeering remark heard by the author in reference to Pearse. He was only a schoolmaster!

Then came Salutation, a fine tribute tho' also at first anonymous. I quote the first and last verse.[7]

Later came Dora Sigerson and Eva Gore-Booth (the latter Constance Markievicz's sister, the former closely associated with Casement). Both helped to clear the air: their poems shone out of the murk – 'Sixteen Dead Men' –

And on the eve of Connolly's execution after John Dillon's scathing speech in the House of Commons denouncing the methods employed to put down the rising, Dublin was surprised by a visit from Asquith. He arrived, strangely true, on the morning of Connolly's and McDermott's execution. He visited the prisoners and made a gesture of sympathy. One story illustrates the temper of the time.

Approaching a lad who looked about 14 years he exclaimed. 'But this is a mere child! He shouldn't be here at all!' The attendant jailer murmured that he was a sniper, captured red-handed.

'Ah,' said Mr Asquith in benevolent vein, 'It cannot be. There must be some mistake!' Turning to the lad, he said: 'I am sure, my boy, you weren't shooting. You are too young to be a combatant!'

The boy looked up and perky as a Dublin gaum can and said with a smile and a military salute – 'I did my best, sir!'

In July I had to cross to London to try to induce Mr Asquith to keep his promise of an inquiry into the Portobello murders.

On my way home at night I saw a small group huddled together on deck . . . to my surprise there floated across to me a familiar strain –

Sons of the Gael, men of the Pale
The long-watched day is breaking –

'The Soldier's Song' never before or since has it roused in me such profound such poignant emotion. It was sung by young prisoners who had been raked up in the general round-up after 1916 and were returning home, the first batch to be released. Whether they went in rebels is doubtful – probably not, for they would not have been released so soon had there been anything against them. But certain it was they had come out rebels. The tide had turned.

My Trip Home Again, July–August 1918[8]
Our boat left New York on June 27, 1918. We were seen off by Liam Mellows & others very carefully searched, had to strip to skin & take down my hair: female searchers of a hard type. This tho' passport seen in order & who warned ahead. I had nothing of importance naturally & my few addresses were camouflaged. I was bringing money from organisation home – later I handed to Collins whom I met for first time in Dublin in August. He came on his bike to my sister's house & collected it. I think it was 5,000 dols but disremember sum. We travelled in a fleet of ships, camouflaged all producing a weird effect. We were cut off at 10 am & did not move out till that night sometime. Accompanied by fleet of ships to escort us on way & some aeroplanes. It was virtually a troop ship, only a few 1st class passengers like ourselves & very few women, chiefly YWCA of aggressive type. We were four (Nora, Margaret,[9] Owen & self) & had a four-berth cabin. Trip was very slow & we went far south on line with Azores it took 13 days. It was very fine. Our quarters were cramped & the company was keyed up & very pro British. One felt sorry for boys from middle west who lay in the hold & on open decks, closely crowded, very seasick & homesick. Some had never before seen the sea. They didn't seem specially keen on the war & knew little about it but the civilians made up for all that. We had to do life-boat drill once a day regularly & were forbidden to go anywhere without lifebelts (or rather jackets, very clumsy & heavy

contraptions) we could take them off but they had to be beside our chair at dinner and in one's bath. The sense of the whole fleet along gave a leisureliness to the trip & an air of unreality: we had to keep the pace of the slowest. There were lectures & a concert – one telling us all about Russia's crime in dropping out of the war & how Lloyd George was helping the 'loyal' Russians. When questions were asked I queried wisdom of foreigners telling the Russians their business. This had a suffocating effect – 'Fancy that woman calling us "foreigners"' said a YW dame to a friend as they left the hall. We did before 'God Save the King'. One felt that the British were in control of everywhere. Owen learned to play chess & was bored one day at being called to look at the submarine infested coast as we approached Ireland. Must I stay? He asked. I thought it better in case a torpedo got us: as we were a troop ship it would have been all in the day's work of course, tho' somewhat of an irony. We were told that Ireland (except the north) was friendly to the submarines & that they used Irish waters & bays to hide in. We saw a flurry on the water in the distance one morning like a stone being hopped along its surface. We were all duly drilled prepared, if necessary, to take to the life-boats but the danger passed if dangers there had been, for it was too far off for us to see clearly.

When we docked at Liverpool the fun began for us four. We were kept apart from the rest & separately searched & our luggage 'combed'. I still remember how a customs man fell upon some chocolate given him as a tip. Sugar & sweets were scarce & adulterated in England then: the belt was tightening what with meat, sugar and milk tickets & ration cards. All that was new to us of course. Liverpool looked drabber than ever after the brightness of NY. Owen said it was 'uncheerful' & so unloved it was. When he was taken solemnly by a military officer to be searched I whispered to him not to know anything if asked questions. He could be a clam on occasion. I was searched all over again, tho' not as scientifically as by the NY woman. They took away some pamphlets out of my trunk by Wilson (some were returned later) & a box of theatrical make-up. I was commissioned to bring it to an actress in London by her brother. When O. was brought along the contents of his overcoat had been gone through & a box of antidote for Poison Ivy found in his mackintosh pocket caused suspicion. Whose was it? What was Poison Ivy? If it doesn't grow here, why the antidote. I asked the officer if before he had his Majesty's Crown had he ever been a small boy? Yes, yes he replied impatiently. Then I say your mother probably went thro' your pockets sometimes & found all kinds of stuff in them – string & catapults (pointing to these), knives & sealing wax & sticky messes. That's the only way I can explain. Small boys collect curiosities! He turned aside with a slow smile – but I never got back the antidote against Poison Ivy. It may repose in some wax museum.

Nora Connolly & Margaret Skinnider were taken separately: they were going to Glasgow & were passed on. I was brought before a tribunal (three officers) & asked where my going out passport & my son's was. Naturally it was not forthcoming for it did not bear my name or family history. I had gone to NY as a Scotswoman with a special family bill for the purpose. So I had left it behind in New York. I said I hadn't it with me. But I must produce it otherwise I would be liable to six months' imprisonment. Well I hadn't it, so they could do what they liked. (It would have got me six months anyhow but I didn't mention that. And it would have got others into trouble too.) I proffered my passport home & said that was all I could do. They deliberated & let it go at that. My address here? I had none. Rathmines Dublin was my home address. That would not do. I could not get permission to go to Ireland. Passports were then required to that country. I must stay in Liverpool for the duration of the war & report fortnightly (apparently as an unfriendly alien) to the police. Where was I staying. Temporarily at the Bee Hotel (that name had been given me years before by Sean McDermott)[10] but I warned them I was going home. I had no intention of staying in Liverpool for the duration. Well I could with notice stay in Sheffield or London or even in Scotland. No, my home & business were in Dublin. Did the same order apply to my son? Another consultation. No – he could go to Dublin and notice was served on me formally, DORA[11] of course.

So I said goodbye to my companions who set off, for Glasgow & I went to the Bee, despatching a telegram to my sister asking her to come for Owen, which she did in a day or two taking him alone. A detective was placed on duty: he sat at a neighbouring table, had a room opposite mine on the corridor & padded after me wherever I went. Till Owen was gone of course I did nothing. He was not perturbed remarking to a query, ah my mother will come – in a week! It took a little longer. First I contacted with Peter Murphy whose newspaper shop in Scotland Rd was like Clarke's tobacco shop in Dublin. He put me in touch with Neil Kerr & other friends & a plan was unfolded. A boat plying between Dublin & Liverpool would take me: men travelled on it frequently & no questions asked. There is a freemasonry of the sea and of the Irish. It was a coal boat plying between Liverpool and Ringsend. I'd have to wait a fortnight or so till inquiries could be made & plan fixed. I was to be ready when the word came. It was harder for women but already Delia Larkin had gone over (later Nora Connolly did). I do not think the captain ever knew 'for certain' – anyhow he turned a blind eye.

But first my 'tec' had to be shaken off. So the net was laid in sight of the boat – I went openly to the station having paid my bill & given a forwarding address. At the station still closely followed I wrote to my father in House of Commons (he was Member for South Meath) saying I was arriving that evening & asking to be met. (The family at home of course already knew this was a blind.) Then I took a single ticket: I had already sent all my heavy luggage home by my sister keeping only a small hand bag. I went along & got into a Ladies Only, wondering whether my attendant would come on the train. He did not: I was apparently passed on to the London police for that night at an Irish pub (the barman was a friend) he boasted his relief saying that it was now up to the London lot to keep tabs on me that I had gone to London & he had wired description ahead.

So I got out at Manchester there was no need. Leaving & facing the possibility that I might be watched I slightly changed my appearance (so as to evade a phoned description) taking off my glasses, changing my hat for a bonnet & veil & donning a macintosh. As one lady in the carriage had children I took charge of one toddler & got by alright. Connolly used to say that it was always a good plan to give the enemy credit for more intelligence than they had & to leave nothing to chance. All day I travelled in trains the length & breadth of Manchester & left quietly by an outside station (not the chief one) taking a ticket to a similar one just outside Manchester. There (Aintree was my desti-nation. I was met with a car, my friends & I rapidly driving off) I think the authorities were successfully mystified for I just disappeared & later the accepted story was that I had taken refuge in a convent & had travelled to Ireland as a nun.

For some time afterwards every religious was carefully scrutinised for the fugitive. I laid low (going out only for a short walk after dark) with friends (good Republican women, Irish of course) in Aintree. Then word came to be ready – dungarees & a cap with a peak were produced, a muffler for the neck & a sweater. These I donned at night fall one evening. I took no luggage. My hair was hitched under the cap & it was pulled down. I smeared my face & neck with coal dust & my hostess sewed a run of hair around the bottom of the cap. Brogues & coarse woollen socks completed the outfit & two sailors from the crew came along one on each side. Liverpool was darkened over the war time so that helped: we had to go on board several hours before the boat started. We were down there by ten. Getting up from top of a tram a funny thing happened, I instinctively stood to catch up an imaginary skirt – such is habit – before climbing the steps. However no one noticed this gesture in the dark. On board I was guided by hand to the top of the stairs steep & narrow leading to the galley. As I was supposed to be one of the crew & familiar with the place I had to go carefully: another friendly hand led me to a berth, a lower one draped in front with a towel & some seaman's underwear & I slipped in clothes & all, pulling the blanket over me. I had been warned that there might *[page missing]*

I doubt if any but my two companions ever knew that I had travelled on the boat tho' of course it was generally known that men on the run do now & then cross. A sort of prerequisite the crew claimed for themselves this privilege of giving 'a lift' to a pal. No questions were ever asked & to the credit of the men I must record that no one lifted that towel or tried to shove aside the hanging underwear which could easily have been done for no elaborate curtain could have been rigged up for fear of drawing further suspicion. They slept, washed & mended their clothes, gossiped, peeled & cooked potatoes in that galley & all respected their pal's secret as he no doubt would respect theirs. And the less anyone knew about such business the better & the safer. For there were heavy war time penalties. I always think with gratitude & warmth at the heart of those sailors on that coal boat. It was nice to feel my feet once more on my native soil as we got in at Ringsend – I was taken off quietly when most of the crew had slipped away home. It was near daybreak on an August morning & the air was balmy. I was taken to a friend's cottage near the docks where clothes had been left for me previously by instructions conveyed by my sister. Mr Fox (whose son was killed in Stephen's Green in Easter Week) came along with me to my aunt's by the canal & took word later to my sister. For 2 or 3 days I lay low as I did not want the particular boat I came on to be suspected. Then I went to my sister's house & applied at the local police station at Rathmines for my sugar card as a test to the authorities, for I did not intend to remain 'on the run' even at home 'for the duration'. I was arrested within a week. But that is another story.

Home Again 1918[12]
Here I was home again after two years. Dublin was not war darkened like Liverpool, food was more plentiful. There were sugar cards, of course, but in general rationing was loose & you could always get things if you knew how & where. Many English refugees – 'fly boys' – had come over & many families had migrated for the sake of the better food & the then greater security. After all, we helped to feed England so why should we not have enough? Jam was rather scarce & much adulterated, bread was coarse, but good, eggs, butter & meat were plentiful. Public opinion had swung to the so-called 'Sinn Féin' side: even the police were glad to avoid being drafted, having the pretext, of course, of looking after us & law & order. They were extra severe on the 'conchies'. I linked up with Michael Collins (his name even was new to me) having an official message to deliver & he called on his bike took over the money (it had been in my name in the bank) & talked intelligently on the situation in America, asking many shrewd questions.

He was then young and sprightly, boyish in fact, looking physically very fit. Had an alert manner, as if eternally on the 'gris vive' though he moved about freely and without disguise. I often sighted him later flying around on his bicycle in the midst of street jams & with danger in the air. Later he became heavier, probably for lack of exercise. He had a dashing way with him and got good service and devotion, was very dependable, a 'driver'. He could be brutal and his language was by no means choice. He rather liked to shock and had the usual soldier's contempt of civilians, particularly of women, though these often risked their lives to help him. He was recklessly brave, full of resource & had a penchant for surprising & for seeming inscrutable: he rather encouraged the myths that sprang up about him. He had a special attraction because of his qualities for the young, particularly for young men. Had a boisterous humour of the barracks type. Could be fun & human & could laugh at himself. Had a touch of the dictator-to-come about him – a 'go & thou goest'. Was not without vanity and the desire for power. I think the Republic he visualised would have been a middle class replica of an English state (certainly not ancient Gaelic Ireland) for he knew no other.

I was left in peace a while but it was only a temporary lull. The papers sent their reporters and there was a good deal of publicity given to my arrival, because it was *[illegible word]* passportless & baffled the Castle & the secret service (they naturally hate to be fooled). Captain Bowen Colthurst (he still held his title) had been released 'cured' from Broadmoor a few months before.[13] The blow fell suddenly about a week after my appearance. As I got off the tram to go to the IWFL office about 3 pm, I was approached by a plain clothes detective & asked to come along. He was presently joined 'unobtrusively' by a colleague & I walked between them to the detective HQ in Pearse St (irony that P. Pearse shd give his name to the street with CID HQ). But even in that short distance & with these precautions for secrecy I was 'spotted'. The brother of a friend (Mary Bourke-Dowling of our League Com) saw me between two obvious detectives, trailed me & then to the police station & gave the word at once. I was removed after the usual waiting interval to the Bridewell, situated in the police courts in vicinity of the Four Courts. There I was kept for 2 nights and 2 days till the authorities decided what to do with me. I started hunger-striking at once, refusing all food from the time of my arrest. (How useful our militant suffragette apprenticeship was to us!) The bridewell is only a temporary jail at most used over week-ends for drunks & poor derelicts of both sexes: it is a filthy hole, with dirt-clogged windows high up in the wall & giving a basement effect, with that stuffy, yet cold air & twilight dusk characteristic to such places. The floor is stone, infrequently washed, reeking of former fugitive occupants, who have been sick there. There is a slab for bed, a deal board fastened to the wall, the blankets look forbidding & there is a lavatory which can only be flushed from the outside. A grill leaves one eternally under inspection & the male police are in charge marching around at night. There is a police 'matron' but she is not in charge & has not authority, having a sort of charwoman status. The first night I was in the bridewell a poor unfortunate in the next cell to me in a fit of melancholia tried to commit suicide. There was no sleep for any of us after that. Luckily for me my friends came in the morning & brought a rug & some comfort. Next day the Lord Mayor, my friend Lawrence O'Neill came to see me. When he arrived I was hastily shifted into the 'solicitor's room': it was actually a horse-hair sofa & was clean & airy. He thought it 'terrible' nonetheless & was under the mistaken impression, poor man, it was my cell! Next day towards late afternoon two wardresses & 2 plain clothes men came along & bullied me into a waiting cab, served on me en route a 'deportation order' to Holloway Jail for the duration of the war, under our old friend DORA. My guard had refused to tell my sister, Mrs Culhane,[14] my destination, but suffrage friends had been posted to Kingstown pier & when one (Miss Maxwell) came forward to shake hands I slipped to her the order. The cops were upset but could do nothing. Secrecy of this stupid kind is the very marrow of officialdom: it always amuses me to prick the bubble. I was glad to have that parting gleam, for, probably on account of my fast, a melancholy descended on me as we left the pier. I wondered how long it would be before I saw that familiar lovely coast line again. It lay basking in an August sun. I leaned against the rails with my guard close at hand – perhaps on the look out for an attempt to give them the slip. When I went below my wardresses came along & sat beside the berth, the men being outside in the offing. Soda water was offered me – they were kind enough – but I refused. I did not want them to report that I had taken some 'light refreshment', I told them. The crossing was smooth with the usual war-time precautions, dimmed light & the rest. At Holyhead a carriage was reserved for us four & when civilians tried to board it, for the train as usual in those times was crowded, my guard intervened. The wardresses looked like nurses so I said 'I don't mind you coming in but it's not in my hands. I am a prisoner & these are my jailers.' It was funny to watch the scared look come into the passengers' eyes as they melted away. Probably they thought I was a murderer waiting to be hanged or a spy on her way to the tower. At Euston the press was in attendance. I got papers, talked to them & told them where I was bound. There were no taxis. We waited in vain & then my guard asked me did I mind walking a bit as far as a bus or train. Of course I didn't: it was pleasant in the early morning. I said I didn't mind if we travelled all day – Holloway was always there & sure there was no hurry. When we arrived in this leisurely manner there was another snag. My committal order had been given away & they had no document to show the governor! So a lot of phoning had to be done & I sat by waiting. Presently Holloway decided to chance it & I was handed over to the relief of my escort. The matron then conducted me to my friends & I got a cordial welcome & a cheer from Constance Markievicz, Madame MacBride & Mrs T. Clarke. They had been here interned also for the duration, since the previous May when on account of a supposed 'German Plot' all the leaders had been rounded up & sent to jails in England. The three women had won, after the usual struggle, political treatment; they had a wing to themselves, occupying a floor set apart: they had their meals in common, had hospital beds, were allowed books, sewing materials & the like & I think, papers to a limited extent. But they were having no letters & no visits at that time so they were very glad of a new arrival. They told me they had been watching a cell being prepared & knowing it was for some other political (& of course being denied information) Constance Markievicz said – well I hope it's Hanna Skeffington for she can tell us all about America! I had not seen her since Easter Week at the College of Surgeons. She looked thin but fit & was busy as usual – painting, embroidering, writing. Mrs Clarke was sitting for her portrait. Madame embellished life with sketches. Mme MacBride I had not seen for years – she had been living in France when the war broke out. We walked around the little exercise ground or sat about in the sun, I returning to my cell when meals came along (one always smells everything more acutely during a hunger-strike): I could smell the tea coming along the corridor. Normally tea is not smellable. The worst (that is most tantalizing) smell of all is that of a frying rasher. Soup is also pretty trying. Madame Markievicz urged me to give up the hunger strike, saying they meant to forcibly feed me, having all the appliances here (it had been done to many suffragettes in Holloway). I thought they would too & I can't say I didn't dread the ordeal, having heard so much of it already from suffragettes. But, of course, I was going to see the thing through. (I think the authorities had hoped that my friends would persuade me; if so they were doomed to disappointment.) When my friends saw I had my mind made up we dropped the subject & talked steadily for hours on end of Ireland, the war & world affairs. I wanted to be as weak as possible to make forcible feeding harder & walked about to tire myself out. Then to bed & to sleep. Next morning we all went to church. I had refused to answer any questions & earlier the English Catholic chaplain came on a courtesy call. He said he hoped I was not a convert. I told him he needn't bother about that.[15] In church we listened to a long sermon & then a lecture was given on the war situation & we were told how well we were doing.

After service I was summoned to the governor's office. Now for forcible feeding I thought & braced myself to mean it. The governor and doctor were there: I was examined & then the doctor announced that I was being released (under Cat & Mouse of course) & was being conducted by a wardress to whatever address I would remain. I gave the Tower Hotel off Euston Rd – I had stayed there once some years before. The doctor gave me my sugar card. My things were fetched: I asked, but was not allowed to say goodbye to my friends. In a short time I was at the Tower. I knew few in London & did not know my way about. The House was not, I think, sitting, anyhow no Irish Member that I knew were there & darkened, khaki-filled London seemed remote indeed. At first I was too weak to care. I knew the hunger strike technique & came back slowly on liquids, fruit juice & milk. But the latter was a difficulty it & other things were rationed. They had forgotten a milk card. A suffragette Scots friend who called offered to procure this from a doctor. She tried two famous women doctors ('suffs' both who had struck & knew all about it) but they were on war work, having offered their services & they both refused to issue a Milk Order, apparently on patriotic grounds. At last a third woman, Dr Inglis, was found, & she had no such scruples so I got the essential milk.

So days passed: my fortnight would soon be up when I was due for re-imprisonment. I of course meant to skip: my two friends had come from Scotland with a plan & we fixed up all details. But meanwhile at home there had been quite a stir about the whole affair: the Dublin press was on my side (at least the 2 nationalist dailies) & there was much indignation. Lord French was bombarded by his sister Mrs Despard,[16] my old friend & colleague & by mine, Mrs Kettle[17] (whose husband, Tom Kettle, had given his life in the war). Mr Shortt[18] sent Mr McMahon from the Castle to assure my friends that everything was being done for me that could be thought of. That my guard was specially chosen from officers who had frequently arrested me before, could anything have been more considerate, then I would not be forcibly fed & so forth. Mrs Short a kindly Scotswoman had the temerity to offer my sister her London house where I could be looked after, but Mrs Kettle explained that as I meant not to be arrested it would be embarrassing to be under her roof. Mr Short had a fortnight to make up his mind & he wisely decided to give in. I was therefore informed that I could return (at my own expense) to Dublin. Mr Short made a final effort at face-saving by writing to Mrs Kettle to say that I was to reside with her, asking that she saw to it that I met no Sinn Féiners there! This she naturally declined so it was dropped. A neighbour, a Unionist, was approached & asked to keep an eye on me but he too jibbed so the Castle resigned itself to the menace & I came home, not much the worse for the experience. My passport was signed by Philip Snowden, an old friend of Labour days. I recall one play I saw in London at his home – Dear Brutus![19]

1918 – Treaty[20]

After I got home I resumed my ordinary life – taking after a few months a house once more, in Belgrave Road. There was a great scarcity of accommodation & Dublin was feeling the war pinch though our streets were not darkened & our food was comparatively plentiful. I was elected to Executive of Sinn Féin almost at once (I had joined it formally about that time). I was asked by Labour Group (O'Brien and C. O'Shannon)[21] to link up with them but as that meant leaving SF I did not do this as I felt that SF was in the foremost ranks of the fighting front. Later I acted as Hon Sec with Ald T. Kelly to SF & remained on its Executive till the Fianna Fáil split (i.e. up to 1925). With 4 (?)[22] other women I stood for Dublin Corporation & served on that body till it was disbanded by Mr Cosgrave, a curious irony as he had first entered public life by that door. Later I was co-opted (& subsequently elected on County Council Dublin when James McNeill dropped out – story) & I served on that body till Raths was incorporated in the city so in each case circumstances put an end to my career as public representative. The Corp election was held at end of 1918 (?)[23] & under PR (alderman & widow). It was only when women were members of Council that its posts (under competitive exams) were thrown open to women & that children's libraries were opened. These women did good service in their repres. capacity. The Treaty split drove us apart, however, not to meet again.

Once that autumn not long after my return I was arrested with M. F. Connery and H. Molony: we were addressing a meeting in College Green for release of Con. Markievicz (then alone in jail, the other two women having been released on grounds of health). We were held a few hours at the station, Pearse St. but not charged or committed.

Next came in Nov the Armistice (Nov 11, 1918) but for Ireland no peace, in fact Britain was then free to send her military & later the Black & Tans to continue the war at home. A more intense & bitter struggle began. About this time the S.F. courts were set up & did great work. My area was South City with D. Figgis, Neill Watson, Mme MacBride, two priests, Barrd and another. We had a panel from which three were chosen. We met sometimes in York St working men's club, sometimes in Hatch St Hall (Court Laundry). We had no knowledge of law, but registrar supplied that & there was appeal to Supreme Court. Many well known lawyers (Reddin, O'H [*illegible name*], etc) pleaded in our courts & firms such as Barnardo applied. Many cases covered dealt with disputes as to housing between landlord & tenant, also cases such as petty larceny & money got on false pretences or by fraud (furniture in instalment plan disputes) moneylending, minor assaults, personal disputes came up. Usually the women sat in cases regarding women. The decrees were respected, fines collected & often agreement arrived at by consensus (in marriage disputes). Courts were cheap, business done expeditiously & they were popular & respected. They did more to undermine British legal business in Ireland.

We could hear lorries of tans flashing by in the street outside as we met & were all liable to arrest were we caught in the act. But we were never given away. We had no real power to punish or to enforce our judgements but they were respected: the SF police functioned under us.

In that time as never either before or after there was an enthusiasm that had a religious quality: everyone was ready to sacrifice & serve in whatever capacity it was thought best. Many of the leaders were still in jail, those at large were on the run. But secrets were well kept. In the end of the year came the General Election & we were all mobilised at full strength for election work, speaking, canvassing, organising voters – the new women voters first voted that year. Fr O'Flanagan, Vice. Pres. governed and J. O'Mara was director of elections & SF offices were a hive of activity & efficiency. I think the little Ford helped more than any single factor to win that election.

Then came the jail delivery the setting up of Dáil Éireann & its Cabinet with Mme M. its first woman Minister for Labour. It was too much an exact replica of the British Parliament even the use of Hon. Member term was tried tho killed by ridicule. The enthusiasm for the work infected everyone, each dept. had its HQ & all were well & faithfully served. Com. Activity was great – the time we wasted in it – & the sessions lasted hours: often I had to walk home, last trams having ceased. I think the IRB kept its grip on the various Coms. & one often had a sense when voting of decisions previously taken – this was notable when De V. escaped from Lincoln Jail & came home. (Details)[24]

All the local bodies gave allegiance to D. E. & declined to recognise the Local Govt. Board: we were surcharged of course again & again (I owed some £1,000 to Britain by the time I was done) & all this helped to undermine British authority & prestige. De V.'s trip to USA *[end of manuscript]*.

2

WOMEN AND EDUCATION

INTRODUCTION

The issue of Irish women's access to university education in the early twentieth century was contentious for many reasons. At first, the few who succeeded in graduating from the Royal University were those who attended Protestant schools, as the Catholic Church viewed girls' education as the preserve of the religious orders; higher education was a male issue. However, as a small minority of Catholic women began to attend Protestant schools in order to be prepared for university examinations, the Dominican and Loreto Orders began to organise classes and women's colleges were formed to prepare young women for Royal University examinations. The women's colleges were not represented on the senate of the university and neither were they taught by university fellows. When the government appointed the Robertson Commission in 1901 to consider the future of university education in Ireland, it provided the opportunity for women to lobby on their own behalf. The Irish Association of Women Graduates and Candidate Graduates was formed in March 1902, with Alice Oldham as its first president and Mary Hayden its vice-president. The Association argued that women should have the best education possible, and that meant full admission to university colleges. The existing women's colleges and the Catholic Church, on the other hand, argued in favour of the retention of single-sex colleges. In 1904 Trinity College announced it was admitting women students, which had the effect of closing down the college department of Alexandra College as Protestant women chose the new opportunity of a Trinity College education. In 1908 the University Act ensured the dissolution of the remaining women's colleges as the new act established two universities, Queen's University in Belfast and the National University with three constituent colleges in Dublin, Cork and Galway. This gave women total equality with men, not only in teaching but also in the appointment of teaching staff. However, the issue of women's higher education continued to be debated as those who favoured separate education of men and women, such as Norah Meade, an alumna of St Mary's, continued to argue their case.

Hanna was a graduate of St Mary's, the Dominican-run college, having graduated with a BA in Modern Languages in 1899 and receiving a first-class MA in 1902. She therefore had first-hand knowledge of the inferior experience of female students. In addition, she had begun a friendship with Frank Skeffington, who felt so strongly about the issue that in 1901 he had published a pamphlet with his friend James Joyce. Frank's contribution, 'A forgotten aspect of the university question' argued for co-education as a means of fostering comradeship between the sexes. Hanna admitted that her understanding of feminism began as a result of coming into contact with Skeffington and the question of women's right to a university education was the first campaign in which they engaged, together with others who would later be active in the suffrage movement.

Hanna's first article on the question of women and education was a reply to an article by Lilian Daly, published in April 1902. In this Daly had argued that it should be left up to women to decide whether they wanted a university education. She maintained that woman was a help-meet to man and women should not abandon their special domestic sphere, although they should have other spheres opened to them. One of the issues that Hanna was at pains to address was what she considered to be Daly's misreading of the philosophy of John Stuart Mill. In later years she was to tell R. M. Fox (who wrote a short biographical study of her), that Frank Skeffington had talked to her about Mill when they first met. So important was Mill to him that he made Mill the subject of his inaugural address at University College Dublin. Frank had been appointed registrar of that institution, but resigned his post in 1904 when reprimanded for having circulated a petition calling for women to be admitted into the college on an equal basis with men. After that time, Hanna became the main financial provider through her work as a teacher of languages. It was her personal experience of teaching at Catholic schools, where well-qualified graduates like herself were given yearly contracts and lowly wages, often to be displaced by a newly qualified nun, that prompted her article in the *Irish Review* of 1912, taking the opportunity of a government review into secondary education, instigated by Augustine Birrell, president of the Board of Education, to publicise her views.

'Women and the university question'
New Ireland Review 17 (May 1902)
Hannah Sheehy BA
In her paper of last month on this difficult and pressing subject, Miss Daly gave, as her reason for writing, the meagreness of the space allotted her in the queries sent recently to women-graduates for the purpose of eliciting their opinions on important points connected with the University Question. One

might, then, not unreasonably have expected from a woman graduate, giving her views upon the subject, that she would deal with the question upon a broad, practical basis, with clear insight and sympathy, and that some original thoughts might be presented, with the object of helping to the solution of the great problem. Instead, under the guise of impartiality, Miss Daly is, on the whole, unsympathetic, and, while contributing nothing directly bearing on the present aspect of the question, she turns aside in order to go over the whole dreary line of argument common to those hostile to women's higher development. That these statements have been refuted again and again seems but to give them a greater hold; like nine-pins, they are put up, and the game recommences, as if in the hope that, in sheer weariness, they would be left standing – as, indeed, does sometimes occur. After all, a man may be pardoned when prejudice, custom, convention, or professional jealously warps his views. But when a woman, who has had, moreover, all the special advantages of trained thought and careful study, reveals a similar narrow tendency, the case is discouraging, and calls for criticism. That is why I venture on something in the nature of a reply, though necessarily, the subject can be treated only in barest outline. Were Miss Daly's paper allowed to go unchallenged before the public, the readers of the *New Ireland Review* might be justified in supposing that the views put forward by her represented those of many of her fellow-graduates, and were not merely the expression of individual and exceptional opinion – that, in fact, the ordinary woman-graduate came forth from the ordeal physically impaired by her efforts to attain to the masculine level of study, and morally tainted by her pushful competition outside her 'special domestic sphere'.

When Miss Daly states, after this depressing estimate, that, after all, it is not for men to decide the question as to whether or not all rights shall be thrown open to women, and that it should be left to women alone to choose for themselves, the conclusion comes as a distinct surprise. How can such a momentous choice be proposed to women unless they are first carefully trained to think for themselves; and how can this be effected unless they have had opportunities for intercourse with the best equipped and most cultivated minds, until their faculties are quickened by stimulating interchange of ideas, until the many latent possibilities of the individual have been touched and developed in the course of a liberal education? And is not such the object of University life, the essence and supreme good of University culture? To regard a material commercial end as the primary idea of University training, is to degrade and corrupt its ideals, and render it powerless for good. Though, probably, Miss Daly does not for an instant uphold this utilitarian standard in University education, nevertheless, many of her arguments tend that way – else how can the 'lowering of wages' possibly enter into the discussion of the University Question as it affects women? The University degree is surely not an investment, a marketable commodity: with a certain net value to its happy possessor! If University education is true to itself, if it constitutes a fitting preparation for Life, a moulding and a discipline of character and intellect, a cultivation of heart as well as brain, a widening of the individual outlook, a deepening of the individual sympathy, then it has most certainly fulfilled its function in the world. To propose to exclude women from sharing equally and to the full these advantages, which can alone be adequately given through the medium of a University, would not only be ruinous to her own higher development, but would materially affect education generally, by cutting off the refining and ennobling influence of woman at a stage where it is peculiarly beneficial and far-reaching.

The distinction drawn between the equipment of women as women and men as men is specious and misleading. What seems more liable to be forgotten is, not that men and women are different, but that, after all, they both 'belong to the same species of vertebrate animals'. Woman is surprisingly like man in most of her feelings, tastes, desires and antipathies, and the evil has ever been that the differences have hitherto been far too much accentuated by education and convention, thereby producing the highly undesirable idiosyncrasies known as 'feminine' and 'masculine' weaknesses. Woman is thus regarded as a being with needs and interests apart from, if not altogether conflicting with, those of man; whereas the fact is that the interests of the whole race are inseparably bound up in both, essentially the same as affecting each, and touching woman in equal degree with man. Everything human is also her province, and nothing that appertains to the interest of man is alien to her sympathy. How the sentiments of a woman with a mind and heart disciplined and elevated by years of serious study and the literary culture of University, can militate against the 'unity of the home', is not obvious to moralists, or even the ordinary people, though Miss Daly dreads it as a threatening danger.

The paper is unfair to Mill throughout – an example of how far want of sympathy may lead one into error. Mill does not regard woman merely as a help-meet to man, but as an individual entity. He looks naturally to the perfection of the race through the development of woman, but, primarily, she is to him a distinct individuality, at liberty to choose her vocation, and his whole book goes to prove that the fact of regarding woman's sole vocation to be marriage is a radical mistake, pernicious alike to man and woman. He expressly states that those women who would choose public life, would be women who had 'no vocation for marriage, preferring some other employment of their faculties'. This occurs, too, in the last chapter, which Miss Daly condemns as inconsistent with the rest. There is no discrepancy here, nor is there any between Mill's ideal and the means he proposes by which it may be realized. Everything that has been done to remove the disadvantages under which women suffer, both as regards their civic disabilities and their private individual grievances, has justified Mill's attitude, and has been carried out on the same lines that he had originally suggested. Yet, while Miss Daly agrees with Mill's idea, she declares that to carry it out would be absurd.

Men will not stand aside to allow woman her free choice as to whether or not she will enter upon their ground. She must herself strive to attain her desire, step by step, using the already attained in the pursuit of the attainable. An organised public opinion, as well as a bond of sympathy between individual workers – which would subsist apart from all differences on other grounds, merely because all were fellow-workers in a common cause – would do much to help and fortify single effort. Thus, by steady and vigorous organized work, we may obtain all that can be realised at every stage of human progress, without ever losing sight of the great unachieved Ideal.

'Women in universities: a reply by Mary Hayden MA ex. junior fellow RUI and Hanna Sheehy Skeffington MA'
Irish Educational Review, 1908

In replying to Miss Mead's article on Women in Universities we desire to say in advance that we do not wish to undervalue the work done by that talented young lady and that with some of her conclusions we wholly agree. From what, however, appears to be the fundamental idea of her essay, namely, that women seeking a degree in a University, although they should be allowed to enter into competition with men-students, at the examinations should be prepared for mainly by lectures and instruction given in separate colleges by women-Fellows of the University, we felt ourselves obliged entirely to dissent.

We assume that in putting forward this scheme Miss Meade had before her mind the probability of the foundation in Ireland of a new teaching University and expressed her views of the conditions under which women students should be admitted to its teaching and degrees.

Her scheme appears to us, not only undesirable, but under the circumstances with which we have in this country to deal, quite unworkable, if justice is to be done to women-students, so as to enable them to compete on equal terms with men.

The objections urged against mixed classes at Universities have been mainly grounded on mere theory, and have not been generally supported by those who have had real experience of co-education.

When, in 1893, the General Association of Irish Schoolmistresses, who were then urging that the lectures of Dublin University should be open to women, addressed to the 18 professors of the University of Cambridge a series of questions regarding the working of mixed classes, these gentlemen, who had taught such classes for periods of from 10 to 15 years, unanimously declared in their favour. Two only expressed the opinion that the men-students objected to the presence of women in the classes; and several considered that, since women had begun to attend their lectures, there had been a marked improvement in steadiness, seriousness, and discipline amongst their pupils as a whole.

The report of the Moseley Commission on American Education (1902), deals at much length with the subject of co-education, both at schools and in universities; and, though a minority report, makes certain objections to it, the general conclusion of far the greater number of the educational experts to whom the question was submitted was in favour of mixed classes. Want of space renders it impossible to make more than a couple of short extracts from the report.

Dr W. T. Harris, St Louis, upholds mixed education on the grounds of economy (a very important matter for us in Ireland), of discipline, and of the production by it of a better-balanced intellectual development for both sexes.

Dr Jordan (President of Leland Stanford University) says: – 'A woman's college encourages womanliness of thought as more or less different from the plain thinking that is called manly. The brightest work in women's colleges is often accompanied by a nervous strain . . . The best work of men is natural, unconscious . . . in this direction, I think, lies the strongest argument for co-education. Each man, by his relation to action and realities, becomes a teacher of women in these regards, as, in other ways, each cultivated woman is a teacher of men. In woman's education, as planned by women alone the tendency is towards the study of beauty and order. Expression is valued more highly than action. The scholarship developed is ineffective. The educated woman . . . may know a great deal, but she can do nothing. Often her views of life must undergo painful change before she can find her place in the world. In schools for men alone the reverse condition often prevails. The sense of reality obscures the elements of beauty and fitness. It is of great advantage to both men and women to meet on a plane of equality in education. Women are brought into contact with men who can do things. This influence affects them for good. In like manner the association with wise, sane women has its value for young 'men'.

Dr Barnard, President Colombia University, New York, deals at length with the question whether women students are specially liable to overtax their strength when brought into competition with young men in their university course, and decides it is in the negative. He also favours the mixed university on other grounds.

The report of the presidents of many other universities is equally favourable to co-education.

The late Monsignor Molloy, in his evidence before the Robertson Commission, made the following statement: – 'I have taken pains to ascertain whether any practical inconvenience has arisen from having women in our Medical school (Cecilia St, Dublin), and I am informed that there has been none whatever, although the difficulty with us has been specially great, on account of the limitations of our space in relation to the number of our students. That I consider very satisfactory.'

Dr Hamilton, President of Queen's College, Belfast, referring to the attitude of his college towards co-education, says: – 'We have solved the difficulty of their women attending the same lectures as men, or rather, we have found, when we have faced it, that there was no difficulty at all about the matter . . . After an experience of nearly twenty years we are able to say that . . . instead of the admission of women being attended with evil results, either to them or anyone, those results have been all the other way.'

Professor (now Sir H.) Reichel, Principal of the University of North Wales, briefly stated his views before the same Commission as follows: – 'Firstly, a dual college can be worked far more economically than two colleges, and, in a poor country like Wales, if the women were not admitted to the University Colleges their total exclusion from higher education would be the almost inevitable consequence . . . The second point is that, as far as my experience goes, the dual system, if rightly managed, is productive of advantage to both sexes, having a civilising influence on the men, and promoting a more healthy tone in certain respects among the women.'

In 1902, in consequence of some reports received by them, the Central Association of Irish Schoolmistresses addressed to the United States Commissioner of Education, an inquiry as to the working of co-education in America and their secretary received in reply a letter declaring that co-education was a complete success in the States, that all statements to the contrary were 'totally unfounded', that the reports received from Presidents of colleges and universities were 'entirely favourable' to it, and that, in the decade 1891–1901, the number of co-educational institutions had risen from 65.5 per cent of all the schools and colleges to 71.6 per cent.

In this same year the Irish Association of Women Graduates, being desirous, in view of the settlement of the Irish University Question which was then supposed to be pending, to ascertain the views of the women graduates of the Royal University on the position which women should occupy in any new University which might be established, drew up a series of queries which were despatched to as many of the 575 women who had graduated in the Royal University up to that date as could be reached (the addresses of a large number it was not found possible to ascertain). One of the queries enquired whether the graduate would desire in a new university (1) that two of the existing women's colleges should be endowed for the university teaching of women, or (2) that the women and men students should compete together in one college, the teaching to be given either separately or together as the authorities might decide. 300 replies were received to the queries, and of these 279 were in favour of the mixed college.

When the Royal Commission to inquire into University Education in Ireland (the Robertson Commission) was holding its investigations, one of us was commissioned by St Mary's University College, the College which numbers Miss Meade among its students, to give evidence before it. In the statement drawn up with the approval of the authorities and read before the Commission, the following passage occurs: – 'The authorities of St Mary's College strongly urge and earnestly request that all lectures in such a college (i.e., any teaching college that may be founded in connection with the new university) or colleges, all professional schools and all scientific laboratories should be open to women equally and under the same conditions that they are open to men.'

The statement goes on to point out the objections to a separate college for women: that the expense would be almost doubled; that lectures would have often to be provided for very small classes, perhaps for a single student, in courses not generally taken up by women; that many of the Fellows, and these too the most distinguished, would probably refuse to repeat their lectures and that the degrees would never, in the eyes of the outside public, have as high a value as those obtained in a mixed university, so that the graduates, when seeking appointments, would find themselves greatly handicapped.

Miss Agnes O'Farrelly, MA, and Miss McElderry, MA, were appointed by the Women Graduates' Association, of which mention has already been made, and of which the majority of the then women graduates of the Royal University were members, to give evidence in its name before the same Commission. The following is an extract from their statement: – (Evidence given by Miss O'Farrelly) 'I think our Association also wishes distinctly to emphasise this point, that we do not wish, even for pass degrees, lectures in women's colleges to count, as it would lower the value of the degrees . . . As to allowing the women's colleges a certain amount of autonomy and having the Fellows repeat their lectures a second time, that plan is in vogue in Glasgow University and has proved a complete failure. Most of the Fellows refused to go to the women's college. No man very good in his subject will repeat his lectures.' She goes on to say that it had become the custom to send the assistant lecturers only to the women's college, so that the women were deprived of the best teaching, and were consequently very much discontented with the arrangement.

Both the authorities of St Mary's College and the Women Graduates' Association asked that a good endowment should be given to some at least of the existing women's colleges, to enable them to be turned into Halls of Residence for University Students alone. It was pointed out that the present arrangement by which these students were mixed with junior school pupils was not satisfactory. Tutorial instruction could also be given in these Halls, and bursaries provided for students of merit whose means were limited.

As against this consensus of opinion in favour of mixed colleges, we must in fairness mention a minority report against them made by some members of the Mosely Commission; the statement sent in by the Northern Women Graduates' Association to the Royal Commission of 1902; and the evidence of two witnesses before the same Commission. Regarding the first we need only say that absolute unanimity on such a point as co-education could scarcely have been expected, and in this, as in all other matters we must take the view of the majority as, roughly speaking, representing the opinion of the Commission as a whole. As to the others, we must remember that the members of the small Association mentioned above were all past students of one or two women's colleges and the great majority of them teachers while the two lady witnesses were themselves heads of important women's colleges: thus, in the case of each, vested interests were involved.

The Irish Women's Graduates' Association consisted largely of teachers, and the interest of the average woman teacher certainly lies in the direction of the establishment of separate university colleges for women. Yet we find the overwhelming majority of the members of the Association and also one very important women's college (St Mary's) disinterested enough to vote for what they considered the system most beneficial to the education of women in general, irrespective of their own individual advantage.

Evidence given in opposition to the interests of the witness is surely entitled to be held as of special weight.

Having dealt so far with the general question, we should like to consider particularly some of Miss Meade's statements.

She is of the opinion that the small number of women students in French Universities is due to the fact that these universities are mixed, yet she admits that 37,000 girls attend mixed universities in America. A simple explanation of the state of things in France is this, that the idea of university education for women is new in France – a very large proportion of the women students are foreigners – and that the conditions of social life in France, which restrict the liberty of unmarried women in a fashion quite unknown in these countries are against its introduction on a large scale. Our home life in this respect differs comparatively little from that of the Americans.

The proposal that only women Fellows should lecture the women students in their colleges would, if carried out, lead to great unfairness. So far, the women in the Royal University have numbered only about 25 per cent of the total amount of students. Could it be hoped that as large a number of distinguished women would be found among these, as of distinguished men among the remaining 75 per cent? In many subjects women have few distinctions to show. No Junior Fellowship, no Studentship, and few Scholarships have been won by women in the Royal University in either Classics or Mathematics. How could really distinguished teachers be at once provided in these branches in which excellence can only be attained as the result of careful training early begun, to which comparatively small attention is given in most girls' schools, and the study of which the present regulations of the Board of Intermediate education do not certainly tend to encourage any girls.

We desire to see women appointed to Fellowships, but wish that they should obtain them on their merits as scholars, in open competition, without distinction of sex, and that they should deliver their lectures to the men and the women students of a mixed university.

The courses of Domestic Science suggested by Miss Meade would, it seems to us, be quite out of place in a University; though lectures on Hygiene would be of advantage to both men and women students. Elementary 'Domestic Economy' is essentially a subject for the Primary and Secondary schools; beyond this, it becomes a technical subject to be dealt with in special institutions. Does Miss Meade think that a University should aim at producing professional cooks, laundresses, dressmakers? And if so, why not tinkers, tailors and shoemakers?

The statement that 'it is generally the profession of teaching that women have in view in entering on a University career' is, we hold, only partially true even now, and is becoming, we think fortunately, less true year by year. The supply of women teachers already far exceeds the demand and we confidently hope that an increasing number of women graduates will adopt other professional careers, or will marry and as the enlightened trainers and educators of their children work for the social and intellectual benefit of their country in the next generation.

That there is any 'essential difference' in the modes of thought of men and women remains, we submit, Ruskin notwithstanding, to be proved, and, even if there were such a difference, it would not follow that they should be educated differently or apart. Regarding this, Dr E. White, in an article in an American paper (*The National Teacher* June 1872) remarks: – 'The physical organisation of the two sexes is diverse. Does it follow that they require a diversity of food? The mere fact of mental diversity no more necessitates diversity of education than physical diversity necessitates a diversity of food and air.'

As against Miss Meade's opinion that, if boys and girls work together the one will keep the other back, we might cite the testimony of numerous experienced teachers, among them the eighteen Cambridge Professors whose replies to the queries of the Schoolmistresses' Association have already been mentioned. The report of the St Louis public schools (1870) declares that by mixed classes both 'the masculine and the feminine extremes' in teaching and learning are avoided. 'The girls make wonderful advances, even in mathematical studies, while boys seem to take hold of literature far better.'

Miss Meade is certainly correct in stating that girls like to carry on discussions regarding interesting points arising out of their work, while boys show this desire in a far less degree. Such discussions, however, are rarely carried on in class, and would indeed not be possible unless the class were very small. In a mixed college the girls could still during their leisure time in their residence halls, amuse themselves, by arguing on the physical peculiarities of Lady Macbeth, or the state of Hamlet's affections. If, now and then, such a subject cropped up in class, it would do the male students no harm, but rather good, to be obliged to listen for a few minutes to the views of the professor, or of their women classmates. The opinion quoted from Ruskin that girls excel in 'precision and accuracy of thought', especially when taken with Miss Meade's own corollary that they have 'a kind of intuition and clear perception of what exactly is important and what is not', is rather startling, in view of the fact that it is exactly with want of clearness in thought, accuracy in expression, and proper perspective in their views of life as a whole that women have been most frequently, from time immemorial, reproached. Our own experiences as teachers leads us to think that, in as far as there is any difference at all (and this difference is usually apt to be unduly stressed) it is rather the contrary of what Miss Meade states. The girl dwells on details, at times, unfortunately, even on inessential ones; the boy goes more directly to the point, often, however, neglecting to consider the circumstances which alter the case. If the feminine mind has really these excellent qualities which are ascribed to it, how can the generally poor record of women in pure science – mathematics especially – be accounted for? 'Precision and accuracy of thought' are what these studies most require.

Miss Meade considers it not unlikely that girls, if proper advantages be given to them, may at some future time become eminent in classical studies, but that boys have so far beaten them in this branch she does not deny. Yet 'it is quite possible to draw a *strong* (italics ours) line of demarcation between the studies in which boys will excel, and those in which girls of the same age will be superior'. If this be so, how can she look forward to a time when girls will dispute the boys' supremacy in classical lore, and even (as she implies) capture this ancient stronghold of the male sex? Nay, on her own showing, it would seem that any competition between the sexes, even at examinations, is absurd. As a matter of fact, upon close examination, her scheme will thus be found self-contradictory in many vital points.

We have already mentioned the necessity for the liberal endowment, under any university scheme, of Residence Halls for women students. In these

Halls they would enjoy all the advantages of university life, as the men would in their Residence Halls. There would, of course, be clubs and societies connected with these Halls, while other societies might belong to the University itself with membership open to both sexes. Social intercourse of this kind would broaden the views both of the men and the women. Women not intending to take a full university course might be allowed to reside in such Halls and even to assist as 'hearers', at general lectures in the University, a practice which avails in many continental universities. It appears to us that the best ways to convince the incredulous woman of 'the capabilities of her own sex' is, not to segregate women in a separate college, but to show them capable of holding their own with their male fellow-students, not in examinations alone, but also in the class-room, the laboratory, and the debating-society.

Miss Meade's statement that in all the mixed colleges of Wales the boys and girls are not permitted social intercourse with each other is entirely incorrect. In the three constituent colleges of the University of Wales the students meet, work, and chat together as they please within the college buildings, join in class-picnics, etc., and in many of the university societies and clubs – the only restriction being that men and women students, though they may stop and talk in the streets, are not allowed to go for walks together. The women students may receive their men friends in the reception rooms of their residence hall, but may not invite them to their private studies. In most American mixed universities the system is similar. There may be exceptions, but we do not ourselves know of any. Victoria University, Manchester, and the University of Liverpool, allow the students of both sexes practically complete freedom in social intercourse, and it is quite common to see them in the library helping each other in the preparation of their work. Indeed we know of no university anywhere in which such a system of, one might almost say, boorishness, as Miss Meade describes prevails, except Trinity College, Dublin, and even there, we believe, the regulations are beginning to be relaxed. They were very wittily held up to ridicule by a clever young girl undergraduate in a poem entitled 'The Maids of Trinity', which provoked much mirth, even, it is said, amongst the venerable Dons.

Of the statement that we are not of the same temperament as the Americans, and that therefore co-education, although good for them, would be bad for us, no proof is given. Miss Meade seems to imply that, if co-education is to be tried at all, it should begin in the Primary school and be carried right through the whole system. But many of the students of the mixed American universities come from separate schools; many even have had their early training in Europe, being the children of recent immigrants. We have seen, too, that in England and Wales, where practically all the schools are unmixed, co-education in the universities has been tried and proved a success.

Miss Meade declares that co-education is not popular, and adduces as proof of this that, when men's colleges were thrown open to women, few women entered them. Now the only colleges so thrown open until lately were those of Cork, Galway and Belfast. The number even of male graduates in the two former is very small (and Catholic women were forbidden to enter them under pain of excommunication). In the case of Belfast, the college had to contend with long-established women's colleges which of course endeavoured to prevent their pupils from entering, and besides the women were not altogether satisfied with some of the arrangements made for them. Trinity College, Dublin, which opened to women only three years ago, already counts over 70 women amongst its students, and University College, which opened fully about last October, has almost forty women students in regular attendance.

How 'there can be no objection to women attending the general lectures of a University' if there are so many to their attendance at ordinary classes, we fail to see. That 'women taught by women have shown that they can reach the highest standard' does not appear to us to prove anything.

So far we have more or less assumed that a choice between the two schemes, that of an endowed University College or Colleges for women alone, and that of a mixed college or colleges, was open to us, but this is scarcely the case. In order to carry out the former scheme properly, a very large sum would be required, if the colleges were to be properly equipped. Each women's and each men's college should have a complete staff of fellows for each branch: several teachers, mere 'jacks of all trades' would not do here. There should be physical and chemical laboratories, dissection rooms, and so forth. Unless these were fully provided for each, either the male or the female students would be unfairly handicapped and deprived of the full benefits of the University. It requires we think, no special gift of prophecy to foretell on which sex the burden of the injustice would, in actual fact, fall.

One solution of the University question contemplates the foundation of three or four University Colleges, namely, in Dublin, Belfast, Cork and perhaps Galway. If the separation arrangement were carried out, six or eight such colleges would be needed. Where could the immense sums required be found? Would the British treasury suddenly abandon its starvation policy and blossom forth in all liberality without parallel in the history of Irish, or indeed of English education? Such a miracle is scarcely to be expected, nor indeed, for our part, should we desire anything of the kind. If women will not consent to eat at a common table provided for men and women alike, it will, we fear, be their fate to go hungry, or to be obliged to content themselves with a few crumbs and husks flung to them in half-contemptuous charity.

'Irish secondary teachers'
Irish Review, October 1912

Mr Birrell's scheme for improving the position of secondary teachers has arrived barely in time to save the profession – in fact, many will doubt whether it is not just too late. The prospect of a minimum £120 per annum for men, £80 (a still wilder dream) for women with the same or higher qualifications, steady, if laborious, work, and the certainty of half a year's notice, are all propositions startlingly revolutionary in character: the idea, vaguely suggested and timorous, of a register for teachers holds out the further prospect of raising the oldest profession in the world to the dignity of that of medicine, religion, or the law. It is not surprising that the vested interests are up in arms, that the Catholic headmasters and the clerical representatives of the convent schools are clamouring. It behoves sound public opinion to range itself behind Mr Birrell and insist that his scheme for the betterment of a sorely aggrieved class be helped to realisation.

Since the establishment of the Intermediate system in Ireland, it is generally admitted, in spite of extreme critics, that the system, though far from ideal, has improved beyond recognition the general standard of teaching in the schools, that it has benefitted the headmasters and headmistresses by its indirect endowments and the pupils by its direct. One factor in the scheme it has degraded: the assistant lay teachers. Their position is undoubtedly the worse for the Intermediate bounty; their salary has been whittled down to one-third of what it was in pre-intermediate days. In Mr Dale's report the average salary for male assistants was estimated at £80, for female at £40. From my experience I would fix the latter sum at a considerably lower figure for the ordinary convent-school teacher. I have known University graduates – exhibitioners, scholars, gold medallists – accept salaries which a competent cook would have scorned.

The moment an educationist attempts to introduce any test for teachers in Ireland he is threatened with the sad examples of Portugal, France, and other countries that have taken the schools under state control. In no country save Ireland does the belief prevail that a religious vocation *per se* is sufficient induction into the teaching profession, and need not, save by way of painting the lily, be accompanied by any training, mental equipment, or experience. Nor are Irish Catholics the most superstitious in faith-teaching: Irish Protestants who go in for being liberal-minded and have an ultra-sensitive horror of being dubbed bigoted are even more a prey to error. Ireland ought to insist, as England, Germany and every other country has insisted – and most of all Catholic countries where the need is greatest that the religious teacher be submitted to the same tests as the lay, and that no amount of saintliness can be regarded as an educational substitute for a University degree, no more than it would be accepted by the Medical Council or the Benchers of the King's Inns in lieu of medical or legal training. On this basis a register should be set up for teachers in Ireland. Such an attempt of a voluntary kind, assayed under the last Conservative Government (I know not by what Chief Secretary), was opposed effectually and finally stifled by clerical boycott, though the register in England is now a matter of course. I expect that Mr Birrell's scheme is an attempt to follow, though more warily, in the footsteps of his predecessor, and that his discrimination between lay and clerical is dictated by the policy of the line of least resistance.

It has been said that the Birrell scheme works out more harshly against the Catholic than against the Protestant schools. It certainly does: to be effective, it must. The Protestant lay teacher has less clerical competition to face, better chances of promotion and invariably better pay; Protestant private schools, entirely under lay control, are abundant and prosperous. In the case of women especially the advantage is altogether against the Catholic laywoman. The Protestant woman-graduate enters the teaching profession with the fair assurance (especially if she has graduated well) that her career opens with a comparatively well-paid assistantship, with the chance of promotion in due course to principalship. For the Catholic, the private school is practically non-existent; attempts at such usually end in bankruptcy, owing to the enormous competition of the religious orders. Unless she becomes a nun she may never aspire to be head mistress, or even to any minor post of authority or per-manence. If she teaches in a convent, she may be engaged in two ways: as an intern or extern teacher. The former may be a pupil-teacher. Many convents take untrained girls on the '*au pair*' system. In return for their teaching services they obtain tuition in University courses or in other branches from extern professors. It is an abominable system, quite indefensible educationally; but, being cheap and profitable, it obtains widely. Since the establishment of the National University it has received some check, for secondary schools are now happily divorced from University teaching. Mr Birrell ought to have his attention definitely drawn to this condemned remnant of the obsolete truck-system.

Throughout the country the intern system prevails. In return for a fixed sum – ranging from £16 to £40 (my experience deals with University graduates, doubtless other women-interns are offered even less) the teacher devotes practically her whole time to her pupils, teaching, or supervising their studies, eating, playing and walking with them. She keeps convent-hours, and is as entirely shut off from the outer world as if she were herself a cloistered nun. Her tenure of office is usually a yearly one, but may be terminated at any time, without notice. Her salary is not increased as she gains experience, or as a recognition of her class-success. Any kudos gained by her pupils as gold-medallists and exhibitioners does not benefit her or confer any additional security; such prestige belongs entirely to the religious house, of which she is but a cipher. Frequently she instructs the nuns, and, having equipped them in certain subjects, she finds her place filled by her pupils. Sometimes her pupils enter the convent and supersede her. Even if neither of these calamities befall, she often sees herself displaced by a cheaper teacher, who is willing to undercut in order to gain experience. Many convent schools adopt the principle of picking new teachers regularly from the ranks of their brilliant head-girls, to the detriment of the senior mistresses who, fearful of such blackleg competition, dare not ask an increase of salary, and continue to slave for years at the same meagre rate for which they started on their teaching career. This is why many convents object to teachers with an MA degree, and drop them as soon as possible for unfledged graduates; the former usually ask higher rates on attaining the higher degree.

The other method of engagement is payment per hour (from 1s. 6d. to 4s., rarely to 5s.). By this arrangement the teacher gets usually a higher fee, her work cannot be suddenly doubled in midterm without a proportionate increase of pay; but on the other hand, she is at the mercy of various breaks for holidays, convent retreats, feast days, and the like, and generally finds at the end of the school year that, though freer and less sweated, she is not appreciably better off than the intern teacher. Her average is usually £50 to £60, and she is subject to the same fluctuation and accident as her colleague, the intern-teacher, while losing financially on every chance holiday or school festival.

The worst blackleg that intern or extern teachers have to encounter is usually a man! This at first sight seems incredible, for men look on themselves, and (what is more important) get other people, including educationalists, to regard them, as the more expensive sex. The men who undercut the unhappy woman Intermediate teacher are not permanent followers of the teaching profession, as, of course, the latter (male or female) could not afford the luxury. They are usually briefless barristers, living at home and earning cheap pocket-money as unskilled workmen, while waiting to come in for their own at the Bar or on the Bench, civil servants, University undergraduates, helping to pay for their keep by earning ten shillings a week, and incidentally keeping the professional out of a living wage. Sometimes they are Professors holding a well-paid chair in some State endowed college and teaching at nominal rates in order to oblige the reverend mother. This latter scandal has somewhat abated since the establishment of full-time professorships at the National University, but no doubt these things still happen. How often have I and my colleagues (struggling by means of friendly private trade unionism to keep up a uniform standard) been undercut by eminent University professors, journalists and barristers whom I could name, now all, happily for themselves, installed in comfortable official posts, many even then possessing ample professorships and just playing at convent-teaching and feeling philanthropic. One is tempted to ask how trained teachers and graduates allow this state of things to go on? The answer is found in the fate of most women teachers. Either they abandon the teaching profession for less sweated work or they emigrate. In my own brief experience I have helped to equip schools in Australia, New Zealand, America, South Africa, England, and the Continent, with Irish women-graduates, very often the pick of their class. Most Irish secondary teachers obtain posts under County Councils in England; Ireland, as of yore, exports her scholars after exploiting them; her saints she usually keeps at home and provides for out of the public funds.

Men teachers, though their position is pitiable compared with that of any other class, even policemen, have not as great grievances as their sisters, and those grievances have, moreover, greater prospect of being attended to. That is why I am chiefly concerned with the problem of the woman secondary teacher. Even the Birrell scheme, though it will, if allowed by the grudging vested interests to come into force, improve her condition and her prospects considerably, doubling and trebling the present convent average of pay, has not the audacity to regard the education of girls as equally important with that of boys. The woman-teacher's minimum is less by £40, though there is no hint that less will be expected of her. Mr Birrell's National University has recognised the equal value of the work of men and women-professors in its appointments. Women-professors are not paid less than their male colleagues, though many of the higher posts are given to men. Girls who graduate pay the same fees and are awarded the same scholarships and prizes for their work as boys. Why, therefore, when they become teachers of men and women, the scale of pay should discriminate to the detriment of the women, remains an anomaly which educationists ought to remove; it is a remnant of old-fogeydom that Mr Birrell should have outgrown. It is noticeable, too, that no male teacher has lifted a voice in protest against this unfair treatment of his woman-colleague. We shall not hear a word of criticism from men of this part of the scheme. They are obsessed by the idea that men are better paid because they have so many 'dependent' on them – as if a male teacher's pay increased automatically on his marriage or on the birth of his children, or fell off when a maiden aunt ceased to encumber him or when his daughter was taken off his hands! Even on this test of providing for dependents it will be found that women have frequently dependents in the shape of aged parents or younger sisters and brothers, yet statesmen take no recognition of the fact.

Three notable improvements are urgently needed in the Birrell scheme – a pension for secondary teachers, some salutary check on the unpaid-teacher and the unskilled worker, and the establishment of the principle of equal pay

for equal work. Even unamended (for when we women get the vote we shall
see about the latter principle, and so shall our statesmen) it ought to be backed
by every educationist in the country. It is the first brave attempt to ameliorate
the condition of the most harassed and exploited class in the country – the
secondary teacher.

3

WOMEN, THE NATIONAL MOVEMENT AND SINN FÉIN

INTRODUCTION

'Women and the national movement' was Hanna's first writing on the role played by women in the Irish national movement. It was the text of a speech first given to the Young Ireland Branch of the United Irish League, the organisation of the Irish Parliamentary Party. It was deeply personal, reflecting her own experience of the organisation. Male members included Frank Skeffington, her brothers Eugene and Dick, and Tom Kettle and Cruise O'Brien, the latter two soon to be husbands of Hanna's sisters Mary and Kathleen. The *Irish Times* later described it as 'one of the most brilliant of Dublin's coteries'. The lack of enthusiasm evidenced by the parliamentarians for women's participation would contribute to her scepticism regarding the sincerity of politicians and add weight to her conviction that women would continue to count for nothing until they possessed the vote. Even more personal is Hanna's categorisation of young women in terms of their interest in political movements. The description of the girl 'belonging to a Parliamentarian family, whose father or uncle went to prison in the days of the Land League' is undoubtedly herself, someone with 'enthusiasm' but 'never made conscious that she has a part . . . to play'.

The history of the Ladies' Land League and the explanation for their demise was, for her, conclusive evidence that women had no power unless they were 'armed with the vote'. Her enthusiasm for the Ladies' Land League was stimulated by her uncle, Father Eugene Sheehy, 'the Land League priest' who had once shared a platform with Anna Parnell and who encouraged both her studies and her political education. In July 1904, when Hanna informed Eugene that she wanted to research the history of women's political involvement, he immediately invited her to his parochial house so that she could work in peace on what he termed 'the illustrious ladies of this land'. Her fond

47

reminiscence of Eugene, written in 1938, shows her enduring love for her mentor (Chapter 13).

'Women and the national movement' was published in the *Irish Nation*, 6, 13, 20 March 1909. When Inghinidhe na hÉireann began their journal *Bean na hÉireann* in 1908, politically active women had a valuable vehicle in which to argue the issues of the day. A debate had begun, stimulated by a remark contained in a speech by Constance Markievicz, that the objective of the Irish Women's Franchise League bore 'the hallmark of an English agitation'. For her, the vote was useless if Ireland did not have its own parliament. Members of the IWFL wrote in response and many other women joined the debate. Hanna had given birth to her son Owen in May 1909, and was out of action for a time, but by November she was back in the fray and writing a lengthy dissertation on the social, economic and political disabilities suffered by Irishwomen, together with an analysis of their roles in different aspects of the national movement. For Hanna, the vote remained 'the keystone of citizenship'. When a reply was published the following month from 'A Sinn Féiner', describing Hanna as part of 'that section of Irish who do not desire separation, but who merely wish to see Ireland growing more prosperous, quiet and resigned under British rule', she soon returned to the attack, declaring that 'the time for patience and resignation is over', and Irish women would not 'submit in patience because the wrong is inflicted by an alien government'. By 1910 therefore, the differences of opinion between those who put the needs of women first and those who put the nation first, were clearly articulated on both sides.

'Women and the national movement'[1]
19 February 1909

When women were desirous of joining the Young Ireland Branch (the first name suggested, as some of you will remember, was the narrower appellation, 'Young Men's Branch'), at its initiation, the doubt presented itself as to whether women were eligible. Officialdom, I remember, was chary of us; some of us were told we ought to form a 'Ladies' Branch', by all means; but we knew that whatever was the case in the glorious days of the Ladies' Land League, (and even then, when women had done the work they were set aside) Ladies' Branches of the UIL chiefly existed for social purposes, their main duty being apparently to present valuable pieces of lace, of Belleek ware, to the wives of leading politicians, they had no voice in the choice of delegates to Conventions or Executive, no powers in the management of the organisation. Besides, most of us Young Irelanders had been brought up in different traditions; in the Gaelic League, for example, as well as in many branches of our education, in medicine and in other careers, women had been accustomed to work side by side with men, and refused to see that any good purpose was served by sex-segregation. Accordingly, after an initial meeting of the YIB, at which there was a good deal of trumpet-blowing (I speak from hearsay; I don't think any women were present), and appeals to the young intellect (altogether male) of Ireland to rally round this new centre of nationalism, this nursing-ground of politicians, a formal business meeting was announced and young <u>men</u> interested were cordially invited to come and join. There has been a rumour lately to the effect that there is nothing in the constitution of the UIL to exclude women from joining the ordinary branches. The exclusion indeed seems to have been one of precedent purely, but that this precedent is firmly established is manifest by the manner of our own foundation. Several of us students determined to put the matter to the test, and invaded the League offices on the occasion of the second meeting, plonked down our entrance fees to an amazed official, who, though visibly reluctant and embarrassed, did not openly refuse us, murmuring something of course about a 'Ladies' Branch', which we ignored. Once formally enrolled as members our position was firmer; still we had a struggle (supported, I thankfully add, by many, though not all, of the men), before our state was assured. I have ventured on this piece of Branch-biography partly for the benefit of the younger members, partly to illustrate the anomalous position of women in the National Movement, or, to be more correct, in the Parliamentarian movement. Our Parliamentary section of Irish politics is, curiously, in this respect the most backward. Women are welcomed in Sinn Féin, in the Gaelic League (and this is probably due to the renascence of older, Irish traditions, wherein women shared as a matter of course every phase of the community's life) they are influential; and their aid is courted in whatever Unionist political life exists, – though here their influence is less direct, and consequently less valuable, for an English tradition is followed. Why women have been so completely ignored in the later phases of Parliamentary nationalism it is not possible to determine accurately. Personally I am inclined to attribute it partly to the absence of the vote (politicians have but little time to waste on the voteless), and partly to the less tangible, but none the less baneful, influence of certain party-leaders who temperamentally are wont to ignore women save as ornamental social factors. Whatever the true cause may be (and I hope in the debate to follow that more light may be thrown on this psychologically dark issue), the growing estrangement between Irishwomen and the Parliamentary Party is now acute, almost to alienation. Possibly the last to realise this will be the leaders themselves; kings, crowned or uncrowned, do not hear the opinion of the people through their courtiers, and, I fear, Haroun-al-Raschids are all too rare in modern days. When I look around among the younger generation of women Nationalists, I am struck by the fact that though according to the Gilbertian dictum: 'Every little boy or girl that's

born into this world alive, is either a little Liberal, or else a little Conservative',
the boy in the parliamentary nationalist family is usually by birth a Parliamentarian (though the defections are many even here, other political parties,
fascinating by their more direct appeal to youthful enthusiasm), the girls, in
99 cases out of 100 fall into one or other of the following categories: (1)
'No-interest-in-politics', – which in Ireland means shoneenism, fashionable
young-ladydom of the castle-haunting, anti-tuberculosis variety); or (2) Gaelic
League, – the type, as admirable one in its way, but not ideal, of 'follow-the-
Irish-language-and-all-these-things-shall-be added-unto-you'; and (3) the
Gaelic League plus Sinn Féin – among the women that I know (and as teacher,
student, and one interested in women as women I think I can claim to know
many varieties) the last is the best type. Then here and there may be a girl
belonging to a Parliamentarian family, whose father or uncle went to prison in
the days of the Land League, whose mother or aunt was one of the young
enthusiastic band who centred round Fanny Parnell and chanted as a cradle
song her 'Hold the Harvest', whose grandfather hid Fenians in hay-lofts or
concealed arms (destined, alas! never to be used) among her spinning-flax, –
such a girl will have had her enthusiasm stirred by the family sagas, but how
can her enthusiasm be utilised ere it be atrophied or is alienated? There is no
place for her in present-day Parliamentarians. She is never made conscious
that she has a part, however humble, to play in the National movement. The
branches of the organisation throughout the country do not recruit for her aid.
She may certainly, if her pocket-money allows her, contribute to the parliamentary party; she may sit in a gallery, if her place is not wanted for more
important people, and look on at a banquet given in honour of some leader (it
is a quaint rule of 18th century barbarians, which survives only among politicians
in this country, and which has often amused us women-spectators as politics,
to refuse to admit ladies as ordinary guests at these party-feasts); and when a
National Convention is held, she is finally made aware of her obscurity and
uselessness by being denied even a spectator's place at national deliberations.
So far, indeed, has the UIL lagged behind the common life of today, that in
one case, at the recent Convention, where a woman was imprudently chosen
as delegate of a branch in Westmeath, though duly accredited, she was excluded
as a woman, and the branch that had the temerity to choose her summarily
disenfranchised for its action! 'pour encourager les autres' we must suppose.

I remember reading of a curious parallel to the above in the treatment
accorded to women delegates who were chosen to represent some American
States at the great Anti-Slavery Convention held in London in 1840. These
distinguished American women, who had taken a prominent part in the
Abolition movement, were, on coming to England, to their amazement,
excluded by the organisers of the Congress, after a fierce debate. This exclusion,

an illuminating object-lesson to women of the slight esteem in which they were held in public life, led to the secession of some delegates from the Congress, and to the formation of the first woman's suffrage society in England.[2] I think the women were wise who straightaway drew the moral from the slight; it was their voteless condition, and no other cause, that shut them off from even a rescuing share in a great humanitarian movement. I should be thankful if, after more than half a century, the Nationalist women of Ireland in their turn realised, while the smart of their exclusion, even as visitors, from the National Convention is still poignant, that until they pass from the ranks of the voteless, until they rise from the category of lunatics and felons, they will not be permitted to take even a dilettante share in national struggles. This I hold to be particularly true of the parliamentary movements, (whether Nationalist or Unionist), because the influence of environment is notoriously all but all-powerful; and members returned to a male Parliament by males, shut in by the male-club atmosphere which pervades the House of Commons, are naturally predisposed to discount the influence of women in public life, and not only to ignore her point of view as the necessary complement to their own masculine outlook, but to doubt her helpfulness as a factor in progress towards national ideals.

Now, Sinn Féiners may ask, if the vote is all-important how have Sinn Féin women held their own without it hitherto? There is much virtue in the 'hitherto'! Sinn Féin is, theoretically at any rate, a revolutionary party, and as such disdains no enthusiasm, no help, whence-so-ever it comes. In revolutionary parties in their infancy and their struggles (in France and in Russia for instance) women have always been welcomed, possibly by reason of their inherent taste for martyrdom, a crown never denied their womanhood once it enters the lists. It is when parties grow circumspect through partial success and line up their ranks after the fight and the dust for the parade that woman falls naturally out of step and is duly left behind. Modern Finland I must in passing point out as the valiant exception that proves this rule. Finnish women fought side by side with their brothers for national independence, when it was wrested from Russia the men of Finland saw no reason why the women who had shared the heat of the struggle should not be admitted to full rights of citizenship. So Finnish women can not only return males to parliament, but can be represented themselves, and are returned to Parliament by the various parties in the state. But this is by way of digression; one swallow, we know, does not make a summer. I personally prefer to take my cue from the more general human experience, and, while I honour the party that admits equality, I too wonder whether Sinn Féin men, if tried by success and forced to more constructive policies, may not, as other advanced parties have done, tend to lose sight of the women who helped when friends were fewer. Perhaps, however, the wilful remoteness from Parliamentarian traditions may serve to prevent this consummation. I hope a Sinn Féin woman, if present, will deal with this point, for it is one of considerable interest. I have of course, heard male Sinn Féiners speak very confidently on the subject, and theoretically they are sound, but one must be pardoned if one is sometimes disposed to question the soundness of their practice. I have met Sinn Féiners and Gaelic Leaguers whose attitude towards women in public life would bear considerable amendment.

Parliamentarians in their palmy days did not neglect the help of women. You all know the story of the brave women of Young Ireland and the women contributors to the *Nation*;[3] but I may be pardoned if I presume that the part played in the constitutional fight by the women of the early Land League is not so well-known to the men and women of the present generation as it deserves, partly because more recent history is ever less attended to, being somehow devoid of the glamour that years accumulate round great fighting figures, partly because of the unheroic end of the early Land League visions in the ignoble Kilmainham Treaty,[4] which proved the death-blow both to the Ladies' Land League and to the forward fighting policy as advocated by Davitt, in contradistinction to the more cautious opportunism of Parnell.

How many of you, I wonder, could recite that 'Marseillaise of the Irish Peasant', as Davitt calls it, Fanny Parnell's 'Hold the Harvest'? A poem which, when read in court at the State Trials of the Land Leaguers formed one of the chief documents against the League.

> Now, are you men, or you kine
> Ye tillers of the soil?
> Would you be free, or evermore
> The rich man's cattle toil?
> The shadow on the dial hangs that points the fatal hour –
> Now hold your own! Or, branded slaves,
> Forever cringe and cower.
>
> The serpent's curse upon you lies
> Ye writhe within the dust,
> Ye fill your mouths with beggar's swill
> Ye grovel for a crust;
> Your lords have set their bloodstained heels
> Upon your shameful heads,
> Yet they are kind – they leave you still
> Their ditches for your beds!

Oh, by the God who made us all –
The seigneur and the serf –
Rise up! And swear this day to hold
Your own green Irish turf;
Rise up! And plant your feet as men
Where now you crawl as slaves,
And make your harvest-fields your camps,
Or make of them your graves.

The birds of prey are hovering round,
The vultures wheel and swoop –
They come, the coroneted ghouls!
With drum-beat and with troop –
They come, to fatten on your flesh,
Your children's and your wives';
Ye die but once – hold fast your lands,
And if ye can your lives.

Three hundred years your crops have sprung,
By murdered corpses fed:
Your butchered sires, your famished sires,
For ghastly compost spread;
Their homes have fertilised your fields,
Their blood has fallen like rain;
They died that ye might eat and live –
God! Have they died in vain?

But God is on the peasant's side,
The God that loves the poor;
His angels stand with flaming swords
On every mount and moor.
They guard the poor man's flocks and herds,
They guard his ripening grain;
The robber sinks beneath their curse
Beside his ill-got gain.

'The reading,' says Davitt, 'electrified the crowded audience, and applause which could not be suppressed burst forth as the last stanza, with its fine appeal to the God of the poor, gave expression to Ireland's awakened hope to wrench the soil in one supreme struggle from the hands of the *[illegible word]* confiscation.' If the gift of writing the ballads of a nation is to be preferred to that of drawing up her laws, Fanny Parnell did more than many of our legislators in her passionate lyric utterance of a nation's agony.

But the women of the Land League did more than write ballads. Hear how the Ladies' Land League came into being shortly afterwards. Again I quote Davitt's *Fall of Feudalism*, abbreviating slightly. Davitt's attitude towards women, as contrasted with that of some of the leaders who survived, is interesting. Coming from the greatest Irish revolutionary of our time, his view of women as ideal stuff for revolutionaries is particularly enlightening. A council of war, he relates, was held after the State Trial by Parnell, Davitt, Dillon, Egan and Brennan. All knew that immediate arrest was in prospect for all the leaders. There would be wholesale proclamation of meetings, wholesale evictions. With the leaders in prison, how was the fight to continue? 'The formation of a Ladies' Land league on the plan laid down by Fanny Parnell in New York was proposed. This suggestion was laughed at by all except Mr Egan and myself (writes Davitt), and vehemently opposed by Parnell, Dillon, and Brenann, 'who feared we would invite public ridicule in appearing to put women forward in places of danger . . . we were engaged in a virtual revolution. No better allies than woman could be found for such a task. They are in certain emergencies, more dangerous than men. They have more courage, through having less scruples, when and where their better instincts are appealed to by a militant and a just cause in a fight against a mean foe . . . The courage and constancy of Irish women could not be better employed than in the task of carrying on this fight after the male leaders were sent to jail.' 'Would you have girls sent to prison too?' was asked. 'Certainly in such a cause, why not? Moreover, what of the effect this would have on the public opinion of the United States and the world if 50 or 100 respectable young women were sent to jail as "criminals" without trial or conviction, by England's rulers in Ireland.'

Miss Anna Parnell was consulted on the plan and approved, and finally Dillon and Parnell gave a 'passive assent' to the scheme. Davitt goes on to relate how the organisation was started, and shows how when the men went to prison the women held the fort and stirred up fresh enthusiasm, carrying out alone the whole weighty work, the housing of the evicted, the keeping alive of agitation, the holding of meetings, the forming of branches. The Ladies' Land League became in time a greater terror than the male Land League, and its leaders inspired Forster with a dread passing in our days even a Liberal Minister's dread of Suffragettes. It is curious, by the way, to observe how parallel these two militant movements are; the Suffragettes acknowledge that their destructive policy was suggested by that of Parnell, but they are perhaps unaware of the closeness of their likeness in methods and inspiration to those pre-Suffragette valiant ladies of the Ladies' Land League. Enthusiasm is immortal, and though the later history of the Ladies' Land League is saddened, and overshadowed, perhaps it too was one of those glorious failures, more illuminating than any 'low success', that lead, phoenix-like, to larger triumphs of a larger day.

To complete the Suffragette parallel, numerous arrests were made among the enthusiastic young women of the Land League – one may always count upon the English Government fostering revolutionaries in this way, without distinction of sex – each arrest bringing, as usual, fresh recruits. Refusing bail to keep the peace (how familiar the device!) women were imprisoned for periods of three to six months. The reading in Hansard of the questions in Parliament on the arrest and prison treatment of those women make one rub one's eyes for wonder, so like are they to modern newspaper reports re the Suffragettes. Take this, does it not suggest our valiant Herbert, Hon Secretary? – it is Forster's answer: – 'Then an action is taken up by a magistrate, it is done on his own responsibility, and it would be a most serious matter to suppose that I, as representing the executive, have power to interfere with the action of magistrates.'

This was in 1881. Truly as of the Bourbons might it be said in 1909 of the Liberals that they have learned nothing and forgotten nothing – by the way our immortal Edward III hereto proves as truly a friend to Liberalism as in the days of *[illegible word]* and Farrells and such like 'rogues' as T. P. O'Connor well says in his 'Parnell Movement', this answer of Forster (I had almost said Gladstone) is 'a trick venerable in the history of despotism. The magistrates who were carrying out his work in Ireland were as much the servants of Mr Forster as the smallest messenger in his office . . . And these were the gentlemen from interference with whom Mr Forster shrank with the delicate respect for constitutional forms which he was displaying in so many ways at that moment.' The women of the Land League suffered far more severely than the men (again I quote T. P. O'Connor) 'The prisoners (male) under the Coercion Act were allowed to have communication with each other for six hours out of every day. The young ladies sentenced by Clifford Lloyd were in solitude the entire day. In the prisons in which they were placed were none but the degraded of their own sex.' Thus we see that Buckshot Forster and his minions recognised, like Davitt, that women were the more dangerous revolutionaries, and dealt with them accordingly. Davitt beheld his tribute justified. To use his own words: – 'Under the very nose of Mr Forster and in utter defiance of his most strenuous application of the arbitrary powers at his disposal, everything recommended or done in the way of defeating the ordinary law, except the holding of meetings, was more systematically carried out under the directive of the ladies' executive than by its predecessor.'

The Ladies' Land League finally brought Forster to his knees, but, unhappily for itself, it had achieved so complete a success that it could be the more easily dispensed with. A fine instrument, so long as a dangerous instrument was needed, it threatened to become a two-edged sword when compromise with England filled the air. Davitt was safe in Portland; more subtle-minded politicians came to a deal in the fatal Kilmainham Treaty, as a result of which the sword was laid too soon aside in sight of the victory, and the Ladies' Land League too prematurely and high-handedly disbanded by Parnell. Then in May 1882 the fatal blunder of the Phoenix Park murders threatened to undo the work wrought by more peaceful and successful methods of boycott and no-rent agitation. England had one of her bad fits of nerves, and found it convenient to associate Parnellism and crisis, in spite of horror-stricken protests from the party itself, all too sensible of the consequences of the fatal step; and presto! Coercion reigned supreme once more in Ireland. But ere this the power of the revolutionary part was broken, and the golden moment for pressing home the victory gone for ever.

What concerns me for the moment, however, is the death of the Ladies' Land League. What a tragedy that the fine enthusiasm, the generous spirit of co-operation revealed by those noble-hearted women should be so lightly diverted, repressed, ultimately lost for ever to the cause of nationalism. For with the death of the women's organisation, there being no effort by a further reorganisation to maintain for Ireland the fine reserve forces so called up, either in a new league under new conditions or (better still) by encouraging women to enter and strengthen the ranks of the male branches, women lost touch with Parliamentarianism and have never since regained it. Since then, as I have already shown, their energies and enthusiasm have been turned to other channels, their force is expended in directions indifferent to or hostile to Parliamentarianism. One is too near to one's own epoch to judge it properly, but it will be a matter of wonderment to a future historian of Ireland to note the silence imposed on Irishwomen from the early eighties down to the dawn of the twentieth century. As to the future, who can say whether the women of Ireland will ever again throw in their lot with parliamentarianism, or devote themselves exclusively to the language movement and Sinn Féin? Perhaps (and better or maybe) they too may realise at length that to make their help and co-operation in any cause permanent and solid, and not a mere parasitic growth on male strength or male weakness, they need before all to build, not on the shifting quicksands of men's sufferance, but on the basic rock of citizenship; that, until that essential to healthy civic life is granted, they cannot count at their full worth in any cause. Till armed with the vote, women, after all, are but timid watchers of the fight from behind buttressed walls; they may make desperate sorties, it is true, but these will be the exception; their position in the fray will continue to be a hazardous and unequal one, subject to more than their share of penalties of the strife, harvesting none of the honours of war.

It will, therefore, be a fortunate thing for Ireland when her women are admitted to full citizenship, aye even though it be by an alien and grudging parliament. The party that enfranchises them, or helps them to attain enfranchisement, may, it is true, be making thereby a blind 'act of faith in the future'; but a party that lives firm-rooted in true ideals of self-government can afford (and it alone can) to make these acts of faith. It will not (in the nature of things it cannot) count all its women new-made citizens in its ranks; – women will divide into political parties as inevitably as men; – but it will have done a great thing for the cause of freedom by widening horizons, throwing open new vistas for endeavour, and its act will ultimately bring its full reward. A party that is truly representative of the people can always afford to appeal to a wider franchise; a party at heart hostile to popular demand, and rooted on force and confiscation, may well be chary of casting down barriers, levelling obstacles.

Will the Irish party be bold enough to make this act of faith and help the citizenship of women? Save for its own sake, it scarcely matters, for that hour cannot now be long delayed. For myself I have sufficient faith in my own countrywomen and in Ireland to look forward to their emancipation as marking a glorious epoch for the nation, and promising a mighty recrudescence of the national spirit, a fresh enkindlement from their new-awakened enthusiasm, that will not lightly suffer extinction, once enflamed.

I cannot better finish my paper (with apologies for my digressions and incoherencies throughout) than by again quoting from the poetess of the Land League one of her finest if most poignant lyrics, 'After Death', written within the valley of the shadow of her early death in 1882. It portrays to me a double wistfulness, that of the ardent patriot hearing at freedom's dawn the call to a shadowland, that of the woman 'whose soul's in fetters too', summonsed by death just as she glimpses a prospect of sex-emancipation. As freedom for Ireland and freedom for women are the gift of the future, the words of Fanny Parnell may strike a sympathetic echo for us even now.

Shall mine eyes behold thy glory, oh my country,
Shall mine eyes behold thy glory?
Or shall darkness close around them, ere the sun-blaze
Break at last upon thy story?

When the nations ope for thee their queenly circle
As a sweet new sister hail thee,
Shall these lips be sealed in callous death and silence
That have known but to bewail thee?

Shall the ear be deaf that only loved thy praises,
When all men their tribute bring thee?
Shall the mouth be clay that sang thee in thy squalor?
When all poets' mouths shall sing thee?

Ah! The tramp of feet victorious! I should hear them
'Mid the shamrocks and the mosses,
And my heart should toss within the shroud and quiver,
As a captive dreamer tosses.

I should turn and rend the cere-clothes round me,
Giant-sinews I should borrow,
Crying, 'Oh my brothers, I have also loved her,
In her loneliness and sorrow.

Let me join with you the jubilant procession,
Let me chat with you her story:
Then contented I shall go back to the shamrocks,
Now mine eyes have seen her glory.

'Sinn Féin and Irishwomen'
Bean na hÉireann, **November 1909**

We all, Unionists and Nationalists alike, live overmuch on our past in Ireland. Our great past condones our empty present, and seems to deprecate, instead of stimulating endeavours. Living thus in our past, one is apt to over-draw one's bank account. This tendency is nowhere more aptly illustrated than with regards the position of Irishwomen in the Ireland of to-day. Nowhere in the pitiful tangle of present-day life does the actual more sadly belie the far-off past. It is barren comfort for us Irishwomen to know that in ancient Ireland women occupied a prouder, freer position than they now hold even in the most advanced modern states, that all professions, including that of arms, were freely open to their ambitions (indeed, 'open' is scarcely the word, for it implies concession whereas the right seems never to have been questioned) that their counsel was sought in all affairs of state. That 'in the humane ideal of Irish civilization' (to quote from Mrs Green's 'Making of Ireland and its Undoing'), 'women were called to public duties of conciliation and peace'. Let the Irishwoman who doubts herself turn to these records for inspiration, but not for mere complacency, for if ever the theory of *'noblesse oblige'* held good in its best sense it is here it ought to be vindicated by the descendants of such ancestresses. Our ancestresses were the state-recognized arbiters in matters under dispute between rival factions, forming a final court of appeal, a permanent Hague Tribunal.

'Where is it now, the glory and the dream?' Does the vision of the past mitigate the abject present? Is the degradation of the average Irishwoman the less real, her education sacrificed to give her brothers ampler opportunities of having a good time loitering through their examinations in the capital, her marriage a matter of sordid bargaining, broken maybe because an over-insistent prospective father-in-law demands a cow or a pig too much, her 'fortune' (the word is significant and the fortuneless had better never have been born) instead of being, in French fashion, sensibly settled on her and her children, handed over blindly to her husband to dispose of it as he may think fit, it may be to pay his racing debts, or, if he is a generous brother, to endow a sister for the matrimonial marker, or to equip an aspiring brother for the priesthood. Whatever its uses, the bride's portion belongs irrevocably to the husband's family.

I have chosen but a few salient examples to illustrate the disabilities Irishwomen suffer today. The result of Anglicization? This is but partly true; much of the evil is, however, inherent in latter-day Irish life. Nor will the evil disappear, as we are assured, when Ireland comes to her own again, whenever that may be. For until the women of Ireland are free, the men will not achieve emancipation. It is for Irish women, therefore, to work out their own 'Sinn Féin' on their own lines, for with the broader, non-party aspect of Sinn Féin – namely, the reformation from within, outwards all Nationalists have always been in agreement.

The Irishwoman has far to go before achieving her destiny. At present she counts for less in her own land than does the Englishwoman in hers (time and again the Englishwoman has forced her point of view on reluctant legislators, and we may expect her one of these days to wrest the vote similarly from her countrymen). First, as the Englishwoman counts less to the nation than the Frenchwoman, and as the Frenchwoman is a harem-slave compared with her American sister, so in the scale of civilization the Irishwoman comes somewhere between the Oriental woman and her more advanced Western sisters.

Many vested interests (notably that of the publican) are openly opposed to any broadening of woman's horizon in Ireland. Public opinion, educational fallacies, convention militate against her assuming her rightful place in public life. In the Gaelic movement, in the Industrial revival and in the Sinn Féin organization she has undoubtedly made her power felt. So much the better for the movement. The reason, however, is obvious; it is not due, as many would have us believe, to a reversion to the older Irish (for the individual in all these movements is as narrow as his presumably less enlightened brother), but rather because of the nature of the work involved. The Gaelic League must make its final appeal to the young, unless those to whom the very beginning are entrusted to take up Irish it will surely perish. So too with the Industrial revival – it is the woman who looks after the domestic budget, her voice can make or mar Irish Industrialism. Therefore, it is primarily in her capacity as mother and housekeeper, not as individual citizen, that these movements have of necessity recognized her importance. After all, as a wag has put it, 'woman is matchless as wife and mother'. No male has ever denied her these onerous privileges, and for that very reason the average male would see her confined to these purely incidental avocations. That is why, doubtless, many worthy Gaelic Leaguers get restive at the thought of women having places on the Executive Body, that is why, too, in spite of theoretical equality, some Sinn Féiners have not yet rounded Cape Turk where women are concerned. One of the leaders afforded an interesting object-lesson to his women colleagues in the move-ment by founding university scholarships from which girls were expressly excluded. Irishwomen may be excused, therefore, if they distrust all parties in Ireland, for what I have said of the Sinn Féin organization applies with far greater force to the Parliamentarian movement which, since the extinction of the Ladies' Land League in the eighties, has steadily ignored Irishwomen, hitherto indeed with impunity. It is for Irishwomen of every political party to adopt the principle of Sinn Féin in the true sense of the word, and to refuse any longer to be the camp-followers and parasites of public life, dependent on caprice and expediency for recognition. It is for Irishwomen to set about working out their political salvation. Until the Parliamentarian and the Sinn Féin women alike possess the vote, the keystone of citizenship, she will count but little with either party, for it is through the medium of the vote alone that either party can achieve any measure of success. This is a fact of which we parliamentarians have long been aware to our cost, but which Sinn Féin women have yet to learn.

'A reply to some critics'
Bean na hÉireann, February 1910
It seems to me that some reply to my recent critics in the December and January numbers of your paper is necessary. I do not think a 'Sinn Féiner' can have given any serious thought, either to the question of Woman Suffrage in particular or to the other problems of democracy raised in the article. A vote, according to this writer, is the last word of British dominion – in registering a vote for a Parliamentary or Sinn Féin Nationalist as against, say, Mr Walter Long, or the Marquis of Hamilton, the voter (male or female) is bartering freedom 'for a mess of pottage, joining with our country's conquerors and worse enemies' and so forth. Such a tissue of inaccurate thinking can only be dealt with by a few straight facts, platitudes, it is true, but platitudes that seem

in danger of being forgotten when flamboyant rhetoric is indulged in to the detriment of truth.

First, the vote does not bear the British hall-mark. It is a mistaken piece of generosity on the part of 'Sinn Féiner' to ascribe its invention to Englishmen, and a true Sinn Féiner ought to be the first to quarrel with that view. The Romans valued the Jus Suffragii as the apple of their eye, the Independent States of America are known to exercise it without prejudice to their liberty, and in most European States where any measure of democracy prevails in the government the free citizen registers his opinion by means of the vote. If Ireland were entirely freed from the Saxon tomorrow (and let me say by way of personal explanation that it is my ardent hope that she will one day be so) we would still, no doubt, until someone devised a readier and fairer method, continue to exercise the privilege. The vote, therefore, is not intimately bound up with the British Empire and is quite distinct from the Union Jack, Rule Britannia, and other peculiarly characteristic features of the Empire on which, as we are aware, the sun refuses to set.

Let me point out also that, waiting the hour of Ireland's freedom, we all see ourselves compelled to submit, however much *à contrecoeur*, to the outward symbols of British rule. The most ardent nationalist stamps his letters with the head of King Edward, pays for his morning newspapers in coin of the British realm, drinks tea which has been taxed so that Dreadnoughts may uphold British supremacy on the seas, and so throughout his day tacitly submits to alien rule. It is regrettable, no doubt, but the machinery of life must run on somehow and we are not strong enough in Ireland yet for a general strike. So the nationalist who would refuse to apply for an Old Age Pension on the grounds of patriotism would be acting in a very misguided manner, just as the woman who possesses the municipal vote would be guilty of a grave dereliction of duty if she abstained from voting under the delusion that the vote was a British institution. In this connection I need only refer unbelievers to the Sinn Féin organ which urged in the recent Municipal elections the duty of voting on every duly qualified woman. Surely then if a Sinn Féin candidate were to present himself for parliament as against, say Mr John Redmond, the woman Sinn Féiner equally with her male fellow-countryman, far from tainting her soul thereby, would help her party more effectively by recording her vote?

A 'Sinn Féiner' goes on to admit that 'Englishwomen are . . . infamously treated, having to obey laws equally with men without the feminine point of view being represented in the Government or the law court', being paid less than men for the same work and so on. But do not Irishwomen suffer precisely the same disabilities? Are we in Ireland tried by female judge and jury, or Irish teachers paid the same whether men or women? In this case the grievances Irishwomen suffer are identical with those suffered in all countries where women have no vote, in France and Germany, as well as in England. True, we Irishwomen suffer a two-fold tyranny, the tyranny of an oppressing race as well as the tyranny of an oppressing sex, but I have never heard that two tyrannies were easier to bear than one. Nor do I think that if Ireland's liberty were to be granted on condition that the present situation between the sexes were reversed, (that Irishwomen alone had the right to vote, the right to sit on juries and on the Bench, and possessed all the privileges that citizenship now confers on men) Irishwomen would care to have it at such a price. And Irishmen would, no doubt, be right. We women know too well the disastrous effect of sex tyranny to blame them.

I think I have shown therefore, that Irishwomen, whatever their political party, are justified in putting Sinn Féin principles in practice and setting about working out their own political salvation first. That achieved, all the rest will be added unto them. Without that, their aid to any party is valueless; their influence, because indirect, is detrimental.

I agree with so much that Mr John Brennan[5] says in his article on the subject of the training of Irishwomen, that I am quite at a loss to discover what his grievance against the Irish Women's Franchise League is. It aims also at political and educational propaganda, and a Tuesday evening spent in the Antient Concert Buildings, our headquarters, would, I think, effectively dispel his doubt as to whether we do anything but 'reiterate our demand for equal rights'. He advises the League to set up a feminine counterpart to St Enda's – a most laudable and necessary work, no doubt, but not within the province of a Suffrage Society. I might as reasonably ask the Editress[6] of this paper to abandon her editor's chair for a rostrum. Besides, I need hardly remind Mr Brennan that the schoolroom is not the only place where ideas are promulgated – in fact, though I myself belong to the teaching profession and cannot therefore be accused of prejudice or ignorance in the matter, I should be inclined to say that it is often the last place to which a new idea penetrates, that, in fact, it is only when the idea has lost the edge of newness it is deemed safe for the youthful intelligence to manipulate.

With an 'Old Fashioned Nationalist' I find myself in complete agreement especially in his denunciation of the ideal sometimes idly held by well-meaning Sinn Féiners of the Kings, Lords and Commons of Ireland and its restoration. But what does he mean by 'the power to vote (but not the English Parliamentary vote) is the hall-mark of citizenship'. As well might he declare under present conditions: 'The halfpenny stamp (but not the English halfpenny stamp) is the key which throws open the postcard to free circulation within the British Isles.' Neither do I entirely agree that the 'barrier to women's freedom is not a legal one, but only ignorant prejudice which will crumble away if women prove that they can take an intelligent view . . . of the needs of their country'. Surely Irishwomen have always abundantly proved a devotion to Ireland equal to that of Irishmen and yet the prejudice as well as a good deal of solid hewing will be needed before these barriers are cast down. It is not the time for patience and resignation (we women are getting a little weary of our monopoly of these much over-rated virtues) when Irishwomen are ranked with the criminal, the infant and the lunatic as incapable of exercising the right to vote, when a woman is not legally recognised as the parent (even part-owner) of her child unless that child bears the stigma of illegitimacy, when legislation is hourly interfering (and because it is British legislation forsooth we Irishwomen are asked by Irish patriots not to interfere, strange paradox!) with her right to work.

Perforce Irishmen are taxed for the upkeep of the British Empire (and as yet no Irishmen, Sinn Féin or others), has refused to pay that tax, though many Englishwomen have had their goods seized as a protest against their unenfranchised condition), but they exercise at least a free franchise, and have some voice in the administration of these taxes, say in the case of the present Budget. Irishwomen have also perforce to pay their share of taxes to keep up a British Empire, which many of them wish at the bottom of the sea; yet, because they are women they have no right whatever to a voice in the administration of such taxes. Englishwomen are stirred to protest against this aggression, and are praised by Sinn Féiners for their protest. But Irishwomen because they suffer a two-fold, and, therefore, a doubly unbearable wrong are told to submit in patience because the wrong is inflicted by an alien government. I hope we have heard the last of this egregious argument.

'Dublin Corporation and women's suffrage'[7]
Freeman's Journal, 8 April 1911
Dear Sir,

In a letter of protest against the Dublin Corporation's exercise of its ancient privilege (won for it by Henry Grattan and now threatened by Captain Craig) of petition to the House of Commons, Róisín Nic Sheamuis makes several misstatements regarding the Irish Women's Franchise League, which I am sure she will regret, as a good Suffragist, when their falsity is shown. The Irish Women's Franchise League is not an Irish branch of an English organisation. It is an absolutely independent Irish body, run on Irish lines, and adapted to Irish conditions. In fact, of the three Irish suffrage societies having their headquarters in Dublin, the Irish Women's Franchise League is the only one that is not affiliated to any English body. Its election policy and general tactics are framed on Irish lines. It has sent an Irish contingent to great Suffrage demonstrations in London, as have the women of other nations, France, Norway, etc. On the occasion of the last march on Westminster, it sent a militant Irish deputation to show that Irishwomen demand the same civic rights as English and Scottish women, and that they are determined not to be excluded from any further benefits wrested by women from the legislature, as they were by tacit consent of the Irish members in the case of the Bill which declared English and Scottish women, but not Irishwomen, eligible on County and Borough Councils. The Irish Women's Franchise League was founded by Irishwomen indignant at the slight thus put upon them, and to ensure that it shall not be repeated. It is strange, indeed, that such an attitude should be pilloried as 'anti-national' – about as reasonable as the Sinn Féin protest against the use by the Dublin Corporation of a privilege wrung from parliament by Henry Grattan.

Though Róisín Nic Sheamuis holds that 'the subjection of half the human race to the other is a greater wrong than the with-holding of self-government from Ireland', she not quite logically thinks 'it will be time enough for Irishwomen to demand the vote when they have an Irish Parliament from which to demand it'. No scheme of Home Rule would be worthy of the name which excluded Irishwomen from the vote. It would give Irishwomen, however patriotic, little satisfaction to be misrepresented in an Irish Parliament by Irishmen instead of at Westminster by Irishmen and Englishmen; in fact, from the national point of view, it would be still more intolerable. Moreover, Irishwomen have confidence only in themselves, being in that sense, as Councillor Sherlock very properly put it in his forcible speech last Monday, the only true Sinn Féiners. We are inclined to be suspicious about the 'wait-till-we-get-Home-Rule' catchword. It rings false, and is usually uttered by the known anti-Suffragist MP, just as in England it is the Conservative 'Anti' who is loudest in his denunciations of Women's Suffrage Bills as 'undemocratic'. It is a cry that would quickly be changed, under Home Rule, to the stock 'Do not embarrass the Government'.

Had Róisín Nic Sheamuis been present, as I was, in the gallery of the City Hall on Monday last, and heard the coarse jibes of some 'extreme' Nationalists in the gallery, who attempted to hound us down, and would willingly have assisted in flinging us out in the interests of 'law and order', she would, I think, have lost some illusions as to the chivalry of nationalist Ireland. Some Sinn Féin women who helped us did, as Sinn Féin Corporators may learn at some future day unless they improve their attitude towards the women who return them.

Hanna Sheehy Skeffington

[There was a comment on Hanna's letter, published in the journal *Sinn Féin*, 15 April 1911: 'If it prefers English government without woman suffrage to Irish government without woman suffrage, it is Unionist and nothing but Unionist . . . If a class-interest or a sex-interest opposes itself to national self-government, that class-interest or sex-interest necessarily becomes anti-national.']

4

VOTES FOR WOMEN

INTRODUCTION

In the second half of the nineteenth century, women in Britain and Ireland were involved in a wide number of movements and campaigns to improve their social, economic and political status. The first suffrage society in Ireland, the Irish Women's Suffrage Society, was formed by Isabella Tod in Belfast in 1873. It was followed in 1876 by what would become the Irish Women's Suffrage and Local Government Association, led by Anna and Thomas Haslam. Most Dublin feminists began their political careers in that group, which by 1911 had grown to 647 members. Hanna Sheehy and Frank Skeffington were both listed as members in 1902, before their marriage in 1903, and they remained with the IWSLGA until the formation of the militant suffrage group, the Irish Women's Franchise League, which they co-founded in 1908 with their friends Margaret and James Cousins. The Haslams were unionist in political orientation, content with the union with Britain, and most of the membership of IWSLGA was Protestant. The IWFL was to be very different. As Margaret Cousins explained, they intended to develop a programme of action 'suitable to the different political situation of Ireland as between a subject-country seeking freedom from England, and England, a free country'.[1] As an Irish-defined organisation they recognised that the colonial relationship between Britain and Ireland would determine the strategy of the Irish militants. Crucially, they declared they wanted 'Home rule for Irish women as well as Irish men'. What distinguished the IWFL from all other suffrage groups, was that it was a militant organisation, following the lead of the Pankhursts' Women's Social and Political Union, recognising that drastic action might be determined necessary to achieve 'Suffrage First – Before All Else'.

As the suffrage campaign developed momentum in tandem with the constitutional crisis around Home Rule, a mass meeting of women from all political persuasions, held in Dublin on 1 June 1912, resulted in the sending of a petition to the leaders of all the political parties in Britain and Ireland. Despite their differing views they were united around the principle that there could be no democratic Home Rule government if it ignored a whole sex. There was no response to their demand. Women's frustration resulted in the start of 'militant militancy', as Hanna, with seven other members of the IWFL on 13 June 1912 embarked on a coordinated campaign of window smashing. She received a two-month prison sentence for attacking Dublin Castle. Four of her colleagues received heavier six-month sentences as they had managed to smash more windows before being caught. In her memoirs she describes her experience of imprisonment and hunger strike, and the visit of friends and family, including Anna Haslam, her husband Frank and son Owen. Hanna recounts a second prison experience in 1913, when the Home Rule issue was becoming critical and the authorities keen to protect Sir Edward Carson from feminist questioning (Chapter 14).

Her brief article on why militancy had been adopted was published by the *Irish Review*, the literary journal, co-edited by Thomas MacDonagh and James Plunkett, two of the leaders of the Easter Rising. As well as emphasising the socio-economic conditions suffered by women, which possession of the vote would help to change, Hanna made it very clear that militant action by women had honourable precedents in Irish history. Through this she made it clear that it was not an 'English campaign' as many opponents of suffrage had claimed.

Suffrage campaigning continued with efforts to have women included within the Home Rule Bill, which was carried in the House of Commons on 25 May 1914. The outbreak of war in August decimated the suffrage groups, but the militants of the IWFL attempted to continue to keep the issue of suffrage and women's exclusion from Home Rule before the public.

The extracts from the *Irish Citizen*, written in the heat of the moment, reveal the increasing pressures experienced by the militants, and their frustrations that militancy and prison had not influenced the politicians, particularly those of the Irish Parliamentary Party, whose role in propping up the minority Liberal government was a crucial factor in preventing the inclusion of Irish women in the Home Rule Bill.

By 1914, with Home Rule about to become law, Irish women redoubled their efforts to reach both John Redmond, the Irish Party leader, and Prime Minister Asquith, but to no avail. They were strongly supported by the United Suffragists, particularly Emmeline Pethick-Lawrence, who had been a supporter of the IWFL since she and her husband Frederick had first met Frank and Hanna Sheehy Skeffington. In her role as treasurer for the Women's Social and Political Union she had provided the funding to establish the *Irish Citizen*. Since that time the Pethick-Lawrences had been expelled from the WSPU by an increasingly autocratic Christabel Pankhurst and in February 1914 helped to form the United Suffragists as a mixed-sex organisation open to both militants and non-militants. In the spirit of the United Suffragists, the Irish delegation was also a united one, consisting of Hanna, representing the Irish militants; Dora Mellone from Warrenpoint, representing the non-militants of the Irish Women's Suffrage Federation; and Margaret McCoubrey, a Scottish woman living in Belfast, who had joined the WSPU when it established an Ulster Centre in Belfast with Dorothy Evans as organiser.

Other extracts, on spreading the suffrage message to the west, and on 'suffragette revels' portray other aspects of the movement – the commitment required to brave often hostile territory in the small towns and villages of rural Ireland, contrasted with a lighter side, when campaigners relaxed and enjoyed social evenings inspired by feminist influences. Hanna wrote *Reminiscences of an Irish Suffragette* a few years before her death, but it was not published in her lifetime. Her friend Desmond Ryan, writing not long after her death, said:

> During the last year Mrs Skeffington undertook at last the task that probably no other living person could do better: to write her life-story. Fortunately she succeeded in finishing more than a third of these memoirs, while over the years she had written and told to many audiences the more important phases of her remarkable and militant life. (*Bakery Trades Journal*, April–June 1946)

Hanna always hoped she would not become 'elderly minded' and her memoirs, despite being written towards the end of her life, are characteristically lively, witty, and completely unrepentant regarding the militant actions in which she was involved. They throw light on personalities of the day and on the difficulties experienced by the suffragettes. She glosses over internal divisions in the movement; perhaps the passing of the years rendered these less important in her eyes. The contrast between her later memoirs and the polemical style used during the years of militancy is notable; together, they provide invaluable insights into the most important campaign for women's rights that Irish women have witnessed and experienced.

Reminiscences of an Irish Suffragette[2]
1941
Anna Maria Haslam, a Quaker rebel, one of the most consistent and ardent feminists I have known, of the old school, the New Woman one, led the movement for Women's Suffrage, ably assisted by her husband Thomas, a libertarian in many fields. The organization founded by them and a few valiant women pioneers (the Women's Suffrage and Local Government Association) did much educative spadework, especially in connection with Local Government.

I first became aware of Mrs Haslam (or, rather, she of me) through Esther Roper (Eva Gore-Booth's lifelong friend) when the latter was organising women graduates in Manchester by means of a gigantic Petition to the House.

I was then an undergraduate, and was amazed and disgusted to learn that I was classed among criminals, infants and lunatics – in fact, that my status as a woman was worse than any of these. Naturally, I signed, and became a conscious suffragist from that hour on. Later, or perhaps that same year, anyhow in the late teens, my education was continued by Mill's *Subjection of Women*, to which I was introduced by Francis J. Skeffington, who made it the subject of a College paper.

The Votes for Women movement in England some years later stirred a responsive chord in some Irish feminist breasts, but, for some years we did nothing to start a fire on our own. Then, in the late summer of 1908, stimulated by English revolt, a group of us got together and planned an Irish 'Suff' group which was to have the same aims – Votes for Women – but to work on independent Irish lines: that was essential, and we were strongly Irish-minded, most of us, realizing that, though the House of Commons was still the arbiter of Irishwomen's as well as Irishmen's destinies, we should have to adopt slightly different tactics and begin at once on our own MPs, pressing to have a clause embodying Votes for Women in our measure of Home Rule. Home Rule Bills were going forward – and backward – battledore and shuttlecock, for years in the House. But no one thought of a change so drastic as Home Rule for women, and the MPs' minds were virgin ground mostly – unreceptive to any feminist ideas. It is remarkable, and a discovery that all rebels make in their time, how watertight the minds of rebels can be. Here were good Irish rebels, many of them broken in to national revolt, with all the slogans of Irish revolution and its arsenal of weapons – Boycott, Plan of Campaign, Land for the People, and so forth, the creators of obstruction in Parliament – yet at the whisper of Votes for Women many changed to extreme Tories or time-servers who urged us women to wait till freedom for men was won. Curiously too, these were joined by many Sinn Féiners – Arthur Griffith being one.

Sinn Féin was then in its infancy, but already it was challenging Parliamentarianism. Its line was that to ask inclusion in the British measure of Home Rule was to acknowledge Britain; this was a view taken by such good rebels as Constance Markievicz, Helena Molony and women whose natural sympathies should have been with us and pitted against English politicians. It is true that later they modified this viewpoint – when the jail gates opened to us in turn.

Meanwhile, we had a rough road to go and our chief opponents were the powerful Irish Party and its machine, backed by such organizations as the sectarian Ancient Order of the Hibernians of Joseph Devlin. To these we were a pestilential red herring across the trail of Home Rule. We had adopted the policy of fighting the then Liberal Government, and Keep the Liberal Out was in its turn the old Parnellite tactic adopted by the Suffs.

A New Organization

We formed a Committee, took an office, held weekly meetings, organized country branches, took our stand on soap-boxes in Phoenix Park, Foster Place, Beresford Place, heckled politicians, and got thrown out of meetings with such frequency that the male organizers shortly banned all women from their gatherings. In 1912 we went to Mountjoy Jail, six of us; that year a weekly paper founded and edited by James Cousins and Francis Skeffington was launched; we had arrived! Our paper was shortly on sale at all meetings, in the street. We had colours (orange and green), a Votes for Women badge, slogans; we made use with feminine ingenuity, of many good publicity devices and stunts, and became a picturesque element in Irish life, the Irish being always glad of any new element, especially one that challenged and took sides. We held parades, processions, pageants (a Pageant of Great Women which went back to Irish history for heroines). The leaders of the movement in England were invited to speak for us, and Dublin's and Belfast's and Cork's largest halls were packed to overflowing to hear them. Mrs Pankhurst had a convincing personality; through her husband she had been linked with English Labour, and had once taken the chair for Michael Davitt; Christabel, her gifted daughter, had an extremely different line of approach: she captured by her close reasoning, her quick repartee, her youthful *élan*. Mrs Despard, even then a veteran, was another persuasive and eloquent speaker who commanded attention and respect; many who came to scoff left convinced. The myth of the hard-faced man-hating spinster was dispelled; these women were charming, they made a pleasing impression; they showed courage and resourcefulness; they were ready to make sacrifices.

Our public was rapidly becoming educated. Women speakers who could hold their own, who could lift their voices in the Fifteen Acres, meeting heckling on their own ground, being good-humoured and capable of keeping their temper under bombardments of rotten eggs, over-ripe tomatoes, bags of flour, stinking chemicals, gradually earned respect and due attention: Suffs were good sports.

Birrell, as Chief Secretary, I collared once when selling the *Irish Citizen* at the corner of Grafton Street. He walked with his plain-clothes officers in attendance. A Press man gave me the word, and I dashed after him, poster in hand. He stopped and asked: 'How much?' I said: 'Anything you like to give, Mr Birrell. It's a penny.' He plunged his hand into his pocket, pulled out a handful of miscellaneous coin and extracted a threepenny bit. On another occasion a colleague and myself waylaid him in Greystones and extracted a promise to receive a deputation on Votes for Women and Home Rule, which he had hitherto ignored. The local dignitaries, including the then MP John Muldoon, were furious, for we managed to get between them and their visitor – and on his other side was the sea – so the *Evening Mail* described the Chief Secretary as between the Devil and the Deep Sea. He advised the deputation (of which Mrs Kettle was one, wife and daughter of MPs and an able exponent) to keep on hammering – a rather ambiguous phrase, perhaps, indeed, purposely so.

The movement was a liberal education for all those who took part in it; it developed a new camaraderie among women, it lifted social barriers, it gave its devotees a new ideal, a revelation as of a new religion, it helped women to self-expression through service, calling forth that spirit of sacrifice strong in most women (too potent perhaps), but this time, for the first time in history, not for a man's cause but their own. When prison followed, and later hunger-strike, a deeper note was struck; many hitherto protected comfortable women got glimpses of the lives of those less fortunate, and became social rebels. Some of the wiser male leaders saw this possibility, notably James Connolly, who (unlike some other Labour leaders) recognized from the first the possibilities latent in the movement and welcomed women rebels wholeheartedly.

Connolly never once failed to respond to a call for a Mass Meeting, a Protest Demonstration; when he went to Belfast he held meetings there for us: I recall one in a Park there held under Labour auspices, at which the rowdies present intervened to drown our remarks with the strains of 'God Save the King'. In Dublin the 'Hibs' (Ancient Order of Hooligans, Francis Skeffington called them) used to close our open air meetings to the strains of 'God Save Ireland' or 'A Nation Once Again'. In Belfast our movement was regarded as tainted with Nationalism (of the Craigs, one brother, later Craigavon, was a suffragist, the other an anti; of the Redmonds, John was an anti, Willie a suffragist), while in the South we were held to be opposed to Home Rule because of our opposition to the Liberal Government then holding back suffrage.

Limerick and Belfast

One memory of a hectic meeting with Redmond in Limerick – I had managed to get on the platform, Limerick being my home town in a sense, when I was recognized too late to throw me off (Mrs Redmond was in the front row). I was begged to give a promise of non-intervention, but declined, unless Mr Redmond promised to include Votes for Irishwomen in the Home Rule Bill. So my protest took place duly, and I was pinioned and rapidly hustled down the steps, a threatening mob accompanying. An infuriated male relative came along, partly to see me off the field, but also to prevent mob violence: his cousinship struggling visibly with his Party feelings. At the gate, the women – they are swift actionists – tore my cap from my head, and the hairpins tumbled down. An elderly 'bum' thrust a dirty face close to me and shouted beerily: 'Are ye a Suff?' I said, 'Yes,' whereupon he spat copiously into my face; my hands were held with cousinly firmness, so I could not ward off the volley. The police intervened to offer 'protection' – they would take me to the station. Was I being arrested, I asked, and, if so, for what? Oh no, just for my own protection. Being a strong disliker of police by nature, distrustful of protection, I declined with an inspiration: 'I will not go to the Police Station. I want no police protection from a Limerick crowd,' I answered. It worked like magic, and I was allowed to go my way in peace, and to clean the spit from my face. Crowds are queer things.

Another heckling is memorable: in Belfast, when Churchill came to a Home Rule mass demonstration. He was then a Liberal – and a Home Ruler of sorts, and the Orange blood was up, so he was refused the Ulster Hall, but the Nationalists had the Gaelic sports grounds engaged instead, in the heart of the Green Quarter. As suffs, we gave no quarter to British visiting Ministers, and two of us (how we secured tickets I know not, but we usually had a friend or two in various camps) travelled to Belfast. They were offering life insurance tickets at Amiens Street that day. Five Belfast women had also got tickets, and we followed the usual plan. Each was assigned her number, being instructed to wait her turn and make her appropriate interruption in due course, a pause being made between each 'Votes for Irishwomen!' and the seven duly distributed in different parts of the tent. It was a dripping day; the grey tent was packed; the orator and his friends duly arrived; there were cordons of police outside, and inside strongly enforced Hibs. I was number three. The first heckler was like a bombshell; she got her word in and vanished, so did the second from another part, and after due interval my turn came – again from another quarter. By that time tempers were breaking – how many more would there be? I brought my Dublin accent along, an extra offence of course. After my interjection, the crowd did the rest; I was seized and hustled to the top of rough flight of steps leading to the soggy field. Two rough and angry stewards held me. One said, 'Let's throw her down the steps', and made a grabbing gesture. I turned and caught the lapels of his coat with each hand firmly, saying, 'All right, but you'll come along too!' I wasn't thrown down; they saw me off the premises, as well as the Irish Party and their supporters.

The Press, both National and Conservative, official Sinn Féin, the clergy on the whole (organized religion generally) were opposed to the militant movement, primarily because revolt of women for their own emancipation is always frowned on by organized males, and partly because the Churches are opposed to any change. Organized Labour wanted women to help them press for Adult Suffrage, ridiculing Women's Suffrage as 'Votes for Ladies'. Some Socialists feared that women, if given the vote (this is still true on the Continent) would prove clerically-minded. So from Right and Left Wing there were critics – even the Quakers, though usually receptive, were opposed to 'violence'. The women's violence was largely symbolic and directed only against property. In Ireland there is always, as in agricultural communities generally, a strong prejudice against women working on independent lines. Bishops denounced the new movement in pastorals: Dr O'Dwyer, Bishop of Limerick, himself a strong individualist, a critic of the Irish Party, later a saint among Sinn Féiners, fulminated against Votes for Women on the usual lines in a Lenten Pastoral, warning his flock against this insidious enemy of the Home. Other clerics, in Co. Leitrim, for instance, so influenced their flock that in Carrick-on-Shannon we could not get a hall or even a soap-box in the town. The younger priests were often favourable or at the least open-minded, as they were on the Sinn Féin and Gaelic movements. It is extraordinary how Church and State, the politicians and the pundits accept and, alas, try to neutralise the ci-devant rebel. Once when a deputation waited upon John Dillon (a fine rebel on certain lines and up to a point), he said sadly: 'Women's Suffrage will, I believe, be the ruin of our Western civilization. It will destroy the home, challenging the headship of man, laid down by God. It may come in your time – I hope not in mine!' It was to come before he died. John Redmond, to another deputation, when a member used the word 'feminism', interrupted sneeringly: 'I do not know what the word means.' He, like Pilate, did not wait for an answer. Davitt, of course, was a feminist, a true equalitarian, but he did not live for the Votes for Women later movement; he had few disciples on the later Irish Party, and strange anomaly, many of those who were greatly in favour of suffrage for English women opposed the idea of its inclusion in a Home Rule Bill. Mr Hugh Law said on one occasion that he opposed giving Irish women the vote because there was no 'noisy demand' for it in Ireland. The Irish Party feared a Conservative vote for women – John Redmond told me he did, and feared clerical domination, but asked me not to publish him as saying this, proving he too feared these forces.

Another enemy to Votes for Women in Ireland was the licensed trade, a powerful, rich and highly organized body: it exercised of late years a strong control over the Irish Party – it still does over our politicians, North and South. Sir Edward Carson and his Party were equally opposed; the Orange Order is exclusively male, humbly served by women in a strictly ancillary capacity. They too wanted no diversion of forces, busy on the Covenant and all that.

The First Stone, and Jail

The first stone was flung (after four years' slow education and preparation) in 1912, when Irish women were excluded from the Vote in the Home Rule Bill. That Bill was never to materialize, played with by the Liberals, till 1914 shelved it forever; but just then it appeared imminent. As a protest, the Irish Women's Franchise League followed a careful plan; then women in the early morning hours, having originally selected their buildings, taking sticks along, smashed quite a goodly number of panes of glass in Government buildings, in the GPO, the Custom House, Dublin Castle. The Custom House gave a splendid front, and two stalwarts covered its four sides, encouraged by a group of dockers, who entered into the spirit of the thing, cheering the ladies on and keeping a look out! They got clean away, and operated next on the GPO, where they were duly apprehended. The idea was, of course, to give the police the impression of a larger force – the Dublin Metropolitan Police was certainly taken completely by surprise and much flurried in consequence. They were to live through much stormier times, but were then a lazy, overfed, on the whole good-natured lot, except where riots were threatened, when, like all police, they could be cruel and vicious, especially to the poor and the defence-less. Educated, articulate rowdyism (as they would call it) from the comfortable classes, from respectably dressed women, stupefied them.

To my lot fell Dublin Castle in the bombardment. I specially asked for it when we were planning our attack – 'the treasured wrongs of fifty years' etc. Ship Street was the venue near the Castle Gate; the panes were small and very dirty (I expect they still are), and the garrison was near at hand, so I did not get far with the breakage (only enough, as it proved, for a three-month stretch[3] – The Custom House-GPO band got six). The policeman who grabbed my arm instinctively seized the right, and, as I am left handed, that gave me a chance to get in a few more panes before the military arrived and my escort led me off.

Thus eight of us were duly arraigned and divided into two lots, and ours was the first to enter Mountjoy – we got excellent publicity from an enraged Press, and mixed feelings from the general public, but on the whole, naturally, condemnation. Not only were we enemies of Home Rule, but rebels as women.

We benefitted curiously by Churchill's forced concession to the English suffragettes that where 'moral turpitude' was not involved offenders might be given a modified first-class misdemeanant status. Wardresses (matrons) and even the Lady Superintendent herself were on our side. I have noticed, then and later, in Ireland at least (England is more starchy) that the ordinary prisoner favours the politicals; she welcomes any flouting of authority. We were quickly on good terms, and we always spoke to prisoners, disregarding silence rules. In the 'Joy' we were given liberties on the quiet, as if, wisely, the Superintendent and others realized that it was better not to look for trouble.

Next the chaplain (Father Waters) came, reminding me that he had been there when my father was a prisoner – 'a stubborn man', he said drily. Visits were another concession. We had them daily, upsetting the prison routine. Countess Markievicz, Helena Molony, Deborah Webb were among mine. Constance rallied to us with the window breaking. Mrs Haslam came, with a difference: 'Don't think I approve – but here's a pot of verbena I brought you. I am not here in my official capacity, of course – the Irish Women Suffrage and the Local Government Association strongly disprove of violence as pulling back the cause. But here's some loganberry jam – I made it myself.' This well summed up the attitude of many of our visitors. I appreciated and understood. My uncle, Father E. Sheehy, once a Kilmainham suspect, my godfather, came of course – one of those dear comfortable relations who condone anything in a favourite. My father did not; he disapproved as a loyal Party member. He was a stoic father and I responded and respected, though I officially disapproved of his attitude as much as he of mine. Mother came (disapproving but fond), when the hunger strike happened that was to terminate our 'stretch'.

Prison Was a Liberal Education
I would not have missed my experience for anything. Our meals came (one a day – the rest we took supplemented prison fare) from Mrs Wyse Power's Restaurant[4] in Henry Street. Sometimes a kindly wardress would leave a mug of coffee or soup, with strict injunctions to hide same should any colleague come along, for mutual distrust is the basis of prison and tale-bearing is encouraged under a universal spy system. Once when a chaplain came I had to hide away two separate mugs. Prison coffee was excellent, given only to long-term prisoners (women convicts served in the day, and we had then a pair of murdresses, poisoners who worked in the kitchen, subdued weak sullen-looking women, I heard their male accomplice had given them away, turning King's evidence). Prisons depend on convicts more than any other class for smooth running, for short-term ones, having hope, give trouble; convicts live long, work well, and are the mainstay, so their food was the best: later in Armagh I noticed that only lifers got cheese or golden syrup on their menu: not caring for either, it hardly seemed worthwhile.

Frank, my husband, came pretty well every day; he enjoyed the experience vicariously, and urged us on even to the hunger-strike. He was never amenable to the Governor's suggestion to advise his wife to be 'sensible'. Owen, aged three, was sometimes brought, and once allowed to come to my cell to sample chocolates, an unheard-of concession, because he had managed to fall on the stone floor of the reception room and raised such a howl that the

Superintendent said it would never do for him to go out roaring, as it might get into the Press!

Frank was editing the *Citizen* – and did he give us good publicity! I had to do articles and book reviews – I recall reading and reviewing *Maurice Harte* in jail. The jail was military, run even for women on military lines: wardresses had to give the military salute and were paraded: they were as much prisoners as we were. Now I expect the military part is relaxed, but men are still Governors, in Ireland North and South, of women's prisons, with all the male limitations and the male delight in red tape. At that time (and still, though now in a modified way) the matrons were dressed in a hideous garb; half nurse, half military, with a sad Victorian bonnet perched precariously on their heads, and huge bunches of keys at their waists; the prisoners wore silly white caps, though forbidden hairpins to fasten them, and at the side a handkerchief which was knotted and hung down beside the apron (different colours for the different grades and broad arrows by way of decoration).

Asquith's Visit

Meanwhile, things were moving outside. Asquith came to Dublin that Summer on one of his 'promising' trips – to offer a 'free gift to a free people'. Party fervour was at its height – at last the Liberals were going to give Home Rule – or so it seemed. Two suffragettes from the Women's Suffrage and Political Union (Mary Leigh and Gladys Evans) came over;[5] Cabinet Ministers wherever they went were their quarry logically, but unfortunately this time they did not leave the heckling in Irish hands (even the best-meaning English have blind spots where the Sister Isle is concerned). Mary Leigh brought a small hatchet – it was blunt and meant symbolically, but that didn't help much. It skimmed between Asquith and Redmond and grazed the latter's ear. There was the devil to pay, of course; the public and press worked up a fine hysteria, women were mobbed, any suspected of being Suffs were mobbed – our Secretary, Mrs Emerson, was seized and about to be rushed to the Liffey and flung over the low parapet at O'Connell Bridge, when she was rescued by some friends; another group, attempting to hold a meeting at Beresford Place, had the platform rushed by a mob and tried to take refuge in Liberty Hall, but the doors were closed upon them. (James Connolly came to Dublin specially to speak for us, against the will of James Larkin, who did not approve.) We were all put in the same boat as the hatchet-thrower. The Irish Women's Franchise League did not repudiate, whatever our private opinion of the timeliness and manner of the act, because we naturally considered the women strictly within their rights. We lost members (the usual 'up-to-this' friends that shook off the tree each time anything fresh was done). My mother wrote to me to the 'Joy' thanking Providence that I was 'safe' in jail. In connection with the Asquith episode, we had a resolution of repudiation from our Cork branch, signed by the Hon. Secretary, Miss Mary MacSwiney – and Cork cut itself off from us, joining the law-abiding section.

Hunger-Strike

Meanwhile, four of us determined to hunger-strike – a voluntary gesture, as I hold, hunger-strike decisions should always be. Our sentence was nearing its close, as it happened, and by the time the law had ground out its course and Mary Leigh was sentenced to three years' penal servitude and her companion to a year's hard labour, we had but a week to go. So we hunger-struck in sympathy, for the two sentenced begun theirs the moment they returned, as we already knew they would.

Relatives were allowed to see us to plead in some cases. Wardresses and the authorities joined their persuasions, but we had our minds made up. Each was, of course, told that all the rest had given in. Hunger-strike was then a new weapon – we were the first to try out in Ireland – had we but known, we were the pioneers in a long line. At first, Sinn Féin and its allies regarded the hunger-strike as a womanish thing; some held that politicals should take their medicine without whining and all that, others more sympathetic regarded the fast as a form of suicide and a waste of life. But the public was, at least, not apathetic, and a feeling began to be voiced that there was something unreasonable in refusing women the vote.

To us, the idea even of a week without food was something of an ordeal, a step in the dark, a plunge into the unknown. But we stuck it, and found, as many were to do later with this and other ordeals, that it was not as formidable as we had supposed. Eating is a habit the body learns to do without, getting weaker in the process until the desire itself passes. Senses are sharpened, one hears steps afar off (we rather dreaded doctors and forcible feeding, but of that there was no question). I think the doctors were puzzled and scared. One hears one's heart pound, and it awakes one tossing in the night. Water applied to one's head evaporates as if a sponge were put on an oven; one gets slightly light-headed. The sense of smell becomes acute – I had never smelt tea before. A dying women craved for a rasher, and it was fried somewhere nearby (perhaps to tempt us?). That was tantalizing. One instinctively skips in books the descriptions of food; I never realized before how much both Scott and Dickens gloat, and how abstemious are the Brontës and Jane Austen. I slept – others could not – and the days passed; news seeped in: we heard how 'Leigh' and 'Evans' were faring. Leigh had been given a book by Winston Churchill, but was disgusted to find the novelist was a namesake. They were to be forcibly fed, but that we did not know till later; for six weeks their ordeal went on till the authorities, wearied out, released them both on the Cat and Mouse Act.[6]

They were removed to a friend's house in Merrion Square and attended to by Dr Lynn. For many weeks after, having trained themselves in automatic rejection of the food poured into the stomach, they could not retain food and looked like living and slightly decayed corpses. Compared with theirs, our strike was easy, and the authorities did not let us off an hour of it; I had lost over a stone in a week, some of the others even more. Other suffragists in Mountjoy and Holloway were to hunger-strike later, and had a harder time, authorities growing callous. Later, in 1913, I got a week for giving out leaflets outside Lord Iveagh's house to Sir Edward Carson. One Sergeant Thomas grabbed my arm as I flung them towards the carefully posing statesman on the steps, and when I tried to wrench myself free, the clutch tightened and the Sergeant, angry, marched me off, entering a charge against me of assault. I was considerably bruised and battered, and tried (in vain, of course) to enter a counter-charge. I was to learn that a Sergeant's word is one that is implicitly believed against any prisoner. 'She bit me, your worship, and tried to throw me,' swore the gallant DMP officer, whose belt came to my forehead. A titter went round the Court, but was instantly suppressed, and the Magistrate offered bail – 'your husband's bail – I see he is in Court' – which was refused. Then came the sentence – 'I am convinced that assault took place, but that it was slight. In view of the fact that it was against a Sergeant, I must pass a sentence of one week. Remove the prisoner.'

Back to the 'Joy' in dark November, alone this time. Another hunger-strike, and this time I was held for five days. Then the Aberdeens intervened and I was released. I promised myself that never again would I go to prison without doing something to justify detention, if I had to throw a stone at the judge's head.

The IWFL, following Mr Birrell's advice, kept hammering; we staged processions, protests, a newspaper campaign, formed country branches, addressed noisy meetings in Boyle, Carrick and elsewhere (the crowd in Boyle turned out to throw us in the river and a priest who was hurriedly sent for told us later that they declared they hadn't had such fun since the Parnell split. Fortunately we happened to be staying at the hotel on the safe side of the bridge, but their windows there were driven in and we were stoned.) We bombarded party leaders, heckled Government officials, and the rare ones that came to Ireland, went *en masse* deputations to Conventions of the National League, crossed to London to lobby there, and had our own detectives who trailed us wearily about and against whom we pitted nimble feminine wits: I learned much during that period of the ways of police and lost any awe (it was never great) of law and its ramifications and absurdities. We organized a census resistance (being duly condemned by Arthur Griffith, but given by Constance Markievicz her mountain cottage for the registration night). Our numbers abstaining did not greatly throw out the census figures, but we led the police a dance, camping on the hills or in empty houses, scattered far and wide.

Dublin saw poster parades, Daffodil Fetes, Pageants of Great Women, a Christmas Fair where our cockshots (sixpence a shot) were figures of Asquith, Redmond and Carson. Grace Gifford and Ernest Cavanagh (both names linked later with 1916) were among our cartoonists. 1913 saw Lansbury, Nevinson, Dora Montefiore, Mrs Despard, the Pankhursts, and Pethick Lawrences among our speakers. Skeffington volunteered for Lansbury's campaign in Bow and Bromley, putting in an intensive fortnight speaking for him (he was defeated). Rebel forces were drawing together, and many who had looked askance were thrown together. Joseph Plunkett, Pearse, MacDonagh, spoke for us and championed our cause. Constance Markievicz had a way of appearing when storms blew, as once when a TCD. Ragging band stormed our rooms and started to break up the place and throw our furniture and literature out the windows (our office and tea rooms were all too close to the University); 'Suffs' were fair game.

'The voice of Irish womanhood. A demand and a warning. Points from historic speeches. The voice of Leinster. The last constitutional chance'
Irish Citizen, 8 June 1912
Mrs Sheehy Skeffington MA (Irish Women's Franchise League) writes:

We recognize that the responsibility in this question is not with the individual Members of Parliament, but with the Liberal Government, which is responsible for introducing the Home Rule Bill. We demand that the Liberal Government shall make itself responsible for this amendment, and we shall not be satisfied with less. We know perfectly well that a private member's amendment would have to pass between the Scylla of the kangaroo closure and the Charybdis of the guillotine closure. We want to go in by the front door, and if this constitutional meeting does not force its way, no doubt women will find other ways. Do not be mistaken. If the Liberal Government refuses to respond to our resolutions, there is no further chance for constitutional agitation. The franchise is deliberately tied up for three years after the establishment of Home Rule. We demand now the safeguard of the vote, not for a minority, but for a majority. The success of the Local Government franchise has been used as an argument for Home Rule by Mr Redmond, Mr Devlin, and others. Mr Balfour has used the same argument in another connection. Under that register women vote. We have helped to build up the house out of which we are now to be shut. If our amendment fails, it will only mean a bitter struggle on the part of Irishwomen to try to keep up with China, whose women have the vote.

'Mass meeting of Irish women: an impression from the platform'
Irish Citizen, 8 June 1912

Some weeks ago – when, in fact, we first learned that we were excluded from the Home Rule Bill – the Irish Women's Franchise League conceived the thought of rallying all Irish suffragists under a common standard to voice our common demand. Suffrage societies and other women's organisations throughout the length and breadth of Ireland instantly responded. Constitutional joined militant – for the day at least; Unionist was allied to Nationalist, party claims (so dear to our loyal women) were for once subordinated to sex principle, and the result was Saturday's delegate meeting, the first woman's congress held in Ireland. Its memory and its inspiration will survive long after its definite purpose – the pressing of a Government amendment to the Home Rule Bill – has been achieved or blocked; long after it has been resolved once more into its individual elements and scattered, the thought of it will abide: Dublin will be inspired by the demonstration of the keenness of the provinces, and the provinces will gain new energy by contact with the centre.

Women possess the genius for organization, for skilled manipulation of effect. Their unfailing attention to detail gives their meetings an element of the picturesque lacking in male-run assemblies. Those twenty shields of plain black and white lettering, bearing the names of the various provincial centres represented at the meeting, those banners and pennants of orange and green, azure and silver, dark-blue and gold that lined the hall, added a further emphasis to the exclusively feminine platform, representative of so many varying feminine activities, from medicine and the law to artistic needlework and craftsmanship. One woman doctor had snatched some moments from her crowded professional day to come, a woman labour organizer joyously told of a strike, happily settled, where her girls had won, another came from a teachers' congress brimful of economic sex-grievances.

The spirt of the audience, as judged from the platform, was throughout deeply earnest and, to my mind at least, stirringly militant. It was a women's audience, one felt, moreover, that every woman present represented many others, as their chosen delegate. It was an audience of experts: every subtle point, every political allusion was at once appreciated; those women were unanimous as to what they wanted and how what they wanted was best achieved. Moreover (and this to me was the most cheering sign of all) they were so strong in their sense of absolute right, of unswerving sex-faith and constancy, that they did not take over seriously the prospect of political wiles and delay. Home Rule or no Home Rule, Westminster or College Green, there is a new spirit abroad among women: whether the vote is reluctantly granted by a Liberal Government or wrested from an Irish Parliament, to women in the end it matters but little.

Politicians and parties (Irish and English alike) if they do push on their Home Rule ship, regardless of warnings, 'full steam ahead', will be iceberged and their male monster will founder – that is all. But the women who are behind this world movement will most surely achieve their purpose. I am almost sorry for the politicians at their party play, those little legislators blindly making little laws for those who make the legislators.

'The women's movement: Ireland'
Irish Review, July 1912

Now that the first stone has been thrown by suffragists in Ireland, light is being admitted into more than mere Government quarters, and the cobwebs are being cleared away from more than one male intellect. As to the method, no one has much to say in Ireland: at the siege of Limerick the women gathered aprons and stockings full of shards, glass and flints, which they hurled upon the Williamites. In Land League times 'Tipperary stone-throwers' became proverbial, whether from the deadliness of the aim or the particular proneness of Tipperary for that method of 'persuasion', I know not. No doubt, in our own days, the followers of Sir Edward Carson, when preparing the last ditch, will not neglect to stock this homely ammunition. So the stone and the shillelagh need no apologia: they have an honoured place in the armoury of argument. So, too, men applaud the stone-thrower as long as the missile is flung for them and not at them.

The novelty of Irishwomen resorting to violence on their own behalf is, I admit, startling to their countrymen who have been accustomed for so long to accept their services (up to and including prison, flogging at the cart-tail, death by torture) in furtherance of the cause of male liberties. There is an element of unwomanly selfishness in the idea of women fighting for them-selves repellent to the average man. Some Celtic enthusiasts hold the average Irish-man very high above petty sex spite and prejudice, and quote ancient Irish traditions of womanhood in support of their theory. One learns, however, to distrust this thriftless Irish habit of living on the reputation of its ancestors, especially when one is faced with the problems of Ireland of to-day. Belfast is notorious as one of the worst centres of sweating in the world, the streets of Dublin at night have been declared by experts to rival those of Buda-Pesth – 'the worst city in Europe', while the 'bargain marriage' is a sordid institution which banishes love from our Irish countryside. In view of these facts, it is not surprising that Mr Redmond, when taunted recently with anti-feminist lean-ings, replied scornfully: ' Feminist! I'm not sure that I know what a feminist is!' An Irishwoman, who has travelled much, told me once that Ireland of all Western countries came nearest to Orientalism in its disregard of woman, its exclusion of her in all public occasions, its scarcely veiled contempt of wifehood, while, with regard to motherhood, the Orientals were ahead of us; for in the East the old woman is venerated, while in Ireland the term is synonymous for imbecility.

These are some of the reasons why we women of a younger generation are somewhat in a hurry with reform, why, if it falls asleep at its post, we shall wake it with a stick. The secretary of an Irish suffrage society wrote the other day, rather proudly, that her organisation goes back to 1876. The Irish Women's Franchise League dates from 1908, and already it has run the gamut of constitutionalism, and is now knocking at the prison door. Weekly, nay daily, meetings, petitions, country campaigns, deputations, open-air demonstrations, processions, resolutions from local bodies, heckling of Cabinet Ministers sojourning in Ireland, election propaganda, have been tried on public opinion and on Members of Parliament. Public opinion has admirably responded, but Members of Parliament are not so easily convinced by the voteless of their own land. Statesmen cry for outrage before they yield, doubtless because they know that mere patient appeal to reason is but 'tickling the dome of St Paul's to rouse the Dean and Chapter'.

This is the point we have now reached: thus closes the chapter of constitutionalism opened at 1876. It was a pretty tale, full of friendship, of election pledges and platform appeals from those who 'have always been our best friends', but who were always fatally debarred from action at 'critical junctures', and who in the sacred cause of party were regretfully obliged to shelve our cause when there was a likelihood of its winning. The chapter might have been a serial in time, but for the 'disgraceful tactics' of the militants. As it is, it will be interesting material for the psychologist working out a research-thesis on Female Patience in the 19th century.

These scattered thoughts are penned on the eve of prison. When I come out I may have more to add.

'Militant militancy'
Irish Citizen, 4 January 1913

One of the supremest justifications of militancy is that willy-nilly it keeps before the public in season and out of season the now literally burning topic 'Votes for Women'. Wherever two or three are gathered together, in tram or train, or golf links or in market-place, the latest 'outrage' comes up for discussion when the weather and other customary amenities have been satisfactorily disposed of. In going over some press cuttings of two or three years ago the other day, I was amused to observe that the same thrills of horror were then evoked by tactics now condoned even by Mrs Fawcett, by the passive militancy of earlier days which took the form of protest by picketing, by deputations, by 'raids' upon the Sacred Houses, and in which the only sufferer was the suffragette herself. Then, as now, we were 'maenads', 'viragoes', 'termagants', 'unsexed hooligans', and the rest; then, as now, the revival of the ducking stool and other obsolete medieval methods of dealing with feminine rebels was advocated. Passive militancy sent thousands to jail and some to death: through it matrons and maidens were subjected to indecent assault; it resulted in forcible feeding and nameless brutalities upon militants. The public criticized and remained cold: these things were terrible, but what could one do? And now the new militancy has arrived: step by step women, as was natural, proceeded to greater and greater violence, assailing the Government through the public that it represents, and passing from the breaking of Government glass to interfering with Government services, the post-office and the telephone.

One is asked what justification is there for pillar-box attacks. There is none – that is precisely the reason of their adoption. Reasonable militancy was regarded as merely playing at being militant. The public comfortably assured itself that cultured sensible women would not proceed to extremes of anarchy, abused them, and turned upon the other side to resume its interrupted slumber. After all, no great harm was done to anybody but the women. Now we are faced with another situation and the public are beginning to realise that the new militancy savours, as a recent able critic has said, of 'anarchy and the final dissolution of all society'. It does. It matters little what name it be called – anarchy, revolt, upheaval. It is for the public and the Government to recognize that this is not a riot, but a revolution, and that if society attempts to stand much longer in the way, society as at present constituted must go.

There are many parallels to the present situation in history. The French Revolution, which we all approve of, in theory, today, created anarchy and chaos before it emerged as a republic. In this case, too, the community at large suffered for the sins of the comparatively few aristocrats. The modern weapon of the strike also affects through the unredressed grievance of the few, the whole community, perhaps most of the class from which the strikers themselves spring. So complex is society that no action of an individual is isolated, each of us reacts a hundredfold upon the whole fabric; therefore it is useless to argue that certain acts of militancy or war are reprehensible because they may injure the innocent.

True, 'once people take to throwing vitriol into pillar-boxes, there is no knowing where the practice will end'. It is remarkable how much of our life is built on trust and mutual faith. If these be sapped, society totters; and if society is rotten at the core through the denial by a corrupt bureaucracy of the rights of half the community, it is better that the fabric should totter. It is precisely when these symptoms of popular discontent appear in riot and disorder, in 'irregular methods of vengeance', that governments are wont to reconsider their position. It is to such regrettable incidents that we owe

Catholic Emancipation and the Reform Bill, just as cattle-driving, boycotting and moonlighting promoted the settlement of the land question in Ireland.

Two recent critics have raised doubts as to the efficacy of militancy in Ireland. It seems to me that, in Ireland especially, no other methods are preferable, for here the soil is especially favourable. Some years ago a schoolboy debating society, discussing the question, came to the conclusion that, 'while warmly approving the methods of the militants, it was doubtful regarding the principle of woman suffrage'. Ireland may be – I do not say it is – in the same case, but certainly the question of militancy per se needs no explaining to Irish audiences.

Irish statesmen in the past were fond of threatening English Governments with making government impossible in Ireland if grievances remained unredressed. Today a section of Irishmen in the North are repeating the same threat, should Home Rule be granted. It is a familiar device, and women are learning by experience how much more effective it is than any peaceful method of propaganda. In an ideal state, doubtless, such a method would stand condemned; but we do not live under ideal conditions: we live under a Liberal Government, run by politicians accustomed to yield only to 'pressure'. For this gentry holding up a state service, obstructing public and private business by a system of guerrilla warfare, is much better business than the resolution-passing, the petition-presenting, the lobbying and wire-pulling in vogue among 'constitutionals'. Degrading to womanhood? That is altogether a matter of temperament and point of view. Many Britishers thought it more unsportsmanlike of the Boer to dress in colourless khaki and lurk behind kopjes instead of donning scarlet and coming out in the open to be shot. These tactics are not magnificent, but they are war. Veteran generals do not court battle, for their mettle requires no proving. So suffragettes, who have faced forcible feeding and the hungerstrike, need not mind being called shirkers because of a change of tactics. Desperate diseases need desperate remedies and if the vote is wrested from Government by methods of terrorism when five and forty years of sweet and quiet reason produced only seven talked-out or tricked-out bills, why, who can say it wasn't worth a mutilated letter, a cut wire, a Premier's racked nerves?

'Tullamore Jail and hungerstrike'
Freeman's Journal, Tullamore, 8 February 1913
Sir,

Allow me to draw public attention to the latest refinement of cruelty shown by the prison authorities towards the suffragist prisoners – namely compelling them to make a journey when they are in a condition urgently requiring rest and care. Mrs Hoskin was released from Tullamore Jail[7] this afternoon, in a state of utter collapse after six days' hunger strike. The natural and humane course to take would have been to hand her over to Mrs Evans and myself, who are in Tullamore for the express purpose of receiving the prisoners on their release, and seeing that they are properly looked after. Instead of this, without any intimation whatever to us, she was hustled away by train to Dublin, in charge of a wardress, and when we met her by accident at the station, and offered to take charge of her, the wardress refused to allow this, saying she had orders to bring her to Dublin and leave her at the house of a friend. The idiocy of this proceeding becomes manifest when I add that the friend to whose house she was brought was Mrs Evans, who was actually in Tullamore for the purpose of meeting her, and as soon as she was fit for the journey, bring her up to Dublin.

There can be no object in this course, except to torture the prisoners, to whom, in the critical condition induced by the hunger strike, a railway journey might easily prove fatal. If the authorities adopt the same barbarous method of dealing with their other prisoners, they will hear more of it, both in Parliament and elsewhere.

Hanna Sheehy Skeffington.

'Towards an Irish policy'
Irish Citizen, 1 March 1913
Mrs Sheehy Skeffington, MA, Chairman of Committee, Irish Women's Franchise League, writes:

The symposium on the question of an Irish policy has proved in itself a valuable indication of the keen insight of Irishwomen into political affairs and their growing mastery of political tactics. As to whether Irish women are right in demanding a Government measure and rejecting all offers of private member's bills, there seems to be almost complete unanimity. Militant and non-militant alike, with two remarkable exceptions, unite in demanding a Government measure of Woman Suffrage. It does not seem worthwhile to labour the point. The experiment of the Conciliation Bill has shown beyond all dispute that under present conditions (whatever may have been the case in the past when party discipline had not yet become a fetish, and when the private member counted for something), no bill that is not backed by the Government and enforced by its Whips, has the slightest chance of becoming law, because the perils it would encounter at every stage would prove insurmountable.

As to the second question, regarding the advisability of adopting an anti-Government policy, there seems to be a greater divergence of opinion. Most of your correspondents, while agreeing as to the necessity of the Government measure, seem to hesitate about what is really the logical outcome of this demand, namely an anti-Government policy. For we must face the situation prepared to meet all contingencies. We are not discussing for the sake of discussion: we are formulating a definite policy. If the Government accedes to our request and puts woman suffrage on its programme with a Women Suffrage Measure, our policy will then be clear. We must support the government and work to keep it in power until its pledge is redeemed. Assuming the opposite alternative, that the Government refuses to grant our demand, and offers us something that we have already repudiated; what then? Do we accept the situation? Every 'politically minded woman' (to use Mr Gwynn's[8] own words) will then 'be bound to work against the Government' and to shorten its days in office, recognising that every hour occupied by it in power is a menace and a delay to the cause she has at heart. It will be her business to weaken and lower its prestige, and to make its continued existence impossible. English-women who put votes before party, will certainly do this, and the future of Irishwomen will largely depend on their action at this crisis. They have an important choice to make: it lies with them alone to decide whether they will be enfranchised with the women of Great Britain or if they will lag behind. If they put party considerations before their enfranchisement they will be told by politicians that they do not show any keen interest in the vote, and they will be passed over. If, on the other hand, they adopt a definite anti-Government attitude – to include the Liberal allies, the Irish Party – they will make it impossible for a Government scheme to leave them out. The Irish Party must be made to feel that the only real danger to Home Rule is the postponement of Women Suffrage, that by alienating suffragists they are wrecking their own and the Liberal cause: otherwise we shall have repetitions of the 'free' vote scenes, with pledged suffragists, like Mr Law, reinforcing the ranks of the enemy, because of Mr Redmond's and Mr O'Connor's solicitude for Mr Asquith's 'prestige'. On the other hand, if the Irish Party wakes up to the fact that the Liberal Government is going to split on the rock of Women Suffrage, and that Home Rule will sink when the ship goes down, and if Irishwomen play their part single-heartedly towards that end, we shall have conquered the coalition, and the same bill that enfranchises the women of Great Britain will enfranchise Irishwomen, the Irish Party, 'anti' and suffragist alike, backing it to a man. Irishwomen have a great opportunity for good tactics: let them see to it that they use it well.

'Mr Redmond and the suffragettes'
Irish Citizen, 14 February 1914
Mrs Sheehy Skeffington writes:

Mrs Jacob[9] asks why suffragettes continue to approach Mr Redmond in view of his famous hostile pronouncement to the deputation from the Irish Women's Franchise League on April 1st 1912. She suggests that as he is opposed to our claims, he should be left alone. Were he favourable, the same suggestion could be made with equal force, and if this view were generally acted upon no one would attempt to reason with politicians at all.

Mr Asquith's position is similar to Mr Redmond's, yet suffragists do not lay down their arms because he has declared himself a convinced opponent. Why? As in the case of Mr Redmond, they hope to be able to bring sufficient pressure to bear on him to make him alter or modify his position, and to make that position untenable, if not intolerable. Politicians have been known to yield to such pressure in the past. Wellington and Peel gave way on the question of Catholic Emancipation; Gladstone altered his views on Home Rule; Sir Edward Carson, an anti-suffragist, has promised Votes to Ulster women under a Provisional Government, because of pressure from influential quarters. Mr Redmond's own record shows that he has frequently changed his mind on important issues, notably regarding the Irish Council Bill, which he personally favoured but found himself obliged to reject at the bidding of the National Convention.

When Mr Redmond realizes that it will be to his advantage to declare himself 'entirely and absolutely' convinced of the necessity of giving Votes to Irishwomen, he will find historic examples to justify a change of front.

Meanwhile it is for us to continue to supply the needed pressure by every means in our power, in and out of season. Politicians are never converted by acquiescence and submission, for they trouble themselves but little about considerations of abstract justice.

Correspondence

Irish Citizen, 7 March 1914

Mrs Sheehy Skeffington writes:

Mrs Jacob, in her first letter, questioned the expediency of 'deputations and heckling' as far as Mr Redmond was concerned. In her second letter, however, she admits the necessity of 'some action' by Irish suffragists, but still doubts the 'effectiveness of heckling in Ireland', suggesting by the limitation that Irish members are fair game for heckling in England.

My reasons for making a parallel between Mr Redmond and Mr Asquith was that Mrs Jacob emphasised Mr Redmond's anti-suffragist pronouncements, and asked why we persisted in worrying him by deputations and heckling, seeing that he was a declared opponent. In this he is similarly situated to the English Premier. I never suggested that the position in Ireland was identical with that of England: on the contrary, the League with which I am associated has always clearly insisted on the differences in the Irish situation and adopted an independent Irish policy.

At the same time, just because there are vital differences, Irish suffragists cannot sit idle and passive under slights and injustice, and are perfectly justified in using every weapon within their power to enforce attention to their claims. One of such recognised weapons is the 'voice' at public meetings: a weapon used in the past with effect at all times against political opponents. The raison d'être of all such methods of pestering politicians lies in the fact that the latter are always affected in the end by persistent pressure, never by motives of abstract justice.

True, if 'Parliamentary pressure, assisted by the fear of a revolution', were at the disposal of women, their claims to justice would be much nearer realisation. But we have to use the weapons at our hand, such as they are: in their way, if slower, they may prove as effective in the end. Mrs Jacob states that Gladstone never gave way to heckling, but to 'public opinion'. Heckling is a method of creating public opinion. Gladstone himself admitted that he was convinced on the Irish Question by a dynamite explosion in Clerkenwell Jail – in other words, by militant methods.

Mrs Jacob declares that, as Mr Redmond was sent to Parliament 'to obtain one special act of justice for Ireland, he has no warrant for concerning himself with any other matter'. Would that Mr Redmond himself held this heroic view! Then Ireland would have no Insurance Act foisted on her against her will to please Lloyd George – to name but one of many measures in which the Irish Party have actively interested themselves and to which public opinion in Ireland was actively opposed. English women would have been grateful had the Irish Party, remembering their 'sole mission', refrained from voting on their enfranchisement. But it was the Irish Party's vote on this matter that did not concern them killed the Conciliation Bill.

Mrs Jacob's constructive policy – namely to devote ourselves for three years after Home Rule (whenever that may be) to educative propaganda – comes years too late. The people of Ireland are already quite sufficiently educated; they are with us, witness the resolutions of the chief Irish City and County Councils in support of the Conciliation Bill, on which the Lord Mayor of Dublin went on a special mission to the House of Commons. It is the politicians that need education, and it is to them we devote ourselves, employing the methods successfully used by men to enforce attention to their claims.

'Votes for women in the west'
Irish Citizen, 14 March 1914
Longford, Leitrim and Roscommon lay long a dark disfiguring blot on our suffrage map, for there no suffrage speaker had ever penetrated, while, with the exception of Clare, every other county in Ireland has now been opened up by some pioneer. Accordingly, Mrs Connery[10] planned to wipe out the stain by holding three meetings, one in the chief town of each county; namely in Longford, Carrick-on-Shannon and Boyle. She organised the tour in advance, visiting the towns one after one, interviewing the local magnates and engaging

halls. In Longford alone did there seem difficulties, the Bishop being hostile, refusing 'to argue with a woman', and using his influence against the granting of the Catholic Hall. As we had heckled the local MPs a few weeks previously, and as one of them, a pronounced 'anti', owns the chief newspaper in the town, we looked for some trouble in Longford. But, as usual, a suffragette's life is full of surprises and in Longford alone did we find everything smooth in our path – a crowded hall, an enthusiastic meeting. Many converts who had come to jeer remained to join. One interrupter, who essayed dubious jests, was sternly quelled, and we were apologetically informed that he was 'no Longford man', an excuse which seems all sufficient to the native.

Next day we passed on to our next halting-place, Carrick, not many miles away – but what a difference! It is a small town of 1,100 inhabitants, containing thirty-two public-houses. It lies in marshy swamps, then half engulfed owing to persistent rains, miles of sodden bog-land stretching to the horizon. Here we experienced the nature and horrors of a sympathetic lockout, a steady boycott. The explanation of the mystery we learned later, bit by bit. The Canon had denounced us at first Mass on the Sunday previous, with other Lenten abominations, including a Patrick's Night dance that the young people were arranging. He advised the women of the town to remain at home, look after their families, and to have nothing to do with Votes; and, to make assurance doubly sure, the local publicans, trustees of the promised hall, were advised by their spiritual director 'to withdraw their permission and break their agreement' the sacredness of contracts apparently not being recognised in Carrick. Everywhere we met with stony silence, any occasional gleam of hope or approval being instantly suppressed with a kind of tremulous fear.

The publicans particularly (whose activity is not impaired by the Lenten season) seemed most afraid of contamination. Some of the younger spirits, railing at the 'rages of old men' seemed interested, but paralysed with a nameless fear: doubtless any help given or sympathy shown would be visited on the offenders hereafter.

Failing to get the Town Hall, which had been duly billed and advertised, we tried to secure one of those under Protestant management, only to find the non-Catholic section equally fear-ridden and evasive. The fiat having gone forth that suffrage was taboo, vestrymen, churchwardens, rectors, freemasons vied in putting us off with futile equivocation and shallow subterfuges, each shifting the responsibility on to the shoulders of someone else. At last, abandoning all hope of securing even a barn, we managed to enlist a journeyman carpenter to hammer a few planks on a couple of soap-boxes, so that we might address Carrick from the Market Square. By this time night had descended upon wet and badly lighted streets: still an open air meeting had possibilities. But true to the tacit boycott, no Carrick shopkeeper would sell a board, or even a nail, for a free platform; no crier would cry the meeting through the town. When the carpenter, at half-past eight, after a weary search for materials, came to tell us, he was followed by a howling, raging mob, led by a drunken virago. In spite of Lent, in spite of the proximity of the church, they paraded the space before the hotel, creating a pandemonium for over two hours with motor-bombs, savage yells and obscene jeers, mock 'suffrage' orations and wild charges across the street. After two hours' vigil they were dispersed at the sight of two policemen. So much for Carrick. A friend told us later that the only way to hold a suffrage meeting there would be to insinuate it into the middle of a picture show, by collusion with the management and without previous announcement. As a matter of 'free speech' it is not to be thought of.

In Boyle a similar fate threatened. Here the local priests were sympathetic. We had secured St Patrick's Hall without difficulty, till a local faction (Boyle is a town of factions and faction-fights) brought pressure to bear to prevent free-speech, threatened to wreck the hall, to cut off the lights, and make the speakers forever silent. A local paper, which had accepted an advertisement, calmly announced, on its own, that the meeting would not take place. The distributor of handbills was suborned to suppress the bulk of them, shop-keepers who had placed them in their windows were bullied into withdrawing them. The local politicians (partly Hibernians, of which there are two opposing camps) had determined that by fair means or foul we should not be heard. But for the kindness of the Rev. J. Watson, in giving us Clew's Memorial Hall, and but for a chance encounter of a brave and public spirited knight-errant, no meeting would have been possible. As it was, we had to collect our audience by house to house canvass in the midst of a pig fair; no crier would give his services, none would hire or lend a chair to eke out the school-benches. Many feared the wrath of politicians, and remained away. Yet we had a goodly meeting in the little schoolhouse, a small charge keeping out the hooligans. We won many converts, and uttered some hometruths to the foul-mouthed 'horse-blocker' from Belfast, who attempted heckling, only to cover his discomfiture with obscenities and to be repudiated by the decent-minded people of Boyle for his pains. Towards the close of the meeting we had red pepper scattered by some boys, and a broken pane from outside, and when the meeting was over the rival factions made use of the occasion for a fight, during which they rolled over the police in the mud of Boyle's chief thoroughfare, and got their heads broken in consequence. Plate glass was shattered as a further diversion: five baton charges took place, stones rained. As one of the combatants said next day, 'Shure, we hadn't such a grand time since the Parnell split!' Who said hysteria?

On our side we had compensations in the shape of a few trusty stalwarts (among the progressive spirits who recognise the bane of faction-mongering), several new recruits, a good collection, brisk sale of literature, unbroken heads, in spite of flints and in spite of police 'protection' (sixty police had been hastily drafted into the town to 'keep order', yet no arrests were made), and, lastly, the luxury of column-long reports, not only in the local, but in Dublin and English papers. Reporters may overlook with impunity enthusiastic meetings, as in Longford, but five baton charges, yards of shattered glass – what journalist could resist these appeals to 'copy'?

Next day the great Horse Fair took place, and we wandered freely among the wild colts from Connemara, and their haggling sellers and buyers, too bent on bargaining to give a thought to the doings of yesternight. In the intervals of sales one could catch snatches of suffrage debate going on all around. Decidedly ground has been broken in Boyle – and glass incidentally.

'Two deputations'
Irish Citizen, 20 June 1914

The Irish deputation crossed on Wednesday, June 10th, to London for the purpose of seeing Mr Asquith and Mr Redmond regarding the inclusion of Votes for Irishwomen in the Amending Home Rule Bill, as a concession which did not 'outrage the fundamental principles of self-government'. We knew that the native obstinacy which some politicians mistake (till too late) for firmness would probably not permit these gentlemen to change their minds and see us, after they had refused to do so on specious pretexts. But we had made up our minds to challenge Mr Redmond and Mr Asquith publicly, and to demonstrate that their professions of desire for concessions all round to secure 'universal goodwill' were not intended to be acted upon.

Before three on Thursday we foregathered in St Stephen's Hall, armed with *Irish Citizens*, and wearing orange-and-green badges. We sent in cards to some friendly members to secure their kind offices to hand a letter to Mr Asquith and Mr Redmond personally, asking whether they would see the waiting Irish deputation. The letters were safely delivered, and while waiting we interviewed or intercepted a number of Irish and Labour MPs. Many we found too busy escorting parties of fashionably-dressed ladies to the inner sanctuary of the House (no woman can pass nowadays without a member, who vouches for her 'good conduct'), where strawberries and cream awaited them on the terrace. One member (he hails from Donegal, I think) told us he could not remember whether he was in favour of or against Votes for Women; another said that militancy was not yet strong enough, and that was why we hadn't got the Vote; a third and fourth found militancy too strong, and said we'd never get the vote till it was stopped; an Irish Unionist MP said we should get the Vote when the Tories returned to power, and under the Provisional Government; an Irish nationalist stated that we would get it from an Irish

Parliament and so on. And so they passed, mildly bored, to resume a tete-à-tete on the terrace, or to help Mr McKenna[11] to decide what to do with the militants.

The party women who were waiting with us (under the picture of the Speaker being held down in his chair) were an interesting study, doing the drudgery for the politicians, buttonholing members on Single-Tax – a 'far wider and more important reform than votes' – on the Mental Deficiency Act, on Welsh Disestablishment. One had got a number of names of Irish MPs to some petition or other, but, as she plaintively declared, 'the worst of it is they often sign without reading.' I said I thought that would be the only way of getting them to sign anything worth signing, and she looked very pained at my cynicism. Another gave me harrowing details as to the physical and mental degeneracy of the militants, which made me thankful I had hitherto escaped committal as a criminal lunatic. Parties of tourists and school-children filed in and out to be conducted, duly awed, over the House. A German lady journalist, in quest of information, asked me to explain in German to her the difference between Suffragist and Suffragette. Meanwhile, not far off, a bomb was being laid under the Coronation Chair.

We had determined to close our vigil after two hours. At five we terminated it by advancing to the lobby to make a speech – our voices rang through the hall in indignant protest and members clustered round steps – among them Captain Craig to whom our Belfast representative[12] said 'They only mind the militants who have guns.' Another cried out 'If we had been men they would have heard us!' The audience was distinctly favourable; the police, taken by surprise, did not intervene for some moments. At length the protestors were forcibly, but without violence, removed from the hall and escorted off the premises, strict orders being issued that they were not to be readmitted!

A protest within the House renders one liable to detention in the Clock Tower but, as it would hardly suit the Prime Minister or Mr Redmond to shut up Irishwomen for the offence of trying to see them, this penalty was not enforced. Mr Redmond had, no doubt, a qualm of conscience as to his treatment of his countrywomen and the press was informed afterwards that he had sent his private secretary with a message. Had we left quietly, we should never have heard of that private secretary, who managed to take two hours to reach us.

On Wednesday night we witnessed Sylvia's deputation of working-women from the East End[13] being broken up within a mile of the House by mounted police, while the band played the Women's Marseillaise. A clergyman in surplice headed it – Sylvia had been snatched away to Holloway just before –

and thousands of workers, men and women, followed. But after a brief glimpse it disappeared: mounted police and ordinary police and plain-clothes men poured out from the side-streets and rode it down, scattering it into fragments. The mounted police drove their horses upon the pavements, on to the steps even of private houses, flinging the crowd, men, women and little children, pell-mell before them, penning them frightened into corners, crushing them together in masses and closing in upon them. One marveled that the patient, fretted horses did not do more damage: the police themselves seemed not to relish their stupid task, the crowd keeping its temper wonderfully; everywhere there were cries of protest against Sylvia's arrest and expression of sympathy with the militants.

We found our way, in spite of the police, to Parliament Square. Here cordons of them were drawn up in bewildering array, while mounted police rode up and down between, clearing the streets and pavements. At times we were hemmed in between two cordons, and though repeatedly enjoined to 'pass along, please', neither cordon would allow us either to advance or retreat. Then a plain-clothes man or an inspector would suddenly issue a mysterious order, and the lines would break up, allowing the crowd to 'pass along'. Sometimes an 'obstructor' was hauled off in custody, but, as far as possible, arrests were avoided. Meanwhile some of the deputation were permitted to enter the House and gain speech with the Chief Whip. So we are getting on – but a short while ago such a deputation usually ended in serious violence and sentences of 'hard labour' for those who took part.

Thanks to the courtesy of the United Suffragists, the Irish Deputation was invited to address an indignation meeting, held in the Essex Hall on Thursday night. Irishwomen attended in large numbers, and a strong protest was made against the treatment, by Mr Asquith and Mr Redmond, of the deputation who had come from Ireland for the purpose of pleading with them for Home Rule for Irish Women. The atmosphere of the meeting was electric: one feels at present that the very air is full of Votes for Women. The papers ring with it – it seems to be the only live issue. One cannot escape the feeling of impending tragedy: one of those brave women will be done to death. And victory will follow in the wake of that catastrophe. Mr Nevinson,[14] an acute observer, said that, in his memory, passion had never run so high over any question, and that the present situation was only paralleled by the Home Rule fight of the 'eighties and the Boer war. Nero played the fiddle while Rome was burning: our representatives eat strawberries and cream while women slowly starve to death in prison. Governments are like the Bourbons, they learn nothing and forget nothing.

'London's welcome: Essex Hall meeting'
Irish Citizen, 20 June 1914
[No author given but one can assume that Hanna wrote at least the bulk of the report.]

On Thursday, June 11th, the question of the enfranchisement of Irishwomen was specially dealt with at a meeting held in Essex Hall, London, under the auspices of the United Suffragists. Representatives from different Irish societies attended, including the Irishwomen's Franchise League and the Irishwomen's Suffrage Federation.

The chair was taken by Mrs Ayrton Gould, who explained that the United Suffragists had offered their platform to the members of the Irish deputation visiting London for the purpose of an interview with Mr Asquith and Mr Redmond.

Miss Mellone,[15] speaking for the Irishwomen's Suffrage Federation, emphasized the strength of the suffrage movement in Ireland, and the fact that even now, in this time of intense political feeling, Irishwomen of all shades of political opinion had united in the demand for recognition as citizens.

Mrs McCoubrey (Northern Representative of the IWFL) referred to the situation in Belfast. The Unionist Council had promised the vote to women under the Provisional Government, but this could hardly be considered as a more than temporary expedient, and Irishwomen demanded more than that.

Mrs Sheehy Skeffington explained the object of the joint deputation, which the Prime Minister and Mr Redmond had both refused to receive. This deputation was of representative Irishwomen, and its purpose was to demand that the Amending Home Rule Bill should be so framed as to allow for the enfranchisement of women. There was a strong demand in Ireland for this reform, as evidenced by the resolution passed by many local Councils, and by the Trades Congress, held in Dublin on June 2nd. On this occasion a strong resolution was passed, not at all a vague expression of belief in the need for the enfranchisement of women, but a definite demand that women should be included in the Amending Bill. There was as a fact no anti-suffrage opinion in Ireland. Irishwomen and Irishmen had worked together in every form of public activity for many years, and there was no need to emphasise the enormous political activity of Irishwomen at the present moment. The deputation, organised by the joint committee, had been refused, on the plea by Mr Redmond that the question should be left to the Irish parliament, and by Mr Asquith that it had been dealt with in his speech on the Manhood Suffrage Bill. The fallacy of both these objections had been too often exposed to need further refutation. Though the deputation had been thus formally refused, the militant section of it had been at the House of Commons that afternoon, and had again asked Mr Redmond and Mr Asquith to receive them. They had interviewed a number of Irish members, but the gentlemen referred to had not thought it worth their while to hear the wishes of Irishwomen in this matter.

The meeting was very well attended, chiefly by Irishwomen residing in London, and the interest taken in the question was proved by the large and responsive audience.

'The Asquith meeting'
Irish Citizen, 3 October 1914

On the two previous occasions of the visit of a Cabinet Minister, or ex-Cabinet minister, to Dublin, I happened to be in prison, once for an assault on Dublin Castle by me, and once because of an assault on me by one Sergeant Thomas. My offence against Mr Bonar Law was that of handing out leaflets; against Mr Asquith – this time it was that of attempting to make a speech within a half-mile radius of the Mansion House. The penalty for the first was one week's imprisonment, for the second some hours' detention.

On the last occasion that Mr Asquith was with us he had a public procession, with torch-light and bands. This time his movements were wrapt in mystery. Half Kingstown turned out to meet him on Thursday; local luminaries, portly clerics, Vicars and Archdeacons, thronged the pier to receive his boat. Suffragists, too, were there, eager to meet him; but at the last moment word came that he had changed his mind – and we were left forlorn! He departed in a special boat, and the hour of his leaving was also a profound secret. Mr Asquith is not as popular as he was.

Long before the great man arrived, the Government spies were busy. The movements of all known suffragists were assiduously followed, their private correspondence tampered with, telephones tapped, visitors at headquarters scrutinised by lumbering 'G' men, who hung around us while we shopped, lunched, or travelled, on the look-out for 'discoveries'. No 'ladies' were admitted to the meeting, lest a suffragist might get in, with the result that many Nationalist and Unionist party-women bitterly resented such exclusion. Suffragists did not greatly mind: they had a heckler there all the same. And besides, there are other ways. Never were more police concentrated on one spot than in the neighbourhood of the Mansion House; the DMPs were reinforced by the RIC, and they in turn by mounted police. Asquith had a bodyguard of 'Hibernian' Volunteers, to make assurance doubly sure, and Larkin's Citizen Army prevented **him** from being arrested. The streets bristled with armed men. Asquith had to entrench himself behind cordon after cordon to escape the general enthusiasm, and to slip up to the Mansion House by a side-street. So great was the relief of the organisers of the meeting at his safe arrival, that volley after volley of fireworks went forth from the

Mansion House, and lighted up the serried ranks of DMP and RIC. And very 'nervy' they all were.

When we advanced on the cordons, armed with leaflets, we were received with a flutter of 'Move on, please', 'Keep moving', 'You must confine yourself to the carriageway', 'None but ticket-holders', etc. Wherever we seemed to be making headway with the crowd – who were practically all sympathetic – police and plain-clothes men intervened to hustle us on. We held little meetings everywhere among the crowd and could have given tens of thousands of leaflets. When an Irish MP assaulted an associate, no one interfered – suffragists were fair game. Fortunately, however, the crowd near the Mansion House was friendly, so the police were busy keeping us away from them.

When our leaflets were all exhausted, shortly after 9.30, we made our presence felt at the Fountain at the top of Dawson Street. Coming up from the back, we took the police by surprise, and were well started in our speech when they awoke to what was up, bore down upon us, arrested two of us, and proceeded to march us down Grafton Street. One of them muttered something about a cab, but he was over-ruled. His superiors remembered the mob on the last occasion of Asquith's visit, and acted apparently in the hope of a repetition on us of its former violence. They would, no doubt, have been not altogether ill-pleased had we been badly mauled ere we reached College Street; our bodyguard was few, and it could have been said that we were arrested for our own 'protection'. But Dublin has greatly changed to suffragists since 1912; the crowd was friendly, if puzzled. Only one hero attacked us; a postman in uniform bravely struck Mrs Connery full between the shoulders, and came round to deliver a second blow on her face, while the police held her hands. She drew the constable's attention to the assault; but, as usual, with no result. That postman is after all, a possible recruit; he may ere this be volunteering for the defence of Belgian women against their foes. The only other 'incident' of note was a stone flung at the constable who held me, cutting his ear. He'd put 'five bullets' in the fellow when he got his gun – he was an RIC man. We told him to be calm, and reminded him how well he bore up when one of us was assaulted, but he was not to be soothed. Next time the police will think twice before they try to provoke an assault on us.

We were a pretty large body ere we reached the station, several friends having joined us en route. At first we were all admitted; presently the goats were divided from the sheep. The station was so full of 'reserves', that there was no room for us, and we sat outside on the cross-bench by the door, interviewing the multitude as it passed. Soon the police got restive, afraid of a 'rescue', perhaps, and we were admitted to the reserve room, where our friends were shortly permitted to penetrate. From 10 till 12 we waited, turning over the possibilities of bail, hunger-strike, forcible feeding, in our minds, and wondering would the charge be – 'Obstructing the traffic', 'Interfering with the police in the discharge of their duty', 'violent and seditious language likely to cause a breach of the peace', 'Assault on the police', 'High treason' – or perhaps all five – when we were summoned to the Charge Room, and solemnly told we were discharged – Asquith, no doubt, having just rung up from the Viceregal Lodge that he was in bed and had double-locked his door. Doubtless, had the orders been to detain us, all the above would have been solemnly sworn to by DMP and RIC before Mr Swifte the next day, and we should now be in Mountjoy. British justice is a funny thing! Legal men tell us that the whole proceeding is quite illegal, and that we could bring a charge of 'assault and unlawful arrest' against the force. We certainly could, but we suffragists know what the result of that would be. The police would leave the court without a stain upon their characters, and we should leave it with a much-lightened purse and a warning from the bench not to repeat the offence. After all, what can we expect? We are not voters, nor recruits, nor even Belgian women.

'Suffragette revels'
Irish Citizen, 5 December 1914

A Dublin paper recently reproached us with unseemly 'fiddling' (and dancing) while 'Rome was burning' – meaning, no doubt, that it was sinful to dissipate while Europe was at war. We might reply variously to the charge as thus: If scribes scribble while Rome burns, why should suffragettes not dance? Or again, had the Dance been linked to a martial purpose – Red Cross, Purple Cross, War Relief, or the like – would our dancing have offended? One surmises, no. Why, then, if to us our great cause alone is glorious, should we not dance for it, just as we have gone to prison for it, hunger-struck for it – aye, and died for it (some of us) when the Call came? Militants might well reply, in the words of a wit who recently defended us against the charge of being 'womanly' just now and dancing: 'After all, now that men have taken over (and extended under new management) the "outrage" department, we women may turn our thoughts elsewhere.' Militants cannot help recalling, too, that not so long ago Rome was fiddling, while they were burning – and getting penal servitude for it, to the great delight of Rome and the Press.

A suffragette's life is essentially a varied and eventful one, and dancing is but one of its many phases. The morning and afternoon of the dance were passed 'Watching the Courts'[16] at a pitiful and poignant case of seduction, for which the Law at its best could do no more for a girl's broken life than assess pecuniary damages to her father for 'loss of her services'. On the way to the

Dance a vision lingered with me of that Court, crowded with gloating males, listening agape to the sordid tale of betrayal: while lawyers bandied innuendoes and judges gibed at suffragettes and their grievances – the change to the ballroom of the DBC, filled with gaily and quaintly-attired dancers, was sudden, and the painful memories had to be switched off. The symbols of the IWF League – orange and green – were around; little flags bore the magic words, 'Votes for Women'; many dancers wore our favours; there were many old friends to greet.

Social functions, apart from their primary purpose of helping to fill the exchequer, serve an almost equally important purpose – that, namely, of destroying hoary old myths. One of our members was warned by her brother-in-law that there would be no men at a Suffrage Dance. He will be surprised to know that the men were so abundant that they had perforce to dance together! I recently beheld, in the rooms of a certain society, a silly caricature of a suffragist – toothless, gaunt, angular, decrepit – bearing the symbol, 'I want a Husband – or a Vote!' Most of the suffragettes at our dance were already equipped with the former alternative, and married and unmarried alike had none of the popular characteristics by which the wary are told to mark down the 'wild woman' or (to parody present Press parlance) the Female 'Hun'. One of the most charming and graceful dancers was a recent bride, whose name figures prominently in our 'Roll of Honour' – ex-prisoner, ex-hunger-striker, and victim of forcible feeding.

Is there, then, no difference between the 'suffragette' and her sister of 'womanly' fame? There is a subtle nuance, and it was quite observable at the Fancy Dress function. The former has the additional charm of self-reliance, of initiative. She is no prude; in fancy dress she frankly favours doublet and hose; her chosen characters mirror her pet virtues – the Rosalinds, the Charlotte Cordays; but neither is she a philanderer. She enjoys herself whole-heartedly with the more zest, because to her a ball is not a thing of every day; in most cases she has been hard at work all day, and her occupations will not allow her to indulge in a long sleep on the morrow. Neither does she don frivolity with her mask; she brings her cause with her, and bears it about with her as part of her being. Her small talk does not reek of ballroom ineptitude; she may even startle her partner with an allusion to incarceration, past and to come! At supper an ex-prisoner was recounting the fact, as the clock struck twelve, that she was in Mountjoy on that day twelve months ago. The table rose and toasted her 'Many Happy Returns!'

The Dance mirrored, as such functions do, the varying phases of the hour. Among Geishas, Pierrots, sailor lads and lassies, fisher-girls, colleens and cowboys, the background of the war furnished a Red Cross Nurse, some Boy

Scouts, some Volunteers in uniform, a dainty impersonation of England and France with flags entwined, and as pendant a radiant emerald and gold 'Irish Freedom' with broken manacles and gyves. In addition, there were Bulgarians, Russians and Roumanians. The MC, as was fitting, was a woman, an efficient and wholly delightful Mistress of the Revels.

Joan

5

WAR AND PACIFISM

INTRODUCTION

The two-year period covered here includes some of the most significant events in both world and Irish history. The Home Rule crisis had become increasingly serious with the formation of the Ulster Volunteer Force as symbol of unionist determination to resist incorporation into an Ireland outside of the United Kingdom of England, Scotland and Wales. In response Irish nationalists had formed the Irish Volunteers in November 1913 and in April 1914 the women's auxiliary organisation, the Irish Women's Council, soon to be known by its Irish name, Cumann na mBan, was inaugurated. The Irish Volunteers' refusal to allow women a place on its executive committee, or to state that women's enfranchisement was included within its objective of fighting for 'Irish liberty' provoked an indignant response from the militants of the IWFL, and Hanna was a leading figure in challenging Cumann na mBan to demand an equality of status for women within the Volunteer movement. Her lengthy letter to the *Irish Independent* (published in part by the *Irish Times*, but omitting some of her criticism on feminist grounds) made it clear that the subordinate position of the women's organisation was her primary concern, but she also objected to the conservative views which had been expressed by Agnes O'Farrelly[1] in her inaugural presidential address, in which the latter implied that the work to be performed would not threaten the social order because it would be simply an extension of women's domestic role – each rifle would represent 'a bolt fastened behind the door of some Irish home' and each cartridge 'a watchdog to fight for the sanctity of the hearth' (*The Irish Volunteer*, 18 April 1914). Suffragists continued to press the issue of votes for women during the first two years of war, despite the increasing complexity and polarisation of the political landscape.

The outbreak of war in August 1914 was a blow to those who believed that if women had political power, they would have been able to act as a force for peaceful negotiation rather than bloodshed. The *Irish Citizen* reacted immediately, with a poster declaring 'Votes for Women Now! Damn Your War!'

and both Hanna and her husband Frank deployed their considerable powers as orators and writers to argue against those who supported the war effort, either directly as combatants or indirectly as workers for war relief. Hanna's despair that the 'map of suffrage' would now be rolled up as women threw themselves into war work led her to plead for the maintenance of 'peace, sanity and suffrage'. Her outspoken statement that women should not be 'mopping up the blood and purifying the stench of the abattoir' but 'clearing away the whole rotten system' (*Irish Citizen*, 15 August 1914) shocked many; she persisted, however, and used the pages of the *Irish Citizen* to address her critics. In June 1915 Frank was sentenced to six months' hard labour as a consequence of his unrelenting campaign to persuade men not to enlist in the British army. He won his release under the terms of the 'Cat and Mouse Act' after a hunger and thirst strike and, in order to avoid re-arrest, went to America until December. Hanna therefore had the additional burden of the *Irish Citizen* (although friends helped with the editorial work), as well as her son's welfare, and her work as a teacher during this period.

The IWFL remained in close contact with the international suffrage movement, and the proposed women's peace conference at The Hague in May 1915 was greeted with great enthusiasm in Ireland. Not only would it provide an opportunity for a united feminist response to the war, but for Irish feminists, who had succeeded after some negotiation in having a separate delegation, it would also provide a unique opportunity for Ireland to be seen on an international stage as constituting a small nation separate from Britain. Hanna hailed this as a victory for the nation as well as for women, 'For the first time . . . Irish delegates take their place as representatives of their own country. It is the hour of small nationalities. Long live the small nationalities of the earth!' (*Irish Citizen*, 17 April 1915). The British government's action in preventing the women from reaching The Hague through denying passports (apart from a few 'discreet' women, who included Louie Bennett) and then closing the North Sea to shipping so that none could travel, came in for ferocious criticism from Hanna, who had had the frustration of waiting in vain in London for an opportunity to cross to Holland. At the subsequent protest meeting in Dublin she articulated a clear link between nation and gender, 'They would send from that meeting a message to Asquith and McKenna that Ireland was still alive; and apt to kick them now and then. If they had had votes they would not have been so humiliated' (*Irish Citizen*, 2 May 1915).

The undated fragment of Hanna's letter written to Louie Bennett, of the Irish Women's Reform League, who held very strong pacifist views, was in response to Bennett's experience of this protest meeting. Louie had proposed the resolution of protest at the meeting, which was seconded by Thomas

MacDonagh, director of training of the Irish Volunteers. She had then been forced to sit in appalled silence as he continued with his description of his duties, including training men in techniques of bayonetting, which he declared would eventually help 'to end age-long wars such as that in this country'. Louie wrote to Hanna 'to let you know that I shall in future take no part in peace meetings which put Irish nationalism above international tolerance and which are embittered by anti-England feuds'. Hanna's response reveals a position more in line with the militant republicanism of MacDonagh than with Bennett, her feminist colleague. From this period, in her speeches and by her actions, Hanna Sheehy Skeffington revealed her conviction that citizenship was not only gendered but raced. Much of her denunciation concentrated upon the nationalist rather than feminist implications of the ban, believing that the government was 'afraid to let Ireland's voice be heard on the rights of small nationalities' (*Irish Citizen*, 22 May 1915).

The hope that Ireland could be included as a small nation in any peace negotiations following the conclusion of war was one harboured by all nationalists and was part of the impetus behind the Easter Rising. During the weekend before Easter 1916 Hanna met James Connolly, a close friend of herself and Frank, who apparently said 'if you are interested in developments, I would not advise you to go away on holiday just now'.[2] He also said that women had been given equal rights and equal opportunities in the republican Proclamation. She was obviously in the confidence of at least some of the leadership, because they selected her to act as a member of a civil provisional government, which would have come into effect if the Rising had succeeded in lasting for a longer period of time.

'Irish Women's Council'
Irish Independent, 6 May 1914
Sir,
    It was made abundantly clear by myself, by other speakers, and by the chair, that I spoke at Saturday's meeting of the Irishwomen's Council entirely as a critic of the new organisation. I welcome the opportunity given me by Miss O'Farrelly's letter to state publicly that I am not connected in any way with the new society. Any society of women which proposes to act merely as an 'animated collecting box' for men cannot have the sympathy of any self-respecting woman. The proposed 'Ladies' Auxiliary Committee' has apparently no function beyond that of a conduit pipe to pour a stream of gold into the coffers of the male organisation, and to be turned off automatically as soon as it has served this mean and subordinate purpose. I ventured to remind these women that the Ulster Unionist Women's Council acted on a different basis, and that Sir Edward Carson had promised them, in reward for their services,

a place in his Provisional Government;[3] and I suggested that the Irishwomen's Council might see to it also that the women were placed on a footing of equality with the men, and given a share in the Executive and in the Council of the men's organisation. I did not raise the question of votes for women at the meeting, but I did ask the Irishwomen's Council to protest against the importation of English Coercion Acts into Ireland in the form of the Cat and Mouse Act. In making those suggestions I had the approval and sympathy of nearly all the women present, and of many of the men. Miss O'Farrelly is inaccurate in stating that I had no permission to speak. I had not her permission, but I had the permission of the meeting. True, some of those for whom rifles were to be procured at the expense of the women's 'fur coats' attempted to howl me down; and some of the ladies on the platform who have relatives or patrons in Ministerial circles objected to my criticism of the Liberal Government in its treatment of women, and tried to closure me; but on a vote being taken, the majority decided to hear me out, and many of the speakers who followed entirely endorsed my view.

Miss O'Farrelly declares that the new organisation will not be 'interfered with or exploited by any person or by any organisation for their own ends'. There are indications that this is precisely what is happening; the enemy is not the outside critic, but the insidious influence within.

Until the Irishwomen's Council repudiates the early Victorian cant of some of its official spokeswomen, and forms itself on proper feminist lines, it will be liable to such open criticism at its public functions.

In conclusion, I would remind Miss O'Farrelly, in the words of Mrs Wyse Power, that 'there can be no free nation, unless the women as well as the men of that nation are free'.

Hanna Sheehy Skeffington
11 Grosvenor Place, Rathmines, May 5, 1914.

'Nationalist women and Volunteers'
Irish Times, 8 May 1914
Sir,

It was made abundantly clear by myself, by other speakers, and by the chair, that I spoke at Saturday's meeting of the Irishwomen's Council entirely as a critic of the new organisation. I welcome the opportunity given me by Miss O'Farrelly's letter to state publicly that I am not connected in any way with the new society. Any society of women which proposes to act merely as an 'animated collecting box' for men cannot have the sympathy of any self-respecting woman. The proposed 'Ladies' Auxiliary Committee' has apparently no function beyond that of a conduit pipe to pour a stream of gold into the coffers of the male organisation, and to be turned off automatically as soon as it has served this mean and subordinate purpose. I ventured to remind these women that the Ulster Unionist Women's Council acted on a different basis, and that Sir Edward Carson had promised them, in reward for their services, a place in his Provisional Government; and I suggested that the Irishwomen's Council might see to it also that the women were placed on a footing of equality with the men, and given a share in the Executive and in the Council of the men's organisation. I did not raise the question of votes for women at the meeting, but I did ask the Irishwomen's Council to protest against the importation of English Coercion Acts into Ireland in the form of the Cat and Mouse Act. In making those suggestions I had the approval and sympathy of nearly all the women present, and of many of the men. Miss O'Farrelly is inaccurate in stating that I had no permission to speak. I had not her permission, but I had the permission of the meeting. On a vote being taken, the majority decided to hear me out, and many of the speakers who followed entirely endorsed my view.

Yours, etc.,

Hanna Sheehy Skeffington

'Duty of suffragettes'

Irish Citizen, 15 August 1914

The present situation offers many lessons to suffragists. There are many pitfalls at our feet. The women of Europe, whose motherlands are engaged in strife, are all alike in their voteless condition. Like us their hands are clean they have no responsibility for this war. Like us, they have to pay the price none the less to the uttermost farthing. They have to deliver up the sons they bore in agony to a bloody death in a quarrel of which they know not the why or wherefore, on the side of the particular ally their Government has chosen for the moment; they have to face starvation at home for themselves and their children meanwhile; many of them are exposed with their helpless daughters to lust and outrage of a war-maddened soldiery. That is what in cold fact war means to women. It is an aspect that the world's press disregards, because it would make war unpopular.

There is one 'bright spot' – and it is a real one, not a will 'o the wisp – in this, namely, the fine solidarity of organised womanhood. With one voice at the International Suffrage Alliance and through the entire suffrage Press it spoke bravely and firmly against the 'insensate devilry' of war. When the Churches of the Peacemaker were silent, womanhood, standing for civilisation and progress, lifted a voice of unanimous protest. But her appeal was as usual disregarded by male statesmen, eager to let loose the yelping dogs of war at one another's throats. Still the protest has been registered: united womanhood has intervened for the first time on a great issue and her message will be remembered when the shouting is over.

At every crisis suffragists must be alive to insidious dangers that threaten to swamp the cause. War is the favourite method employed by governments hard pressed at home and eager to shelve their responsibilities. The rock of party politics on which so many suffragists in the past suffered shipwreck they now, thanks chiefly to the militants, have learned to avoid. We smile now when we are told to put the needs of the party first, not to embarrass the Government or Home Rule or the Union by pressing our claims 'at this crisis' (and this 'crisis' is a chronic state). We now know by bitter experience that the women who heed these cries are traitors to their cause, and that it is their supineness which is largely responsible for our voteless condition.

Now the 'wreckers' are at work again. This time attempts will be made to induce women to abandon propaganda, to roll up the map of suffrage with the map of Europe, to forget their own pressing economic and political grievances (now more acute than ever) because of the 'national crisis'.

Now will the test-stone be applied to the soundness and sex loyalty of every one of us; do we really put Votes for Women above everything, or does it fall into second rank? Are we women first of all?

Note how we women are being worked upon by a Press that advocated lynch-law for us but a few weeks ago. We are inundated with invitations to be up and doing 'to help the men'. They have not yet forced Conscription upon us, not because they desire to spare us the horrors of war – for these we suffer as non-combatants to the full – but because it is our function to replenish the nations decimated by fire and sword, to continue to supply 'food for cannon'.

But, short of facing the enemy's guns in actual warfare, every other duty is expected from us. Here is a list compiled from the daily Press of things that we may do to show 'we are not unworthy of our soldier brothers'. We are to knit 'soft woollen comforters' for the departing soldiers, to replenish their cigarette-cases from our pin money, to see to food supplies at home, so that no unseemly riots take place among the starving poor to disturb the progress of affairs, to accompany the troops as Red Cross nurses, helping to patch up the shattered victims of machine-guns and torpedoes, to fill the places of reservists and conscripts at a lower wage at home, to till the fields and garner the harvests left by the labourer, and contrive the weekly budget on a diminished allowance, so that our menfolk may not have cause to grumble at their dinner, though society totter. Some of these tasks are noble, some ignoble, but all end for suffragists in a cul-de-sac. When the war is over we shall be gently but firmly put back in our place once more – on our pedestals.

While some invitations to suffragists are a flattering admission of the efficiency and public spirit of organised women, they constitute none the less a grave danger. How often have we been invited to drop our troublesome propaganda, to show our fitness for citizenship by 'being good', by slumming, by playing at municipal reform, by devoting ourselves to poor-law work, by any and every imaginable side-issue. Anything but Votes for Women!

Again it behoves us to reply to all those who would enlist our services – Suffrage First! Every suffragist will take to heart the lesson of present happenings. We see more clearly than ever what humanity loses by refusing to enfranchise women throughout Europe. May Europe's, England's, difficulty be Womanhood's opportunity! A truce to tinkering with reform while the very bulwarks of society are being swept away. It is not for us to mitigate by one iota the horrors of war; such attempts, however laudable, are but 'casting snowballs into hell to lower the temperature'.

To humanise war is to perpetuate war: once seen in its naked hideousness, the glamour of romance gone, its sway is over.

Women are eminently practical: they realise the futility of fiddling with symptoms while the disease rages unchecked.

If male statesmanship after all these centuries has nothing better to offer by way of adjusting differences than a universal shambles, then in heaven's name let men allow women to lend a hand, not at mopping up the blood and purifying the stench of the abattoir, but at clearing away the whole rotten system. Until then it is our duty to press on with unabated energy, to increase our activities at this crisis, to preach peace, sanity and suffrage.

War must not devastate our ranks: this at least it is in our power to prevent. Our guns must be directed not against the Germans (from whom, by the way, we have much to learn) but against our common enemy – the warmongering politician, the pledge-breaking Government, now so sentimental over the wrongs of oppressed nationalities, while it continues to sweat and bully with impunity the women of the land. These are the enemy: it is these upon whom we wage war until they offer terms. The suffragist who turns aside from the cause of Votes for Women at this hour is, indeed, helping to put back the clock. By redoubling energy in pursuing our propaganda, in war as in peace, we suffragists shall find ourselves when the war is over – and may it be sooner – not in the position of a disbanded army for whom there is no more active service, but as eager and strenuous in our campaign as before, as determined to have a voice in the councils of the nation in order to avert in future the evils of a Man-run State. All the rest is vanity; it is but pandering to the war fetish. Retro Satanas![4]

Letter
Irish Worker, 15 August 1914
Although in times of peace women are ignored by the politicians of all parties, they are nevertheless expected as a matter of course, and without question, to make untold sacrifices whenever the follies or the crimes of male statecraft

have plunged the nations into war. Women are denied all voice in deciding for peace or war, for arbitration or for massacre; yet it is upon the women that most of the horrors and burdens of war inevitably fall. Interested primarily in the welfare of the race, the guardians of civilisation, they recognise more clearly than men, who are easily blinded by war-passion that a war is an unmixed evil; that womanhood, a passive participant, pays its bitter toil in rapine and destruction, in famine, in horrors unnameable, wherever the monster leaves its devastating track. The sympathies of suffragists, of all thinking women, go out in this hour to the stricken womanhood of Europe, in every country that is the victim of war. Women, like us, aliens in their own land, powerless to stem the tide of barbarism, yet compelled to sacrifice all they hold dear at the bidding of male autocrats and warmongering bureaucracies. With them we hope and pray that sanity may shortly be restored and the peace of Europe re-established before her civilisation suffers eclipse. We realise more acutely than ever our parlous state, deprived of all safeguards, yet forced to expiate the crimes of governments, which we are powerless to prevent. We trust that women will lay to heart the moral of the present situation by insisting that their claims for citizenship shall no longer be swept aside. If we are good enough to help in emergencies like the present, let us see to it that those who now beg our assistance recognise our equal rights as human beings. We are good enough for all and every service and responsibility till the war is over. When peace is restored, we shall again be reminded of our inherent disabilities; we shall be told by carpet-warriors that because we do not fight, we may not vote. While suffragists do not deny the usefulness of many such good works as are now enthusiastically recommended to women, they remember first of all that the chief duty is to their common womanhood. They have happily no responsibility for war and its bitter consequences; and they will permit nothing to divert their energies from the achievement of their purpose. The war makes it more than ever imperative that women must be given a voice in the councils of the nations, that they may exercise a salutary check upon male aggression and militarism.

Hanna Sheehy Skeffington. Chairman of Committee. Irish Women's Franchise League.

'Emotional nursing'[5]
Irish Citizen, 21 November 1914

Were Florence Nightingale alive today she would see her life-work being set at nought, and the profession that she devoted herself to uplift at the mercy of the amateur. Of all women who have suffered directly or indirectly through the war, the last, one should imagine, would have been trained nurses, for, with millions of men suffering hideously, the services of such healers must surely be at a premium. But such is far from being the case: Florence Nightingale, with all her genius and devotion, did not extirpate 'Sairey Gamp',[6] who, on the contrary, occupies an honoured place at the front tending the Tommies, while her trained sisters, who have volunteered for active service, sit at home waiting to be called. And the soldiers die of tetanus and rot of gangrene, while unskilled duchesses and influential ladies, athirst for a new sensation, usurp the functions of the skilled worker, and are photographed in half-penny papers bending tenderly over their victims, with jewels ablaze at their breast and favourite greyhounds by their side.

In many cases these ladies have constituted themselves Lady Superintendents of hospital units on a few weeks' training: one of them offered herself recently to the matron of a large hospital, asking for 'a week's training on any terms you like, but only a week, for I want to go to the front then'. Cholera, smallpox, fever epidemics will cheerfully be left to the trained to cope with, but these society ghouls fasten themselves on the wounded soldier or officer, not realising that the proper treatment of wounds demands exceptionally high training. Many of these women are but schoolgirls: one, a girl of eighteen, died at the front the other day. One is not surprised that one such unit, marshalled by a fascinating society hostess, was instantly deported from Belgium by orders of the German Emperor, and that the German Surgeons have refused to allow these half-baked amateurs to work in the field hospitals in Germany, for there, too, the plague of the amateur threatens the soldiery.

The nursing journals at home are full of the scandal, but the war office heeds not their protests. Just as at the beginning of the war fashionable ladies rushed to form sewing-parties until firmly checked by the leaders of organised labour, who persuaded Queen Mary to deprecate all such encroachments on the work of dressmakers and seamstresses, so now the nursing profession is the happy hunting ground of these blacklegs, and here there is no one to make effective protest, for nurses have no trade unions, and their societies are usually too timorous for organised protest, acquiescing silently in the abuse. The hospitals in Dublin particularly are being flooded by ladies wanting to learn, in a course of four to six weeks, an art which the professional, however skilful, must devote three to four years to master. By means of a weekly payment of one guinea, a short cut to nursing is made; in many hospitals the volunteers are relieved of various irksome duties, the 'dirty work' falling to the ordinary nurse; ladies are allowed their pet dogs, visitors are permitted them practically at all hours, and many disciplinary regulations are in abeyance, the nurses being in some cases turned out of their quarters for their accommodation. The extra work entailed by this invasion falls on the ordinary nurse, who has to do it as well as her own as best she may. And for the further confusion of the public these outsiders are allowed to wear the hospital uniform of the trained nurse, without any distinction whatever. Many of these amateurs are the sisters and daughters of doctors; some have left husbands and children in the pursuit of this latest fashionable fad (what an outcry there would be if this desertion of the hearth were due to enthusiasm for suffrage!) because they are influential, and because of their fees, the hospital authorities have supinely condoned this incursion of hordes of the untrained into their ranks. In one case only in Ireland, as far as can be ascertained, has an hospital refused to admit these amateurs – Belfast would have none of them. The Belfast hospital authorities apparently put efficiency first, even in time of war. It is impossible to ascertain the exact figures of the various offending institutions, but the plague of 'emotional nursing' seems pretty extensive in Ireland: I have heard of only one institution where any attempt was made to check it. In certain convalescent homes for the wounded the whole management is in the hands of untrained volunteers, while trained nurses are out of employment. These helpers are under the Red Cross or the St John's Ambulance Societies, both wealthy organisations, which ought to be able to pay their staff and secure the services of the highly trained instead of 'this mob of disorganised workers'. The other day in Sussex, the Red Cross ladies took up the post of a night nurse in an hospital, and their kindness, as the *Nursing Mirror* pointed out, has been the means of depriving a trained nurse of the post and the poor of a skilled attendant. This case is but one of many: these ladies undertake the nursing of convalescents 'for practice' at nominal rates, heedless of the wrong they are inflicting on those who depend upon such work for a livelihood, and who have devoted years to training. No doubt many are well-meaning and devoted, if thoughtless: they fail to realise that their action, far from being truly patriotic or likely to be of any use to the State, is helping to degrade a great profession, by flooding it with unskilled workers and lowering its standard and prestige; they need to be told that, if they really are desirous of helping, the best assistance that they can render would be to pay for trained nurses at the front and stay at home themselves. Florence Nightingale underwent a stern apprenticeship in training at various establishments before she embarked on her life-work: she insisted on adequate training for her helpers, and packed home any nurses who fell short of her high standard, no matter how influential their connexions and how sublime their aspirations. Has 'the lady with the lamp' lived in vain?

Today the very abuses she strove against are rife. The War Office permits the untrained to usurp the place of the trained because the former, organised by private individuals, pay their own expenses! Meanwhile it shuffles out of its responsibility by decreeing that it shall send only trained nurses to the front (and keeping hundreds of nurses on a waiting list) and connives at the abuse by allowing private enterprise to do its work free of charge, while it smothers in its own red tape. Busy getting war grants of hundreds of millions passed purely for destruction, the Government depends largely on private enterprise and haphazard individual schemes for the care of the wounded, and will doubtless go on doing so till plague has decimated the troops and frightened away all but the trained professional.

The present scandals would have been impossible under a system of State Registration of nurses. Where such registration is operative (needless to say this is so in Australia, where women vote), the nurse is safeguarded as well as the doctor. For over twenty-five years nurses in these countries have agitated for this reform, and have been baffled by the machinations of the vested interest, sometimes the hospital authorities, sometimes the doctors, who not infrequently are given to exploiting the mere nurse, and like keeping her carefully in her place. In Dublin no single hospital (not even those for women and children) possesses a woman-governor, hence 'many influences are at work unfavourable to the trained nurse'.

Had nurses possessed the vote their agitation for recognition would have been successful years ago: it is more than doubtful whether they will achieve their purpose until they are enfranchised. Their Bill has had the usual fate of measures for women, shelved by its 'best friends', blocked and obstructed by those whose object it is to keep women cheap and unorganised. Just as no doctors would tolerate young men rushing through a few weeks' training and proceeding to set up as medical practitioners, so under State Registration it would have been impossible for any amateur to find a 'Red Cross short cut' to nursing. No hospital authorities, no medical men would have dared to risk their prestige by encouraging 'emotional nursing', or allowing a noble profession to be degraded by silly society women or well-meaning, if misguided, senti-mentalists. It is for nurses to take the lesson to heart, to organise and to insist on their profession being recognised. And now that they are most of all necessary to the State is the time for them to act.

Correspondence
Irish Citizen, 10 April 1915
Mrs H. Sheehy Skeffington writes:

Mr Haslam's letter comes to me as a revelation: through it I realise why the agitation of constitutional suffragists in these countries has not achieved its purpose in all these weary years. The cause that relies only on appeals to conscience and to reason, that takes no account of selfish interests, or of the driving force of fear, is one that statesmen will continue to believe in piously, and as piously to ignore. The franchise was won in the past by what Mr Haslam would describe as horrible 'bullying'. O'Connell did not achieve Catholic Emancipation by praying for it; the negro slaves were not freed by appeals to the reason or conscience of their owners; and the methods employed to-day against Prussia cannot be described exactly as relying on philosophic argument. To come nearer home; Home Rule has not been placed on the Statute Book as a result of an appeal to reason and conscience, and Sir Edward Carson's policy of armed resistance and civil war to prevent its enactment, is not one that relies solely on moral suasion and sweet reasonableness. If history teaches anything it is that great causes achieve their purpose finally only when they are driven home by force of some kind: the only argument that statesmen listen to when deaf to reason. It is no doubt soothing to male vanity to lay down the law that men never yield to bullying, above all, never to the bullying of women. Unfortunately for male superiority, we know that they do constantly. They hardly ever yield to anything else.

Mr Haslam objects to women bargaining over the vote, though he admits they are justified in holding out for fair wages: surely if they are right in the one case, they are equally right in the other. But this view of the vote as something to be conceded by men to us if we are good – and not until we are all equally good – is fundamentally wrong. The vote is not a reward for virtue: it is a human right. We do not ask it as a boon to promote our own well-being merely, but because we hold its possession to be for the good of the whole State, which, without women's guidance and co-operation, is being crippled. It is bad for men that we remain unenfranchised, for the evil reacts on them equally. Therefore, for men to refuse us citizenship because we do not bow to all their whimsies, is as if a man were to say to his wife: 'You shall not cook my dinner or darn my socks until you are in a better frame of mind!' He might punish his wife by such a course, but would certainly punish himself much more.

Mr Haslam's view with regard to the Peace Congress shows the same fear of rousing the resentment of 'statesmen' to our everlasting damnation. Fortunately, 'in the Nature's copy not eterne'; the proud politicians of to-day may be execrated or forgotten to-morrow, and their good opinion either way is not worth bothering about. They have not the keys of liberty, and their petty resentments and vindictiveness will never bar the onward march of the Women's Movement. If women line up against the war they will be doing a service to humanity that will not be forgotten, and if they are the first to raise a voice for Peace, they will be doing a great world-service that future generations will estimate at its true worth. Let them go ahead, firm in the consciousness of Right and regardless of the frowns of 'statesmen', who, after all, have always recognised how useful wars are for shelving reforms at home.

Mr Haslam, in his defence of wars of self-defence as opposed to wars of aggression, must remember that every war is regarded by each country engaged in it as a sacred and holy war. It is always the other side that is the aggressor. We are always fighting for religion and freedom; the enemy (the ally of yesterday, the friend of to-morrow) is always the foul foe of civilisation and progress. Unconsciously, no doubt, Mr Haslam is using all the cant phrases by which military castes are wont to cloak their hideous doctrines. Women must rid their minds of such cant by cultivating a necessary detachment which will regard war in itself as a crime and a horror unspeakable.

'Suffrage and the Volunteers'
Irish Citizen, 10 April 1915

Easter Sunday was a field-day for the IWFL. A special leaflet was prepared for Volunteer consumption, and was eagerly consumed by thousands. In it the fact was emphasised that, though Home Rule is on the Statute Book, Irishwomen are still without civic rights – the countrywomen of Maeve, Granuaile, Brigit, Fanny Parnell, are on the level of the criminal and the outcast. The Volunteers took the lesson well; they took our handbills eagerly, and everywhere there was a friendly word for us and for our cause. The *Irish Citizen*, with its placard, 'John Redmond's Record', had a record sale, one member alone buying nine dozen. Among the buyers was Lieutenant Kettle,[7] who told us to wait till the war was over. He was reminded that formerly he said wait till Home Rule – wait always for something else. Jam tomorrow, never jam today!

When it was announced that Mr Redmond was to appear in Dublin on Easter Sunday to review the National Volunteers, a vow was registered that Mr Redmond should not leave Dublin without being reminded of his treachery to Irish women in their fight for political freedom, a freedom which Mr John Redmond has in his power to grant, but which he persistently refuses to do. Being well aware that no woman would be allowed within speaking distance of him, that there would be no speech and, consequently, no chance of heckling, another plan had to be devised. Suffragettes usually find a way. The platform from which he was to take the salute was guarded on four sides by Volunteers armed with rifles, supplemented by a large force of DMP men.

On the very outside of a large crowd of people, the prospect of getting in a protest or reminder seemed pretty hopeless at first. Nothing daunted, the Suffragettes edged their way inch by inch to the line of guards. This was by no means an easy passage, as at this point the crowd was thickest; but it was livened up by the snatches of sounds from portions of the crowd. Now it was 'Who fears to speak of '98', then 'Sergt Johnny Redmond'. Mr Redmond has lost much of his glamour of late.

As good fortune had it, as the guarded line was reached, there was a break in the procession, and then came the Suffragettes' opportunity. In the pause between two Volunteer corps, a Suffragette broke the lines, bearing aloft a flag with the words – 'Irish Women demand the Vote!' and the crowd cheered her lustily as she unfurled it and swung it proudly over her head, right under Mr Redmond's eyes as he stood on the front of the platform. The cry, 'Irish Women demand the Vote!' was passed from lip to lip, and Votes for Women was heard on all sides, the crowd hugely enjoying the dramatic coup. The men around where the flag was hoisted made a circle round the woman who held it, and kept the curious element in the audience from pressing in on her. The flag was fluttering in the breeze several minutes before the disturbers of the peace – the police – bore down, a dozen strong, and wrenched the flag out of the woman's hand, flinging her violently to the ground. The sympathy shown by the crowd was most marked, and cries of 'Shame!' were mingled with 'More power to you!' 'Good luck to you!' 'What courage she has!' and 'I wish the men of this country knew as well how to fight for their liberty as the Suffragettes!' Refusing police 'protection', the Suffragettes stood their ground, backed by the crowd, who eagerly helped them to fling their leaflets broadcast over the heads of the Volunteers towards the platform. They remained talking in the centre of the friendly on lookers until the demonstration was over, noting with satisfaction the changed temper of that same crowd which, but two years ago, wrenched the placards from our poster paraders and violently assaulted them on Home Rule Sunday.

As in the city, the crowds in the Phoenix Park were equally sympathetic to the Suffragettes. None of the workers experienced the least hostility; and from the demeanour of the crowd it would appear that the general public in Ireland are awake to the justice underlying Irishwomen's claim to a share in the government of their country. Two paper-sellers were cheered by a detachment of Volunteers who were passing through Westmoreland Street on their way to entrain for the country. Needless to say, this act of friendliness on the part of the men was much appreciated by the women, who returned the 'salute'.

Next day, at the Volunteer Convention, the Suffragettes were again in evidence – selling papers, giving out handbills, and holding impromptu suffrage meetings with the waiting knots of Volunteers. The opinion prevailing seems to be that Home Rule is not as sure as Mr Redmond would have us believe, and there is a militant note, in the attitude of the younger men especially, that awakes sympathetic response to a militant appeal from women. We succeeded in interviewing not only several members of the rank and file, but the three leaders themselves. Mr Redmond was presented with our leaflet, and reminded that Irish women are still voteless, while another suffragette bore the placard, 'John Redmond's Record', before his eyes (and conscience, let us hope). Mr Dillon had similar reminders thrust into his cab. When Mr Devlin[8] was being approached, the Belfast Volunteers (smoking large cigars, though 'on duty') rushed up to assault the women and prevent their leader from being 'molested'; but they were too late, for Mr Devlin did not pass unchallenged, and would probably have preferred to be spared their officious 'protection' which was not extended to the senior leaders. It was not a nice sight to see Belfast bullies holding up a woman on the Mansion House step because she wanted to remind Mr Devlin of his duty, especially as Mr Devlin is the only one of the leaders who calls himself a suffragist. It recalled the old days when Mr Lloyd George had similarly to be protected at Llanystumdwy from suffragette reminders.

Altogether, suffragists have reason to be satisfied that Irish politicians were effectively reminded of their claim, and conscious that (whatever may happen elsewhere) there is and can be no truce among Irish militants until Votes for Irishwomen is also on the Statute Book.

H.

'Irishwomen and peace'
Irish Citizen, 17 April 1915

It is remarkable how small nationalities seem to be coming into their own. Hitherto, at International Congresses, held for various purposes, Ireland came in merely as (in the unflattering phrase of a Continental journalist) England's 'backstairs'. Delegates, if they attended, came not to represent their own island, but had to be content with being merged in Great Britain, Ireland being regarded as but a province. Now, for the first time (and Irishwomen have a right to be proud of the fact, and to use it as a precedent on all future occasions), Ireland has a separate entity, and Irish delegates take their place as representatives of their own country. It is the hour of small nationalities. Long live the small nations of the earth!

But apart from this outstanding feature of this Peace Congress, there is another that must be considered of almost equal importance. After all, if Irishwomen had no special contribution of their own to offer to the International debate, the desire for separate recognition might be considered as a purely sentimental one. If we had no message of our own, if we were but an echo, having no individual vote to contribute to the great world-harmony, then it would matter little what we would call ourselves. But just because we come from a small nation, we, like the Bohemians, the Alsacians, the Poles, have a definite point of view of our own. We see with clearer vision the baleful effect of rule by force, of coercion by the stronger of the weaker. For this reason, too, we realise that the safety of the subject nation comes not from armaments, but from peace; not from the arbitration of the sword (for there the weaker arm may always fail), but from the arbitration of the plebiscite. We aim at Peace through Justice and Liberty, inasmuch as we are Irish (and therefore under the shadow of age-long government without consent), and inasmuch as we are women (members of a subject sex, also governed from without and having to submit to the tyranny of the predominant male). It is curious, moreover, to consider that at a time when Ireland is sending its women-envoys to counsel peace to the warring nations, Irishwomen at home, even under the latest 'Charter of Liberty', as Mr Redmond fondly calls it, should still be kept outside the pale of citizenship, should still be deemed not to form part of that 'free people' from whom Mr Asquith expects 'free gifts'. The Parliament of Women at The Hague may yet be able to give lessons in justice and freedom, not only to the Parliament at Westminster, but to the Parliament at College Green.

'Irish militants and the war'
Irish Citizen, 1 May 1915, from *Jus Suffragii* for April

It may be of interest to the readers of Jus Suffragii *to know the attitude towards the war of the Irish Women's Franchise League, the organisation of Irish Militant Suffragists.*

The Irish Women's Franchise League regards war as the negation of the feminist movement, and in a special manner of the Militant Suffrage movement. The underlying spirit of the Militant Suffrage movement, when it destroyed property in order to call attention to the importance of life-values, was a protest against the rating of a property at a higher value than life; the essence of war, on the contrary, is the destruction of human life and the devitalising of the human race in the pursuit of property. That being so, the Irish Militant Suffragists feel themselves bound in a special manner to war upon war. Women, not having been consulted, directly or indirectly, in any of the belligerent countries, as to the war or the policy which led up to it, have not even that indirect responsibility for it which rests upon the mass of male voters. Women are accordingly not called upon to endorse this war or its conduct in any way. As Suffragists (whatever our individual feelings) it is our duty to preserve an attitude of neutrality with regard to the merits of war, to concentrate upon our demand for votes for women, that we may have a weapon with which to prevent future wars, and to do all we can to bring about a speedy and lasting peace.

Taking this view, the Irish Women's Franchise League has, since the commencement of the war – (1) carefully abstained from expressing any opinion as a society, on the merits of the war or the responsibility for its outbreak; (2) taken no part whatever, as a society, in any scheme of relief in connection with the war; (3) continued its agitation for votes for women, especially in the Amending Home Rule Bill promised by the Government to satisfy the Militants of Ulster; and (4) given special attention to the manifestations of British militarism which have been evoked by the war. We regard it as the duty of every woman to fight the militarism which is nearest to her; and we regard

British militarism as more immediately dangerous to us and our cause than German militarism – with which the women of Germany may be left to deal.

Some comment has been caused by our abstention from all relief work. We cannot, however, regard such work as any part of the functions of a Suffrage society. During the great Dublin strike of 1913–1914, which came much more keenly and closely home to the people of Dublin than this war has yet done, many of our members, as individuals, helped in the relief of distress; but it was never suggested that we should divert to such work any portion of our corporate energies or of the funds and organised power which we had built up for a definite object. Our attitude towards war-relief schemes is precisely similar.

Taking these views, we are naturally keenly interested in the various peace movements which have been initiated by Suffragists, and which specifically recognise the citizenship of women as an essential condition of any lasting peace. Accordingly, we have decided to be represented as an organisation at the forthcoming International Congress of Women in Holland.

H. Sheehy Skeffington, Dublin

'Irishwomen and The Hague Congress'
Irish Citizen, 8 May 1915

'You will find,' said a friend many weeks ago, when the question of The Hague Peace Congress was mooted, 'that the Government will be extremely sympathetic, but that at the last minute some apparently unforeseen little accident will occur to prevent your going to Holland'. He was a man experienced in the ways of governments, and his words have been most accurately borne out. The tale of how most of the British delegates were blocked has been already told. First, Government refused all permits to British and Irish women, thinking in its lordly way, that the Congress would thus be killed outright. It was borne in upon the official mind, however, that, in spite of Britannia's fiat that none of the women under her free flag would be allowed to leave her shores, the women groaning under the yoke of foreign oppression would be permitted by their Governments to attend the Congress. The authorities then determined to modify their attitude and give permits to a certain number of those certified by Mr McKenna to be discreet, and finally, when permits and passports were duly granted, the North Sea was suddenly closed to all traffic 'for about a week', and kept closed till the Congress was over.

On coming to London I found myself, with all the other Irish delegates but one, excluded from the list of the 'discreet'. I cannot say that the exclusion in any way surprised us – we should have been deeply pained if we had been so soon forgotten. We had fought tyranny at home: for some of us had been devised the terrors of forcible feeding and the Cat and Mouse Act. Mr McKenna is stated to have said that on no account could he be induced to allow certain names on their list to go to Holland. Presumably any of those who ever 'gave trouble' to the authorities in peace, who refused to be diverted from their goal in war, were taboo.

The action of the Government is the best argument for Peace and Suffrage. The authorities were obviously frightened at the thought of 180 women (most of them representing thousands in various societies) joining in with their sisters to ask for peace. Afraid to face the clamour in the open, they pretended to negotiate, first by holding up the permits; secondly, by holding up the boats. In this way they saved their face and gained their end. They successfully fooled women from day to day by holding out hopes that a boat would leave: otherwise they might have had 180 women besieging the Home Office and holding up the traffic. Many of these women, especially those with a non-militant past, believed all that they were told from day to day, however absurd and contradictory the tale: their law-abiding instincts shrank from even a mild protest. Mr McKenna drove a wedge in the pacifist forces, dividing the militant from the passive. All kinds of rumours were rife: a battle in the North Sea, Holland 'coming in' (on both sides), the danger that we should all be 'interned' in Holland till the war was over. One lady, who had changed her nationality within the last few weeks by the simple process of marrying an American, found that the passport and permit, refused to her as a British subject, were readily granted to her as an American. An indiscreet clerk in the Home (or Foreign) Office told her that they considered it unpatriotic of British women to go to The Hague Congress, but that, of course, they would not interfere with Americans, and added, with a twinkle, that the stoppage of boats was 'not unconnected with The Hague Congress'.

We held that the case of Ireland deserved special consideration. Instead of being tacked on to the tail of a British list, we should have been considered separately. Out of twenty-four delegates, plus four 'alternates', plus half-a-dozen officials granted permits, only one Irish name was chosen.[9] The North was excluded entirely, and all Irish suffrage societies were overlooked. Finally, owing to the 'no boats' trick, Ireland was deprived of her one delegate, while Great Britain had two[10] at the Congress. This was not all mere coincidence. The Government was obviously afraid to let Ireland's voice be heard on the rights of small nationalities. The only small nations we are allowed to sympathise with are those chosen by Mr McKenna.

The Irish delegates determined not to take their exclusion tamely, regarding the 'no boats' device as a Government dodge. For a week we besieged the House and the Home Office. We put the case of the exclusion of Ireland to the Irish members, and to some Liberals, and a few of them took it up. Mr

McKenna's replies were various and diverse, as usual. To some he stated that, as no boats were running, the matter was of no practical interest (though he was still holding out hopes to others that boats would be running before the Congress was over); to others that the Admiralty had forbidden him to interfere in the matter; to others again he maintained that one in 25 was quite a fair proportion for Ireland; while others he referred to 'the answer already given to the Hon. Member for North Somerset'. Mr Birrell left the matter entirely in the hands of Mr McKenna, and Mr McKenna was entirely under the sway of Mr Churchill, while he, for 'naval reasons', found it impossible to raise the embargo imposed on passenger traffic. Meanwhile the mails got through, and, though an attempt was made to hold up the American delegates, the Channel was ultimately found safe enough for them. We telegraphed to Holland: 'Irish delegates, prevented attending Congress, send greeting. Small nationalities interested in Peace,' but 'naval reasons' may have prevented this message from getting through.

Before the Congress we Irishwomen had congratulated ourselves on the fact that at last Ireland was to be granted separate recognition, a place of her own in the sun, at this great World Congress. But we reckoned without our McKenna. No doubt such an opinion would be regarded as evidence of a highly dangerous independence. So our nation is once more denied a voice in International Councils. The Swedes, the Poles, the Belgians, the Norwegians, the Dutch all are there, the gallant little nations; the British, the Americans, the German, the Italians – but for Irishwomen there are neither votes nor boats. Neither in the affairs of their own land, nor in international ones, may their voice be heard. They are only good enough to knit socks for soldiers, to replenish the population drained by war, to work under male guidance at less than male pay on any and every 'war service', from tram-conducting to agricultural labour. But let them suggest constructive methods of doing away with war and they become noxious busybodies or unpatriotic rebels, interned for 'naval reasons' in the British Isles.

Irishwomen, however, are not content with this role, and they cannot submit to being McKennaised out of their proper place in The Hague Congress. This initial effort may be followed by others, more and more extensive, until Peace is achieved. It behoves Irishwomen to take to heart the lesson of The Hague Congress, and see to it that they are not tricked again. A protest meeting will be held in Dublin on the question. The excluded Irish delegates will be invited to attend to emphasise the views of Irishwomen regarding peace, thus holding a supplementary Peace Congress of our own. In this way we may effect in Ireland as much for the cause of Peace as if we had been allowed to attend the Congress.

'Ireland and The Hague Congress: Dublin protest meeting'
Irish Citizen, 22 May 1915

On Tuesday May 11th, a Public Meeting was held in the Trades' Hall, Dublin by kind permission of the Dublin Trades' Council, to protest against the Government's prohibition of Irish delegates from attending the Women's International Peace Congress at The Hague. The meeting, which was arranged by the Irish Women's Franchise League, was largely attended and enthusiastic . . .

Mrs Sheehy Skeffington then made a statement as to the circumstances in which the Congress was called. Irish women had gladly responded to the call of the Dutch women, eager to do something for peace and also to seize the opportunity of getting Ireland a place in the sun – to get Ireland separately represented at the International Congress, along with Denmark (which had just given votes to its women) and all the other gallant little nations, instead of being swamped in Great Britain. They went through the medieval process now necessary to obtain passports; they made no concealment of the object of their journey; and then the Government, thunderstruck at finding so many women in Great Britain and Ireland keen about peace, refused all passports and permits. Then the British Committee brought pressure to bear, and convinced the Government that the Congress was actually going on, whether the Government liked it or not; and then the Government agreed to let a certain number of women go, who were selected by Mr McKenna. The selected twenty included Miss Bennett, who was discreet; she (the speaker) notoriously was not (laughter). All militants were excluded from the select list; Mr McKenna had a good memory, if some other people had short ones. Mrs Despard had been refused a permit; she had refused to address recruiting meetings for the Government. Olive Schreiner was refused a permit; she had given too much trouble in South Africa. But among the select twenty, there were some admirable women, and they would all have been delighted if even these twenty had got through, and if Miss Bennett had been present to represent Ireland. However, when all the passports and permits were issued, the Admiralty stopped the boats! Mr McKenna was 'desolated'. Did they believe that? ('No'.) Apparently the British Committee did, for they would not make a protest. That was the British Committee's own affair; but they were determined to register the Irish protest, and show that Irish women would not be trampled on, even though the war was on. They had agitated in London, and had stirred up even some of the Irish members, and some independent Liberals, on the question. One of Mr McKenna's different answers was, that one in twenty-four was a fair representation for Ireland. No doubt the Government thought it was – except when there was fighting to be done. The fact that Ireland was going to speak on the subject of small nationalities doubtless had something to do with it. It was indiscreet to speak of Ireland as a small nation. The women groaning under the yoke of German tyranny – even the Belgian women – were allowed to attend the Congress; but the British Government was afraid to let Ireland's voice be heard. Ireland had a particular grievance, because two British delegates got through, while Ireland had none. They would send from that meeting a message to Asquith and McKenna that Ireland was still alive, and apt to kick every now and then. If they had votes, they would not have been so humiliated. They had just seen how those Irishmen who were interested in the drink traffic had used the power of their votes most effectively to protect their interests.

Fragment of letter to Louie Bennett n.d. (1915)[11]

. . . the Boers for instance were justified under present conditions in resisting the (British) invasion of their country, so are the Belgians now. But a terrible war for reasons of commercial jealousy admits of no defence. There are pacifists who hold with Tolstoi that resistance to all violence is wrong – I quite see the extreme logic of the position and if you hold that view of course all war is equally hateful to you. But there are other pacifists (and I am one of them) who hold that while war must be ended if civilization is to reign supreme, nevertheless there may still be times when armed aggression ought to be met with armed defence. If I saw a hope of Ireland being freed for ever from British rule by a swift uprising, I would consider Irish men justified in resorting to arms in order that we might be free, and I should still be radically opposed to War and Militarism. This is of course my personal view and in no way represents the League. But I hold no such hopes. I think that freedom for small nations lies in Justice by Arbitration and there is one of my strongest motives in standing for Peace. The whole matter is a very complex one and I know we differ very widely and we must agree to differ. My feeling is (and I put it to you with all respect for I know that you are not only perfectly sincere but perfectly tolerant) would you be as unsympathetic to expressions like: 'I am not for Peace at any price, because I hold that the allies are fighting a sacred fight.' Or 'I want Peace but the Germans must first be cleared out of Belgium' or 'We British women recognise that now that we are in the war we must go on, nevertheless I wish a speedy peace' and the like? I writhe under expressions like the above and do not consider them really pacifist at heart. They are just as one-sided as those you object to but one must pardon them as an attempt to grope after an ideal. They are better than blatant war-mongering.

The way of Peace Propaganda in Ireland must lie along totally different lines from that of England, just as Dutch or Danish methods would be different. And the only way to rouse people here for Peace is to stir up feeling against this particular war by every appeal to Irish sentiment. That is why a protest meeting succeeds where a purely peace meeting would not. I see you don't like that way but you will never get a crowded and enthusiastic meeting like Tuesday's by dealing with us as if we were British. May I say at the end of this over-long letter that I was very glad to have your doubts cleared up as to our attitude towards your going to the Congress. As I told you I was very glad you were chosen and I quite agree that it was best for you to even as one of twenty. I think the British . . . (end)

'The IWFL and the war'
Irish Citizen, 31 July 1915, in reply to Violet Crichton, 24 July
Mrs Sheehy Skeffington writes:

Mrs Crichton finds it 'hard to understand the attitude of the IWFL since the war began'. It has been, nevertheless, a perfectly clear and logical one – concentration upon the one object of our existence as a society, Votes for Women. We take no sides as an organisation on any issue of peace or war until that end is achieved. It would be just as improper for us to divert our energies to War Services as it would have been to work for or against Home Rule, or to devote ourselves to any issue outside Suffrage. No one pretends that this war (however much it may be supposed to be concerned with Civilisation and the Defence of Small Nationalities) is a fight for Woman Suffrage. Therefore, as suffragists we have no concern with it: as individuals we are free, of course, to hold whatever opinions we choose on the matter, provided always that we remain true to our policy of Suffrage First.

As women, we have no responsibility for the war: nowhere in all the belligerent countries were women consulted, directly or indirectly, as to war policy. Had Great Britain chosen to ally herself with Germany against Russia, had she adopted a neutral attitude the women of these countries would have been equally powerless to express a preference. Had Sir Edward Grey and his Cabinet so decided, we might even now be sending our sons to kill Frenchmen and Belgians, and German women might have been our Allies instead of 'alien enemies'. In view of our utter impotence as women in the deciding of all matters affecting our life and liberty, is it to be wondered that we should put all else aside save the fight for the Vote and all it means to us?

Mrs Crichton condemns our resistance to the census instituted last year for war purposes. She 'fails to see the connection between suffrage work and the military census'. So do we! Such a census is a register of citizens, asked to co-operate in war service by those legislators they have chosen to represent them. Women, not being citizens, being ranked politically with the incapables and degraded, refuse as a protest to take part in any such census or register, and are perfectly justified in such refusal as long as the Government denies them the rights of citizens. They resist the military census just as they resisted the official census of 1911; in each case they act on the strict suffrage principle, No Vote, No Census. Such action, far from being 'wrong and treasonable in the highest degree', is but the natural outcome of a consistent militant suffrage policy: the protest of the voteless against Government without consent. As a policy it is neither the monopoly nor the invention of the IWFL. Many British suffragists are taking the same line: they, too, are refusing to co-operate in Government schemes: they are resisting the imposition of taxes. The only militant society which has diverted its energies entirely to War Service has abandoned Suffrage.[12] Yet Mrs Crichton very wisely disapproves of such desertion, for she honours 'the ideal of keeping the flag flying'. Unfortunately, she cannot have it both ways: either Suffrage must come first or War Service must. The organisation that attempts to court two conflicting ideals can adequately serve neither.

The reproach of being 'narrow and selfish' may be levelled against any policy of concentration on one definite goal. We militants have always had to hear such censure from male politicians: we were told by statisticians that we were guilty of a crime when we resisted the census: we have wrung the hearts of Mr Asquith, Mr Redmond, and Sir Edward Carson by refusing to sink suffrage and concentrate all our energies on Home Rule, on maintaining the Union, on the abolition of the House of Lords, or whatever happened to be the 'one and only' vital issue of the moment. But the vote is not to be won by such unselfishness and easy broadmindedness. It will be won only by fierce and steady concentration of energy on that issue to the exclusion of all others.

If we believe in our cause why should we not work for it as whole-heartedly as men work, and fight, and die (if necessary) for causes which they hold sacred? We may ask women, too, to die for Suffrage: we do not ask them to kill for it. That is the main and vital difference between the militant and the militarist ideal. Who shall say that the latter is the holier? And if the cause of free womanhood is righteous, why should we lay down our arms and surrender to military exigencies?

Mrs Crichton is grieved because 'a body of suffragists could be found to withstand any effort to serve our national existence'. Waiving altogether the question as to what particular nation is meant (and we Irish Suffragists are primarily concerned with the Irish nation), suffragists hold that the most effective service they can render to their nation is the emancipation of its womanhood. A nation that denies its women elementary human rights is not, and never has been free. To be worth fighting for it must set its own house in order first. If it really needs the help of women in its hour of trial, let it liberate them from bondage by giving them the keys of their own house. Mrs Crichton is a sincere and earnest suffragist, who has done valuable service to the cause, and who feels passionately the need of enlisting and arousing the enthusiasm of Irish suffragists. I would suggest to her that it is time for governments to expend some of their superfluous energy in conciliating women, and that as long as they continue to treat the mothers of the nation as aliens, they must accept no help from self-respecting suffragists.

6

DEATH OF A PACIFIST

INTRODUCTION

On Easter Monday, the first day of the Easter Rising, Frank Sheehy Skeffington was near Dublin Castle. He risked his life trying to help a wounded British soldier, then walked around the centre of Dublin, pleading with rioters to stop the looting of shops which he feared would damage the idealism of an insurrection whose aims, if not methods, he supported. He returned to that task the second day, attempting to organise a civic police, while Hanna went to the GPO, headquarters of the insurgents, to offer her services. She had collected food from IWFL members and brought this to the College of Surgeons outpost, where Constance Markievicz later remembered her appearance through bullet-swept streets, adding 'I have nothing but pleasant and happy memories of the Sheehy Skeffingtons. They always instinctively took the right side and were always ready to help' (*Irish World*, 3 May 1924). On the afternoon of that day Frank and Hanna met in the IWFL offices before Hanna made her way home, anxious for the welfare of their son Owen, leaving Frank to follow her after he had waited (in vain) for volunteers for his Citizen's Defence Force. On the way home he was arrested and taken to Portobello Barracks. That evening he was taken from his cell by Captain Bowen-Colthurst, hands tied behind him, and used as a hostage on a raiding party, where he witnessed the cold-blooded shooting of a young man. The following morning Frank, together with two other journalists, were taken from their cells and summarily shot dead in the barracks yard by firing squad. Hanna learned on the Wednesday that Frank had been arrested, but it was not until the Friday that she discovered he was dead. When she asked for the release of her husband's body she was informed that he had already been buried. Captain Bowen-Colthurst that evening led a raid on her house, removing many of Frank's papers, in an attempt to justify his murder. With the support of Sir Francis Vane, a British officer stationed with Bowen-Colthurst, who had demanded the latter's immediate arrest and who condemned the conspiracy of silence surrounding the murders (being dismissed from the army as a result), a court martial in Richmond Barracks found Bowen-Colthurst 'guilty but insane' and he was sent to a mental asylum. With much evidence of the army's conduct during the Rising omitted, Hanna travelled to London in July, using all her contacts in a campaign to demand that the government hold a full inquiry into the events surrounding the Portobello Barracks murders.

She met Prime Minister Asquith in the cabinet office in Downing Street, who pressed her to accept compensation of £10,000. She rejected this 'hush money' but Asquith granted her request. As a result, Sir John Simon presided over an inquiry in Dublin that August and Hanna had the opportunity to speak of her terrible ordeal. The indiscriminate shooting of unarmed civilians, the dismissal of Sir Francis Vane and the planting of evidence on Frank's dead body were all matters that were made public. The report of the Simon Commission was issued in November. Although it did not satisfy Hanna, Tim Healy, acting as her lawyer, believed that 'We have thrown new light on events . . . There will be little esteem for martial law or for soldier's decisions after the Skeffington disclosures.'[1] As the government refused to publish the report of the Commission Hanna sent it to all those who had given their support to her campaign. At the same time she decided that she would bring the facts of the case to the American public. Her pamphlet *British Militarism as I Have Known It* reproduced the speech she gave throughout America. In the first months she would tell her audience: 'I am not here just to harrow your hearts by a passing thrill, to feed you on horrors for sensation's sake. I want to continue my husband's work so that when I meet him some day in the Great Beyond, he will be pleased with my stewardship.'

That second sentence was omitted from later editions of the pamphlet. It was an indication of the grief she was experiencing, and of her growing strength, no longer needing the crutch of an unlikely heavenly future to sustain her. In her conclusion, as America entered the war on the British side, she argued forcibly for Ireland's right to be classed as an independent small nation and urged her audiences to give their support for this.

The fifth and final version was published by Hanna shortly before her death. Her reasons for doing so are given in the foreword, reflecting her mood in the aftermath of the Second World War. A shorter version of the pamphlet was published in Roger McHugh, ed., *Dublin 1916* (London, 1966).

BRITISH MILITARISM AS I HAVE KNOWN IT

Foreword to Fourth Edition

This pamphlet is a reprint of a lecture delivered in the United States during my stay there, from December, 1916 to 1918.

The text was banned in England and in Ireland during the 1914–18 war, but the pamphlet had a wide circulation at the time throughout Canada, in South America, and in Australia. I have (with the exception of a few minor alterations) left the text as it stood. The facts referred to have already appeared in the press here, having been published during the Colthurst court martial and at the subsequent Simon Inquiry. The chief features of the Skeffington Case have been referred to by Mr T. M. Healy, Sir Francis Vane, General Crozier and others who have since written on 1916.

There is sufficient data here to dispose forever of the myth (widely circulated by British writers and military apologists) that the murder of Sheehy Skeffington was the isolated act of a demented British officer.

H. S. S. Dublin, 1936

Foreword to Fifth Edition
I have decided to issue a fifth edition of this 1917–18 lecture for two reasons. First, several requests for copies of the 1936 reprint have reached me from Irish men and women working in Britain during the 1939–45 war. Finding themselves plunged in an atmosphere of British self-righteousness, which was protected by a dense wall of ignorance about British crimes in Ireland and elsewhere throughout the Empire, these Irish exiles remembered the story of my husband's murder, which official circles had striven hard to conceal – it is significant that, though the murderer was found guilty by a British court-martial of a triple murder, the press in Britain still camouflages the term as 'shooting without trial'. So I was written to frequently for the facts; but the '36 edition was already exhausted and I doubt whether the censor would have let the booklet through during the recent war any more than his predecessor did in the first.

The second consideration which prompted me to reprint is the present smug attitude of Britain and the victors generally towards 'war criminals'. I believe that a saner outlook might prevail if the nations sitting in judgment were a trifle less complacent in their conviction that they are fit to cast the first stone.

Francis Sheehy Skeffington's murder was but one of many. It was not an isolated case, even in 1916, and it was followed several years later by the long trail of murders, reprisal-burnings and other atrocities by Britain's Black-and-Tans, sent us after the war in Europe was over, the War to end War. The Tans were indeed the early Blackshirts and Brownshirts who formed the spearhead of Britain's answer to Ireland's democratically-expressed desire for Independence in the General Election of December 1918 (the 'Hang the Kaiser' one, as it was called in Britain).

One might indeed argue with reason that, since Britain claims to be a democracy, the average Briton was really more responsible for the crimes of His Britannic Majesty's Representatives in Ireland, than was the average German for the subsequent Nazi imitations thereof in other countries. Possibly it may have been a sense of common guilt that prevented the trial of any British war criminals in 1922, though it will be recalled in Ireland that Irish

Juries brought in verdicts of Murder against Premier Lloyd George and others in connexion with the murder of Limerick's Mayor, of Lord Mayor MacCurtain, Cork, and many more.

As I look back, across the space of thirty years, on the events narrated here, one impression emerges more clearly than ever, namely, that it is not the brutality of the British Army in action against a people in revolt (we learned to take this for granted and indeed it is part of war everywhere) but the automatic and tireless efforts on the part of the entire official machinery, both military and political, to prevent the truth from being made public. This was wholly characteristic of the British regime in Ireland: it is this more than any individual crime or atrocity which damns beyond redemption the whole apparatus of British Imperialism.

H. S. S. Dublin, 1946

British Militarism as I Have Known It

When first I learned the facts about my husband's murder I made up my mind to come to America and tell the story to as many audiences in the United States as I could reach.

Francis Sheehy Skeffington was an anti-militarist, a fighting pacifist, a man gentle and kindly even to his bitterest opponents, who always ranged himself on the side of the weak against the strong, whether the struggle was one of class, sex or race domination. Together with his strong fighting spirit, he had a marvellous, an inextinguishable good humour, a keen joy in life, great faith in humanity and a hope in the progress towards good.

F. Sheehy Skeffington's Last Days

At the beginning of the outbreak on Easter Monday, April 24th 1916, my husband was in Dublin. At the assault on Dublin Castle, a British officer (Captain Pinfield) was reported gravely wounded and lying bleeding to death near the Castle gate. As there was considerable cross-firing no one dared to go to his aid. My husband, learning this, persuaded a chemist to go with him to the rescue, and crossed the square under a hail of fire. He found, however, that some of his friends had managed to drag the officer inside the Castle gate, there being left only a pool of blood. When I remonstrated that night with my husband on his running such a terrible risk, he replied simply, 'I could not let anyone bleed to death while I could help,' – characteristic of his simple heroism, cool courage and horror of bloodshed.

All Monday and Tuesday he actively interested himself in preventing looting by British sympathizers. He saved various shops, posted civic guards and enlisted the help of many civilians and priests. He talked to the crowds and held them off. But by Tuesday evening everyone was afraid. He called a meeting that evening to organize a civic police. I met him about 5.30. We had tea together and I went home by devious routes, for I was anxious about my boy. I never again saw my husband.

Because of my husband's work on behalf of the freedom of Ireland his arrest was desirable, from a British standpoint, and his description had been circulated at the bridges, which he would have to pass on his way home. Accordingly, when, between 7 and 8 he passed Portobello, Lieut. Morris, who was in charge, had him arrested. He was unarmed, carrying a walking stick and was walking quite alone in the middle of the road. As he came to the bridge some of the crowd shouted his name. He was arrested and taken, without resistance, to Portobello Barracks, and was searched and questioned. No papers of an incriminating character were found on him. The Adjutant (Lieut. Morgan) reported the arrest, with that of others, at headquarters, saying that there was no charge against Skeffington, and asking whether he would release him, with others against whom there was no charge, that night. Orders were given to release the others, but to detain Skeffington. The charge sheet was produced at the Simon Commission hearing, and I saw it. Against my husband's name was entered, 'no charge'.

When told he was detained, he specially asked that I should be informed, but this was refused. No message was ever allowed to reach me, no notification of his death, of his first or second burial was ever issued, and every scrap of information with regard to his murder has had ever since to be extracted bit by bit from the reluctant authorities.

Hostage Incident

About midnight, Capt. Bowen-Colthurst came to the captain of the guard, Lieut. Dobbin, and got him to hand over his prisoner. This was an illegal act. The captain of the guard is supposed to hand over no prisoner under his care (in what they call the 'King's Peace') without a written order from the commanding officer. My husband was taken out as a hostage, his hands bound behind him with a rope. He was then taken out with a raiding party in charge of Capt. Bowen-Colthurst and Lieut. Leslie Wilson. As they went they fired at various houses along the Rathmines Road to prevent anyone appearing at the windows.

Coade Murder

Opposite Rathmines Catholic Church they saw two boys (one a lad called Coade, 17 years of age). They had been attending church that evening and were going home. The captain questioned them and asked them did they not know that martial law had been proclaimed, and that he could shoot them 'like dogs'. As Coade turned away, Colthurst said, 'Bash him' and one of the underling officers broke his jawbone with the butt end of his rifle, knocking him senseless. Then Colthurst whipped out his revolver and shot him as he lay.

He was left lying in his blood (the stain marking the spot for several days); later he was taken by the ambulance to the Barracks, where he died that night without ever regaining consciousness. My husband protested against this horrible murder, and was told by Colthurst to say his prayers (Capt. Colthurst, like Cromwell, was a very religious man), as he would likely be the next.

A few yards further down another murder was committed by Capt. Colthurst, but we have not been able to elicit any facts. The Simon report states, 'The evidence of the different witnesses can only be reconciled by inferring that more than one case of shooting occurred during the progress of Capt. Colthurst's party.' It goes on, 'None of the evidence offered to us afforded any justification for the shooting of Coade; it is, of course, a delusion to suppose that martial law confers upon an officer the right to take human life, and this delusion had in the present case tragic consequences.'

The evidence as to the above atrocities was carefully omitted at the military court-martial held in June on Colthurst. It was only against the strongest protest from the military that Sir John Simon insisted on this case being investigated at the Commission. We have evidence that at least two other murders by Colthurst later in the week were perpetrated but this was ruled out at the Commission as 'not within their scope'.

Taking Hostages: 'A Common Practice'
My husband was then taken as far as the bridge and left by Colthurst in charge of Lieut. Leslie Wilson. Colthurst said a prayer over him (O Lord God, if it shall please Thee to take this man's life, forgive him, for Christ's sake) and left instructions that if his party was sniped at during their expedition Skeffington was to be shot forthwith. Leslie Wilson testified that he saw 'nothing strange' in the order and would have carried it out, and it was in fact a common practice with these parties engaged in suppressing liberty in Ireland to take such 'hostages'.

Capt. Colthurst then bombed Alderman James Kelly's premises (they mistook him for his namesake Alderman Tom Kelly, a Sinn Féiner). They sacked the premises and took prisoners the shopmen, and two editors, Dickson and McIntyre, who had taken refuge there. They flung live bombs into the house without warning and wounded one of the men. I have seen the house; it bears the marks of the bullets and bombs yet. As there was no resistance from the unhappy people, my husband was escorted back alive to the Barracks with the two other editors. Dickson was a cripple. He was the editor of *The Eye-Opener*, McIntyre, editor of *The Searchlight*. By a strange irony both had been loyalist papers and Alderman James Kelly had helped to recruit for the army, but owing to the initial mistake, protests were useless. The soldiers confused *The Searchlight* with a paper called *The Spark* (a volunteer organ) and editors' lives were cheap during those days. Dead editors tell no tales – though sometimes their wives may. Again my husband was flung (according to some, still bound) into his cell. Whether he was further tortured that night I shall never know. Capt. Colthurst spent, according to himself, the rest of the night in prayer. At three o'clock he found a Bible text which seemed to him an inspiration – from St Luke – 'But those mine enemies, which would not that I should reign over them, bring hither, and slay them before me' (Ch. xix 27). He interpreted 'I' to mean the British Empire, the message as a divine command.

The Murder

Shortly before ten o'clock the next morning (April 26th) Colthurst again demanded my husband from the guard, together with the two editors. Lieuts Toomey, Wilson and Dobbin were present in charge of the guard with 18 men. He stated that he was going to 'shoot Skeffington and others, that he thought "it was the right thing to do"'. They were handed over accordingly, and the rest of the story we pieced together from the evidence of the other unhappy civilian prisoners who were in the guardroom and heard what was going on, for the military naturally do their best to prevent anything being known.

It seems, according to the account, that my husband was taken out from his locked cell by Colthurst. As he walked across the yard (the yard was only about 12 feet long by 6 feet wide) he was shot in the back without any warning whatever by the firing squad. While he lay, the two other editors were marched out also and murdered in cold blood without warning. The other prisoners listened eagerly the while, and as they heard volley after volley ring out, said, 'Another poor fellow gone', and thought their own turn would be next. Then (after the second volley) they heard Dobbin say, about my husband, to Sergeant Aldridge, 'That man is not dead.' My husband moved as he lay on the ground. Dobbin then reported this fact to Colthurst, who gave orders to 'finish him off'. Another firing squad was then lined up and my husband's body was riddled as he lay on the ground. After that the other prisoners heard washing and sweeping going on for about two hours and when they were allowed into the yard it still bore the marks of the murder. The wall was blood-stained and riddled with bullets. No surgeon was called to examine the bodies; one stated that 'about noon' (two hours later) he visited the mortuary and they were transferred to the mortuary. Up to the present moment I have never been able to find out how long my husband may have lingered in anguish, or whether the second volley did its work more effectively than the first.

Inquest Refused

The British were careful to prevent my seeing the body or having it medically examined, and later, when I attempted to have an inquest held, permission was refused. At eleven Major Rosborough again communicated with the garrison adjutant at headquarters and with Dublin Castle. He was told to bury the bodies. Capt. Colthurst sent in his report (as ordered by Rosborough), but he was kept in command, and no reprimand made to him.

Other Murders

On the same day Capt. Colthurst was in charge of troops in Camden street, when Councillor Richard O'Carroll surrendered (one of the labour leaders in the Dublin City Council). He was marched with his hands over his head to the back yard and Capt. Colthurst shot him in the lung. When a soldier pityingly asked was he dead, Capt. Colthurst said, 'Never mind, he'll die later.' He had him dragged out into the street and left there to be later picked up by a bread van. Ten days later O'Carroll died in great agony. For six days his wife knew nothing of him and when at last she was summoned to Portobello, he could only whisper in her ear his dying statement which she repeated to me. The authorities, as usual, refused all inquiry. Three weeks after his murder, his wife gave birth to a son.

On the same day Capt. Colthurst took a boy, whom he suspected of Sinn Féin knowledge and asked him to give information. When the boy refused, he got him to kneel in the street and shot him in the back as he raised his hand to cross himself. Inquiry into this case has also been refused – it is but one of the many.

My husband was buried on Wednesday night, secretly – in the Barrack yard – his body sewn in a sack.

My Search

Meanwhile, from Tuesday night, when he did not return, I had been vainly seeking him: All sorts of rumours reached me – that he had been wounded and was in a hospital, that he had been shot by a looter, that he was arrested by the police. I also heard that he had been executed, but this I refused to believe – it seemed incredible. I clung to the belief that even if he had been condemned to die he would have been tried first, at least before a jury, for martial law did not apply to non-combatants – and that I would be notified, as were some of the wives and families of the other executed men. Of course, the reason of the silence is now clear. It was hoped that my husband would 'disappear' as so many others, that we could never trace his whereabouts, and that it would be taken for granted that he had been killed in the street. My husband's murder was but one of the many – the only difference being that in his case the murder could not be kept dark. On Tuesday, May 9th (13 days after) Mr Tennant stated in the House of Commons in answer to a question, that '*no prisoner had been shot in Dublin without a trial*'.

All Wednesday and Thursday I inquired in vain, and on Friday horrible rumours reached me. I tried to see a doctor connected with the Barracks, but was stopped by the police, for by this time the police had been restored and were helping the soldiers. I was watched, as I have since been, carefully under police supervision. Houses were being raided and pillaged. Mme Markievicz's house was broken into on Wednesday, and all her pictures stolen, and other valuables taken and the door was left broken open. Whole streets were ransacked and the inhabitants terrified while the soldiers thrust their bayonets through the beds and furniture.

On Thursday evening, about seven, I met Mrs MacDonagh (the wife of one of the Irish prisoners shot by the firing squad) wheeling her two babies to her mother's house; the soldiers had turned machine guns on her house. Soldiers sold their loot openly in the streets – officers took 'souvenirs'. While the volunteers were holding their stronghold their wives and families were thus tortured.

My Sisters' Arrest

On Friday, to allay my growing anxiety, my two sisters, Mrs Tom Kettle[2] and Mrs Culhane,[3] went to the Portobello Barracks to inquire. They were at once put under arrest and a drumhead court-martial was had upon them. They afterwards identified the officer who presided as Colthurst. Lieut. Beattie and other officers were also present. The crime they were accused of was that they were 'seen talking to Sinn Féiners' (to me, probably).

They were refused all information by Capt. Colthurst, who said he knew nothing whatever of Sheehy Skeffington, and told them, 'the sooner they left the Barracks the better for them'. They were marched off under armed guard, and forbidden to speak till they left the premises.

It being then clear that we had information, the next step was to try and find my husband guilty on *post facto* evidence. That afternoon I managed to see Coade, the father of the murdered boy. I got his name from a doctor – and he told me that he had seen my husband's dead body with several others in that mortuary when he went for his son. This a priest afterwards confirmed, but he could give me no other information.

The First Raid

I went home shortly after six and before seven was putting my little boy to bed, when the maid noticed soldiers lining up around the house. She got terrified

2 The Sheehy sisters. From left to right, Hanna, Mary, Kathleen, Margaret. Image courtesy of the Sheehy Skeffington family.

3 Father Eugene Sheehy and household in Limerick. Image courtesy of the NLI.

4 Irish Women's Franchise League activists 1912/3. Front row, from left, Eva Wilkins, Hanna, Meg Connery. Back row, Margaret Cousins, Cissie Cahalan, Hilda Webb, (unknown), Kathleen Houston. Image courtesy of the Wilkins family.

5 IWFL meeting in Phoenix Park, *c.* 1910. Meg Connery speaking, Margaret Cousins seated
behind her. Image courtesy of the NLI.

6 Hanna and Frank Sheehy Skeffington in 1912 at the height of
the 'Votes for Women' campaign. Image courtesy of the
National Museum of Ireland.

7 Hanna with her uncle, Father Eugene Sheehy, and Frank on
the day of her release from Mountjoy Jail after hunger strike in
1912. Image courtesy of the NLI.

8 A *Daily Sketch* photo of Hanna addressing a protest meeting by the walls of Mountjoy Jail, where
suffragette Kathleen Houston is imprisoned in 1914. Image courtesy of © RTÉ Stills Library.

9 Bill advertising protest meeting against the 'Cat and Mouse Act'. Image courtesy of the NLI.

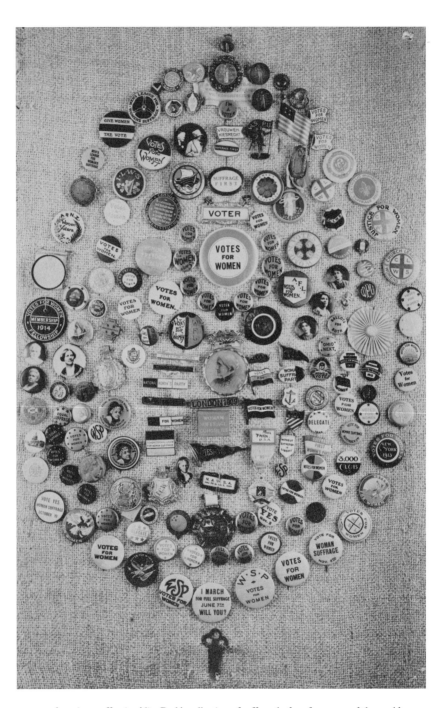

10 American suffragist Alice Park's collection of suffrage badges from around the world.
Image courtesy of the NLI.

IRISH REBELLION, MAY, 1916.

FRANCIS SHEEHY SKEFFINGTON,

11 A memorial leaflet for Frank
Sheehy Skeffington. Image
courtesy of the NLI.

12 Frank's IWFL badge taken
from his coat after his death in
1916. Image courtesy of the
National Museum of Ireland.

13 Hanna, far right, with her sisters, from left, Margaret Culhane, Mary Kettle and Kathleen
O'Brien, after the murder of Frank, May 1916. Image courtesy of Library of Congress, Prints &
Photographs Division (LC-B2- 3962-9).

14 Hanna and Joseph Kirwan Bridgeman BL going to the court martial of Captain Bowen-Colthurst, 1916. Father Eugene Sheehy is on the far right. Image courtesy of the NLI.

15 Press clipping from 8 June 1916, showing Captain Bowen-Colthurst and Hanna among figures from the court martial. Image courtesy of the National Museum of Ireland.

and dashed out with Owen by the back door. I went to call her back, for I knew that the house would be guarded back and front, and feared the boy, especially, might be shot if seen running. When I got to the foot of the stairs a volley was fired in front of the house at the windows, followed almost directly by a crash of glass which the soldiers shattered with the butt-ends of their rifles.

They broke in simultaneously all over the house, some went on the roof, and Capt. Colthurst rushed upon us, the maid, Owen and myself, with a squad with fixed bayonets, shouting 'Hands up!' to the boy and me. The boy gave a cry at the sight of the naked steel, and I put my arm around him and said, 'These are the defenders of women and children.' That steadied them a little. The party consisted of about forty men and was in charge of Col. Allett (an officer of 29 years' service), Capt. Colthurst (16 years' service) and a junior officer, Lieut. Brown.

We were ordered all three to be removed 'under guard' to the front room and to be shot if we stirred, while they searched the house. This was done: Soldiers with levelled rifles knelt outside the house ready to fire upon us, and inside we were closely guarded by men with drawn bayonets. This lasted over three hours. The house was completely sacked and everything of any value removed – books, pictures, souvenirs, toys, linen, and household goods. I could hear the officers jeering as they turned over my private possessions. One of the soldiers (a Belfast man) seemed ashamed, and said, 'I didn't enlist for this. They are taking the whole bloomin' house with them.' They commandeered a motor car in which were women, and made them drive to the Barracks with the stuff – ordering the men to keep a safe distance 'in case of firing'. They left an armed guard on the house all night. Colthurst brought my husband's keys, stolen from his dead body, and opened his study (which he always kept locked). All my private letters, letters from my husband to me before our marriage, his articles, a manuscript play, the labour of a lifetime, were taken. After endless application I received back a small part of these, but most of my most cherished possessions have never been returned, nor was any attempt made to find them.

The regiment took with them to Belfast as a 'souvenir', my husband's stick, and an officer stole from his dead body my husband's 'Votes for Women' badge. For days my house was open to any marauder, as none dared to come even to board up my windows. Capt. Colthurst later falsely endorsed certain papers as found on my husband's body.

Second Raid

On Monday, May 1st, another raid was made during my absence, and this time a little temporary maid was taken under soldiers' guard to the Barracks. She was detained in custody for a week, the only charge against her being that she was found in my house. Why I was not taken I never knew, but one of the officers (Leslie Wilson) publicly regretted 'that they had not shot Mrs Skeffington while they were about it'. It would have saved them (and me) much trouble if they had. Colthurst continued in charge of raiding parties for several days.

On May 1st, Major Sir Francis Vane, the second in command at Portobello, was relieved of his command by Lieut. Col. McCammond, for his persistent efforts, (unavailing) to get Colthurst put under arrest. He was told to give up his post (that of commander of the entire defenses of Portobello) and hand it over to Capt. Bowen-Colthurst, who was thereby promoted six days after the murders. Later (on May 9th) he was sent in charge of a detachment of troops to Newry, and not until May 11th, the day of Mr Dillon's speech, was he put under 'close arrest'. I leave it to American intelligence to decide whether these facts once proved before a Royal Commission were consistent with the theory of lunacy.

Sir Francis Vane is the only officer concerned who made a genuine effort to see justice done. He went to Dublin Castle, finding that the Portobello officers would do nothing. He saw Colonel Kinnard and General Friend, as well as Major Price (head of the Intelligence Dept). All deprecated the 'fuss' and refused to act. Major Price said, 'Some of us think it was a good thing Sheehy Skeffington was put out of the way, anyhow.' This was the typical attitude of the authorities. On Sunday (May 7th), also by order of Colonel McCammond, bricklayers were brought to the yard to remove the blood-stained bricks, stained with the blood of my murdered husband, and carefully replaced them with new bricks.

Sir Francis Vane, thoroughly horrified at the indifference of Dublin Castle to murders committed by an officer (they were busy trying 'rebels' for 'murder'), crossed early in May to London, interviewed the war office, and on May 3rd, saw Lord Kitchener and the latter was reported as sending a telegram ordering the arrest of Colthurst. This was disregarded by General Maxwell, then in command in Dublin. Instead of anything being done to Colthurst, the only result of Sir Francis Vane's efforts was that he, himself, was dismissed from the service ('relegated to unemployment') by secret report of General Maxwell, deprived of his rank of Major and *refused a hearing at the court-martial*, although he had previously been favourably mentioned in the despatches by Brigadier McConochine, his superior officer, for bravery.

Second Burial

On May 8th, my husband's body was exhumed and reburied in Glasnevin, without my knowledge. That day I managed to see Mr John Dillon and told him my story. I never saw a man more moved than he by the tragedies of

Easter Week. He read my statement in the House of Commons on May 11th, and his wonderful speech on the horror he had seen, compelled Mr Asquith to cross at once to Ireland. Mr Asquith said of my statement, 'I confess I do not and cannot believe it. Does anyone suppose that Sir John Maxwell has any object in shielding officers and soldiers, if there be such, who have been guilty of such ungentlemanlike, such inhuman conduct? *It is the last thing the British army would dream of*!' I do not blame him for his disbelief. He went to Ireland, found every word I said was true, as verified at the Commission – he found there other horrors – the North King Street atrocity, for instance – surpassing even mine. *Yet he did his best to help the military to shield the murderers and hush all inquiries.* In a few short days secret court-martials had condemned to death no less than sixteen Irish leaders – whose crime was that they had wished Ireland as free as is your country, a 'free republic'. Early in May a Royal Commission was appointed to inquire into the causes of the rebellion, but all inquiry was refused into the atrocities committed by the troops while in Dublin.

Courtmartial

The courtmartial was presided over by Lord Cheylesmore and consisted of twelve senior officers – a more wooden tribunal it is impossible to conceive. All the witnesses were military, and all were drilled to tell a special tale. They were sworn, and yet at many points their story later to the Commission flagrantly contradicted the previous one – yet they have never been brought to book for perjury. I was not allowed to present evidence. Mr Healy said of the courtmartial: 'Never since the trial of Christ was there a greater travesty of justice.' Its findings were afterwards completely discredited by the Royal Commission; the evidence was doctored and all legal forms violated, the prosecutor and defender playing into each other's hands. Dr Balch, who had refused to certify Colthurst insane, was not questioned, and he was afterwards sent to Sierra Leone, and would not be produced at the Commission. Sir Francis Vane was not called, no evidence of the other murders was given, or of the part played by Dublin Castle in cloaking the murderer. Colthurst was under no restraint during his trial. He stayed at a well-known hotel in Dawson Street with his family during the days, and, though found insane later, was not shut up for several weeks. Finally, when feeling ran high, he was transferred as a 'patient' to Broadmoor, England, and was allowed to continue to hold his rank as captain and to draw half pay for several months. Later he was 'retired', *but has not been dismissed from the service.* He is detained 'during the King's pleasure' and will be released when 'cured'. As has been the case of the perpetrator of the Bachelor's Walk murders, in July, 1914, he will probably be given some important post when this trouble blows over.

Asquith Interview

In July I went to London to interview editors and members of Parliament to force the Government to administer justice. On July 19th I was sent for by Mr Asquith, who had, with his 'wait and see' policy, been shuffling and evading a direct answer for months – I brought a witness with me, a well-known suffragist, Miss Muriel Matters.[4] Mr Asquith saw me in the room where the Cabinet meets (Downing Street). The wily statesman explained to me the difficulties in the way of keeping his pledge, regretted that no adequate inquiry could be given: The House, he said, would refuse a sworn inquiry, and that alone could be satisfactory. Would I be satisfied with an inadequate inquiry, which was 'the best they could do'? I told him I would not be satisfied with any inquiry that he told me in advance would be unsatisfactory and inadequate, and that, while I must accept the best he could give – I would not be 'satisfied'. I said I would take further action if I wasn't – for even then I had in view a visit to America to tell an honest country what British militarism could do. Then Mr Asquith carefully approached the question of 'compensation' in lieu of inquiry – proposals had previously been made to me, unofficially, from various sources (my boy's future at stake, etc.). I was told that no inquiry could be given – that the military wouldn't allow it but that 'adequate and even generous' compensation would be assured. Mr Asquith now put this point ever so delicately (it was clearly his object in sending for me) tapping his fingers on the green baize table – he sat with his secretary at the middle, and my friend and I at the end – and glancing sideways at me, for he never looked me straight in the face throughout the interview. He is mellow and hale, with rosy, chubby face, and silver hair, a rather Christmas air about him. He explained that the other injured people were asking for compensation, would I not consider it too? He said nothing could undo the past, etc. I told him that the only compensation I would ask or take, was the redemption of his promise, viz: a full, public inquiry into my husband's murder.

I inquired, 'Were the military blocking him?' 'No, no,' he replied, 'the military *court inquiry*!' 'In that case, Mr Asquith,' I said, 'will you say yes or no? It is time that I had an answer.' He would reply on Thursday to Mr Dillon, and so our interview ended. He is an able, astute politician, the ex-Premier, but his pitiful little traps and quibbles and his 'hush money' suggestions were hardly worthy of a great statesman.

Scope of Inquiry Restricted

He finally granted the Commission of Inquiry with Sir John Simon at its head, and a judge and well-known lawyer to sit with him. But Asquith, as usual, broke faith (unbroken record) as to the scope of the inquiry, by narrowly restricting the terms of reference. The court could not produce or examine

Colthurst, the chief culprit, because he was in England – evidence was voluntary, other atrocities were carefully ruled out. The military had purposely scattered important witnesses. Several were at the front, some had been killed in the interval, some were afraid of vengeance.

The Military refused to produce others, Colonel Allett had died mysteriously in the interval – according to some he committed suicide in Belfast when Colthurst was condemned, saying, 'The game is up.' Every device was used by the Government and the Military to defeat the ends of justice. Yet, in spite of all, the Inquiry Report established many important facts – the promotion of Colthurst, the failure to take any disciplinary measures against the other officers, the dismissal of Sir Francis Vane, the raids on my house for incriminatory evidence after the murder. Doubt was cast upon the insanity of Colthurst and grave censure passed on the Military.

Exposure

As a public exposure the Commission had a great effect, and the attitude of the Military under the searching heckling of Mr Healy and the questions of Sir John Simon showed them at their worst. One officer actually fainted in court and his cross-examination had to be suspended. Francis Sheehy Skeffington could not have imagined any more damning exposé of the militarism he detested and under which he perished. No writer of fiction could have imagined a more harrowing story of unrelieved brutality than may be found in the cold and lawyer-like language of the Simon Report. But all these officers still enjoy favour. Major Price still rules in Dublin Castle.

'A martyr fights in death more terribly than many warring saints. He is entrenched, you cannot reach him with your heaviest shot.' My husband would have gone to his death with a smile on his lips, knowing that by his murder he had struck a heavier blow for his ideals than by any act of his life. His death will speak trumpet-tongued against the system that slew him.

'Pogrom', Demoralisation, Other Atrocities

Nor was it, as I have shown, the one mad act of an irresponsible officer. It was part of an organized 'pogrom'. We possess evidence, sworn and duly attested, of at least 50 other murders of unarmed civilians or disarmed prisoners (some boys and some women) committed by the soldiers during Easter Week. The North Staffords murdered 14 men in North King street, and buried them in the cellars of their houses.

A coroner's jury of the city brought a verdict of wilful murder against these men, who could be identified, but Sir John Maxwell refused to give them up, and they are in Dublin at the present moment. Pits were dug in Glasnevin Cemetery and bodies piled up were carted off and buried in a common trench.

In various cases the soldiers stated that they were under definite orders to kill civilians and prisoners.

Over three hundred houses were looted and sacked in the suburbs and the city. Thousands of men, hundreds of women, were arrested all over the country and deported in cattle boats to England, some to jails, some to internment camps. Most of these had no part whatever in the rising, but the police and soldiers had a free hand to arrest all, and exercised their powers to the full. Time does not permit me to dwell any longer on the treatment accorded to the prisoners. In Kilmainham, in Richmond Barracks and later in England, they were brutally ill-treated.

State of Ireland
Ireland is still under martial law, threatened with famine and with conscription; death by hunger or in the trenches. But Ireland's spirit was never stronger, never was it more clearly shown that no nation can be held by force, that the aspiration after liberty cannot be quelled by shot or shell.

The Volunteers
A word as to the Irish Republicans. 'Treason doth never prosper; what's the reason? For if it prosper, none dare call it treason.' When the United States of America set up its republic, it declared its independence of Great Britain; it happily won, and maintained its independence. But if it had lost – would its leaders have found quicklime graves? Surely.

I knew the Irish Republican leaders, and am proud to call Connolly, Pearse, McDonagh, Plunkett, O'Rahilly and others friends – proud to have known them and had their friendship. They fought a clean fight against terrible odds – and terrible was the price they had to pay. They were filled with a high idealism. They had banks, factories, the General Post Office, the Four Courts, their enemies' strongholds, for days in their keeping, yet bankers, merchants and others testified as to the scrupulous way in which their stock was guarded. A poet, AE said,

> Your dream, not mine,
> And yet the thought, for this you fell,
> Turns all life's water into wine.[5]

Their proclamation gave equal citizenship to women, beating all records, except that of the Russian Revolutionists, and their Revolution came later.

Conclusion: A Dream
It is the dreamers and the visionaries that keep hope alive and feed enthusiasm – not the statesmen and the politicians. Sometimes it is harder to live for a cause

than to die for it. It would be a poor tribute to my husband if grief were to break my spirit. It shall not do so. I am not here just to harrow your hearts by a passing thrill, to feed you on horrors for sensation's sake.

The lesson of the Irish Rising and its suppression is that our small nation, Ireland, has a right also to its place in the sun. We look to the United States particularly to help us in this matter. The question of Ireland is not, as suggested by England, 'A domestic matter'. It is an international one, just as the case of Belgium, Serbia and other small nationalities is. We want our case to come up at the Peace Conference, if not before – to the international tribunal for settlement.

Democracy for Europe?
The United States Government has declared that it is entering this war for the democratization of Europe. We do not want democracy to stop short of the Irish sea, but to begin there. If Great Britain is in good faith in this matter, she can begin now, by freeing our small nation, and this can be done without the shedding of a single drop of American blood, and the whole world would applaud the deed.

We look, therefore, to America to see that her allies live up to their professions and that the end of the war will see all small nations of Europe free. As my husband said, in an article in the *Century Magazine*, February, 1916, on a 'Forgotten Small Nationality', 'Shall peace bring freedom to Belgium, to Poland, perhaps to Finland and Bohemia, and not to Ireland?' It is for America to see that Ireland is not excluded from the blessings of true democracy and freedom. In this respect America will be but paying back the debt she owes to Ireland. In the day of her struggle for independence, before she set up her republic, she was aided by Irish citizens – many of whom gave their lives for her freedom. And in the Civil War thousands of Irishmen died that your negroes might be free men. It is for their descendants, the beneficiaries of those old wars of yours for freedom in '76 and 1861, now to pay back the debt, and to help us set up an Irish republic, as independent of Great Britain as is your own.

At the end of the war we hope to see a 'United Europe' on the model of your own United States, where each state is free and independent, yet all are part of a great federation. We want Ireland to belong to this united Europe, and not to be a vassal of Great Britain, a province of the British Empire, governed without consent. Unless the United States is as whole-heartedly in favour of the freedom of Ireland as she is of the emancipation of Belgium, she cannot be true to her own principles. Her honour is involved and we look particularly to the Irish in America to remember the claims of the land of their fathers when the day of reckoning comes.

I shall conclude by quoting from William Rooney's poem, 'Dear Dark Head', which embodies in poetic form Ireland's life-long dream for freedom.

Speaking of the men who died for Ireland, he says:

> And though their fathers' fate be theirs, shall others
> With hearts as faithful still that pathway tread
> Till we have set, Oh Mother Dear of Mothers,
> A nation's crown upon thy Dear, Dark Head.[6]

New York, 1917

Appendix

The following letter has recently been sent to me by a friend. It has not before been published, I believe. It was written in 1917 by the late Major Sir Francis Vane (referred to in my Lecture) and was addressed to a Dublin woman, who had congratulated him on his courageous efforts, against powerful forces in high places, to have the truth made known and justice done.

I think it will be read with interest to-day, and will even be found to have some strangely topical allusions.

March, 1946. H. S. S.

10 Pembridge Gardens,
London, W2.

My dear Madam,

I cannot thank you too much for your kindly appreciation of my poor work in Ireland, and for the honour and credit of British Administration there.

For this at least I have nothing to regret, for I could not have done other than I did. Militarism, which is the vulgarisation of Patriotism, is a universal vice (to talk of Prussian Militarism is as stupid and illogical as to talk of English, or Irish Catholicism) for we find as much of this sentiment to-day daily expressed in the Senior United Service Club in London or in the Kildare Street Club in Dublin, as in any Military coterie in Berlin or Dresden.

Mind you I have seen it in action in two wars, in South Africa and in Dublin, and in both I have equally opposed it – not mainly on account of its cruelty – but chiefly on account of its impolicy. (See my book – *Pax Britannica in South Africa*.)

But in Dublin last Easter this evil was pretty clearly crystallised. The forces of this evil were out to work destruction, and Colthurst was only a neurotic instrument of these. There exists in Ireland a de-nationalised and unnatural clique of persons, Irish at least in name I fear, who are in every way unpatriotic – as patriotism is known to the average honest man. These persons are there, for their own interests, to make the most of every 'émeute' which Irish unrestrained patriotism may exhibit. They desire to prove their case against the Catholics and the Nationalists, by driving these into Rebellion, by harsh and unjust measures of repression. Most of us know the story of Wexford!! As a matter of fact the party of Czarism, within a few weeks of now, practised the same methods in Petrograd, but they were countered by the mutiny of the men of the Guards who were sent to shoot the populace – and who refused to shoot their brothers – and incidentally shot some twelve of their own officers who tried to force them to do so. In Dublin last Easter week the same methods were in execution – The men who rose up against us were at most 1,500 – and probably not more than 1,100.

The people, as I know, through personal experience, were against the gallant folly of the rebellion. Yet the unpatriotic clique in and around Dublin Castle – wished to make the most of the 'rebellion' by exasperating others into joining in – so that it might be said that 'their prophecy was fulfilled' – and that Ireland was disloyal at heart – and Home Rule could never be wisely given to them.

Colthurst was their emissary in Portobello Barracks – a neurotic bigot. It was a very fortunate accident that I happened to be there – if it is not egotistical to say it – because no one who knows my record could suppose that I would countenance such methods. It was not within my power, to prevent the murders of Skeffington, McIntyre, and Dickson, for I never heard of these until 12 hours afterwards – but when I did hear of them, I stopped further murders. I made it known that I would report the matter – I gave a lecture under authority to all the officers on duty, as to their responsibility under Martial Law, and I took every available precaution to prevent a recurrence of such, by having the prisoners reported on every three hours. However the complicity of the clique in Dublin Castle is proved beyond any measure of doubt.

Within an hour of the murders of Skeffington et cetera, Major Rossborough telephoned to Dublin Castle for instructions what to do with Capt. Colthurst (this was extremely weak of him, because as Colthurst had committed a Military crime he should have been placed under arrest at once, but Major Rossborough is a kindly officer, and was much worried) and he received a message to the effect that Colthurst was to be left in command of his men. When I saw Rossborough and demanded that Colthurst should be placed under arrest – I was countered by direct instructions from Head Quarters. I then said that I would not hold myself responsible for the defence of the Barracks if he were allowed to go outside in command of men. This Major Rossborough agreed to.

Yet without the knowledge of Major Rossborough, and of course of mine, the day after, Capt. Colthurst was taken by Colonel Allett to raid Mrs Skeffington's house. Colonel Allett being senior to both of us and not an officer in Barracks.

On Sunday the wall against which these unfortunate men were shot was most carefully bricked up, to prevent detection – without our knowledge – and on Monday, 1st May – I was ordered to hand over the command of the Defences to Captain Colthurst – an officer who should have been arrested for Military crime – 6 days before.

I then proceeded to the Irish Head Quarters – and, as by my sworn declaration, reported the murders of the 26th April; and was told that 'men like Skeffington are well out of the way' – And then, and then only, I applied for leave to go to London.

As is generally known now, on the 2nd May I reported to Mr Tennant at the War Office and on the 3rd May to the late Lord Kitchener at 10 Downing Street – and on the latter occasion Lord K. sent the telegram placing Captain Colthurst under arrest. He was placed under arrest 10 days after he had committed the crimes – and only then because I went to London to report them.

You will realise therefore that there was a conspiracy of silence – and I think of murder – more clearly emphasised perhaps in the fact that I was recommended for promotion owing to my relieving a convoy and commanding in the attack against the South Dublin Union on the 7th April – which recommendation was held back by Sir John Maxwell, and, while I was the only senior officer recommended for action in the Field against the rebels, I was relegated to unemployment, while Colonel Allett, Major Price and Sir John Maxwell were all honoured by the King.

Now they have refused to allow my book to be published – though all the facts are quite well known in America, as witness the long letter sent to me from Ex-President Roosevelt, and which I have answered at equal length.

Believe me I am very truly grateful for your sympathy; it is always pleasant to know that strangers appreciate one's actions – none the less so a lady, and one who now writes from but a few doors from the house in which I was born (10 Great George's Street).

I remain,
Dear Madam,
Yours sincerely,
FRANCIS FLETCHER-VANE of Hutton.
9th April 1917

7

AFTER THE RISING: IN AMERICA

INTRODUCTION

Hanna and her son Owen arrived in America in December 1916, having travelled under assumed identities because the authorities refused to give her a passport unless she pledged herself not to discuss Ireland, Great Britain or the war while in the United States. In her 18-month stay she spoke at more than 250 meetings, not only to Irish Americans but to many other interest groups. The first event took place in Carnegie Hall, New York, on 6 January 1917. After America entered the war in April 1917 Hanna began to call for American recognition of the Irish republic in order for Ireland to have a place as a small nation in the Peace Conference to follow the end of war. The title of her lecture changed from 'British Militarism as I Have Known It' to 'What Does Ireland Want?' The Department of Justice took an interest in her and agents working for the Bureau of Investigation took notes at her meetings, concluding that although she was pro-Irish and anti-British, she did not attack the United States and therefore could not be prosecuted. On 11 January 1918 she succeeded in meeting with President Wilson and presented him with a petition signed by Cumann na mBan which put forward Ireland's claim for self-determination and appealed to the president to include Ireland among the small nations whose fate would be considered in future peace negotiations. While denounced by those who supported the war effort, she was widely praised by American radicals and the Irish-American community. The veteran Fenian, John Devoy, bestowed high praise in his newspaper, the *Gaelic American*, 'Mrs Sheehy Skeffington has done more real good to the cause of Ireland during her short stay in America than all the Irish orators and writers who have undertaken to enlighten the American people for the past twenty five years' (3 March 1917). Hanna's familiarity with Devoy and her confidence in dealing with those at the highest levels in political life is evident in her letter of 9 March 1918, as is the fact that the industrialist Henry Ford thought her a person worth meeting with. Her success in obtaining an interview with President Wilson was a triumph that no other Irish republican was able to emulate.

Her pamphlet *Impressions of Sinn Féin in America*, not published until 1919
due to war-time censorship, provides a vivid account of her experiences and the
fevered atmosphere within American political circles as the country prepared
to enter the war. As a declared Sinn Féiner she insisted that full independence
had to be granted to Ireland as a small nation, given the evidence of British
misrule in Ireland, the heroic efforts of Irish republicans to achieve independence through force of arms, and because the war was supposedly being
fought on behalf of the small nations of Europe. Her oratory and ability to stir
her audience are vividly demonstrated in the report of her last meeting, in
Madison Square Garden, which powerfully conveys her fury regarding the
murder of her husband, the machinations of British agents and others in the
pro-war lobby. She was undoubtedly a propaganda asset to the republican
movement, all the more so as she was also eminently capable of writing well
argued, erudite responses in newspapers and journals, as demonstrated by her
riposte to Shane Leslie,[1] who wrote in the journal *America* of Irish Home Rule
rather than complete independence.

On her return to Ireland, discovering the impoverished state of one of the
widows of Easter Week, the young Grace Gifford, she immediately used the
contacts she had made in America to plead on behalf of Gifford, urging Joe
McGarrity to provide financial support to Plunkett's widow rather than
erecting a memorial to the Easter Week martyr. This example demonstrates
the practical, non-sentimental side of Hanna's character, as a woman who
would put the welfare of people before any symbolic display of national pride.

*Impressions of Sinn Féin in America: An Account of Eighteen Months' Irish
Propaganda in the United States*
Publishers' Note:

We regret that, owing to circumstances beyond our control, this pamphlet,
hastily compiled in December last for the General Election, could not be
published until now. And that the proofs have not been corrected by the author;
in view, however, of the present Irish campaign in the United States it is now
of even more vital interest.

The Davis Publishing Co.

When I first learned the facts about my husband's murder by Captain Bowen
Colthurst on April 26th, 1916, I made up my mind – and this intention was
strengthened after the abortive inquiry forced from Mr Asquith in connection
with the case – to go to America and to tell that story of British militarism to
every audience in the States that I could reach. After the wholly unsatisfactory
report of the Simon inquiry in September of that year, I approached a friend
of mine – a politician – and asked him to take steps with a view to obtaining

for me a passport in my own name to the United States. Upon inquiry he was told that no passport would be given me except on certain strict conditions. When I inquired what these conditions were, I was told that I must pledge myself in writing not to discuss Ireland, Great Britain, or the War, while in the United States, even in private conversation. I told my friend that I could accept no such conditions, but that I would pledge myself, while in the United States, 'to tell the truth and nothing but the truth about Ireland, Great Britain and the War'. When I said this my friend laughed and replied: 'Truth in war time – impossible!' and it was only afterwards while in the States that I came to realise the profound truth of his words.

A great writer once said: 'Truth is the first casualty of war', and as far as the truth with regard to her relations towards Ireland, and with regard to Easter Week, Great Britain has been most chary of that export; so much so that I found subsequently that the fact that one had been able to obtain a passport from the authorities discredited one as far as propaganda was concerned in the United States, because people felt that those provided with pass-ports had a duty imposed upon them beforehand to tell only such portions of their story as would be acceptable to Great Britain. The refusal to grant me a pass-port, however, strengthened me in my conviction that good work could be done in the United States by telling the truth about Ireland and that the more the authorities desired to block me, the more imperative it was to go. I made up my mind, accordingly, to go all the same, and, the front door being barred to me, I took the side door, and took what used to be called 'French' leave, but what we may now more properly call 'Irish' leave, of the authorities. How this was done, unfortunately, I may not yet say. My former experience as a militant suffragette served me now to some good purpose; I took my boy of seven with me, and he was also sufficiently 'camouflaged' to pass muster. I arrived in the United States in December, 1916. Feeling was then running very high. About the time my boat arrived I was missed at home and the long arm of the British authorities was stretched out across the sea after me; word was sent through the American authorities on Ellis Island to detain me with my boy, with a view to having us deported by the next boat as offenders against the Defence of the Realm Act. The American authorities, however, did not see their way to take such action; it was not the first time that the United States has welcomed political refugees; in fact, the then mayor of New York (John Mitchel) was himself the grandson of a famous political refugee who escaped to the United States with a price on his head. The Americans were rather 'tickled' at the idea of evading DORA, and the American Press made the most of the episode in its picturesque way.

Things were very ripe for propaganda just then in America. Other Irish refugees had got over during the months following the Easter Rising, and had done splendid work in telling the tale of Easter Week. Miss Nora Connolly, daughter of James Connolly, Mr Liam Mellows, Miss Nellie Gifford, Mrs and Mr Padraic Colum,[2] later Dr McCartan, Captain Monteith, and others, had helped to enlighten American public opinion, always open-minded, eager to learn, and always interested in Ireland and Irish politics. Several books had appeared: *Ireland's Tragic Easter*, edited by Mr Padraic Colum; *The Sinn Féin Movement*, by Mr Frank Jones; again, later, Miss Margaret Skinnider's book entitled *Doing My Bit for Ireland*,[3] Miss Nora Connolly's *The Unbroken Tradition*. In addition there was great demand for every scrap of writing by the men and women of Easter Week, and America seemed to have awakened to the fact that there was a new Ireland, that Irish-Americans had every reason to be proud of. The effect of the Easter rising, and, above all, of its suppression, had revolutionized public sentiment in America and had stirred up all the slumbering fires of revolt hidden away in the Irish-American heart. Not only did this affect Irish-Americans, it touched profoundly Americans of whatever nationality; for, after all, your only real American today who can absolutely dissociate himself from the hyphenate is the Red Indian. Europe, not Great Britain, is the mother of America today. The same tales of horror and militarism, and the crushing of oppressed people woke responsive echoes in the hearts of Russians, Poles, Germans, Belgians, Jews, Italians, and even of the few inhabitants of the United States that are of English or Scottish descent. One of the facts that struck the Americans most profoundly was that the leaders of Easter Week, afterwards executed, were men of such outstanding intellectuality – poets, writers, painters, sculptors. As an American writer said, speaking of Joseph Plunkett and Padraic Pearse: 'In Italy they blind nightingales – in England they kill poets.'

There are in the United States, it is estimated, twenty millions of Irish birth or descent – that is to say, a fifth of the entire population is of Irish strain. The Irish in America, in addition, cling to the thoughts of Ireland, with its traditions, with a tenacity that is shown by the descendants of no other country. One can imagine therefore the effect upon public opinion of an Irish Rising in the midst of a war alleged to be on behalf of the small nations, followed by so many executions, deportations, murders. It is my opinion – and that is shared by many in America – that the United States would have entered the war in 1916 but for Easter Week. Another effect of the Easter Rising is to demonstrate more clearly than anything else could have done the fact that Ireland is not satisfied to be a province or colony of Great Britain; up to that time British propaganda had been busy, creating the impression that Ireland was loyal to Great Britain, that Ireland cared more about the freedom of Belgium than she cared about her own, that in fact the Irish Nation had become snug and comfortable, prosperous through the war, and glad of the 'protection' afforded her by the British fleet, that the dreams of old of an independent Irish Republic were dead. It is not surprising that this should be so, because of the open support given by Mr Redmond and his party, by Mr William O'Brien and his party (that is to say, by all save one, Mr Ginnell,[4] of the Irish Nationalist representatives at Westminster) to the war policy of Great Britain. Great Britain was able to point out this fact in America to demonstrate that the Irish at least were loyal, and that Ireland was, in the words of Sir Edward Grey, 'The One Bright Spot in the British Empire.'

Some of the Irish papers in America, notably the *Irish World* and the New York *Freeman's Journal*, which had hitherto supported the Irish party had broken away from it at the beginning of the war, but there were many other controlled and syndicated papers left, and all these, including the weekly organ, *America*, subsidised for that purpose, spoke of Ireland's new-found devotion to the British Empire. The guns of Easter Week helped effectively to kill that calumny.

Most of the leaders who perished during Easter Week were well-known in America, especially Padraic Pearse, Sir Roger Casement, Thomas Ashe, and James Connolly. The effect of their deaths was more powerful in swaying American sentiment to sympathy with Ireland than all the efforts of the syndicated press. Moreover, President Wilson had just been re-elected as President of the United States on the issue that he had 'kept America out of the war'. He was still working very hard to preserve America's neutrality, and he was backed by strong sentiment in Congress and the entire pacifist movement of the United States. On all this movement the story of Ireland's Easter Week had a powerful effect. The murder of my husband especially, told in all its naked horror, was used by pacifists as a powerful indictment of militarism, tending to show that militarists are all alike. In the first days after my arrival in America I succeeded in having an interview with ex-President Roosevelt, and of laying the facts before him. He informed me subsequently that he had proved the truth of my statements, and had correspondence with Mr Lloyd George on the subject. I also met Colonel House, and informed him in detail of the terrible Portobello murders, of the court-martial, the shielding of the guilty parties, of the shooting of James Connolly. On him and other leaders of America that story of Easter Week had a profound and salutary effect, and helped, as I have said, the case for Ireland. About that time (December, 1916) an enormous Irish Fair was held in Madison Square Gardens, New York, for the purpose of raising funds for the victims of Easter Week. New York was placarded with huge posters depicting the shooting of Connolly, Irish propaganda being taken over and strengthened by a new organisation called 'Friends of Irish Freedom'. For the first time Americans of other nationalities began to interest themselves in Irish Freedom, and many of them joined the organisation.

The American press, notably the *Hearst Papers*, the *New York Evening Post*, and various radical organs, took up the case for Ireland. In fact, so huge was the demand for information on Irish questions that an army of writers could have been kept busy long after the Rising. I was told that accounts of the state of things in Ireland occupied more space in American journals during April and May, 1916, than any other matter.

My first meeting was held in Carnegie Hall, New York, on January the 6th, 1917. Before that I had been inundated in characteristic style by American newspaper men, photographs had been taken of us both (my boy and myself) until I dreaded the process as I would have dreaded a visit to the dentist. Even my little boy had been 'interviewed' by an enterprising young editor, eager for copy, while many newspaper women insisted on making what are called 'sob-stories' out of the case. The Americans, like the Germans and British, even perhaps to a greater degree, are incurably sentimental. They like rather blatant appeals to the emotions, and are very eager for 'thrills'. The human interest, as they call it, particularly appeals to them and usually, as everywhere in America, a woman has a good show and is more sure of sympathy and kindliness in the States than usually would be the case in any other country. I had heard many weird tales of the unscrupulousness of American interviewers, but in my entire experience of them – and it was pretty wide before I left the country – I never once found them unfair or unkind; even when their papers were hostile to our Irish propaganda, it often has happened that the reporter was Irish and managed in spite of editorial blue-pencils to give our story a good show. Invariably they were particularly 'tickled' by the story (such as could be given) of the escape from the clutches of DORA without a pass-port, and the game way in which our little nation stood up alone against the world, and dared to rise and try conclusions with the greatest, most powerful Empire in the world appealed to the sportsmanlike sense of the Americans.

At Carnegie Hall I delivered my lecture under the presidency of Mr Bainbridge Colby, an influential American (afterwards put in charge of the American Shipping Department) and a personal friend of President Wilson's. The gathering was not entirely Irish – in fact, every section of the American Republic was represented – pacifists, suffragists, Russians, and a large sprinkling of newspapermen, judges (most of them New York judges or Irish), socialists; in fact the papers on the next day noted the cosmopolitan character of the gathering, New York being, of course, the most international of American cities. The Irish element was also naturally strong, for many Irish emigrants never go beyond New York – as it is popularly said: 'there are more Irish in New York than in Cork.' My lecture was entitled 'British Militarism as I have Known It'. Fortunately, I was well primed as to documents, having managed to get various documents bearing on the case out before me; I confined myself entirely to facts without personal comment, and allowed the Americans to draw their own conclusions; I dealt not only with the story of my husband's murder but with the North King Street shootings, the death of the boy Coade, of Councillor Richard O'Carroll, the deportations and raids, and of the horrors that have become the platitudes and the every-day happenings in a country under military occupation. It was this address which I delivered mainly throughout the entire tour, though on other occasions for special meetings I dealt with the Ulster problem and with the labour movement in Ireland.

Subsequently we printed the story in pamphlet form and it was circulated not only throughout the United States, but in Canada, the Philippines and South America. When in the following April America entered the war on the side of the Allies, I continued to deliver the same lecture through the States, and it is a remarkable fact showing, I think, the strong feeling there is in America for Ireland, that Irish propaganda, except in one or two slight incidents, was never interfered with, though it was continued, if possibly, more intensely and more passionately after the United States had become associated with Great Britain. We also reprinted my husband's article, 'A Forgotten Small Nationality', published in the *Century Magazine*, February, 1916.

Immediately under the auspices of 'The Friends of Irish Freedom', and of various other Irish or Pacifist groups, a tour was organised for me throughout the New-England States. In connection with this, an interesting episode occurred. The British Agents in the United States are naturally very perturbed at the Irish propaganda on behalf of our small nation. They dislike particularly propaganda of such Irish exiles as myself who had come directly from Ireland, and could speak with first-hand knowledge. As one of them rather pathetically observed: 'My objection to Mrs Sheehy Skeffington is that she has a lot of damaging facts.' Accordingly, a trap was laid for me. I was invited by a Women's Society in Toronto to cross the frontier and lecture there on Woman's Suffrage. I realised that Suffrage was being possibly used as a bait to get me on hostile ground, where I might be interned, and politely refused the invitation. On my journey, however, to Buffalo I was intercepted near the Canadian Border by a small group of men and women who wore green badges, and who represented themselves as a local committee sent to meet me, and to be my escort. They invited me to board a train, and I was about to step into it unsuspecting, when, happening to look down the platform, I saw in the distance an agitated group with waving umbrellas and handkerchiefs, and trying to draw my attention. I waited for them to come up, in spite of the urgent insistence of my green-badged escort that I should board the train at once. When they came up I discovered that they were the genuine committee sent to meet me, and that the train which I was about to board was one bound for Canada, which would have got me safely across the border in half-an-hour!

While these explanations were going on I looked around for my first escort and found that they were rapidly disappearing, having succeeded in escaping the clutches of the local committee. We were never able to discover their identity, but the conclusion was obvious, that they were sent to decoy me into Canada, and after that incident I was usually on my guard, and careful when near the Canadian frontier as to the trains and routes I should take. The British Agents, however, still continued busy, and I frequently found my luggage was tampered with, the contents of my desk ransacked, doubtless with the object of connecting me with some bogus 'plot' or other. As my propaganda courted publicity I was not embarrassed by these little attentions. We in Ireland are quite inured to them. Sometimes, locally, attempts were made by the British Agents to interfere with the letting of halls for Irish meetings, but usually the local committee was able to deal effectively with such attempts. In fact adverse newspaper talk at a meeting engineered for hostile purposes usually helped us. As American slang has it: 'A knock is a boost' – in other words, an attack is very often a free advertisement! One of the many such free advertisements given was afforded by the President of Harvard University. I was invited by the students to lecture there in the early months of 1917, when America was still a neutral country. President Lowell is well-known for his strong pro-British sentiment. A week before my lecture Major Ian Beith Hay had been lecturing frankly for British recruiting purposes and was not interfered with in any way. The President, however, woke up to the fact that my propaganda was pro-Irish, and suddenly, on the day of the meeting, took it into his head to forbid the students the use of the hall. The students resented this action, and promptly engaged a larger hall over which the President had no control, with the result that we had an extremely successful meeting. Much indignation was expressed in the College paper, as well as in New York and Boston papers, on the President's attempt to suppress free speech. Other Presidents profited by the example, and I was not interfered with in lecturing at Columbia University, New York, Chicago University, Madison University, Wisconsin, Wellesley Women's College, and others. In general, I may say, schools, colleges, and universities in America as well as Women's Clubs which are a special feature of the country, afforded a very valuable ground for Irish propaganda – a ground hitherto almost untouched because, unfortunately, many Irish speakers who visit the States make the profound mistake of devoting themselves exclusively to addressing Irish audiences. I made it a point of never refusing an invitation to address any society on the question of Ireland, from the most conservative and reactionary to the most advanced and democratic, because it was my object to expose British hypocrisy to as wide a circle as possible throughout the entire States.

Great Britain was ever astute in her propaganda. From the time of the outbreak of the war she turned a regular army of lecturers into the United

States, instructed, not only to put her case for the war before American audiences, but to vilify, wherever possible, those nations that did not agree with her in the Imperialistic ambitions. Her lecturers were chosen with care, schooled to appeal to every section of the community. There was, for instance, Major Ian Beith Hay, notorious for his book on *The Oppressed English*, a jovial, soldierly type camouflaged to represent the bluff, military man who takes 'no interest in politics'. He was sent to every town in which I lectured to conduct counter-propaganda. He told delighted audiences: 'How jolly it was to be in the trenches, don't you know,' and explained how we Irish were paid emissaries of the Kaiser. Then there were radical lecturers of the *Manchester Guardian* type, such as Mr Radcliffe, formerly connected with that paper. Their line usually was to 'regret profoundly the tragic errors' made by the British with regard to Ireland, but to indicate that the British democracy was sound and only desired to do the right thing towards Ireland, if but 'the Irish would unite among themselves'. Mrs Pankhurst, ex-Militant suffragist, was sent to make an appeal specially to the women of the States. Alfred Noyes, the minor poet, poured out war poetry by the ream of the school of 'Poppies in Picardy', favoured by such trench sentiment as Patrick Magill favours. Then there were English priests who lectured at fashionable Women's Clubs on the 'Anti-Catholic' atrocities of the Germans, and who stated that the Sinn Féiners were all atheists, who fired on churches and murdered Nuns and lived immoral lives. Some of those lecturers, however, worked unconsciously on behalf of Ireland. Mr Balfour, Lord Northcliffe, Sir F. E. Smith, did us a world of good by showing the American people what we Irish have to suffer. It is no secret that Lord Northcliffe's propaganda created a very favourable impression in the United States, and that Sir F. E. Smith received a polite hint from the American Authorities that he should cut his visit short. Both of these gentlemen served only to stir up bitter race feeling in the States, and to inflame public sentiment against the cause that they advocated. For example, a distinguished Washington Journalist (a member of the Bureau of Public Information) told me that he had been converted into a Sinn Féiner by listening to Sir F. E. Smith. After hearing the after-dinner oratory of 'Galloper' Smith he said: 'I have become a convert to Irish Independence – I have just been listening to Sir F. E. Smith, and I now understand at last what you Irish have to put up with!'

On the occasion of the visit of Mr Balfour to Washington he was invited to address Congress. Americans in general were very much repelled by the haughty superciliousness of the Balfourian style. Bluff and jovial Marshall Joffre produced everywhere a favourable and friendly impression, but Balfour, with his haughty aristocratic air froze up American sympathy. His speech fell flat in Congress for the morning on which he appeared to address it on behalf of the Small Nations every Congressman found mysteriously placed upon his desk by some unknown agency a little leaflet bearing the heading: 'Who is Bloody Balfour?' giving a brief life history of Mr Balfour and of his regime in Ireland, and an account of his famous Mitchelstown telegram to the Police on the occasion of the riot there: 'Don't hesitate to shoot.'⁵ The Congressmen, as I was told by a spectator, were more profoundly interested in the little leaflet than in Mr Balfour's careful periods which, as a consequence, fell flat. Americans are puzzled at the curious specimens of British 'democracy' that Great Britain exported to the United States to be her spokesmen. It seemed as if only Imperialists of the *Morning Post* brand were furnished with credentials. For instance, while Mrs Pankhurst's campaign, Anti-Russian and Anti-Irish, was facilitated by the British Government Mrs Pethick-Lawrence, the distinguished Suffragist and Pacifist leader, was refused pass-ports to America where she was invited by American Suffragists to help in their campaign. Margaret Bondfield, who represented British Labour, was similarly refused permission to travel to America to attend an important Labour Congress. In a like manner the more progressive labour papers of England, as well as, of course the entire Sinn Féin and pro-Irish papers continued to be excluded from the mails even after America had entered the war. Such papers as *The Herald*, *The Labour Leader*, the Glasgow *Forward*, *The Workers' Dreadnought*, *The Irish Citizen*, *New Ireland*, etc., are not permitted to circulate in Canada or the United States. All these signs go to show that the British government is afraid of American public opinion finding it out for the sham that it is, which while preciously guarding every degree of liberty in certain sections of Europe would like to curtail and 'Hooverize' these dangerous commodities as far as possible elsewhere. Now that the war restrictions are largely lifted from the American Press, and that the censorship can no longer continue to be so rigid in Great Britain, it will be more and more possible for the Progressive elements in all countries to get into touch with one another.

Yet in spite of this British Anti-Irish Propaganda, in spite of the daily misrepresentations of a controlled press, the most popular Small Nation in the eyes of the United States is still, as it always has been, Ireland. The reason for this is obvious. Americans have been worked up to an interest in Belgium and in Poland; they are beginning to find out about the Czecho-Slovaks and the Jugo-Slavs: they are learning to place the Rumanians and the Siberians on the map, and to pronounce the names of the various little new republics, such as the Ukraine and Estonia – but Ireland – well, there have been enough Irish exiles and refugees all these years to keep America fully informed about the wrongs of one Small Nation, Ireland, which has given over one-fifth of its entire inhabitants to the Republic. The demand for an Irish Republic is also readily understood by the Americans. There are, in fact, only two views in America with regard to Ireland, namely: the view of Sir Edward Carson and that of Sir Roger Casement – the view that regards Ireland as an English Shire and the view that regards Ireland as a separate Nation. That is why at present the Sinn Féin Movement is more popular and more comprehensible than the Home Rule Movement, and that is why, probably, Mr T. P. O'Connor's[6] mission in America was such a huge failure: he never succeeded during his nine months in the States in addressing a single public meeting in any town on the Irish Question; while, on the other hand, Republicans were everywhere eagerly welcomed. This is but natural in a country which is itself Republican in Government, and is so far the one of the British colonies that has been fortunate enough to throw over the yoke of Empire and set up a free Republic. Washington in fact may be claimed as the first Sinn Féiner. Last April on the anniversary of American's entry into the war a little group of Irish delegates from the Irish Progressive League of New York, gave expression to this sentiment by laying a wreath upon the tomb of George Washington, bearing the colours Orange, White and Green, of the Irish republic with the inscription: 'To George Washington, half of whose army was Irish and whose ideals and principles inspired the men of Easter Week.' Washington's tomb has been a place of pilgrimage since the war from all the Small Nations, all of them, from Japan to Belgium, have laid wreaths and scrolls upon the tomb of the father of the American Republic. Mr Balfour and General Joffre paid their tribute to democracy also by floral emblems, but none is more appropriate than this last which lies upon the tomb of another great rebel. George Washington also was a traitor to the Empire, the only difference between his treason and the treason of Easter Week was that his treason succeeded. As the poet says:

> Treason doth never prosper.

What is the reason? When treason prospers none dare call it treason. One wonders what would have been the fate of George Washington if his treason had not prospered – no doubt he would have found his answer in a firing squad and a quick-lime grave.

Entry of America into the War
With the entry of America into the war on Good Friday, 1917, there was naturally a certain change of front towards European problems, but, as the vested interests – the big-money trusts, and so forth – had never really been neutral, the change was not as great and by no means as far reaching as might have been expected. This was particularly so with regard to the Irish, for the German element had less cohesion and was more easily swamped. True, many of the Irish politicians for whom the Irish Question was mainly a political asset, a trap to catch votes, at once dropped their Irish propaganda like a hot

coal and suddenly discovered that they were 'Americans first, last, and all the time', whatever that may mean, and lectured us Irish on the iniquity of not standing in 'now that the United States had come into the war'. In fact, I would say, in general, that the Irish-American politician is one of the worst obstacles Ireland has to encounter. It is perhaps just as well that the 'Hot Air Harps', as they are picturesquely called in American slang, have been found out for the sham that they are. The bulk of the people, however, in the United States still remained sound on the Irish Question. This is particularly true of the middle west and the western states. Indeed, had a referendum at any time been given on the question of America's entry into the war, there can be very little doubt but that the United States would have as a whole decided against it. Even upon America's entry and ever since, President Wilson has always made it clear that he regards the United States, not as an Ally of Great Britain and France and the other Allied Powers, but as an 'associate', and once went the length of publicly correcting the Food Controller, Mr Hoover, on this important point. Mr Hoover having used the word 'ally' on his public posters when referring to the United States and Great Britain. In the west it must be remembered that the serious problem is the question, not of German militarism, but of Japan's Imperialistic ambitions. Therefore the war-enthusiasm of the west is tempered by a shrewd suspicion of Japan. There was, of course, the usual war hysteria in a pretty virulent form when America first decided to go in. I encountered some of it in a rather amusing form in a little town in the middle-west, where I had been invited to lunch. There was much patriotic talk at the table. Noticing that I was somewhat silent a vivacious lady opposite me – the president of the Local Ladies' Club – and a social leader – said, I suppose with the intention of stimulating me conversationally: 'And how do you think the war will end?' I replied solemnly: 'I think it will end in peace.' She started as if stung by a serpent and she exclaimed, in tones of horror and consternation: 'Oh, I had no idea you were a Pacifist!' her exclamation illustrates well the attitude of some war-mongers in America. To them the mere suggestion that there should ever again be peace on earth savoured of rank blasphemy, and of course, as many of these 'patriots' were engaged in the production of munitions or in other ways making huge sums out of the war, their attitude was not surprising. There was, therefore, pretty much the same ebullition of surface war hysteria in the States as there was in Great Britain in August 1914, and, with the characteristic exuberance of a young people, the Americans have indulged in many extravagant and childish exhibitions in the much-abused name of patriotism. For instance the children in the schools have to salute the flag as a morning exercise; German music was banished; prayers in German were declared illegal in some States by Governor's proclamations; public libraries made bonfires of all their German books, while harmless German words like 'Sauerkraut' and 'Frankfurter' had to change their name into 'liberty cabbage' and 'liberty sausage'. One no longer was permitted to suffer from 'German' measles, only 'American' measles being officially recognised. Of course, one might still drink German beer under another name, and the flavour, I believe, is not impaired.

There were, moreover, less harmless ebullitions of war sentiment, such as the lynching of the German Praeger in Collinsville, Illinois, and the tarring and feathering of suspected pro-Germans in the west. Many of these outrages were, however, the result of local press propaganda of a ferocious kind, while others, like the brutal lynching of Frank Little, a Labour leader in Butte, Montana, and the tarring and feathering of the Rev. H. Bigelow, distinguished preacher and Social Reformer of Cincinnati, Ohio, had their origin, not in any Pro-Ally feeling, but in economic and social causes. Just as in the case of the 'frame up' of Tom Mooney[7] (The Socialist Labour Leader of San Francisco) by the Anti-Labour Corporations, so too in the case of Frank Little – it was not entirely an accident that he was organising the strike of miners for decent economic conditions when he was murdered; while Bigelow had aroused the hatred of the vice and drink interest in Cincinnati some years before by his plucky fight and subsequent victory over them, and his life. The war is thus often made a pretext for vengeance against the Socialist reformer – a war 'activity' by no means confined to the New World.

We Irish exiles in the United States at America's entry into the war at first thought that all Irish Propaganda on behalf of self-determination for our Small Nation would have been made impossible, that our meetings would have been suppressed, and that we ourselves would be sent to prison or deported. To our great surprise nothing of the kind happened. Irish Propaganda went on, if possible, more strongly than ever. In my own case my largest public meetings in the largest halls of the United States – one of them, the Auditorium in San Francisco, holding twenty thousand people – were held after America's entry into the war. It was about that time I started for the west, and realised for the first time the enormous size of the States to be covered: San Francisco is in many respects as different from New York as Petrograd is from London, and no one can estimate the strength of Irish sentiment in the United States who has not included the west in his observations. Butte, Montana, and San Francisco, are more enthusiastically Irish, and now more enthusiastically Sinn Féin than any town in Ireland is. Moreover, in the west particularly the Irish blood holds the strings of government in their hands – judges, lawyers, policemen, are usually Irish to a man. A large percentage of Irish among the soldiers and in the camps of California and in the State of Washington is a factor to be reckoned with. In fact, generally, American soldiers are extremely susceptible to Irish propaganda. They flocked to our meetings and many of them told me that America's entry into the war, far from changing their sentiment towards the problem of Ireland's freedom made them feel more intensely than ever that the United States has a duty to perform to Ireland as well as to other Small Nations. 'Now that we are in it,' they said, 'we shall see to it that you get your full share. Ireland must be free as well as Belgium!' During the year and a half of my stay in the United States I spoke in the following States: – New York, Connecticut, Massachusetts, New Jersey, New Hampshire, Rhode Island, Pennsylvania, District of Columbia, Oregon, Illinois, Minnesota, Michigan, California, Washington, Montana, Texas, Colorado, Wisconsin, Ohio, Kansas, Missouri, from Texas to the Canadian frontier, from New York to San Francisco, to Montana miners, to the Professors at Harvard, to the Congressmen and Senators in Washington, to Socialists and Pacifists, speaking in all at over 250 public meetings. At two of these – one in Washington's largest hall, Madison Square Garden,[8] which holds 10,000 people, one in San Francisco's largest hall – there were interruptions from women 'vigilantes' – as the extreme patriots are proud of calling themselves – but it was interesting to observe that the interrupters, not the speakers, were removed by the police for 'disturbing the meeting'! On another occasion in Los Angeles a police man, whose family hailed from County Clare, said to a Canadian woman who demanded my arrest on the spot for 'sedition': 'Sure, ma'am, this is an Irish meeting – we are all for Ireland here, and if you don't conduct yourself I will have to put you out.' As Liam Mellows observed at a New York meeting: 'Blood is thicker than water and Irish blood is the thickest in the world.' America is not blind to the fact that Ireland up to the present hour is a country governed by force, held by an army of occupation under martial law. The authorities in America might speak on this with authority, for more than any other race they have given their sons in this war. While their loyalty to the land of their adoption is unshakeable and most touching, their loyalty to the land of their fathers is also strong, and they ask insistently: 'Is Ireland the only country that will not be safe for Democracy?' If peace is to see Belgium free, Rumania, Poland, the Czecho-Slovaks and Jugo-Slavs, and the others granted self-determination, while Ireland alone continues the victim of alien militarism, the people of the United States will realise that their republic will have abandoned her own principles to her lasting shame, and that the sacrifices of her sons in the war will have helped but to rivet Ireland's chains. The problem is one of which President Wilson is fully aware, and he is, I am convinced, prepared to press it as vital at the Peace Conference for the sake of the future peace of the world, as well as for the hour of the United States. A striking proof of the strength of sentiment was seen in New York's Mayoral Election in November, 1917. The late ex-mayor of New York, John Mitchel, had been returned four years previously. He was the grandson of

John Mitchel, who had been imprisoned and exiled perpetually from Ireland after the '48 Rising. That record was enough to make every man of Irish birth or descent in New York vote for Mitchel, but once elected, Mayor Mitchel, like other politicians, forgot the Irish, and denounced and repudiated all Irish-Americans who dared to ask for fair play for Ireland as well as Belgium. He posed as the one and only patriot, wrapping himself in the American flag, while patriotism of the most Jingo kind was his platform. He had behind him all the New York dailies with one exception, while the monied interest of the Morgans, the Vanderbilts, and the trusts backed him up. The Vanderbilts, as his friends proudly boasted, called him 'Jack', but he was mistaken in suspecting that he could dispense with the Irish, and was beaten by an overwhelming majority. The fate of Mayor Mitchel had been a salutary lesson to the politicians and the patriots. At the last Congressional Elections the Irish made Ireland a test question wherever the candidates standing had a strong Irish vote in their constituencies. Hitherto the Irish have supported the Democratic Party, but the recent defeat of many of the Democrats is probably an indication that their support is only conditional and that they will, if necessary, defeat the Democrat unless he is prepared to stand for freedom all round. There were last year six resolutions on the Irish Question before Congress, all, with one exception, framed by Republican Congressmen. One of them was from Jeannette Rankin – 'The Lady from Montana' as she is called – the only woman representative in Congress. Miss Rankin is returned by the Irish vote of the Montana miners, and the flag of the Irish Republic occupies the place of honour over her desk in her office in Washington. She is of Scotch and French extraction, without a drop of Irish blood, but she told me that her French mother had always taught her to love Ireland.

On the Eve of St Patrick's Day of last year, the veteran leader (since dead) of the Republican Party in the Senate – Senator Gallagher of New Hampshire – brought in a resolution laying down as a principle Ireland's right to self-determination and suggesting a referendum of the adult population of Ireland as to what form of government the Nation will accept. This resolution had the effect of a bomb on the British Embassy in Washington and was described by the *Washington Post*, a hostile and reactionary organ, as one 'loaded with dynamite'. It was an open secret in Washington that the President favoured the suggestion of a referendum for Ireland. For a time he trusted that Mr Lloyd George's Convention[9] might bring forth some satisfactory solution, but when the Convention collapsed it became clear that there could be no settlement of the Irish Question as long as that settlement remained in the hands of Great Britain.

The 'Friends of Irish Freedom' in the United States arranged a monster petition – which has been signed by over two and a half million American citizens – for presentation to President Wilson, claiming also Ireland's right to self-determination.

On St Patrick's Day last year 50,000 Irishmen and women walked in procession down Fifth Avenue, New York, bearing side by side the American and the Irish Republican Flags, while an effective 'sticker' (poster) was being widely circulated throughout the United States bearing entwined the Irish and American Republican Colours, with underneath the words from President Wilson: 'We fight for the rights and liberties of small nations,' with the addition: 'Ireland is a nation and must be free.'

Last October an important Congress of 'Small and Subject Nations' was held at the Hotel McAlpin, New York, and sat for three days. At it were represented not only those subject and oppressed nationalities that were under the yoke of Germany, Austria or Turkey, but also those under the British Empire – Ireland, India, Egypt and the Boers. A powerful effort was made to suppress the Congress and influences were set at work in Washington to have it declared seditious and to have certain of its speakers – the Irish and the Indian – arrested. No official action was taken, however, against the Congress, which proved to be a great success. I had the honour of putting the case for Ireland, while the case for India was put by a distinguished Indian exile, Lajpat Rai, the editor of *New India*, an ex-Boer General, a friend of De Wet and De La Rey, General Pierson, represented the Boers. It was notable at the Congress that all the representatives of the small and subject peoples felt united by a common bond of sympathy against their oppressors. A resolution was sent to President Wilson – it was afterwards recorded in the Senate Record by Senator Borah – once more laying down the now famous principle of self-determination for all peoples. Professor Masaryk – who went to Washington as a representative of the Czecho-Slovaks to plead on their behalf, and who has since been made President of the Czecho-Slovak republic – when interviewed by an Irish deputation on the subject of Ireland, warmly expressed the sympathy of his people for the claims of Ireland. He himself was then under the sentence of death as a Rebel against the Austrian Government. He declared that Ireland had always been a beacon-light to the subject peoples in Austria – our struggle being largely parallel to their own.

All these instances (I mention but a few) are indications of the large and growing feeling in the United States that the case of Ireland must be included in the Peace Conference. It is significant that the British Press has carefully suppressed all mention of this propaganda, fostering steadily the calumny that the United States has been alienated by Ireland's attitude towards the war.

President Wilson
Since my return to Ireland I have often been asked my view as to President Wilson's personality. It is an extremely complex one, and one that has been

variously judged from every possible angle. I think the President's attitude towards progress may best be illustrated by his action upon a matter of internal American policy, namely: The Women's Suffrage Federal Amendment. It tends to show that while President Wilson is not of the type of lone pioneer who would push ahead on a forlorn hope against any odds, he is guided usually by what one may call a policy of enlightened expediency, and there is no statesman in the world to-day who knows better the exact time to come in on the right side and to press a reform home to a successful issue, when the demand becomes imperative and insistent. When America decided to enter the war the same situation was created with regard to the Women's Suffrage Movement as occurred in Great Britain in 1914. Many of the so-called Constitutional Suffragists turned their backs on Suffrage and preached to their followers the urgent duty of winning the war before all else. Their leaders – such as Dr Anna Howard-Shaw, Mrs Chapman-Catt – put Suffrage on the back shelf as did some of their British sisters, and told their followers that to ask for a vote just then, when their country was in a war to make the world safe for democracy, was to be unpatriotic, if not Pro-German. *The New York Times*, and other violently anti-Progressive organs, adopted this argument. A comfortable and decent burial was accordingly arranged for the Suffrage corpse, and the internment would have taken place duly but for the Militant Section, known as 'The Nationalist Women's Party', headed by Alice Paul, a Quaker, and Lucy Byrne, an Irishwoman. These women were not content to bury Suffrage till the war was over, but on the contrary showed a most insistent desire to have it 'right now'. They asked inconveniently: 'How could America help to make the world safe for Democracy, when she herself was not a democrat, and while millions of her women were then denied citizenship?' They asked that America put her own house in order, before reforming the world outside, by immediately putting through the Federal Amendment, granting Suffrage to the women of the entire United States at one stroke. Hitherto Suffragists had mainly confined their attentions to winning the vote State by State – a slow and weary process which has succeeded in winning the vote in 13 out of the 48 states. There then arose a situation extremely awkward for the politician, for there is nothing that your politician dislikes more than this harping upon painful questions in an hour of crisis – and there always is an hour of crisis for the politician, which furnishes a convenient excuse for shelving reforms. The chief obstacle to the passage of the Federal Amendment was the Democratic Party, headed by President Wilson, who was known to be opposed to the Federal Amendment, though personally a Suffragist. The National Woman's Party had opposed the Democrats and President Wilson's candidature in 1916, on the principle adopted by the late Suffragist, Christabel Pankhurst, of 'Keep the Liberal Out' – in other words: turn out the government responsible for blocking the measure. Such a policy was used on more than one occasion, unfortunately, by Parnell, when he turned the Irish vote in favour of the Tories. This did not mean that the Republican Party in America was necessarily regarded as the more progressive, no more than the Tory Party was by the British Militants or by Parnell; but the women felt that they could only secure reform by using one party effectively against its rival. All this, from the politician's point of view, was of course more deplorable, but the women wrote upon their banners: 'Suffrage first', and acted up to that principle. On America's entry into the war in 1917, there came a clamour for a truce. The Constitutionalists in a body rolled up their banner and handed it over for the duration of the war. It was hoped that no more would be heard of the Federal Amendment until Europe was safe for democracy, but the Nationalist Women's Party, whose motto was 'Suffrage now', decided otherwise. Accordingly they directed their attention to the Head of the Democratic party, President Wilson, and they inaugurated a State-wide campaign, starting with the White House. They placed peaceful pickets with suffrage banners – purple, white and yellow – to stand at the gates of the President's official residence. On these banners they wrote up many of President Wilson's historic and epoch-making phrases, such as: 'We fight for those things which are nearest our hearts,' 'This is a war to make the world safe for Democracy,' and under these lines they wrote such comments as: 'America is not a Democrat while she denies votes to half her citizens.' Once when an Irish deputation went to lay the case for Ireland before the Senate, the pickets seized the occasion for propaganda and a friendly alliance. The pickets are warm friends of Ireland, and once when the Russians came to Washington and were received by the President, the pickets informed the Russians that American women were not free – as Russian women are today, the Russian and the Irish Republics being the only Republics that in their Proclamation had given equal rights to men and women. The pickets were also in attendance when Mr Balfour came to Washington. It must have seemed like old times to him, to see Suffragists demonstrating once again. Finally, the authorities, who had pretended to ignore the women or to kill their cause by ridicule, changed their tactics and began to persecute. Curious how alike these authorities always are in their methods. After the Russian incident the pickets were arrested. They could not be charged with picketing, for this is legal. They could not be charged with wanting a vote or wanting women made safe for Democracy, for so far that had not been made a Statutory Offence: so they were charged – again how like some others – with unlawful assembly and with obstructing the traffic. Pennsylvania Avenue is as wide as O'Connell Street and two small pickets at the White House Gates could hardly be said to create a block, but the usual police methods of finding a crowd, and blaming you for it, of creating a disorder and arresting you for it, were forthwith employed – again with the usual result. Picketing became popular. Hundreds of women were arrested. The local gaols became congested and lo! The new criminals were found to be the wives and sisters and daughters of prominent Government officials, Senators, Judges, Professors, Lawyers, Editors – pillars of the State and shining jewels of the Democratic Party. Then the women hunger-struck, and the authorities – the good old authorities who always did accept forcible feeding – they beat them, locked them up 'incommunicado' in vermin-infested cells, refused them lawyers, tooth brushes, and other essentials of civilization, and for some days the daily bulletins from the prisons thrust the Western Offensive off the front page of the newspapers. Prominent officials – supporters of the Government – like Dudley-Malone, the brilliant Irish lawyer – resigned their posts in protest. Personal representations were made to the President, who expressed his horror at prison brutalities. The warden of the Workhouse resigned his post, and at Christmas, 1917, a general release took place, and a brief truce was negotiated with a promise that after the holidays something would be arranged. Accordingly, early in January of this year, Congress voted on the Federal Amendment – introduced by the woman representative, Jeannette Rankin – and passed it by the necessary two-thirds majority. Before the voting President Wilson gave an interview to the heads of the Parties, and urged them to drop their opposition to the Federal Amendment – thus showing by his conversation that he is statesmen enough to change his mind when sufficient cause is shown – unlike some of our home brand – and his pronouncement had the desired effect, turning the votes necessary to secure the passage of the measure. Recently the President again personally urged upon the Senate the full need of passing the Amendment, so that it will not be long before the necessary technicalities are gone through before all the women of all the States who have attained the age of 21 enjoy equal rights with men.[10] I have dwelt upon this story largely for the sake of its moral – it contains a valuable lesson for all reformers on the need of persistency and courage and on the mutability of politicians, *mobile quale puma al vento*.[11] When the gale blows these straws are swept before or swept away entirely. Similarly on the Irish and other questions – persistence and solidarity will win out no matter how strong the opposing forces.

Interview with President Wilson
Sometime in January, 1918, I received a mysterious paper (smuggled over, I cannot tell how, but certainly not 'passed by the Censor') from Cumann na mBan in Ireland, with a message that I was to deliver the paper 'personally into the President's own hands'. It was a petition signed by Constance de Markievicz, President, Cumann na mBan, by Mrs Pearse, Mrs Wyse Power, and many other distinguished Irishwomen. It put forth the claim of Ireland for self-determination, and appealed to President Wilson to include Ireland among the Small Nations for whose freedom America was fighting. I regret I

have not an exact copy of that historic document, and of others that would have also been of much value to me in this brief survey. It was impossible to bring any papers with me from the United States, but later I hope to retrieve omissions when circumstances again permit free speech and freedom of the Press.

At first, the message that this petition was to be presented personally rather dismayed me. In January, 1918, President Wilson was overwhelmed with work, and he has always been, even normally, one of the least accessible of Presidents. Still it was 'up to me' to formulate the request for a brief interview, and to work hard to get it. It was through the intermediary of Mr Bainbridge Colby, President of the Shipping Department and of Mr Tumulty, the President's Private Secretary, that that request was granted. Three days after President Wilson formulated his now famous 'Fourteen Points', and on the day after the passing through Congress of the Federal Amendment for Women Suffrage throughout the States, I was accorded my interview – I was the first Irish exile and the first Sinn Féiner to enter the White House, and the first to wear there the badge of the Irish Republic, which I took care to pin in my coat before I went. The President had been busy all the morning receiving American suffragists who came from all over the country to thank him in person for his advocacy of their cause, and as it is generally admitted that the women of the West, enjoying a franchise, had cast an almost unanimous vote for Mr Wilson's election, it was appropriate that they should congratulate him on their further step towards the general enfranchisement of women.

The White House tradition is one of simplicity and democracy. Theoretically at least the first citizen of the Republic is at the service of the poorest and humblest citizen, and though in practice, and from the very nature of things, Presidents nowadays cannot emulate the simplicity of George Washington or Abraham Lincoln, still, enough of the tradition remains to permeate the White House atmosphere. Mr Asquith's butler, and possibly even Sir Edward Carson's, shows more 'side' and self-importance than President Wilson, who removes all embarrassment by a cordial handshake, and a pleasant smile. His general appearance is much less 'dour' than his picture would lead one to suppose. His manner is that of a Professor in a good humour, academic tempered with amenity. A glance from his spectacled grey eyes is shrewd and penetrating, yet not unkindly. Our interview was private – in fact, there is in the United States an unwritten law precluding any report of an interview with the President, save that sent out by himself. The fact, however, of his 'friendly gesture to Ireland' in granting an interview to a declared Sinn Féiner was widely commented on by the friendly and the hostile press of the United States of America, also that he received a document unsubmitted to the British censor, and that he consented to discuss and consider Ireland, was significant.

At the time of the interview the President, I may say, had in mind a possible settlement by the Lloyd George Convention then sitting in Ireland. It was clear to me that he had been given hopes, if not definite pledges, that the Irish question would then be settled. The President would not probably be dissatisfied to find the thorny question of Ireland out of the way before the Peace Conference, so that Great Britain could say to America: 'This question between me and Ireland is adjusted to our mutual satisfaction,' and pass to the more congenial atmosphere of Jugo-Slavs, and Esthonians. We Irish Republicans had, of course, no such faith in the Convention, recognising as we did that it was largely Lloyd Georgian 'camouflage', got up for the deception of the United States. A fortnight after my interview with the President it collapsed like a badly-built house of cards, as was bound to happen sooner or later, leaving once more the Peace Conference solution of Ireland the alternative policy. From my experience of the President, from what he said and what he left unsaid, I am convinced that while he might have preferred the Irish question settled 'domestically', he will now see the force of having it settled internationally for the sake of the peace of the world. President Wilson is not the type that will lead, pioneer-like, a forlorn hope, or stake all on a desperate enterprise; but, on the other hand, he is one who by tradition (he has Irish blood in his veins) and by temperament, will see the need of self-determination for Ireland as well as for other nations. There will be sufficient pressure at home to keep the Irish question well in the forefront, and 'if only Ireland shows herself strongly for this solution', President Wilson cannot turn a deaf ear. As an American his view is naturally more sympathetic than even the most enlightened English view. Moreover, America is out, as he says, to see justice done all round, and it would be therefore a point of honour to see that such even-handed justice is meted out to all alike. A free Belgium, a restored Alsace-Lorraine, a free and unpartitioned Poland, a free Serbia, a free Bohemia, and a coerced and oppressed Ireland would be a blot for ever upon the honour and national integrity of the American Republic, and a menace to the future peace of the world, on which America is building.

Another factor that we Irish must not forget is that but for America's coming to the rescue the Allies would have sustained a crushing defeat. America is, therefore, in the strongest position to make Ireland's case an essential – the final decision has passed for ever out of Great Britain's hands. President Wilson is known in Washington to favour a referendum on the Irish question – America is now in a position to enforce such a settlement.

After seeing the President I spent several months in Washington interviewing Senators and Congressmen on the Irish question, and everywhere I was met with friendliness and sympathy, the atmosphere of Congress being more democratic and kindlier than the Tory clubdom of the British House of

Commons. Most of all, it is an atmosphere more human and more courteous where women are concerned. I found every Senator and Congressman I approached, from Champ Clark, the veteran speaker of the House, to the newest recruit accessible, all eager to talk of Ireland – indeed, there was but one, a Bohemian Jew who told me that the 'Irish vote' did not count in his State, and who, therefore, took merely an academic interest in Ireland's freedom. For not only is the Irish vote a factor almost everywhere, it is in addition so highly organised that even where small in number it can make its influence felt, and can sway a large number of other votes to its side. Every Congressman is aware of this fact, and the recent 'slump' in the Democratic Party at the Congressional elections last November is due largely to the turn-over of the Irish vote to the Republican side. Hitherto the Irish were usually Democrats but many voted anti-Democrat as a protest against the indifference or veiled hostility of the Democratic Party on the Irish question. Many Democrats were defeated recently because, like John Mitchel's grandson, they forgot Ireland.

My experience in Washington, therefore, further strengthened my conviction that the question of Ireland's freedom is a by-factor in American politics, and that those who ignore it do so at their peril. We held a large meeting in Washington in April, 1918, to wind up our campaign, and it was attended largely by Congressmen, Senators, and leaders of opinion in both Houses. At it was passed unanimously a resolution in favour of Ireland's claim to independence. John Devoy, the veteran Irish leader, spoke stirringly and addresses were also delivered by Liam Mellows, Dr McCartan and Padraic Colum. Flags of the American and Irish Republics entwined decorated the hall, and the whole was a striking demonstration, in the very capital of the United States of America, to the strength of Ireland's demand. That and a final meeting in New York – the Irish Peace Convention – were the last meetings I addressed. On June 27th, 1918, I left for home, only to be held up at Liverpool. That story and the story of my subsequent internment in Holloway, I may not dwell upon just now, the exuberance of Lord French[12] and Mr Shortt[13] having nothing to do with the present narrative. My American mission was accomplished, and I could return home satisfied that I had tried to put the truth before the American people, and that I might trust to the international situation to do the rest.

'What does Ireland want?'
America, n.d. (1917)
In his article under the above title in *America* for April 28, Mr Shane Leslie pleads for colonial Home Rule, 'a workaday gift of autonomy based on the free dominions in the Empire', and the ideal solution for Ireland, setting aside as

'extreme' the other schemes, an Irish republic on the one hand, and coercion on the other. He is an able exponent of the case for moderation. While admiring his great qualities and admitting that his scheme has possibilities – it is better than coercion – may I be permitted to put the case for Ireland's independence? I have the advantage of a more recent and intimate knowledge of present conditions in Ireland, impossible to one who knows of the Irish rising and its sequel only through foreign sources.

Ireland, like Russia, is a country of surprises. In '48, after the abortive rising, Charles Gavan Duffy left Ireland 'a corpse on the dissection table', yet in '67 there was a resurrection of the Fenian movement. W. B. Yeats declared in our own day: 'Romantic Ireland's dead and gone. 'Tis with O'Leary in his grave,' he sang, referring to the death of the great Fenian veteran. A fortnight before the uprising last Easter, George Bernard Shaw wrote, deprecating Irish Nationalism, saying with a cynical shrug, that no one bothered nowadays about a 'little green pocket handkerchief' of a country. Yet, almost before the type was dry, the Irish Volunteers had seized Dublin, hoisted the Irish tricolour over Dublin Castle and managed to hold the capital for a week; and it took 40,000 British soldiers to dislodge them. As a result of the uprising, Ireland, even Belfast, is now governed by martial law under a military governor with an army of occupation estimated as three times the size of the Canadian standing army. Moreover, Great Britain has considered the rising of such magnitude that, exclusive of military murders, she found it necessary to execute sixteen Volunteer leaders, to condemn to penal servitude 136 men and one woman, to deport about 6,000 men and several hundred women. If all these steps were necessary for the 'defense of the realm', it is clear that one must not minimise the strength and power of the Irish republican party, or pass over as negligible the arguments in favour of the Separatist solution. It was the tragic mistake of Mr Redmond and the Irish party to ignore this important factor in Ireland; a disaster to constitutionalism has been the result.

Mr Leslie deprecates revenge. True, 'Vengeance belongeth to the Lord'. It is regrettable that the principle is not regarded as practical politics by all governments, for if it were, we should all be at peace. Logical Irishmen do not see why the wrongs of Belgium should alone be worth dying for, and why the doctrines of liberty for small nations should stop short at the Irish Sea. Mr Leslie also says that 'Republics are for countries like Russia and France which have discovered the art of putting up successful revolutions'. In other words he favours the principle of revolution. One must remember, however, first, that Russia and France finally succeeded in establishing republics after repeated failures and, secondly, that, judged by the standard of success, Belgium, Serbia, Rumania and Poland, nay, even Alsace, have forfeited their right to independence, for they all have been overcome by greater force, yet the world is in arms for their right to independence.

Laying aside, therefore, mere word-weaving and sophistry, there remain logically but two solutions of Ireland's grievance, government by force, the present solution, or government by consent within or without the British Empire. There are supporters of all three solutions and it would be idle and futile to wait until there is perfect agreement among all, for that will never be. In the end that party will triumph that can enforce by arms or by methods of peaceful persuasion its special panacea.

The first method, government by militarism is that favoured by the ascendency or Tory party. It was employed by Mr Arthur Balfour during his regime in Ireland in the eighties when his method during riots and evictions was crystallized in the famous telegram sent to the police of Mitchelstown: 'Don't hesitate to shoot.' That method was employed last Easter to put down the Irish Volunteers and it is the method by which Ireland is now governed. It has the merit of logic and extreme simplicity and has always commended itself on that account to the military caste. Its rule of government is: 'Shoot – after a trial, if you must, but shoot, anyhow – imprison, deport all inconvenient critics, buy the others. Make a solitude and call it peace.'

As to government by consent within the Empire, it is the solution favoured by Mr Leslie and by supporters of the Irish party. The difficulty with the present generation in Ireland is that the scheme is now passé. To mention Home Rule in Ireland at a Nationalist gathering is to be greeted with derisive laughter. The Home Rule act now on the statute book is recognized by the Irish party itself as inadequate and unsatisfactory. It is unacceptable to the people of Ireland, for it creates an Irish parliament entirely subservient to Great Britain. By its provisions we are unable to levy taxes, to impose a protective tariff. We have no control over customs or excise, over our police, army or navy, and Great Britain maintains her right of final veto on measures passed by the Irish parliament. Yet, even this restricted and purely local government measure Great Britain, bullied by Sir Edward Carson's swash-buckling threats of 'civil war' in Ulster, refused to pass into law. And now the Irish party itself tacitly rejects the act and asks for more, realizing that England's difficulty is Ireland's opportunity. But even colonial Home Rule, based on the government of Canada and Australia will not satisfy modern Ireland. Gladstone wisely declared that 'No government, however good, can be a substitute for self-government'. Thirty years ago Ireland might have accepted a Home Rule parliament under England as an installment, though even Parnell wisely said that it could not be regarded as a final solution, for 'No man can set bounds upon the onward march of a nation'.

In times of peaceful development and natural slow evolution toward better government such a solution might have worked happily. But a war that is changing the entire map of Europe, leaving its altering mark on all the

Governments of the world and shaking empires and dynasties out of their ruts, will not leave Ireland unchallenged. When the fate of other small nations is being decided, the fate of Ireland too must be considered. Ireland from being a national problem is now international, and it is unlikely that America, entering this war as she states 'for the democratization of Europe', will jeopardize her own honor and the future peace of the world by closing her ears to the voice of Ireland pleading among the small nations for her independence. Hence it becomes important for America to know what Ireland wants so that there be no mistake about the final settlement. It is the policy of Great Britain to regard Ireland's case as a 'domestic' grievance, and accordingly some attempt at a patched-up 'settlement' will likely be put forward. Such a solution even on the lines of 'colonial Home Rule' will not, however, satisfy the Irish people. Their demand at the Peace Conference will be for complete and absolute independence. There can be no tinkering with a demand based on the principle of nationhood: anything that falls short of this is neither freedom nor true democracy.

The Irish Separatist or Republican party is not a party of 'dynamiters' relying upon 'outrages' and methods of terrorism to enforce their views. The only 'outrages' committed during the Irish Rising of Easter week were those perpetrated by the British militarists, the only assassins those of Irish editors, of unarmed civilians and disarmed prisoners, were the so-called upholders of 'law and order'.

Ireland recognizes that complete independence is the only policy that will give her self-respect and abiding peace, that any system that unites her even by the slightest thread to the 'predominant partner' will never be administered for her own good, where interests clash, but only for the good of the Empire whose subject she remains. She will continue to be but a pawn in the game, a land exploited for imperial ambitions, plunged into wars with which she has no interest or sympathy, a victim of secret diplomacy and entangling alliances, taxed for the upkeep of imperial armies and navies whose protection is problematical at best, an alien province misgoverned by absentees. This is the grim reality behind the glowing version of colonial or other Home Rule. The 'dreamers and visionaries' are not those who died for an Irish republic, nor those who live now for it, but those who fondly fancy that the lion can lie down in peace with the lamb, that the British Empire will ever give Ireland a free and equal status within its boundary. So far is it from being true that 'Ireland wants less than any other small nationality in Europe today', no self-respecting Irishman or woman would see her sink beneath the level of any other small nation. Ireland has a stronger claim racially, geographically, historically to independent nationhood than Belgium, Serbia or even Poland. She will not sell her birthright for colonial Home Rule.

Henry Ford and the Irish Republic[14]
Washington DC
9 March 1918

Dear Mr Devoy,

Am much disappointed at failure to call Convention. Had delayed my plans hoping to be here for it and to be able to take some cheering word home, but as there seems no prospect of its being called, and as things at home need all my attention, I have decided to leave at end of this month for Ireland. I am trying to have meeting arranged here before I go, and should be glad if you will have invitations sent for delegates from NY, and other cities, as we want a good gathering. Pittsburgh and Phila. will send people – the former wanted me to go there, but I suggested they come here instead and they have promised. Nothing is fixed yet, but we hope to have word shortly. The local people, of course, will help. My opinion is that action here in this town is now most important, and as the Convention won't sit, this seems the next best plan. One meeting here is worth *ten* in NY, where, as you rightly say, one can always get a good meeting for Ireland.

The Dr (McCartan) will tell you about our Phila. meeting and also about my interview with Henry Ford. I was delighted to find him in favour of an Irish Republic, and he said so to T. P. (O'Connor, MP) and to (Lord) Northcliffe to their amazement. I gave him our flag which he put in his coat. We talked in his home for over two hours on Ireland and he asked a lot about tillage and so forth. He is keen on Ireland's freedom and says that we'll surely get our independence, and that we'll never thrive until we do. The interview, of course, was private, but there could be no objection to your mentioning his views as he expressed them to T. P. without giving my name, of course. He didn't give a cent to T. P. and said he had no use for his type, and that any help he'd give to Ireland would be to the people themselves, and to a free Republic. Wasn't that fine? You see we have more friends than we realise.

He also told me that the 'unseen hand' as he calls it is hampering his work in supplying his tractors to Irish and English farmers. He has no illusions about 'British greatness'; says their time has come and that they'll get more democracy than they bargain for.

Did you see the article in *Metropolitan*? I see to-day, *March 9th*, that the paper is 'denied the mails', but they conveniently allowed over a week for it to get to the public first. I bought it in Chicago at end of February. I think this ought to be pointed out as a contrast.

I shall see you at end of month before I go home. Shall stay here till then, as I want to lobby and push, if I can, that resolution. So far it's blocked by Flood.

Yours sincerely
H. S. Skeffington

Speech Delivered by MRS HANNA SHEEHY SKEFFINGTON at Madison Square Garden on the Evening of May 4, 1918[15]

Mr Chairman, ladies and gentlemen, at this late hour I am not going to keep you by making a speech. I feel that I have spoken so often already in this country that I would now prefer to leave it and go home to help keep Ireland free from conscription and safe for democracy (*applause*). This was to have been my last meeting in New York but the British Government has decided otherwise. I learned last week in California that my passport to Ireland has been withdrawn. I think I know the reason for that, as you know, Mr Preston, the Federal Attorney in San Francisco, was very anxious to lock me up in Angel Island (*hisses*). Mr Preston, however, did not succeed and it seemed to me that England would like Uncle Sam to lock me up, and therefore she has refused a passport, but I have confidence that Uncle Sam will not lock me up (*applause*). And it seems to me that if it is to be decided in this country that it is treason to the United States to talk against conscription in Ireland, then I think the best place for any self-respecting man or woman is prison (*wild applause*). And my friends, if enough of you, as apparently you do, agree with that sentiment, there will not be prisons big enough to hold us Irish in this country (*applause*). The ground has been amply and ably covered by the other speakers. I am not going to weary you now by going over reasons against conscription. People have said to me 'But the British Empire may depend upon Irish conscription'. Now, I say deliberately this, – and I hope the Secret Service men are listening to me and have their pencils sharp (*wild applause*). I say, if the continuance of the British Empire depends upon the life of a single Irish conscript, then I say, let the British Empire be wiped out (*wild applause*). And I for one, and there are a good many others who think like me; they may be aliens, but they are friendly aliens. I for one will lose no sleep at any time over the extinction of the British Empire (*wild applause*).

I read in the *New York Tribune* yesterday (*hisses*) – Oh, I don't think these papers are worth any demonstration – I read that Ireland was greatly placated, and why do you think? Because Mr S. was sent to us as a Chief Secretary instead of Mr Duke. You wouldn't be surprised, would you, if Belgium refused to be placated if they sent Ludendorff instead of Hindenberg? One rotten liberal instead of another rotten liberal makes no difference in Ireland. And the people who write that kind of stuff for Americans to read well deserve all they get. And I can say that if you read these kind of papers, you are also criminals after the act (*applause*). We are told in Ireland again by the omniscient American press, – we are told that Ireland ought to accept conscription in return for home rule (*cries of 'Never'*). We say, my friends, as you say, 'Never, Never, NEVER!' (*loud applause*); not for any kind of home rule that Great Britain, in her hour of crisis, was prepared to cough up! What would be said if

Belgium was offered home rule in return for conscription by Germany? Belgium would very probably reject that offer with scorn; and will Ireland. There will be no bargaining with Great Britain; she has broken her words too often; she is nothing but a discredited bankrupt today (*enthusiastic applause*). Who knows whether any check that she is prepared, in her hour of extremity, to write, will ever be honoured internationally?

I am interested particularly in the anti-conscription movement in Ireland because it was my husband Francis Sheehy Skeffington who first advised that pledge which has since been administered generally throughout Ireland. I heard him at many meetings in Dublin administering that pledge to thousands of Irish men, and it was on account administering that pledge that he was done to death at the bidding of the Liberal Government (*hisses*). And I heard these men swear with uplifted hands in P., as he administered the oath 'If England should conscript us, we swear we will not go' (*applause*). and that is the spirit that is winning today. We Irish were never more attacked and maligned than we are at present; but, for my part, I am proud of Ireland today (*applause*). She is standing practically alone in her fight, and she is the only country in the world today that says that she will choose her quarrel and know what she is dying for if she is to die.

You need not worry about the psychology of the Irish people. Everyone knows that the Irish love a fight; but everybody who respects the Irish race know that we like to choose our fight (*applause*). We are not going at this hour. Who will dare to blame us or to deride us? We are not going to be driven to that slaughter-pen in Flanders at the bidding of a government that is dripping red with the blood of our best countrymen (*applause*).

And now a word about American responsibility, America has not yet definitely and officially pronounced on this question. It is time that the American Government do so. You are told my friends that secret messages have been sent over telling Mr Lloyd George (*hisses*) that this is not the opportune time to conscript the Irish. I thought we had enough of secret treaties and secret diplomacy. You ought not to be satisfied unless there is an unmistakable official pronouncement from your government on this important question, which concerns the very life of our nation. President Wilson has stretched out a hand to Russia: He has said to Russia in her hour of crisis, – and has said it finally, – that America is not going to desert Russia, – that America will help Russia all she can. All we ask him is that he say just the same on behalf of Ireland to the British Government. And we think, – and who shall dare to say us 'Nay' we think that Ireland has fully as big a claim on the Government of the United States as Russia or any one of the other nations. That is for you to demand, and if you do not immediately take steps and this Government does not take steps on the question of conscription for Ireland, then I say deliberately that this Government is an accomplice in one of the foulest crimes in the foul history of Great Britain (*applause*). There is one remarkable thing that that charlatan from Wales, Premier Lloyd George (*hisses*) who said apropos of conscription and home rule 'Conscription is going to be held out like a club with one hand'. Lloyd George said, in order that you may realise, in the House of Commons, that it was necessary that England placate America on the question of Ireland; he said it was necessary that the Irish Government be settled. And why do you think he said it? Do you think he said it for the sake of justice or humanity, or freedom? He said it was necessary for England to settle the question of Ireland. Why? Because, he said, we must have the good will of America. As you say here, 'Here is the nigger in the wood pile' of America. Do you think that Mr Lloyd George would waste his time talking about securing the good will of America if he felt that he had really got that commodity? That is exactly the spot on which to meet Mr Lloyd George. Otherwise it should be forever silent, – forever silent on the question of liberty. (*Commotion caused by interruption of speech by two loyal American women, Dr Eleanor Keller, 55 East 75th Street, New York City and Mrs John Oakman of 3 West Sixteenth Street, New York City having members of the family fighting for the United States.*)

I remember a story of a woman in Ireland which reminds me of the Irish question today. The Irish question has now become, as Mr Lloyd George confesses, an international one, and we thank God for that, because there is not a nation in the world, with the exception of Great Britain, that would not willingly see Ireland free. This old woman in Ireland had an important law suit on, and she engaged no lawyer; and after a time when her friends came to her and said 'You are very foolish; why do you not engage counsel?' And she said 'No! I will not engage counsel; I do not need them.' And her friend said 'Why?' And she smiled knowingly, and she said 'I have got a few friends on the jury.' No, we feel exactly like that in Ireland today. We feel if our case comes up before an international tribunal of nations, we are all right; we need no one to plead for us; we have got a few good friends on the jury.

And I for one am convinced that the United States is one of these friends. And I am convinced that the plot of Mr Preston in San Francisco, – Mr Preston, by the way, is of English descent, and that is significant, – the plot set on foot by him to interfere with the Irish meetings has been badly defeated in San Francisco. And quite an interesting thing happened there a week ago that you in New York will also be interested in. I was arrested for an interrupted meeting on Wednesday and told that I was not, by orders of Mr Preston, to discuss any question in California, – conscription or anything else. I was arrested; I was taken away; I was not detained. Mr Preston worked himself up into a fury of indignation in the papers the next morning so grinding that it wiped out the Western Offensive for the time being (*laughter and derision*). And Mr Preston said he was going to stamp out sedition, as he called it, – in other words, Irish meetings. Then he added, by way of after-thought, – because he is not yet a czar, – that he had asked for instructions from Washington as to how he was to proceed in this question. I waited for a week in San Francisco in order that those instructions would have plenty of time to reach Mr Preston. The following week after my interrupted meeting on last Wednesday, we held a magnificent protest meeting in San Francisco, and I delivered every word of the interrupted speech at the meeting (*howling applause*).

I do not mention it for any personal bearing, but I think the result of that is instructive everywhere. It means that if you stand out and know that you are right, – stand out for a principle, whether it is that of free speech or any other such principle, – that you will be able to drive the Prestons and the politicians under cover pretty quickly (*applause*).

I congratulate the Irish Progressive League in the face of many obstacles, – untold obstacles, – for having held this magnificent gathering. I think they are doing wonderful work for Irish freedom just now, and I hope that American public opinion will be so aroused on this question of Irish conscription that the British will shortly get into a second line trench, as you call it, on the matter (*applause*).

We are told that this conscription act which was rushed through Parliament, – rushed through both houses in a few days, – that this Conscription Act is going to be held up for the time being. We may find that it will be held up, as the saying is, for the duration of the war. However that may be, if conscription is defeated in Ireland, it will be defeated by the spirit of Sinn Féin (*wild applause, waving of rebel flags and hats, stamping of feet, etc.*). I want every one of you men and women to do your part now to see that the question of conscription will never be mentioned by a British statesman again.

Widow of Easter Week[16]
1 May 1919

Dear Mr McGarrity,

Some time ago Mrs Joseph Plunkett (Grace Gifford) got a cutting sent her from a Philadelphia paper called *Catholic Standard*, about a suggested memorial of Joseph Plunkett and herself (to be a group of statuary) for which donations were acknowledged. The report went on to add that this would be the best form of memorial as the family of course did not need money.

I think it would be well for the committee to know that Mrs Joseph Plunkett is unprovided for and that therefore the most suitable memorial to her husband ought to be some provision for his widow. I know you will agree with this and I write you because of my confidence in you personally. I feel you can take steps in the matter, which is delicate. Mrs Plunkett received £200 in all from the National Aid Committee and that is exhausted. It is quite inadequate as a provision. She receives no help from her people-in-law and is now therefore without provision of any kind. She is an able artist but cannot live on that work as orders are few and precarious. If therefore any society or committee in America is interested in her and her husband it would seem more fitting that a memorial should most properly take the form of some financial provision for his widow. I feel if these facts were known to the committee that they would agree with this view, as they seem to be under the mistaken impression that Mrs Plunkett is already well off. Her own family are not sympathetic with the cause and do not help her in any way. I enclose a brief statement from the National Aid Committee to show you that the facts as stated are correct. I feel sure I can leave the matter confidently in your hands and that you will take such steps as seem advisable to put the facts before this committee. I know that the Irish in America would not tolerate the thought that the widow of one of the executed leaders was suffering hardship while a marble memorial was being erected to him. With sincere regards to you and your family and to all my friends in Philadelphia.

Hanna Sheehy Skeffington

PS I would like to impress upon her friends that the matter is urgent and that any steps taken should be at once. Address 9 Belgrave Road will reach her – if you have any good news perhaps you would kindly cable on receipt of this.

8

THE WAR OF INDEPENDENCE
AND THE TREATY

INTRODUCTION

Before she left America Hanna wrote an article for the *Suffragist*, praising the progressiveness of the Proclamation of Easter Week, with its promise of women's enfranchisement, while comparing unfavourably the British promise of votes to women over 30. She believed the vote was not to be extended to women in Ireland and that women would still be unable to stand as candidates for election, but the Representation of the People Act 1918 included the whole of the United Kingdom and the Parliament (Qualification of Women) Act 1918 enabled women to be elected to parliament.

On her return to Ireland Hanna resumed editorial control of the *Irish Citizen*, assisted by Louie Bennett. As nationalists regrouped in the aftermath of the Rising and the release of the prisoners, the political side of the movement came to the fore with the re-organisation of Sinn Féin. In the election of December 1918, the Irish Women's Franchise League worked with Cumann na mBan to ensure the success of Constance Markievicz. Hanna herself had been offered the chance of standing for Sinn Féin, but refused on the grounds that North Antrim, a unionist stronghold, was not a winnable seat. She made her delight at the win of Markievicz plain in her editorial 'Bravo, Dublin!' and all through this period, dominated by the war between Ireland and Britain, her commitment to both nationalist and feminist causes was much in evidence.

In May 1919 she was appointed organising secretary for Sinn Féin and between that time and the truce of July 1921 was extremely active as a propagandist and activist for the republicans. She spoke at many meetings in England and Ireland. It was now much more dangerous to be a public figure in Ireland as by October 1919 all nationalist organisations were outlawed and by the start of 1920 martial law, curfew, raids and arrests had become the norm. In August 1919, while speaking in Kilbeggan, County Westmeath, Hanna was struck several times on the head by the butt end of a police carbine, which incapacitated her for a few weeks. Apologising to the readership of the *Irish Citizen*, she hoped they would 'forgive any editorial shortcomings' (September 1919). Investigations into conditions in Ireland and the impact on the civilian population were made by the British Labour Party, by the Women's International League and by an American Commission on Conditions in Ireland, whose members included the suffragist Jane Addams. Witness statements were taken, and additional information supplied in the main by women activists. Hanna's statement would appear to be compiled for the American Commission, and focused mainly on the impact of war on women and children, with a particular focus on sexual assault.

A Committee for the Relief of Ireland was formed in America and in Ireland a White Cross was established in February 1921 to distribute those funds. Hanna was appointed a member of the executive committee, together with Maud Gonne MacBride and Kathleen Clarke. Áine Ceannt, widow of Éamonn Ceannt, was the paid organiser.

This was a hectic period. Hanna was sometimes 'on the run', and had her house raided, but maintained her commitment to the democratic process by winning a seat to the Dublin Corporation in January 1920, one of five women elected to the Corporation. She refers to her experiences on the Corporation in an article in the *Irish World*, 4 July 1925 (Chapter 9).

While the *Irish Citizen* continued to be published, first as a monthly journal, by March 1920 it had become bi-monthly and then quarterly. The last edition was in September 1920. Sometime afterwards the Black and Tans smashed the typeface and it did not re-appear. During the truce of July 1921, trying to ensure that the imprisoned Markievicz was released from jail was one of Hanna's preoccupations, as evidenced in her correspondence with Eva Gore-Booth. Fearing that the period of the truce might be short, Hanna encouraged Gore-Booth to campaign on behalf of her sister. She was uneasy at the lack of women involved in the peace negotiations with Britain, and the refusal of the victorious pro-Treaty side to allow a revision of the electoral register in order to enable the younger generation (particularly young women between the ages of 21 and 30) to vote crystallised her dislike of the Treaty. Together with other feminists, she lobbied members of the Dáil to extend the franchise, supporting Kate O'Callaghan who had introduced an unsuccessful motion in the Dáil to that effect, following the main vote on the Treaty.

In November 1922 Hanna was sent to America by Éamon de Valera, together with Linda Kearns (a nurse and republican activist who had been part of a Cumann na mBan escape from Mountjoy Jail in 1921) and Kathleen Boland, the sister of Harry Boland, who had been shot dead by Free State troops. They were the 'Irish Women's Mission', there to raise funds for the relief of families and prisoners in Ireland. They travelled to 25 states during their tour, returning in May 1923. Hanna's familiarity with America can be seen in her correspondence with American feminist Alice Park as well as her article in *Freeman* (New York) and letter to the *Nation*, reprinted in *Éire, the Irish Nation*. Hanna was sent as an emissary of the republican forces to Geneva to lobby against the Free State entry to the League of Nations. Despite her protests, it was admitted to the League of Nations on 10 September 1923.

'How suffrage stands in Ireland'
Suffragist,[1] 30 March 1918
We Irish women are proud of the fact that the Irish Republic proclaimed in Easter week, 1916, just two years ago, was the first in the world's history to lay down from its inception the principle of equal suffrage for both sexes. It declares for a national government representative of the whole people of Ireland and elected by the suffrages of '*all her men and women*' and 'guarantees religious and civil liberties, equal rights and equal opportunities to all its citizens'.

On this point the Irish Republic surpasses in its Proclamation the Declaration of Independence (a document which in many respects is its basis) because the Republic of the United States did not unfortunately lay down the principle of equal suffrage from the beginning, though it has now practically accepted it.

Neither did the French Republic, the French government even of today still denying citizenship to women. The Russian Republic, proclaimed nearly a year later than the Irish, also embodied the principle of citizenship for women, and Finland has already done likewise. Great Britain lies behind her own colonies with respect to the franchise, both for men and women, being the only great power whose franchise is still based upon a property qualification.

True, the British Parliament has recently considerably widened its franchise, and at the next general election (which is expected to take place in the coming summer) boys of nineteen will be enfranchised provided they have served in the armed forces during the war. In addition the franchise is being further widened to include about six million women voters. A new anomaly is being introduced at the same time to make the franchise a still more patched-up one, it being laid down that only women of thirty years and upwards shall be deemed worthy of the ballot.

In Great Britain a girl may marry at fourteen; she may agree to prostitute herself at eighteen (the age of consent being eighteen); she may bestow her property as she pleases at the age of twenty-one (the law protecting character- istically her property for three years longer than her person), and when nine more years have passed she may be deemed capable of deciding whether Mr Lloyd-George or Mr Arthur Balfour shall represent her in Parliament.

Even then, though she may be Queen of England, Empress of India, head of the Established Church or Mayor of London, no woman may become a member of Parliament. It will need another long agitation and another act of Parliament to make women eligible to sit in Parliament, and our time may not see a 'Lady from Montana' gracing Westminster.

It is generally admitted by such anti-suffragists as Mr Asquith and Lord Curzon that it is largely owing to British women's cooperation that Great Britain has been able to 'carry on' in the present war. Many suffragists completely gave up the struggle for citizenship in order to help the men, in the fond belief that the politicians would grant them the franchise later on as a reward of virtue and patriotism – only to find after nearly four years that boys of nineteen, because of their war service, are ranked above them.

The reason for this new sex barrier is diverting; it is stated that adult women may not be enfranchised because women are in the majority! It would be too revolutionary in a democratic government to allow the majority sex to vote on the same qualifications as the minority sex! Truly British statesmanship works in a mysterious and inscrutable way its wonders to perform.

Irishwomen are (to judge from the latest reports which have reached me) to be excluded entirely even from this fancy franchise: Irishwomen, no matter what their age, are not permitted to vote, the older male property qualification being also continued in Ireland because of the fear of the British politicians that any widening of the ballot in Ireland would open the doors more widely to those dangerous elements called 'Sinn Féin', which desire to see operating in Ireland the hazardous and terrible experiment of a 'Government of the people, by the people, for the people'.

So we Irishwomen have the interesting contrast before us of an Irish Republic giving full and free citizenship to all adults, men and women, and a British Parliament timidly opening its doors to British women of thirty and excluding all Irishwomen. Is it surprising under the circumstances that we hanker after the Republic and an independent Ireland!

True, all the signers to the proclamation that emancipated us have been executed. Patrick Pearse, the first President of the Republic, did not live to see his dream fulfilled. But we Irishwomen still hope that the western Republic will befriend us and maintain our rights when the time of settlement comes.

In conclusion may I pay humble and heartfelt tribute to the National Women's Party? In my opinion it is to them and their plucky fight for democracy that the recent victory for suffrage in Congress is due. It is those dauntless women who make one glad for women in these dark days – one feels that with them the future of the race is secure.

When history comes to be written the names of those women who 'carried on' for suffrage will fill as bright a page on honour's roll as that of any man who died for liberty or suffered persecution for justice.

Election of Countess Markievicz[2]
Letter to Nancy Wyse Power n.d. (1918)
*[This letter is a reply to Nancy Wyse Power of Cumann na mBan, who had written
to apologise for a meeting being cancelled at short notice, explaining that a message
had been sent both to Hanna's house and to the League office. There was no room for
blame, she wrote, as 'such trifling inconveniences are irritable in press of general
election'. Canvasser books had been given out before the Irish Women's Franchise
League called, and so nothing could be done. In an emotional letter Wyse Power
describes Hanna as 'highhanded' in her approach, complaining 'if every body of men
or women which supported Madame were to act in this way, great confusion would
result.' In response Hanna wrote that she had spoken for five candidates in the
election.]*

. . . and in no case have arrangements been called off except in Madame
Markievicz's case. Complaints have gone out not only from our members but
from Cumann na mBan members and outsiders. Nonsense about books being
given out. We applied at the first and day after day. Dozens of people called
and one of the men was always away and he had all the books and another was
drunk. Now I hear one has resigned and one dismissed . . . I hear new management to take over from tomorrow . . . it's the worse managed constituency in
Dublin – every other constituency has had more frequent meetings (many
nightly) and has been better canvassed. The committee can't play 'dog in the
manger' so, finding them hopeless in cooperation we decided as I told you a
week ago, to have our own meetings in future. All first week only one set of
meetings (Wed) and so far today we had offer of Mrs Connery who wanted to
speak for Madame. There are 4 meeting places we have taken 2. Committee
can take them and take ours by having a different hour.

   As a woman's organisation we feel we have a duty in this matter and think
it is a disgrace to the women's organisation if Madame Markievicz is let down
by an inefficient committee – consider committee not interested in her success
. . .

'Bravo, Dublin!'
Irish Citizen, January 1919
Dublin leads in feminism and deserves congratulations as the only place that
elected a woman candidate during the recent General Election. All the British
women candidates (and they ranged from Independents to Coalition and
Labour) were rejected in spite of the admirable record of many, notably Mrs
Pethick Lawrence, Mrs Despard, and Mary MacArthur.[3] Their rejection is
but another sign of the present hopeless state of reaction prevailing in Britain.
Miss Christabel Pankhurst, even with Lloyd George's benediction, failed to

get returned – there is blame in Gilead. And by a strange irony the one woman elected to Parliament refuses on principle to attend and lies at present an untried prisoner of war in Holloway jail. St Patrick's returned her by 4,000 majority to show how highly it prized this rebel and jail bird. And so Ireland again leads the way, and while Britain wallows in reaction and turns her back on woman MPs Ireland proudly writes Progress on her banner to show the world how much in advance she is of those who would rule her. It is fitting that this should happen; the wider and more democratic Ireland's franchise the more she will reveal herself progressive and a foe to reaction and cant. Dublin, as we learn from the Life of Sophia Jex Blake,[4] was the first to receive women medical students, and to throw open its college to them freely; the Dublin University is the only one of the older Universities that grants degrees and other honours freely to women still barred out from Oxford and Cambridge; the National University was the first to establish in its Charter absolute equality for women and men within its walls. And now it is Dublin, also, that returns the first woman member of parliament. Bravo! Dublin! 'Hail to thee, Constance, in thy cell!'[5]

'Sex-bias in language'
Irish Citizen, September 1919
In a recently published work, *Footsteps of Freedom*, by the distinguished feminist and poet, J. H. Cousins (the founder of the *Irish Citizen*), discussing the 'limits of brotherhood', he quotes a sonnet by C. Egremont, which begins as follows:

> Let us be men, my brothers, men are more
> Than nations.

Mr Cousins makes the deserved comment: '"Would not a few women be useful?" Very probably the writer of the sonnet is a suffragist who has not yet found a way out of the limitations of a language that has been brought up only by its father. To the sonneteer this linguistic masculinity may mean little or nothing; but words have a curious way of influencing one's attitude when one is not looking, and the majority of mankind do not often take the trouble to look or listen, in the deeper sense of these operations, it is incumbent on those who possess the dangerous responsibility of utterance, to be constantly on the watch against verbal fog and mud. It is bad enough to use speech for the transmission of a false thought, but a falsity that is alive will carry a challenge with it, and stimulate contradiction: it is something less than worthy of intelligent beings to put their necks into the noose of a word or phrase . . . that must ultimately lead to narrow ways of thought and action unless the temptation to acquiescence is broken.' The reproof is sorely needed; of Mr Cousins, at any rate, it may be said, as of few men, or even women, writers, that he never truckles to the anti-feminist bias of language in any of his writings. He is too good a humanist, too pure a stylist to indulge in loose and misleading expressions, he realizes as a poet the profound immorality of action. Would all our stylists were as pure!

So saturated is the English language with masculinity that it has no definite word to translate 'Homo', the human being, as distinguished from Vir, the male person. 'Man' is used, sometimes to include 'man and woman', sometimes to mean only the 'male', and the result of this defect of language has been many a legal disability that has had to be broken down after long agitation – so may language betray woman. French is equally defective and goes one worse, for while, like English, it has only one word, 'homme' for mankind and for the male portion of mankind, it misuses 'femme' by making it mean sometimes 'woman' and sometimes 'wife', characteristic of the male arrogance which only recognizes a woman in her capacity as wife. German is more human and logical, for 'Mensch' means 'man and woman', while 'Mann' can only be used of the male.

Even in religion, as the poet William Watson aptly observed in his poem on 'The Unknown God', we 'narrow the Supreme with sex'. Obviously, the Supreme Being must be feminine as well as masculine in essence, but, such is the influence of a false masculinity on Religion, as on language, most people, in thinking of the Godhead, employ masculine phraseology, as if God were merely male.

So error flourishes. Even though women have come partly into their own (at least, women of thirty) at election time, when campaigning for the Republican party in Ireland, the only party that ran women candidates, I observed that nine speakers out of ten referred exclusively to 'men' in their speeches and, like a recent writer in *New Ireland* (a professor who ought, by his calling, to be careful of his language) seemed to think of 'the people of Ireland' and the 'men of Ireland' as synonymous. Many speakers (lawyers, soldiers, and the clergy are naturally the worst offenders) still address mixed audiences as 'gentlemen'. Nor are parliamentarians and reactionaries the only offenders: Sinn Féin and Labour are equally liable to such lapses in language. Recently De Valera had to be reminded by a polite note sent up by a woman in his audience that his hearers were not all males and that women, as well as men, were eligible for any office on the Sinn Féin executive. True, he smilingly corrected this slip, saying as if in excuse, that 'it was an old fault of his to forget the women' – and the audience sniggered as if the thought were highly hilarious, while a later Sinn Féin orator (a good feminist at heart) made the groundlings laugh by the stale mof 'that man embraced woman in such cases', whereupon a young priest remarked, sotto voce, that 'women should all wear trousers in future instead of petticoats'. I recall this incident because it is unhappily typical of the way in which language is perverted, even by progressive speakers, and to show how necessary it is to correct such a false attitude of mind lest there be worse lapses. Some will say, 'Why fuss about such a trifle?' It is, however, as women know to their cost, of such trifles that our disabilities are woven. Sex-bias in language creates unconsciously sex-bias in thought, which in turn easily passes to sex-bias in action.

Even in the sex-biased English language it is possible to pick terms so that when male and female are intended a common term can be used. 'Member', 'voter', 'person', 'human being' carry no sex-exclusion and are more precise. Socialism has chosen 'comrade', which, fortunately, may be of either sex. It is for women, the educators and mothers of the race, to insist upon, as far as possible, purging the language of such crudities and adapting the older moulds to the needs of the younger generation. For it is the task of the women and the poets to fashion language to fit the new thought, to clear it of its dross and to make it embody new ideals. Just as woman in the past has been the civilizer, the refiner of manners and morals, checking the ribald, pruning speech of its ancient coarseness, so in the future it must largely be her task to see to it that language be not misused against her and that, from being unduly masculinized, it be humanized to fit the Newer Thought.

'Our policy and our critics'
Irish Citizen, October 1919

From time to time it seems to be necessary to restate one's position and re-formulate one's policy, for public memory is short and liable to confusion. The *Irish Citizen* was founded in May 1912, to further the cause of Woman Suffrage and of Feminism in Ireland; as its name implies, its ideal was to urge 'For men and women equally the Rights of Citizenship, from men and women equally the Duties of Citizenship'. In addition it has stood for the rights of Labour, especially of the women workers (often overlooked) and for the rights of small peoples, beginning not with the far-away Balkans but at home in Ireland. During the war in the almost universal stampede of British (and even some Irish) suffragists and feminists who prostituted their movement to militarist uses, the *Irish Citizen*, under the guidance of Francis Sheehy Skeffington, stood firm for Peace, believing that the cause of Woman and the cause of Peace were inextricably bound together. When partial franchise to women of thirty was granted during the war some British suffragist papers ceased activities and left the struggle for complete emancipation, 'for the suffrage on the same terms as it is or may be granted to men', to valiant papers like *The Vote*[6] and to the more conservative *Common Cause*.[7] Other papers like the *Woman's Dreadnought*, edited by Sylvia Pankhurst, became socialist, changing the title to the *Worker's Dreadnought*. The *Irish Citizen*, like *Vote*, still continued its feminist and suffragist propaganda, and hopes to do so until **all** women have the vote equally with men and until women have secured the other rights that enfranchisement involves, of which the vote is but a small part and but a symbol. We want equal pay for equal work, equal marriage laws, the abolition of legal disabilities, the right of women to enter the hitherto barred learned professions, women jurors and justices, in short, the complete abolition of various taboos and barriers – social, economic, and political – that still impede women's progress and consequently that of the race.

There is much need in Ireland, as well as in most other countries (for women can hardly be said to be fully emancipated in any country today) for a distinct feminist organ devoted primarily to the advancement of women and holding a watching brief for their interests. It is obvious that such a paper must not belong to any party; one set of critics would deflect us entirely to Republicanism or to Labour, while another would have us 'non-political' in the unionist sense of the word, which means non-Irish. With both sections of these friendly critics we differ. We stand for the rights of all Irishwomen as women, independent of party or sect. But, at the same time, we recognise the right of the majority of the Irish people to mould its own destinies and accordingly, like Irish Labour, we stand for self-determination for Ireland – accordingly we are anathema to some Belfast women 'loyalists' to whom the mere word 'Irish' in our title is an offence. The cause of Woman in Ireland has suffered too much from party rancour; it is time that women tested these party shibboleths for themselves. No party, unhappily, is yet quite free from sin where women are concerned. It is to hold the mirror up to the failings and shortcomings of each in turn that the *Irish Citizen* exists, and we reckon it a sign of grace that we are blamed in turn by each party for not becoming mere camp-followers of this or the other side.

While we shall always be glad to publish divergent views, our editorial policy must remain feminist and non-party on the lines that we have stated. We hope that we have made this clear. We shall be glad of our readers' views on the question. It is good for women from time to time to do a little mental stock-taking and spring cleaning, to tot up gains, estimate improvement or deterioration, to clear out rubbish and to sweep away cobwebs. If we have assisted the process, even at the risk of raising a dust, we shall be satisfied.

Statement of Atrocities on Women in Ireland, Made and Signed by Mrs Hanna Sheehy Skeffington, n.d. (1920)[8]

I have been asked to furnish details for your convention on atrocities and terrorism of women in Ireland. It is impossible at present to send sworn statements but I send pamphlet on Cork which embodies some and deals incidentally with terrorism of women. For the rest my material is drawn from Irish or British press (of latter *Daily News*, *Manchester Guardian*, and *Herald* notably) from investigations by members of Irish Women's Franchise League, from Irish Bureau for propaganda or from my own personal experiences or observations at first hand. I can only take typical cases in this brief statement and group these under various headings.

Terrorism of Wives, Widows, Mothers and Sisters of prominent Sinn Féiners, many of whom are 'on the run'. For last three months over 79,000 raids of private houses, usually at curfew hours (often between 1 and 4 am) of armed and often drunk soldiery or police. When the man on the run is not found his wife, sister, etc., frequently threatened, separated for hours from her terrified children and sometimes compelled to stand in the street under the rain barefooted in her nightdress while her house is being sacked and dismantled or even burned. Recently blood-hounds accompanied these searches and added to their terror. Among such cases I mention the frequent raids upon Mrs Maurice Collins, Parnell Street, Dublin (see Erskine Childer's pamphlet *Military Rule in Ireland*), Mrs Kent, widow of Eamon Kent shot in 1916, Mrs Pearse (house at St Enda's destroyed as 'reprisal'), Mrs Cathal Brugha, wife of speaker of Dáil Éireann (Irish Parliament) (To her house blood hounds brought), Mrs Wyse Power, member of SF executive, etc.

Wanton Terrorism of Young Mothers – Two pregnant women Mrs Quinn, Gort, County Galway, Mrs Ryan, Tipperary, shot dead. First shot by lorry of Black and Tans (auxiliary police) and left to bleed to death. Mr Lloyd George described the murder in the House of Commons as a 'precautionary measure'. Mrs Ryan owned a shop in Tipperary and all the traders were ordered to close their premises during the funeral of some officers killed in outlying district as form of compulsory mourning and trade reprisal. After the funeral had passed Mrs Ryan ventured to open her door to let out a friend and was instantly shot dead. She was within a few months of her confinement. Mrs MacCurtain, Lady Mayoress of Cork, was also within two months of her confinement when police invaded her house and killed her husband who died in her arms. She was delivered shortly after of still-born babies, two boys. Instances of this kind could be multiplied (v. Evelyn Sharp on Terrorism of Women, *Daily Herald*, February 7). Medical doctors report terrible effects to have resulted from constant strain on young wives and mothers. Two women (friends of my own) have gone mad as a result.

Curfew Restrictions on Women – Curfew now prevails in most Irish towns. As civilians without permits are liable to be shot dead, it is often impossible to summon doctors and nurses to maternity cases and many babies and some mothers have lost their lives in consequence.

Murder of Children – Annie O'Neill, aged twelve, shot dead while playing outside her mother's house; a five-year old boy killed while walking with his mother in Camden Street, Dublin; a boy of ten bayonetted to death in Croke Park at football match, etc.– such cases occur almost daily, the results sometimes of wanton 'reprisals', sometimes of carelessness or cruelty when soldiers or police fire at random from lorries when passing through towns or villages. These men carry their rifles at the ready, are often drunk (v. Labour Reports) and frequently highly hysterical. Many of the Black and Tans are proved to be recruited from the jails of England, 'pardoned' on condition that they join the Black and Tans. Mr Nevinson in *Herald* reports shooting of a girl of sixteen in Ardfert as result of bet between two Black and Tans as to which was the better shot. She was 'potted at' as she crossed the road with a child in her arms.

Wholesale Arrests of Women – ranging in age from girls of fourteen (Maria Bowles, Cork) to women of seventy-three and seventy-six (Mrs Devine and Miss Martin now in Mountjoy jail, Dublin – v. *Manchester Guardian* Report enclosed). Many of these are teachers and University lecturers (six arrested last Saturday in Dominican Convent, Dublin). Miss Eileen McGrane, lecturer in National University,[9] Countess Markievicz sentenced lately to three years' penal servitude, a woman editor of paper in Donegal, etc. These women are usually taken (by men only) in military lorries from their homes at night and their destination unknown to inquiring relatives for several days. They are often kept in military barracks under entirely male guard (often drunk) for days. (Maria Bowles for three days thus during which she never undressed or lay down, then sent to Cork female prison, where she collapsed for lack of sleep. Investigated by Mrs Despard and Mrs MacBride, former the sister of Lord French). Similarly the old ladies of 73 and 76 mentioned above kept for days in barracks and finally sent to Athlone Infirmary where one was anointed. Now both in Mountjoy Jail, Dublin. Countess Markievicz told me that during her court-martial she asked to be shown the lavatory with her attendant wardress. They were marched by an armed guard of military to an open lavatory while military lined up outside. The lavatory seemed to be a general one and was in a filthy condition. Mrs Annan Bryce, sister-in-law of Lord Bryce and wife of Annan Bryce, ex MP had similar experience of filthy conditions. In those cases where women are taken they are now under male military guard and no accommodation is provided for them, though there are female prisons available. Before being sent to these they are usually detained by the military for some days.

Nuns – recently two Bon Secours sisters coming from Armagh to Dublin were detained part of the evening and all following night in Dublin Castle. They were searched, no charge made against them, but detained nevertheless.

Kept in military guard-room, with no chance of rest or sleep no lavatory accommodation and refused a drink or any refreshment. Nuns have been seen in lorries under military guards going through Dublin, but except in above case we have no details about them, and convents are usually most reticent. It may be that they are being taken round as hostages, now a common practice with men. At any rate they have been seen in lorries under armed guards.

Searching of Convents (v. Cardinal Logue's pastoral) – This is now a common practice, Convents of Marie Reparatrice, Merrion Square, Dublin, Carmelite Convent, Ranelagh, George's Hill Convent, Dublin, Dominican Convent, Eccles Street, Dublin, have all been searched recently. Many of these are cloistered nuns. They are invaded in small hours of the night by soldiers and police, the nuns searched, their cells visited, nuns in infirmary not even spared and in case of Carmelites in Ranelagh the newly made grave of a nun, recently buried, dug up and coffin opened in search of 'arms and ammunition'. In Merrion Square Convent the door was battered by butt-end of rifles, because presumably the nuns did not open at once. The raid took place at 1 am.

Assaults – There have been many cases of girls' hair cut, girls beaten, etc. In West, near Galway, two girls were made to stand for some hours waist deep in a pond, in their nightdresses and troops searching their houses. Miss Daly, Limerick, had her hair cut and her hand gashed by a razor while defending herself against the military. I have myself suffered from concussion of brain as result of blows from butt-end of rifles of RIC while addressing a meeting in Kilbeggan last year on 'Ireland and America'. On that occasion an old woman of 70 was clubbed into unconsciousness.

The Case of A. Fitzsimmons. (Please do not publish name in full.) Dundrum, County Dublin, is typical of what is happening throughout Ireland. (Investigated by Labour Commission.) She was taken in her bedroom by Black and Tans. Her room and personal linen, etc. searched. She was caught by the throat in the search and her night-dress ripped from throat to hem. She was obliged to dress (under protest) while the men invaded her room. Then taken in a lorry with drunken police and kept all night in Dublin Castle listening to obscene jeers and drunken rivalry. She is young and pretty but was a complete nervous wreck for weeks after this experience.

Mrs Clerkin Wife of A. Clerkin had her house searched an hour after her baby was born. The military dragged her from her bed which, with all the linen they searched, and so great was the shock to her and her baby that the little boy died after a fortnight. Mrs Joseph Clarke, wife of Councillor Clarke had a similar experience.

There are now over 2,000 men interned without any charge in Ballykinlar and other camps. In addition hundreds in jail, two-thirds of these have dependents all unprovided for – their women are suffering privations. When

Germans were interned in war, the Government paid their families an allowance, but the Government at present is actually seizing funds subscribed for these victims and confiscating same.

Further Cases of Attempted Rape have been reported on Miss McShane and Miss Murphy, UCR whose house was entered by four officers of the 15th Hussars (Lieutenants Sinclair, Poppleton, Templeton and another). After a prolonged struggle during which shots were fired and one woman wounded the man escaped and got the police (it was curfew time). The officers were arrested, but as usual nothing further has been heard of the case. (Sworn statement published) and policemen (Middlesburgh) in Limerick got a sentence of two years for attempted rape (cases appeared in court).

Case of the rape of a girl in presence of her father reported in Galway near Gort but not yet investigated fully.

Case of girls at County Tipperary, who refused to 'walk' with soldiers taken forcibly and kept three days in barracks. (Reported by a nun in Ursuline Convent, Thurles.)

Case of girl in Cork stripped naked by Black and Tans and made to stand so for several minutes but not (I hear) violated. This girl is being brought secretly to Dublin to testify to committee of women. Cases of this kind very difficult to verify as victims shamed and terrified. A special committee of women is being appointed to procure testimony.

Finally – Under curfew prostitutes alone are free presumably as a 'military necessity'. They are at large in Dublin and are taken about by military police in lorries and often kept in barracks for days (this happened recently in Portobello Barracks, Dublin, and at Rathmines Police Station, to my own knowledge). The officers take the better class for 'joy rides' at curfew hours also. English societies are taking action in this matter in the interests of public health and morality. Many of these women are paid to act as spies and recently one testified in a murder case against an Irish Volunteer. She was supposed to be a servant in an officer's house but was a prostitute in Secret Service Army.

I send also two reports of Irish and British Commissions which shed light upon general conditions.

(signed) Hannah Sheehy Skeffington

PS Owing to Government withdrawing grants to local bodies of local rates, the school-children in Dublin, Cork, etc., can no longer be fed and 30 per cent of the children have to be kept at home owing to hunger at present. Child starvation is becoming general and hospitals, sanatoria, asylums, etc., are being closed owing to lack of funds.

H. S. S.

'Current comment'
Irish Citizen, September–December 1920
Haircutting Outrages
We are convinced that the monopoly hitherto enjoyed by alien militarists of terrorizing women and children will not be interfered with by anyone claiming to be a Republican. If the 'Black and Tans' or their agents indulge in the practice of "reprisals" by cutting off the hair of girl Sinn Féiners we trust that there will be no counter-cutting of loyalist hair. The practice of cutting off the hair of terrified girls is not one to commend itself to any decent citizen of the Republic; it is base and cowardly as well as futile and degrading. Let the monopoly continue to be enjoyed by those who kidnap little children and murder Lord Mayors in the presence of their wives and sisters. In the olden days in Ireland a maiden could travel alone through the length and breadth of the land with the proud boast that 'no true son of Érin shall offer me harm'. Even a state of guerrilla warfare enjoins decencies at least upon those fighting in the righteous fight.

Women Judges
Recently many Irish women have been appointed judges in Sinn Féin courts and have been made chairmen of various local boards and councils. A woman, Councillor Wyse-Power, has been elected to the chairmanship of the Richmond Asylum Board, an appointment which she will fill with distinction, notable as she is for splendid public service. In other countries we hear of women entering the diplomatic service and it is possible there may be a woman in the next American Cabinet. But 'after all' as the *Irish Independent* pathetically observes, 'all that was to be expected from the moment they got the vote'. In fact, one might go further back and say once they learned to read. That was the time to nip in the bud. Now the days for nipping are for ever past.

America's Victory
Congratulations to our American sisters upon their full enfranchisement throughout the United States. Theirs is a suffrage wider than the British, for it is given to all women of twenty one; theirs is a real equality with men citizens, not a tardy dole for women of thirty and their victory is due largely to the militant women of the Women's Party, under the leadership of Alice Paul. We hope after this that a woman candidate will stand for Presidency in 1924.

'Do you want the *Irish Citizen*?'
Irish Citizen, September–December 1920
The future of a woman's paper in most countries is uncertain – in Ireland, at least, it is not doubtful, but the element of certainty means rather the certainty of despair and difficulty rather than the certainty of promise. Since 1912, that

is for eight long and difficult years, half the time being consumed in a world war, the *Irish Citizen* has championed the cause of women's emancipation. We began as a weekly, in 1916 became a monthly, and now, in order not to drop out entirely, we have decided to become a quarterly. Owing to increased prices of printing and postage, and owing to the extreme shortage of voluntary workers and writers for the paper, this step is necessary.

In Ireland at the present crisis, we are in a state of war, and all the conditions prevailing in other countries during the late European war now apply at home. Just as then the woman's movement merged into the national movement, temporarily at least, and women became patriots rather than feminists, and heroes' wives or widows, rather than human beings, so now in Ireland the national struggle overshadows all else. We as women may sometimes regret that militarism in any form, native or foreign, has little use for women, but however we may repine, we are compelled to acknowledge facts, even though we may hope that our cause may emerge from the struggle stronger, and reach in a few big strides the ground either partially lost or yet to be conquered. Meanwhile we can but mark time. There can be no woman's paper without a woman's movement, without earnest and serious-minded women readers and thinkers – these in Ireland have dwindled perceptively of late, partly owing to the cause above mentioned, and partly because since a measure, however limited, of suffrage has been granted, women are forging out their own destiny in practical fields of endeavour.

We had recently the choice offered us of becoming the organ of a section (an important section, but yet a section) of women workers. But the experiment has not encouraged us to continue, because we feel we ought to be the organ of all women, not of the few. Then there became evident a tendency to make part of the paper a sort of 'Home Chat' affair, and that we regarded with disfavour. There are enough such papers for those who need them – the *Irish Citizen* has other interests to serve. We still believe that we have a mission and a message for Irishwomen as a purely feminist paper and emboldened in that belief we shall carry on. It will be for our readers and supporters to help us by an increase of their support so that when time and conditions permit, we may return to our former strength.

Ask yourselves, dear readers, do I want the *Irish Citizen*? If the answer is in the affirmative, then write to us, contribute to the paper, talk about it to your friends, get us new subscribers, and make it your business to help us build up our little paper. Its life in the end depends upon each of you.

Sinn Féin Report on Organisation, n.d. (1921)[10]

In accordance with the express desire of President de Valera a campaign of intensive organisation has been initiated through the country, so as to take advantage of the present opportunity afforded by the truce, to put Sinn Féin Clubs everywhere on a properly working basis. For obvious reasons, which need no stating here, the organisation has suffered grievously during recent months, our organisers one after another being imprisoned or otherwise put out of action, the local Clubs left leaderless their funds and literature seized, their halls burnt, their social and other activities banned, their Members marked, so that there was no possibility of their functioning or even meeting. The result has been naturally that the activities of many clubs have dwindled and almost entirely ceased while many others were only kept together with greatest difficulty and with considerable sacrifice.

As the Sinn Féin Organisation is the political backbone of the movement, it now becomes imperative that every branch be put at once into proper working order, and it is accordingly incumbent upon all secretaries to get busy without delay upon the work of the re-organisation. Several Organisers *one woman (about 20 at present) [handwritten addition]* have been recently appointed and are at present engaged in getting into touch with branch Secretaries, through the country, for this purpose, and it is hoped that everywhere their efforts will be warmly supported, that the old branches will be revived and their membership increased and that new branches will be formed, where possible.

Keeping the machinery of Sinn Féin working, helping the work of Sinn Féin Courts, enforcing the Boycott, and maintaining an effective electoral machinery are the proper functions of the Sinn Féin organisation. It is essential to the well-being of the movement that this, the civil side of the organisation, be as perfect and thorough as the military side. *Ought to be no strife [handwritten addition]*. It is therefore the duty of every Republican man and woman to be a working member of a Sinn Féin Club and to see that the local clubs are properly functioning and maintaining the high standard of efficiency which should mark Sinn Féin in every department.

Hanna Sheehy Skeffington
Director of Organisation
(shall welcome any suggestions from delegates present) [handwritten addition]

Letter to Alice Park [11]
Dublin, Ireland
25 February 1922

We are all pretty disillusioned just now. I strongly dislike the treaty but I think it will be accepted at the elections. There is a regular stampede for it of all the moderates, and the 'safe' people with stakes in the country, of the press, and the clerics.

Women in the main are against it, and as a result, there is great bitterness against us all just now and a decree to extend the franchise was beaten at the Dáil the other day. To fight for this absorbed all my energies, and it seemed like old suffragette times again.

Enclosed are some leaflets we gave out to members of the Dáil. But for the present we are beaten, tho we are promised Adult Suffrage in the new Constitution – 'Jam tomorrow, but never jam today.'

The treaty is a bad compromise and I fear we are in for some decades of reaction under a temporary false prosperity, reinforced by our native militarism! It's a queer jumble, and needs some explaining, but I merely give you the general lines so that you know where I am.

Justice for Irish Women (Gaelic)[12]

The will of the people. Are Irishwomen under 30 people? British law says no. The Republican proclamation, 1916 says yes! What does Dáil Éireann say? A general election is at hand. The will of the whole Irish nation must be consulted on this issue. We demand government by consent. Women must vote in this election on the same terms as men.

(Irish paper. Irish ink. WUL)

'The Irish electorate'
The Freeman,[13] 10 May 1922
SIRS:

The *Freeman*, which is singularly well-informed on the Irish question, commented recently on the exclusion of the young women from voting at the coming election and asked, 'Can it be that they [Messrs. Collins and Griffith] believe a majority of women to be in favour of the Republic?' The answer is in the affirmative and, in that connexion, perhaps some of your readers would be interested to know some of the facts about the present register in Ireland.

Although we have proportional representation in practice at Irish elections (the British having tried the experiment first on the Irish dog, are as yet hesitating to apply it to themselves) we are still wedded to the antediluvian property-franchise, with all its anomalies and rottenness, its plural votings and university electorate. In the coming Irish elections there will be electors with four and more votes due to the fact that they hold property in various parts of the country, or that they are university graduates. This will naturally be to the advantage of the vested interests, for the propertied classes, the people that boast of 'stakes in the country', are all in favour of the Free State. These will all vote at the elections.

On the other hand, by the strange irony of fate, those who have done most to bring about the present offer of terms of peace, are cut off from voting by their very activities. In 1918, at the 'khaki' election, as it was called, which took place immediately after the great war, British soldiers, still undemobilized, were given special facilities for voting on the issue of 'hanging the Kaiser' and 'making Germany pay'. In Australia during the war, when the issue of conscription was before the Australian electorate, soldiers in the trenches and women serving at the front were allowed to register their votes. In Ireland, however, this right is being denied to the soldiers and the young women, for Arthur Griffith has peremptorily refused to consider the question of putting their names on the register in time for the next election.

Mr Griffith states that it would take eight months to add to the register the women between twenty-one and thirty (they number about 280,000). The Government Act itself prescribes three months, but both the young men and the young women could easily be registered before the time of the election. Americans, whose register is, I believe, revised yearly in a much shorter period in spite of the difficulties due to a large floating population, will readily see that the question of time does not present a real difficulty. Even if it did, it would be statesmanship to defer the elections the necessary number of weeks in order to register the entire adult population, since the question involved is not the usual Tweedledum and Tweedledee of politicians, but one which concerns the future destiny and status of the nation. True, adult suffrage is promised in the Constitution and, at the election after next, we are told that every one shall vote; a case of 'Jam yesterday, jam to-morrow, but never jam to-day'. We may not vote for the Free State or the Republic, but we may vote later when others have voted us into the Free State.

The present register is at least two years old. Apparently no male in Ireland has reached the age of twenty-one and become eligible for voting, no woman has become thirty within the last two years, while all those who have died within the period are still on the list and may be resurrected for voting purposes. One name in every six on the old register is wrong, according to the testimony of election experts who have examined it. In many districts the 'register' consists of blank pages, marked 'no information available'.

During the last two years, events in Ireland have not been propitious to so peaceful an affair as getting one's name on a Parliamentary register. In order to do this, a man on the run or in the army (then engaged in guerrilla warfare) would have had to risk being tracked down, imprisoned and perhaps put to death. It was therefore customary to ignore the preparation of registers, and only loyalists bothered about them. Most of those thus unenfranchised are, therefore, those who would vote against the treaty.

The women have a twofold grievance. The original Constitution of the Republic granted them equal citizenship with men, but they have been excluded from citizenship by the fact that Ireland had to conform to the Parliamentary laws of Great Britain. They feel, however, that on such a vital question as the treaty, the Dáil should have declared a plebiscite of the entire adult population. This is also the demand of Labour, definitely refused by Mr Griffith. The young women between twenty-one and thirty number one-seventh of the total electorate. It is upon these women that much of the brunt of the Terror fell: upon their morale depended, in effect, that of the entire Republican army. Many of them played a very active part in fighting for freedom, many suffered imprisonment, torture, deportation for their principles. Being under thirty did not exclude them from court-martials and convict cells, but now excludes them from voting at the coming election. I know a young university professor who served a year as a convict in Britain. Released in the recent amnesty she is now deprived of the right to vote! She is against the treaty, although for her its rejection would mean re-imprisonment, for she had received a three-year sentence. There are many such cases.

In the main, the women are opposed to the treaty, especially the young women. All the six women deputies in the Dáil voted against the treaty and their action is typical of Irish womanhood generally – I exclude, of course, loyalist women, and others who were not Sinn Féiners. Almost all the young women I know in the movement are against the treaty: their organization, *Cumann na mBan*, rejected it by more than seven to one. There are families in Ireland in which wives, daughters and sisters are in one camp (Republican) and their men-folk in the other (Free State). This difference of opinion along sex lines is significant. As Michael Davitt said of the women in the land-war of the 'eighties, 'Women are more uncompromising than men.' It is not surprising, therefore, that there is hot resentment among the youth of Ireland because they are shut out from voting next June: it is a resentment that no true statesman should attempt to ignore or minimize. I am, etc.,

HANNA SHEEHY SKEFFINGTON
Dublin, Ireland

'Mrs Skeffington controverts the *Nation* (New York)'
Éire, the Irish Nation, **Saturday 11 August 1923**
To the Editor of the *Nation* (New York).

In a recent editorial you refer to de Valera's 'content' with the 'substantial measures of self-government obtained by Ireland under the new constitution', but doubt his conversion to this 'content'. Apropos of de Valera's 'last word' to Free Staters and England, you observe: 'Saying one's last word may appear a less heroic attitude than dying in the last ditch, but the friends of Ireland will hope that, after all, the controversy may reach its final stage of speeches and manifestos rather than in deeds of violence.'

The real friends of Ireland cannot see a 'substantial measure of self-government' in the new constitution. That such an expression can find a place in the columns of the *Nation* is a tribute to the thoroughness with which pro-British propaganda in this field has worked. We have the word of a British authority in the latest edition of the Encyclopedia Britannica that 'indifference to truth is a characteristic of propaganda, that it is to promote the interest of those who continue it – (which) differentiates it from useful knowledge'. The so-called Treaty divides Ireland arbitrarily into two hostile camps, with an army of occupation in each. No referendum vote has been taken on the Treaty.

Status of Slave State
The constitution gives 'Southern' Ireland but the status of a slave state. We have no control over our Parliament, our Judiciary, or even over the spending of our money. Our judges are appointed by the King's governor-general. The Parliament is called and dismissed by the King, who has a veto on all legislation. As for the 'deeds of violence' of the Republicans, would it not be more to the purpose to emphasise the deeds of violence of the British Government which has precipitated all this? When it is realised (as it ought to be) that the Free Staters are and have been all along simply the tools and puppets of the British Government, one will be able to get something like a real perspective on the situation.

It is only from each perspective that one can write or speak fairly or even effectively of the Irish situation to-day. One is reminded of those profoundly true words of Mahatma Gandhi of India: 'Great Britain is the worst menace to the peace of the world, if only for the fact that her best men think she is keeping the peace. An armed peace is no peace.' It is British injustice, caused by greed and self-interest which is to blame for what some people like to call 'Republican violence'. It is British Imperialism that has been at the bottom of a good part of the trouble in the world for the last 100 years. Witness Egypt, India, Ireland, Turkey and the Near East.

Mr Bennett (an Englishman), writing in *Foreign Affairs* last month, says:

Even amidst the debased standards of international morality to-day the diplomatic record of England is unsurpassed for impotence, greed and shameless lying. For the various secret treaties with respect to Turkey there was not even the excuse that they were made in order to secure allies in the time of desperate need. They were simply instruments for international loot.

Ireland, too, is a part of this 'international loot'. The Free Staters do not see this, or they are willing to take 'half-loaf', together with the half-loot. But the

Irish people will not be satisfied with anything less than complete independence. Why should they? The United States demanded entire freedom and would not now revert to Colonial status. We are of different racial stock, different ideology, different aspirations. I only echo the thoughts of the best minds of England when I say that, with such manifestations of territorial greed there will always be deeds of violence somewhere in the world. It is regrettable that your paper, usually characterised by its broad vision, one, too, which did valiant service to Ireland by exposing the Black and Tan regime, should now show such regrettable, one might almost say, wilful, blindness on the Irish situation.

HANNA SHEEHY SKEFFINGTON
New York City

'Protest to Geneva'
Éire, the Irish Nation, **Saturday 15 September 1923**
Geneve, le 3 Septembre, 1923.
(To the delegates to the League of Nations and to members of Sixth Commission now considering question.)
Sir –

As delegate of the Irish Republic (proclaimed in 1916, ratified in two subsequent elections, and not since disestablished by any vote of the Irish people) I beg to make the following representations to you regarding the plea shortly to be put before you by the so called 'Free State' for admission to the League of Nations. These facts (which can be verified readily from the files of the Irish and British Press) should be borne in mind when the matter is being formally considered, so that no premature decision, taken on insufficient data, may mar the prestige of your assembly or expose your deliberations to the reproach of over-haste.

(1) The Irish nation has never been consulted on the question of entry into the League. Even the Free State Parliament and Senate have admitted that the question was opened up *proprio motu*[14] by one of the Ministers. The Irish Press has commented unfavourably on the indecent haste of the executive in attempting to force the issue without proper debate or consultation. The Senate has also recorded disapproval of these tactics on the grounds of un-seemly haste and insufficient information. Both of these bodies, it must be remembered, are part of the Free State machinery itself, no Republican taking any part in these assemblies. This demonstrates that, even in the Free State, opinion is adverse to this premature application for entry into the League.

(2) The so-called 'Free State' does not represent the whole of Ireland, which has been partitioned arbitrarily by Great Britain prior to the Treaty, all requests made by our people to decide frontiers by referendum or commission

having been persistently refused. The 'Free State' boundary is, therefore, fixed by a foreign nation contrary to the express will of the Irish people, and it consists only of 'Southern' Ireland.

(3) The Treaty, recently imposed upon the Irish people, has not been voted on by the electorate. It was a treaty signed under duress and under the threat of 'immediate and terrible war' on the part of Great Britain. It does not represent the free choice of the people of Ireland and in no sense can be said to confer freedom. All acts of its judiciary and legislature are expressly controlled by Britain. Similarly the Constitution of the 'Free State' has never been voted on by the Irish people. Both Treaty and Constitution have admittedly been forcibly imposed.

(4) Ireland, on the admission of the Free State Ministers themselves, is still held to be in a state of war. This fact is assigned as a reason for detaining without trial of about 16,000 prisoners (some hundreds of whom are women). Trial by jury and the right of Habeas Corpus have been suspended on the ground that a state of war existed, and the Government of the Free State have virtually suspended their own Constitution, a military oligarchy taking the place of civil government.

(5) During and immediately before the recent elections the same plea of war was held to excuse wholesale raids on private houses, murders of Republicans (taken from their homes by armed forces and shot out of hand), the arrest of election agents, the imprisonment of candidates, the seizure of election literature, of voters' lists, the non-issue in many districts of the election register, even the arrest, last Monday, at the polling booths of presiding officers and of many Republican voters, and in Cork, the holding up of Republican voters by armed forces (see the Irish Press of last week). Yet in spite of all this military intimidation the 'Free State' has been considerably weakened at the polls. In fact, the *British Morning Post* (an ultra-Conservative organ), in its issue of August 31, states that 'the number of seats won by Republicans entitles them to claim a moral victory'. At the present time the Free State Party is actually in a minority in its own Parliament.

(6) The 'Free State', according to its arrangement with Great Britain, has not the right to enter into direct relations with any other Governments without Britain's permission. It is evident, then, that the admission by the 'Free State' into the League would, therefore, merely have the effect of strengthening further the influence of one already powerful member of the League, at the expense of all the other members. Such preponderance of any one factor is undesirable in a body claiming to be international, and would expose your assembly to the reproach of partisanship.

(7) The Irish Republic, in the name of all Ireland, accepts no responsibility for the debts of the 'Free State', which functions only by virtue of the military

and financial backing of Britain. Were this for an instant withdrawn, the 'Free State' would collapse like a house of cards.

(8) The recent refusal (dictated by the British representative) of the International Red Cross to institute an impartial inquiry into the conditions of war and political prisoners in Ireland is but another proof of the impossibility of Ireland being afforded any fair dealing even on so-called international bodies, as long as these are British-controlled. Every regulation supposed to apply to the treatment of prisoners of war by the Geneva Convention has been violated by the 'Free State,' with the connivance of Britain, yet even as refused at the mere *ipse dixit*[15] of a British representative, the Irish side being refused even a hearing.

From the foregoing I hope it has been made clear that Ireland is not yet in a position to decide on its merits for herself as to whether or not she should apply for membership of the League of Nations. If she should ever so desire, it will be in the capacity of a free nation, acting independently, and not in that of a puppet-State. The inadvisability of considering the question now is apparent. Under present conditions to admit the 'Free State' to membership would be to be guilty of a slur upon your prestige, would justify those who maintain that your League is a one-sided assembly and not truly representative. You are, therefore, respectfully requested to postpone your decision in this matter.

I remain, on behalf of the Irish Republic,

Yours respectfully,

HANNA SHEEHY SKEFFINGTON

9

OPPOSING THE FREE STATE

INTRODUCTION

The main source for Hanna's writings in the 1920s was the *Irish World and American Industrial Liberator*, more commonly known as the *Irish World*, founded in New York City by Patrick Ford in 1870. His sister, Ellen Ford, was a member of the New York Ladies' Land League and the paper gave huge coverage to the work of Anna Parnell and the Ladies' Land League in the 1880s, even supporting their more radical agenda over that of the parliamentary party. After Ford's death in 1913 his son continued the paper's tradition of active propaganda on behalf of the Irish national cause. In July 1923 Hanna was appointed a 'special correspondent and news reporter' and was paid an average of $15 per week, which was an important part of her income at this time. Frank Gallagher, former director of publicity during the War of Independence also contributed a column.

Hanna was closely involved with Constance Markievicz at this time as they were part of a concerted campaign to oppose the Free State. For example, the *Irish Times* (21 November 1923), in reporting the arrest and subsequent hunger strike of Markievicz, arrested while she and Hanna were organising lightning meetings around Dublin to exhort people to sign a petition for the release of the republican prisoners, quoted directly from an indignant Hanna:

> Mrs Sheehy Skeffington said that ever since last Wednesday Madame Markievicz had been circulating literature and addressing meetings at various parts of her constituency, using a lorry as her platform. Her meetings never lasted longer than twenty minutes, and she endeavoured always to avoid obstruction. Yesterday she mentioned the death of Denis Bray at Newbridge and gave the lie to President Cosgrave's statement that the hunger strike was merely a fraud.
>
> Mrs Sheehy Skeffington went on to say that she offered to go with Madame Markievicz but, the detective not allowing her to do so, she later went with Madame Gonne MacBride to the G Division office. There she was assured it was an official arrest but that no charge had yet been made.

She was allowed to write to the prisoner, who sent back a note stating that she would accept warm clothing, but not food, and ending, 'I have gone on hunger strike.'

In the bitter period following the end of the Civil War, with many still imprisoned, Hanna's column reflected the mood of those times. While she tried to highlight women's issues as much as she could, her main focus was often to attack the Free State government for its continued repression and to highlight the growing development of the republican opposition, in particular the rise of Fianna Fáil. Some articles are given in full, some have been edited. Some other *Irish World* articles appear in chapters dealing with European travels and her friendship with Constance Markievicz. References made within articles are sometimes to long-forgotten events, reflecting the pressures of writing on an almost weekly basis at times, but overall they provide a vivid impression of the tense period in the aftermath of war, when full political independence continued to be a contested issue. We can also see women's citizenship rights beginning to be challenged, as in their removal from jury service, an issue covered by Hanna in her newspaper articles, letters to editors and involvement in concerted lobbying by women's groups.

The Women's International League for Peace and Freedom Congress in 1926 was held in Ireland and was a significant landmark, not only for the international women's movement but also for post-Civil War Ireland. Helena Swanwick, one of the English delegates, thought Cosgrave's government 'fairly established' but added that 'one could sense more than a mere parliamentary opposition to it'.[1] Hanna's speech to the Congress conveys this most powerfully as she delivered a wide-ranging indictment of Free State policies, and followed up her speech with an account of the proceedings of the conference for readers of the *Irish World*.

Although she joined Fianna Fáil on its inception, leaving Sinn Féin, and was a member of the Fianna Fáil executive, the party was not a natural home for her. Fianna Fáil's decision to enter the Dáil before the Oath of Allegiance had been abolished prompted her resignation from the party in May 1927. She would never again be a member of a political party, although she began to hope for the creation of a women's party. For the next decade Hanna found herself closer to the republicans centred around *An Phoblacht*, which from May 1926 was edited by Peadar O'Donnell and reflected the views of the IRA. The *Irish World* was a strong supporter of Fianna Fáil and Hanna's articles for the paper became less frequent, ending in 1929.

'Review of recent events in Ireland'
Irish World, 19 January 1924

As I cabled you last week, Constance Markievicz, TD, the last woman prisoner to be detained, was released from the North Dublin Union Military Prison on December 27 having been held in military custody without any form of trial since November 20. Whether the large building formerly used as a poorhouse, then as a Free State military prison for women will be now used to relieve the congestion in Grangegorman Lunatic Asylum and its military garrisons disbanded or whether these will be kept on and provided with fresh occupation in the new year through further arrests of women is a question still on the knees of the gods.

Though considerable clearances in jails and camps were made during the week preceding Christmas – (over 1,000 in all), fresh arrests are being made daily, while prisoners are also being transferred, when the camps are emptied, to Kilmainham in large numbers, apparently with a view to indefinite detention such as the extended Public Safety Bill provides.

Government by Jails

In the Northern area, prisoners just released by the Free State are almost at once re-arrested and transferred to Northern jails. A Sinn Féin club in Derry City was raided last week and several members (some newly released prisoners) were thus taken. It may be that Cosgrave provides his friend and ally Craig with lists of 'suspects' as was done to the British Home Secretary by the Free State Spy Department in the case of the deserters from Britain. In some cases the Northern internees are being offered conditional freedom in the form of tickets-of-leave. Otherwise the condition of prisoners in the Northern area continues unchanged, and no effective pressure can or will be exercised by the Southern 'Government' to have these (some of them supporters of the treaty) released as long as the Free State detains so large a number in its own area.

It is difficult to estimate the exact number of prisoners now in jail, for official figures lie and are hard to check sufficiently – it is stated, however, that there are still in jail between 3,000 and 4,000. The Free State actually admits over 2,000 in its official figures. So it will be noted that Cardinal Logue's advice to clear camps and jails by Christmas has been disregarded and the Cardinal seems to have no reproof to offer though his terms were taken as an informal basis of agreement by Republicans and the people generally when the hunger strike was called off.

The Hunger Strike

Constance Markievicz spoke at the weekly meeting held in O'Connell Street on the day following her release and was accorded an enthusiastic reception. She is thin and pale as a result of the hunger strike, but is as undaunted as ever and as full of plans for future work. She detailed the story of how Tom Derrig (blinded, it will be recalled, as a result of a Free State beating in jail, when he lost one eye and had the other injured) came to the women hunger strikers (some were fasting for nearly 40 days) and explained the situation. Two men having died and the Free State, like Pharaoh, having hardened his heart, the leaders felt it incumbent on them not to advise a continuance of the strike which would involve the deaths of over 100 men and women, and therefore decided to call off the strike for all.

It was a hard step, declared Constance Markievicz, and one requiring great moral courage because 'to order a retreat is always the hardest thing a soldier may be called upon to do'. But, soldier-like, they all obeyed in the same spirit they had entered into the long strike. This was the first account at first hand of what had happened and explained the real reason of the cessation of the strike.

The following TDs are still in jail: Éamon de Valera, T. Kilroy, Gerald Boland, Ernie O'Malley, Barney Mellows, while many public representatives, including the Mayor of Limerick, are still being held. Ernie O'Malley, though better, is, it is feared, permanently invalided. Kilmainham is quite unheated and the prisoners, weak from their long fast, suffer intensely from the cold and from the miserable conditions in the jails generally. Many of those recently released are still in nursing homes.

The Sligo Men

I saw just two days before Christmas a group of some 40 men and boys leaving the little canteen in Harcourt Street,[2] where prisoners came on arrival in Dublin. There they are provided with a meal, with clothes, with a temporary billet, if needed; a little hospital has been fitted up on the premises for them and they are tended with loving care by a committee of devoted women. These boys from Sligo were leaving hours in advance to catch the Western train. They were singing blithely and their eyes shone with the glad light of freedom regained. All were without hats or caps, many without even collar or tie: they carried pathetic little bundles – little gifts for those at home, made out of all sorts of odds and ends, carved photo-frames, rude rings, network, bags and the like. When asked why they were leaving so early, they said they 'wanted to be walking', and 'sure, they'd feel they were on their way home and nearer home in the station, just to be looking at the train!' I wish those good friends in the United States who have helped our prisoners so generously could be there to see the pleasure in the faces of those boys at the little simple comforts provided for them!

For those still in jail the committee also arranged to have Christmas parcels sent in, while toys and children's gifts came from various friends in America to cheer the homes of prisoners or ex-prisoners. Many of these men had spent every Christmas since 1916 to the present either in jail or on the run. Truly the war in Ireland has lasted longer even than the Great War!

Meanwhile the Free State machinery grinds on. In the new year a general holocaust of rural councils and a possible demolition of some city councils and other public bodies is expected. Our doped press is attempting to stampede the public in this direction under a false and deliberately misleading cry of economy. The *Independent*, with a 'furtive leg on the other side of the fence', as the *Morning Post* puts it, has already realised that it may have gone too far and now rather deprecates the abolition of rural councils though it would fain sweep others away. There is a demand for cutting down of representation on certain bodies so that democracy may be pruned of its popular elements and cut down to a loyalist, withered stump. This, we are told, may be done in Dublin City, and for this purpose, the propertied townships such as Rathmines and Pembroke may be thrown in with Dublin. Rathmines has a Unionist majority – the only one south of the Boyne – and Pembroke, Blackrock and other townships have also a considerable quota of 'true blues' so Dublin may thus be watered down and its Labour and Republican elements largely eliminated. Then if any such are perchance returned, the Public Safety Bill can always be requisitioned to reduce them further by putting some members out of action.

The Senate proposes to disenfranchise electors at the coming elections who may not have paid their rates – such an amendment to the Local Government Electors' Registration Bill was recently inserted. One genius, Senator Lenihan, desired to go still further and introduced an amendment favouring quadruple voting, that is giving four votes according to property qualifications. Those who had property valued at £100 were to get four votes, at £50 two and so forth. This fancy scheme was defeated after a debate but the proposal and backing show clearly the Free State 'Upper' House tendency. In both Houses property holds sway over democracy, hence the lust for abolishing local boards, for appointing in their stead 'paid' commissioners, preferably relatives of certain ministers and deputies, for centralisation schemes which so ill fit native Gaelic tradition, and while piling up huge salaries for ministers, secretaries, judges and police, ruthlessly cutting down old age pensions, teachers and meals for poor children.

Cosgrave's largely nominated Senate can be counted on to react according to type, and already I have heard grumbles coming from Free State and Labour TDs to the effect that Senate members had not to face the bother and odium of election and envying their happy lot as contrasted with members of the Lower House who have to go to the people! So ere long some luminary may propose abolishing votes as dangerous to Public Safety. One critic has aptly suggested that a commissioner might be appointed to supersede both Houses doing the work now performed badly by amateurs and saving the considerable expense of deputies and ministers' salaries and thus promoting efficiency. Such would indeed be the logical sequel to the abolition of public bodies. Formerly, before the recent war for freedom, such a commissioner superseding democratic and elected bodies used to be called a Czar – a bureaucrat by any other name may smell as sweet.

Recently the Pope sent a message referring with gladness to the 'settlement rapidly approaching' in Ireland. The source of such cheering news is not given but may be guessed, for British influence is, as ever, strong in Rome. Acting President Ruttledge[3] sends a reply which appears on Page Eight of this issue to this alleged 'good tidings', stating that Republicans are 'absolutely unaware of the approach of any settlement or of any intention to remove the cause of all our troubles, vis, England's unwarranted interference in our national affairs'. While I expect the American press generally may have given space to the Pope's message, probably the *Irish World* will be among the few papers that will chronicle the reply of our Acting President giving the lie to British-inspired propaganda about Ireland being 'settled' at last! How often have we been 'settled' since the advent of the Anglo-Norman? How often 'pacified' since the days of good Queen Bess or Cromwell, Edward the Peacemaker and George of the Tans!

Next year (1924)[4] we are threatened with a visit from the arch-royal, the Prince of Wales. J. J. Walsh is again getting ready for the Tailteann Games,[5] and we are promised if we are very good, that the venue for the International Motor Race may be fixed for Kildare. As the French cynic said, 'Life would be tolerable but for its amusements.' Certainly Prince's visits, Olympic games and motor races look like the modern version of 'fiddling while Rome is burning', or like giving the people circuses without the bread that even Rome's emperors also supplied. This with over 40,000 (plus their dependents) unemployed within 'Free' State area, with thousands untried in jail, their dependents also in want outside, with a recently demobbed army used to bring down the scale of wages for labourers further, with over 70,000 persons in Dublin alone living in single-room tenements in the heart of festering slums! George Bernard Shaw once said that our planet, the earth, is the lunatic asylum for the universe. Well, if so, Ireland of the Free State must be its padded cell set aside for its most violent cases of 'lunacy'.

Raids and Murders by Tans
We have had around Christmas a crop of armed hold-ups in and near Dublin – in many cases where robbers have been caught red-handed, they are found to be army or ex-army men. In Monaghan and in the Curragh drunken soldiers have broken out and caused mutiny and have fired on one another, fatally

wounding. Coroners holding inquests upon the victims have commented on the lack of discipline in the army. There have been the usual number of cases (now becoming a regular feature) of guns going off 'accidentally' and killing comrades or friends. The notorious Lieutenant Gaffney, who is involved in the killing of Sergeant Woods of the Civic Guards and young Tom Bresnan is still at large.

Yesterday our Dublin press had the quaint caption 'Civic Guards Raid Military Barracks'. Some soldiers and officers were raided by the Guards looking for Gaffney and an army officer has been arrested on suspicion of 'harbouring' the fugitive! But Gaffney continues to remain at large. Neither has anyone been apprehended for the brutal murder and torture of Joe Berain, referred to in my last article. It is remarkable that the 'unprecedented wave of crime' referred to by O'Higgins as an excuse for his Safety Bill is largely due to his National Army of violence. The danger of the demobilisation of so many dangerous and lawless men who have been used by the Free State ministry to commit unheard of outrages upon Republicans is now being borne in upon the Staters themselves. In fact, it is a matter of common knowledge that the Ministers are scared of their own murder machine, and would now fain be rid of this Frankenstein that they themselves have created.

As Deputy Gorey of the Farmer's Party recently declared in Parliament, the danger now is not from the Republican side, since Republicans have loyally obeyed since the 'cease fire' order last April, but from the arms and ammunition in the hands of Free State soldiers turned bandits. The government has more to dread from these arms than from any other quarter.

Even Sir Horace Plunkett's own organ, the *Irish Statesman*, an ultra-government paper, waxes uneasy at the failure of the Free State to quell their own banditry and looks askance upon the O'Higgins Safety panacea and demands that trial by jury be restored.

Destroying Trial by Jury

On this point, O'Higgins recently made a very damaging admission when he declared in excuse for his internment without trial policy that juries generally in Ireland would not convict in the case of political offences! Long ago the British used to make this fact a reason for their jury-packing system. Things are now admittedly much worse for O'Higgins cannot even trust packing and has to abolish juries altogether in political cases. In his Judiciary Bill, now being considered, he further proposes to make a unanimous verdict of 12 unnecessary. It will be enough to have nine found in agreement for a verdict – another of the many subtle attacks upon democratic safeguards by the Free State.

Recently the Irish Labour Party in Parliament made a great display over the introduction of a railway bill, the effect of whose provisions would be, if acted upon, to nationalise our railways. A case for this, as well as for land nationalization, has been repeatedly made by reformers, and Labour haltingly and mincingly tried to follow on their path. But even this tentative and hesitating scheme, as fathered by Johnson,[6] proved too much for the Free State and its mechanical majority, and so the entire bill was quietly scrapped. Johnson, in fact, seemed to imply by his subdued undertaker's manner that he considered he was attending a funeral, not a birth of a new order of things. So unwept, unsung the Railway Bill went to the cemetery and we are told as a consolation that the Free State will 'shortly' deal with the problem, tackling it, of course, as becomes conservatives in a less drastic spirit and one more friendly to 'Big Business'. As the railroads by way of bribe contributed to the recent loan we may feel certain that their monopolies will not be interfered with. Meanwhile railwaymen are having their wages cut.

Cosgrave, too, carried his scheme for parliamentary secretaries, though he felt obliged to cut the number to four, instead of seven, as at first intended. This means of course providing further highly-paid jobs for his followers in Parliament. Mr Cosgrave (or rather, Mrs Cosgrave, his wife) succeeded in obtaining a fancy sum of £7,000 in 'compensation' for the bombing of his house. It was quite a surprise to the public to know the number of art treasures and precious objects that made the total for a very modest and sparsely furnished dwelling rise so high, but naturally the Free State judge did not question the 'President's' own figures, and gave practically the entire sum claimed, though usually such figures are drastically reduced. Thus, a tax is added to the already burdened taxpayer to pay Mr Cosgrave's exorbitant 'compensation' for losses most fictitious.

Edward Martyn

Events outside the political arena to be noted are the recent death of Edward Martyn, one of the greatest patrons of art, music and the drama that modern Ireland knew. His work in establishing Palestrina choirs, his subsidising a theatre for the production of foreign masterpieces, his plays produced by the Abbey company would, any one of them, have made him famous. Politically he was an ardent Sinn Féiner and a staunch upholder of our nation's right to absolute independence. His large fortune he freely gave to many causes; his charity to the poor was inexhaustible. His death too showed his love of the lowly, for he directed that his body be handed over to the College of Surgeons for the cause of science and medical research, as are the bodies of the nameless dead. After, he directed in his will, that he be buried in the plainest deal coffin and put into the pauper's grave at Glasnevin without any ceremony save that accorded to the poorest and most friendless. His choir boys alone chanted his requiem. Thus even after death he set an example of true humility and of love of Lady Poverty seldom emulated by those devoted to her service.

The Nobel Bill

Another notable happening was the award of the Nobel prize to Senator Yeats, awarded apparently rather to the present Senator and loyalist than to the poet of Cathleen ni Houlihan who in the *King's Threshold* glorified the hunger strike through the mouth of the Irish rebel bard. Mr Yeats is credited (or rather discredited) with a flamboyant after dinner utterance glorifying imperial Britain and declaring in the fullness of his heart that 'Britain's enemies can never be Ireland's friends'. Just as Cosgrave recently discovered Geneva and Bobbio in his 'Innocents Abroad' tour of Europe, so now Yeats appears to have discovered Stockholm and his Norse ancestry. It is interesting to note that in spite of Mr Yeats' fulsome flattery of the British, their press is somewhat sore over his getting the Nobel prize which, it points out, ought not to go to a mere Irish poet as long as any British writer remains unrewarded.

Meanwhile Dark Rosaleen still has poets in her service – and in jail. Harry Stuart,[7] who was imprisoned for over a year, has just been released after a lengthy hunger strike, has won the 'Young Poet's' prize for his lyrics. The award is an American one, and I understand his lyrics appeared (forwarded by his wife, Iseult Gonne) first in the American periodical *Poetry*. The title of his volume is, appropriately, 'We Kept the Faith'.

'Review of recent events in Ireland'
Irish World, 16 February 1924

. . . Motor cars and typewriters are still dangerous to public safety and the Free State seize them. (During my absence in America as part of the Irish Women's Mission, raising funds for the relief of the prisoners) my husband's machine was seized, with various other things, by Free State raiders and carted away. Subsequent on my return I was told the machine was in Island Bridge barracks, but the Colonel added it was 'not deemed advisable' by the authorities to let me have my property. Since then a correspondence has developed, beginning dutifully 'A Chara' and ending 'Mise le meas', for at least the Staters must begin and end in Gaelic . . . My typewriter, like our prisoners, seems on each occasion to be located in a different barracks . . . I seem to be collecting autographs of various colonels and adjutants, but so far with no tangible result. My Remington is still in the hands of the enemy.

'Trying to hoodwink with explanations'
Irish World, 3 May 1924

An instance of how the Free State protects its gunmen came to our knowledge last Sunday on the occasion of a monster meeting held by the Dublin Trades Council in O'Connell Street to demand the release of the prisoners. The meeting was addressed by Jim Larkin and other Labor leaders and by various republicans. Though other parties were invited by labor's Left Wing, the platform being non-political, they did not attend for obvious reasons. While the meeting was in progress – I was a witness of this episode from No 1 platform – a motor car attempted to force a way through rather aggressively. Larkin appealed good humoredly to the crowd to 'let the fellow through, maybe he's a Free State General', when suddenly the occupants got impatient and one pulled back the flap of the hood, brandished a revolver threateningly and fired two shots in rapid succession in the direction of the platform. The man was at once recognised by the crowd as Superintendent O'Driscoll, formerly at Oriel House, now one of the heads of the Detective department, a man notorious for his vile record as torturer of Republican prisoners. He is said to have initiated the practice of tying up prisoners by the wrists and other fiendish devices for trying to wring information out of prisoners. When the police recognized their superior officer they immediately intervened to protect him from the wrath of the crowd, an inspector getting mauled in defending O'Driscoll. The car got away and no attempt was made by the police to disarm the gunman. Incidents of this kind happen daily. They will be instructive examples of law and order to any American visitors who may choose to visit this 'Free' land this summer.

By the way, the Northern area still imposes curfew. In Dublin we are freer – entirely at our own risk. Last week here in the suburbs of Rathmines a block or so away a man returning home was clubbed into unconsciousness and left bleeding on his doorstep. He was not robbed and was apparently mistaken by the murder gang for a well-known neighbour, a lawyer who has had recently to prosecute some demobbed Free State officers for such crimes as criminal assault, embezzlement. The murderer of Free State Deputy Coyle, North Mayo, has just got a sentence of three years' penal servitude for passing a false check. The Free State has tried hard to hold up the case, fearing a by-election.

In another case an ex-officer got five years' penal servitude and some strokes of the cat for criminal assault of a young girl and robbery with violence. Such are the forces now loose among the Free State demobbed and active forces. No wonder O'Higgins etc. are fearful. The Dublin City Council has led the way again in the matter of the prisoners. By a large majority (the Free Staters abstaining from voting), the council passed a resolution demanding the instant and unconditional release of all political prisoners interned or sentenced now in British, Free State or Northern jails. A plebiscite is now being taken by Sinn Féin on the question so that the British Labour Government can no longer allege that there is no demand for the release of prisoners or that the Free State would regard such a step as an 'unfriendly act'.

MacDonald must be shown, as Baldwin and Churchill were in their time, that it does not pay to keep political prisoners in jail and that labour will lose if it persists in acting as jailer for Irishmen.

'Review of recent events in Ireland'
Irish World, 4 October 1924
[In referring to the news that the bodies of Erskine Childers and other republicans executed during the Civil War were being exhumed from Beggar's Bush Barracks and secretly reinterred, Hanna made a strong reference to her personal experience.]

The Free State fears if the bodies were handed over the Irish people would flock in their thousands to give them full honours. I well recall how the British in Portobello disinterred my husband's body from the hole in the yard where it lay in a sack on condition I should not be informed and that my father-in-law would promise not to allow any 'demonstration'. These reinterments are right to fear the dead.

'Review of recent events in Ireland'
Irish World, 31 January 1925
A report of the death in Spain of Mlle Lydia Ducondon, who taught for many years in St Mary's Dominican College. Later, Mlle Ducondon came to New York where she became actively interested in every movement connected with Ireland – she knew many of the women in the Sinn Féin movement in Ireland, having been their professor at college. I remember on my first visit to New York, in 1916, hearing with joy the well-known voice over the phone of my former professor of French and pouring into her eager ears all the news of many of her old friend and pupils, some of them today professors in the university and in various colleges abroad. Later, in 1922, when I came to the United States once more, on behalf of the Prisoners' Dependents Committee, I found her unwavering in her allegiance to the republic.

'Republican reconstruction'
Irish World, 21 March 1925
Kathleen Barry[8] and Linda Kearns are in Australia on behalf of the Irish Republican Reconstruction Committee. The committee in charge of the Irish Republican Prisoners' Dependents Fund is now turning its attention to reconstruction. £36,000 was administered in the last few years, by mostly voluntary help, so the overheads have not been more than 2%.

'Review of recent events in Ireland'
Irish World, 28 March 1925
[Hanna was travelling through the west of Ireland with de Valera, 'Scelig', and Fr Michael O'Flanagan, speaking at fairs and markets and at after-mass meetings in towns and rallies at night. In Roscommon and Sligo they were asked if there was famine in the west. They said no, but that it was a bad season and the sheep got fluke from the sodden fields.]

It is important to be accurate. The Free Staters say there is no distress in Ireland, and thus we have two opposite currents – one that exaggerates, the other that minimises, and both acting not in the interests of the Irish people, but of their own vested interests. It is only when a Republican government functions again that the whole question can be properly dealt with.

'Cardinal Mannix civic reception in Dublin'
Irish World, 14 November 1925
[Cork-born Cardinal Mannix of Melbourne, banned by the British government from entering Ireland in 1920, eventually arrived in 1925. Close to de Valera, his presence was seen as endorsing those anti-Treaty republicans who would go on to form Fianna Fáil. Hanna was present at his civic reception in the Rotunda. Seán T. O'Kelly, as Dublin's senior alderman, presided.]

Cardinal Mannix's address was a masterpiece, one of the finest, his appeal to the intellect rather than the emotions. To hear him develop his theme is a rare pleasure in these days when it is the habit, rather the pose, of the military type of speaker to begin by announcing with a swagger, that he is 'no orator' but a plain, blunt man of action, the implication being that oratory is something second rate, not to compare with knocking your man out, or blowing him up . . . When a real orator appears, the pleasure is all the greater because it is now so rare.

'Proceedings of the Ard Fheis explained'[9]
Irish World, 3 April 1926
The following is the official interim report of the first two days of the Ard Fheis session, which took place in the Rotunda, Dublin, this week. Father O'Flanagan's amendment having been passed by 233 to 218 votes, it was put as a substantive motion. A number of amendments were then put and rejected. It was finally proposed in the following form:

> That it is incompatible with the fundamental principles of Sinn Féin to send representatives into any usurping legislature set up by English law in Ireland.

And rejected by 179 votes to 177.
    The report of the last day's proceedings are as follows . . . The President was compelled to regard the vote as one against his policy, the adoption of which he considered necessary at this juncture. He tendered his resignation accordingly as President of the organisation.
    It was with great regret that the Ard Fheis accepted the resignation of the President, which he could not see his way to reconsider.

The chair was subsequently taken by the senior Vice-President, Miss Mary MacSwiney, and the Ard Fheis adjourned to enable those who supported and those who opposed the resolutions to meet separately.

Those two bodies then appointed committees to meet jointly and discuss and decide on the future work of the organisation and the basis of co-operation.

The Ard Fheis re-assembled at 2.30 pm and the following resolution was adopted: That the joint committee be given full powers, on behalf of the Sinn Féin organisation, to deal with all matters arising out of the present situation, and to make all necessary arrangements for co-operation, etc.

Meantime, the Cumainn and Comhairlí Ceanntair will carry on work as usual.

The important message which goes from this Ard Fheis is that the division within our ranks is a division of Republicans who are unanimous on this fundamental issue; that in no circumstances can any Republican take an oath of allegiance to an alien King, or assent to the partition of our country.

The delegates expressed determination to work together for our common objective is every way consistent with the opinions expressed as to principles and methods during the Ard Fheis.

Before the adjournment of the Ard Fheis, Father O'Flanagan proposed that the Ard Fheis should express its feelings of admiration for President de Valera.

Miss MacSwiney, in seconding, declared that one could only choose the shortest possible form of words since no words could express what the Organisation and the country owed to Éamon de Valera. Several delegates having supported in fading terms, the Ard Fheis, by a rising vote, tried to express by acclamation the deep love and gratitude which each member feels for the man who was described as the greatest Irishman for a century.

It will be seen from the foregoing that, while there is no split in the Republican ranks on the essentials, namely the refusal to acknowledge allegiance to a foreign king or the acceptance of partition, there is a definite difference of opinion as to immediate future policy. For, though Father O'Flanagan's amendment (taken first so that the President's resolution never really came to be discussed), passed by a small majority of five, some not voting, nevertheless later, when put duly as a substantive motion in final form it was rejected by two votes, so that the assembly cannot be said to have made a decision either way in the end. None the less, as stated, President de Valera (who, of course, remains President of the Republic, though no longer President of the Sinn Féin organisation) declared on the morning of the third day's session, after the inconclusive vote of the previous day had been recorded, that he must resign from Sinn Féin as such, feeling that his suggested policy had not been accepted or endorsed by that body. He could not naturally (and such is the position of those supporting him on the executive and elsewhere) logically remain head of an organisation that declined to subscribe, if even by a narrow vote, to his policy.

. . . The warmest tributes were paid to him, his almost superhuman patience and toleration. It was a scene of deep emotion and many eyes were wet with tears of affection, mingled with sorrow at this even temporary parting of the ways.

. . . From now on, President de Valera with his party will bend his energies to solidifying Irish opinion on the removal of the oath, while Sinn Féin proper will continue its ordinary activities. All Republicans, of whatever shade of opinion are prepared to welcome the abolition of that barrier, and to regard its removal as a victory, though some would not, even were it abolished, enter even as active opposition either the Free State or the Northern Parliament.

. . . As President de Valera so aptly put it in his speech, he feels that the left as well as the right arm, the constitutional as well as the military, should be tried. Since the Cease Fire order the military arm has had perforce to be inactive. It is now time to start about trying to wield the other arm in its full strength against the Treaty. For this purpose the bond confining it must be severed, the obnoxious oath must go! That is what he and those who support his view must now put to the Irish people; for it is the Irish people that must and can take the initiative in this matter. If the united people declare that the oath to a foreign king must be destroyed, then Republicans can be free to enter a subordinate assembly in order to use the leverage of amassed and active opposition to destroy the fabric created by the foreigner.

Personally, I hold this view. It is no 'recognition' of a building to enter it with a bomb in order to blow it to pieces . . .

There are strong Republicans to be found in both groups now operating and these may be relied upon to keep the movement sweet. The women differ as strongly as the men – to give an instance – while Mary MacSwiney, Mary Comerford and Dr K. Lynn are on one side, Mrs Pearse, Mrs Tom Clarke and Countess Markievicz are on the other.

. . . Éamon de Valera's personality has accomplished the miracle that we may differ without bitterness, and may choose a new path without losing the comrades who have marched on the same road with us thus far – for the new path and the old road lead eventually to the same destination – that of a united and independent Republic.

'A week's events in Ireland's capital'
Irish World, 10 July 1926

One of the things that strikes one most when abroad is that Ireland has completely dropped out of the world's news. Britain has got her propaganda across that Ireland is no longer an entity. 'North or South?' is the parrot query when one announces that one is from Ireland. Beyond this, Ireland has ceased to exist. Thousands of pounds are spent in consul camouflage; a Free State representative has, I believe, an office in Paris, but no inquiry could place it. It was represented at no official gathering, and the only activity that its young men engage in is, I believe, dancing. That it is not even Irish dancing one may be sure.

If there is a passport difficulty, it is the British consul who attends to it; and frequently he confiscates as spurious the Free State passport. In international gatherings the British do not permit the so-called Free State flag, or permit it only as part of the Union Jack, like the other colonies. Egypt is the only country that insists successfully on its right to its own flag, green with white stars and crescent.

As to tourist traffic, Ireland is not catered for. In Paris I looked in vain at Cook's, at the American Express office for any booklet about Ireland (north or south). Even in the 'British Isles' booklet, no route was given that included Ireland, though copious literature, profusely illustrated and temptingly set forth, abounded for every country on the globe. The *Leader* fittingly dubbed Irish manufacturers once the 'Dark Brotherhood' – certainly the description pointedly applies to the Free Trade representative abroad. In Paris I heard that, but for the Republican office, there would be no link between Ireland and France. Yet over £45,000 was recently voted in the Free State parliament for the 'Department of External Affairs' . . .

At Mountjoy

On Saturday, June 28th, a group of Republican women assembled in the early morning outside Mountjoy jail, to welcome to liberty Sheila Humphries and Bride O'Mullane, after their two months' imprisonment.[10] As the big gate swung open for them, a ringing cheer went up – Mrs Despard, Mrs MacBride, Mary Comerford, the executive of Cumann na mBan, Mme Markievicz, members of the Defence League, your correspondent and many others from various groups were present.

The prisoners told us smilingly that the authorities after the usual struggle had conceded certain rights, that of association of exercise, for instance, though at 4.30 each evening (these long June evenings) they were locked up for the night in solitary confinement! The military had, they said, given military honors by putting on a sentry specially for them, so that in effect, the government recognised their political character.

Their imprisonment had been lightened by the glad news of Keogh's gallant rescue,[11] though at first this was kept from them. They declared that after that nothing mattered; for they knew that it was worth while to risk liberty so that the facts of his case should be known and actions taken accordingly.

And, as they left the prison, they were asked (by some of those inside) to call attention to the case of a poor woman condemned to hang within a week for infanticide and not yet pardoned by the Governor-General, though clearly not responsible for her action. Once again even jail authorities recognise that it is only 'politicals' who will get prison wrongs righted, prison grievances redressed.

Our prisoners were released in time to do honor to Tone's memory by taking part in the Bodenstown annual pilgrimage, to which Republicans were all flocking on June 20th.

'A week's events in Ireland's capital'
Irish World, 17 July 1926

An Irish bishop's voice, that of Dr O'Doherty, Bishop of Galway, has at last been raised in condemnation of the Free State Executive. His Lordship speaks with refreshing candor, on the occasion of an indignation meeting held last Friday in Galway, to protest against the government drive against Galway University College. What executions, treason acts, boundary betrayals, wholesale emigration, and unemployment did not achieve, has at last been accomplished by the government plan to starve out University College, Galway; and, on the scriptural principle of the heart being found where the treasure is, there is a cry upraised from Connaught that has proved strong enough to deafen and stupify Mr Hogan, Minister for Agriculture, who, as a local deputy, attended the protest meeting, trying, in vain, to shift the blame onto the absent shoulders of Mr Blythe, the bold, bad Minister for Finance.

Galway College

Mr Blythe following his usual Cromwellian traditions by way of bettering his predecessor's slogan of 'Hell or Connaught', had determined to close down Galway College, establishing in its stead a station for 'Marine Biology'. Connaught was to become the limbo where professors, deprived of government patronage, were to sit in the darkness of deep-sea exploration, shut off from the Merrion Street paradise so freely opened to their colleagues in Dublin and Cork.

Behind the suggested closing-down of Galway is decidedly the desire to aim at the Irish language; for those who wish Galway College expanded would fain have the City of the Tribes made the centre of Gaelic civilization, fed with students and scholars from the Gaeltacht.

German professors are once more in the West (one is now in residence on the Blasket Islands) making a comparative study of Irish phonetics from various living Irish dialects. In the Sorbonne, Paris, are students specializing in the study of Celtic languages, particularly the Irish tongue. Here at home, in response to the Anglomaniacs now in control of affairs to whom anything Irish is taboo, the plot to shut down Galway is but the natural sequence of the move to dismiss teachers of Irish throughout the country by imposing on them a test of 'loyalty'.

Apparently, however, Mr Blythe and his colleagues have over-reached themselves and have succeeded at last in getting the 'West awake'; for several voices, that 'like thunder spake', were uplifted last week to make 'England (and her Colonial Ministers) quake'. All Connaught rallied against the Government and easily routed Mr Hogan, who declared himself convinced that a case had been made for retaining the College, repudiating Mr Blythe's references to a 'toy University' as 'unfortunate'. I quote Dr O'Doherty's indictment verbatim, refreshing as it is rare:

Bishop's Criticism
'Proposing the resolutions, most Rev. Dr O'Doherty, Bishop of Galway, who got an enthusiastic reception, said that when he spoke of the Minister of Education he wanted it to be understood that he was speaking of the Government as a whole. It would not do when questions of this kind arose to say that the Minister for Finance blocked the way. Whatever had been done or left undone in regard to Galway was the doing or undoing of the Government as a whole. Mr Blythe said they had not been in earnest, but since the first whisper of tampering with the college they had been deadly in earnest. We can tell the Ministry of Education and the Executive Council as a whole that we have our college, that we want to keep it, and that we will keep it and develop it,' added his lordship, amid applause.

'The Government satirically suggested for Galway a marine biological station. He confessed he did not know what that meant. He learned however, that it had something to do with the counting of fish.'

'Our answer to the Government was that we did not want that,' continued His Lordship. 'What is the use to us of this marine biological station, when foreign trawlers are reaping the harvest of our seas and raking the spawning beds along the Irish coast?'

Matter for Minister
'What is the Minister for Fisheries doing that he cannot take up this marine biological station? The boat for the protection of our fisheries, as far as I can learn, is used largely as a House boat.'

'If the Government wanted us to take an interest in marine biology they must first protect our shores, they must first show an interest in the people trying to make a living out of the fisheries, and then when the fish were available they might even in the University examine the habits of the fish,' added his Lordship amid laughter and applause.

In the matter of Irish he thought there was little sincerity on the part of the Government, who were neglecting the largest Gaeltacht in Ireland – in the West.

The suggestion in the proposal at one of the conferences that Galway should be governed like the other universities but should remain under the Ministry of Education in case Dublin and Cork were converted into separate and district universities, was, said his Lordship, that no body of men could be found in Connaught to govern the college honestly – that there would be corruption and that the wrong men would be appointed.

It was an astounding proposal, coming from Mr Blythe or anyone else, 'and a man in his position should not make a statement like that,' said his Lordship. 'He has had reason since to be careful about throwing mud. You will remember that as a director of the Land Bank he has been frantically engaged in sweeping mud from his own door, and he is the last person who should throw mud.'

Gaelic League Support
Frank Fahy TD, Republican representative for Galway, (secretary to the Gaelic League) pledged the support of the Gaelic League for Galway; and so many different voices were raised that, when Mr Hogan appeared, it was as a criminal in the dock, a convicted criminal who has not been recommended to mercy. He threw Mr Blythe overboard immediately; and amid derisive interruptions, proceeded to give definite and humble assurances that Galway would be permitted to develop, and to work out its own destiny, unimpeded.

The moral of the demonstration is obvious; that, when the Government is faced by a determined and united opposition, not a mere perfunctory one, it can be forced to yield. Galway offers a warning and a precedent. Connaught has put Mr Blythe and the Ministry on the run: it is for the sister-provinces to follow up its action by similar massed attack on national lines, for a natural objective, not a mere saving of vested interests.

'A week's events in Ireland's capital'
Irish World, 24 July 1926
Éamon de Valera has just completed a successful tour of the West and part of Southwest (Clare and Kerry). Conferences and public meetings have been held in Roscommon, Ballaghaderreen, Ballina, Balla (Mayo), Tubbercurry (Sligo), Ballinasloe and Loughrea (Galway), at all of which the new organisation was got under way, preparatory to the election campaign which may take place within the year. Everywhere Éamon de Valera was warmly received: and, as his car went from place to place, the people, recognising him, passed the word along, and pressed forward to shake his hand and pass a kindly Irish

greeting to him in the old tongue. In Ennis he expounded his policy, (of getting rid one by one of the shackles that fetter) from the self-same spot where nearly three years ago, in August 1923, he started his election address to his constituents, and was interrupted by the murderous volley of the Free State soldiery that proceeded to take him prisoner with every show of violence.

The speech was never finished: it did not get beyond the first words: and now, in the fullness of time, he came again before his people in Clare to lay down his plan of campaign, this time with no armed forces intervening. From Clare he went to his native county, Limerick, where his youth and early manhood were spent, addressing a large meeting in Abbeyfeale and a conference of delegates at Newcastle West. Shamus Colbert, TD, chairman of West Limerick Organising Committee, presided. T. McEllistrom, TD, General Michael Kilroy, TD, P. J. Rutledge, TD, Frank Carty, TD, were his chairmen in Mayo, Sligo and Galway: while Gerald Boland, TD, accompanied him during his Roscommon tour. In Ennis, in spite of the fact that Bishop Fogarty's influence had the local Feis cancelled, and consequently that there was no opportunity to run special trains, the meeting was a huge success, while many came from Limerick to attend it and to hear for themselves de Valera's message to his constituents.

Later a big rally took place in Tralee, attended by delegates from various parts of Kerry: while on his return to Dublin, last Sunday, Éamon de Valera spoke at a large open-air gathering held in the grounds of Roebuck House, Clonskea.[12]

Women's Congress
An important International Congress of Women of the League of Peace and Freedom, is being held this week, in Dublin, in the National University Building. Twenty-four nations have sent delegates. The International President of the Congress is Jane Addams of Chicago, the distinguished internationalist and pacifist. Dublin has stretched out both hands to receive these women from far-off countries, and to show them honor during their stay among us. Such vital problems as Imperialism and Militarism, the Rights of Minorities, the Next Steps to Peace, are to be discussed. The Republican Hostesses Committee are taking charge of the delegates for a one-day excursion through the historic valley of the Boyne, rich in archaeological interest. The distinguished Republican musician, Arthur Durley, is giving a special lecture and recital on Irish music; and an Irish Ceilidh will conclude the Congress. The occasion affords a valuable and much needed opportunity for lovers of Ireland to show to friendly foreigners, centers of thought in their own lands, how far short this ancient nation, British partitioned into two military Crown Colonies, falls of true freedom; and how great a menace to world peace is British militarism, holding nations in unwilling subjection.

Eva Gore-Booth

A true lover of peace and freedom, Eva Gore-Booth, sister of Constance Markievicz, TD, has just passed in London. She will be remembered by every lover of poetry as a writer of poignant Irish lyrics (the 'Waves of Breffny' has a place in every anthology). To lovers of peace she will be known for her beautiful poetic drama, the *Death of Fionavar* (illustrated during her long imprisonment, in Holloway, by Constance Markievicz); and to lovers of Irish freedom she will be recalled as the friend and champion of Roger Casement, of James Connolly, and of every Irish rebel from 1916 onwards. She, with Dora Sigerson[13] (also dead) was one of the first to visit us after 1916, while the fires of Dublin were still smouldering and the graves of the men of 1916 still red-sodded. Her heart and sympathy went out at once to Ireland; and she was one of the first to voice her sympathy in the hostile British press. Her passionate plea was raised later for Casement, for MacSwiney, for Kevin Barry, for Erskine Childers. She never wavered nor faltered in her sympathy which extended to every oppressed people. But a few weeks ago when last I spoke to her, she spoke of the Fascists in Italy, and expressed her revolt against the new tyranny that the Italian people are suffering under, saying that she could not visit Italy, while the Fascists reigned. Then she spoke of the locked-out miners, and their struggle in Britain for decent conditions, picturing graphically various scenes during the brief general strike. She was one of those rare, fine souls, the true internationals, to whom no suffering people or class is alien, in whose heart any cry raised against injustice or wrong found a ready echo. I quote from her dedication of the *Death of Fionavar* ('To the many who died for Freedom and the one who died for Peace.')[14]

> Poets, Utopians, bravest of the brave,
> Pearse and McDonagh, Plunkett, Connolly,
> Dreamers turned fighters but to find a grave,
> Glad for the dream's austerity to die.
> Oh, bitterest sorrow of that land of tears,
> Utopia, Ireland, of the coming time,
> That they true citizens through weary years,
> Can, for thy sake but make their grief sublime!

Message from Maryborough Jail (extract from a Republican prisoner's letter, recently to hand)

'We wish to thank all who assisted in bringing Jack Keogh's case to the notice of the public, particularly those who sacrificed their liberty in so doing.

'There is separate treatment here for political prisoners who have demanded justice have always been ignored and treated with contempt by the Governor and the Board. The enemy hates with a vengeance the IRA men, especially those who left the chapel on account of the Bishop's political pastoral in 1925. If the ordinary prisoners got any encouragement they would make a strong fight to bring the conditions of this prison to the level of the English ones. Many of them are prepared to create trouble over existing conditions.

'Patrick Dunleavy is supposed to be in Hospital here-an ordinary cell. His wound is suppurating and is worse than ever and his general health is very bad. Dr Dwane told him on the 19-5-26 that he would report his condition immediately to the Board. He hopes to get him removed to Mountjoy or released. This is the only prison in the civilized world without a hospital. Dunleavy's is a vital case, and should be brought to the notice of the public.

'Since writing last our position here is unimproved. Life here is becoming more unbearable every day. They are constantly making new regulations and renovating old ones to make things stricter and more severe. Patk. Dunleavy's plight is appalling. I believe Dr Dwane failed to influence the Board to do anything for him. He is now out of "Hospital" (an ordinary cell), where he was locked up for 22 hours out of the 24 and is working in one of the shops. His wound is suppurating worse than ever.'

It is further reported by a released prisoner that the water supply in the jail is contaminated and that there is danger to health from drinking it. Prisoners who showed sympathy with Jack Keogh and protested against the system that drove him and eight others mad in less than a twelve-month, have themselves been isolated in dungeons previously condemned as unfit for habitation.

Congress of Women's International League for Peace and Freedom[15]
July 1926

I must apologise for the fact that I have no written report and I must throw myself in a sense, therefore, on the mercy of this Committee, because there has been some confusion regarding procedure.

Ireland is, as you are doubtless aware, the worst example in the world today of a victim of imperialistic capitalism or of economic imperialism. Personally I find it, as other speakers have found it, very difficult to disentangle imperialism from militarism. We must consider both together. Ireland is an agricultural country. Great Britain is an industrial country. It has always been the policy of Great Britain to use Ireland as her 'back garden'. As a writer has described it – an English writer – it has been Britain's ideal that Ireland should be 'the fruitful mother' – not of human beings – but 'of flocks and herds', that is, that Ireland should produce beef and other food for the neighbouring country. The result is that, very naturally, Ireland has been the victim of economic exploitation. The keynote of this economic position is that our interests have never been consulted when these happen to be contrary to those of the

predominant partner. Although Britain has free trade generally, she has
warred against Irish industries whenever in our history they have seemed to
threaten her own, so we have suffered both from her Free Trade and her
Protection. (I would ask those interested to read the works of Mrs Stopford
Green).[16] Thus our woollen industry was almost wiped out, because British
manufacturers in the past became jealous of its prosperity and succeeded in
getting restrictive measures passed to restrict the industry. The remnants that
you see still surviving of this great industry are those that struggled on under
this handicap. So with our mines and our mineral resources – none have been
allowed free development. Similarly in the past in the days of the Plantations,
when the native Irish were driven to 'hell or Connaught' and British settlers
placed in their stead in north-east Ulster, Britain established and subsidised
the linen industry for their benefit, having crushed the woollen industry in the
South. Briefly, it has been Britain's policy to keep Ireland largely agricultural
and develop it only so far as suited her imperialistic scheme. Ireland has in
consequence, decreased in population, although our birth rate is very high.
We have the extraordinary example of a large birth-rate and a decreasing
population, drained by emigration. Ireland had at the beginning of the 19th
century over eight millions; today she has about three millions and her population is still slightly decreasing. We gained, curiously enough, in Ireland in
population during the war owing to the fact that Ireland resisted conscription,
man power being kept within Ireland and, as Lord French put it, in speaking
on one occasion during the war, we had 'too much man power in Ireland' and
that it must be Britain's policy to get rid of it by emigration so as not to be a
danger to Britain. We would, I think, normally develop along agricultural lines
and cooperative lines, like Denmark, which is at present our chief agricultural
rival. Denmark, in many respects, resembles Ireland and we have much to
learn from her, but, unhappily, we are not free, as she is.

A word with regard to the recent phases of war. Ireland has suffered from
three war phases since 1914. In the beginning of the war a great many Irishmen
volunteered and fought and died, believing that this was a war 'for the freedom
of small nations'. Others did not believe that and they stayed at home, making
any attempt to impose conscription impossible. The Republican Rising took
place in 1916 and from then till 1923 we have had almost continuous war in
Ireland on the part of Britain. We have had what you know as the 'Black and
Tans', the British Army of occupation, and, recently, an acute phase of Civil
War when Great Britain lent arms and ammunition to those who supported the
Free State to aid them in fighting the Republicans. Look round our buildings –
the ruins speak for themselves, war ruins, all representing the various war
phases. We have now Partition of Ireland by Britain, dividing the country into
the Six-County (or Northern) area and the 26-County (or Free State). We
have two parliaments, both under Great Britain, with British-appointed

Governors-General and an arbitrary frontier, settled without consulting the Irish people, either through a referendum or any other way in which a people can be consulted directly. I want to stress the fact that the frontier which cuts 'Southern' Ireland from 'Northern' Ireland is an artificial frontier, presented to us by Britain as un fait accompli and in whose making the people had no voice. We in Ireland would like to see one Ireland, because the island is too small to support these two governments and two armies. I shall give you one example of this crazy patchwork frontier. The most northerly point geographically in Ireland is Tirconaill (Donegal). Yet it belongs politically to 'Southern' Ireland for the purposes of this new frontier. Tirconaill is a county in the extreme north and, if you want to go there from Dublin, you must pass through the Six-county area – have your luggage examined at the Customs, etc., before you proceed further and return to Free State (or Southern) territory. I emphatically agree with the delegate from Great Britain who spoke in her report of the setting up of arbitrary frontiers as a dangerous menace to the peace of the World. All these barriers make for friction and for the necessity of keeping up a standing army. Great Britain has her army in Northern Ireland. We have the Free State Army in the South. We hoped that the method of referendum might be employed in order to ascertain what form of government Ireland would desire. The settlement of the treaty is one imposed on the Irish people – not given as of their choice but given as an alternative to 'immediate and terrible war'. The Irish people have not had the opportunity of settling freely for themselves what form of Government is wanted.

There is the question of minorities and that is always a difficulty. I think yesterday Mrs Swanwick said that sometimes Great Britain opposed the majority and not the minority. It is so in Ireland. Certainly when concessions are made they should be made rather to the minorities than have force imposed on the majorities.

We have, therefore, in Ireland a situation arising out of economic imperialism and militarism and these students who are studying world problems cannot do better than study conditions in Ireland, where, like Egypt and other countries suffering from imperialism, we have these same problems to face.

I shall be glad to supplement my report further by giving any information in my power to those students who would like to follow the subject up further and place at their disposal any literature available.

'Congress of Women's International League for Peace and Freedom'
Irish World, 7 August 1926

For the last week the event that looms largest in our news, and that has created the biggest 'stir' in our Dublin public generally, is the Congress of the Women's International League for Peace and Freedom, now holding its fifth session in our capital. This gathering of women first assembled some years ago at The Hague, inspired by Miss Jane Addams and a group of internationally-minded women from various countries. In 1915, in the height of the great war, they were called together for an attempt at promoting peace. At that time, however, Britain refused passports to some of the Irish delegates (I happened to be one), and all boats between Britain and Holland were stopped for the week, so that even British women, supplied with passports, did not succeed in crossing, while French and other women were similarly prevented by various groups or governments. Since then the Congress has met in Washington and in Vienna, and, by a remarkably fortunate chance, Dublin was chosen as the gathering place this year. Here, too, governments got busy – Italy refused Italian delegates permission to come, Ukrainian women were not allowed to pass through Poland (and hence could not get through); while Britain or the Free State (each laid the blame upon the other) blocked one American women, Mrs Lloyd of Chicago, refusing to give any coherent reason for its action. Eventually she was allowed through: but her younger children (minors both) were prohibited, and had therefore to be left behind in France. One theory is that Mrs Lloyd's name happened to be on the British secret service list as having been friendly to the Irish Republic, and that, Britain's enemies being now the Free State's, she was naturally barred. Congress unanimously passed a resolution, calling upon all governments to abolish the passport system as one of the evil heritages of the war, condemning strongly also the system of Secret Service Archives maintained by governments and used by officials to block certain persons whom they may happen to dislike. Other resolutions passed by Congress included one calling for amnesty for all political prisoners held by various governments, one claiming industrial equality for prisoners and others of a like international character. A proposition embodied in a report laid down the self-evident axiom that uprisings by natives against foreign governments should not be classed as 'rebellious', a proposition that Britain for one has never yet accepted in her relations with her oppressed nationalities.

The most important effect of the Congress was, however, the throwing a flood of light and truth upon conditions in Ireland, such as no counter-camouflage on the part of the Free State could obscure or avert. At last informed and representative women from the world outside were enabled to penetrate our gloom. Journalists, doctors, teachers, world leaders among women, saw Ireland for themselves – saw it 'steadily' and saw it whole! They eagerly welcomed information regarding industrial and social conditions, regarding prisoners, partition, imperialism, emigration and various other problems; and they as eagerly demonstrated their sympathy with us and their desire to help us to real freedom. As Marcelle Capy, the French editor, declared with passion, 'Peace cannot exist without justice', paraphrasing the words of Pearse, 'Ireland unfree can never be at peace.' Mlle Desjardins (the Belgian leader, imprisoned during the war for three years because she helped Belgians to escape) at a meeting held for our prisoners, declared that Ireland had been 'put under lock and key' by Britain and no news of her allowed to penetrate to Europe, but she promised that as a result of her visit, Belgium would now be better informed. French, Belgians, Germans, Americans, Czecho-Slovakian women addressed open-air meetings held by the Irish Women Workers' Union and by the Political Prisoners' Committee, supporting eloquently our plea for freedom for prisoners and better conditions for workers. A delegation of the unemployed waited on Congress, and were heard and addressed later by Jane Addams and others. Later, German, French and American women declined to attend a Viceregal Party given by the Governor-General, arranging to visit the poor of Dublin instead. They later paid a visit to St Ultan's Baby Hospital with Dr Kathleen Lynn, its founder and that night Mme Capy came before Congress to make a passionate plea for the poor and the unemployed of Dublin, calling for a subscription as a gesture, not of pity, but of sympathy for the suffering and the exploited. This was generously responded to. One day was allotted to the Republican Hostesses' Committee for an excursion to the historic Boyne Valley; it proved the happiest and most successful day spent, and each delegate bore away with her a beautiful little souvenir, with quotations from Tone, Pearse, Connolly, Terence MacSwiney, Sheehy Skeffington. Again at the University Buildings a reception was held, at which the Chancellor of the National University Éamon de Valera was a guest of honor, delegates from every country pressing forward to greet one whose name was known to all and honored by all. He took the opportunity of thanking the American delegates (Jane Addams, the International President, Ann Martin and others) on Ireland's behalf for the work that they had done on the Washington Commission of Inquiry to expose the atrocities of British militarism in Ireland.

It will be remembered that Jane Addams was one of the commissioners appointed on that occasion to hear evidence presented on conditions in Ireland, embodied later in a valuable official report. Mary MacSwiney, Muriel MacSwiney,[17] the Lord Mayor of Cork, the Chairman of Thurles Council and many others appeared before the Commission and gave evidence at first hand as to what was happening in Ireland. Éamon de Valera recalled this fine work done by women internationalists, paying a tribute to their courage and public spirit. The delegates later in the week were entertained by Mrs Seán T. O'Kelly,[18] Hon. Albinia Broderick,[19] Mary MacSwiney and others. Much literature was distributed among them, dealing with the Republican position and events since the Treaty, and many came to us to ask for further data.

The general effect of the visit of so many thoughtful and enlightened women was 'to clear up' any of the British-sown propaganda against Ireland, so common throughout Europe. Some who came, believing that Ireland was free and had freely accepted the Treaty, went away wiser. Madame Drevet, a Parisian editress, said with a smile, pointing to the Free State stamp: 'Why it is a lie! They claim the whole of Ireland, but part of the north is not under them, and why do they pretend Ireland is not partitioned?' Jane Addams in her opening speech in the Mansion House quoted the words of Francis Sheehy Skeffington and endorsed them:

> I advocate no mere servile lazy acquiescence in injustice. I am, and always will be, a fighter. But I want to see the age-long fight against injustice clothe itself in new forms, suited to a new age.

'A panic run for "safe" seats'
Irish World, 4 September 1926

Now that the Dublin Horse Show (which, under the auspices of the 'Royal' Dublin Society, keeps up its Imperialistic tradition as of yore) is over, and Dublin has once more subsided into its usual jog-trot, Indian princes and British captains having departed after the usual wining and dining at the Viceregal Lodge, and in strike-picketed restaurants, we are permitted to hear the 'perturbing news' that the gulf between imports and exports steadily widens, and that our adverse trade-balance now amounts (in the Free State) to considerably over nineteen million pounds sterling.

Decline in Trade

Even the much talked of 'invisible exports' cited to prove that all is still well, do not afford the usual consolation; for as Mr George Russell's organ, the *Irish Statesman*, plaintively puts it 'the available material only stretched a little over half the way'. In plainer English, we do not make ends meet. Mr Russell cries for a Mussolini to solve the problem by imposing a drastic dictatorship, or for Bishop Berkeley's panacea, a 'wall of brass round Ireland' a thousand feet high. One thinks of Swift's trenchant advice in these days of coal-rationing and threatened shortage, 'Burn everything English, except their coal'. This is the official report (if these were not cold government figures they might be deemed Republican propaganda).

'For the year ended June 30 imports from the Saorstat into Britain and exports from Britain to the Saorstat formed smaller proportions of Britain's total trade than the year before, while the actual values of imports and exports were both about one-eighth lower.'

This fact is revealed in figures published in the British Board of Trade Journal, which show that British imports from the Saorstat for the period amounted to £41,669,000, against £47,717,000 for the previous year, being 3.34 p.c. of the imports from all countries against 5.47 p.c.

Exports to the Saorstat of British produce and manufacturers were valued at £37,136,000, against £42,228,000 or 5.17 p.c. of the exports to all countries, against 5.28, and imported merchandise at £10,675,000, against £11,1551,000 or 7.44 p.c. against 7.77 p.c. of the exports of imported merchandise to all countries.

The value of British exports to the Saorstat per head of the population of the Saorstat for the year ended June 30, was £11 14s. 10d.

Nor are things better in the Six-County area, Britain's spoiled darling. Here there is a marked decrease in the linen export (Britain's subsidized industry), owing to competition with Belgium and France, where, on account of the present low rate of exchange, foreign linen is sold at much lower rates. The adverse trade balance in the Free State is ascribed largely to the coal crisis in Britain. Formerly, it was attributed to the 'menace of Republicanism'. It grows since the 'Treaty' every year more marked; but, of course, it would be considered almost blasphemous to put it down to the latter.

An American Critic

It is amusing to note that ex-Judge Cohalan, formerly so loud in extravagant eulogy of the Free State, now strikes a critical note. In a recent interview to the press, he made stress on the contrast between the manner in which British representatives in America boasted their country as a tourist's resort on every possible occasion, while Ireland is neglected in spite of 'the capable minister at Washington'. 'Why,' he asked, 'does he (Mr Smiddy) go round to the Chambers of Commerce, Boards of Transportation meetings and the learned societies, and place before them the real conditions in Ireland?' Surely ex-Judge Cohalan knows the answer to that riddle. He has also discovered what your readers are already fully aware of, that 'landing in Ireland is made as difficult as possible . . . a case of 500 people having to wait in a stormy sea at Roche's Point, near Cobh, while baggage and mails were put on. There should be at least the same facilities for landing as there were at Cherbourg.' Thus his lament. It is but a confirmation of what has been stated again and again in these columns – yet even now this new critic does not draw the obvious moral.

Éamon de Valera, speaking last week at Castlepollard, Co. Westmeath (Lawrence Ginnell's former constituency); emphasized the fact that Ireland was self-supporting economically, and could support a much larger population. He dealt also with the enormous and ever-increasing cost of the Free State government as compared with that of other countries; showing how the Army is kept, not to defend Ireland against the foreigner – it is not large enough for that – but to hold the Irish people down.

Ireland was neither a pleasure resort for tourists nor a bullock farm for England. Her prosperity depending not upon the success of the Horse Show, but upon the work of the small farmer, the labourer, the artisan. Empty pockets, poorly stocked farms and crushing taxes do not spell prosperity.

It is curious to note that while the Free State government is, even on the admission of supporters like George Russell and ex-Judge Cohalan, lacking in many respects in its duty towards the people, lax in looking after their interests or safe guarding their material welfare, it should be rallying with all its might to the protection of the foreign usurers in its midst.

Under the 'Treason Act'

As a sequel to the fifty raids made upon Republicans in search of documents seized in money lenders offices, several Republicans were brought up for trial – among them Michael Price, D. O'Donoghoe, Fiona Plunkett, (daughter of Count Plunkett, sister of Joseph Plunkett), Roisin O'Doherty. The descent upon the usurers when their books were taken for examination, is described as 'conspiracy and armed robbery' and the Treason Act is drawn upon for various high-sounding and terrific expressions, 'maintaining an unlawful military force', 'carrying military dispatches', 'organising a military body not established by law', and so forth. Two youths of fifteen, are also among the arraigned. The police appear to be the only witnesses against the prisoners, the money lenders themselves being denied testifying or identifying. The prisoners refusing to recognise 'the court by law established' (the British recognised one) were sent to Mountjoy on remand, to await trial later. Previously they were bestowed for a night in the filthy Bridewells which are vermin-infested and foul. So bad were conditions that the prisoners, on arriving at Mountjoy, had to send out their clothes to be disinfected. The Free State, in its zeal to protect the usurers, is doing its best to make a State trial out of the cases and may be relied upon as in Treason Act cases usually, to pack juries and intimidate witnesses.

The women are specially indicted for 'concealing treasonable correspondence upon their persons', the police apparently gaining in some occult way from their appearance the presence of such documents, for Superintendent Ennis, on arresting Miss O'Doherty on suspicion, declared that he 'had reason to believe' she carried 'treasonable documents'. Under the Treason Act almost anything against the government may be so classed.

Scurrying for Shelter

Now that the talking-shop is closed, all mid-November ministers are turning uneasy eyes to their constituencies with a view to 'mending their fences' between this and the General Election, now looming larger on the horizon. We are told by a government organ that there is much perturbation in the ranks, and much inquiry as to the relative safety of certain seats, formerly deemed thoroughly reliable. The game of 'general post' may be resorted to, ministers changing places with the rank and file so as to secure some safer berth, the said rank and file parting with their security naturally for a consideration in the shape of some government post where elections cease from troubling.

Monaghan is said to be 'through' with Mr Blythe and he is already rumoured to be turning his eyes to the west; though whether there is safety there for him must remain to be seen. Lynch, in Kerry, Desmond Fitzgerald in Dublin, Burke in Tipperary, even Cosgrave himself in Kilkenny – none are deemed sure of re-election. In fact, it is only in a Unionist constituency that a minister may hope for victory; even there, not an easy one. As a weekly organ (non-Republican) admits (*The Irish Statesman* itself), the 'star politicians who invaded their constituencies with the idea that their part was merely to wave a fiery cross came in for a bad shock. Their job would be more like that of a man trying to kindle a fire with sods of wet turf.'

Australia

Happier (for the present at any rate) is the lot of the Free State Delegates allotted at public expense to attend the Empire Parliamentary Conference in Australia. Two senators and two members of the Lower House are chosen – Senator Sir E. Coey Biggar, Senator O'Hanlon (Farmer's Party), Major Bryan Cooper (Unionist pro-Britisher) and O. Esmonde, TD. The British and Irish delegation left Southampton together (the notorious Arthur Henderson 'representing' British Labour, Lord Salisbury and other British Conservatives) and were fittingly 'blessed' officially on their departure by Mr Amery, British Secretary for Colonial Affairs.

'O'Kelly and de Valera speak in Dublin'
Irish World, 16 October 1926

On Friday, September 24th, Fianna Fáil held its first open air rally in Dublin's largest thoroughfare, O'Connell Street, about six months after the opening campaign which Éamon de Valera inaugurated in La Scala Theatre.

A Great Meeting

It was well that the organisers of last night's meeting planned an open-air demonstration; for, apart from the fact that such a gathering always strikes a more popular note and makes a wider appeal than an indoor one, last night's assembly could not have been fitted into Dublin's largest hall. It almost filled the space between the Father Mathew Statue and the Parnell monument; and it completely jammed the street across, leaving but the narrowest passage for the trams to pass on one side, all traffic being barred on the other. From windows all around, there was a listening gallery; many climbed on statues, lamp standards and every jutting space available to catch a sight of 'the Chief', and to give him a ringing ovation.

The contrast with the Government's admission-by-ticket, police-protected indoor gatherings is striking – a spectator at the Listowel meeting for Mr Cosgrave and Mr O'Sullivan told me that the crowd did not number 800 in all, counting in police and plain-clothes detectives!

Last night a special lorry held the press, and a large number of foreign correspondents were in attendance. The meeting was primarily held in honor of Alderman Seán T. O'Kelly, TD for North Dublin (which area, as he reminded us he represented in the Dublin City Council for over 20 years, being the city's senior alderman), to welcome him home from his mission as Republican Envoy to the United States. The meeting afforded him an opportunity of addressing his constituents once more, and of explaining the Fianna Fáil programme to which he had pledged support.

Seán MacEntee, ex-TD Hon. Treasurer of Fianna Fáil, presided. The meeting lasted from eight till nearly eleven; and though the first touch of Autumnal frost was in the air, it gathered in numbers and enthusiasm as it went on. The audience numbered three or four thousand; and it was composed almost entirely of the workers of Dublin, the same men and women who rallied to James Connolly in the GPO, Countess Markievicz, TD, Connolly's disciple, representing Dublin in the Dáil from 1918 was on the platform. So were Gerald Boland, TD, brother of Harry Boland, Dr McCarville, TD and other deputies resident in or representing Dublin.

Mr O'Kelly's Speech

Seán T. O'Kelly dealt in his lengthy address with the history of the movement from the early days of Sinn Féin through 1916 onwards, covering the Black and Tan period, the Truce, the Pact after the Treaty vote, the Provisional government, the Civil War, and, finally, the last three years of the present administration. It was a story of high hopes blighted, of sacrifice and struggle (the word that seemed to occur oftenest in his speech was 'sacrifice'), from Wilson's failure at the Versailles Peace Conference to Griffith's and Collin's failure at the Downing Peace negotiations. Even after the disastrous acceptance, 'under duress', of the Treaty, he showed how things could have been made good had Collins and Griffith been true to the Pact arrangement, namely, to run a Coalition government until the Irish people had an opportunity of voting on an Irish-made constitution and on the Treaty. He had himself been offered by Michael Collins the post of Minister for Finance or Local Government under the Provisional government; but had refused, because he rightly held that it was for his Republican colleagues to make the choice of their representatives, not the Treaty Party . . .

While Seán T. O'Kelly declared that he had no regrets and no apologies to offer for his part in the past, he hoped that another fight would not be necessary; because he believed that, under Fianna Fáil, a separatist movement could be launched and brought to realization without the further shedding of blood. For that a united people was necessary – the whole people of Ireland, to use Mitchel's phrase, must be rallied in order to end British domination, the source of all our political ills.

He reviewed in conclusion the situation in America and stated that it was his belief that we could rely, as of yore, upon America's assistance and support to rid the country of the present incubus, the oath and to 'organize the general discontent' of the country with the present usurping junta.

De Valera Speaks

Éamon de Valera then spoke, receiving ringing cheers of welcome from the large crowd. As he spoke the meeting grew larger and more densely packed. He was heard with sympathy and close attention, and there was not a single interruption, not a note of dissent, while every statement of principle, every argument of unity against the common enemy, was applauded again and again, with cries of 'we'll follow you!' 'Up the Republic!' and, at the end, three lusty cheers were given for a 'Free Ireland under an Irish Republic'.

The keynote of the speech was optimism – it ended with the words, 'I have more hope in Ireland today than at any time since the Treaty.' Basing his principles on the bed-rock of Wolfe Tone, Connolly, and Fintan Lalor, to the right so well expressed by all of these of Ireland to her own soil 'from the sod to the sky', for her own people for ever, he showed what a mockery the claim of the Free State was for 'sovereignty' when at every point they were hemmed in by foreign interference. Every promise held out by the supporters of the Treaty – no Oath of Allegiance, an Irish Constitution, the Revision of Partition by a referendum in the Six-Counties, the Evacuation by the British – none had been kept. The Oath of Allegiance stood as a barrier to each elected deputy, the Irish-made constitution had been scrapped, and a British-made document substituted; the Boundary Commission had come to nought, no vote being allowed to take place on the issue; and as to the evacuation by British troops, why but the other day in Cobh he saw British troops in Khaki walking about the streets, while in the Six-County area they were entrenched. So much for the statement accepted by so many who ought to have known better that 'the Treaty could be interpreted as Ireland wanted', so much for the 'stepping-stoners'. The army of the Free State, costing us millions each year, was there to help by means of the Treason Act to prevent any step being taken to achieve that freedom.

As he warmed up into his speech, one could see the listening faces lighting up with the old hope, with a wistfulness and a yearning; and many of those faces looked pinched and wan, for in every crowd gathered in Dublin's streets today there are hungry men and women, workless and homeless, yet clinging to a grim hope that things may yet mend and that their dreams of better days are not entirely vain.

'Neutrality'

Éamon de Valera showed that the Oath is no 'mere symbol', as its apologists would have it; that the King means the British Cabinet; and that allegiance to King George means allegiance to British politicians and obedience to their behests.

Dealing with the Imperial Conference, now exercising the minds of politicians (at which Cosgrave, O'Higgins, Blythe and MacNeill, it is stated, will be present), he showed how utterly futile was the discussion about the Free State's 'neutrality' in time of war, when already a clause in the Treaty has laid it down that 'in time of strained relations between Britain and another country' certain facilities must be given to Britain in Ireland, involving her as a belligerent whether she chooses or not. The Treaty disposes of any claim Ireland could put forward to neutrality.

As to those who make little of the oath, they are but as the fox in the fable, whose tail was cut. Éamon de Valera explained further at length how he envisages the removal of the oath – from without, rather than from within. He does not expect it to come from the action of any party in the Parliament, but from the people themselves at the polling-booth as a definite mandate, accepting only candidates who refuse to serve two masters, and who own but one allegiance, namely to the Irish people.

Strong Hope for Ireland

Dealing with the Shannon scheme, he showed the alternative scheme which the Dáil had already prepared before the Treaty, with a view to keeping at home as many of the Irish people as are now drained by emigration. He reviewed in detail the census revelations, about which the Free State politicians and their press are maintaining an uneasy silence. (These have been fully dealt with already in the *Irish World*). He showed how Dáil Éireann could, had it been allowed to function freely, have provided work for the population now fleeing the country. Since the Treaty a quarter of a million have gone. But it is part of Britain's scheme of things that Ireland be her grazing ranch, providing cheap food in a near market for her industrial centres. She is our 'best customer', not for 'our beautiful eyes', but, as Lloyd George admitted to Griffith across the table at the pre-Treaty pourparlers, for the sake of our 'beautiful butter'. When a people leave a country en masse, as the British economist Stuart Mill puts it, something is wrong with its government. Something is wrong with ours; and as de Valera puts it, they are now asking 'to be returned on their record'. Well deal with them on their record – and put them out! They have carried out Lord French's behest, which he himself could not do; they have got rid of our 'surplus manhood and womanhood', by emigration. The 'poisonous insects' as he called our youth, are gone or going. They have carried on unconstitutionally since the Treaty. They claim to have 'restored order' – but it was they who destroyed it. As well claim to cure a patient on whom a needless operation was forced, and who was by a miracle recovering from the ill-effects. Finally, he said as quoted above, that he had more hope in Ireland today than ever, since the Treaty had been signed – hope in the possibilities now offered of getting rid of our year-long nightmare, of forming all who loved Ireland into one party, with one objective. For as Davis said, there are only two parties in Ireland (call them what you will) the party that stands for Ireland and the party that stands for the British connection. No one can serve Ireland and England at the same time. And the time for choosing will soon be at hand.

'The renegade's return'
Irish World, 25 December 1926
The Safety Act, rushed through, without ever a vote, by the subservient Upper and Lower Houses and now, 'Law' (having obtained King George's imprimatur through his representative the Governor-General) has proved a damp squib. The Crumlin raid which occasioned the final 'emergency' proclamation is now well-known to have been arranged by the CID themselves, with government connivance, it was immediately disavowed by the Republican Army through *An Phoblacht*.

'Working' the 'Safety' Act
The arresting near Kilmessan of two armed 'amateur detectives' by the local police caused a flutter at headquarters for those official or unofficial investigators (since released) appear to have been a part of the 'murder gang' sent out to kill Republicans after the manner by which Noel Lemass[20] and many others were disposed of.

It is a significant commentary on the safety of the new Safety Act that men, admittedly armed and actually arrested can be pulled aside and be at once released, apparently still armed.

A dump also found near Kilmessan, on a Republican's field was the subject of investigation. The Republican, against whom the frame up was engineered, was acquitted by the Free State Court, the evidence being insufficient to convict. He was at once re-arrested under the Safety Act, upon leaving the court.

This formula is now, in fact, becoming stereotyped. Any Republican who is cleared of some trumped-up charge or against whom 'informations' are refused, because no evidence is forthcoming, is at once 'interned' under the Safety Act, before he leaves the court precincts. The official procedure appears to be as follows. A band of armed CID select certain well-known Republican houses; raid them during the small hours; arrest those found on the premises, trump up some charge or other, (it hardly matters what, because the same need not be sustained subsequently by any evidence whatsoever); next bring the men up for trial; and when they are duly acquitted of burglary, possession of arms, murder of policemen or the like, they are interned before they leave the court under the 'Safety Act'; the only evidence against them being that they were declared innocent of the offence with which they were charged. The police notion apparently is that, being proved innocent merely argues great cunning and depravity, making the accused too dangerous to be longer at large. Many men taken in the first round-up and released have since been re-arrested and interned. One noticeable feature of the arrests in Munster is that men, prominently connected with the GAA and largely responsible for the recent revival of general interest in Gaelic Athletic football and hurling contests are among the first victims of the government's malice, John Joe Sheehy, Captain of the victorious Kerry team, and Mr McCarthy, chairman of the GAA are examples. As a protest, the Kerry team cancelled a match in Waterford last Sunday, refusing to travel.

As to the number now arrested, it is impossible to estimate, for daily, more are being added to the list, while a few releases have taken place, apparently also on no particular principle.

Hundreds of raids have taken place throughout the country; and, as usual, the ordinary police duties are being neglected because the police are busy on political activities. As an example of this, it is noteworthy that, though under the recent School Attendance Act, the police were supposed, from November 1st, to take over the duties of school attendance officers, (local officials and local committees being disbanded), it is now found that the police are 'not ready' to assume this duty and the local committees confined to function as heretofore. The police, always a political and semi-military force in Ireland, are too busy raiding and arresting Republicans to attend to anything else just now.

For a Panic Election
Yet, as I have stated above, the act has proved a failure, as far as its primary object is concerned, namely, the return on a panic 'safety' issue of the present

junta to power. Already rumour is again rife that we shall not have an early election (though anything is possible) because the country is not a whit excited about its safety, still regarding the Government as its chief enemy. So the junta may, after all, decide to hang on till the eleventh hour, continuing meanwhile to arrest and intern key Republicans (both Fianna Fáil and Sinn Féin), so that its only serious rivals may be crippled.

The floating of a new loan is mooted, a new commission (the Tariff commission) has been appointed; and various feelers have been put out for possible allies in case a coalition government should be set up. In spite of all the industrial prostrations at the London Imperial Conference, the party funds are reported low; Big Business like the sibyl of old demanding an ever higher price. The Chamber of Commerce Banquet at which the Governor-General's indiscretions proved such a scandal has not helped matters. The more concessions that were made to the vested interests and the imperial connections, the more are exacted.

The Anti-Irish Church

Having found the government hitherto amenable to pressure, the Ascendancy party now wishes to remove from its path 'compulsory Irish' as it is called, and requires government assurance that it be dropped from its party platform at least as far as non-Papists are concerned. The Protestant Party of the *Irish Times* finds something incompatible with sound Protestantism in the speaking or teaching of any language save English, and just as Mr (now Dr) Cosgrave found refuge in the election cry, 'the country is in danger', so too the 'church of Ireland' (as the Episcopalian Church of the Anti-Irish minority quaintly mis-calls itself) has raised a sectarian cry, 'the Church is in danger!'

Whether the government will drop Irish overboard in response to clamor, or will be content, as heretofore, to impose it upon the groundlings and to ignore it in the highest branches of civil service, Judiciary, and the Administration generally, remains to be seen. The Ascendancy objects even to the merest camouflage, and has of late been showing its teeth.

Then the Protection – Free Trade issue is causing trouble within government ranks, and a certain cleavage even among members of the executive. All of which considerations have again given pause to the Junta, and may yet succeed in postponing the election; though it is said that some members in the inner counsels of the government would like to rush the issue, notwithstanding. As at present advised (and the situation shifts almost hourly), it looks as though the 'wait and see' counsels would prevail, it is certain, as I have already stated more than once, that, whenever the Junta does make up its mind, it will rush the election; consequently Republicans must be prepared for this contingency any time from the New Year onwards. The Safety Act, launched in the hope of winning a panicky population for the 'saviours' of the country, has failed. These stunts, once so effective, no longer work.

Suppressing the Light

The Junta, however, is by no means tired of its new toy. Last week *An Phoblacht* (the official Republican organ), was reduced in size to four pages, and came out late, owing to difficulties in printing. This week it is back to war days, appearing as a single sheet, just as the *Republican Bulletin*, edited by Erskine Childers, used to appear in the Black and Tan days. As the British used to do, the present regime does not suppress, but puts the responsibility upon the printers of having their machinery broken up; accordingly it has become increasingly difficult to get the paper printed. It will be remembered that, in the later days of the war, *Éire* had to be brought out in Glasgow, later in Manchester, no Irish printer being in a position to take the risk; or, if willing able, for other reasons to do so. *An Phoblacht* will, no doubt, overcome its present difficulties and is even now bravely endeavouring to cope with them; for its little type written sheet preserved continuity, and at the same time gives in 'stop press' form, latest news. The editor[21] and assistant editor[22] are both being sought by the forces of the crown; and this too had made production difficult.

Under the heading 'Your Majesty Subject', the current issue has the following item, worth recording:

Before Kevin O'Higgins crossed to Dublin on Tuesday week to preside over the Proclamation of a State of Emergency, he signed in London, an address to the British King, containing the words:

> We ... desire before we separate, to express once again our fidelity and devotion to Your Majesty and her Majesty the Queen ... The foundation of our work has been the sure knowledge that to each of us, as to all Your Majesty's subjects, the Crown is the abiding symbol an emblem of the unity of the British Commonwealth of Nations.

Kevin O'Higgins's house has for some time been heavily guarded; in fact, up to last week, it was the only ministerial residence under police protection. Since their return from the Imperial Conference, all the ministers have been under special police guard; and their houses have had police in uniform put on them, in addition to the plainclothes men of the secret service. This attention has also been given to the Speaker of the House, Mr Hayes, who for purpose of police protection, is apparently regarded as coming within the meaning of the 'Safety Act', though at other times he is represented as 'non party', like Mr Healy,[23] the King's Representative. Last Saturday night the windows of Mr Cosgrave's and Mr Blythe's houses were broken – hence the reinforced guard.

This week at the Gaiety Theatre, Mr Healy, attending with Mr Monroe the Newfoundland premier (his first public appearance since his late intemperate Banquet Speech, as one of the weekly press organs aptly phrased it), met with a hostile reception which had hastily to be drowned in music. A storm of booing and hissing through the house drove the King's representative behind the curtain of the Viceregal Box, while the Colonial Premier looked as if he expected a bomb to be thrown at any moment. Mr Healy summoned a special squad of police to conduct him to his carriage, fearing further popular hostility.

'Further details of atrocities'
Irish World, 22 January 1927

On Monday, December 20th, at College Green, Art O'Connor, and Éamon de Valera spoke at a large meeting, called by the Political Prisoners' Committee, to demand the release of George Gilmore, now fighting for the rights of political prisoners. Judge Byrne, (who sentenced him to eighteen months hard labor, for his part in the rescue of the nineteen Republican prisoners from Mountjoy), has had a special armed guard on his house ever since, being raised to Ministerial rank, for, since the Imperial Conference speeches and commitments all the Free State Ministers have had double guards, who challenge any passer-by who seems to look like a Republican. Mr Cosgrave, apparently, takes no chances, for motor-cars appearing on his street are stopped and searched. The Emergency Act has thus turned back history's pages, and we have once again Emergency men, as they used to be called in the days of Buckshot Foster.

The Gilmore Case

George Gilmore,[24] as Éamon de Valera pointed out, is being singled out for specially vindictive treatment because of the neat and daring jail delivery which set Ireland laughing at the Treason Act, and because, also, of his defiant challenge in court, when he declared that no judge would make him do hard labor. The warders, who also owe a grudge because they were out-witted on the former occasion, told Mrs Gilmore, George's mother, that they would yet 'tame' him, as they had 'tamed' others, so the process is now in full swing.

He has been beaten so that the sounds could be heard by other prisoners, flung, without his clothes, into basement cell, (refusing to wear felon's clothes, his own were carefully removed), put on punishment diet of bread and water, and later, when other methods failed, forcibly put into a strait jacket and the hose turned on him.

It will be remembered that the savage hosing of prisoners led to the general hunger-strike of prisoners two years ago. It was only after two prisoners had died as a result of a strike, extending over nearly forty days, that proper treatment was granted to the politicals. For this principle, Thomas Ashe and others sacrificed their lives – in earlier days John Maindeville died, a victim of prison savagery, while William O'Brien and John Dillon, in the eighties – and Michael Davitt still earlier – fought in their turn for decent prison treatment, the first named refusing also to don convict clothes in Tullamore, and finally winning a victory over his jailors by getting a suit of 'Tullamore Tweed' smuggled into his cell. Each new set of prisoners seems, in turn, to have to fight over again the battle for political treatment, for Britain, almost alone among the civilized nations, makes no distinction between politicals and criminals, save indeed, that at times the former fare worse than the latter at the hands of the authorities.

So the 'Free' State, subservient in all things affecting 'rebels' to Britain, also refuses any distinction between the vilest criminal offences and those involving no 'moral turpitude'. When the renegade Judge Byrne, who loads the dice against Republicans, gave his sentence (the maximum) and added 'hard labor', he meant therefore, to take it out on Gilmore – a Protestant Republican from the North – and to spare him nothing. Previously, for months, Donal O'Donoghoe and Michael Price had, too, been fighting the same battle. They had just won out, and were at last, after several months, during which Price had not left his cell for exercise, granted the 'boon' of association, which the women prisoners had also successfully claimed and won, being allowed to exercise and work together.

Mary Comerford, after over ten days' hunger strike, was informed of this by The McDermott, member of the Prison Board, who came to visit her. He had functioned under the British previously and was one of those in authority when Thomas Ashe was done to death. He promised her that if she discontinued her protest, these concessions would be granted, and told her further of the releases of the internees. Satisfied that the principle had been won, she agreed to come off the hunger-strike, not knowing that George Gilmore, the latest victim, was even then fighting the same fight, and is still fighting it. Like Sisyphus of old, whose task it was to roll a stone to the top of a mountain and to see it ever tumble down again, recommencing his labor at the foot, each prisoner has to fight the battle over again. It was hoped that, as a result of the agitation, Gilmore might also have won out, but up to date, his grim and lonely struggle still goes on. An unconfirmed rumor has it that he has just been removed to hospital.

A further prisoner scandal has been partially exposed, concerning the brutal ill-treatment by the Civic Guards of suspected Republicans who fell into their hands in Waterford. Mr O'Higgins himself, as I stated last week, has had to make some very damaging admissions and to promise an inquiry into the matter. One prisoner has had to be removed to hospital as a result of police beating, and kicking – a fractured skull, some broken bones and some grave internal injuries are reported. The promised inquiry is being held behind closed doors, and it is not likely that much will emerge therefrom. Those conducting it are all strong supporters of the government, some of them holding official positions, so it is hardly likely that they will do anything drastic, though if one victim dies, there might be some minor scapegoat selected to bear the sins of the force – and like Sir David Harrel of Bachelors Walk fame, to retire, in order later to be rewarded with some government post. *An Phoblacht* states that Mr O'Higgins was wishful of making an example – he likes to pose as a sea-green incorruptible at times, though his own record hardly justifies that pose – but that Commissioner O'Duffy, backed by Cosgrave and others, willed otherwise, not daring to allow the police to be tried in the ordinary criminal courts before a jury, however carefully selected. There has always been one law for the police and the big law-breakers in Ireland, and another for the common folk. Accordingly police are tried in secret, and no breath of publicity is allowed to blow upon their misdeeds.

. . . Meanwhile the war on the Republican press continues. This week *An Phoblacht* is printed once more by a Dublin firm (a different one from the former Dublin one) but in a reduced size, a two page broad-sheet. *Irish Freedom*, the new Republican organ, appears as a monthly, issuing its second number in December, like the first, which aptly synchronized with the Armistice Day protests, a spirited and out-spoken number.

The Christmas Aonach
This Christmas the Aonach, the annual exhibition of Irish goods, was held as usual, being run and patronized largely by Republican or Irish-Ireland supporters. Among the stall holders were Mme MacBride, whose shell-flowers are a beautiful and unique industry, creating things of beauty from Irish sea shells as ravishing as any from France, Mrs Despard whose jams and preserve factory gives much needed employment, Hon. Albinia Broderick, whose Kerry tweeds and rugs, home-spun and home-dyed, were much sought, Miss McDermott, whose leather and enamel work is singularly beautiful. The Christmas cards and calendars with verses from Eva Gore-Booth (poet-sister of Countess Markievicz), Susan Mitchel, James Stephens, Joseph Campbell, were never so beautiful, or so varied as this year. Among the old Gaelic sayings illustrating the strong, simple philosophy of the people, were such gems as 'God's help is nearer than the door.' 'God is strong and He has a good Mother.' – I would like every Irish-born American to have one, and every lover of beauty and color to compare these exquisite cards with the cheap banalities of the mass-production specimens. Many Americans, I am glad to

note, have introduced the custom of importing their Christmas cards from Ireland – it is a happy thought and should commend itself to all.

This Christmastide, too, saw an Irish version of the Cinderella pantomime produced by a specially trained group of school-children for the benefit of St Ultan's Hospital, Dr Lyon's splendid institution for saving of the babies of the poor. This pantomime, entirely in Gaelic, was a great success from every point of view – it is the first attempt to introduce a Christmas pantomime in Irish. John McDonagh's revues are now as regular a feature of Dublin stage-life as the Abbey Theatre itself. All these efforts have sprung from Republican sources and are interesting illustrations of the many phases of the Republican revival. They point a curious contrast to the Anglicized life of the official 'Free' State – the imported fashions, the Bacchanalian orgies, the banquets and junketings with never an individual or distinctive note struck, which might mark them off as different from London and Paris entertainments, nothing to show that they are Irish save here and there an Irish accent that has escaped Cockneydom.

Scullions to the King!
The British Broadcasting Company announced just before Christmas (and the news came over the wireless to us in Dublin) that representatives of the 'Free' State and of the Colonies were present and helped to stir the plum pudding, being prepared for King George and his household in Buckingham Palace – to such vile uses have our representatives abroad descended, to serve as scullions in the Royal kitchen! It is only Republicans that can save the nation from this slough into which our new Imperialists have sunk her. Perhaps, in the new year that is dawning, we may see gleams of a better day.

'More government by outrage'
Irish World, 29 January 1927
An Phoblacht has successfully weathered its recent crisis, having sourced an Irish printer impervious to threats of sabotage and having increased its circulation because of the government challenge, its normal size is restored this week; and next week; the editor tells me he hopes to have all the ordinary features of the paper resumed. Apart from its general Republican activities, the paper will devote itself to pursuing a militant policy regarding the drive against payment of land annuities and the constant seizure of cattle by government agents shall cease to be a paying proposition. For the collecting by the Free State machinery for the benefit of Britain and the landlords of these annuities is as bad a feature as the rackrenting of the old regime; and any resistance to this tyranny can count upon the same popular support.

The movement is growing in Tirconaill, Kerry, Tipperary and the West. Recently the Dublin County Council by resolution protested against the continuance of the clause in the Land Purchase Act, making the County Councils responsible for defaulting annuitants, and calling for its repeal.

Fianna Fáil has started a regular weekly Bulletin, the first number of which appears this week. It will be circulated by the publicity department, and will contain news of the various activities of the organization, which the ordinary Dublin press boycotts or misrepresents as far as possible. The provincial press, on the other hand, has of late awakened to the growing importance of the new movement; and many leading papers in the provinces now afford the fullest hospitality of their columns to Fianna Fáil, even when not directly committed to the movement.

Removing Barrier to British Dumping

The *Derry Journal* is a striking example of a recent change of heart in this respect. In Britain, the *New Age* (the organ of Guild Socialism), a weekly of considerable influence and prestige among intellectuals devotes a special article to the economic and banking policy of Fianna Fáil, which it endorses.

An agricultural conference dealing with matters of vital interest to farmers is being called for February 3rd under the auspices of Fianna Fáil. Prominent local representatives and farming experts are being summoned to attend with a view to framing a national policy. The National Executive of Fianna Fáil is extending invitations to all those interested in such problems, irrespective of party politics. Attention is thus being focused upon the special needs of the farming community, agriculture being Ireland's most important asset.

While a deal is on for the exploitation of Ireland as a tourist resort, one of the conditions for a suggested loan for this purpose being that the barrier between the Free State and the Six-County area be removed, and that British goods may again be freely dumped on us through the Northern ports, there is no 'let up' on the persecution of the Republicans, victims of Craig's deportation orders. There is, in fact, a free exchange of information as to the movements of Republicans visiting their northern homes, the Free State CID informing the RUC on the other side of the boundary whenever 'dangerous' men or women cross the line; so that they may be arrested as soon as they touch Orange soil.

No Titles

Recently a Gaelic League function was being held in the North at which Éamon de Valera was expected to speak, or rather the rumor got abroad that he was to attend. Immediately the Free State authorities conveyed the tidings across to their sleuth comrades in the Six-County area, and the entire police and military force available, was forthwith mobilized for instant action, a police cordon being literally drawn up along the entire 'front', waiting in the hope of being able to arrest the member for Armagh. At Christmas, a teacher, now stationed in Dublin, but whose parents' home is in Belfast, went for his Christmas holidays to that city. Word was passed along by the CID, so that he was at once arrested and held for trial. This week, he was brought before a Belfast magistrate; and, because he refused to obey the order prohibiting him from his home city, saying that he would go to Belfast whenever he chose, he was sentenced to six months' imprisonment. Such is the 'law' in the Orange Free State. By such deeds does Sir James Craig earn his Viscountcy, recently conferred upon him by a grateful monarch.

In this connection it is interesting to record that the only recipient of New Year honors from King George within Free State territory, is the notorious 'Tommy' O'Shaughnessy, late recorder of Dublin, and ex-judge under the Free State. His title, too, was earned for Imperial service, for signing proclamations supressing the Volunteers, the Gaelic League, Sinn Féin, and Cumann na mBan, during the Tan regime; and recently for his savage sentences upon Republican prisoners, such as Jack Keogh, Carolan and others. O'Shaughnessy, was recently pensioned off, his place being taken by the subservient O'Byrne (ex-Volunteer). As titles are taboo by Parliamentary decree (yet unrepealed) in the Free State, the point arises whether King George, before 'ennobling' ex-Judge O'Shaughnessy, consulted his Premier Cosgrave, or whether the Colonial Government is not asked its advice in such matters. There is, of course, little likelihood that Mr Cosgrave would refuse his sanction; yet, to confer a title in a state that does not approve of such, shows the usual British imperviousness to local feeling.

It is stated that many of the Ministers of the 'Free' State would gladly forget the self-denying ordinance banning titles, and would fain possess other 'handles' to their names besides the mere academic ones of honorary degrees; but the decree still stands on paper at any rate. If King George continues to ignore the fact, we may yet have the O'Shaughnessy precedent followed, though (as the *Daily News* says, commenting on some of the recipients of honors, 'there are some whom no title can ennoble'.)

The British traffic in titles is notorious, having been bitterly exposed by Hilaire Belloc, Shaw, Wells, and others. Any wealthy brewer or soap-boiler, any entirely undistinguished nonentity, who is prepared to pay the price of a contribution to the secret party fund (Liberal when a Liberal Government is in power, Conservative when the Tories are in, as now), can secure a title. And, as far as Ireland is concerned, any renegade Irishman who has helped his country's enemies is eligible.

No wonder, therefore that our Ministers feel sore that a ban enforced at a time when they still paid lip-service to democracy and Republicanism, should prevent them receiving the award which Britain's King would gladly confer. Then we might have a Lord Mountjoy or a Viscount Merrion or Sir Kevin of Maryboro'.

Police Outrage

As to the prisoners in Mountjoy, there has been a series of protest meetings, poster parades and jail demonstrations during the past week, in and around Dublin, to press forward Gilmore's fight for political treatment. He is still, according to the latest information deprived of his clothes; and, because he will not wear the convict garb, he is confined to bed, only bed-clothes or prison clothes being available.

All over the city there has been an extensive publicity campaign, boardings, walls, shop-shutters being chalked up with the slogan 'Gilmore fighting for political treatment: George Gilmore no criminal.' The police, after trying in vain to get a shopkeeper or householder to prosecute (for a chalk inscription is regarded as no permanent defacement), at last arrested a man and a woman, and charged them with chalking up certain premises, for which crime both prisoners are now in Mountjoy jail. Both decline to give their names; and, on the woman protesting against the verminous condition of the cells, at the Bridewell, her face being swollen and disfigured almost to blindness from bug-bites, the magistrate merely reproved her for refusing her name, stating that, had she given it, he would have telephoned for her release pending trial. Apparently vermin are regarded as part of the punishment that arrest entails, part of the ordinary prison routine, like skilly on the Black Maria.

Since the torture of prisoners in Waterford and Tipperary by the Police, and, no doubt, as a result of the recent publicity given to this scandal, a secret circular has been issued by General O'Duffy,[25] head of the Civic guards, to each station, warning the men that a serious view will be taken in future, of such offences; and that policemen who are guilty of beating prisoners will be liable to be tried in the ordinary criminal courts. Apparently, however, a policeman, like a dog, is allowed by the authorities the 'first bite'; for hitherto such offences have been condoned, nay even officially sanctioned, and even now no policemen are being handed over for trial to the civil authorities the inquiry into the recent atrocities being secret, and its report confidential.

The Political Prisoners' Committee are striving to have a test case tried in the 'Free' State Courts, however, in order to expose, as far as possible, the conduct of the police and of the higher authorities; and a defence fund is being specially raised for this purpose.

Ned (Eamon) Reilly of Tipperary, recently taken by armed police from his home at midnight, his whereabouts being concealed for some days, is being charged with the shooting of the Guard Ward. He denies the charge, and declares that he spent the particular evening in question at the home of Father O'Mahony. He is obviously merely selected for attack because he is a prominent Republican whose record of service extends to the days of the Black and Tans, when his parents' home was burned by the British forces as a 'reprisal' after an ambush in the locality.

An Phoblacht exposes police 'identification parades' in the following statement: 'Previous to the identification parade, O'Reilly was asked to stroll in the
barrack yard, while his cell was being fixed up. He was induced to wear his
top-coat and cap going out. When he returned to his cell, it was unchanged.
he was still wearing the top-coat and cap when put on the identification
parade.' Identification made easy!

On Saturday, January 8th, Fleadh na Nodlag (Christmas festival) was held
by the Ard Craoibh at the Gaelic League Headquarters. Éamon de Valera,
President of the Branch (of which he and Mrs de Valera were among the
earliest members), delivered the address of welcome, which was broadcast
from the Dublin Wireless Station. It was a notable gathering, including Mr
and Mrs de Valera, Cormac Breathnach, President of the Gaelic League; P.
O'Fataigh, TD, Secretary (with de Valera, one of the Easter Week leaders,
being in charge of the Four Courts area); An Buaichillin Buighe, president of
the Fainna, who has adopted as his pen name the yellow 'ragwort' which
flourishes in every field in Connemara, Cu Uladh (T. P McGinlay), well
known to *Irish World* readers; and many other well-known Gaels.

Éamon de Valera received a hearty ovation at this, the greatest social gathering of the year, given over to Irish dancing – and song – among the former, the
very names suggesting the old-time steps and tunes, the 'Waves of Tory', the
'Walls of Limerick', the 'Siege of Ennis', 'The Bridge of Athlone'. It was
recalled by one present that it was at this Branch (where Sinéad O'Flanagan,
now Mrs de Valera, was one of the most able and successful teachers of Irish),
that Éamon de Valera and his wife first met; it was here they both studied
Irish together; here, too, Éamon Ceannt, Cathal Brugha, and many others afterwards famous for their share in Easter Week, used to foregather. The Branch
is still true to its fine tradition: and its president, Éamon de Valera, never fails
to attend its various functions, in spite of the many calls upon his time.

Meeting the President
When in London recently, Mr de Valera consulted an eminent eye-specialist,
concerning some trouble of old standing, which he has had with his right eye.
He was reassured by the specialist diagnosis, which happily confirmed that of
his own doctor, the trouble being definitely pronounced as not likely to increase,
and requiring merely a stronger pair of glasses.

An amusing story is told of a distinguished Irish American who recently
visited Ireland. He met during his stay persons representing various groups;
and once, at a dinner given in his honor, he met General Richard Mulcahy,
who inquired, 'have you met the President yet?' 'No,' replied the visitor, 'I have
unfortunately not yet been able to see him, but, of course, I met him during his
visit to America.'

'Oh,' said General Mulcahy, puzzled, 'I think you must be mistaken. President Cosgrave was never in America.'

'Cosgrave? Who is Cosgrave?' asked the American, now puzzled. 'Never heard of him. I'm talking of Éamon de Valera!' The silence around the table was eloquent, following this bombshell, Mulcahy looking extremely uncomfortable and nonplussed. Whether the visitor was quite so innocent as he seemed is a matter of doubt; but he successfully kept his imperturbable air of childlike simplicity.

'Sex equality: a reply to Victor Hall'
Voice of Labour, 12 March 1927

Mr Hall's letter in the current issue of the *Voice of Labour* falls into the common error of males who from the time of Adam to our own day complacently put the blame of all misdoing upon Eve and her successor. Because one women's union decides, being doubtful of the potency of parliamentary agitation, not to take part officially in election activity, women have failed and deserve to be excluded from jury service, if not the vote itself. 'Not proven' should be the answer to his contention. What if the Labour and other parties (for none is blameless) set about cultivating men's favour, instead of alternatively ignoring or berating her.

I am concerned, however, mainly with the paragraph relating to women and jury service (for others can and no doubt will reply to the other charges, being fully competent to do so from the point of view of the IWWU). Here Mr Hall states (taking his own information unquestioned, from the pure well of truth, Mr O'Higgins himself) that 95 per cent of women refused to serve on juries, and therefore 'it is but natural that these rights should now be interfered with by those in authority'. On this reasoning no males would serve either, for males have shown no eagerness to serve.

Mr Hall is not aware that for over three years practically no woman has been allowed by the State to serve on criminal cases, women being ordered *en masse* (as Catholics used to be in John Mitchel's day) to 'stand aside' when they answered their names in court. Mr O'Higgins was asked during the debate (and by a deputation of women who interviewed him) to produce figures showing how many women answered their names when called for service. He replied that no such figures were available, knowing full well already that it is the court practice not to allow women to serve because, to use his own words, 'women in certain cases are loath to convict'. There is no record available being taken of the number of women challenged by either State or prisoner, and Mr O'Higgins' statement, therefore, that women do not serve is based on a deliberate misrepresentation. I have seen a recent panel of the Criminal Court (Green Street). On it were eight names of women. Six of these answered in court, two did not appear. Not one of the six was permitted to serve.

It is quite true that many women (as well as men) are reluctant to serve, but it is also true that a proportion of women was ready to serve, but not permitted to do so. Every obstacle was put in the way of their serving, every discouragement and discourtesy shown. Kept in court for days, they were steadily ordered to 'stand down', and then informed that 'no woman jurors were required'. Many women though eligible for jury service since 1919, have never once been summoned, so that one wonders how the panel is chosen, and why certain names appear to have been overlooked, just as one wonders, if attending in court while a political case is on, at the extraordinary number of foreign or English names on the panel, and the peremptory challenge issued to those bearing Irish names. No woman regards Mrs Collins O'Driscoll as anything but a party henchwoman. She was chosen by men because of her relationship to Michael Collins, just as Lady Astor was chosen by British Tories because of her husband's wealth and standing. Men prefer to select women of this type, faithful to party, selected because of sentimental reasons, and because the party machine is still for the most part controlled by men, these are the types of candidates put forward. This is true not only of Ireland, but of other countries as well, for women have not yet had sufficient time since their emancipation to organise to realise their full strength.

The majority of the active women in Ireland were opposed to the Treaty, and are still opposed to the present Free State Parliament; consequently they have remained aloof and may continue to do so. Personally, I would like some day, when certain barriers have been removed, to see women returned pledged to women's interests solely; but with the present tangled issues and with a mixed vote and masculine party control that is merely a Utopian dream.

I have often wondered why Labour did not (as Republican and even Conservative and Governmental groups have done) run women candidates for local bodies (I know only of one such). In this matter the Sinn Féin party years ago took the lead, returning five women for the Dublin City Council and later six for the Republican Dáil. Perhaps Mr Hall's letter indicates that Labour is at last waking up to the importance of women in its councils. Hitherto the door, though nominally open to them, has been rather grudgingly guarded. I remember being sorely disappointed more than once (in the City Council and elsewhere) at the reactionary attitude of Labour on feminist questions. I suppose I made the mistake of thinking in terms of James Connolly, and expecting Labour leaders to live up to his standard.

I quite agree with much of what Mr Hall says regarding the need of fuller education in citizenship, though I cannot accept, especially inasmuch as they affect women, most of his conclusions.

'O'Higgins on the run'
Irish World, 19 March 1927

Today is announced officially (through O'Higgins in a speech in North
Dublin)[26] that the General Election will take place in four months. This
follows a semi-official statement published last week, placing the date on 21st
or 27th of June, a date convenient to agriculture and big business, for there is a
slight lull about that time in farming operations, while Big Business will not
have yet departed on holidays, July and August being holiday months for the
city and suburban vote, which many of the Ministers are now clinging to as to
a raft in perilous seas.

It is stated today that dissolution of parliament may take place in mid-
May, four weeks or so before the Election, so as to give deputies a chance of
campaigning in their constituencies unimpeded by parliamentary work. This
is all that appears on the surface of things, of course; as if Irish affairs and Irish
interests alone were being considered.

Other factors, Imperial ones, however, form an important feature, the date
of our General Election depending largely upon British circumstances. It will
be recalled that a statement was made in these columns, sometime ago, that
the election date was fixed for February, Mr O'Higgins preferring that date.
The Emergency Act was rushed through: the cry of the country is in danger
was raised, hundreds were arrested; intensive raids took place; secret service
men got busy; agents-provocateur fired on police barracks; 'dumps' were
alleged to be found in alarming quantities – the stage was set for the election.
But fate willed otherwise.

Ministers were summoned to London, receiving orders from Downing
Street to wait until the Naval defence question for 'these islands' was settled;
the ideal being to have Great Britain magnanimously declare – when good and
ready, that she was prepared to take over (for a slight consideration of course)
the pleasant task of 'protecting' us as part of her Imperial charge. At the same
time the 'customs barrier' was to be removed, and an arrangement entered into,
for the North, under most advantageous conditions, to come in, Craig (now
Viscount Craigavon) to be dumped upon some far-off colony as Governor, and
other dispositions of Orange demands to be made. Unfortunately, just as the
deal was being concluded, Chinese complications occurred to postpone the
final settlement of the Irish question; and all the press-machined 'victory'
celebrations. Mr O'Higgins suddenly got word to reverse his engines; the
Emergency Act was scrapped; the dumps stored away, to be 'found' again at
election eve; and the ordinary members (as well as most of the Ministry who
have not Mr O'Higgin's prospect of a safe Unionist seat) breathed a sigh of
relief that the evil day of facing the country was postponed . . .

It is a sad commentary on the temperance crusade of the earlier Sinn Féin that a government that came into being as the result of the sacrifices and ideals of Easter Week should now be at the mercy of the vested interests of King Bung.

The truculent O'Higgins, whose hands are red with the life-blood of his former friend Rory O'Connor; who gloried in an orgy of executions that no protests could stop or check; who boasted of his adamantine will, whenever fresh coercion was in question, now stands at bay before the angry clamor of the organised drink interests, cringingly flinging them sop after sop, to be perhaps at last flung to them himself. Even if his fall came at such hands, it would be welcome; but it is probable that he has found his match in a foe equally merciless and unscrupulous; and that he will truckle under in the end. Either the Liquor Bill will be proceeded with after such drastic alterations as will render any good in it void, or the government will decide upon dropping it for good and all.

It is a sad comment upon the corruptions of the time that the liquor interests have such a grip upon the nation that they can dictate to the Junta itself. All this is but another testimony to the need of a really national government; or even of an effective opposition.

The Juries Bill,[27] another of Mr O'Higgins' bureaucratic motions, which excludes women from jury service, reached another stage last week, passing its third reading by a majority of 37. As usual, the government whip was made effective, many deputies being practically forced to vote as Mr Higgins dictated. Labour, Farmer's Party, Redmondites, Clann Éireann and some Independents were opposed. The whole tenor of the debate revealed the low standing of respect for women which the government and its supporters, the Trinity College unionists, hold a contempt that was scarcely concealed pervading the discussion. The Junta fears women upon the juries of the Free State, especially its political cases; and would fain wipe them off the jury panel. Mr O'Higgins may inadvertently have done the women of the nation a service by attacking them in the open; for he has roused a surprising volume of protest against him by his Juries Bill. Several of the women relatives – sisters, wives, mothers – of the deputies and some even of the Ministers are up in arms, and were responsible, I understand, for certain 'absentees' from the division lists last week. Mr O'Higgins here too has thrown out a sop to the women – though it is but a poisoned sop – by agreeing to a Trinity College deputies' suggestion for a voluntary jury list for women. It will readily be seen that such a proposal for a hand-picked jury is as bad, if not worse, than complete exclusion as far as women are concerned; consequently the women's organisations have emphatically rejected it. Eventually the Senate may hold up the measure, which the intervening general election may eventually kill.

'Forty-six deputies exclude forty-five'
Irish World, 16 July 1927

On Thursday at parliament's opening the 48 members who compromise the Junta excluded by force one-third of the elected deputies from entry into the chamber because these refused to take the oath of allegiance to King George of England.[28]

To do this the entire police force available was mobilised, military reserve being also at hand within the building. By police proclamations a wide area in the very heart of Dublin was declared taboo for either vehicular or pedestrian traffic; and no one was permitted to enter the area around Merrion Street without a preliminary investigation by the police as to identity, business and the rest, just as if martial law had been proclaimed and as if the Parliament were in a state of siege.

. . . The new assembly, like the old, prostituted itself on the first day it met, to its lasting disgrace. Its deputies meekly endured police investigation, passed through cordons, military sentries, secret service spies and the rest, allowed their privileges as to admission tickets for the public galleries to be taken away arbitrarily (the galleries being practically closed to the public), and allowed within the precincts the doors to be locked and barred against deputies elected by the same machinery as themselves, many of whom had stood at the head of their poll in their respective areas, while those who excluded them barely scraped in without a quota. Last Thursday was a day of shame and acquiescence in shame on the part of the oath-bound deputies whether Government or alleged opposition.

The Opening Day

Republicans mustered early outside headquarters. From every part of Ireland, from the North as well as the South, contingents came, some by tram, some by char-a-bancs, some marching, many bearing banners, tricolours and streamers with the slogan 'No Oath!' which many thousands wore as a tag in their coat as a popular symbol. Outside the offices of Fianna Fáil, the 45 deputies elected on the 'no oath' ticket lined up headed by Éamon de Valera. Daniel Corkery, elected as Independent Republican, had, by the invitation of a unanimous North Cork convention, joined the Fianna Fáil deputies, making their number but one short of the Government's total. The procession moved in good order across the city swelled to huge proportions on the way. Dublin lined up to see it pass or moved joyously along with it till Kildare Street corner was reached. There under the frowning, imposing portico of the Kildare Street Club (chosen haunt of the anti-Irish clique) it met the police cordon that blocked its passage. But the police were quickly swept aside by the dense throng which broke easily through the lines. In vain, the police tried to hold back the crowd, drawing their batons, flinging off their capes and preparing to charge. Lorry loads in covered vans drawn up in side streets and alleys were ready to reinforce these at a gesture; while plainclothes men, it is said, were there carrying arms, ready to provoke a riot if necessary.

The situation was becoming tense when Fianna Fáil members stepped in and quietly took charge, giving the armed forces no excuse for a riot. Linking arms, these quietly held back the eager crowd, the Republican deputies asking them to wait there while they proceeded on their way. The crowd obeyed without demur; the police replaced their capes and batons; and 'order' was restored, not by them, but by the Republican volunteers. . .

Past the cordon the 45 deputies marched up to the Parliament Building, Leinster House, and passed its portals. Inside they were halted almost immediately by the armed guard and informed that unless they took the oath they could go no further. Various officers came forward to parlay, but none could cite any authority beyond that of force. Inside, the doors of the assembly had been locked and barred to prevent a rush, and the galleries emptied (save of wives and near relatives of the ministers) lest Republican visitors might take possession. De Valera, Seán T. O'Kelly, Countess Markievicz, Mrs Tom Clarke and others were forcibly held back, technically assaulted by the police guards.

Republicans, as part of their formal protest, were determined to demonstrate thus that it was force alone that kept them from taking their places as elected deputies in the assembly. Having made this clear, they withdrew and left the building to its state of siege. Outside, the crowd had been patiently waiting for them; and it now accompanied them back to headquarters where a mass meeting was held addressed by Éamon de Valera, Ruttledge and others.

Here it was made clear that the campaign was now begun to sweep away the barrier of the oath and to bear down with the pressure of public opinion the forces of reaction responsible for its retention. The referendum will be demanded if necessary, so that the Irish people can repeat its election mandate more clearly than before for the issue will then be 'oath or no oath'. Prominent lawyers as well as the organs of the British press already hold that Thursday's parliamentary proceedings were, even according to Free State law, invalid because the oath is not mandatory even under the treaty itself. All speakers made it clear that this was but the beginning of the fight; and that other protests would follow, other demonstrations take place, and that whenever occasion should arise the Republican deputies would again attend and again demand their rights.

Resignation from Fianna Fáil[29]
11 May 1927

Chairman, Fianna Fáil,

Owing to certain decisions taken by the majority of the Executive at its last meeting, which I must regard as equivalent to a vote of 'no confidence', I feel obliged to resign membership of that body. The justification of Mr Briscoe and others, the reversal of previous vote re Mr Belton and other vital decisions recently taken made it impossible for me to accept any further responsibility as member of the Executive for its collective action.

I still, however, believe firmly in the policy and constitution of Fianna Fáil, I shall continue to be a rank and file member of the organization and shall sincerely rejoice if my present fear regarding its management should prove to be groundless.

It is with deep regret that I sever my long connexion with a Republican Executive and with colleagues with whom I have worked for many years in the same cause. They will not, I am sure, misunderstand my present attitude, even if they may differ with me. For my part, I fully realise the difficulties they have to face in shaping present policy and I hope that the movement for unity with Sinn Féin will be successful. In courtesy to Mr de Valera, seeing that the situation causing my resignation arose during his absence, I have withheld same until I could place it, with the reasons which caused it, in his hands. Please note that a vacancy will arise on the Prisoners Com. and on Publicity Com. by my resignation.

Sincerely,
Hanna Sheehy Skeffington

Letter to Éamon de Valera[30]
16 August 1927
France

Dear Mr de Valera,
The detailed accounts in the home press, just to hand, of the recent step taken by your party, indicate so complete reversal of policy on the part of the Executive of Fianna Fáil that it is impossible for me to remain any longer a member of that body or of the organisation. I beg, therefore, to tender my resignation and shall be obliged if you will communicate same to Executive at its next meeting.

Sincerely,
Hanna Sheehy Skeffington

'Every British resource against the Republic'
Irish World, 24 September 1927

Some years ago in England, when even Tory politicians grew weary of Arthur Balfour, there was called a general election on the slogan 'BMG' (Balfour must go!) So now the slogan in the present election should be CMG (Cosgrave must go!), for should he and his junta return we shall have the worst coercion since Cromwell.

Twice within six months a general election is called, the Government and its anti-Irish allies hoping by a 'snap' election to steal a march upon its opponents. It is now known that the coup was planned by the inner ring of the 'Free' State Cabinet on the advice of Beaverbrook and Healy. Cosgrave, Blythe and McGilligan decided to rush the election without even consulting or informing their colleagues in the cabinet, who were faced with the 'fait accompli' and were, it is said, not a little taken aback.

. . . On Saturday 263 candidates were nominated – 113 less than at the last election. Trinity College alone returned its faithful trio of 'Government Independents' unopposed. Sinn Féin in a manifesto issued by Art O'Connor, decided not to contest any seats (though one woman, Miss McCarry, is standing in Tirconaill as an Independent Sinn Féiner), while Clann Éireann, whose nominees were defeated last time, did not stand as a party either, two of its former members running as Independents. Individual Clann Éireann and Sinn Féin supporters have nominated and are assisting Fianna Fáil, apparently feeling themselves free to do so as against the Government, now that Sinn Féin itself is not standing. Others are abstaining from any part in the elections. The issue is knit between the two outstanding parties – Government and Fianna Fáil – these alone putting up sufficient numbers to carry on the Government if elected.

The Government has 89 nominees, Fianna Fáil 37, both slightly less than before. The Farmer's group (Government allies) are reduced to only half their former numbers, running but 19 candidates, while Labour instead of 45 is now proposing only 29. The greatest reduction, however, is in the National League group, these having shrunk to six (from 30), two of those elected with big majorities the last time standing down, another passing into the Government ranks, while the notorious Mr Jinks[31] is now emerging as a camouflaged Independent.

The Independents number 31 – some of these too, have thrown off the mask, like Major Cooper and Dr Myles Keogh and joined the Government. Others still retain the label of Independent but are Government supporters in all but name.

Government-Farmer-Independent are massed against Fianna Fáil-Labor and National League (though a few Independents may be counted as in the opposition). Among the surprises of the contest are the candidatures of Jim Larkin and his son, Jim Larkin Jr, in Dublin City and County, respectively, and the nomination of Lord Mayor O'Neill for North Dublin (City). The oath presents apparently no difficulty to Jim Larkin, though the question of taking it will probably not arise in his case, it being improbable that he will be returned. Only three women are going forward (instead of 10 last time); Mrs Collins-O'Driscoll, for the Government, one (Mrs Tom Clarke) for Fianna Fáil, and one Independent Sinn Féin, Miss McGarry . . .

The struggle is more definitely than before one between the Government and Fianna Fáil. Now that the Oath has been subscribed to, it is no longer a live issue in the election, though its abolition is still urged. The Safety Act is really the issue, hence Republicans are voting for the group pledged to smash it.

The editor of *An Phoblacht* in this week's editorial urges as a duty upon Republican voters to drive the Government out. In an article entitled 'Our Attitude Towards the Elections' this course is advocated as the immediate duty though ultimate reliance is placed upon an armed rising or revolution. The slogan would appear to be 'Vote Against Cosgrave and keep your powder dry!' Indicting Cosgrave and his party as arch-plotters against Ireland's peace, who are even now striving to force further turmoil on this country because such is Britain's will, the editor of *An Phoblacht* concludes 'that party should be swept aside at the coming election', and that, once that end is achieved the movement enters once more upon its educational phase on the lines of Pearse's ideals, for he says, 'The influence that made Cosgrave and Co scoundrels will not be without danger to those who succeed them.'

The above advice and attitude represent very fairly the general feeling of most Republicans at present. The junta realise very clearly that for it this election is practically the last ditch, and is straining every part accordingly, it has been widely and authoritatively stated that the Government coffers have been replenished by a huge subscription to the party fund from Mr Healy's and Mr Cosgrave's old friend and ally, Lord Beaverbrook.

'How Cosgrave's boomerang came back to himself'
Irish World, 15 October 1927

Ireland is again settling down after the recent strenuous election campaign and politicians are taking stock preparatory to the launching of their several party policies at the opening of the new Parliament on October 11.

The new loan, we are informed, is to be raised by December. Mr Cosgrave's 'bold move', hailed by his admirers in the press, has proved somewhat of a boomerang. He has increased the number of his party – from 46 to 61 as between the June and September position – but Fianna Fáil has still further increased its strength – from 44 to 57 – having won the uncontested Sinn Féin seats and having acquired others from Labour, Government, National League and Farmers' parties.

The calculation on which, no doubt, Mr Cosgrave and his advisors built, namely, that his allies would also increase their strength at the cost of Fianna Fáil and its allies has failed, for all the smaller parties, as has been shown, have suffered at the expense of one or the other of their stronger rivals, leaving Mr Cosgrave a sadder, if not, a wiser man.

Mr Johnson, also, sadly miscalculated. He advocated in his pre-election speeches the wiping out by the voters of the two 'factions', for and against the 'treaty' and their replacement by a 'middle party', presumably his own. So little did the electorate heed his warning that they declined to elect himself, the exponent of the middle way. The election result gives Mr Cosgrave and his party no new lease of life – he has technically a majority of four over the next biggest party, that of Fianna Fáil, and the relative strength of the then allied groups, Government-Independent-Farmer versus Fianna Fáil, Labour, National League and Communist, is as 79 to 73.

Of the first preference votes, while 453,064 were cast for the so-called 'Government' party, 411,833 were cast for Fianna Fáil, and compared with the June election each big party increased its poll, while all the other parties lost members.

The Communist Party is represented by James Larkin, the only candidate returned. He may be the nucleus of a new left wing Labour group, though how long the greatest individualist of all will remain in any party, except a party of one, is problematic. At present, there is doubt as to which James Larkin (James Senior or 'Young Jim', his son, a merry youth) will claim the North City of Dublin seat. Should the elder be likely to be disqualified as a bankrupt, his son may appear as the elected TD. All the public knows is that two 'James Larkins' stood for Dublin seats and that one was returned.[32]

The By-Elections

There are some by-elections pending. Mr Cosgrave does not appear to have yet definitely made up his mind as to whether he would be safer in retaining his Cork or his Kilkenny seat. Should he vacate Cork, J. J. Walsh may again be a candidate, this time either as head of a new group or as a new recruit for Fianna Fáil. It is rumoured that Mr Walsh has presidential ambitions and that a section of his former Cumann na nGaedheal organisation, which he has been largely instrumental in building up, would break away with him into a 'whole hog' protectionist party.

In Limerick, a by-election may result from a petition to unseat one of the Government candidates, Mr O'Connell, for irregularity. According to report, he voted twice in the election.

In the case of Mr Leonard (North City) another petition is also pending, he too, having been accused of infringing the election law.

Mr Johnson is mentioned as likely to go forward for one of the above vacancies, his loss being acutely felt by his party. But by-elections under provisional representation are chancy – they usually fall to the Government, more especially when the vacancy is caused by a Government casualty.

Sinn Féin's abstention policy apparently operated effectively only in the National University, where the Fianna Fáil candidate lost by about 40 votes. It will be remembered that Professor Tierney (Eoin MacNeill's son-in-law) declined to stand for his former Western constituency because of his professorship, finding his 'Greek students' to be likely to suffer from his Parliamentary duties. His critics are now amusedly wondering what is to happen to his Greek students, now that Professor Tierney has chosen to go back to the Parliamentary arena.

Many Changes

The number of new deputies, especially in the Government and the Fianna Fáil ranks, is noticeable. Out of the latter's 57, no less than 21 are newly elected. Of the Government's 61, 16 have not been returned to the last Parliament though some have sat before in previous ones, while some others have changed their labels.

Of the anti-'treaty' TD's, but seven or eight remain in Fianna Fáil, members of the Second Dáil – de Valera, Ruttledge, Seán T. O'Kelly, Fahy, Dr Ryan, Seán MacEntee, Buckley. On the present Government panel of those who were members of the Second Dáil and voted for the 'treaty' the numbers are approximately 12 – such are the many swift changes to personnel that a few short years have brought.

Of the valiant little band of women deputies who voted unanimously against the 'treaty', not a single one remains. These were (it is right to recall their names) Madame Markievicz (Dublin), Mrs Pearse (Dublin), Mrs O'Callaghan (Limerick), Miss Mary MacSwiney (Cork), Dr Ada English (National University) and Mrs T. Clarke (Dublin).

The effect of the election on the anti-Irish press, both at home and abroad, has been distinctly chastening. In all the dovecotes, recently so fluttered, there is a universal cooing of peace. Had the junta won a majority over the other parties in Parliament we would have had, to change the metaphor, a sharpening of the hatchet. Now that the junta's life is precarious indeed, there is a general cry from press and politicians that the mandate given by the country is to bury the hatchet.

Coalitions of an impossible and undesirable type are preached in the name of brotherly love and fraternity and Irish-Ireland and parties lusting for the blood of their enemies are now talking about our common heritage and about 'giving politics a rest', whatever that time-worn phrase may mean in this particular context, since Parliaments are pre-eminently political institutions and politics the very essence of government.

The London and Irish *Times* both seize the occasion to deliver homilies to the 'Roman Catholic Church' in their best 'Pecksniffian' manner. According to these organs of the British public, the result of the recent election and the failure of the junta to come prancing home at the polls is entirely due to the inaction of the 'Roman Catholic Hierarchy', one that may one day be 'vigorously exploited by ultra-Protestant critics of the Church'. Seeing that the individual bishops would appear almost to a man to have been ranged on the side of the Government, the above is a typical example of the ingratitude of 'perfidious Albion'.

The *Morning Post*, the organ of die hard Toryism, declares that 'the vote clearly shows that the Irish electors sigh for the good old days of British rule'! The old people, who are addicted, it would seem, to this sighing business did not vote, so hopeless have they become, while the young people voted for the opposition because it promised 'more excitement'.

The Communist organ, the *Sunday Worker*, acclaims in its poster, 'Johnson's Defeat a Victory for Labour'. A group of self-appointed intermediaries, amateur peace-makers, aided by a section of the press and encouraged by big business elements, is striving to create an atmosphere favourable to certain unity proposals on coalition lines. Their idea would appear to be a sort of working alliance between the Government and Fianna Fáil in the manner of the 'pact' election of 1922.

Feelers are being put out already in this direction. Mr Cosgrave has declared his willingness to 'carry on' even with his unstable majority and between now and the date of the opening of Parliament it may be expected that strenuous efforts will be made to rope in as many forces as possible on the Government side.

Mr Cosgrave has solemnly issued Ten Peace Points, declaring his willingness to enter into an alliance on this basis. He has been advised, however, by his opponents to apply three principles – one of them is for an independent judiciary and comes ill from the head of an executive that has by the 'Safety' Act superseded its own judges in favour of military tribunals – to themselves first, as being primarily most in need of their application. The atmosphere is full of political finessing, and for the present the general public is rather in the dark as to what to make of the rumours as to possible alliances, new alignments, a new protectionist drive, and Irish-speaking ministry and the rest of it.

It would appear as if all sides are sparring merely and playing for time. Mr Cosgrave, Mr de Valera and Mr J. J. Walsh (still in Padua, the city of St Anthony, the patron whose aid is invoked when things are lost) are all mentioned as likely to be proposed as president of the executive. A conference has just been held at Cork City, called by the Harbour Board, which contains adherents of both parties. Its sessions were private, but it is reported that no agreement was reached and that Fianna Fáil has declined alliances.

Hitherto the 'peace-terms' offered would appear to be those of the boa constrictor with its prey, namely, the peace of complete assimilation. Those who do not favour such 'unity' are termed by the Independent as 'aggressive' and 'intransigent'.

Meanwhile the political prisoners still continue to pine behind prison bars and the 'Safety' Act's victims remain interned. Two of those arrested last week have been released, but E. Horan, ex-brigadier of the Free State Army, is still held in Limerick Jail under the Treason Act. Eamon Horan is one of those who resigned from the National Army as a protest against the Government's imperialistic policy.

Leader's Death
Harry O'Hanrahan, brother of Michael O'Hanrahan, executed by the British in 1916, has just died in Dublin. Harry served in Boland's Mills in 1916 and was sentenced to death, but his sentence was later changed to penal servitude for life. He was released with the other internees, served on the Sinn Féin executive, was candidate in the 1923 election and was, until his health finally broke down, an active and strenuous worker. His early death was probably due in large measure to prison and other hardships – his and his sister's home having been repeatedly raided and wrecked by the British, by the Black and Tans and later by the Staters. He lived not far from Mountjoy Prison gates, consequently the house and shop became a war centre whenever reprisals were ordered for a prison rescue or whenever a jail gate protest, meeting or a hunger striker's death took place.

Death has been busy among Republicans. Witness, since 1916, the large number of those cut off in the prime of manhood or womanhood, victims of the strain and stress of war conditions. The Republican Plot has almost always a red earth grave – ere one little mound grows grassy green, another's sod is lifted.

The Union Jack Again
Last week was inaugurated in Dublin the function of Civic Week. The City Commissioners paid officials nominated by the Government to supersede the elected representatives – the 'City Stepfathers', as they are called – in cooperation with the Chamber of Commerce launched the enterprise, and accordingly the city was 'en fete'. The Government staged an imposing military display in Lansdowne road with a tattoo and fireworks, illuminated aeroplanes, military bands and all the panoply of war. Trinity College threw open its stately portals and handed over its beautiful park grounds for a pageant of Dublin's history. There was an industrial parade organised by the IDA, picture and photographic exhibitions, library exhibits of Dublin's rare book treasures, an alluminated 'whale' on the Liffey, accompanied by musical parties in gondolas. The old house in College Green hung itself round with gaily coloured festoons and its outlines were traced in electric lights. Six Union Jacks floated from buildings

and banks to Dame street and from Trinity College – the largest number ever seen together since the 'treaty', testifying to the Ascendancy spirit again lifting its head among us of late.

The pageant shown in the streets, in College Park and in the Mansion House, was interesting, and in the main, in spite of its auspices, it provided excellent material. It showed the high lights in our history – the many invasions of Dublin ('Ford of the Hurdles') by Norsemen, Danes and Normans. Tableaux were shown of Brian Boru, of St Lorcan O'Toole, the protector of his people, scenes from the life story of many of Ireland's heroes – Finn and the Fianna, Art MacMurrough, Cavanagh, Hugh O'Donnell and Art O'Neill, Hugh O'Neill, O'Sullivan, Beare, Eoghan Ruadh O'Neill, Sarsfield, the fight for the bridge at Athlone, the field of Aughrim, scenes from the penal times, the Volunteers of 1788. Three prominent literary Republicans were in charge and the setting was worthy of all praise – no committee of management could near its effect, although the '98 period was entirely passed over and the rebels, Tone and Emmett, not to speak of those of 1916 and later, did not appear.

In the procession, by a touch of unconscious irony, we had the Lord Mayor's gilded coach, but its rightful occupant was not in it, though an O'Neill, actual Lord Mayor of Dublin, was seven times re-elected to that high office before Mr Cosgrave arbitrarily abolished the office.

Within the Mansion House one noticed that the crests and coats of arms of Dublin's lord mayors had all been removed from the historic Round Room, where once the Dáil used to meet. But in the place of honor in the hall one beheld the life-size portrait of Queen Victoria, who reigns there undisturbed, just as her statue (a terrible monstrosity from every point of view) still has pride.

'A woman's view of censorship: "ridiculous and impossible"'
Irish Times, 23 November 1928

Mrs Sheehy Skeffington, speaking to members of the Women's Freedom League at the Minerva Club, Bloomsbury, WC yesterday, on the subject of Free State censorship and its effect on women in Ireland, said that the legislation which was shortly to be imposed was as ridiculous and impossible a legislation as bidding cocks to crow at certain times in certain districts.[33]

'The Minister for Justice apparently is to decide for us what is good and what is bad,' she said. 'We are not to be allowed to use the free will which we are all supposed to enjoy. But we are to have this grandmotherly, or rather, I should say, grandfatherly, legislation imposed on us; for it seems we are always to be legislated for by the other sex. This is one of my main grievances: that we should be legislated for by men who in their prudish way think that women should not be allowed to serve on juries because it is not nice (Laughter). For the same reason women stenographers have been removed from the Court, although they are usually far more skilful than men. But the men, who are jealous of the women's superior skill, have to find some excuse, so they say that it is not nice for a woman to hear some of the things in Court.

Negative Legislation

'It is this fussy, negative kind of legislation that we are up against, instead of the constructive kind of legislation which is so necessary. Then again, there is the question of pensionable posts for women. But these are only open to women with drastic legislation and such ridiculous provisions as insisting that they can only qualify for such posts if their vaccination marks are visible (Loud laughter).

'This bill, of course, was fathered by a lawyer, and anything that comes from a lawyer's brain we women have learnt to distrust.'

Referring to the drastic banning of books and advertisements by the bill, Mrs Skeffington remarked that parts of the Bible, particularly the Song of Solomon, as well as Shakespeare's *Romeo and Juliet* would certainly come under the ban as being described as the literature which would excite sexual passions (Laughter). Advertisements dealing with birth control or venereal diseases would also be banned, and, therefore, some of the best papers, including the *Observer* and *Spectator*, which contained advertisements dealing with such subjects, would also come under the ban.

Anti-Feminist Origin

'Such legislation,' she added, 'is fostered or suggested by the monastic, celibate type, to whom women are not only dangerous and explosive, but also a rather indecent quantity (Laughter). They linger on the shortness of women's hair or her skirts, and seem to regard such things as just a little immoral (Laughter).'

'What we want is free, pure air to blow over Ireland as it does in other countries, instead of the hothouse atmosphere prevailing at present. I do not say necessarily that this air should blow from Great Britain; for in some respects Great Britain in the matter of censorship is rather behind-hand, but this air might be wafted from the Continent or America.'

'Yet,' concluded Mrs Skeffington, 'I think as far as we women are concerned, we may let them go ahead with the Censorship Bill; for we shall probably read in the end exactly what we want.'

'Working overtime to smash the Republic: "Free Staters" hysterical campaign of mad brutality'
Irish World, 4 May 1929

The campaign of raids and arrests after a temporary lull over Easter while the CID were in the country tracking Republicans speaking at Easter commemorations, has been resumed. As usual the offices of the printing press of *An*

Phoblacht are visited daily, so are the offices of Sinn Féin and Cumann na mBan and certain private houses like Cullenswood House (home of Pearse's first school, St Enda's, in Ranelagh and the property of Mrs Pearse) being also visited frequently. This week, too, the private house and shop of Senator Mrs Wyse Power were twice raided in search of a girl in her employment, Miss Margaret Lally. The intensive war on women now going on illustrates even more clearly than in the case of the men how provocative the campaign of persecution is and how utterly futile from an ordinary police point of view.

Last night (April 11) an elderly woman, Mrs Doyle, in whose house two old revolvers were found, was arrested and has been sentenced to two months imprisonment. The authorities cannot expect the public to believe that Miss Broderick, Miss Coyle[34] and the others arrested almost daily are criminals that must be 'hounded down' and 'stamped out'. In fact they do not believe this themselves, otherwise they would produce some evidence and would not release these suspects after a few hours' detention each day. Once a CID man called this week at the Dawson street offices and explained that he had missed his pals who were raiding somewhere and that he would wait there until they came, as they would be sure to come about sometime! Seventeen men (and two women) were arrested in the last week – many of these have already been repeatedly taken. They have all been again released, but will probably be arrested again next week. Even the hostile English press describes this state of affairs as abnormal in any country as well as dangerous. Several English papers have sent over their 'mis-representatives' to write up the annual Easter rising, for the British always feel creepy about Ireland's condition at this season. One correspondent who humorously calls himself 'Ketchum' and writes for Beaverbrook's organ, the *Express*, a paper that always gets exclusive news for the 'Free' State Junta, has this time also been primed by the Department of Justice itself, and certainly his tale is in the best dime-novel tradition. He has discovered a whole series of murders and outrages and states that loyal citizens are fleeing the country in horror of the Black Hand Gang whose device is a 'skull and cross bones'. He also makes the curious statement that Mr Cosgrave is inundated with letters 'demanding reprisals' for the many murders he alleges have taken place. This is reminiscent of the best Hamar Greenwood style and would suggest that the same hand that used to pen the lurid 'Hue and Cry' of that gentleman's time is still busy in the government service, and he winds up by telling his British readers that the Department's official asked him to remove his 'monogram' from the notepaper on which he supplied these wonderful notes lest he himself suffered the death penalty from ghosts![35] We are told, of course, that the women are the worst conspirators of all. One of the women alluded to – the grey-haired widow who presides at the secret conclaves of the 'League of Ghosts' in a slum attic would appear to be meant – wrote to the

Express, pointing out some of the more glaring errors of the correspondent Ketchum, but the *Express* suppressed the letter.

An interesting outcome of all this is that the Tourist Association has made a protest to the government, stating that this kind of thing would frighten wealthy tourists from Britain in this our emancipation centenary year, and the government having first supplied the 'facts', now furnishes the disclaimer. The explanation, of course, is that there is no cause for alarm for the 'plot' is now 'stamped out'. Mr Fitzgerald Kenny declared that the attack is now all over!

In Cork as well as in Dublin the terrorist campaign is proceeding. Among recent arrests are Seán MacSwiney and several Fianna members, for the only Scouts allowed in Ireland are the Baden-Powells. They and the British Fascisti, both foreign military organizations, are approved, while the Irish Fianna corps as well as the IRA are banned as 'illegal'.

Collections for prisoners' dependants and sellers of Easter lilies were also interfered with and knocked about by CID men. Yet 75,000 lilies and 100,000 leaflets were sold over Easter in every part of the country.

In Cobh, Youghal, Midleton, Fianna boys were 'deported' by CID men, being forcibly seized and put outside the area. In Clare, a most brutal series of police (CID) outrages is reported throughout the entire month of March. Men were beaten and kicked, some on their way from Mass, either being detained in local barracks for several hours, their homes smashed into, Easter lilies flung down and trampled. (In an office in Dublin a copy of Mitchel's *Jail Journal* was seized as seditious and its pages glued together by industrious CID men who apparently were shocked at its contents.) In spite of all suppressions, raids and threats, the 'mosquito' press manages to appear twice weekly, the *Dublin News* and the *Irish Bulletin*. The police have hunted in vain for copies, though newsboys manage to provide themselves with bundles for sale, these being quickly sold out.

And one of the men constantly sought far and wide – Proinsias O'Riain, Frank Ryan, not only was present to unveil the 1916 memorial at Glasnevin on Easter Sunday, where he delivered the oration at the Republican plot, but he also travelled to Birmingham to attend there, as Honorary Secretary of the Irish section of the Anti-Imperialist League at the conference held by that body!

The question of the latest CID terrorists campaign against Republicans was raised in the Dáil by Mr de Valera and Mr Lemass on the reopening of Parliament. The 'Free' State Minister for 'Justice', Mr Fitzgerald Kenny, took the extraordinary position of refusing any information whatever as to the raids, arrests, re-arrests, numbers of prisoners taken. He only unbosoms himself to Mr Ketchum of the *Daily Express*! It was mentioned in the debate that one man by these repeated arrests has lost a well-paid post in Guinness and that he, his wife and his six children are now destitute. Fitzgerald Kenny was full of his usual cheap jibes and taunts, and in the end refused to make any reply whatever. Mr Johnson, in the Senate, speaking on the minister's powers as conferred in the forthcoming censorship measure – this has now passed the Senate – described the speech of the Minister for Justice on the prisoners as 'full of the atmosphere of tyranny and in the best vein of Hamar Greenwood, without any sense of justice and regardless of the liberty of the subject. A man with such mentality was dangerous.'

HANNA AND SEÁN O'CASEY

Hanna's objections to Seán O'Casey's *The Plough and the Stars* are well known. In not only protesting during the performance of the play, but in tackling O'Casey in public debate afterwards, she came to symbolise republican woman-hood's determination to oppose any criticism of the idealism of those who fought in the Easter Rising. The protests have to be seen in the context of the times: a bare two years after the end of a Civil War, one that had left many on the anti-Treaty side out of work and impoverished, bitterly resenting the 'subsidised, sleek old age' of the Abbey, where those who were victorious now occupied the prime seats. However, Hanna's misgivings regarding O'Casey's antagonism to republicanism predates the Civil War, as her review of his pamphlet on the Irish Citizen Army makes plain. While moved by O'Casey's tribute to her husband, she disagreed strongly with his insistence that Frank Sheehy Skeffington was a socialist martyr who was ignored by nationalists. For Hanna, Frank Skeffington and James Connolly were good friends, both martyrs because of their ideals, and she refused to separate them into different camps because both believed strongly in national self-determination as well as in socialism. This prior encounter with O'Casey, and her knowledge that O'Casey was hostile to Connolly and his role in involving the ICA in the Rising, helped to inform her later attitude to his play. There was a cruel irony in the fact that O'Casey wrote about the Dublin working class and those who looted during the Rising. It was in an attempt to prevent looting for fear this would damage the reputation of the insurgents that Frank Sheehy Skeffington found himself arrested and summarily shot without warning.

The Story of the Citizen Army, by P. O. Cathasaigh. Maunsel and Co. Price 1s.
Irish Citizen, September 1919
This little volume gives an account of the rise and growth of the Irish Citizen Army during the Dublin Strike of 1913, and the part subsequently played by it in the Rising of 1916. It contains interesting pictures of the notables of the

time, of Countess Markievicz, James Connolly, Jim Larkin, and Captain White. It is not without the prejudice at times of the special pleader, and contains inaccuracies that mar it for the future historian. Already about the figure of James Connolly a dispute rages as to whether he was primarily a martyr to Nationalism or to Socialism, and the writer of this little book prefers to regard him as dying for the National Ideal. To those who admired Connolly it seems a minor matter; both ideals for him were so intertwined that it would be impossible to disentangle them. I think he died a martyr to the twin-causes of Irish freedom and of economic freedom, in other words, he died for the idea of a Workers' Republic. But I suppose controversies will continue to rage about the point and each side will attempt to decide it favourably to itself. James Connolly himself would be the first to smile at all these academic disputes.

The writer pays a touching tribute to Francis Sheehy Skeffington. It is one with which I do not altogether agree, but it is worth quoting none the less:

> In this new wine a lowly life, like a pearl, had been dissolved; a life untarnished by worldly ambition, or selfish perception; a life of mourning struggle and valorous effort sacrificed humbly and fearlessly for the general good; sacrificed under circumstances that stripped the offering of all the impressive draperies of martyrdom. Unwept, except by a few, unhonoured and unsung – for no National Society or Club has gratefully deigned to be called by his name – yet the ideas of Sheehy Skeffington, like the tiny mustard seed today, will possibly grow into a tree that will afford shade and rest to many souls overheated with the stress and toil of barren politics. He was the living antithesis of the Easter Insurrection: a spirit of peace enveloped in the flame and rage and hatred of the contending elements, absolutely free from all its terrifying madness; and yet he was the purified soul of revolt against not only one nation's injustice to another, but he was also the soul of revolt against man's inhumanity to man. And in this blazing pyre of national difference his beautiful nature, as far as this world is concerned, was consumed, leaving behind a hallowed and inspiring memory of the perfect love that casteth out fear, against which there can be no law.
>
> In Sheehy Skeffington, and not in Connolly, fell the first martyr to Irish Socialism, for he linked Ireland not only with the little nations struggling for self-expression, but with the world's Humanity struggling for a higher life.
>
> He, indeed, was the ripest ear of corn that fell in Easter Week, and, as it is true that when an ear of corn falls into the ground and dies it bringeth forth much fruit, so will the sown body of Sheehy Skeffington bring forth, ultimately, in the hearts of his beloved people, the rich crop of goodly thoughts which shall strengthen us all in our onward march towards the fuller development of our National and Social Life.

Francis Sheehy Skeffington and James Connolly would not worry either about individual or joint laurels. I fancy they would smilingly deprecate all the glories and the haloes of martyrdom. Neither craved nor obtained, what is called 'popularity', and once the former declared, when warned that his pacifism might impair his 'popularity' with nationalists: 'If I thought I was in danger of becoming popular, I would examine my conscience!'

It is curious to think that he was the first to die and Connolly 'the last to cast his torch upon the pyre'. In Connolly's last interview with his wife he sent a special message to his old friend asking him to look after some of his work for him – only to learn for the first time that he had already gone.[1] And when he learned the news he turned away his head with a sigh, I believe. And murmured that, as all were gone, he might too, follow, or some words to that effect. So in their deaths, too, these good friends were not divided. What matter which is the Socialist or National hero: both died as they lived for their ideals. Personally, as Eva Gore-Booth says, I prefer to think of Sheehy Skeffington as 'the one who died for Peace', while the others 'died for Freedom'. Nathan Hale, the American boy patriot and martyr of the revolution, said before he was shot: 'I regret that I have only one life to give for my country.' Possibly, if Connolly and Skeffington had more than one life they might have sacrificed the others for the other causes with which their lives were bound. Having but the one, they gave it, one to Peace and one to Freedom, and neither looked for fame or laurels, in death or in life.

Joan

'*The Plough and the Stars*'
Irish Independent, 15 February 1926
Your editorial misses what was apparent in your report regarding the Abbey Theatre protest. The demonstration was not directed against the individual actor, nor was it directed to the moral aspect of the play. It was on national grounds solely, voicing a passionate indignation against the outrage of a drama staged in a supposedly national theatre, which held up to derision and obloquy the men and women of Easter Week. The protest was made, not by Republicans alone, and had the sympathy of large numbers in the house. There is a point beyond which toleration becomes mere servility, and realism not art, but morbid perversity. The play, as a play, may be left to the judgment of posterity, which will rank it as artistically far below some of Mr O'Casey's work. It is the realism that would paint not only the wart on Cromwell's nose, but that would add carbuncles and running sores in a reaction against idealisation. In no country save in Ireland could a State-subsidised theatre presume on popular patience to the extent of making a mockery and a byword of a revolutionary movement on which the present structure claims to stand.

I am one of those who have gone for over twenty years to performances at the Abbey, and I admire the earlier ideals of the place that produced *Cathleen ni Houlihan*; that sent Sean Connolly[2] out on Easter Week; that was later the subject of a British 'Royal' Commission; the Abbey, in short, that helped to make Easter Week, and that now, in its subsidised, sleek old age jeers at its former enthusiasms.

The incident will, no doubt, help to fill houses in London with audiences that come to mock at those 'foolish dead', 'whose names will be remembered forever'.

The only censorship that is justified is the free censorship of public opinion. The Ireland that remembers with tear-dimmed eyes all that Easter Week stands for, will not, and cannot, be silent in face of such a challenge.

'The Plough and the Stars: a reply to Mr O'Casey'
Irish Independent, 23 February 1926

In his letter Mr O'Casey sets himself the task of replying to certain criticisms of his play. Since receiving Mr Yeats's police-protected 'apotheosis' Mr O'Casey appears to take himself over-seriously, not sparing those of us who decline to bow the knee before his godhead. His play becomes 'the shaking of the tinsel of sham from the body of truth'; an over-statement surely, for of the body of truth as portrayed in *The Plough and the Stars* one only discerns a leprous corpse.

As Arthur Griffith wrote nearly twenty years ago, when last police assisted at an Abbey production: 'If squalidness, coarseness, and crime are to be found in Ireland, so are cancer, smallpox and policemen.' But because these are to be found it would not be true to claim that nothing but these are present in Ireland. Because Mr O'Casey has seen the tricolour painted on a lavatory wall he claims the right to parade it in a public-house as typical of the custom of the Citizen Army and the Volunteers. Because indecent and obscene inscriptions are similarly so found one may not exalt them as great literature.

Mr O'Casey's original version, as is now generally known, was pruned before production. One wonders on what basis certain parts were excluded and others retained. This may, indeed, be the reason for the lop-sidedness of some scenes, suffering, as sometimes the picture plays do, from a drastic, ill-concealed cut. Will the original version now appear in London and elsewhere, benefitting by the réclame of a 'succès de scandale', a réclame that is usually ephemeral?

As to Mr O'Casey's ransacking of literature to find soldiers that show fear or vanity, all that is beside the point. Whether the sight of men parading before an action that will lead many of them to their death is 'damnably funny', or whether it might be pitiful and heart-rending, is also a matter of presentment and point of view. The Greeks, who knew not Mr O'Casey, used to require of a tragedy that it evoke feelings in the spectator of 'pity and terror', and Shakespeare speaks of holding the 'mirror up to nature'. Submitted to either criteria, *The Plough and the Stars* is assuredly defective. But no doubt Mr O'Casey would regard such standards as sadly out of date.

A play that deals with Easter Week and what led up to it, that finds in Pearse's words (spoken in almost his very accents) a theme merely for the drunken jibe of 'dope', in which every character connected with the Citizen Army is a coward, a slacker, or worse, that omits no detail of squalid slumdom, the looting, the squabbling, the disease and degeneracy, yet that omits any revelation of the glory and inspiration of Easter Week, is a *Hamlet* shown without the Prince of Denmark.

Is it merely a coincidence that the only soldiers whose knees do not knock together with fear and who are indifferent to the glories of their uniform are the Wiltshires? Shakespeare pandered to the prejudices of his time and country by representing Joan of Arc as a ribald, degraded camp-follower. Could one imagine his play being received with enthusiasm in the French theatre of the time, subsidised by the State?

I learn that Mr O'Casey's personal knowledge of the Citizen Army does not extend beyond 1914–15. To those, however, who remember the men and women of 1916 such presentation in a professedly 'National' theatre seems a gross libel.

Mourning for the men of Easter Week is not incompatible with sympathy for the suffering survivors. The Ireland that is 'pouring to the picture houses, the dance halls and the football matches' is the Ireland that forgets – that never knew. It is the Ireland that sits comfortably in the Abbey stalls and applauds Mr O'Casey's play. It is the Ireland of the garrison, which sung twenty years ago 'God Save the King' (while Mr Yeats then, too, enforced the performance of *The Playboy* with the aid of the police). These do not shed tears for the navvy on the Shannon nor for the men of Easter Week nor for the sores of the slum.

Mr O'Casey accords me as a critic in a shrieking paragraph or two the 'charity of his silence'. Unfortunately for his play, the professional critics are for the most part on my side, justifying my opinion that his latest play is also his poorest. For (pace Mr Yeats) the police do not necessarily confer immortality, nor is it invariably a sign of a work of genius to be hissed by an Irish audience.

Arthur Griffith wrote thus in *Sinn Féin* of a similar episode: – 'Mr Yeats has struck a blow' (by calling in police and arresting certain members of the audience who protested against *The Playboy*) 'at the freedom of the theatre in Ireland. It was perhaps the last freedom left to us. Hitherto, as in Paris, or in Berlin or in Athens 2,000 years ago, the audience in Ireland was free to express its opposition to a play. Mr Yeats has denied this right. He has wounded both art and his country.'

May I suggest that when Mr O'Casey proceeds to lecture us on 'the true morality of every woman' he is somewhat beyond his depth. Nora Clitheroe is no more 'typical of Irish womanhood' than her futile, snivelling husband is of Irish manhood. The women of Easter Week, as we know them, are typified in the mother of Padraic Pearse, that valiant woman who gave both her sons for freedom. Such breathe the spirit of Volumnia, of the Mother of the Gracchi.

That Mr O'Casey is blind to it does not necessarily prove that it is non-existent, but merely that his vision is defective. That the ideals for which these men died have not been achieved does not lessen their glory nor make their sacrifices vain. 'For they shall be remembered for ever'[3] by the people if not by the Abbey directorate.

'*The Plough and the Stars*'
Irish World, 13 March 1926

Last week saw history curiously repeating itself at the Abbey Theatre, at a performance of Seán O'Casey's much boosted *Plough and the Stars*, the subject of which was the movement that led up to Easter Week. It is now the fashion of our new aristocracy to sneer at ideals, and to belittle everything Irish as synonymous with everything that is sordid and mean.

The Abbey stage has shifted from the 'mud walled cabin' of its earlier peasant drama to the fetid slum, and oscillates between pub and tenement. The language of the western peasant, the Kiltartans of Lady Gregory or the Arran of Synge, has given place to the 'soldier's language' of the back lanes and brothels. A new audience, sleek and smug in after dinner mood, now haunts the show and indulges in ribald laughter at the sallies of tenement drolleries. Such was the setting of O'Casey's former play, his *Shadow of a Gunman*, and *Juno and the Paycock* drama is not without power, with a grim and sinister humour of their own that made their creator popular if not famous. The Abbey directors, having for years turned down Mr O'Casey, suddenly discovered him and acclaimed him as a new Synge. His cynical vein fitted their mood: for he, being an eternal grouch, saw everything through warped vision, holding not the mirror up to nature but indulging rather in those mirror-shows which distort and disfigure whoever stands before them.

Mr O'Casey was found to have a particular grudge against the Citizen Army and the Volunteers (he is said to have been expelled by James Connolly from the former in 1914–15, and nourishes a grievance ever since against both organisations), and he, accordingly, chose for his theme, Easter Week. I do not propose to detail the plot of his drama (if his successive scenes can be said to have a plot), stating merely that the effect of the whole and of every part is to hold up to derision and obloquy Pearse, Connolly and the men and women of Easter Week. Not a single character has a gleam of nobility or idealism; the men are all poltroons, drunkards, slackers or criminals, inspired by no motives save that of vanity, greed or empty boastfulness, while the women are back-biting harridans, half-witted consumptives, neurotics and prostitutes.

One scene introduces a 'pub' where a prostitute and bedraggled crone hob-nobs with tipplers, while Pearse's splendid words are heard outside speaking to a gathering of Volunteers in 1915. The public house crowd cry jeeringly, 'Dope!' and two uniformed captains, bearing the flags of the Citizen Army and the Irish Republic, swagger in a call for drinks. Later, there is a coffin, wherein lies a dead girl and by its side on the door are gathered men playing cards. Again there is a looting scene where men come in with jars of whiskey and shrews fight over the spoils; while afar off are heard the guns pounding the city. Then two Republican soldiers in uniform enter, bearing a snivelling comrade, wounded and whining. All are trembling with fear, and their knees knock together as they cower in the doorway. The only brave men shown are the British 'Tommies' of the Wiltshires, who come to raid. The moral of the piece appeared to be the 'foolishness of it all!'

The Abbey Theatre enjoys from Mr Blythe a subsidy of £850 and the Minister sat with Mr O'Higgins in the stalls, and applauded every thrust at the men of Easter Week. Even some prominent Free Staters in the audience showed their approval; and I have heard that the Lord Chief Justice O'Kennedy left before the play closed, as a protest; while individual protests were also made during the first nights.

On Thursday Cumann na mBan attended and made an effective demonstration. The women, all of them having lived through Easter Week, and knowing the men that fought and died in 1916, accompanied by some men of the old Volunteer and Citizen Army, rushed the stage, and compelled the management to stop the play and lower the curtain. Then Mr Yeats appeared, shutting himself in a room at first until he had a speech prepared, and then, having sent for the police and being thus fortified, issued forth. His careful periods were, however, unheard; and had to be handed with an official report to the press. He glorified the author . . . Then, in a police protected house, to the few that still remained, the rest of the play was given, any interrupter being violently ejected.

Even then the drama did not continue harmoniously. That night the police slept on the building; and cordons of them outside kept away the crowd on the following nights; while on Saturday the actors remained locked up between the performances.

Mr Yeats threatened to continue the play for another week; but hurriedly changed his mind and is now preparing for London instead. Later it is intended to take the play to America. I think I know how the Irish will receive it there.

As, after the *Playboy*, George Russell wrote in parody of *Kathleen ni Houlihan*, so now one may write of the Abbey directorate and their plays, 'the police shall protect them forever'.

I I

TRAVELS IN EUROPE

INTRODUCTION

For Hanna, possessing a BA and MA in Modern Languages and specialising in French and German, travel in Europe was a great pleasure. In a radio interview in 1945 she remarked it was 'a mighty good thing to travel when young'. Incipient tuberculosis had sent her 'roving to the Rhineland' when she was 18 and after that she enrolled as a first-year language student. She maintained contact with her French teacher in St Mary's even after the latter moved to America and at University College Dublin, she and Patrick Pearse shared the same French teacher. Hanna also studied in Germany during her student days and returned there and to France frequently throughout her life. Her knowledge of European literature was extensive, as is evident in her writings, particularly in the *Irish Citizen*. She was therefore an ideal person to act as the Irish representative for international events. Her column for the *Irish World* afforded her scope to publicise the work of the international suffrage movement and the growing move to enfranchise women on a global scale, while also allowing her free rein to criticise the Free State, for its enforced dependence on Britain and for its regressive policies regarding women. She attended the International Woman Suffrage Congress as a representative of the International Women's League for Peace and Freedom, not as an official representative of either the 'Northern' or the 26-county state, as she was careful to point out. Her subsequent interview with Madame Pacha, leader of the Egyptian women's delegation, was obviously conducted in French as she noted approvingly that Madame Pacha spoke 'little or no English', which Hanna hints was a result of her commitment to Egyptian nationalism. While in Paris she visited James Joyce, an old student friend of both hers and Frank's. Although she did not mention this visit in her newspaper articles, her pride in Joyce and other Irish writers is evident in her 1929 article in *An Phoblacht*, when she visited Prague while attending the Sixth Congress of the Women's International League for Peace and Freedom. It is noteworthy that her focus by then was on 'Middle Europe' and the political and economic difficulties countries were experiencing, particularly those that had suffered defeat in 1918. Post-war Europe now required passports, visas, and custom searches, in great change to her early travels as a young woman. While it would be another decade before the beginning of the Second World War, Hanna's observations convey a mood of disquiet. There are sinister undertones, even in small points, such as the refusal of Mussolini's Italy to grant passports to women.

In August 1930 she was part of an Irish delegation to Russia, along with Charlotte Despard, Helena Molony, Sheila Dowling and other radicals. A party of British communists was also on board their ship and during that time Hanna was, according to Charlotte Despard, active in putting forward an Irish republican view to the British comrades, as a result almost exhausting her stock of Irish revolutionary mementoes. Hanna enjoyed the journey, and life on the Soviet ship, with its very different food and politics, 'brown bread and red pamphlets' as she put it. From the evidence of the different note pads and pieces of paper that she used to jot down impressions, the visit obviously inspired her with hopes that a more egalitarian future could be possible. Her anxiety (as a 56-year-old woman from Ireland) to fit in with this new world can be seen in her decision to leave her umbrella behind, dismissing it as a relic of a 'bourgeois' past. Women's release from 'the tyranny of the pots and pans' was a phrase she would use from now on, even in her last writing before her death. She admired the freedom granted to children, communal life, free welfare and no unemployment. The visitors were not shown Soviet prisons, so took on trust the assurance that prisoners were not punished but trained for citizenship. While delegations such as this were criticised for their naivety and blindness to the growing totalitarian state, what comes out of her jottings is her hope for the future, and her enjoyment of escaping for five weeks from the consumerism of the west. After this visit she gave five lectures – to the Contemporary Club, the Dublin Literary Society, the Rotary Club, Rathmines Library and to Friends of Soviet Russia, for a Russian Anniversary meeting. The first four talks used items from the notes she made during her tour, tailored to her audiences, but do not have the immediacy that the scrawled notes, on a variety of pieces of paper and notepads have. The speech for the Russian Anniversary meeting consists of four and half handwritten pages and provides us with a sense of Hanna's power as a public speaker.

'International Woman Suffrage Congress 1926'
Irish World, 26 June 1926
I am writing this in Paris, where I am attending an International Woman Suffrage Congress. Forty nations are here represented, and women from the five continents are gathered together – from Iceland to the far North of Peru, from Japan to California. For the first time the various little nations sprung up

in Europe under Republics as a result of the World War (for 'freedom', as we were so, often, told) of separate representation . . . Jugo-Slavik, Czecho-Slovakia, Hungary, Finland are here with their women senators, delegates, ministers and so on. The women of Turkey too for the first time are given representation, though (officially) in Turkey women are not permitted by their government to mention 'suffrage'; and forming a suffrage society would be equivalent to a breach of the Turkish Treason Acts or whatever their equivalent in Turkey may be.

Female Suffrage
There is a large delegation of women from the German Republic – members of the Reichstag of the Prussian Landtag and a Minister of Public Instruction from one of the local states. These have been warmly received in France, and are helping the women of France to win suffrage for themselves. It is a curious commentary on French freedom that no French women are allowed to vote (even for a municipal council) while the 'oppressed' German women, of whom we heard so much, have got every right under their Republic which they help to administer. German women and those of other European countries are, in fact, better off in this respect than British women or Irishwomen in the Six-County area; because the former have equal suffrage with men, while the latter cannot exercise the vote until they arrive at the age of 30, though they may be elected as members of Parliament at 21![1] One of the resolutions of the Congress called for the extension of the vote in Britain and Northern Ireland and urged the governments responsible to remove this disability. For Britain (with the Northern Irish ally), as usual, lags behind; being too busy administering 'justice' and 'civilization' to less favoured peoples to attend to its own affairs. Britannia being, in fact, the international Mrs Jellyby, immortalized by Dickens as a benevolent matron too preoccupied with the fate of uncivilized savages abroad to attend to her domestic problems.

If women in so-called Southern Ireland now have a wider franchise than the British, it is because Republican women have insisted upon their rights; forcing Griffith and Collins to accede to this by stressing the Proclamation of the Irish Republic in 1916, which granted this. Willingly would our present rulers have revoked this, had it been possible. As it is, the Free State Junta has since filched many rights (such as admission to juries, equal rights in civil service, etc.,) previously given to women.

The Congress in Paris
Two delegations were present at the Congress, one from the 'Northern' area, one from the Twenty-Six County. Personally I belong to neither, getting my authority as fraternal delegate from an international body, the International

Woman's League, which recognises no frontier. I noted with regret that the general tendency of the Suffrage Congress was to favour the League of Nations as an instrument for peace. On the whole, the Congress was right wing and non-revolutionary; one of its first acts being to decline to recognise the National Woman's Party of America, whose leaders, Alice Paul and others, have always been friendly to the cause of Ireland's independence. These were only granted a 'fraternal' delegacy, which precludes one from voting or taking any direct part in the deliberations of Congress.

It was noticeable that, among the flags of the various nations, there was no recognition of the Free State, in spite of the vain boasting of the Minister for External Affairs. Both Northern and Southern Ireland were merely 'colonies' of Britain; and the official delegates were apparently quiescent. As a Republican, I was naturally indifferent; because no Republican would wish to see the flag of the Republic paraded as a Free State emblem; a piece of mere camouflage which deceives no one. We do not wish to see our Republic emblem degraded, and it may not be used internationally until Ireland is free and independent.

Another fact I noted was that everywhere Partition is taken for granted, one is at once asked, when Ireland is mentioned: 'are you Northern or Southern?' British and Free State propaganda is to that extent successful, that Ireland now no longer means one entity, but two fragments. I was glad of the opportunity of explaining the situation (as it was) to women of various nations, eager for information on the subject.

I believe the Free State has some unknown and carefully concealed representative in Paris. He did not show up at the Congress; nor was his presence indicated in any way, yet Mr Fitzgerald, as Minister for Foreign Affairs, got only last week a vote of over 230,000 dollars passed for the upkeep of his various consuls abroad! The representative of the Republic, Mr Kerney, furnishes a more valuable link abroad; and has been able steadily to keep the French press (or rather such sections of it as are friendly) informed on the Irish situation.

In this Congress we have been in touch with the Egyptian delegation and others through him – for our case and Egypt's present remarkable parallels just now. Even though Mr Kerney has, unfortunately, been stricken with a serious illness, obliging an operation, he has, none the less, almost single-handed, been able to achieve a good deal. His office is the only one where Ireland as a nation is recognised and remembered. It is a growing scandal that in the League of Nations' headquarters at Geneva as well as at various capitals in Europe as well as in America the expensive department of 'External Affairs', as it is humorously named, is a mere adjunct of Britain; and that no effort is attempted to do any real propaganda for Ireland. It is in fact a costly farce, whose only reason for existence appears to be the furnishing of comfortable posts for various hangers-on of government.

Mr Lindsay Crawford, the representative in New York, is now visiting Ireland, and handing out the usual glowing speeches for publicity, praising the present regime as heaven sent, and professing to find Ireland 'great, glorious and free'. One could only imagine that such men, who ought really to know better, have their tongues in their cheeks, and are wilfully misleading the American people. As for our 'External Affairs' Minister, he is really, (as a deputy reminded Mr Fitzgerald) usually Mr T. M. Healy, the King's governor-general. It is he who signs all passports abroad, not the Minister – but a while ago really they were signed by a British Minister. In some cases, these passports have been discredited and confiscated by British officials abroad, as Mr Fitzgerald himself was forced to admit in the course of a recent debate on his Ministry. Usually, when one shows such passport and answers 'Irish' to the query of nationality, one is waved aside with: 'Oh, British, it's the same thing', and the passport is regarded as merely British.

The Power Behind
When delicate negotiations are under foot with Britain, it is Mr Healy who conducts them or Mr O'Higgins or, sometimes, Mr Cosgrave; while Mr Fitzgerald of 'External Affairs', remains in the background discreetly. For, after all, neither he nor the other Ministers of His Majesty, King George, dare regard Britain as 'External', being part and parcel of the British Empire. When the 'Northern' government was recently approached on a delicate mission about customs, it was Mr Duggan (sole survivor of the Free State Treaty signatories), who went officially to Belfast. This note is struck in a long letter sent to the press this week by that indefatigably pro-British polemicist, Rev. Dudley Fletcher, Rector of Cooltanagher, who declares, referring to a recent speech at Cork of Éamon de Valera:

> I must add that I regard King George V as no "foreign ruler", but as the greatest blessing which the British Commonwealth of Nations possesses as a guarantee of unity and peace and prosperity. We saw the consequence of a mere partial and temporary paralysis of the King's authority in Ireland. God save Ireland from a repetition of Mr de Valera's policy!

However, Mr Fitzgerald remains in blissful ignorance, and draws his salary unperturbed; and when challenged as to the attitude of his Department on the Imperial Conference, declares airily, 'There is no predominant partner where there is a commonwealth partnership', and the debate ends thus with 'progress reported', things being left in the usual misty state as far as the Free State Parliament was concerned.

The Russell Incident

In another direction, the Free State External Affairs has been busy – blocking the entry into Ireland at Cobh of Mr Charles Edward Russell, the well-known American publicist.[2] Britain, 'acting on the advice' of the Free State, also excluded him, and has got itself into bad odour in consequence; and is now desirous of mending its hand, and allowing him to Britain but not to Ireland. In reply to queries Sir Joynson Hincks, British Home Secretary, stated that the 'Irish Free State were in friendly relations with them, and they had, in their discretion, decided against Mr Russell landing there. They communicated that fact to them, and asked them to take the necessary steps to prevent him landing in Ireland.'

No Objection

'I have no objection to his landing here,' he added, 'and when he arrived at Plymouth he was requested to go on to South Hampton, but he went on to Cherbourg instead, and made no further request. If he desires to do so, there is no reason whatever why he should not enter England.'

Mr Wedgwood asked why, if the Irish Free State wanted to keep him out of Ireland, they could not do their own work, instead of asking the British police to do the work for them. 'There is very easy transit between England and the South of Ireland,' said the Home Secretary, 'and arrangements have existed for a long time between the Irish Free State and us by which they should stop undesirable aliens coming here and we should do likewise for them.'

In other words, the Free State cannot of itself, without agreement with Britain and Northern Ireland, exclude anyone, because the Free State and Britain are one and a foreign visitor is not required to produce a separate passport (a British one covering all). Therefore, the usual government's agreement has to be entered into, and naturally Britain is only too willing to oblige her subordinate by excluding a Republican. When that Republican has Mr Russell's standing and reputation, and when a fuss is made, Britain somewhat lamely, seeks to mend her hand. Here, no doubt, Mr Fitzgerald of External Affairs, had got busy – for an American friendly to the Irish Republic becomes an alien enemy forthwith! Mr Russell is now in Paris, having refused, quite rightly, to submit to any conditional entry into Britain. It must be a somewhat grim reflection to him to recall his services to Britain during the war; for he was, it will be recalled, one of those Socialists who favoured America's entry into the war to make the world safe for democracy. Britain's memory for past services is proverbially short, for eaten bread is soon forgotten. For those who give her service or who decline to follow her blindly, no gratitude tempers her judgment. Erskine Childers once served her: so did Roger Casement: but when they turned their backs upon her for a noble cause which they felt that she was betraying, her vengeance was swift and relentless.

'The revival of Egyptian nationality'
Irish World, 3 July 1926
After the International Suffrage Congress was over, I sought an interview
for the *Irish World* with the leader of the Egyptian women's delegation,
Madame Hoda Charaoni Pacha,[3] who had been elected on a new board of the
International Suffrage Alliance, who edits a feminist paper for the advance-
ment of Egyptian women, and who has been prominent for the part played by
her in her country's struggle for independence.

On the last night of the Congress, Madame Pacha gave a reception to her
women colleagues from various nations, to which our Republican Envoy, Mr
Kerney, was specially invited, and at which I was present. Next morning, I
met her by special appointment at her hotel, where, with Mr Nassif, she was
busy all day interviewing correspondents of the Continental, American and
Australian press. Just before I came she was carefully explaining to two
Australian women journalists that Egypt was ready to be friendly with Britain
as with all countries; but that she wished to be completely free from her
control – 'friendly to all, but dependent on none'. She was detailing the
arguments for British withdrawal, explaining how Egypt was suffering, and
how Britain was interfering in her affairs to her detriment.

As far as I could gather, the Australian journalist was doubtful. It is the
Colonial mentality to regard Britain as synonymous with freedom. When my
turn came, I said that she need not begin to explain to an Irish woman why a
country wished her independence, and that we could begin just where she had
left off. She smiled and replied with animation that she knew that she greeted
a representative of another oppressed people in many respects similar to her own.

A Plea for Equity
She is a very beautiful woman, with a Madonna-like face, with hair drawn
simply back from her broad brow; her eyes dark and flashing; with magnetic
charm in her personality. She is the daughter of Sultan Pacha and wife of the
first President of the Egyptian Parliament. Her message, addressed to the
Congress, on behalf of Egyptian women and in support of universal peace,
draws attention to the fact that Egypt is excluded from the so-called League
of Nations. It states: 'the women of Egypt desire peace as much as the
other women of the world do – they desire it all the more because their own
unfortunate country has been the prey of so many successive ambitions on
account of her geographical situation, her riches, and on account of the pacific
disposition of her people. All future wars would injure us as all the wars of the
past have done. But there is no lasting peace except that which is founded on
justice (a principle which the League of Nations has always professed). On
that account, Egypt asks that the problems which concern her vitally should

also be resolved in a real spirit of equity. As women the Egyptian women know that there can be no peace without justice.'

This moving message was applauded by thousands that gathered into one of the largest halls in Paris to hear the women of the world deliver their addresses. 'Peace built on freedom and justice' – how the small nations have in vain clamoured for such a peace; and how indifferent the great powers have been to their cry, save when it seemed to suit their imperialistic purpose. In the midst of much recent boosting of the League of Nations, one reads the calm announcement in the Continental press that, as a result of the recent elections in Egypt (unfavourable to Britain's occupation), Britain has sent war cruisers to Egyptian waters to 'dominate the population by a display of force, which (says the *Daily Mail*) we hope may not be necessary'. Yet Britain is a member of these League of Nations which professes to be opposed to force.

The story which Madame Charaoni Pacha told of Britain's occupation was one strangely familiar to me in the smallest details. Substitute Ireland for Egypt, and Lloyd George's Black and Tans for the British Army or occupation – and the story is exactly the same. Another ancient nation with a glorious history, a great civilization, a tradition all its own, exploited by foreign force, impoverished, degraded, robbed of its wealth, ground down by the imperialistic despot: forty-four years ago, said Mme Pacha they came – to stay a week or two, in order to help us to 'restore order' (familiar phrase) and they are still planted in our midst and refuse on one pretext after another to pack their bags and go – which is all we ask them to do! They declare when deputations of men and women wait upon them (Mme Pacha headed one such delegation) that order is not yet restored, and we reply that, if they have not restored it after 44 years it is clear that they are incapable of doing so at all!

Under the French protectorate, she explained, education was fostered. French savants, professors of world standing, came and gave Egypt of their best. The French are (even in India) no better colonists than the British. They set up no religious antagonisms, they raise no color bar, they are genuinely interested in the people among whom they come. Mme Pacha spoke French as fluently as a native speaker, and significantly, seemed to have little or no English – she is a woman of the wider culture, and of large vision. Desiring neither French nor English interference in Egyptian affairs, she would feign see her country free to develop into nationality, with complete control of her internal affairs. Britain has starved education systematically. Her irrigation works have been she admitted, good; but these were in her own interest; and so it suited her to develop them. Her grant up to recently (out of Egyptian money, be it remembered) was but one hundred thousand pounds for a country of over 14 million inhabitants. Recently this has been slightly increased, but a scheme of compulsory education was refused for over thirty years. Britain desires the natives to be ignorant and poor. The professors and teachers she sends to Egypt are the failures at home. A man, said Mme Pacha scornfully, need only be 'a good boxer or tennis player to be put in a responsible official position'. Here Mme Charaoni Pacha made a digression to pay a warm tribute to the Irish Republican delegation, set up in Paris under Seán T. O'Kelly and Gavan Duffy, whose help she remembers (and Egypt remembers still) with lively gratitude. There was from the first the warmest sympathy between the delegations and she declared that it was the Republican Envoy who first helped Egypt to get world publicity for her case, and to pierce the 'wall of paper' that surrounded her. It was pleasant to have the help of the Irish Republic remembered.

Mme Charaoni Pacha then traced for me with vivid eloquence the recent history of Egypt, so like our own. Up to the great war the people were peaceful and submissive, waiting for their unbidden guests to keep their promise – and go. The British were treated courteously as guests, though as the years went by, the people murmured – when will they depart? As Britain, however, still declared that her occupation was purely temporary, and that she meant to go very soon, the people believed her at first, and accepted each pretext she put up for postponing imminent departure.

Egypt in the World War
Then came the Denshavi affair (one recalls George Bernard Shaw's vivid story of it in the preface of one of his plays, *John Bull's Other Island*, if I remember rightly). Next came the great war. Egypt was then too a sort of 'bright stop' in the Empire, and was promised much, and told that all would be well when once the war (for freedom, of course; of all oppressed people) was over. Then Britain would leave; and she only asked that the country remained tranquil and at peace. Nothing would be expected of Egypt. Years passed; all practically commandeered and conscripted. Over a million Egyptians went. Britain then took whatever she needed, at her own price, and much lower always than what the market price happened to be. If it had no corn, it had to procure it at a high price and resell it at Britain's 'fixed price'. Mme Pacha saw, for instance, that her property was in cotton, and that she had no corn; but such reply was waived aside, and she was levied for a certain huge amount, which she had to procure. Deputations waited upon High Commissioners, one after another, to plead with them. Once in the burning sun she stood for over two hours with Britain's guns fixed upon her, leading a group of women – and their deputation would not be received. Then came the armistice – and armistice day in Egypt was a day of brutal riot, or rampant militarism, when the victorious Saxon saw red, flushed with victory. The 'native' were treated as mere dirt beneath the jack-boot of the conqueror. Egyptians suspected of sympathy with the Turk were

openly reviled so that the pacific people were gradually goaded into rebellion. She told me of women violated by the British soldiery in sight of their husbands, who were then murdered. In some places the men had to build a kind of deep, dry well without light or any access by way of door or window. Into this the women were lowered by ropes, that they might remain hidden while the soldiers swept by. She spoke of their flag (Egypt's flag was raised at the Congress; it is green, a crescent and three stars, then it was red) being held in the hand of a woman leader at a national demonstration. She saw the woman brutally beaten, her veil torn from her head, the staff that held the flag broken in her grasp – but yet she held to it and would not let it go. A man, who intervened to protect a child from the brutality of the soldier's, was savagely set upon and beaten. When complaint was made, the British reply was to the effect that a native should feel honoured by being touched by a Briton.

The people (unlike the Irish, said Mme Pacha) were unarmed; and at one time not even butcher's knifes were allowed, while stones were even removed from the reach of the people, once the British even, 'massacred our trees', cutting them down (they are rare in Egypt and need cultivation and care) lest the youths use them as staffs to protect themselves. They went again in deputation – 'to ask the British to have mercy upon our trees' and to spare these at least. But the British declared that they were 'diseased' and must be felled! Until the people had broken some branches to use as sticks, no one had perceived the disease, she said gently smiling, and outwardly the condemned trees seemed as healthy as could be! But lest they be used in self-defence they had to go.

These incidents, the murders, the sudden 'riots' savagely quelled read like the 'reprisals' we endured. And then when Sir Lee Stack is killed – seven are killed by way of reprisal after 'trial', half a million fine is imposed and the Sudan is annexed, all for the life of one English official. The Sudan is Egypt's lost province – her unbidden guest has taken it over.

In the recent elections but 2 pro-government candidates were returned, with 240 against; a situation like our 'Southern' Parliament farce, when only four members (from Trinity) formed the Parliament, the rest being Republican. Whatever, however, the result of the elections, the British Junta continues to ignore the Egyptian people's demands. The Parliament is simply 'closed' whenever it suits the British; and the High Commissioner reigns supreme.

As to the future? Mme Pacha is hopeful. Egypt will survive, 'the country remains', the forever passes. Such has been her fate throughout the ages, such the effect of her ancient civilization. 'Free for ourselves, hospitable towards all' is her device. An international highway, her Suez Canal, internationally owned, with the British gone forever, and Egypt free to control her own destiny in peace. All parties are now united in Egypt according to Mme Pacha, against the foreign occupation which blocks everything 'entrava tout', as she expresses it. Eventually this break must be lifted, and Egypt must have her freedom restored. That is the message of this remarkable woman; and then, she said, smiling, 'we shall be free to be her friend, which now we cannot be.'

I have endeavoured to give the gist of her wonderful message. Its passionate eloquence I cannot reproduce; for it was enhanced by the force of her magnetic personality. But the moral at least is easy and obvious – that neither Egypt, Ireland, nor any other country, can thrive under foreign occupation; or, in Joan of Arc's own words, when she was asked for terms with the English: 'the only peace that I can make with the English is that they return to their own country.'

'Ireland off the map'
An Phoblacht, 28 September 1929
This is the impression that I sadly register after four weeks in Germany, Austria and Czecho-Slovakia. I had not been in Germany since the year before the war. Comparing memories, I find that Ireland was better known and understood then than she is now. Now she is regarded as a divided colony attached to Britain, or she is confused, even by intelligent foreigners (and at the WIL Congress we met representatives of over 30 different countries and of four continents) with Scotland, or even Iceland.

Consuls and Passports
This, though the Free State has 'consuls' abroad – for all the good they do as far as advertising Ireland as a separate country, they might be bulked in with the British, with a considerable saving of expense and no loss whatever save to the individuals themselves. Getting one's passport for Prague one found that even these unobtrusive gentlemen do not exist for Czecho-Slovakia. The London Czech consul pockets one's fee for the necessary visa! Yet we found in interviews given to the Czech, German and American press at the Congress that the passport was a distinct help. 'We Timothy Healy', – it was in his reign mine was issued – 'one of His Majesty's Counsel, Governor-General of the Irish Free State, request and require in the name of His Britannic Majesty' – and so forth. 'Certainly,' said one pressman to me, 'that is proof enough that you are not free! But why then call it the "Free" State?' Abroad one is classed as 'British' and when, returning home, at Ostend – in 'gallant little Belgium', for whom Irishmen died not long ago, with an Irish Cardinal's blessing – an official at the customs asked: 'What nationality? – British?' and the reply was 'Irish', one was surprised and relieved to find another, his colleague, adding with a smile: 'It's not the same, is it?' Thankful for small mercies!

Two Outstanding Figures

In Germany and Austria two figures stand out in recent Irish history – those are Terence MacSwiney and Roger Casement. In the case of the first, his name was sometimes stumbled over, but he was always correctly referred to as the 'Lord Mayor of Cork', and his prison martyrdom at Britain's hands was remembered. 'Casement, hanged by Britain', was also known. I found in France some years before that 'le lord maire de Cork' was also generally known and honoured. It is interesting to note that this instance of supreme sacrifice, of purely spiritual resistance, is more widely remembered than any other, bearing out Terence MacSwiney's own prophetic words: 'Victory will rest, not with those who can inflict the most suffering, but those that can most endure.'

Joyce, Shaw, Wilde

As to Irish names in literature that of James Joyce is most widely known in middle Europe. He is, I am told by an Oriental scholar, being now translated into Hindustani by an admirer. His works are already translated into most European languages. Professors and writers were eager to know anything at first hand of 'your great countryman', for, like him or not, as the reader may, Joyce is Irish in the very warp and woof of his mind, and Dublin at that. As he once remarked when reference was made to his many allusions to Dublin, 'there was some British queen who said that Calais would be found written on her heart. Well, Dublin will be found on mine!' Other Irish writers, Shaw and Wilde are placed as Irish too. Shaw has great vogue in Germany – they pride themselves there on appreciating Shaw and Shakespeare better than the British do and while in Dresden I noted that Wilde's *Importance of Being Earnest* was being played. In Vienna there was a comedy entitled *Linen from Ireland* at one of the theatres, but how far Ireland came into the theme beyond the title I cannot tell.

Tipperary

At a German school where French and English songs were sung in honour of the visitors, the teacher got a bright notion, on hearing that we were Irish and said 'Tipperary is in Ireland! We shall sing "Tipperary".'[4] Luckily, we were able to stop that atrocity and a harmless substitute about a 'boat and a ferry' was provided, with the assurance that it was Irish. If it was, we had never heard of it! Ireland is frequently confused with Scotland, and one professor assured me that he had got much delight and inspiration from the writings of Fiona McLeod, under the impression that he was referring to a compatriot. Of Fiona McLeod – or, rather, William Sharp – any country might well be proud, but Gaelic Scotland has the right to claim this great mystic as her very own. Two German writers have written on recent Irish history in sympathetic vein –

Der Frau des Feindes (The Wife of the Enemy) is a novel by Thurston and *Patria*, by Federer, were cited as evidence that Ireland's story has had echoes in German literature as in French, Spanish and Italian. I have not been able to procure, so far, either of these works, so cannot verify the statement for myself.

WIL Congress
The Sixth Congress of the Women's International League for Peace and Freedom, held at Prague, the capital of Old Bohemia and of the new Republic of Czecho-Slovakia, had some interesting and notable features. Delegates attended from over 30 countries, from four continents and the chief European states with the exception of Russia and Italy. The latter were refused passports by Mussolini, while the delegates from Ukraine had to come by an indirect route. Women from the East, from China, Japan and India were also represented, as well as coloured women delegates from Philadelphia, USA. Jane Addams presided over the polyglot assembly – where there were three official languages for all business – and is such an excellent and impartial chairman, so scrupulously fair, so business-like and brief, that I wish some men I know and under whose chairmanship I have groaned, would but take lessons from her!

India's Indictment
The 'high point', as the press put it, of the assembly was reached when the Indian delegate spoke – her address an impassioned and telling indictment of British Imperialism that starves and exploits suffering India – spending £43,000,000 on militarism to £1,000,000 on education. Many wept to hear her – she spoke in faultless English, even with an English accent, for she had studied in an English university – and some of the British delegates hung their heads in shame at her story. Later, Ellen Wilkinson, MP,[5] at a public meeting, denounced British Imperialism in frank terms, delighting the foreign press with her refreshing un-English candour. She stated truly that England at the League of Nations is a hypocrite as long as she maintained her stronghold upon other nations. Imperialism is a standing menace to the world's peace to-day as in the past.

Peace and Freedom
In Dresden, at a public meeting in the Capital theatre on September 1st, delegates from France, Germany, Austria, Ireland, Belgium, Canada spoke to the theme 'A World Without War'. Ireland's position was explained, that of a partitioned colony on whom an enforced Treaty was imposed. Her ideal was stressed as being that of an independent nation, part of Europe's commonwealth, and not a subject race dominated by foreign imperialism. Her objective, that of no peace of the graveyard ('Frieden des Friedhofs') but a peace of

freedom, compatible with the ideals of Peace and Freedom of the Women's international League.

Europe's Problems and Ours
Next week I hope to deal with some of Europe's present problems, particularly with reference to home conditions of a similar nature. For middle Europe, like Ireland, has passed through two phases of war, foreign and domestic, and while some states have emerged victorious and thus come into their own again, like Czecho-Slovakia, others have known the bitterness of defeat, with its slogan: 'Woe to the Beaten!' . . .

'The Bloody International: Post-War Europe Visited'
An Phoblacht, 12 October 1929
This is the name of a pamphlet written by a German scientist, Dr Lehmann Russbuldt, dealing with the scandals and ramifications of the armaments industry of the world. The author shows and his brochure is fully documented with every fact proved to the hilt, that all through the Great War the makers of armaments plied their trade with both belligerents indifferently, concentrating always on the best markets for their wares and shipped those *via* neutral countries. Thus, many Germans were shot by German bullets supplied by Krupp to Britain, and similarly the rubber, oil and other material used in munitions, explosives and war machines and serving to blow up English women and children were supplied in many cases to Germany *via* Switzerland, Sweden or Holland by Britain. Dr Lehmann Russbuldt told the whole story at the WIL Congress.

Gold for Iron
I noticed many German women wearing dull-looking iron rings, replacing their marriage ring. On inquiring I found that they had given in their gold ones in the war to be melted down when gold had run short. In return for their sacrifice of the precious metal, or the jewels that they gave, they received plain iron rings, bearing the date and the motto: '*Gold gab ich für Eisen*' (I gave gold for iron).

Pensions in Czecho-Solvakia
The Czech Republic grants no pensions to teachers or public servants who live outside the country, unless a clear case can be shown why such official must live abroad. If a teacher, having served the necessary number of years in a public school, decided to go away and live in England, his or her pension would automatically cease. The contrast between this practice and that of the Free State towards judges, RIC members and others needs no comment.

Europe's Wheel

I purchased an ingenious toy called 'Europe's wheel' in Vienna. It has spaces for thirty-four European countries in its radius, and by means of a pivotal device a pointer can be shifted to each in turn, showing simultaneously the number of inhabitants, size, chief town, highest mountain, form of government, and flag of any country selected. Andorra, the smallest republic, with 600 inhabitants in its capital: San Marino, Iceland, all were included. But in Europe's wheel there was no Ireland. We are lumped with the British Isles.

Carrageen Moss

Once I saw a mention of Ireland, in a large wholesale chemist's shop in Vienna. Here products (exclusive ones) of various countries in the world used in pharmacies were linked up on a world map by means of tapes and an arrangement of saucers with the country from which they were derived – gums, oil, spices and various drugs. And reposing in one saucer with tape attached to part of the Irish coast was carrageen moss! It was the one and only time I came upon a separate entity for Ireland in my travels. I feel an affection ever since for Carrageen.

Masaryk

The President of the Czecho-Slovakian Republic (which now comprises 60 per cent of the former territory of the Austrian Empire) is Masaryk. Railway stations, boulevards, social centres, housing schemes are called after him. His bust adorns various public buildings, his head is upon Czech stamps. I recall an interesting interview I had with President Masaryk in New York early in 1918. He was then a refugee from Austria with a price upon his head. I was speaking and lecturing in USA on 'British Militarism as I have known it'. When we met he chatted freely upon the world situation and showed a keen and intimate knowledge of Irish history and of our struggle to throw off the yoke of the foreigner. By a happy turn of events Masaryk has come into his own: the hunted, refugee and rebel is now head of an independent state.

Heimwehr v. Schutzbund

For all its seeming peace, there is danger at any moment of civil strife in Austria. It has at present two armed forces, the Heimwehr (or militia) and the Schutzbund (or official army). The Government at present in power has apparently not the force to disband and disarm the former, and clashes between the two organisations are of daily occurrence. The Catholic party (and it is said the Church too) backs the old regime and favours the chance of a *coup d'état* which will overthrow the present government. Austrian women delegates to the WIL told me that sermons were preached in the churches urging the

people to rise and overthrow the government. Yet the latter is now elected by
the will of the people. The government is largely socialistic: those who would
overthrow it, conservative and monarchical.

Political Prisoners
In Czecho-Slovakia, in the Ukraine, in Roumania and other Balkan states
there are to-day numbers of political prisoners, and their lot is like those at
home. I have material regarding the Ukraine and Czecho-Slovakia, pamphlets
dealing with prisoners that read like pages from the *Phoblacht*. Overcrowding,
bad food, no ventilation, brutal guards and jailers. In Prague, at a meeting
held by the Howard League regarding prison conditions, Camille Drevet, the
French writer and publicist, spoke upon her experiences in various countries
where she had gone to try and investigate prison conditions, particularly the
lot of 'politicals'. Her tale was a harrowing one. As she finished, the government representative from the Ministry of Justice arose and said, in Czechish,
that of course nothing of that kind could happen in Czecho-Slovakia. A German
journalist who was present later supplied me with data to the contrary. These
Ministers for Justice would appear to be strangely alike in their methods and
their official denials.

'The new Europe: a trip of scenes, sights and impressions'
Sunday Independent, 27 October 1929
I had not been to Germany since 1912, and then only to the Rhineland and the
North. This year it was my good fortune to go further afield to the fringe of
Slav territory in Old Bohemia, to Vienna – 'Little Paris', as she is still fondly
called – to the Styrian Alps, and to the lovely capital of pleasant Saxony,
Dresden, now centre of a new Free State. By the Danube, the Moldau, and
the Elbe I was able to indulge to the full my natural roving propensity, and all
who feel the urge of fitful spasms of 'wanderlust' will sympathise and envy. I
added three new countries – brand new from Europe's war melting-pot – to
my list. I like collecting them and comparing impressions. Already I had
visited thirteen, including more than half USA, Mexico, Canada, as well as
the still dis-united States of Europe.

First Impressions of Mittel-Europa
Getting into a train at Ostende one afternoon, one arrives in Vienna about
10 on the following night: in the same train one may continue to Buckarest
or Istanbul. There was poetry in the very names painted along the trans-
continental express –

> Though I fly to Istanbul,
> Athens has my heart and soul!

Sighed romantic Byron in his day. Nowadays to fly to Istanbul is a mere commonplace of travel, for all the capitals of Europe are linked-up by air routes, and one can fly from one to another with the greatest of ease. It is fascinating to see at Cook's in Vienna or Dresden the miniature airships in model on the counter and to study the air map. But for obvious reasons I indulged in no such venture, the train still being my magic carpet.

Travelling Companions: A Polyglot Trainful
Just as Ireland begins at Euston, Belfast at Amiens Street, so at Ostende the entire Continent spreads before one, even to far-off Turkey. The train itself speaks six or seven languages: one is warned in Dutch, French, Italian, English, German and modern Greek of the dangers of leaning too far out the window. The compartment in which I travelled contained an earnest Hungarian, who spoke all languages with ease, a voluble Russian refugee – she gave the impression of being at the very least a princess, but may never have got beyond the role of lady's maid – travelling with a mute, inglorious American business man husband – a suave and debonair Roumanian, returning home from a fashionable Ostende beach; a bridal pair, Swedes, and, at one period, a Czecho-Slovakian couple. On the corridor was a be-turbaned Oriental, travelling with four wives in a specially reserved coupé. The mixture of tongues and dialects – American-English, Roumanian-French, Czech, Slav, Turkish, Viennese-German, was international indeed. And that is the first thing that strikes one in new Europe: more languages, more frontiers than ever. The war has added fresh complications, set up fresh barriers.

Coins and Customs: A Contrast
Compare, for example, the United States of America with Europe's anything-but-united peoples. To reach San Francisco from New York, a distance of over 3,000 miles, one entrains on Monday and arrives at one's destination on the following Friday night. One may, by phone, from one's room in a New York hotel not only book reservations in the train, but may also dispatch one's trunk from one hotel to another across the Continent, and by means of a magic 'baggage check' system find it waiting in one's room on arrival in San Francisco. No customs, no frontiers, and one language: travel reduced to simplicity itself. Contrast this with European travel. From Ireland to Prague five examinations of luggage at customs, five different coinages (six, in fact, counting our new Free State currency) to be shifted and changed from frontier to frontier, passport or visa productions, complicated further by the rapid change of language – for English is no use beyond Ostende, French beyond Belgium, and to speak German in Czecho-Slovakia is to give national offence. Yet all the territory covered would nearly fit within the bounds of Texas, USA, a State that covers an area equivalent to the old German-Austrian

Empires. And post-war Europe has now about 34 different independent states or statelets. If Napoleon once declared that the map of Europe could be rolled up and put by until he was through with his campaign, so the World War lords in 1914 rolled up the map as we knew it, and unrolled it, in 1918, a very different one. How far that too, may be only in a transition stage, who can tell?

The European Wheel: The Missing Spoke
In a shop in Vienna I came upon a dainty toy called 'Europe's Wheel'. From a central pivot radiated spokes representing 34 different European countries, from Andorra, in Spain, to Latvia and Iceland in the far North. As one shifted the pointer to each European State in turn one moved corresponding discs showing its chief town, population, river, highest mountain, national flag and form of government. It was an ingenious and delightful geographic device. Studying its chart one realised at a glance the complications of modern Europe and its diversities. Andorra I had first made acquaintance with – it is still merely a bowing and aloof one – during a cross-word puzzle spell. But it is a Free State of Europe for all that though its capital contains but 600 souls. And I turned the wheel in vain for Éire – under Ireland or even its lordly Shannon. And the nearest I got to it was 'Gross-Britannien' – for its capital, its flag 'Free State'. I think Germany might have done better. The Irish spoke is missing still in Europe's Wheel.

A Visit to Russia[6]
August 1930
[Notes on 'Russia as I see it', brief jottings on a variety of papers, some very faded and illegible, in no particular order.]

Purpose – friends of Soviet Russia delegation – do not get truth. Over 5 weeks from Leningrad to Baku – still in making – roads, transport etc. Few general impressions, highlights. But a great hope and a great guest – making world better for the workers, letting them into their heritage. 'To be yourself'.
Week in Leningrad. 6 days in Moscow. The long trek across into other Soviet Republics – 5 in all – into Baku on Caspian Sea. 10 days in travel from one end to another. 5,000 miles.
Six weeks – out on Soviet Ship
Brown bread and red pamphlets
Land of intensive education and propaganda
Ship an autocracy – yet worked well
Dictatorship of proletariat in every detail
No need to insult workers by 'tips'
Preconceived notions got a shake
Leave umbrella behind – it's bourgeois

That and counter-revolutionary – the hardest words that can be used.

First impression – sense of security with hope and dignity – those who do not work shall not eat.

First reaction – smell of *[illegible word]* – Russian leather of bus

Sundays gone – effect

Travelling soft or hard – all Russia on wheels, freights and grain come first.

Language that reads from right to left – address that is upside down.

Complete comradeship in responsibilities too

Women an asset – for enthusiasm

An enthusiasm like a religion – 5 year Plan.

Workers' conception of life, – emancipating women from pots and pans and freeing children from the parental bondage as well as Church.

Cult of open air and sports. Sunshine, fresh air and water best friends.

Efforts to uplift – fighting drink, illiteracy, frivolity.

Acid test.

Shortage and rationing – when short all go without. No shop displays – cabbages piled.

Breakfast – meals – cold meat, boiled eggs and coffee in glass.

Lunch – meat and cheese, vermicelli and cutlet (veal) and peas. Russian tea.

Cheese and sardines breakfast – Friday.

Hammer and sickle everywhere. Waitress with kerchiefs around heads. Flat shoes, like sandals, pleasant.

Purges – only 1/4 million

Prisons not punishment – holidays, radio

Three classes – murder – 10 years greatest

Social pressure – boycott

Adoration of machine – a phase? Why – liberation

Folk dancing – no jazz

Chess – no cards

Sports – no professionalism

Churches a bad habit like drink or dope
  – work and pray
  – live on hay
  – you'll have pie in the sky
  – by and bye!

Freedom from tyranny of fashion and clothes, effect a liberatory one if you regard these as a fuss and a bore. Women with head scarves universal and greater diversity for men and women. No stiff collars anywhere!

Effect of seeing 'bourgeois tourists' – like seeing people dressed up for filmmaking á la Hollywood.

Children – no punishment – sports – pioneers

General liberation of women and children, women from the pots and pans, housework taboo – factory pride instead. Women encouraged to work outside home, communal life.

Talk with 2 re women.

'we are human beings, but not animals', attitude. Allowances accordingly. One partner can divorce (or even at Soviet Consulate in Russia?) for few kopeks. Prostitution illegal but it happens. Murder not always heavily punished. Circumstances considered.

Social pressure and removal from trade union the greatest stigma and a serious loss.

Lesbian love in Berlin – loose period in war.

Motherhood. 3 million population increase a year.

Social pressure strongest.

Treasures of art and beauty. Lovely gardens – palaces of labour.

Shortages and rationing – principle explained when short all go without.

No shop displays, no cafés, no race courses, no professional sport.

Much still a state of transition – a phase.

But what is permanent is real and a great <u>contribution to civilization</u> – two forces, fascism and Bolshevism.

Anxious for peace within borders.

Back into another world – and another century.

Attitude to national language and culture.

'Open Gate' says Lenin.

Artist has to produce 4 pictures per annum.

'Intellectuals' and 'intelligentsia' terms of reproof.

Because all at present serves propaganda.

Russia in state of siege – First things First.

But whole army of writers at her service. Anna L. Strong, Jack Reed, Lermenov.

Russian Anniversary Meeting[7]
November 1930

Greatest pleasure and privilege to propose Resolution greeting in your name to workers of Soviet Union and wishing them good luck. It was here in this very place that in 1917 the Irish workers – then in the majority still revolutionary and with Connolly's words still in their ears – first hailed the Russian revolution. 13 years have passed <u>but</u> experiment has not yet come off, but the Soviets have stabilized theirs and every year, every month that passes strengthens their Proletarian State. This is the third year of the 5 year Plan. Luckily, when in the SU this year – it was an experience that none of us who enjoyed the unique privilege can ever forget – <u>come what may we have lived to see it with</u>

<u>our own eyes</u> – we saw <u>Plans and Pledges</u> in many of the farms and factories showing them to be ahead of the Plan. 'The 5 year Plan in 4 1/2 years', in '4 years' or even less was a common slogan.

One saw the different spirit there, so different as to be almost unbelievable. No unemployment, 'unemployment and illiteracy liquidated' as they put it. 'Bread and work for all' and no bread for those who will not work. Hope for all – that wonderful security enjoyed in the SU alone in the world today, when the worker owns the state and the product of his labour and where he or she are insured against want, against sickness or loss of work. Where each new rationalization process lightens the work and betters the lot of the toiler, where the state is run by the worker for the worker. It is the workers there who have stakes in the country.

To those of us who saw the great achievement there can be no doubt of its ultimate success. But there is a duty upon us of the FOSR particularly and on all workers everywhere to help the SU by making the truth known and to launch a counter-offensive to the campaign of lies now being coordinated against it by the massed forces of capitalism. Capitalism, tottering itself into bankruptcy and general dissolution is prepared to fight in the 'last ditch' – that last ditch of the Diehards of which we heard so much in the past! It is determined not to loosen its hold and to bring down the Worker's State in Ruin if it has to go. Therefore all the catch cries of the politicians and the bourgeois are being used. A Hymn of hate is being intoned by the smug pharasees that prey on the workers. Just as millions were duped in the Great War by similar slogans, so now too the Lords of the earth are getting ready to fool the simpletons once again. Will they succeed this time? It is for the workers to see that they do not get away with it again. The SU is an object-lesson to all workers. What they can do we also could. How often, when showing us their crèches and schools, their cultural parks their pleasant guesthouses, their Soviet Farms did they say 'Why cannot you do this in your own country?' Why? Why? It is our duty to break down this paper wall, this conspiracy against the Workers State and to do it now, not to wait till too late. Messages are being sent tonight, by organizations all over the world to the SU. Let Ireland's Voice be heard there too.

12

MEMORIES OF COUNTESS MARKIEVICZ

INTRODUCTION

The popular image of Constance Markievicz, militant in her Irish Citizen Army uniform and revolver, contrasts strongly with that of Hanna Sheehy Skeffington in sober academic gown, as one of the early women graduates, a suffragette who insisted on 'Suffrage First'. Hanna's early polemics in *Bean na hÉireann*, in reply to Markievicz, would also convey the impression of women who might have occasionally worked together, but who would not have been personally close. The opposite was the case. As Hanna states, they lived near each other and their lives interlinked in many ways. Markievicz herself paid tribute to Hanna's role in the Easter Rising, welcoming her as she carried supplies to the garrison in the College of Surgeons. After that watershed and with the removal of any difference of tactics on campaigning for suffrage, with the granting in 1918 of suffrage to women over 30, both worked to achieve a shared ideal of an independent republic. The letter written by Hanna to Nancy Wyse Power of Cumann na mBan, during the campaign to support the election of Constance Markievicz,[1] reveals some of the determination of the feminists of the Irish Women's Franchise League to ensure that a woman (and particularly one whom the League regarded as a friend) would be elected.

Correspondence concerning the continued imprisonment of Markievicz after the truce of July 1921 demonstrates Hanna's concern for the wellbeing of her friend, and her realisation that without Markievicz's release, negotiations between the Irish leaders and the British government would lack the voice of the one woman who was an elected representative. It is highly revealing of a political arena indifferent to women's concerns and gives us a glimpse of the growing friendship between Hanna and Eva Gore-Booth, sister of Constance, whose feminism, socialist commitment and support for the Irish revolutionaries she admired and appreciated.

'Memories of Markievicz', an undated typescript in the personal papers of Hanna Sheehy Skeffington, contains lively vignettes of Markievicz and the times in which she lived. She gave this to Esther Roper, the life-long partner of Eva Gore-Booth, who incorporated much of it into her introduction to the *Prison Letters of Countess Markievicz*, first published in 1934. The typescript was a source that Hanna mined for various newspaper articles over the years, highlighting the woman who had been the first to be elected to parliament and Ireland's first female government minister. A selection of these are contained in this chapter, together with some correspondence between herself and Esther Roper. Eva Gore-Booth died in 1926, the year before Constance

The most powerful article written by Hanna about her friend was unquestionably her description of her funeral, as 'the People's Idol', written in the bitterness of the aftermath of civil war, with grief for one who, like so many others, had died too young. Hanna was appointed executor of Markievicz's estate and in the succeeding years she ensured that her memory was not forgotten.

Memories of Markievicz[2]
Surrey House
I lived in 1908 round the corner from Surrey House, Leinster Road. Madame, though not a feminist ever and only a mild suffragist (she held that suffrage would come with a lot else when Ireland was free), was always interested in direct action of any sort against authority. She was also keenly interested in people: her home was a meeting place for rebels of all sorts. She would rush in and say 'Come along tonight; I want you to meet so-and-so. The gas is off and the carpets are up – but you won't mind! Tell Frank to come along.' Then we would meet the particular 'lion' and talk round the big fire, sitting on her large divan in the big bow-window, by the light of innumerable candles stuck around.

It was to this house Connolly was brought after his hunger strike, when Lord Aberdeen hastily released him. It was from here Jim Larkin went forth disguised to address the multitude (in August, 1913) from the windows of the Imperial Hotel, O'Connell Street, owned by William Martin Murphy who had locked out the tram workers of Dublin.

No Fixed Home after 1916
After 1916 her home at Surrey House, Leinster Road, Dublin, was raided and wrecked by British military – pictures, lace and valuables were looted. The crowd came later and finished this business, until a friend intervened and had the place padlocked. Many of Madame's possessions found their way as 'souvenirs' into soldiers' and officers' kits and were given to their lady-friends. A hand-press was found there too and smashed up. A manuscript for an article Madame was writing (or reading for some friend) on Catherine de Medici

caused anxious query among the soldiers. 'Who was this woman? A Sinn Féiner?' They were only partly reassured finally when told that the lady was dead for several centuries.

From that time on Madame never had a home of her own. She was 'on the run'; raided, imprisoned, travelling for the movement and held merely two furnished rooms as her temporary place of abode. Her large pictures and few personal belongings, silver and the like, she stored in the houses of friends. Though she loved beauty and possessed even then, out of many wrecks, some exquisite pieces of old furniture, valuable pictures, first editions, autographed copies of verses, etc., all that she had was literally at the disposal of friends. I never knew a person with less sense of property or less attached to possessions. Her linen and other effects went as a presentation to St Ultan's Hospital, founded for babies of the poor by her friend, Dr Kathleen Lynn (who had served with her in the Irish Citizen Army and had been deported after 1916). I have seen her when someone admired a vase, a picture, say: 'Do you like it? Take it,' and literally force the thing upon an embarrassed acquaintance.

I first saw Constance Markievicz on the stage at the Gaiety Theatre, Dublin, where she was acting as Eleanor in George Bonningham's comedy, *Eleanor's Enterprise*. The play was produced by Count Markievicz, himself a dramatist and producer of no mean parts. Constance also played in his drama, *The Memory of the Dead*, a play of '98 in which the role of rebel heroine was written and cast for her. As an actress her high pitched voice and English accent, and her short sight which in later years entailed the wearing of glasses, were disabilities.[3] But her temperament suited rebel and heroic parts, and these she shone in. later, too, her acting gifts helped her with various disguises, necessary when she was on the run, a much-wanted Cabinet Minister. She often chose the role of an elderly and rather feeble old lady, with Victorian bonnet and cape. It was all right as long as she did not speak. But her voice instantly gave her away! During all the time that she was on the run, staying a night here and there with a friend (we all had lists of friendly houses where, if pressed, we might pass the night), though Constance was well known to tram conductors, newsboys, basket-women, and all over Dublin, none of them ever gave her away, or even pretended to recognize her as she passed. 'The Countess', as Dublin called her, (accent on the second syllable) had the freedom of the city, literally.

She herself wrote plays, all of a rebel and propagandistic character – *Blood Money*, *The Invincible Mother*, *Broken Dreams*. The Fianna and the Cumann na mBan or Republican Players staged these and she herself helped to produce them. Owing to the haste with which they were thrown together, feverishly dashed off like her sketches and poems, they did not rank as literature, but there is fire and quality in them for all that – and, of course, propaganda.

Madame ran a roneo paper, writing, printing and circulating it herself, during '22–'23. She was a good cartoonist, and many of her sketches and lampoons were printed in the current republican press.

She had always by her a pad on which she drew pen-and-ink or pencil sketches and portraits. She had the gift of seizing a salient feature, and would dash off sketches of her colleague round a Sinn Féin Committee table or at an Ard Fheis or public meeting, in court, or at a courtmartial, even. Many of these are preserved; some excellent likenesses of friend and foe. She did men's heads and profiles better than women's. Her sketches of Éire or Banba or Dark Rosaleen were conventional.

Her favourite recreation of late years was to take out her little Ford car (a secondhand 'bargain') to the mountains, take lunch along and her sketch book and paint all day.

She loved to fill her little car with children and take them.

I had this from a woman friend arrested and put into Kilmainham Jail with Constance Markievicz. This woman was a member of a rebel women's group founded by Maud Gonne, of which both were members. Perolz was in an adjourning cell when one morning by the friendliness of a wardress she was allowed to get a glimpse of her neighbour. Constance was sitting on her plank bed and looked radiant. She asked P. for the loan of a comb, and when it was handed to her – a pretext to get her inside the cell – she said: 'Oh, P . . . did you hear the news? I have been sentenced to death!' This with such a radiant smile of rapture that it sounded as though she was announcing some tidings of great joy.

A Good Prisoner

Later she was to see the inside of many jails, Mountjoy, Aylesbury, Holloway, Cork and again Mountjoy. She was to be twice courtmartialled and conveyed once in a battle-ship with no female escort over to England. Aylesbury was the hardest experience. A convict, a lifer, alone amongst the most hardened criminals, with murderesses and worse. Wearing convict clothes with the broad arrow, shut away from the world. She was put in the kitchen to help with the cooking, and was given the hardest, most menial tasks. But even here she won friends, and her good spirits and comradeliness broke down barriers. 'Chicago May' tells in her memoirs later how she learned to know Countess Markievicz when both were serving life sentences and what a good sport the latter was.

Madame was what was known as a good prisoner, that is, she did prison work and kept the rules. She never hunger-struck in protest (neither did de Valera, who is said to have scruples on the matter) until at the very end in 1923 when a sympathetic strike was initiated. While in Mountjoy and Cork she did gardening for her health's sake and helped to lay out the Governor's garden and border-beds. She was an enthusiastic gardener and had a 'lucky' hand. Most of her friends, rich and poor, have still plants that 'Madame' planted for them – Madame's rose, Madame's lavender bush or rosemary, Madame's rockery bloom still, and are remembered for her.

She also helped in the prison library, helping to catalogue and make selections. She was in prison for three Christmas times running (1916, '17 and '18) and used to say plaintively: 'I wonder if I'll ever be out for another Christmas!' She helped while in Holloway to prepare ornamental sketches and scrolls for her sister's book.

In Holloway she and the other women interned for Mr Short's German Plot were accorded special treatment, being internees rather than regular prisoners. They had cells set apart on a special landing with separate bathroom for themselves, and took exercise separately. They sewed, embroidered, wrote or painted all day. They were refused letters or visits, however, and saw no newspapers. When, therefore, one August morning they saw a cell being got ready for some new inmate on their corridor they were full of curiosity and conjecture as to whom it could be. 'Well, I hope it's Hanna Skeffington,' said Constance, 'for she'll tell us all about America!' (I had just returned, and having broken the passport regulations by crossing from Liverpool to Dublin without a permit, was arrested in Dublin and sent to Holloway 'for the duration'.) She was right, and soon afterwards I arrived. I had been hunger-striking since my arrest some days before, and I continued to fast, though Madame advised me to discontinue for she feared I would be forcibly fed. I was not weakened yet, however, and we talked and walked about all day together exchanging news; – we had not met since 1916 in the College of Surgeons. After two days I was released and conveyed to a hotel in London. The others were held for many months afterwards.

Madame, who loved the fresh air, sunlight and freedom, must have suffered a lot from prison. It must have shortened her life by many years.

In the Soup Kitchen at Liberty Hall
The next big event in which Madame Markievicz played her part was the great Lock-Out of 1913, when she helped the struggling labour leader, Jim Larkin, in his big fight against the heartless capitalists of Dublin. Twenty thousand men were locked out by their employers sworn to break the Union, their families threatened with starvation. Church and State were ranged, as usual, on the side of the big Battalions, ready to starve the workers out to break their resistance through the hunger of the children of the slums. Constance Markievicz at once stepped boldly into the breach, organized a Soup Kitchen, a communal kitchen, and fed the poor of Dublin for weeks, raising a fund, sub-scribing herself, collecting from her friends, and, better still, tucking up her sleeves, donning a big overall and presiding personally over the *[illegible word]*

16 Hanna and her son Owen after their arrival in the USA,
December 1916. Image courtesy of Library of Congress,
Prints & Photographs Division (LC-B2- 4085-15).

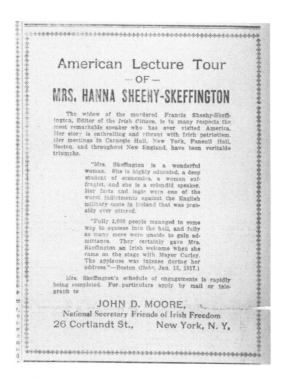

17 An announcement for Hanna's lecture tour of the USA in
the *Gaelic American*, 10 March 1917. Image courtesy of Digital
Library@Villanova University.

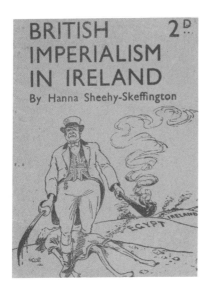

18 The cover of Hanna's pamphlet *British Imperialism in Ireland* (1936). Image courtesy of the NLI.

19 A studio portrait of Hanna at the time of her American tour. Image courtesy of the NLI.

20 Hanna and the National Woman's Party, Washington DC, *c.* 1917. Hanna, second from left. Image courtesy of the NLI.

21 Hanna seated with a large costumed group in America, c. 1917. Image courtesy of the NLI.

22 Hanna and Mrs Pearse, *c.* 1921, possibly during the Treaty debates. Image courtesy of the NLI.

23 'Irish Women's Mission' to America, 1922. Front row, left to right, Linda Kearns, Hanna, and
Kathleen Boland. Image courtesy of the NLI.

24 The Sinn Féin executive 1922. Hanna on extreme right, front row. Also in front row, Kathleen Clarke and Dr Kathleen Lynn. Mary MacSwiney is in the second row. Image courtesy of the NLI.

25 Mary Thygeson, American suffragist Alice Park, and Hanna, outside Hôtel de Nice, Paris, June 1926, attending the International Women's Suffrage Congress. Image courtesy of the NLI.

26 Hanna seated at the top table of a St Patrick's Day banquet, Paris, 1929. Image courtesy of the NLI.

27 Hanna on far left with delegates from France, Germany, America, Canada and Belgium in Dresden, September 1929, where she was a speaker at a public meeting called 'A World without War'. Image courtesy of the NLI.

28 Coverage of Drogheda meeting of welcome to Hanna after her release from Armagh Jail in *The Irish Press*, 22 February 1933. Image courtesy of the NLI.

29 Hanna, third from left, seated beside Seán MacBride at the inaugural meeting of the Students'
Literary and Debating Society, November 1940. Also present are Kathleen Clarke, centre, and
Maud Gonne MacBride second from right, front row. Image courtesy of the NLI.

30 Studio portrait of Hanna in the 1940s. Image courtesy of the
Sheehy Skeffington family.

of Irish stew in the big kitchen at Liberty Hall. Milk depots, clothing centres, fund-raising committees – she looked after them all. Thanks to her, the children of the poor were fed and the homes of those locked-out men were provisioned during the long siege.

Truce and Prisoner Release[4]
Letter to Eva Gore-Booth n.d. (July 1921)
My dear . . . I rang up press and Castle and prison. No news, but apparently it was they thought C might be out shortly. Since then nothing. Position briefly this. Dev and Grif. are not asking <u>any</u> releases – didn't ask G's or Barton's.[5] These 'happened' just. G and McM were unsentenced and two other Dáil members were released with these – apparently under mistaken notion that these were Cab. Ministers. They aren't. Duggan and Staines (latter IRA). Then we thought no sentenced MPs would be let out when to our surprise Barton was. He only got 1/2 hour notice. Now as far as I know Con is the <u>only</u> minister in, but the govt may not even know this as they are stupid. Any other Mins. I know are 'on the run' – Stack, Blythe, Cosgrave, Collins. Con was seen last Sat by Miss Gifford ('John Brennan' y know)[6] who went in as 'typist' with solicitor (Noyk) to witness her will. (This was commonplace) now Miss G. reports her anxious to get out and very eager about it, hoping for news. She (Con) didn't know that no one was being asked for and hoped Dev or Mick[7] would move. As Lab. Min. she wants to be there at any conference . . . There may be Cab. Meetings . . . Now my personal opinion is that Barton's relatives put pressure on unofficially – else why select him? he got 5 and she only 2 years – and so I'd say send letters to press just pointing out that Cab. Min. for Labour is still locked up, get questions in Parliament – all done <u>individually</u>. She said perhaps their woman would but when our League tried that before, you know, we were snubbed by C. herself and told to stop! So it makes it difficult especially as I think if she knew these other details that she mightn't care for any society to move. And besides I don't know how you feel – myself I'd say get her out because it's her desire to be out and if B. and rest are out why keep her in? But I know she hates being treated as a <u>woman</u> so it ought to be as 'Lab. Min.' I also hear your family (Sligo) doesn't want her out but not for <u>your</u> reason – again of course I can't say if this is true. Anyhow if not out soon it may be too late. She is reported thin and rather nervously excited, inclined to fidget etc. though of course <u>not ill</u>. But naturally she must be straining at the leash just now.

I give you details and leave it with you to take any action. Let me know if I can help in any way. *Freeman* has been specially mentioning her and pressing for her release in its leaders. Our side haven't much hope of peace though one important person (not SF) is going to London tomorrow – I think to see Smuts.[8]

In haste
H.

Letter to Eva Gore-Booth[9]

17 July 1921

Dear Eva,

Of course I would love to call you 'Eva', rather than 'Miss' and am glad of the privilege. I delayed writing because of all kinds of misleading and contradictory rumours, but now it's as well for me to sum them up and you can act accordingly. First, I was correct in guessing that, though no names were asked for specially for release, there were unofficial pourparlers and the persons since released were specifically mentioned. Macready promised at the Mansion House to let out all the 'better educated' shortly – miserable snob that he is! As soon as things got underway, the 23 (or 25) Dáil members were to be released and a general jail delivery to follow. Desmond Fitzgerald had his bag packed for some days, being told to await news. Others are being prepared similarly – he is, as you will have seen, now out. I don't see why they haven't pressed for Con: her name was mentioned by a woman (Mrs Kent) to one of the unofficial go-betweens on our side (I don't know whom but a man who had got Barton and other's names) but he didn't follow it up, she says, merely adding that all would soon be out and I can't help feeling that and I heard this only two days ago, but felt it was so instinctively, had she been a man, she would be out, but then she herself so hotly resents that imputation that it impedes our doing anything qua woman. But there it is. I mentioned her to Griffith and Dev but was told (as I wrote you) that no names were asked. It's clear that if things move at all, they will all be out shortly and if they don't – well nous recommencerons! I think the militarists or British rule would like to keep her in, as they have always hated her specially. Mrs Power[10] says (and gives Dr Lynn as her authority but the doctor is away now) that the family in Sligo want her kept in. But you would know that – your brother she specially mentioned. I think it's probably not accurate but these things get about – Dr Lynn is herself from the West and had I seen her she might have thrown light on things. Mrs P is not very accurate and is include to get wrong impressions and to pass them on, unconsciously coloured.

There is strong feeling here that there will be peace as outcome, with some concessions and possibly a plebiscite on terms. But there are many who would regard Peace short of Independence as a defeat – and in spite of my desire for Peace, I am one of these. It's a very difficult matter and one of responsibility either way. Of course, if the country votes Peace on a plebiscite there is nothing to be done, but accept for the time being. And a lot depends on how the leaders put it as to how the people will vote. Democracy to many is only a name and people in masses do as they are told. It's very critical and even on very eve of truce there was danger of something untoward. But that is now over for the present at least while official truce is on. You will I expect have seen our people ere this and may have some news from them. There are a few women over but only as typists or private secretaries. Still even that breaks the monotony! I wish C. had been there.

With love,

Affectionately, Hanna.

'The people's idol: the state's head'
Irish World, 6 August 1927

[This was written for the American newspaper, the Irish World. *It was a tale of two funerals, one that of a government minister, the other that of the woman who had achieved international fame for her militant role in the Easter Rising and who opposed those who had taken the Treaty side. Hanna paid tribute to the political career of her friend Constance Markievicz, while using the opportunity afforded by the assassination of Free State Minister for Justice Kevin O'Higgins, to make pointed remarks regarding the repressive nature of the Irish Free State. The funeral of Markievicz saw a spontaneous demonstration of popular grief and celebration of a life that had been devoted to working for political and economic freedom. Her death, at the age of 59, was a shock to many. Markievicz was a member of Fianna Fáil, which had done well in the election of June 1927, polling only three seats less than the government party.]*

Constance Markievicz is dead – after a sharp fight against death in which she seemed to have emerged victorious she suddenly collapsed, dying peacefully at midnight (1.25 new time), July 14, the date of the storming of the Bastille. De Valera spoke yesterday at her grave her appropriate epitaph as follows:

> Madame Markievicz is gone from us. Madame, the friend of the toiler, the lover of the poor. Ease and station she put aside and took the hard way of service with the weak and the downtrodden. Sacrifice, misunderstanding and scorn lay on the road she adopted but she trod it unflinchingly. She now lies at rest with her fellow-champions of the fight – mourned by the people whose liberties she fought for, blessed by the loving prayers of the poor she tried so hard to befriend.
>
> They would know her only as a soldier of Ireland, but we knew her as a colleague and comrade. We knew the friendliness, the great woman's heart of her, the great Irish soul of her, and we know the loss we have suffered is not to be repaired. It is sadly we take our leave, but we pray High Heaven that all she longed and worked for may one day be achieved.

In Tense Contrast

Within one week we have had two funerals – a State and a National one, presenting the sharpest of contrasts, illustrating in silent pageant most forcibly the truth of Thomas Davis's saying: 'There are only two parties in Ireland, the party that stands for the imperial connection and the party that stands for Ireland.'

On Wednesday the vice-president of the Free State, Kevin O'Higgins, was buried in Glasnevin. On Sunday Constance Markievicz, first woman MP, Minister for Labor in the Republican Dáil, was brought to Glasnevin also and laid next day in the Republican Plot beside Harry Boland and O'Donovan Rossa. The first was a State funeral, made impressive by military and police pomp, at which were marshaled all the forces of the Crown. A public holiday was enforced, all Government and public departments being closed, every Government official and supporter being mobilized, in addition to police, military, the judiciary, the churches of every denomination, headed by State cavalry. Foreign consuls, the British and Northern Government representatives, the Fascisti, Big Business – aeroplanes circling overhead: in short, the Big Battalions were all present, in full array, together with the oath-bound members of the Upper and Lower Chambers. Lord Birkenhead, to his regret, was prevented by a dense fog from flying to Dublin for the ceremony.

Previously there was a solemn lying-in-state in the Mansion House (home of the Republican Dáil in earlier days), which was elaborately draped in black for the occasion. Every effort was made, the cost being levied on the public purse to make the funeral as full of pomp as possible. For the stacks of flowers piled upon gun carriages and lorries every Government department had an enforced levy.

The cortège was four miles long. Flags flew at half-mast from court-houses, halls and public buildings, and from Trinity College the Union Jack flew side by side with the Tricolor. The coffin had military honors, being borne upon a draped gun carriage. At the graveside the firing party gave the soldier's last salute. 'Britain's youngest colony' as the Imperialists are fond of calling the Free State, gave an imposing military display. But the people were absent. As an onlooker quaintly summed it up, 'It was a professional funeral.'

At Constance Markievicz's funeral, official pomp and pride were absent. She who was a soldier, Ireland's Joan of Arc, as she was called, had a civilian funeral, while the lawyer vice-president of the Executive Council had the honors of war. In her case every effort was made by the Junta to boycott. City Hall and Mansion House were refused curtly by the Government-appointed commissioners (O'Donovan Rossa's body in 1915 had lain within the stately City Hall, guarded by Volunteers).[11] The lying in state took place, none the less, for the management of the historic Rotunda put it generously at the disposal of the committee.

Idolized by the Poor
The Fianna Éireann (the Irish Boy Scouts organization, founded by Constance Markievicz, of whom she was chief scout at the time of her death) mounted

guard, and thousands of the poor of Dublin flocked to her bier from early morning throughout the long summer day and during the entire night; watch being kept all night by the Fianna boys and by her women comrades. Her coffin, draped in the tricolor which she helped hoist over the College of Surgeons in 1916, on which lay the green tunic and belt that she wore as second-in-command under Michael Mallin, was borne from the hospital mortuary to the church, and again to the Rotunda, not on a gun carriage, but on the shoulders of her comrades and brothers-in-arms – de Valera, Art O'Connor, Barney Mellows, Patrick Ruttledge being among those who carried it.

Along the line were no mounted chargers, police or uniformed military, but a band of Volunteers who clasped hands, forming a living cordon to let the procession pass. No bishops walked, and but few priests, two Franciscan monks, Father Sweetman, Father Ronayne (Rome) and Father O'Ryan, Dublin (widely beloved also by the poor and the prisoner, whose friend he is).

In the cortège were the TDs, oath-bound only to the Irish Republic, the Cumann na mBan, the 1916 Club, the Prisoners' Defense League, the Republican Executives, Fianna Fáil and Sinn Féin, the rank and file of Labor and of the Republican movements. A notable feature (another contrast with the official funeral in which women were almost entirely absent), was the number of women who walked – many of them working women, street traders and the like, for as one of them said, 'Madame was a friend of the women with the shawl.' By her bier they pressed, kissing the glass that covered her face, so serene, so remote in death, touching the wood of the coffin as a sacred relic, 'the friend of the poor' was their epitaph. I stood there hour after hour and watched them pass – the women with their babies that they lifted up in mute farewell, comrades of 1916 and later; nuns, 'little sisters of the poor'; sandaled friars of St Francis; dockers, whose families she had fed in 1913, when the Big Battalions were bent on starving the workers out; families whom she had supplied with turf, and timber last winter during the fuel famine, ex-prisoners, relatives of the executed men – in short, Dublin's proletariat, her constituents.

'For she gave all; he took all,' as an old woman picturesquely phrased the difference between Constance Markievicz, revolutionary, and Kevin O'Higgins, Imperialist.

The room where she lay had been lovingly draped by the Cumann na mBan and the Republican women's organizations, and filled by them with pine-branches, laurel and sheaves of wild flowers, heather, willow herb, laurel and ivy. Ere long it was a bower of flowers, wreaths and trophies coming from friends abroad and at home. From the Republican Army, from her 1916 comrades, from her God-daughter, Constance Partridge, whose father[12] fought under her in the College of Surgeons, from 'AE' (George Russell), her old friend, and fellow artist, from Maeve Cavanagh, woman-poet of the 1916 Revolution, from American friends in New York, Boston, Philadelphia, San Francisco, from Éamon de Valera, from suffragists, 'to our first woman MP and Minister for Labor', from her daughter Maeve and her stepson, Stanislaus Markievicz, from her fellow players, the Republican Actors, from the 'poor street traders of Camden street', whose cause she championed, from factory girls and box-maker, from Jim Larkin – to read over the inscriptions alone was to realize how wide-flung were Constance Markievicz's sympathizers, how deeply-rooted her place in the hearts of her people.

One pathetic chaplet of water lilies fashioned from Irish shells was brought by Madame MacBride. Memorial wreaths from shells are a new industry started at Roebuck House by Mme MacBride to give work to unemployed Republican girls.[13] As was her wont, Constance Markievicz took up the scheme warmly, first with its artistic possibilities as well as its practical value, for those memorial chaplets are delicately beautiful and ought ere long to replace those hideous glass-covered monstrosities hitherto used. The shells in the little wreath were gathered by Constance Markievicz herself but a few weeks ago along Portmarnock's silver strand. Eight motor lorries were piled high with these tributes: they now cover over the entire Republican plot.

Ireland's Joan of Arc

The official world was represented to a man at Mr O'Higgins's funeral. While the people were absent; at Constance Markievicz's the reverse took place. Officialdom stayed away and the people turned out en masse. The friends of Empire mourned at the one 'the pillar of the State', to use Mr Cosgrave's own words, while the friends of Kathleen ni Houlihan wept at the bier of the other, who, in Grace Plunkett's apt phrase, had 'surrendered place and pleasure for the service of Ireland'.

No sharper, more dramatic contrast could have been staged than these two funerals, typifying, as they did, the two forces ever at war with each other for the possession of Ireland: the one that would hold the nation for the foreigner, the other that would free her forever from his hated yoke.

On Wednesday the massed battalions of England's faithful garrison in Ireland assembled to pay their last tribute to Kevin O'Higgins – 'unsurprised are her sons till they learn to betray'. On Sunday Ireland's Citizen Army and Volunteers mobilised the entire republican movement as in one unit in honor of Ireland's Joan of Arc.

George Russell, moved by the 1916 Rising and Ireland's tragic Easter, wrote this of Constance Markievicz and the women of Ireland. Though he has lapsed, like others, from his earlier dreams, his lines are worth recalling:

Here's to the women of our blood,
Stood by them in the fiery hour;

Rapt, lest some weakness in their
Mood
Rob manhood of a single power –
You, brave on such a hope forlorn,
Who smiled through crack of shot
and shell,
Though the world look on you with
Scorn
Here's to you, Constance, in your
cell.

Here's to you, men I never met,
But hope to meet behind the veil,
Thronged on some starry parapet
That looks down upon Inisfail;
And see the confluence of dreams
That clashed together in our night,
One river born of many streams,
Roll in one blaze of blinding light.

Journalists present at both funerals testify (and this estimate is confirmed by the unfriendly *Manchester Guardian*) that, for all the pride and pomp of the official funeral, that of Constance Markievicz by far exceeded it numerically, taking four hours to pass.

The Shadow of Evil
One final strange contretemps took place, which resulted in the burial being postponed to the next day and the coffin being stored overnight in a temporary vault. Owing to trade union red tape the Glasnevin gravediggers, members of the Transport Workers' Union, decline to bury anyone on Sunday and were unable to relax this rule for Constance Markievicz, even so far as to allow Volunteers to take their place.

The State, unaware of this obstacle, rushed a large contingent of military, CID and police to the Republican Plot. These waited at the graveside, ready to rush it and to make arrests were military honors paid, this aggressive act being now part of the usual routine observed by the State at all republican funerals. When it was announced that the coffin had been placed in the vault overnight the military withdrew – to return next day and repeat the indecent performance. Police stood by as the coffin was lowered to its last resting place and military with fixed bayonets formed up near-by. The Fianna boys sounded the Last Post – and once again the military and police withdrew after their futile display, no excuse being given for violence and bloodshed at the grave of Constance Markievicz.

One American journalist, puzzled at the sight, asked the officer in charge whether he had been sent by the Government as a guard of honor to the dead Republican commandant. He replied emphatically: 'Not at all.' But he seemed, none the less, somewhat perturbed at the query. Outside the cemetery four lorry-loads, reinforced with machine guns, were drawn up – all this military display was marshaled to prevent a young Fianna boy from firing a blank shot over his commandant's grave.

Yet from the official point of view the entire procession of yesterday, being in military formation, was illegal, and all those who took part in it were liable under the Treason Act, the Safety Act and the Emergency Act of the late Kevin O'Higgins. We are now promised another act (I do not yet know its title), a sort of super-treason-cum, Safety-cum Emergency Bill which will further extend and enforce the powers of the military to repress popular manifestations. Yet it is a strange and ironic comment on all their coercion and treason measures, and on all their irrelevant displays of armed force, that the vice-president of the Executive council should be shot within sight of his home. And that none of all this militarism availed to protect him at the end from the bullets of armed men. The love and loyalty of one's own people are a better armour than all the machine guns ever made; a securer protection than all the treason and safety acts ever devised.

Having this shield, Constance Markievicz needed no further weapon; without it, the vice-president of the Free State's Executive Council perished.

'Constance Markievicz – died July 13, 1927 – what she stood for'
An Phoblacht, 16 July 1932

Monuments to the dead are often misused – sometimes, no doubt, unconsciously – by the living to misinterpret what those whose memorial is unveiled truly stood for. Constance Markievicz, whose bust has been unveiled in Stephen's Green, where she fought, as Commandant in the Citizen Army, has suffered similarly. It is due to her memory that an attempt be made to place on record what she was and what she stood for.

Constance Markievicz was primarily and essentially a revolutionary, an iconoclast, with the direct vision, the divine discontent of a Joan of Arc, whose impatience with half measures and compromises she shared to the full, a direct actionist, no respecter of persons, however highly placed or respectable.

The picture painted by Éamon de Valera of Labour's revolutionary heroine is conventionalized beyond recognition. It resembles those portraits by 'studio artists' that improve away the real features of the sitter, smoothing out the wrinkles and furrows for a touched-up image of their own, the image of a chocolate box heroine. It is an apologia where none is needed.

In the speech at the unveiling Constance Markievicz is thus described: 'To many she was simply a strange figure, following a path of her own, not following accustomed paths, but the friends who knew her knew that she did that because she was truly a woman . . . She put aside wealth and position that might have been hers.'

'Love of her kind caused Countess Markievicz to join the ranks of the Citizen Army with James Connolly twenty years ago.' 'Ideas which were common today were then regarded as revolutionary . . .' Then follow references to helping the poor and oppressed to earn a livelihood.

Connolly's ideals, so far from being realized today by any parliamentary party are as 'revolutionary' as ever – and as unattained. Both Connolly and Constance Markievicz stood for a Workers' Republic.

Constance Markievicz was a disciple of Connolly, a member of the Irish Socialist Party. One of its objects was the ownership of the land by the people, who were to have control of the right of production, distribution and exchange; nationalization of canals and railways, abolition of private banks – those and other 'revolutionary' ideas were her ideals. Not a word of uplift, of doing good to the poor in all this.

The interpretation of 'Madame's' attitude to the 'poor and lowly' is one which she herself would have laughed to scorn. For the poor 'who are always with us' were not to Constance Markievicz a fixed, inevitable part of the eternal scheme of things. She challenged the capitalist system under which the dispossessed toilers of the world are exploited. She stood for nothing less than scrapping the 'sorry scheme of things entire to mould it nearer to the heart's desire'. She has left us unmistakable evidence of her attitude in her writings, notably in a pamphlet written in defence of James Connolly, in response to the challenge of a clerical anti-Socialist critic.

Constance Markievicz was associated intimately with the formation of the Citizen Army arising out of the Lock-Out in 1913. When 'Christian' employers were banded together to starve out the families of the locked-out, it was she who rallied to their support, going down to Liberty Hall to minister comfort to them, in person; she was no patronizing Lady Bountiful, no well-meaning philanthropist, but a rebel, meeting challenge with challenge, giving back blow for blow.

'Madame' was, above all, a bonny fighter: her militant spirit was that of Queen Maeve or Granuaile, her countrywomen. She had no early Victorian repressions and inhibitions, none of the sheltered femininity of the drawing-room type. Where there was work that appealed to her to do she did it, whether it was carrying up bags of coal to a tenement back-room in the fuel famine of Cosgrave's late régime or shouldering a gun and sniping at the enemy from the roof-tops in Stephen's Green in 1916 or in O'Connell Street in 1922.

It would take a Connolly or a Mellows or one of the valiant women of the Citizen Army, her comrades-in-arms – to have appraised Constance Markievicz at her real worth. It is a matter of history that Boland's Mill was the only rebel fortress in Dublin where no women were permitted to assist in 1916.[14] Cumann na mBan members were in other Volunteer-manned areas, the Citizen Army women shared command and responsibility in theirs. This fact sufficiently illustrates the radically conflicting viewpoints of Connolly and de Valera – both consistent, both divergent – towards women and towards class distinctions and revolution, as distinguished from evolution and constitutionalism. To the one, woman was an equal, a comrade; to the other, a sheltered being, withdrawn to the domestic hearth, shrinking from public life. Each viewpoint has its exponents, but no one will deny the self-evident fact that Constance Markievicz, Ireland's Joan of Arc, belongs to the former category. As typical of resurgent Ireland's revolutionary womanhood, she has her place in history and all those who pass her memorial in Stephen's Green, near Mangan's Dark Rosaleen monument, will salute her as one of Ireland's revolutionary leaders.

Letter to Esther Roper[15]
15 July 1933

Dear Miss Roper,
  – Thanks so much for Eva's poems – it was a joy to read those I had once seen once again. That one to F. S. S. I specially prize from her. I liked your Foreword very much – it recalled her so vividly.
[Letter continues by sending articles, cuttings, and typed lectures given by Hanna.]
  PS Today, strangely, is the anniversary of Con's death.

Draft of letter to Esther Roper n.d. (1936)[16]
[Explains why she cannot stay in London when en route to France and mentions her article on Markievicz published in the Irish Press *below, 'it's not much either, but still a memory'.]*

. . . am getting horribly sad stories of pacifists and Jews persecuted in Germany. What a time we live in! Here we are rapidly becoming a Catholic statelet under Rome's grip – censorship and the like, with a very narrow provincial outlook, plus a self-satisfied smugness. Result of a failure in revolution really. I have no belief in de Valera. Well meaning, of course, better than Cosgrave, but really essentially conservative and church-bound, anti-feminist, bourgeois and the rest. A sort of professor-type, like Wilson and enamoured of phrases and abstractions.

Sorry your asthma troubles you – and I suppose Ireland would be bad for it? Yes, I wish you could see Con's portrait in Gallery. Thanks for what you say about Owen,

Sincerely,

H. S. S.

'"The Countess": some memories'
Irish Press, 4 February 1936

Constance Markievicz was born on February 4, 1868, she died in July 1927; what a full life was compressed into that comparatively small space! Her memory is like a fragrance which time but intensifies. 'Madame', or 'the Countess' (accent on the second syllable) has her name inscribed in the hearts of the poor, as Pearse wished his to be, in that of a child, not as a remote Lady Bountiful, but as a neighbourly comrade. Today even her enemies – like every active spirit that has bumped up against smug privilege, she had these – now recall her with kindliness, forgetting how bitter and unfair they once were.

May I recall a few odd memory-flashes of her? She lived near us, in 1908, in Surrey House, Leinster Road, just around the corner. We swapped lions when they came a-visiting Dublin. Labour leaders, Indian rebels, writers. She would come flashing in to invite one to an impromptu party, to meet Eva, her sister, pacifist, feminist, poet, to talk to Liam Mellows, taking a weekend breather from his Fianna organizing, or Margaret Skinnider, over from Glasgow, one of the women who later was to fight under Madame in the College of Surgeons, in the ICA, and to be wounded, or James Connolly, up from Belfast, in 1913 planning to help for her soup kitchen in Liberty Hall.

Again rushing in to cheer and wish one luck when, in 1912, a group of us broke Government windows in Dublin Castle, the Custom House, the GPO in protests against the omission of Votes for Irish Women in the then Home Rule Bill. Only indirectly interested in the struggle (she put other things first) she rallied at once when women showed signs of revolt. That stone in the cobwebbed windows of the Castle won her! Years before she had similarly gone to the help of the Manchester barmaids that a Puritan-minded Government was trying to deprive of employment on the hypocritical grounds of morality.[17] When she was heckled by an interrupter with the query, dear to the Victorian male, 'Can you cook a dinner?' she flung back, 'Yes I can. Can you drive a coach-and-four?' She was doing this at the time, so he was nonplussed, and she had the ready sympathy of the crowd.

Another scene. The day of a TCD 'rag', when the students poured into the IWFL premises in Westmoreland Street (the headquarters of the Irish

Suffragettes), their object being to wreck the place for 'a bit of fun', for we were fair game. Madame was in the rooms when the invading band burst in. She had a knack of being on the spot when there was trouble. They flung open the windows, throwing out banners, bunting, pictures, draping themselves in our colours, orange and green. When a ringleader seized a green, Irish-inscribed poplin flag (made for us in Dun Emer, our dearest treasure), Constance Markievicz called a halt, seized the pole, crying, 'Come, boys, not that! That's our best flag. Be sports! You can have the bunting and ribbons, but leave us our flag.' And they did; it hung on the walls intact, above the wreckage. Later, when the leaders were hauled before a police magistrate (the same who not long before had sentenced some of us) charged with riot, Madame, called as witness, declined to recognize any of the youths, like the good sport she was. They had offered to make good the damage, so we saw no reason why they should go to jail in addition.

Another suffrage memory is of a night spent by her making armour for Joan of Arc in a Women's Pageant we were staging. What fine fifteenth century pieces she contrived out of cardboard silvered over . . . and what a characteristic Joan she was. And how she toiled over old pictures of the time to get it just right. She posed as Joan, appearing to a suffragist prisoner in her cell, to cheer her. Her alert, gallant bearing was well set off by her silver armour, helmet and uplifted sword. She flung herself with her usual zest into the part, making a magnificent Joan. When, years later, one April day, 1916, I beheld her in action in the College of Surgeons, wearing the uniform of the Irish Citizen Army, that earlier vision of Joan flashed upon my mind's eye. They were not so far apart.

Another memory. This time a debate between Constance Markievicz and Francis Skeffington, in a hall in Parnell Square, in February 1915. The topic, 'Shall We Make Peace Now?' He pro-peace, she for a longer war, as she held Britain was being beaten. After a warmly-contested word-duel, just before the vote was taken, James Connolly, who had been a quiet on-looker, suddenly intervened, on Madame's side, swinging the meeting round. When Skeffington laughingly reproved him for throwing in his weight at the end, he replied, with twinkling eyes: 'I was afraid you might get the better of it, Skeffington. That would never do.'

After Easter Week the waters closed over her. We met no more till one early August morning, 1918, when I was shown into Holloway Jail, where she, Madame MacBride and Mrs Clarke had been interned from about the previous May in connection with Chief Secretary's Shortt's famous 'German Plot'. I came under DORA for having, on my return from USA, crossed to Ireland without a passport. All four of us were 'for the duration'. (She was actually held until March, 1919.) It was a strange meeting . . . we talked till cells were locked. And in spite of grim surroundings we were quite happy, merry even at times, as we exchanged news.

Later her triumphant return to Dublin, her Ministry, Committee meetings, most of us 'on the run', Madame disguised as an old, feeble lady, but always recognizable by her voice, so she had to be dumb as well. At the Treaty debate her impassioned plea, lit up with rare flashes of humour, other arrests . . . till one midnight I am summoned to her death-bed, only in time to see her die.

Eva's birthday poem, written to her in prison February 1917, best expresses her bright spirit:

> What has time to do with thee,
> Who hast found the victor's way
> To be rich in poverty,
> Without sunshine to be gay
> To be free in prison cell?
> Nay, on that undreamed judgement day,
> When on the old world's scrap-heap flung,
> Powers and Empires pass away,
> Radiant and unconquerable,
> Thou shalt be young.

'Christmas in prison: how Countess Markievicz spent it'
The Distributive Worker, December 1938
Christmas Day is, of all the 365, the loneliest in prison. Sundays and Feast days are the days prisoners – politicals most of all – dread as the most monotonous, for one is shut in one's cell all day, save for morning church service and a brief spell for so-called 'exercise' (and that only if weather permits). No visitors are allowed those days – why, I know not – and, as there is no work, the prisoner sits with his or her own thoughts the live-long day. One gets up, of course, at the same early hour; so the slow hours drag interminably, and unlike the rest of the world, one actually welcomes Monday.

Christmas Day has all the above drawbacks, with some peculiarly its own. For all of us, as we grow older, it is a lonely day often, for vacant chairs are thought of wistfully, and absent loved ones missed as 'Auld Lang Syne' is sung at the end of the festive day. But in jail there is no recognition of Xmas, save on the calendar and in one's heart. There is no change in the dull diet-Christmas ranks just as a Sunday, and you get a sort of suet pudding to mark it. On Coronation Day, under the British, one got an atrocity called plum duff, a sort of treacle pudding, only found in jails. I don't suppose they get that, however, in Éire, and the menu on Xmas Day is probably still as it used to be. Once, when I was a political, I tried on my release to get some recognition of Xmas Day into the heads of authorities but to no purpose.[18] There is a concert, it is true, during the Xmas season, but not on Xmas day. The officials are themselves desirous – who can blame them? – to get home to their Xmas turkey and the rest.

I remember Constance Markievicz saying wistfully 'I do wish they let me have an Xmas at home!' It was her fate after 1916 to spend three or four Xmas days in jail (though she was out at intervals in between), and even her happy, resilient spirit began to feel the strain when Xmas day came. Here is a little poem she wrote for her sister, Eva, around Xmas, 1916, from Aylesbury Jail, where she was serving a life sentence and treated as a convict:

> We're folded in a sheet of rain,
> Clasped to the heart of things;
> My spirit slips its yoke of pain,
> And one with nature sings:
> I am the cloud that floats so free,
> The boundless space, the deep blue sea;
> Of Heaven and Peace I hold the key,
> And poise on golden wings.

She writes of receiving Xmas Cards, but apparently not on Xmas day itself! One rough sketch by her sister was actually held up for several days, as the censor suspected a plot for escape in the innocent greeting! 'The Home Office had to be consulted,' she wrote explaining the delay. And this is her Christmas card – 'for all her friends' –

> The wandering winds of Xmas time,
> The twinkling of the stars,
> The messengers of hope and love
> Defying prison bars.
>
> The birds that fly about my cage
> Are vagrant thoughts that fly
> To greet you all at Xmas time –
> They wing the wintry sky.

'I have all the cards arranged upon my bed, and they are the greatest joy,' she writes. On one Christmas Eve her sister wrote her: –

Do not be lonely, dear, nor grieve,
This Christmas Eve.
Is it so vain a thing
That your heart's harper, Dark Rosaleen;
A wandering singer, yet a queen,
Crowned with all her seventeen stars,
Outside your prison bars
Stands carolling?

This was the poem, with its sketch of a waiting angel, that suggested an escape plot to the watchful Home Office! She was in Holloway Jail on Xmas 1918. In 1920 she was in Mountjoy again – she was also in Cork in the 'Tan' period, and in the Civil War in the North Dublin Union Internment Camp, 1923 – the prisoners were released after the mass hunger strike just in time for Xmas that year. And it was from jail also that she once wrote to Eva: –'Remember, no one has it in his power to make me unhappy!'

[Another article, 'Markievicz: memories and reflections' was published in The Distributive Worker, *February 1940. One additional piece of information was contained in that article, namely that the proceeds of the 'Do We Want Peace Now?' debate of 1915 between Markievicz and Frank Sheehy Skeffington were divided between Cumann na mBan and the IWFL, an example of cooperation between the two groups.]*

13

THE 1930s: FEMINIST REFLECTIONS
AND FEMINIST FIGHTBACK

INTRODUCTION

Many of Hanna's writings in this period are well-informed, measured reflections regarding the position of women, not only in Ireland and Britain but internationally. They were published in Irish, British and American journals. The depth of detail they contain is an indication of the wide scope of her reading and the extent of her networks, providing us with extremely useful compendia of the global status of women during the last decade before war. Hanna continued to travel extensively and, as she explained to her feminist friends in the Minerva Club, wherever she went, she looked out for the women's movement and sought to discover what successes it might have had. She visited Prague, Dresden, Russia, France, England, America and Canada, attending women's congresses, earning money on American lecture tours, and visiting friends and family. This inter-war period was a dangerous time and she saw clearly the growing backlash against women and the continuing growth of fascism. She was foresighted in her recognition that there was no political will to strengthen the role of the League of Nations, and no desire on the part of countries to curb the production of arms.

Hanna also made it clear that she believed the Irish Free State still had to be opposed for its betrayal of the ideals of the revolutionaries of 1916. Her memories of some of the signatories of the Republican Proclamation, while written many years after the tumultuous events of 1916, provide a glimpse of a more carefree time when the lives of future republicans and feminists criss-crossed, as fellow students, as audience members at cultural events, as friends and comrades. Now, Hanna worked with Maud Gonne MacBride and other women members of the Women's Prisoners' Defence League, challenging the Free State. When Frank Ryan, editor of *An Phoblacht*, was jailed she became editor of its temporary replacement, *Republican File*, which sought to escape censorship through publishing clippings from other papers. It was a time of danger and considerable hardship for many. Together with Charlotte Despard she acted as joint treasurer of the Irish National Aid Association, supporting unemployed republicans. While the victory of Fianna Fáil in 1932 saw the release of political prisoners and a hope that political life would finally stabilise, Hanna remained openly critical of de Valera, particularly for his conservative views on women.

She remained uncompromising in her opposition to partition, occasionally defying a banning order imposed by the unionist government in order to visit Skeffington relatives in the north. In early 1933, when she crossed the border to speak on behalf of women imprisoned in the north, she knew that she was in danger of arrest. Her month of imprisonment in Armagh Jail is included in Chapter 14. The civic receptions and guard of honour she received on release indicated her importance within radical circles and of the esteem and affection in which she was held.

Hanna and Frank Ryan both resigned from *An Phoblacht* in 1933, finding their blend of socialist republicanism out of favour with the physical force advocates now dominating the IRA. It was a significant departure – from then onwards, her focus was once again the fight for women's equality at a time when feminist voices were badly needed.

The strengthening influence of the Catholic Church on Irish society continued inexorably with the Censorship of Publications Act in 1929, the ban on married women in the civil service in 1932, the ban on contraceptives in 1934, and the restriction of women in industrial employment in 1935. The first act of the Free State government had been to restrict women's right to jury service, through the 1924 Juries Act, followed up with the 1926 Act. Hanna, as we can see from her writings, opposed all of these measures and was actively involved in women's opposition. The final insult was the 1937 Constitution, promoted by Éamon de Valera, head of Fianna Fáil, a party that Hanna had joined on its formation, only to leave shortly afterwards in favour of the radical republicans gathered around *An Phoblacht*. The Women Graduates' Association, with which Hanna had been involved since 1902, was the leading organisation in the campaign against the draft Constitution. They organised an open air meeting on 21 June 1937, where resolutions condemning articles prejudicial to women were condemned. Hanna proposed a resolution calling for the formation of a women's party, to protect women's political, social and economic interests.

In her criticisms of de Valera Hanna rarely failed to mention his refusal to allow the women of Cumann na mBan into his outpost of Boland's Mill during the Easter Rising. It was an indication, she maintained, of his 'mawkish distrust of women'. Her warm recollection of his mother, Catherine Wheelwright,

written on her death, stands in sharp contrast. *Prison Bars*, a small news sheet
edited by Maud Gonne MacBride for the Women's Prisoners' Defence League,
was the only women's paper since the demise of the *Irish Citizen*. It published
objections to the Constitution from women who had been prominent in the
nationalist movement, including Kathleen Clarke and Kate O'Callaghan, but
the article written by Hanna was the longest and most comprehensive in its focus.

Hanna was more than a single-minded revolutionary. Her interests were
wide, as were her networks of family and friends. She remained an avid reader,
as her talk on Irish women writers to the Minerva Club confirms. She began
to include recollections of her childhood and youth in her analyses of past
movements for Irish freedom. She recalled her uncle, Father Eugene Sheehy,
who had been an enormous influence upon her, both personally and politically.
Her son Owen, with whom she had an extremely close relationship, married
the daughter of an old French friend in Paris, and the addition of her daughter-
in-law Andrée to the family was a source of great happiness to her. Her sister,
Mary Kettle, became chair of the Women's Social and Progressive League
and Hanna a member of its committee. By the end of the decade, full of
foreboding, Hanna warned of the insidious tendency towards fascism, in both
Ireland and Europe, and lamented, again, that the likelihood of Ireland's
unity being restored was as far away as ever.

'Memories of the suffrage campaign in Ireland'
The Vote, 30 August 1929

The votes for women movement here received, as in England, a new impetus
and inspiration from the suffragette or militant phase. When the staid form
'Woman Suffrage', so ladylike and so academic, merged into the war-cry,
'Votes for Women!' we of the younger generation in Ireland – now in our turn
growing old, but not forgetful of pioneer dreams and adventurous, crowded
hours – took up the cry and flung ourselves joyously into the fray. The
suffragists of earlier days – the venerable Mrs Haslam, that Quaker pioneer
who did so much to shape feminism in Ireland as far back as 1860 or thereabouts,
and who lived to vote when she had almost attained her century – did much in
Ireland also to break ground. But their methods of very peaceful and rather
slow penetration did not do more than touch the fringe of things. They concentrated on drawing-room gatherings, on lobbyings, petitions, deputations,
on the use of the local government franchise, and on returning women for
local bodies. Much they accomplished in educative work and, as for local
government work and the like, why, men (and Irishmen are quite human in
that respect as in others) had never any great objection to women doing spadework, provided they had no direct power and that they were interested in
ameliorative and limited reforms having to do with children, poor law, and

the like – the kind of things that men generally 'really have not time for'. These women suffragists, too, were mainly Conservative, or at best mildly Liberal. They did not touch the people and were in the mass even opposed to Home Rule or to any nationalist advance. They were frankly unprogressive, and one of the favourite arguments used for suffrage by them was, 'My gardener and my butler have the vote. Why shouldn't I?!'

Then votes for women came and militant methods. Following the example of the Women's Freedom League and the Women's Social and Political Union, the Irish Women's Franchise League came into being in 1908. Offices were taken, a paper started (the *Irish Citizen*, founded in 1912 by James Cousins and F. Sheehy Skeffington), meetings were held, not now and then, but weekly, almost daily, not in drawing-rooms, but in Phoenix Park, in O'Connell Street, on soap boxes at street corners, everywhere. Protests against the exclusion of Irishwomen from votes in the Home Rule Bill ended in jail. Government buildings had their glasses shivered, and politicians who shelved or derided were heckled and harried. Those MPs who used to tell women year after year that they were our 'best friends' and 'had always voted' for our Bill, began to see that this was not nearly enough unless their party pulled its weight. And both John Redmond and Sir Edward Carson were alike in one thing – namely, their opposition to votes for Irishwomen. And how angry they were when reminded of the fact and opposed accordingly! In Dublin we used to be told that votes for women was a Tory device to spoil Home Rule and that we were 'playing the Tories' game', while in Belfast, during a meeting I spoke at in Ormeau park, the Orange crowd drowned our voices with the strains of 'God Save the King' (always a party tune in Ireland) and scornfully told us to 'go back to Dublin,' as one might tell someone to go to Hades!

But militant methods, especially 'agin' the Government', won us Irishwomen much sympathy and support, especially among the revolutionaries. James Connolly was always a friend of women, as all his writings show. He never failed us even when some of his own right-wing supporters tried to trim. He believed, as he used to say, that as long as women were 'the slaves of slaves', there could be no real freedom for men. He was one of those all too rare revolutionaries whose doctrines of freedom apply all round. It was James Connolly who wrote into the proclamation of the Irish Republic in 1916 the enfranchisement of women, and the document, signed by the seven men who afterwards gave their lives for Irish freedom, is the corner-stone of our liberty. It is the only instance I know of in history where men fighting for freedom voluntarily included women. The French revolutionaries, for all their prating of the Rights of Man, meant thereby only the Rights of Males, so the Americans in their Declaration of Independence forgot to make their women citizens, and the great George Washington owned slaves. It was left for James

Connolly to write Equality for Women upon his tricolour – had it been recognized and allowed to function peacefully, the Irish republic would have been the first to give its women votes; Britain only did this in 1918 – partially.

Workers, men and women on the Clyde and elsewhere should not forget James Connolly. Were he alive today he would be in the forefront of the Equality campaign.

These are but a few stray jottings of our earlier campaign in Ireland that may have interest for feminists today. They are intended as a tribute to the spirit of militant feminism, whose campaign is still being conducted and whose struggles will go on until the equality of men and women is fully recognised all the world over. For, as long as there is a single woman unfree, so long we all remain enslaved.

'Gay recollections: the lighter side in Ireland's fight for freedom'
An Phoblacht, Christmas 1929

There is a wealth of material, a regular gold-mine of anecdotes, adventure, drama, regarding the last thirteen years awaiting historians, memoir-writers, dramatists, poets and novelists. A few Irish writers, some British, American, French and Germans have already picked here and there among the treasure-trove; most, however, lies still unexplored. Much will probably never be worked out, for it will perish with those who lived it through: much indeed has already disappeared. For those were years of swift action, of strife and peril, on the run, in jail: such are not propitious to writing or leisurely narration.

Tales told around the camp-fire, by some cottage hearth, in internment compound, adventures lived through under these conditions vanish like smoke, their only immortality being in the ear of those that hear them. So I pity the poor bewildered historian of the future when he tries to get down to business. His material will be too scanty for proper reconstruction. Already most of those who write have done so from an enemy angle, putting their pro-British twist upon facts, garbling, suppressing.

When recently I was asked for data by an American research-writer, who took the Irish struggle for independence as his thesis (one of the finest of such University theses, on preparations on modern Ireland, hails from Columbia University, New York). I set to work to compile a bibliography only to find, alas, that most of the works upon Easter Week were written by anti-Irish writers, so that straightaway the student would have to check up his data, having a choice between no material and enemy production. The list was scanty and all too meagre. I had not forty books in all, including even ephemeral and flimsy ones.

True, we cannot all be historians, but everyone who has lived through the war period has experiences that should be jotted down ere memories fade. I would like to see every reader of *An Phoblacht* take this to heart and write down some personal narrative. One cannot have too many such accounts and impressions.

Fugitive Impressions

There are many fugitive impressions that seem slight and hardly worthy to be recorded. Yet these too go to the making of history. In this brief Christmas article let me rummage in my memory for a few of these in the hope that others may perchance follow me up and do likewise.

First, a few stories of children's sayings. I recall hearing of a little girl who, steeped in an atmosphere of shooting, first heard the tale of the Passion and her childish heart torn with sorrow, hastened to tell her mother about Christ's Agony, as children love to record a tale just heard.

'And then, mother, what do you think those wicked men did? They took out Christ – and *shot* Him!'

Naturally she could only think of one form of death in the Ireland of those days – taking one out and shooting him.

Similarly, when Michael O'Callaghan, Mayor of Limerick was raided, a drunken Tan said, on someone mentioning God: 'God? Oh, He is dead.' 'Shot while attempting to escape, I suppose?' retorted the Mayor, with a smile. Such deaths were the Tans' usual alibi.

Another child, a little boy, asked what he would be when he was grown up, proudly replied: 'I'll be shot.' And a youngster, hearing that a church in the neighbourhood of her home had been destroyed by fire during the night, asked at once: 'Who shot it?' A psychologist of childhood would find interesting and curious sidelights here on the child-mind in Ireland during the Black and Tan Terror.

Liam Mellows: A Memory

Recently I read in the interesting leaflet published by Cumann na mBan on Liam Mellows a reference to his strange experience while on the run in 1916 after Easter Week, in Clare, with three companions. The tale is usually referred to as that of the 'Fourth Person', from the fact that during their wanderings on the hills, the three comrades were conscious all the time of some unknown presence whom they used to speak of as 'the fourth man', who warned them of certain dangers and at last guided their steps to safety. Dorothy Macardle tells the tale finely in *Earthbound*. I heard Liam himself tell it in New York when he came over early in 1917. His impression, however, was that the fourth man was Padraic Pearse.

I remember asking Liam what he found the hardest in his 60-day journey (for he had to come *via* the Bermudas) from Ireland to America, working his way as a stoker. His reply was, smilingly: 'The language! I never knew that men could talk so vilely.' The reply was characteristic of the man.

I remember also how when Liam was arrested in New York, when trying with Dr McCartan to escape to Ireland, after the US went into the war, the American Press made great capital out of the name of the prisoner. It was explained that 'Liam' was Turkish, proving the close sympathy between Sinn Féin and the Turks, then allies of the Germans and consequently alien enemies! So young 'Liam' was evidently a terrible Turk.

As an instance of the remoteness and indifference of the common people of the USA towards the war, and the confusion of nationalities in the popular mind, I recall in New York being stopped in the street by a puzzled old woman who asked me who those soldiers were that had just passed? I said, 'Australians.' 'Oh,' she replied, with shocked horror, 'I thought we were fighting *them!*' She confused Australians with Austrians. Can one blame her or reprove her ignorance when the daily press that she read mixed up Sinn Féiners with Turks?

Fire-Brigade Arrested

To come back home, I remember, during the 'Tan War, how one Sunday morning in Rathmines, when folk were wending their way to church, there was a fire-alarm raised. Cullenswood House was being set on fire by a party of British soldiers (the Wiltshires, if I remember rightly). The reason? Oh, reason enough. An ambush had taken place early that morning in Terenure and Richard Mulcahy was said to have ordered it. He was supposed to be staying at Cullenswood House (he had a flat there) consequently the logical British were engaged in burning it down as a 'reprisal'. I managed to phone the fire-brigade – they responded to the call, turned out duly, and were promptly put under arrest! Mrs Pearse's house burnt out unchecked, the Dublin and Rathmines fire-brigades being prevented from doing their duty.

A Novena

About that time, when Black and Tans were running riot in Dublin, there was a raid in Oakley Road. Lorries stood about full of 'Tans, in command of a dapper officer with an eye-glass and cane very spic-and-span. He jauntily perched upon the end of the lorry, watching operations and airily swinging his cane, as he hummed a British music-hall ditty. Presently the lorry started forward with a jerk, pitching him face forward into the mud. He arose a much-battered object, eye-glass broken, cane snapped, uniform coated in Dublin mire. An old woman on the opposite side of the road paused to chuckle gleefully over his condition, eyeing his rueful countenance as he wiped off the mud and muttering to herself: 'Praises be to St Joseph! The first result of my novena!' Her prayers had been heard: British pride had had a fall.

Constance Markievicz

Constance Markievicz used to say that she had spent most of her Christmases after 1916 in jail. In 1917 she was in Aylesbury, in 1918 in Holloway (taken up in May of that year by Mr Shortt in connection with his bogus German Plot).

Again, under the Free Staters, she was arrested in December, but released (if I remember rightly) just before Christmas. And most of the time in between she was on the run or on active service. She loved a Christmas at home, and used to say wistfully: 'I hope they'll not take me this Christmas!'

This year the collected poems of her sister, Eva, have appeared. The following, written to Constance in Prison, is worth quoting:

Christmas Eve in prison.
Do not be lonely, dear, nor grieve:
This Christmas eve.
Is it so vain a thing
That your heart's harper, Dark Roseen,
A wandering singer, yet a queen,
Crowned with all her seventeen stairs,
Outside your prison bars
Stands carolling?

'Irishwomen's place in the sun'
The Vote, 15 August 1930
Anti-Feminism in Irish Political Parties
Professor Mary Hayden declared the other day that Irishmen were anti-feminists all. There is much to be said in support of this statement, both of Irishmen generally and of politicians in particular.

When I stated at the Minerva Club, to the Women's Freedom League, that our three political parties are anti-feminist, I gave data in support of this opinion. Interviewed by a special correspondent in Dublin, certain members of these parties subsequently stoutly denied the allegation. They naturally would. Now that women possess the vote, politicians can no more safely own up to anti-woman bias than would they agree to be called reactionary or obscurantist. Pressed on facts they fall back on Father Adam's alibi: it is all the fault of the women themselves.

A Double Dose of Original Sin?
As a race we Irish used to be credited by our enemies with a double dose of original sin. Has this now shifted to Irishwomen? When women, in other countries, now emancipated, are playing their part in world affairs, are we alone, through our own fault solely, still ingloriously mute? What are the facts?

Irishwomen's Part in Revolution
Irishwomen received full franchise before the women of Britain. An Irish constituency was the first to return a woman to Parliament, when the

Harbour Division, Dublin, elected Constance Markievicz in 1918. She was
then in Holloway Jail. On her release she was appointed Cabinet Minister for
Labour in the Republican Dáil, Ireland again leading the way by putting a
woman in its Cabinet. At one time there were seven women Deputies in the
Dáil, while Britain had only one woman MP. Britain has now fifteen women
MPs from all parties. During the stormy years between 1917 and 1922 women
played a prominent part in public affairs and in revolutionary activities. They
were appointed mayors, councillors, aldermen, judges, arbitrators, heads of
executives, some even holding military posts. Five Sinn Féin women were
elected to Dublin City Council, holding office during its stormiest sessions:
Irishwomen were voted the freedom of our chief cities on the one hand, they
were jailed, deported, shot (by both belligerents) on the other. Then came the
Treaty. The women deputies (then six in number) all voted against it, and the
present government has never quite forgiven our sex ever since. Sinn Féin –
which stands outside the Free State Parliament – still alone maintains the
earlier attitude of equality for women, from which Fianna Fáil and Labour,
the official Opposition have fallen away.

Revolution's Aftermath
Women in Ireland still suffer from the effects of the revolution that missed
and of the subsequent reaction. What was given at first with gladness has been
gradually filched away. Equality has ceased to be accorded to us, save on
paper. There is now but one woman Deputy in a Parliament of 153. She is anti-
feminist, voting with her party against her sex when occasion arises. Fianna
Fáil, since its entry, ran one woman candidate – in the same area, North Dublin,
as the Government's doubtless for the same reason – in the last election. Labour
has never put up a woman candidate for Parliament. As there is Proportional
Representation in the Free State, facilitating a panel arrangement, and as the
sexes are nearly equal, in Dublin the majority of the voters being women, all
three parties could, if so minded, run a woman on their tickets in each electoral
area without undue feminism. One out of 153 cannot be described as 'consistent
inclusion in their panel of women candidates' – no, not by any stretch of the
imagination.

Upper House Women
Fianna Fáil has one woman in the Senate (the former candidate for election to
the Lower House),[1] the Government, four (one, the Countess of Desart, a
pronounced and unrepentant anti-suffragist, by the way), and Labour, none.
Some of these women were nominated, some elected on party lines. It is
unlikely that their numbers will be added to. In fact, last year when a woman
Senator, Mrs Green,[2] died, it was only by a sharp struggle with the Government

Party that another woman was accepted for the vacancy,[3] and women were then given firmly to understand that they would be eligible only on the death of a woman Senator. As the Senate has practically no power beyond that of a temporary veto, as its sessions are short and infrequent, and as many favour its abolition or reduction; the concession of five women Senators out of sixty is no proof of feminism. Indeed, with one exception,[4] the women Senators vote not as women, but according to the policy of the party that nominates or elects them.

Local Representatives

On local bodies, city and county councils, the paucity of women is still more marked. Here, as with Parliamentary candidates, the machinery for selection and running of candidates (the party clubs and caucuses) is almost entirely male, women members being discouraged, save in strictly subordinate capacities or for social functions, to raise funds. There are, it is true, a few women on the party executives but their influence on party policy is negligible. Fianna Fáil has at present only one woman representative upon any public board. Labour also has one, the Government two or three. As the number of members elected to public boards is over twelve hundred, it may be fairly deduced that no party greatly favours women. The women at present serving on public boards belong either to no party or to the Republican (Sinn Féin) group. The one woman-chairman of a council in the Free State belongs to none of the three Parliamentary parties.

Government's Anti-Feminism

The Government party has the worst record of anti-feminism. It has deprived women of the right to act on juries, a right possessed in Britain and Northern Ireland. On marriage, women are dismissed from public services, technical teaching, and other posts; posts for women usually carry less salary; women are excluded from certain higher Civil Service appointments. No scheme for widows' pensions operates. No women justices or judges have been appointed even for Children's Courts. Even the few so-called policewomen in Dublin have not the power of arrest, nor the status of their male colleagues. There are about half a dozen peace-commissioners as against hundreds of men. Female prisons are in charge of male governors. Women court-stenographers were abolished a year or two ago. Parliamentary Committees and Government Commissions frequently include no women – the Commission on Unemployment and the Committee on Legitimacy, both intimately affecting women, have no woman member. Legislation for the protection of girls has been delayed for over seven years. These are but a few instances of Government anti-feminist bias: the list is by no means complete.

Controversial

When Miss E. Rathbone, MP,[5] visited Dublin recently and gave an address to the Women Citizens' Society in reference to Family Endowment and the position of women in public affairs, she was not permitted to broadcast her talk because the authorities considered her subject 'controversial'. Women are apparently considered controversial, so fearful are our rulers of our holding 'views'.

Fianna Fáil and Labour

The Government is the most serious offender, because it can translate its anti-feminist leaning into deeds. But all parties are culpable. Mr Lemass, Secretary to Fianna Fáil, is a declared opponent of votes for women, having stated more than once that he would like to see woman suffrage repealed. In his opinion women should vote as their husbands, brothers or fathers, so their vote is either a duplicate one and unnecessary, or the reverse and so pernicious. Mr de Valera, in a recent interview in Boston, stressed his preference for the domestic woman, who is content merely to inspire her men folk to high deeds. While not anti-feminist in theory, he would fain save us from the care and stress of the political arena, which he considers detrimental to womanly charm. He would like to 'save women' from politics.

A Gentleman's Agreement?

It has been stated authoritatively, recently, that the two big parties in the Irish Free State have entered into a gentleman's agreement to run no women candidates in the next election, there being the difficulty that, if a woman appears on one panel, the opposition feels obliged to run a rival or run the risk of losing votes. As hitherto these parties have run but two (one against the other in the same electoral division) and as one of these is now in the Senate and the other is said to be retiring, the decision would be merely the natural outcome of their anti-woman policy. We shall have to await the next General Election to see if the agreement stands.

The Unknown Quantity

In short, none of the male parties in Ireland, North or South, has yet awakened to the woman factor in elections: it is as if no Irishwoman yet voted, as far as campaign appeals, meetings, or candidates go. When parties do wake up, there will be some surprises, and the first one that awakes will reap the benefit. The political Irishman is like the leprechaun. If you catch him and hold him firmly, he will lead you to the crock of gold at the rainbow's end. But if you take your eyes off him for a moment he slips away and his golden treasure with him.

'Christmas in my lifetime: memories of war-years'
An Phoblacht, Christmas 1930

Asked by the Editor for 'something Christmassy', I set about sorting out my recollections – how far back they go in the calendar, those outposts of memory! – of other Christmas-tides. As they focus and take shape, it seems to me that there is a curious resemblance. They hang upon some happening in the Irish world outside that makes them memorable.

The Home Rule Xmas

There was that General Election of 1886 when Parnell and Davitt, as a result of the Land War, had sent the Irish barometer very high and the largest number of Irish constituencies ever known – before or since, until one came to 1918 – had returned fighting nationalists. North and South when Thomas Sexton represented Belfast, when Tyrone, Fermanagh, Down, Derry and Armagh had considerable Home Rule contingents, so that with the successful obstructive tactics, smashing the complacency of the British House of Commons, Home Rule suddenly loomed near. And my father,[6] one of the fighting band that rallied round Parnell and Davitt, wrote his first letter home with triumphant prophecy that he would not be long in exile in the land of the Saxon, that he expected to be back 'to eat his Xmas turkey' – in 1886 – and that he would bring Home Rule along to cheer his Christmas dinner. That letter is one of my earliest recollections.

In the Nineties

That high hope remained unfulfilled. Bloody Balfour continued to wage war with his Mitchelstown slogan 'Don't hesitate to shoot' to cheer on his RIC. The fighting members of the Irish Party answered the challenges and were in turn met with the coercionist retort – the time-honoured British method of the jail, the fight for political status, the eternal round of law and order on the one side, sedition and treasonable conspiracy on the other. Another Xmas Day in the nineties stands out: and Sligo Jail holds one parent, while the other with the rest of the young family, is down with German measles (as they called it before the war). Balfour with the generosity of the jailer breed offered his prisoner freedom at Christmas time to be with his sick wife and family – 'if he gave an undertaking to be of 'good behaviour'. The undertaking was not forthcoming – and the six months' sentence was duly insisted upon. That was a stark and lonely Christmas. But we youngsters got a good object lesson in British methods which some of us never forgot. And Bloody Balfour was the bogey-man of our childhood.

Xmas 1915

Years passed, as the novelists say. Came the war, with Britain heading the band for the freedom of small nations. Recruiting propaganda rampant, an Irish cardinal calling upon Irishmen to fight in defence of Catholic Belgium, St Patrick pressed into war posters. Who does not remember that time to smile at the lunacy of it all? But then it was serious, any criticism of the war-mongers meant, as usual, jail under the all-embracing DORA. Still a few met the challenge and the jails opened to receive them. Francis Sheehy Skeffington, jailed May 1915, got a year's sentence for speeches hindering recruiting, entered upon a hunger and thirst strike, was released under the Cat and Mouse Act, went to the USA and returned on Xmas Eve, 1915, the re-arrest threat still hanging over him. Thinking that he might be removed to some unknown destination and shoved into . . . camp in England for the duration, I travelled to Liverpool to await events. Seán McDermott and Tom Clarke gave me some name and addresses there in case of contingencies. When the big liner came in with its Xmas freight I was told that Skeffington had been fetched by the military, with his trunks, and removed before any other passengers were allowed off. Followed a day of quest, aided by the friends above-mentioned, from barracks to various police-stations, with all the usual police mystery. Then the prisoner was at length released late that evening – though his baggage was held for further inspection – and informed with unconscious humour that he must immediately leave Liverpool for his destination or that he would be again arrested. He smilingly explained that he would have been already in Dublin, had they themselves not prevented his departure. And so home – to spend the last Christmas that he was to see in Dublin. And the toys that he had brought along had to undergo detention in military custody till the New Year, to the disappointment of a certain youngster of six, who thus in turn received one of his first lessons on British militarism. Others were to follow.

Xmas 1916: New York

Next Christmas Day for that youngster and me was in New York, after the Portobello murder, the Simon inquiry and its white-washing findings, another chapter in British militarism that needs no re-telling here. Without orthodox passport we had managed to tell that story in the US arriving a few days before Xmas.

The next Xmas Day that stands out was in 1920 with curfew clamped on so that one had to spend the night wherever one happened to be or be 'lifted' by some passing lorry. And, last of the series, stands 1921, the Xmas after the Treaty had been put over, while yet its acceptance by the Dáil trembled in the balance. An unfortunate 'recess' caused, alas! by Christmas which gave British press and pulpit time for Treaty propaganda in intensive form. Had Xmas not fallen just then, that debate might have ended otherwise. I cannot forgive that delay. Better have met on Xmas Day, if necessary, and rejected the foul thing. Ere another Xmas dawned Harry Boland, Cathal Brugha, Childers and the four of December 8th had gone, the executions were in full swing. Xmas for our generation is a time of wistful memories, of might-have-beens. It needs the redemption of an Easter resurrection.

'New Year reflexions'
The Vote, 9 January 1931

Reading last week *The Vote*'s admirable summary of the achievements of woman in 1930 in various fields, I am struck chiefly by her accomplishments in sport, in aviation, in endurance swimming tests, and the like. And this for two reasons: first, because once again these successes blow to pieces many of the old myths and cherished male superstitions as to the frailty of woman's physique, as to her lack of staying power, as to the devastating effect on her and her children (and these might be male, of course, too, and have to suffer for mother's sins) of physical exercise; and, second, because aviation, motor races, and speed tests are new fields both for men and women, and so it seems to me that these sports give a fair opportunity on the whole to competing women. But a little over a century ago, be it remembered, Michelet, writing on 'Woman', dubbed her the 'Eternal Invalid' and got a lot of satisfaction and sentiment from the idea. It has often occurred to me when reading of feats of lone pioneering, like Amy Johnson's, that had aviation been opened up, say, a century ago, a male taboo would have been instantly automatically established, barring all women out from the very start. I doubt if women would even have been permitted as passengers on airships. Some male pundit would have declared *ex cathedra* that going up in the air had a disastrous effect on woman's physique, that God never meant woman to soar, 'because of the angels'. Statistics would have been forthcoming to prove that air-travel would affect alarmingly the health, or even the existence of offspring. Similarly, no woman would have been permitted to learn to drive a motor-car: she must at all costs be protected from such a 'dangerous' occupation. And, even if a stray 'genius' got away with day-time driving, night driving would be forbidden on grounds of health and morality.

To the reader, who may think this far-fetched, may I recall the agitation over cycle-riding for women and all the predictions then made. Or the convenient male superstition that it is 'unlucky' for all on board for the captain's wife or any other woman to travel on a male-run ship. In fact, if the reader ponders the matter, he or she will find plenty of examples of quaint masculine prohibitions on similar lines. The hardened smokers, for instance, who declare that smoking is 'far worse' in the case of 'women, that night-work is bad for morality', and so forth.

So it is fortunate for us all that the flying woman and the woman who competes in motor-races, drives, and repairs her own machine, swims the Channel or the Hellespont, has, thanks to the pioneer work of earlier feminists, a clear run. There is no depressing 'No Thoroughfare' sign to bar her passage, because the trail has already been blazed. Henceforth in other openings that will be made, arising out of future inventions and initiative, there will be a fair field and no favour (of the latter we may be assured!) for woman, conquering new worlds of exploration and research.

But against the old callings there will still be the continuance of taboos. Medicine, Law, Teaching, the Civil Service, may be said to have kept the door of admission but grudgingly ajar and the door of advancement practically shut and even bolted. Woman has not yet the right everywhere to her own name, her nationality is but an accident of marriage, and marriage itself blocks her professional path and indeed automatically closes it in many cases, unless she happens to be a charwoman, to whom a husband apparently is 'a thing apart', making no difference in status.

Socially, woman is still in the pre-Middle Ages. Honours are still withheld from her for public service, and though fifteen ladies sit in the Lower House, not one may penetrate to the Holy of Holies, the House of Lords. When candidates are chosen for Parliament the acceptable party woman is still preferred to the feminist. The male, who still controls party machines, has a touching belief – whether he be Liberal, Labour, or Tory – that widows of MPs are somehow 'safer', that daughters of politicians, or sisters, or wives, are more dependable and docile than freelances. All the more credit to these women MPs later when they develop feminist tendencies. None the less, the hard fact remains that they do not invariably do so: that party is sometimes stronger than the woman in them. Virginia Woolf finds that to be really independent and to do creative work a woman should be in possession of at least £500 a year and entitled to a room of her own. But even that in the present state of the world does not solve the problem completely and for ever. However, stock-taking and counting our blessings at the threshold of 1931 is heartening on the whole. One echoes old Galileo's 'And yet it moves!' even if at times it does not move as fast as it might and could. And we still need *The Vote* to point the way.

'Scotched, not killed: the anti-feminist snake'
The Vote, 14 August 1931

The virus of an anti-woman complex still poisons the body politics: the anti-feminist snake – though the Biblical promise lays down that woman shall crush the serpent's head – is certainly scotched, but also, most certainly, not yet dead. It is a consolation to those subject to depression, arising from this fact, that reforms of a sweeping character, like the franchise, take a generation or even two, to soak through the community. When the agricultural labourer first acquired the vote in these countries, he did not wake to his power for twenty-five or thirty years. Still more so is this the case with woman suffrage, that revolutionary gesture that lifted, at least women over thirty for a start, out of the category of imbeciles, infants or criminals. Those born and reared in sex, class or colour prejudice retain their obsessions and inhibitions to the end of their days, while the new generation, growing up in their shadow, may also be tainted. Women themselves, bent under the weight of prejudice, have hardly yet in the mass learned to stand upright. The fight for the vote did specific good to those who waged it and to their generation generally, for the militants especially were up against all that crude male hostility and beheld it unmasked.

But when women got the vote nurses did not forthwith stop telling Master Jack, when he bawled, not to be a little silly girl, to remember that he was a man; parents of both sexes did not stop longing for boy-babies and celebrating their arrival as specially splendid achievements. Women themselves are not free from chain-loving slavishness and those in contact with the young seem specially subject to sex inferiority-complex. Even getting from skirts to trousers in the youngster is made a subject of pride, though donning academic, priestly, or kingly robes, or even sporting a military kilt is not a theme for glorification, man still being prone to get into flowing robes whenever he wants to be really impressive.

So right through school and college, shop, work-room or factory, still runs that streak of prejudice. In the Army, the Church, in the British House of Lords, and in the learned professions it flourishes almost as strongly as in pre-suffrage days. The Law still grudges its favours, the Church bangs its door, and the State sets up barriers, in spite of its previous legislation removing sex disabilities. Society still regards the woman as merely the hanger-on, the parasite. Even her highest achievements, her record-breaking in various departments, are honoured but slightingly as compared with those of a big brewer or some powerful male party hack.

In Parliament the women selected are still chosen by the party machine, predominantly male. Though nominally free citizens, women are still unfree when it comes to choosing careers, for many are closed to them, mainly the most lucrative: they are, as a rule, obliged to choose between marriage and their career; in the marriage relation they still suffer from disabilities. In short, it is still largely a man's world that we women live in, run by man for man.

I remember reading some years ago in the American *New Republic*, a little sketch by a woman, entitled 'A White, White Rose for Mother'. It dealt with the reactions of three modern New Yorkers – and American men are about the best natural feminists known – to the Mother Ideal. All had perfectly competent, self-supporting, up-to-date mothers: an actress, a business woman, and a writer. Yet all three at a cinema-show wept over the Dream Picture of an old-white-haired woman, sitting in the twilight, knitting, thinking long thoughts and yearning over her far-off son. And the scenario writer advised each son to send there and then a white, white rose to his old mother – she is always better somehow for these purposes if she is old and frail, wearing a filmy shawl upon her bent shoulders or lace on her white hair. The writer's moral was that men still 'kind of' hankered after their secret picture of such a mother, no matter how well provided they were with a totally different, yet thoroughly satisfactory working type.

There is a good deal in that idea. You can apply it also to the wife or the daughter. It will be some time before these visions give way and get replaced. For they have taken long ages to form in man's brain. Let us take comfort, meanwhile, from the progress, however small, that has been made, say, since Florence Nightingale's time. But let us not forget either that the snake still lives. And will take many a vigorous blow before he is finally crushed.

'Catherine Wheelwright: an appreciation of her services'
An Phoblacht, 25 June 1932
The death in Rochester, New York, of Éamon de Valera's mother recalls vividly a memory of how I first met her, in April 1917, a few days after the United States had entered the Great War on the Allies' side. Rochester, though in New York State, is not far from Canada and was then much influenced by British feeling: British influences were felt in business and banking circles and among the wealthier citizens, many of whom, they had lived in USA for many years, remained British subjects in heart and in fact. There were not many Irish in Rochester, and some that were Irish, were ashamed of the fact.

British Militarism in Ireland
I had been speaking under the auspices of the Friends of Irish Freedom and kindred groups from my arrival in USA in December 1916, the title of my theme being 'British Militarism as I have known it', covering 1916 and the Easter Rising. Until the USA entered the War (on Good Friday 1917, with Wilson's Fourteen Points policy) the Irish and other race-groups in the United States, arranged many meetings, being eager to hear at first hand of Irish conditions. Rochester happened to have already booked a meeting for me in the City Hall: to follow one by Major Ian Hay, one of Britain's propagandist lecturers. The date had been fixed well ahead – it fell on Easter Monday, three days after USA ceased to be 'neutral!' The Committee – the Chairman, a certain judge with an Irish name, a politician who liked to parade Irish

sentiments when these were safe and helpful to his career – had no time to get in touch with our New York Committee: I was already on the way, and their frantic wires and phone-calls did not reach me.

The Runaway Committee

Panic seized them: the judge was hurriedly 'called away' out of the town for the day, leaving his poor secretary to explain matters as best he could. The rest of the Committee had likewise mysteriously scattered. At the hotel where rooms had been booked, the proprietor was embarrassed and could only supply addresses of the absentees. The secretary said that His Honour the judge had left word that the Irish meeting was cancelled. True, the City Hall had been booked; the street-cars and hoardings had been posted with prelimi-nary announcements, for there had been no time to cancel these, but that could not be helped: the meeting must be abandoned. I did not see it in that light myself, and was wondering what could be done with only a few hours left to do anything, and in a strange and unfriendly town.

Mrs Wheelwright to the Rescue

Then a phone bell rang: a lady called me up. It was Catherine Wheelwright. Her son was then serving a life-sentence in a British convict-prison. I took a taxi to her home: we discussed the situation and formed a joint plan of campaign. Together we visited a few citizens, but shortly gave up the effort as vain. Then to the City Hall, where we were told that the fee must be paid down in advance and in full – it was 80 dollars and it cleaned out the treasury. But the blue-eyed white-haired lady said with a smile that we would collect that much in the hall later. We did and more. Then in a taxi to the press: we had a 'good press', for it was a good story, of the judges and bankers who ran away and the meeting to be held notwithstanding. It all came out in the evening editions and 'tickled' the town. When we reached the hall we found a throng waiting outside. We two had the platform all to ourselves, but we managed. Mrs Wheelwright took the Chair. And the 'real Irish' came along, took off their hats and collected in them more than enough to defray all expenses. The meeting was a success: the stampede was stopped: no other town followed Rochester's bad example. I suppose the judge and the others eventually returned.

Her Later Years

That was my first meeting with Mrs Wheelwright. She inquired for news of her son, but was not unduly worried, for she had feared that he would be executed. So she could wait and be patient, she said. A serene, placid woman, Irish to the core, full of memories of Ireland and of her own Bruree, which I happened to know very well from my own childhood days. Later, in 1922, I met her again, frailer, but still the same. She had no use for the Treaty. In national affairs she had a true instinct: in judging of men a native shrewdness, a kindly sense of humour. She helped our mission for the Republican Prisoners' Dependents Fund, came now and then to New York to attend Republican meetings. A quiet and steadfast worker, and one that could be depended upon in a crisis to stand firm. Such is my memory of Catherine Wheelwright.

'The seven who signed for death'⁷
An Phoblacht, Christmas 1933

The Seven Signatories to the Proclamation were intensely individual characters, revolutionaries rather than militarists. It is indeed remarkable that not one was a military type. A schoolmaster – essentially a teacher and propagandist – a labour leader and Socialist, a poet, a musician, a university professor, whose hero was the 'great Florentine', Savonarola, a prison-scarred Fenian, a youth with a golden voice, whose words stirred crowds, yet who was partly crippled, too lame for military action – such the Seven – Pearse, Connolly, Ceannt, MacDonagh, Clarke, McDermott (or, as he preferred, MacDiarmada). Had Fate sorted out her chosen victims she could not have done better. Even in the distribution of counties there was a balance: all the provinces were represented – Pearse, Dublin; Connolly, Monaghan; MacDonagh, of Tipperary stock; Clarke, born outside Ireland, but whose childhood was spent in Co. Tyrone; MacDiarmada, from Leitrim.

Pearse and MacDonagh

Pearse I recall in college – the old UCD. We sat under the same French professor, the cheery, whimsical and lovable Dr Cadic. Pearse brought to his studies a deliberate concentration of purpose, a sort of earnest devotion and though Irish was his first love, his French too had a quality of scholarship. My impression is one of gravity, of solemnity. His exact opposite was the debonair, carefree 'Tom' MacDonagh, full of quips, an excellent mimic, an expansive, sociable soul, ever ready to give a hand, to speak at an impromptu debate, to act or write a play, to discourse learnedly, on occasion on metrics (his thesis was on the learned and little known Campis), to wear a kilt, to dance a jig, or *[illegible]* . . . his brown eyes flashed with merriment, of life, as if he knew *[illegible phrase]* is the most characteristic – he argued with his judges at the court-martial and won the argument. He had a touch of D'Artagnan as he went 'to join the goodly company of those who died for Ireland'. Farewell, gallant Tom MacDonagh!

Ceannt and Clarke

Next to Pearse, perhaps even more passionately steeped in Gaelic culture and tradition was Éamon Ceannt, whose wonderful playing of the bag-pipes at ceilidh and concert is my chief memory. He was eminently the musician of 1916. He expressed his soul best through that medium. Otherwise he was silent and somewhat shy in company: he had come into the movement for independence through his love of the Gaelic.

The veteran of the band, out of another generation, set in an earlier mould, was Thomas Clarke. His sad, set features, in repose almost grim, had the marks of prison. His was the strength of tempered steel – through the tortures of solitary confinement he kept his sanity and hope. He links up with the felons of Our Land.

The Poet Plunkett

In sharpest contrast with him was young Joseph Plunkett, founder of the *Irish Review*, poet and visionary. I remember Frank Harris in New York deploring his fate bitterly. He said, 'In Italy they blind nightingales to make them sing sweeter: the English murder nightingales so that their songs are sweeter in remembrance.'

Connolly the Man

Lastly, James Connolly (whose hand, with Pearse's doubtless fashioned the Proclamation remembering even in that moment to bestow equal citizenship on women) he was the internationalist who gave his life for Ireland, 'the last to cast his torch upon the pyre'. He too was of an older generation, though not as old as Clarke's. Editor, author, leader of men, Connolly ere he died had expounded his creed in his works. His social philosophy links with Fintan Lalor: the worker's worker. Personally in those years from 1908–1916 *[illegible phrase]* . . . in Liberty Hall, the Citizen Army around him – and women by the way – in old Great Brunswick Street giving his weekly talk on some problem, chatting at a friend's fireside, foregathering at Constance Markievicz's in Surrey House, talking, writing, expounding, organising. He also had the great gift of humour, of relishing a joke, even against himself, of hitting off a situation in a terse, racy phrase. Essentially a kindly nature, he could hit out from the shoulder when the situation required. But, even at his sternest, his eye retained its twinkle: he had most of all a tolerant smile of understanding for human weaknesses. Tolerant even to the end to 'all brave men who do their duty', as he waved goodbye to his executioners.

Such the Seven who signed the Proclamation and their death sentence.

'How does she stand? Woman in 1933: a review and a stocktaking'
The Distributive Worker, January 1934

'I don't know the meaning of the word,' said Mr John Redmond some years ago, about 1912, to a suffragist deputation, whose spokeswoman ventured the remark, apropos of votes for Irishwomen, that she hoped he was a 'feminist'. Today the Oxford dictionary defines feminism as the extended recognition of the claims of women. It is something to get into the dictionary at all, though the definition, like most dictionary ones, leaves one guessing.

The First Woman MP

After the war (and during it, when woman burst into so many hitherto firmly barricaded masculine preserves) woman achieved the vote in many countries hitherto barred. Under the 1916 Proclamation Irishwomen had their claims written indelibly into the Irish charter of liberty – the first time revolutionaries, setting up a Republic, remembered women, hitherto equality and fraternity being entirely male. Britain, true to her compromising habit, gave the vote after the war grudgingly, only to women over 30. Germany and Russia granted full equality to women, following Scandinavia, Holland, the US, New Zealand and Australia. Italy gave a partial vote only to take it away under her Fascist dictatorship. Spain, in her recent revolution, gave full equality to women in every sphere. They voted the other day for the first time. France still denies suffrage to women, the Senate barring the measure steadily, though with decreasing resistance (last time it was 175 to 118). In those provinces of Canada, such as Quebec, while French influence dominates, women, though they may vote for the Federal Parliament, may not do so in local elections. Belgium gave women the right to be elected while denying them the right to vote! And the male voters actually elected a woman – a pacifist and Socialist. There is also one woman on the Belgian Senate. Those countries that admitted women to parliament immediately put up and elected a number of women. Constance Markievicz was the first woman to be elected to the British House of Commons. She became, under PR member for the Harbour Division, Dublin, in 1918, while yet under a life sentence in Holloway for high treason. She never attended the British Parliament, so Lady Astor, elected a year later, was the first woman to take her seat.

Now there is evidence of a set-back to women, especially in countries such as Germany and Italy where fascist power is strong. In England recently many of the women MPs went out in the last election, though there are 15 in the present House of Commons. The Free State has three women Deputies – it once had six. It has four women in the Senate, the recent vacancy caused by Countess Desart's death, being filled by a man. The Six County Parliament has now no women deputies. The Isle of Man has one woman representative in its House of Keys. South Africa, which recently enfranchised women, has two. New Zealand, which gave votes to women some 40 years ago (the first country to do so) returned for the first time, in September, a woman to parliament. Brazil women voted for the first time last May, and promptly elected a woman doctor to parliament, Dr Carlotta de Queiroz. Greece is slowly enfranchising its women: they have the municipal vote, not the parliamentary vote, and by a recent law are eligible to be aldermen (each Greek city has a mayor and 12 aldermen). In Britain, many women have held the post of mayor (Liverpool had a woman mayor), but in Ireland, save once where a woman was deputy mayor (Mrs O'Donovan, sister of Mrs O'Callaghan) during the Tan period, none has ever been chosen.

Outstanding Women
In USA the Speaker of the North Dakota House of Representatives is a woman, Mrs Minnie Craig, and a woman, Miss F. Perkins, was appointed by President Roosevelt Secretary for Labor, the first woman to hold cabinet rank. Jeannette Rankin, 'the lady for Montana', US's only woman Deputy, in 1917 cast her vote against the entry of the US into the War.

A Novel Protest
In the island of Bermuda (one of the British possessions, with Trinidad, that still withholds the vote to women), there are stirrings of revolt, the disenfranchised refusing to pay taxes as a protest against lack of representation – 'taxation without representation is tyranny,' said Swift long ago – and are turning the sale of their seized goods into funeral auctions. Thirteen women in heavy mourning attend the sales and at the conclusion lay tax wreaths on the steps of the forum 'in memory of departed justice', A picturesque form of protest against a real grievance! In the Free State jury rights (granted under the British Parliament) were taken from women under the late Kevin O'Higgins; in England and in the Six Counties they still exercise these rights.

In Diplomacy
Reviewing the field generally, women have won their spurs in the diplomatic service, Dr Ruth Bryan Owen (who visited Dublin last year for the Teacher's Congress) being now US Ambassador to Denmark. Soviet Russia, Turkey and Spain have also women in their diplomatic service. In the Law, in Science, in Medicine, Education and Literature women have made progress; women aviators have made successful world records in that perilous sphere. Dame Ethel Smyth,[8] after years of opposition, now conducts her own orchestra in London, producing her own works, a veteran of 76, amid universal applause. And, at the other end of the scale, a woman in France has recently won in an

agricultural competition the prize as the best ploughman – drawing her furrow straight and guiding her team with the best of them.

'Eternal vigilance is the price of liberty.' Man is like the leprechaun: if you take your eyes off for a moment he slips away, and takes your hard-won liberties along with him. So, women should hold fast to all that pioneers and martyrs have won – and conquer fresh fields in addition. The old world, man-run for so long, and not over well at that, needs their enthusiasm, their hitherto untapped resources of power and energy, their co-operation in human evolution. That is the meaning of true feminism. May 1934 bring further triumphs, remove more age-worn barriers!

'Mrs Sheehy Skeffington at the Minerva Club'
The Women's Freedom League Bulletin, 5 April 1935
High Holborn, London.

President: Mrs Pethick-Lawrence, Hon Treas: Dr Octavia Lewin, Hon Fin Sec: Mrs Gerard, Hon Org Sec: Mrs Whetton, Sec of Minerva Publishing: Miss Reeves, Gen Sec: Miss F. A. Underwood

Minerva Club – Brunswick Square. Public restaurant open to non-residents.

More than thirty members and friends came to dinner at the Minerva Club last Saturday evening to welcome our old friend Mrs Sheehy Skeffington and to listen to her account of her recent visit to Canada and the USA.

From the Chair, Miss Reeves declared that the suffrage struggle was still 'news' and that it would be 'on the films' during the Jubilee celebrations. She introduced Mrs Skeffington as a very dear friend and one who had shared in our fight for Votes for Women.

Mrs Skeffington told us that when she went to another country she always looked out for the forward part of the women's movement. She was eager to note women's successes and to report on successes at home. She liked to recall that a woman had been appointed to the Chair of Law in Dublin, and that the National University of Dublin would soon be conferring a high Honorary degree on her distinguished countrywoman, Professor Mary Hayden. Mrs Skeffington had visited Quebec where women still had no vote for their local parliament although they had a vote for the federal parliament. But these women had their own means of propaganda and everywhere they were putting up a fight for their political liberty.

In the USA she was pleased to find that five women had been elected to Congress and that 130 women were serving in the various state parliaments. Throughout the country women were sharing in the spoils of office with men. Child labour was being abolished largely through the efforts of women, and women doctors were working in the new relief schemes. Under the New Code there were regulations for women's work which feminists opposed; the wages of women were lower than those of men; the dismissal of married women workers was general. Women's position indeed was as difficult in the states as in other parts of the world. But women were alive to those difficulties, and that was the thing that mattered.

Mrs Skeffington told us of a group of statuary depicting notable American women of the past. She told us, too, that the Heterodoxy Club,[9] to which she had been elected in 1917, was still active. The qualification of any member was that in some way she must have stepped outside the current conventions. Everywhere Mrs Skeffington had met women friends, many of whose names are household words in this country.

The meeting concluded with a very cordial cote of thanks to Mrs Sheehy Skeffington and a message of love to our first president, Mrs Despard, whom we are eagerly looking forward to having with us in June, to celebrate the 91st anniversary of her birthday.

'Conditions of Employment Bill', to the editor
Irish Press, 14 June 1935
Sir,

Women in the Co. Dublin area are in the majority, I believe, among the voters. There is now an opportunity for them to register an effective protest against recent anti-woman proposals by the Government by declining to vote for the Fianna Fáil candidate and I hope they will avail themselves of the opportunity. The new Employment Bill out-Hitlers Hitler; under section 12 it gives the Minister for Industry (already well-known for his anti-suffrage views) the power to limit the number of women in industry, or to remove them altogether. If such arbitrary power is not checked this may extend to other callings driving women to the lowest-paid drudgery. I do not ask former Fianna Fáil women voters to support Mr Lavery, for his party is also reactionary, having deprived women in the Free State of jury rights exercised in Northern Ireland and in Britain, among its many coercive and undemocratic measures. But I do ask women most earnestly not to cast their vote for the Government candidate as a way of marking their profound dissatisfaction. Hitherto, I have voted Fianna Fáil, not because I always approved of its policy, but as a choice between bad and indifferent. In future I shall no longer support Fianna Fáil in any way and shall abstain from voting, unless there is a third party, or a genuinely Independent candidate that I can vote for. I know many Republicans who for many reasons will do likewise.

'Peace and freedom: the Women's International League'
Irish Press, 11 May 1936
Women first organized internationally for peace during the World War, though previously many women interested themselves in peace, notably the

Baroness von Suttner, whose novel, *Lay Down Your Arms* (*Die Waffen Nieder*) on the 1870 Franco-Prussian War made the same world appeal against militarism that *Uncle Tom's Cabin*, by Harriet Beecher Stowe, did against slavery.

In 1914–15 the Women's International League for Peace and Freedom was founded, with Jane Addams as first President. It met at The Hague in 1915 and issued from there its famous and stirring manifesto, calling upon the women of the world to take mass action against war. Some of the belligerent countries (including Great Britain) prevented delegates from attending. (Britain actually stopped all boats between her shores and Holland for a week, after refusing specifically passports to some Irishwomen delegates.) But Mrs Pethick-Lawrence, who happened to be in USA, did get to Holland, travelling direct from America.

Jane Addams

Jane Addams made a personal tour of Europe after the Congress, visiting neutral and belligerent countries alike on her mission of peace. She was met sympathetically by various statesmen, notably in Austria – she was called 'a great world statesman without a portfolio' – but the war machine was then too strong for any merciful intervention by women.

The League continued its work, and its organization grew; it ran a paper, *Pax*, which still appears (edited in Geneva), and established its headquarters in the Maison Internationale there, from which it has ever since carried on active peace propaganda on the world front, concentrating on whatever country seemed likely to become a centre for war, and sending abroad various peace missions and investigators of conditions, now to China and the East, to India or to Mexico, as occasion called.

World Peace Congresses are held by the WIL every three years or so in various capitals – one was held in Dublin in 1926 attended by women from over 40 countries and from every Continent and presided over by Jane Addams – and these assemblies had a wonderful educational value. In Dublin, I recall, the 'peace ladies', as they were popularly called, created a great stir.

The Arms Traffic

In USA recently it was owing to the initiative of the WIL that the American Senate set up its famous inquiry into the Traffic in Arms Industry (or racket as some called it), the revelations were startling and other countries have since been urged to set up similar inquiries with a view to international action against the Armaments Ring.

Under Fascist and Nazi dictatorships the WIL has suffered sadly, many of its Italian and German members being banned and in some cases their goods confiscated: some have had to settle in Switzerland, England, or France, exiled from their own land and the W.I.L. in Italy, Germany and Austria has to carry on its work underground. But it nevertheless continues to function. Last September, Madame Duchêue, one of its Vice-Presidents, organized a huge peace procession to the League of Nations in Geneva, in which many thousand women of various nationalities marched. (Ireland was represented by three delegates.) This was one of the most striking anti-militarist demonstrations ever held.

While the WIL is a purely woman's organization, there are many others – such as the War Resisters, the various pacifist youth movements, the Peace Council – in which both men and women take part. Some, like the League against Fascism, link up pacifism with opposition to both the Fascist and Nazi regimes, both being regarded as antagonistic to peace, being militaristic and anti-feminist.

Sanctions

In Britain pacifists are divided on the question of the morality of sanctions. Some, like George Lansbury, and Dr Maude Royden, are against sanctions, regarding these (at least as understood by the League of Nations), as likely to lead to war. George Lansbury has just started for the USA on a peace mission and Dr Maude Royden has relinquished temporarily her ministry in London in order to throw all her energies into the World Peace campaign.

In USA Mrs Roosevelt is one of the peace leaders and it is in response to her invitation, backed by various peace groups in USA that George Lansbury, Dr Salter and Dr Maude Royden have crossed the Atlantic. During the Black and Tan regime here, Maude Royden, who is one of the foremost speakers and preachers in England today, was one of those who actively intervened to protest against British Militarism in Ireland, being a member of the Peace with Ireland Council.

Peace Ballot

The Peace Ballot, carried out in Great Britain, helped more than any other factor to organize and make articulate public opinion against war. This ballot was largely organized by pacifist organisations in which women are foremost. It forced the hands of the then government and is even now massing opinion against the armaments race indulged in by the Government since the last general election. The people's mandate to governments for peace is its more recent work. The text of this mandate runs: –

> War settles no problems, brings economic misery, suffering and death to us and to our children.

The WIL has also directed public attention to the futility of gas-mask drill for school-children and on such semi-militaristic ritual.

There is much dissatisfaction felt at present among the plain people in England at the Government's apathy regarding peace, and its warlike preparations under the guise of self-defence, and especially its recent huge Navy and Army Budget. Peace films are being shown in many British cinemas, both frankly propagandist, and like that of H. G. Wells' *Shape of Things to Come*, of indirect approach. Weekly peace meetings are being held at the Friends' House, London, addressed by leading men and women, and in Trafalgar Square there was the other day a mass meeting for Ethiopia. At the annual conference of the Women's Freedom League, held last week in London, a resolution was passed condemning the murderous attack upon Abyssinia by Italy, and declaring that public confidence in the good faith of the League and its members has been greatly weakened by the failure to take effective collective action for peace. Such are the 'straws in the wind' that blow just now.

'Women in the Free State: a stocktaking'
The New English Weekly, 19 March 1936

Has our positioned worsened since the setting up of the Free State? The time is ripe for stocktaking. When the Free State was set up English laws, franchise and the rest were automatically adopted here and in Northern Ireland. Though Irishwomen were given citizenship and equality under the Proclamation of 1916 this did not operate. Up to the Treaty and after it, until Britain revised her own limited franchise, Irishwomen had to keep step with the British. In 1918 women over 30 got the vote, and, when the Treaty election took place (the 'Pact' election) in June, 1922, the younger women were still debarred from voting. Delegations of women waited upon Arthur Griffith, asking him to have the franchise extended at that time, so that all citizens over 21 could vote, but he declined to move in the matter.

In 1918, at the first election under which women were eligible to vote and stand for Parliament, the only woman returned, by a strange irony, to the House of Commons was Constance Markievicz, then serving a life sentence in Holloway. Ireland, as in 1916 when equal suffrage rights were given, led the way then, and also later, when Constance Markievicz was made Minister for Labour in Dáil Éireann. She was the first woman MP and first woman Cabinet Minister in these islands. There has been no woman in our Cabinet since.

There were then six women deputies in Dáil Éireann. Now there are but three. In the Senate, at the time of its going out, there are three and in the Dublin Corporation also three – mystic number! On public boards today there are hardly half a dozen women. From 1916 throughout the Anglo-Irish war there was a goodly number of women representatives and once, when it was dangerous to be a mayor, a Republican woman was appointed Deputy Mayor in Limerick. There has been no woman mayor in the Free State.

The Universities are the only bright spots: women are on the Senate and governing body of the National University, women hold professorships and lectureships, are members of convocation, have complete equality within the colleges as to admission to societies. In the other University they are still barred from most of the college societies. They must not enter TCD portals after six and the quaint caption in the College Historical announcements of public lectures: 'Public (Men only)' still prevails. The door which was opened to women some twenty-five years ago in the Dublin University is still ajar – it has never been pushed wide open.

Almost the first thing that the Free State did when it started to function was to set about depriving women of the right to sit on juries. A measure was put through by the then Minister for Justice (Mr Kevin O'Higgins) which deprives women prisoners to this day of the right of trial by their peers. There was considerable opposition both in Dáil and Senate (by the then opposition) and a voluntary panel was offered as a compromise under which women could offer themselves for jury service. This, however, has never been anything but a dead letter. So women in the State are at a disadvantage when compared with their sisters in the Six Counties and in Great Britain. In cases of infanticide and of offences against women and girls this is a distinct disability that calls for immediate redress. On the other hand, equality in the matter of hanging operates: during Mr Cosgrave's period of office one woman suffered the death penalty. During the present administration, however, though there have been cases of women condemned to death, no woman has been hanged.

During the Anglo-Irish war many women served as justices in the Sinn Féin courts, an honorary position (to which one was elected) roughly corresponding to that of justice of the peace. That was also swept away with the setting up of the Free State and the re-establishment of the courts. In Britain there are many women justices and some women magistrates: we have none. Even the number of women PCs (Peace Commissioners) is infinitesimal, while the children's court is presided over by a man. (Under Sinn Féin the Court of Conscience, an ancient Dublin tribunal, was presided over for some time by a woman councillor.[10] That court and office are now abolished.

There is yet no woman justice or District Justice in the Free State, though one would have thought that a sufficient time had elapsed to entitle a woman barrister to promotion, there being a number of distinguished women lawyers, though these do not actually practice in the criminal courts, which is to be regretted. There are also women solicitors and a number of women probation officers, but as yet only a few women police (without uniforms and without power to effect arrests). In Great Britain there is a regular corps of women police under their own officers; in London alone the number has just been increased, being now 142.

Thus in general it may be said that, while the Free State has taken over from Britain, whereas the latter has advanced with regard to the position of women, we have either remained stationary – or have retrogressed.

This is particularly the case with regard to married women. In the Free State married women are now definitely barred for the future in primary schools so that when the present holders of such posts retire primary education will be entirely in the hands of unmarried women teachers: a distinct drawback that Irish mothers who are qualified teachers should not be permitted to teach. The same holds in technical schools and for the most part in secondary teaching. It is only when the Universities are reached that marriage does not make retirement compulsory. There is still room for mothers at the top of the educational tree!

In Great Britain local bodies (notably the London County Council) have recently reverted to their earlier practice and now again employ married women. In France and the USA there is no ban on married women teachers, rather the contrary. Other things being equal it is considered good from the educational point of view to have as teachers women who are themselves mothers of families.

Throughout the Civil Service the ban on married women operates and it is stricter in this country than in Great Britain. Our women civil servants have had their position much worsened within recent years. Women are the lowest paid, they have less opportunity of promotion, they are often housed in worse quarters and are, in short, the Cinderellas of the service. Men with less experience are promoted over their heads and all the 'plums' are reserved for males. Though other countries have promoted women to posts in the diplomatic service – women are specially skilled, being as a rule better linguists and having often a better social sense – the Free State has hitherto ignored women, though here again in 'the troubled period', as it is euphemistically called nowadays, Republican women often acted (without fee, of course, and often under difficult and even dangerous conditions) as Republican envoys abroad, in USA, France, Germany and Australia. Mr Cosgrave's government once appointed a woman delegate (a distinguished woman graduate in the Civil Service) to represent it in Geneva, but since the present Government took office such posts are exclusively male.

In Great Britain widows may be (and frequently are) taken back into the Civil Service, where their training and experience is an asset, while in certain cases married women are retained. In the Free State widows are permanently barred and no woman can hold her post after marriage.

There are about two or three women factory inspectors in the Free State, though factories are springing up daily.

The Government usually makes a gesture of appointing one or two women on its various commissions and Trade Boards. As these posts are purely honorary (though often onerous) married women are not barred. But no woman has ever been made chairman of such a body.

Yet marriage is not popular in the Free State, if statistics are to be believed. We have (practically alone among the older States) the anomaly of a greater population of males, as census returns show, as well as one of the lowest marriage rates and a tendency (for men especially) to late marriages. There is at least one village in the West which is a sort of male Cranford, where practically the entire population consists of bachelors housekeeping for themselves. And yet, though the Finance Minister racks his brains to tax every commodity, luxury, amusement, there is as yet no proposal to tax bachelors, or any enquiry, as a rule, when appointments are made, as to whether male candidates are married. Probably the dullness of rural life, especially for women, drives out our girls, for the census returns show that more women emigrate or migrate than men. Conditions and prospects for women being better and brighter elsewhere, can one blame them for going?

'Does war pay? Peace problems of to-day'
The Distributive Worker, December 1936
Sir Norman Angell has devoted three books, *The Great Illusion* (written before the World War), *Preface to Peace* and *The Unseen Assassins*, written in 1932 and 1935 respectively, to explain the main causes of war and dealing with their elimination. *The Great Illusion* is the fuller development of a pamphlet published in 1909 which caused a sensation – namely, *Europe's Optical Delusion*. This and the book that followed dealt in a then startlingly novel manner with the Anglo-German chase for armaments. At that time, and indeed long afterwards, the theory was generally accepted (it still is in certain quarters) that military power gave the nation possessing these many commercial, social and economic advantages. This universally-rooted belief the author challenged, showing that it had its origin in a pure optical illusion. His book set out to prove that no such advantage existed, that in fact it was impossible for one nation to destroy the wealth of another or for one nation to become richer by conquering another, because wealth in the modern world is founded upon credit and, if this is tampered with, the collapse involves the victor. The same is true with regard to the annexation of territory. International finance is dependent on trade and industry; international politics have changed with modern conditions, yet mankind still remains hide-bound, still coerced by principles long discarded in practice. The trade *per capita* of the small nations is in reality found to be in excess of the trade *per capita* of the great Powers. The economics on which Bismarck and Tamerlane relied have, happily, no relation to the world of to-day.

The author examines the indemnity futility, showing how a state differs in this respect from an individual collecting a personal and private debt. After 1870, France, instead of being worse off than Germany to the extent of huge indemnity enforced by the latter, had not only a higher standard of comfort, but financially the whip-hand over its victor. The spoils of war are then but another illusion, the terminology of the past.

The author does not, of course, hold that it is impossible for one Government to pay a large indemnity to another in case of war or for the said Government to benefit therefrom. He holds, however, that the population as a whole of any nation receiving such indemnity must suffer from financial disturbances in the credit of the paying nation. All this was new and paradoxical to the generation just before the World War. Now, many of the tenets of *The Great Illusion* are accepted: had they been realised and acted upon in 1914, the folly of four years wastage of human life and treasure might have been prevented. For history after the Treaty of Versailles blundered into exactly the same error (with the parties in the case reversed, the victor of 1870 being now the vanquished) in the matter of even huger indemnities that were in the years that followed to prove even more futile. The question of the 'owning' of colonies is also considered in *The Great Illusion* and the same conclusion is reached with regard to these. England's experience as the oldest and most astute colonizer in history goes to show that colonies in effect are not a source of fiscal profit, and that England is really in a worse position to her own colonies than in regard to foreign nations. The colonies erect severe tariff walls against the 'Mother' country. No British Indian is permitted to enter Australia, though British India is the greater part of the British Empire. It is true that there are other advantages gained by the possession of colonies – but these are not to be reckoned in terms of ownership and direct financial benefit. The 'loss' of her colonies, contrary to the belief of Conservative politicians, will not involve Great Britain in ruin. This fact was also startling when the author first enunciated it. Nor did its realisation penetrate the mind of later peace-makers at Versailles when the German colonies in South Africa were annexed by Great Britain as part of the spoils of conquest. In Sir Norman Angell's other books he touches once more upon these points, with further facts to draw upon, garnered from the disasters of the World War. In the second part of *The Great Illusion* the author states (and demolishes) the psychological case for war, the arguments based on the immutability of human nature, of the pugnacity of man, on the inherent viciousness of whoever happens, for the time being, to be the enemy.

Even when material interests are shown to yield no profit from war-waging there are these other factors to be taken into account. There is still a whole range of ideas, the outcome of old conditions, that continue to make for war. There is an immense array of testimony to be found in all the literature that glorifies war, not only from the Prussian militarists (and these were rampant in the pre-war period when this book appeared) but from many other writers. According to such authorities war is an ordeal, instituted by God Himself, to try mankind, an essential and permanent feature of the state. 'God holds his assizes and hurls the people upon one another' is how one writer puts it. The idea of substituting international arbitration for what was regarded by many as a natural law seemed fantastic. 'Without war the world would degenerate in a morass of materialism.' Moltke, Frederic the Great, Cromwell, Napoleon, even enlightened Ernest Renan, the great French historian; famous churchmen like Charles Kingsley and Dean Farrar glorify war in extravagant terms that to-day sound absurd. In the Psychological Case for Peace Sir Norman Angell meets the arguments of the war-glorifiers. He shows that physical force as an arbiter of quarrels is a constantly diminishing factor, that human nature does change and radically (with regard, for instance, to the duel, to slavery, treatment of prisoners and many other matters). Cannibalism was a common characteristic of early man: killing and eating one's prisoners in war-time was a regular ritual of the tribe – but human nature modified this as time went on. The fact is, not only does human nature change, but it is constantly in a state of flux. In the last 2,000 years man has changed more than in the unknown years preceding, and in one hundred more than in the preceding two thousand. In fact, as is shown by an analysis of various new factors in our life of to-day as compared with the time in which (30 years ago) Norman Angell first wrote, the tempo of change in human nature has been greatly accelerated by various external conditions, so that between 1914 and 1934 there has been swifter change than in the century previous. So much then for the argument that human nature does not change, therefore, there will always be war! Conflict there may be, other outlets for man's pugnacity (if that is, indeed, a permanent part of his make-up, which may be doubted), other channels for his acquisitiveness, his love of adventure, and of new things. But these need not be war no more than they need to be duelling, nor trial by ordeal. Whether warlike nations survive – Norman Angell shows they actually do not – taking examples from history, is another of the fallacies discussed and disposed of, another of the rootlets of war nipped, as is that of the physical force factor. 'Though,' as Bacon says, 'men love danger better than travail, travail is bound – despite ourselves – whether we win or lose to be our lot.' Lastly, new conception of the state is considered, it no longer being a personification, a 'she', again the outcome of modern conditions which tend to weld states together through certain common interests, in groups, in strata rather than as separate divided masses: as society is more and more fully organised states will merge into federations.

The author holds, however, in all three volumes, for his viewpoint in this and other matters has been strengthened by the war and its sequel, that armaments cannot at once be dispensed with, for, if they were, states might revert to chaos and anarchy. Only by a scheme of general rationalism can we emerge to reasoned order. There are no royal roads to Peace and short cuts are dangerous. Education is the weapon which must be reforged: he hopes that England may lead the way.

In the later books he concentrates upon an endeavour to interpret and clarify the mind of John Smith, the average male voter, and to disentangle from the jungle of election problems certain guiding lines that should be followed by him in his search for Truth. For, on the man in the street depends public opinion, and on it depends in the long run the question of the displacement of War by Arbitration. There is still much confused thinking in Press, in Parliament and Pulpit, and 'Truth comes out of error more easily than out of confusion'. Yet, Norman Angell is an optimist – and he has been watching, checking up and stocktaking on the public mentality in its reactions to war for over thirteen years, so his findings should carry weight. The simplest truths are often curiously obscure: that is why, doubtless, the war mentality still survives in a changed world. The author deprecates the emotional attitude of certain anti-war writers: his appeal is to common-sense as the safest guide, to a new spirit to face old problems. The Universities and the schools should play their part – they have not swung in so far.

The Kellogg Pact[11] he considers to have been a good move as indicating a deep change of attitude towards the idea of the 'inevitability' of war, which used to be regarded as much part of the scheme of things as bad weather or old age, the one great evil that man for all his wit and skill could not eliminate. In other respects the Kellogg Pact is considered too sweeping and may cause a swing back of the pendulum: it is not enough to repudiate war as vile: concentrating on that aspect alone obscures certain others that are still dangerous – even the danger element in war, as in sport, has its appeal to the heroic in man. War has thus many disguises: its horrors may sometimes act not as a deterrent, but as a stimulus when man is persuaded that it is necessary.

The Unseen Assassins recalls those fallacies that still create war in various disguises – the Assassin of Justice, the Sovereign Assassin and the rest, the invisible assassins and the visible, still more dangerous because unsuspected. Although all nations are theoretically for peace war still has glamour, war slogans can swiftly create a war atmosphere. Such are the contradictions and the inconsistencies that beset the path of peace and afflict and confuse John Smith: we can only secure Peace when we are prepared to pay the price of Peace as we now do of war. We cannot unscramble the eggs in the omelette after they have been broken up. Socialism, Capitalism, and Peace as well as national illusions are considered in *Preface to Peace*. The author holds that the elimination of the Capitalist competitive system will not necessarily mean the abolition of war. In a chapter called The Short Answer he gives the counter-argument to various popular errors regarding war such as, 'What would you do if a brute attacked your sister?' some of these seem childish thus set forth but they recur constantly and impede the way to Peace. The author believes firmly in the League of Nations as an instrument of securing World Peace, and would have it strengthened, developed, perfected to this end. It is for the expert to point the way and for the John Smiths to follow. For war is a world-wide scourge, its roots in mankind are so deep-set that they will need all man's energy to destroy. As long as he is uncertain with himself as to what he wants nothing effective can be done. All the great states still retain their armed forces; after ten years of Disarmament Conferences they will not surrender one inch. Therefore, these books have concentrated upon the task of clearing up first principles and making the alternative clear, the author believing that only thus can any real progress towards the abolition of war and the final scrapping of armaments be accomplished.

'The Irish Constitution'

Prison Bars 3 (July 1937), published monthly by the Women's Prisoners Defence League, 44 Parnell Square, Dublin

The New FS Constitution

We have had already two Constitutions. In the first, which could fit on a fair-sized sheet of notepaper, citizenship for women and equal rights and equal opportunities were guaranteed. Had the Irish republic been set up then, Irish women would have had votes years before their British sisters, who got partial suffrage only in 1918. As it was, Constance Markievicz was the only woman elected in 1918 for the British House of Commons, and she later held the post of Cabinet Minister for Labour under Dáil Éireann.

Following the acceptance of the Treaty by a majority of seven, a new Constitution was published on the day of the election (1922). As far as women were concerned, it carried out, if more formally and not quite so wholeheartedly, the intention of the 1916 Proclamation. Mr de Valera's Constitution runs:

40. All citizens shall, **as human persons**, be held equal before the law. This shall not mean that the State shall not in its enactments have due regard to difference of capacity, physical and moral and of social functions.
41 (2) 1. In particular the State recognizes that by her life within the home woman gives to the State a support without which the common good cannot be achieved.

2. The state shall therefore endeavor to ensure that mothers shall not be obliged by economic necessity to engage in labour to the neglect of their duties at home.

45.4. Sub-section 2. The State shall endeavour to ensure that the **inadequate strength of women** shall not be abused and that women or children shall not be forced by economic necessity to enter avocations unsuited to their sex, age or strength.

There is no woman in Mr de Valera's Cabinet and but two in his party. No woman appears to have been consulted by him. Now he and his party are up against the entire body of organised women. From all sides, from the Women Workers' Union (consisting of women trades unionists) to the Women Graduates at both Universities, the joint Societies of various Women's organisations, the National Council of Women, a clamour of protest has arisen. Many supporters of Mr de Valera have bombarded him and his party. The opposition (whose record towards women is in the main no better, but oppositions are politicians and naturally exploit their opportunities) has taken up the matter.

Never before have women been so united as now when they are faced with fascist proposals endangering their livelihood, cutting away their rights as human beings. The outcome will probably be the formation of a Woman's Party; meanwhile a special emergency committee has been set up and a fighting fund inaugurated.

Mr de Valera is thoroughly angry and full of declarations that his words do not mean what they seem. He says he only means to honour mothers in the home and that there is now no need to emphasise equality, as we have it! When pressed upon the 'inadequate strength reference' he says it means women should not be miners or navvies.

Mr de Valera shows a mawkish distrust of women which has always coloured his outlook; his was the only command in Easter Week where the help of women (of the Cumann na mBan, women's auxiliary to the Irish Volunteers) was refused. He sent the women home; some went to other areas and were welcomed, and de Valera, as I heard him say somewhat sheepishly years later, 'lost some good men who had to be cooks in their place' . . . Connolly, in his Citizen Army, would have welcomed women as soldiers were they so minded, and he saw to it long before that those that were, had military training.

De Valera has refused to alter, except that he has restored 'without distinction of sex' for voting purposes. He has refused to restore 1916 Equal Rights and Equal Opportunities for Women.

'Irish women writers'
Bulletin: Women's Freedom League, 3 October 1937

The Minerva Club was crowded beyond its capacity last Monday evening to hear Mrs Sheehy Skeffington speak on 'Irish Women Writers', and very regretfully several of our friends had to be turned away for want of standing room.

Miss Kate O'Brien, who had come prepared to be a 'dumb' chairman, told us very charmingly that she had only promised to take the Chair because of her great affection for Miss Reaves, the Minerva Club, the Women's Freedom League, and Mrs Skeffington, and carried out her duties admirably. Those who were present had a real treat. Mrs Skeffington grouped her women writers into poets, novelists, dramatists, scholars and historians. She said that, compared with the volume of output by English women writers, that of Irish women was but a streamlet to a flood, still it was not negligible, for the Irish brook had a music, a liveliness of its own; and when the speaker proceeded to read some of the poems, those who were merely English experienced a sudden catch in the throat as the music of our language with its sweet Irish undertone of wistful dreams and accent was lilted to our ears. Some of these poets, too, are propagandists and rebels of the first order – they include Alice Milligan, Lady Gregory, Maeve Cavanagh, Doris Sigerson and Eva Gore-Booth.

Among the biographers, Mrs Sheehy Skeffington sketched the work of Alice Curtayne, who specialises in Saints, of Dr Helena Concannon, one of the three women deputies of the Free State Dáil, and Nora Connolly O'Brien, whose *Portrait of a Rebel Father* is the outstanding book of the year. Among the scholars the work of Dr Mary Hayden and Dr Sophie Bryant was of special interest to the audience.

As to the novelists, Mrs Skeffington said that Miss Kate O'Brien is in the foremost rank and has been called the Irish Galsworthy. She also has the distinction of having had one of her books banned in Ireland. O. E. Somerville, too, has an abiding place in Irish literature; A. Romily White, an Ulster woman, portrays in *Gape Row* a sort of Northern Irish Cranford. These and others were dealt with by our speaker, as well as the dramatists Dorothy Macardle, Margaret O'Leary and Maura Mallory.

There were questions and discussion, and Mrs Pethick-Lawrence voiced the warm thanks of everyone present both to our old friend, Mrs Sheehy Skeffington, and to Miss Kate O'Brien for giving us a most delightful evening, and one which will long live in our memory. A collection was taken for the funds of our League – amounting to £2.16s.od.

'A feminist warns of a new revolt in Ireland: Dorothy Thomas interviews Hanna Sheehy Skeffington'
Independent Woman, March 1938

Again the question, 'Is woman's place in the home?' arises in Ireland, though the Proclamation of the Irish Republic which gave women citizenship rights in 1916 was thought to have settled the matter. Now certain clauses in the new Constitution as framed by Éamon de Valera, which went into effect in January, are thought by large groups of Irish women to be potentially dangerous to the women of their country.

Mrs Hanna Sheehy Skeffington, well known Irish lecturer, editor and writer, worker for peace and woman's rights, is in the vanguard against this threat to the hard-won independence of Irish women.

'You'd think a woman was born with a home on her back – like a snail – just because she's a woman!' was Mrs Skeffington's colorful exclamation. In America on a lecture tour, she was explaining her views for *Independent Woman* readers.

'When the average woman leaves her home it is usually for the paradoxical reason of keeping it. She takes a job in order to eke out the family budget, or because her husband is ill or dead and she must become the sole support of her children. Or in order to give money to her old parents or her young sisters and brothers. She might even have a worthless husband to support!'

Mrs Skeffington has direct, fearless blue eyes. She is grey-haired, motherly and soft-spoken. But you know she will fight for her convictions, as a mother will fight for her young. She has been imprisoned because she battled for woman suffrage, for peace, and because she joined Mr de Valera in his early efforts for a free Ireland. Her husband, a pacifist, was executed in 1916 during the Easter Rebellion because he urged men not to leave Ireland to fight in England's wars.

Mrs Skeffington believes in a workers' republic and regards the Ireland of today as merely another domain of Great Britain, like Canada and Australia. As things stand now, she declares, in case of war it would be practically impossible for Ireland to remain neutral; England can re-occupy Ireland and there is danger of conscription.

The political situation is not simple. The Fine Gael is the conservative party led by Cosgrave and is pro-English. The Fianna Fáil (de Valera's party) has the majority now. This party controls the twenty-six counties, the Free State. Northern Ireland (six-county area) refuses to acknowledge de Valera's Free State (Éire or Ireland) and remains loyal to England. The Republicans – not to be confused with our own GOP – are radical in Ireland, and are for a republic, not a monarchy. As they believe in complete independence of all of Ireland, naturally they are considered by the North as traitors to 'Ulster' and to England. They enter the six-county areas in Ulster under pain of arrest. Many great Irish writers and editors – including Mary MacSwiney, Mrs Skeffington, and Mr de Valera himself – are under this ban and are constantly watched. However, now that Mr de Valera is doing all right for himself, he is, Mrs Skeffington explains, growing more conservative. He now belongs to the Fianna Fáil or middle-of-the-road party. Mrs Skeffington believes that de Valera has compromised himself so much that he has put himself in the position of

Kerensky who too was once a rebel. The formerly powerful and militant Sinn Féin party (this means 'ourselves') still declines to recognise the present parliament to the extent of not voting at all.

'I believe in using my vote while I've got it,' Mrs Skeffington said. 'We republicans believe in trying to reform parliament from within.'

She then went on to explain that in 1923 it was proclaimed in the earlier Constitution that women should be given equal rights and opportunities. Then, in 1937, along comes the de Valera constitution stating: 'All citizens shall be held equal as human persons before the law' but qualified by the next phrase – '*This shall not mean, however, that the state shall not in its exactments have due regard to the different capacities physical and moral and of social function.*' Even those women who gave up personal careers and went to prison to work for de Valera are dissatisfied with the implications of that phrase, she said.

They also resent: 'The state recognizes that by her life within the home woman gives to the state a support without which the common good cannot be achieved. The state shall therefore endeavour to ensure that mothers shall not be obliged by economic necessity to engage in labor to the neglect of other duties in the home.'

Women like Mrs Skeffington feel that – though the latter is a lovely ideal – until it is achieved in actuality, women should not be barred from earning money. Men may not much regard feminine logic, but it does seem that the gentlemen are putting the cart before the horse when they prevent a married woman from holding a job before they give her husband sufficient economic security to support the home himself. And as for the 'different physical capacities', Irish women have for centuries been considered – and still are considered – robust enough to do the hardest work in the fields. 'I believe work is too important a part of life to be legislated according to sex,' said this mild mannered militant. 'Some women are not fitted either by temperament or native ability to work either in the fields or in the home. They have a right to choose what work they will do. There is a psychological as well as an economic necessity for every human being to find some work within his capabilities.'

Recently a bill has been proposed in Ireland which will bar women from the clothing industry. This is a highly skilled and well paid trade to which women have proved themselves singularly adapted. Efforts have also been made to force women clerical workers out of the Irish Sweepstakes offices. However, this is not a government run business, and women are found so highly capable in this special work, that so far the ouster has not been successful.

Women are dismissed from government and teaching jobs upon marriage. And there follows, of course, the tendency toward this procedure in private

industry, too. Newspaper advertisements quite frankly quote 500 pounds as a salary for a man, and 350 pounds for a woman. The same job of course.

The women of Ireland did a great deal to further de Valera's cause. He never spurned their vote. Now who can blame women for feeling that 'Vel' – as de Valera is popularly called – has wronged them? When women within his own party pointed out that there were certain ambiguous clauses in his Constitution which might restrict them, de Valera denied that they were dangerous, and refused to make any changes. Now he is being warned that if he remains adamant he will lose a large part of the woman's vote. One wonders how many women will have an opportunity at the next election to say, 'I told you so!'

Organisations are being formed to fight this tendency of the present regime to force women back into the home. One of the most militant is the Women's Social and Political League which is recruiting members to fight for equal pay for equal work. One of their slogans is: 'The State is the Home writ large. Women demand their place in it.' This organization dedicates itself to better working conditions, to prevent encroachments upon dearly won rights and to get women representatives on all public boards. Cartoons are now appearing in newspapers and magazines taking sides in this controversy. Mrs Skeffington explained that the real dynamite back of this woman scare is the insidious but strong tendency of the present regime toward fascism.

Should Women Serve on Juries? [12]
1938

In 1916 Irishwomen under the Proclamation of the Republic were granted equal citizenship with men, the Irish Republic claiming our allegiance in return. But, as we remained *de facto* under Great Britain, the vote was not legal under her laws until the 1918 election – and then only for women over thirty. Later it was given on equal terms and with it, at the same time, jury service was included. To this day women in Britain and Northern Ireland are called upon for this duty. But from the setting up of the Free State many difficulties were raised, chiefly owing to the opposition of the late Minister for Justice, Mr Kevin O'Higgins. There were various reasons for this. The outstanding one was political. There was generally a certain 'edge' in the minds of politicians of the period against women. Mr Kevin O'Higgins stated that he feared that 'women would be loth to convict'.

Another grievance was official. Officials hate innovation, Court officials most of all: women jurors would have had to be provided for in various ways in Courts that, save for the dock, had hitherto been exclusively masculine. The question of 'locking up' juries also loomed larger than life – for most juries are not held over night and, if they are, hotel accommodation is provided. Lastly, the women themselves, like most, if not indeed, all men, object to jury service. Some had good reasons, young married women in charge of children (whom their husbands had, perhaps, put down as house-owners in order themselves to escape the onus of jury service), delicate women and so on. The women 'bothered' the officials sorely, clamouring for exemptions. Instead of having the matter straightened out properly and certain exempted lists made for women (as there are for men) it was obviously simpler to exempt the entire sex.

Another factor that irritated both women and officials was that the women were more liable to be challenged as such, or ordered to stand aside: both plaintiffs and defendants in many cases feared this new class, so, when women attended for jury service, they spent hours and days in court, only to find that they were never sworn-in as jurors and thus had their time spent to no purpose. Probably in addition to all this they had to face grumbling male relatives when they got home.

Time could have regulated all this, had there been sufficient good will on the part of legislators and officials. This has been done in both Britain and Northern Ireland, where women jurors are accepted now as part of the scheme of things, their presence taken for granted and indeed approved, Six-County as well as British judges frequently paying special tribute to their good sense and good citizenship. I cannot believe that women in the Free State are peculiarly perverse, had they been given a reasonable chance in this matter. However, by stages their jury service was whittled down, first, in 1924, by an exemption granted to all women jurors for the mere asking and then, in 1926–7, by the passing of the Juries Act, in which women jurors were automatically 'relieved' of jury service in criminal cases, a clause being inserted as a sop, however, owing to much parliamentary opposition in Dáil and Senate, under which a so-called voluntary panel of jurors was to be established. This was to include men as well as women – that is men in certain cases automatically exempted could apply to serve. Sir James Craig, Senator Browne,[13] the late Sir Coey Bigger and others favoured this way out. In practice, however, this panel never really worked for obvious reasons. First, many women who would have been willing to serve when called upon could not by nature of their work offer their services, for employers and others would have regarded such volunteer work as unnecessary and an irksome interruption. Many families also declined to send in their name on principle, regarding the setting up of such a panel as a futile compromise. A certain number – small, it is true, for reasons assigned – did send in their names for some years.

I happened to have been one of those who believed in 'testing out' the panel, but, though my name went in regularly (I gave up after three or four years), I was never once summonsed, though my turn must have come round periodically. Other women who volunteered were called, attended court, but were never once sworn-in, being challenged or called upon to stand aside. The panel was a dead letter from the beginning. It is interesting to note that no men ever volunteered on this panel, though expressly invited. Now it is expiring, a certain number of years having elapsed, but the fact of its existence or elimination makes no difference in the principle namely, that women should not be deprived of their right of jury service in the Free State, a right freely exercised elsewhere.

For it is not a question of pleasing officials by relieving them of embarrassment or of letting women off: it is the right of every woman or girl charged with an offence to have on the jury that tries her certain members of her own sex. In cases of infanticide it should be a matter of course that mothers are represented on such juries: this is a case that calls for the experience of women. A provision should also be made that where a certain woman is challenged by either party another woman should take her place, that is, ruling out of juries on grounds of sex should be illegal.

The whole question of jury service for women should be opened up once more. When the present Government was in opposition Fianna Fáil members during the last stages of the Juries Act professed sympathy with the demand of the United Women's societies. At that time and later during the passage of the Criminal Law Amendment Act there was a strong feeling among social workers and clergymen of various denominations that the presence of women on juries dealing with certain cases was a real safeguard where girls were concerned. There can be little doubt but that, were women eligible for jury service here as in other countries, they would acquit themselves as good citizens just as American, British and Irish women of the Six-County area are doing. I refuse to believe that women in the Free State are more backward and selfish than their sisters elsewhere.

Jury service has, as it is, for men too many exemption-doors. It falls now too heavily on the few, chiefly on business men, who are called over and over again within short periods. It is nearly ten years since Mr O'Higgins' Juries Act became law: it is time for an amending Act – how many measures hastily passed by the late Administration have needed such: – removing certain anomalies and restoring to women the right to sit on juries and to women prisoners that of trial by their peers.

'Censorship in Éire'
The Saturday Review, New York, 18 March 1939

Americans, I found, during a recent visit to USA, were much puzzled by the vagaries of our Irish censorship board and its odd manner of behaving. So, when I got back, I gathered up a number of facts concerning it, in the hope of being able to clarify the situation.

Under the British regime, that is, before the setting up of the Free State (now rechristened 'Éire', but still covering only twenty-six out of thirty-two counties of Ireland) we came under the British censor's rule as far as books went. We never had in Ireland, by some curious oversight, a censorship of the stage – nor have we one now, though we have a specially appointed Irish censor of films, who in turn may be appealed against to a higher tribunal. Shaw's *Blanco Posnet*, banned by the English Lord Chancellor, was proudly produced by the Abbey Theatre. Under the British censorship came Joyce's *Ulysses*, for instance, and Radclyffe Hall's *Well of Loneliness* – this was a matter in the domain of morals and therefore a police affair. In Northern Ireland still (that is the Six-County area) this is what prevails and there they show visitors proudly in shop windows books 'banned in the Free State'. Our Censor Board consists of five men – of whom four are Catholics – two from the National University, one from the Dublin, i.e., TCD, with a Catholic clergyman for chairman. It is curious to find the Protestant University (founded by Queen Elizabeth) lending itself to what is virtually a Catholic censorship. The formula governing the censor is to prohibit books 'whose general tendency is indecent'. Books on sex, dealing with marriage problems or with birth control, are similarly banned, while weeklies like the *New Leader* that merely carry birth control advertisements or even announcements of birth control discussions are also banned.

How are books banned? First, a public informer reports to the Board that a certain book is objectionable. The book has to be purchased by the informer and sent to the Board. But, before it reaches the members, a Civil Servant immune against corruption presumably, is expected to note and blue pencil certain offending passages. Then the Board has to read and report – probably the members divide up the books for reading, otherwise their task would be too onerous. (The members act in a purely honorary capacity, by the way.) Then a majority decision decides the fate of the book in question, and there is no appeal against their decision. It will be seen that the process is lengthy, slow, and extremely inefficient. The Board is entirely in the hands of these picked persons with a nose for the unpleasant. It often takes two or three years for a book to be pounced on – in many recent cases the volumes had actually been issued in the Penguin 6d edition before being discovered. (*Fontmara* is a case in point.) It also means that often high-brow books are marked down because a particular 'informer' reads these rather than popular novels. A case in point is Aldous Huxley's *Point Counter Point*. Hervey Allen's *Anthony Adverse* was likewise marked down, but later, to complicate matters, the motion picture version successfully passed the film censor and was shown widely.

We are quite international in our banning: Mikhail Sholokhov's *And Quiet Flows the Don*, Stefan Zweig's *Amok*, Erskine Caldwell's *American Earth*,

Sinclair Lewis's *Ann Vickers*, Aldous Huxley's *Brave New World*, Somerset Maugham's *Cakes and Ale*, Colette's *Chéri*, Ethel Mannin's *Common Sense and the Child*, Mae West's *Constant Sinner*, Signe Toksvig's *Eve's Doctor*, Francis Hackett's *Green Lion*, Vera Brittain's *Honourable Estate*, Hemingway's *Farewell to Arms*, are a fairly typical list. The unusual, the daring, any criticism of the Catholic Church generally, or of individual clerics, indictment of marriage, sex, hygiene, medical views of birth control, sex education for the young, all these are marked down, Marie Stopes, stock, lock and barrel, and writers like Bertrand Russell (*Marriage and Morals*) and Havelock Ellis (*Essays of Love and Virtue*) as well as Jules Romains's *Men of Good Will* are lumped together under the absurd formula 'in general tendency indecent'. Another strange feature is the fact that only English versions are banned – you may apparently read with impunity the original German, French, Russian, Spanish, Italian.

Irish writers suffer heavily – Seán O'Faoláin, Liam O'Flaherty, Kate O'Brien, Austin Clarke, have had one or more books censored on a principle that would certainly ban Shakespeare, the Bible, Goethe's *Faust*, and Victor Hugo's *Les Misérables*, were these writers alive today. Dead masterpieces have not come in under the ban, for some unknown reason. Recently more and more American books are being 'discovered' by the common informer, as his reading widens – some of these very poor stuff, some masterpieces. And we, the general readers, have usually read any that are worthwhile long before the ban falls.

Among the most recent books banned are Eric Linklater's *Impregnable Women*, Elmer Rice's *Imperial City*, Fannie Hurst's *Back Street*, Louie Paul's *Hallelujah, I'm a Bum*, George Schwarz's *Almost Forgotten Germany*, *The Way to Happy Marriage* (by a Workaday Mother). About one thousand books have been censored since the setting up of the Board under the Censorship Act, in 1929, nearly ten years ago.

Lately the machinery has, however, slowed down. Of course, there is 'book-legging' as AE predicted there would be. Most readers belonging to circulating libraries and *au courant* with reviews, have already anticipated the censors and are rarely caught napping. Then, if you have acquired a book before the axe falls, you pass it dutifully on to your friends and go up in their esteem. Or you get it when you are next in London or Belfast or Paris or New York. And there are other ways still of circumventing our Comstocks[14] that I may not tell, lest I, too, play an informer's thankless role. Many are the yarns told of how censors are fooled. After all, we Irish have a long and honourable tradition in law-breaking and law-flouting. For all that, the Censorship Board is a blot on the vaunted freedom Éire has won, an ironic development, illustrating man's proneness to chain up freedom. But the censors answer no criticism and, short of bringing them into court, there would seem to be no way of bringing them to book. And it is highly doubtful that any court in Éire would have the nerve to find their ban unjustified. And so the vicious circle is complete – and only a martyr can break it by openly breaking the law and defying the consequences. We have had many martyrs for many causes in Ireland, but none, so far, for literature.

'Is the Irish question settled?'
The New Republic, 15 June 1938

There is not a word about restoring Ireland's unity as a result of the recent *pour-parlers* in London that have culminated in a Trade-cum-Defense Pact. Once again (the second time within the last few months), it is announced in the American press that the Irish question has been finally and at last amicably settled. Yet nothing is really finally settled that leaves Ireland partitioned, cut into two Dominion pieces, the twenty-six-county area and the six-county area. There is still a 'Lost Province' (at least six counties of it) detached from the rest, still a substantial and aggrieved minority, wedged in the northeast corner of the island, native Irish in an alien and privileged group.

The cut-off portion is wrongly named Ulster, for three of the counties of that province – Cavan, Monaghan and Donegal – belong to the twenty-six-county area, formerly called the Irish Free State, now called Ireland or Éire. (Éire is the Irish name for Ireland; in English, therefore, the word 'Ireland' is correct.) The six counties arbitrarily partitioned off are Antrim, Armagh, Tyrone, Fermanagh, Derry and Down.

This area (Northern Ireland, as it is loosely called) got its Parliament, Governor-General and separate status before the negotiations that led to the Treaty of 1921–22 were opened. King George V opened the Parliament personally during the vice-royalty of Lord Fitzalan, the last Viceroy of Ireland. Later, the British government paid a million pounds for the magnificent palace at Stormont which houses the 'Wee Parliament', as it is called locally, reigned over by the Duke of Abercorn and Lord Craigavon (the former, Governor-General, the latter, Prime Minister). The Northern area receives from Britain also a substantial annual subsidy – one million pounds.

There was a clause in the treaty which set up the Free State saying that within a term of five years a *county plebiscite* could be taken to permit the inhabitants of the six-county area to vote themselves into the rest of Ireland. Had such a plebiscite been taken, Tyrone and Fermanagh (which have had nationalist majorities) would have thrown in their lot with the rest of Ireland; so would South Armagh, South Down, Derry City and West Belfast. So the 'clenched fist' of Orange opposition would have lost some fingers: even Antrim would not have been intact. Previous to partition, out of thirty-three members of Parliament returned, seventeen were nationalists. It would have been found impossible to carry on with such a reduced area. For this reason, the clause providing for a county plebiscite was never carried out and a hugger-mugger bargain was entered into which prevented the electorate's being formally consulted. This hope of a plebiscite was the main inducement which obtained the support of Arthur Griffith for the Anglo-Irish treaty. He felt that the unity of Ireland was all-important.

'The Land League priest: memories of Father Sheehy of Kilmallock'
Irish Press, 18 July 1938

Two Father Sheehys played their parts as rebels and patriots in their time: the earlier, Father Nicholas, hanged at Clonmel, was called 'The Whiteboys' Friend': Tipperary is for ever associated with his name and story. Father Eugene Sheehy, the Land League Priest, belongs to the later, no less strenuous period of the Land War: his name is linked with Limerick, for he was CC of Kilmallock and later PP of Bruree, where the boy, Éamon de Valera, used to serve his Mass in the little village of Bruree, where he lived with his uncles, the Colls, during boyhood.

Eugene Sheehy was born at Broadford, near Drumcolligher, Co. Limerick, on Christmas Day, 1841: his earliest memories were of the scenes during the Black Famine of '47 and of the Levellers tearing off roofs in his native village during their ruthless evictions. He was educated at the Jesuit College, St Munchin's, Limerick, where he was one of its first pupils. In the early sixties he went to the Irish College, Paris (Rue des Irlandais, as it is still called). At that time the compulsory oath of allegiance to British rule exacted in Maynooth sent young clerical students of rebel hearts to Rome, Spain or France, where no such restriction was imposed.

His first curacy was in Kilmallock: it fell upon stormy times – Kilmallock was a Fenian centre in '67 and the embers were still smouldering. Here Father Eugene Sheehy became President of the local Land League, a very dangerous body in those days: he was shortly to come up against the notorious coercionist Clifford Lloyd, sent to the 'disaffected' district as Removable Magistrate with special plenipotentiary powers from Dublin Castle. The story is told by Clifford Lloyd himself, in his book, *Ireland under the Land League*, of which he naturally is the hero. This frank account of the methods employed by a ruthless Government has its amusing side for present-day readers, though it must have been grim enough to those who lived and fought in those battles long ago. The author did not lack the courage of the Bull Dog breed. He urged the arrest of the rebel curate and the Castle obligingly furnished troops to assist thereat, so at 5.30 am one bright May morning, 1881, a drive was made on the priest's house by the Limerick flying column. Father Sheehy was, to use Clifford Lloyd's own words, 'a great favourite with the lower classes and the poor people to whom, I believe, he was kind and sympathetic'. He walked to the local barracks with an imposing escort, military and police, the crowd following and (to the RM's horror) the PP, Father Doynes, led the procession to demonstrate his sympathy with his hot-headed curate.

It was a memorable scene. 'The people,' says Clifford Lloyd, 'fell upon their knees and seized his hands and the skirts of his clothes, begging his blessing before he left them.' He was sent first to Naas Jail, thence to Kilmainham, where he joined the other Suspects rounded up there, Parnell, Davitt, Dillon among the number. One of my earliest recollections was a snatched, entirely unofficial visit there when I went with the Ladies of the Land League, a chit of four, and escaped under the counter where the lunch baskets were being unpacked, running across the huge reception hall to acclaim my uncle, walking soberly at exercise with tall John Dillon.

From May till September Father Eugene Sheehy was detained (he got into trouble with the Authorities for, I believe, omitting the ritual prayer for the Queen and those in high station, so was not permitted after the first Sunday or two to do more than assist at Mass). Released with the rest he returned in triumph to Kilmallock, Clifford Lloyd sadly recording the tale of his homecoming. In the meanwhile the Castle functionary for all his missions had been sent on the run, being boycotted out of the district: he notes mournfully that it was the women of the town who led the campaign. Brave women of Limerick. Later that year Father Sheehy went on a mission to America for the Land League, T. M. Healy, the youthful secretary of Parnell, accompanying him: they had a lightening tour of the States. In the following years he visited the USA and Canada many times. The churches of Kilmallock, Rathkeale and Bruree (for all of which at various periods he appealed for funds) bear witness to his efforts in the Missionary field among his people in America. His political activity was for the Land League: he helped many a time to raise funds for its campaign, being a close friend of Patrick Ford of the *Irish World* and of John Devoy of the *Gaelic American* in the hey-day of the New Departure.[15] He was a member of the Irish Republican Brotherhood and for a time on its Executive, I am informed. One of his famous speeches delivered in New York, on The Men and Principles of '48 is preserved in A. M. Sullivan's Penny Readings: it is typical of his fervid and passionate oratory. His glowing tribute to Davis and Mitchel is a fine example of his style and must have gained a hundredfold from its delivery in his characteristic quick and fiery manner, that of the born orator whose words quicken the pulse of his hearers. Well do I recall his declaiming of that beloved poem the Fenians –

See who comes over the red-blossomed heather
Their proud banners rising the quick mountain air
Heads erect, eyes to the front, stepping proudly together –

Ending with the dashing refrain:

Out to make way for the Fenian men!

His was (as friends who first heard the phrase from his lips have testified) the first utterance of the now immortal phrase, adopted at once by Parnell: 'No man can set bounds to the onward march of a nation.' It was first used at a banquet in Cork (it was at that time that the friends, Parnell and Eugene Sheehy, were photographed together). Parnell made the phrase at once his own – and there was nothing its original coiner would have liked better.

Father Sheehy was later actively associated in Limerick with the early Gaelic Athletic revival and was on its first Committee. He spoke Irish fluently from boyhood days, his father being a sound Irish scholar. He was a passionate enthusiast of the game of hurling and used to lead his team into the field himself. Well I remember the cry: 'Back it up, Bruree!' with which he would cheer his men on. He and his team took part in a memorable protest against a local evicting landlord, who loved the hunt. He led his men and they lined the ditch, hurley sticks in hand, preventing the rural autocrat from entering the lands. Never after did the landlord hunt in or around Bruree, a telling demonstration of solidarity between people and soggarth against aggression that was not lost upon the landlord.

In later days as health declined, he lived in Dublin, becoming the close friend of Thomas Clarke and Seán McDermott, and often taken into their councils in that now historic little newspaper shop in old Great Britain Street. In 1916 he went straight to his old friend in the GPO to 'administer spiritual consolation' and to cheer on the valiant little band by his presence.[16] He left the building only when it was burning over their heads and the Order to evacuate was issued. He died in the July following at 76, one of his last utterances being: 'I am sorry I did not die with Tom Clarke!' What he said of Mitchel might well serve as his own epitaph:

Never had Ireland a truer lover, never tyranny a more inexorable foe. To Ireland he clung fast through weal and woe: to her his thoughts were given and all his labours, and they were labours of love . . . All these to live unrequited, yet unrepining.

And he passed on that torch of love and devotion to many of the younger generation who were proud to follow in the footsteps of 'the Land League Priest!'

14

PRISON EXPERIENCES

INTRODUCTION

As a suffrage militant, Hanna experienced two terms of imprisonment. These would not be her only prison experiences. She received a two-month sentence on 20 June 1912 for her participation in the first wave of suffrage militancy, on 13 June, when she broke window panes in Dublin Castle. Those imprisoned with her were Marguerite Palmer and Jane and Margaret Murphy. On 12 July Marjorie Hasler, Kathleen Houston, Maud Lloyd and Hilda Webb, who had been arrested at the same time, were sentenced to six months' imprisonment as a consequence of the greater damage they created.

The Irish suffragist experience of imprisonment differed considerably from that of their English counterparts. The first four prisoners received concessions regarding letters, visits, and the right to associate during exercise. The second batch of prisoners, despite their activities, in facing a longer sentence were recommended by the judge to be treated as first class misdemeanants. The prisoners were not confrontational, and therefore relations between officials and prisoners at this stage were generally harmonious. The *Irish Citizen* believed that this was partly because of the particular Irish experience as 'a country many of whose foremost politicians passed through prison to prominence' (13 July 1912). And of course, Hanna's father, David Sheehy, was one such, having been a Fenian prisoner and now an MP.

Hunger strike was only adopted by Hanna and her colleagues because of the complication of English suffrage prisoners, who travelled over to Ireland on 18 July in their separate pursuit of Prime Minister Asquith and who undertook much more extreme militancy. They had thrown a hatchet at Prime Minister Asquith, travelling in a coach with John Redmond, and had attempted to set fire to the Theatre Royal, which was to be the venue for the Redmond/Asquith meeting. In consequence, the three WSPU women – Mary Leigh, Gladys Evans and Jennie Baines – received punitive sentences ranging from seven months with hard labour for Baines, to five years' penal servitude for Leigh and Evans. They did not qualify for first-class status or special privileges and on 14 August they went on hunger strike, putting the Irish prisoners in a difficult position. After smuggled letters between Hanna and Frank, the IWFL agreed that the four prisoners with shorter sentences would go on hunger strike in solidarity with the WSPU women, but that those with six-month sentences would not. Once Hanna and her three companions began their hunger strike their privileges were removed. They were only released on 19 August after they had completed their sentences. Baines was also released, on health grounds. Leigh and Evans continued with their hunger strike and, eventually, the authorities decided to begin forcible feeding. This dreadful process continued until Mary Leigh was released on licence on 20 September and Gladys Evans on 3 October. Both women's physical and mental health were severely affected.

Hanna's account of this period glosses over the reason for her hunger strike, other than to imply a solidarity with the WSPU prisoners. In reality, the Irish women were greatly concerned at the repercussions this development could have on their own campaign. They were right to be concerned, as the authorities were much less lenient in the future. It was decided that suffrage prisoners would now be sent to Tullamore Prison, 60 miles outside Dublin. The next group of prisoners, Meg Connery, Margaret Cousins and Barbara Hoskins, were each given a month with hard labour for window smashing. They went on hunger strike in a demand to be given political prisoner status. After Barbara Hoskins was released the authorities agreed to grant privileges and the strike was called off. Given the isolation of prisoners in Tullamore, their friends travelled to ensure that they were not left alone but had the regular support of their colleagues. It was for that reason that Hanna was in Tullamore when Barbara Hoskins was released. Three other suffrage prisoners were imprisoned in Tullamore in May 1913.

When Hanna found herself arrested again, in November 1913, she was not sent to Tullamore but to Mountjoy, where she immediately went on hunger strike, not for concessions on her status, but as a protest at what she considered was a gross injustice, sentenced for supposedly having injured a police officer while she and Meg Connery had been attempting to give leaflets to Sir Edward Carson and Bonar Law. The centrality of Mountjoy enabled the IWFL to mount effective protests on her behalf. At one stage this ended up in a riot, as football supporters on their way home after a match clashed with the suffragists. Hanna's message of December 1913 in the *Irish Citizen* makes mention of this occasion, referring to police actions in breaking up protest meetings.

While the IWFL wanted the status of political prisoner, in recognition of their cause, there is no hint that they considered themselves superior to the ordinary woman prisoner. On the contrary, there is great sympathy for their plight, and for the reasons that they were in jail, a sympathy evident in Hanna's letter to Lady Aberdeen, calling for amelioration of conditions, and again in evidence when Hanna wrote of the prisoners she encountered when serving her final prison sentence in Armagh in 1933.

Hanna also had a brief period of imprisonment in Holloway Jail, in August 1918, when she was arrested after smuggling herself back to Dublin after having being refused permission to go to Ireland when she arrived in Liverpool on her return from the United States. She was released after hunger strike and returned to Ireland, leaving Countess Markievicz, Maud Gonne MacBride and Kathleen Clarke still in jail, victims of the 'German Plot'[1] arrests. There was no guarantee that Hanna would not have been re-arrested at a future date, given war-time conditions. John Dillon, MP wrote to her to urge her to stay out of political life for the time being as he feared if she was arrested again she would not win release. Her angry reply is included in this section as it is highly revealing of her state of mind and attitude at this difficult time.

Her final prison experience was in the north, in Armagh Jail in 1933, when she defied a barring order from the northern authorities to speak in support of republican women prisoners.

'In Mountjoy: my prison experiences'
Irish Independent, 20 August 1912

On arrival at Mountjoy gates we had some document gabbled to us by some male officials – the purport, I understand, being that our bodies were handed over to the Governor for a certain stipulated period – one month – with an additional month should we refuse bail. We at once declared that we did refuse, but the officials suggested that we might change our minds. We didn't – but then they had had no suffragettes before, so could hardly be expected to understand our point of view. I since learned that the entire conviction sheet (or whatever they call the document) was informal, and had to be cooked up by the Attorney-General and other legal luminaries a month after committal! Convenient, these Attorneys-General.

Registration

Clutching bag, bouquet and cherry-stick that broke those Castle windows, which a policeman pressed into my hand, I followed a uniformed matron (dressed like a hospital nurse), and had the colour of eyes and hair, place of birth, religion, age, and various miscellaneous items of information entered duly in a ponderous volume, together with the name and address of some 'friend'. This puzzled me – it looked quite human, as if the officials meant to dispatch daily bulletins to my anxious relatives; but I learned later that the friend was expected to fetch my body from the Governor in case death cut my sentence short of the time laid down by Mr Swifte. Next came weights and measures, also duly noted, and height recorded. We gave up money and stamps and proceeded to our cells. They were of the dimensions of a good-sized bathroom, about 12 ft x 6 ft.

My Furnished Apartment

In No. 5 of Wing B I reckon I spent 1,236 hours, so I shall remember it when pleasanter impressions have vanished. It was whitewashed (as a result of petition the whitewash was mitigated by green) tempered with tar. On pegs hung copies of prison rules. Two corner shelves held regulation mug and plate in enamel, comb, slate, wooden salt-cellar, horn spoon, a small table, a low, backless stool (devised, like the chapel benches, specially to induce backache) and the plank bed completed the furniture – no, I forgot the prison tins arranged in symmetrical row of unvarying pattern. There was a small window with muffled panes near the ceiling, with frame fixed in the wall, with a slight opening at the top and protected outside by heavy iron bars. This could be reached by means of certain gymnastics. It looked out on the prison green, with concrete rings for prisoners to walk on at exercise. In the iron door (like that of a respectable family vault in Glasnevin) were two peep-holes; a large and a small, cunningly contrived to open only from the outside, and so arranged as to give a glimpse of the occupant at any hour of day or night.

Agreeably Impressed

Later we Suffragists, aided by kind friends, managed to impart some variety and a modicum of comfort into these cells – an armchair, flowers, books, pictures, cushions, helped to take away that deadly uniformity which is one of the dehumanising elements of prison. Outside our door was affixed a card bearing registered number, name, and crime, religion, age, length of sentence, and prescribed diet, with the letters RW in case the victim is not illiterate.

On the whole, I was quite agreeably impressed by Mountjoy. Unlike some English prisons of which I have heard, it is a model of cleanliness, quiet, and good management, its floors scrubbed to a polish, its corridors blue and white with fresh paint, its baths inviting. The prison food is wholesome, if plain, and everything from the neat-robed, pleasant matrons (the ugly word 'wardress' is superseded) down to the shining tins and brasses, would compare favourably as to staff and equipment with some hospitals and pretentious nursing homes I know. The structural arrangements recall those of an aviary, for there is an endless network of bar and wire, designed to prevent suicide. Everywhere the precautions against self-destruction are elaborate and suggestive – knives and cords, pins and scissors, are banished, so that this final contempt of Court may be avoided.

The Prison Oligarchy

We soon made the acquaintance of the oligarchy that runs a prison – the Lady Superintendent, doctors, Chaplains, Governor, Deputy-Governor, Visiting Justices, Prisons Board, and, over all, the Lord Lieutenant, supreme pontiff. Their powers are strictly confined in their own sphere, and one generally found that the particular potentate applied to never had any. If you want soda-water (a 'medical comfort') or an extra hour's exercise, the doctor is the person to approach; if gas in your cell at nightfall, the Governor; if you pine for a friend's visit only the Justices can give any relief; if you are unreasonable enough to want your own doctor (and that a woman-doctor) only the Lord Lieutenant can grant the boon. And so on.

A Demoralizing Restriction

We waited a week without exercise until the rightful machinery was set in motion, in order to allow us to speak to one another at exercise! This rule of silence is another of the demoralizing and meaningless restrictions of prison. There are many others, some of a vindictive character (such as the odious 'visiting box', through which ordinary prisoners see their friends in a sort of cage), others part of the elaborate espionage system – all relics of barbarism. There is no privacy in prison, the very decencies are broken down. You never quit the sight or surveillance of an official for a single moment. You are escorted to your bath, which has but a scanty half-door. You receive visits under super-vision: you see your doctor or the chaplain with some official in the offing; your letters are opened; your newspapers initialed before they are passed on. If the officials are humane and kindly, it is in spite of the system. If they were true to the letter and spirit of prison regime, they would become monsters.

Nature Asserts Itself

As first-class misdemeanants we did not, of course, dip deep into the prison life – save at chapel one saw little of ordinary prisoners, who were carefully kept away from the 'politicals' for fear of mutual contamination. One caught glimpses at prayers of many appealing faces under those neat prison caps, and many pretty ones, some sick, some sad to death, some very old and miserable, some half-crazed. I think the only bright inmates are the prison pigeons that bill and coo all day in the prison yards and nest defiantly outside the barred windows, and – the prison babies. One caught glimpses of the little toddlers 'exercising' with their mothers, having probably a better time and more undivided care than is ever their lot outside. And those 'criminal' mothers dearly love their little ones, and nature, expelled with a fork, re-asserts herself – even in prison.

The Greatest Hardship

The greatest privation in prison? The 'goodly earth and air are banned and barred – forbidden fare'. That, as Byron divined, is, to the 'first-class' at least, the greatest hardship. On bright June or July evenings to say good-night at five – prison ten-hour, after which is general 'lock-up' – is a trial.

Twenty hours out of 24, the first-class prisoner enjoys unmitigated solitude. For the others the laundry, the kitchen, the work-room afford a limited variety. The enforced solitude of prison is harsh and spirit-subduing; it finds out the weak joints in one's armour, and brings into play all one's philosophy and resourcefulness. Stead said that every Judge should go through the ordeal of 'serving time' before assuming office in order to help his imagination to realise the penalties he was inflicting. The salutary suggestion, if enforced, might deplete our jails, and would surely transform them. Yet I have many happy memories of Mountjoy – of pleasant companionship through hours of exercise and associated labour with my fellow-suffragists, of kindnesses from friends who paid us daily pilgrimages, of studious hours far from the madding, mobbing crowd.

Hunger Strike

Towards the end of our sentence we were startled by the action of Judge Madden imposing penal servitude on the English Suffragists. We Irish prisoners sent eight memorials from Mountjoy to Lord Aberdeen on the day after sentence was passed, and the English prisoners also forwarded theirs. Hearing that a week was the interval during which we might expect a reply (in our own case the reply had come sooner) we decided to wait a week, and did not protest until after the English Suffragists had entered upon the hunger strike. Official delays are dangerous, so on Thursday, we decided to wait no longer. I have heard of cases where answers to memorials have been delayed until the day of the prisoner's discharge, when word arrived to the departing one that the 'law must take its course'. The hunger strike is a method of passive revolt that was initiated in Russian prisons where 'politicals' adopt it when all else fails. In Russia they do not add the further refinement of cruelty – forcible feeding; it has been reserved to civilized England to adopt that method of 'persuasion'. On Thursday morning we refused exercise and at noon we declined dinner. Immediately all privileges were withdrawn. There were no more visits, letters, newspapers, as result of our 'misconduct'. We were not unprepared for this, for one finds in prison that while no one apparently has any power to grant privileges, which only come in the most devious ways, almost every official has the right to curtail or withdraw.

A Fast for 92 Hours

The long fast began, and except in the initial stages, for me who am robust it was not unbearable. The habit of fasting 'grows by what it's fed on'. At first one misses the break of meal-time in prison, and one does not, if one is wise, let one's thoughts dwell upon dainties. In novels one skips the allusions to food hurriedly. Then one ceases altogether to reflect upon the fact that if one has occupation the revolt of the body against starvation is not regarded, and the body learns to acquiesce. Water, which the hunger-striker indulges in liberality, is a mitigation. The prison meals, by regulation, reposed neglected in a corner, intended, no doubt, to tempt, but one can master the temptation to prison fare at all times. We were fasting 92 hours before release. Had the strike lasted longer more unpleasant symptoms would have, doubtless, intervened, and forcible feeding would have dragged in its element of agony. This was, happily, spared the Irish prisoners – it will not be spared the English – and but for loss of sleep and gradual weakness, languor and numbness, the experience was not intolerable. At any rate, not when one was braced by the consciousness that no choice remained for those who could essay the desperate remedy but the 'sympathetic strike'.

Hanna Sheehy Skeffington

'Message from Mrs Sheehy Skeffington'
Irish Citizen, 13 December 1913

Mrs Sheehy Skeffington is making favourable progress towards recovery after her five days' Hunger Strike. She is under the care of Dr Kathleen Lynn, whose report (read at the IWFL meeting on Tuesday) states that Mrs Skeffington's heart shows signs of improvement, and that the sleeplessness which at first caused anxiety is disappearing. Mrs Sheehy Skeffington, who is ordered absolute quiet for some time, has sent the following message to her friends through the *Irish Citizen*:

> I desire through the medium of the *Irish Citizen* to thank most heartily all my friends in the Franchise League who worked so strenuously during my imprisonment, and who organised the fine series of protest meetings outside Mountjoy Prison on my behalf. Their splendid enthusiasm and matchless energy were the battering ram that forced open the jail gates! It is gratifying to realise that Sergeant Thomas, by his assault on me, and the police who illegally attempted to break up the protest meetings, have unwittingly rendered us a great service, and given a fine impetus to our movement by rousing public indignation against police methods and the ways of police magistrates. I congratulate the IWFL on its victory over the police, those arch-disturbers of the peace, who were afraid to face even a Police

court judgment of their disgraceful conduct. During this period of enforced inactivity I am happy to know that our work goes forward unimpeded, and that the Franchise League keeps its flag flying, no matter how many of us fall by the way. Later I hope to be able to acknowledge more adequately, and in person, the many messages of sympathy and the many acts of kindness of my friends during my illness – just now I must ask them to take the will for the deed!

I wish also to express my thanks to the sister suffrage societies, the IWSS[2] and the IRL,[3] and to the ILPI,[4] for their resolutions and help on my behalf, and to all those who have rallied to us at this juncture with generous financial support.

'Mountjoy re-visited'
Irish Citizen, 3 January 1914

'Boast not of to-morrow, for thou knowest not what the day to come may bring forth,' 'Let the milk of the goats be enough for thy food,' these were the texts that first caught my eye on opening my prison Bible in Mountjoy on the night of November 28th. They met the situation, for I had little dreamt that morning that the plank was to be my portion that night, while if for the milk of goats the water of Vartry were substituted, there could be no more appropriate scriptural sanction of the Hunger-Strike. As the door of No. 1 cell in Wing B was double-locked on me, I had a last time to review the scenes of that surprising day, the gay sallying forth from League HQ, with the customary sheaf of leaflets and the *Irish Citizen* placard with its appropriate legend 'Questions for Bonar Law', held apron-wise, the group of students outside the house of Lord Iveagh – that pillar of anti-suffrage and Bungery – the ever-growing crowd of cameras awaiting the emergence of the Ulster Rebels on their way to lunch. What came we to see? What were we doing in that galley? We were the uninvited, undesired Banquo – Irishwomen whom Mr Bonar Law had refused to receive in deputation, in spite of his Chief's concession of Votes to Irishwomen – If and When. The leader of the Opposition found time for addresses yards long from loyalists, men and women of North and South – we saw them pouring down the steps, their faces radiant from the presence – but for the three Irish suffrage societies he could not spare a moment. Hence our presence as a reminder that the Irish Women's Franchise League is not accustomed to take 'no' for an answer from Tory or Liberal, from Nationalist or Labour. There was a long wait while the cameras stood at attention. One eager Englishman in charge of the arrangements came to me to express the hope that I would not interpose at the critical moment, lest the film might be spoiled, and, as the desired guarantee was not forthcoming, I heard a voice mutter gruffly beside me, 'I'll look after her, sir!' It was the voice of Sergeant Thomas (5B), with whom I was destined to be better acquainted. Then the conquering heroes came – Bonar Law falling to me. Advancing towards him with my leaflets, I found myself instantly caught in an iron grip that closed like a steel trap over my left arm. (The Sergeant's autograph, one purple thumb-mark and four red angry finger-nails, did not fade from that arm till Christmas.) I made an attempt to move forward and fling some leaflets with my disengaged right, only to find both arms caught and crossed, the leaflets strewn about the pavement, and myself shaken to and fro, as I have seen a terrier shake a kitten, until one of the superfluous cameras was seen lowered to catch the scene, when the Sergeant's grip automatically loosened, and I found myself under arrest! At Lad Lane Police Station I vainly pressed to get a counter-charge against the Sergeant; later in Mr Swifte's court I renewed the effort – also in vain. Mr Swifte's loyalist soul was wrung by the thought of 'our English visitors' being molested, his heart was grieved (while the Court rocked with laughter) at the Sergeant's lurid tale of how he 'was seized, your worship, and pummeled repeatedly with clenched fist!'; he still felt the ache from the blows. Mrs Connery's evidence of the assault on me was entirely ignored – what avails a civilian's oath in the Police Court? I got a week for being assaulted by a Sergeant. I may be thankful that an Inspector or (horrible thought) Superintendent did not hit me, for then no doubt my sentence would have been proportionate to the dignity of the offender.

Nothing remained but the protest of the Hunger-Strike, which I at once adopted, with the result that I was able to 'determine my own sentence' (a thing which Mr McKenna is fond of telling us suffragists are never to be allowed to do), and emerge before my time was up. Had the Cat and Mouse Act been working in Ireland, I might have been a Mouse, but Dublin Castle has not dared (after its first disastrous experiment) to enforce that coercion Act in Ireland. Going to prison for a second time is like having a second tooth out. The novelty is over and one knows exactly how much it hurts. Those banging doors, that ever-watchful spy-hole, the plank, exercise round and round in that concreted circle, the oppressive solitude, broken only by the still more oppressive routine – the experience repeated grows stale even to nausea. And one tries to remember the former hunger-strike – was it on the third day that hunger no longer gnawed? On what night did your heart waken you with its jumping? It is a merciful dispensation most of the great things of life are not repeated, that death happens only once. It would add another pang to the executed to remember former hangings.

A Hunger-Strike is rather worse in cold weather, because as I understand 'oxidization is then more rapid' (or is it less?), and pneumonia is to be dreaded – in spite of which, I had, until I protested, to receive my visitors in a draughty shed in the prison yard. Unless you are in hospital your visitors are not permitted to come to your cell – such is the regulation. As before, the three meals reposed all day untouched in a corner of the cell – tea and dry brown bread, potatoes and prison soup, and later a pint of milk was mysteriously added. The smell of tea or soup slightly aggravates the situation, for the hunger-striker's senses grow sharper by starvation. I believe the hunger-strike is growing common among ordinary prisoners, but it has been found that the poor things always succumb when food is left in their proximity. As I was repeatedly warned against the danger of breaking my fast after release on anything but the lightest and more special fare, it is hard to understand why such solid and dangerous fare should be left within reach, save on the supposition that the authorities know perfectly well that there was not the slightest danger that the food provided would be touched. It is a quaint side-light on prison psychology.

True, I enjoyed many mitigations on this occasion – why, I know not. The hunger-strike was not, as on former occasions, regarded as a piece of 'misconduct', so I continued in possession of all the privileges of a 'bail prisoner' – newspapers, the daily visit and letters, a pillow, a mattress, and a chair with a back. They don't seem much, but they bulk large to the prisoner. A visit from my own doctor was conceded by the Chairman of the Visiting Justices after much argument: it is a privilege to which a bail prisoner is entitled, but red tape usually prevents the regulations framed for the benefit of prisoners being carried out in their favour. Militant methods are as useful inside as outside prison for compelling justice.

Another great privilege I enjoyed (and one not usually accorded even to bail prisoners or first-class misdemeanants) was being able to attend personally, if from afar, the meetings held outside the prison wall to protest against my imprisonment – an unforgettable experience, a joy that helped to clear away the mists of pain and brought messages of cheer and hope, penetrating through the megaphone across the prison bars like a ray of sunshine in that wintry place of shadows.

So time wore on till Monday night, when cold water ceased to be palatable and sleep entirely forsook me. On Tuesday evening I was removed to hospital, and was grateful for the change to an airier, brighter cell with a bedstead – for, these details apart, 'hospital' is but a jail 'writ large'. At half-past seven the next morning, the sixth day, the joyful tidings of release reached me – but for some technicality it might have happened the night before, but the authorities were afraid I might get cold if released at night – ye ironic gods!

Throughout the time of my imprisonment one thought disturbed me more than any physical discomfort – the knowledge that I was suffering unjustly on the false testimony of a police officer, who, having lost his temper and ill-used me, sought to save himself from censure by inventing a counter-charge. The helplessness of the victims of the law, the folly of expecting justice from police magistrates, the power of the bully in uniform to swear away the liberty (and how often the reputation and the livelihood) of his victim – these are the thoughts that create anarchists. For myself, I hope that I shall never again have to suffer imprisonment for an offence of which I am innocent. Such a sentence makes every turn of the jailer's key an outrage, and burns into the victim's soul a searing hatred of the whole infamy of our prison system, whose victims cry to heaven for vengeance.

Letter marked 'private' to Lady Aberdeen[5]
17 December 1913

May it please your Excellency!

When recently in Mountjoy Prison I heard of a great act of kindness on your part some few Christmases ago to the prisoners, which they greatly appreciated. On that occasion after visiting the prison you ordered that a special dinner (of beef and plum pudding) be supplied to all the prisoners for Christmas Day. So you obviously are aware, there is no variety whatsoever in ordinary prison for any day of the year, except on the occasion of a Coronation: prisoners get their gruel, dry bread or whatever it may be on Christmas Day, as any other day. Your simple act of humanity and thoughtfulness made that Christmas comparatively joyful and was a source of pleasure to many poor captives. I can estimate fairly well what such a treat must have meant – a break in the terrible loneliness and dreary monotony, something that drew Christmas Day nearer and made it more real. I feel sure that such a spontaneous act is worth a hundred sermons on peace and good will – and you are the one person who can exercise this power for good. I venture to write to you recalling this act of kindness to those who are without friends in the hope that you may perhaps see your way to do something similar this year. I feel that you may at any rate consider the suggestion, even though – or perhaps because – it comes from one who has lately been herself a prisoner in Mountjoy.

I have the honour to remain,
Yours faithfully,
Hanna Sheehy Skeffington

Draft of letter to John Dillon, MP after release from Holloway Prison[6]
24 August 1918
Portmarnock

Yours marked 'Confidential received' – you are, of course, aware that all my letters are read before reaching me & nothing of mine can be 'confidential' to the government. I was surprised & rather amused at your advice to 'avoid politics' until some safer time, because next time Mr Shortt will let me die if I fall into his hands! Had I meant to give up public activities I would have given the guarantee Mr Shortt first desired & so saved all concerned a good deal of trouble. It is not likely, having wrung the right to live in my own country so dearly, that I shall give up the right to do what I think fit in public matters unconditionally.

You must remember, my dear Mr Dillon, that I am over forty years of age and convictions of a life time are dearer to me than life. Even if my arrest, as you suggest, leads to my death at the government's hands, I do not on that account intend to give up any of my activities & after all my last adventure might also be the last adventure of my assassins. If our militarists think they can dispose of me by letting me die in prison, it only shows how stupid they are. Life is not such an exhilarating adventure that I would not gladly relinquish it if called upon – as others before me.

Of course I read in your letter the implication that 'next time' you wash your hands of me. In that case I can only assure you that your future neutrality will not wipe out my former sympathy. I have explained to my sister and my friends that you are not to be disturbed should I fall into the government's hands again.

Meantime, believe me, sincerely yours. . .

'Arrested and on trial in Newry'
Irish Press, 25 January 1933

Mrs H. Sheehy Skeffington, MA, Assistant Editor of *An Phoblacht*, daughter of the late Mr David Sheehy, MP, and widow of Mr Francis Sheehy Skeffington, the pacifist writer, who was shot dead by British soldiers while a prisoner at Easter 1916, was sentenced to one month's imprisonment at a Special Court in Armagh today in default of giving bail. An armoured car and military with revolvers were on guard at the Courthouse.

Mrs Sheehy Skeffington, who appeared in good spirits, sat between Mr J. H. Collins, MP, Newry, and his wife. She was accompanied by Miss Rosamond Jacob, the Dublin writer.

The case was heard before two resident Magistrates, Mr F. C. Austin and Major J. D. M. McCallum.

Arrested on January 15, at Newry when addressing a public meeting convened to protest against the holding of political prisoners by the Six-County Government, Mrs Sheehy Skeffington was charged with entering County Armagh in contravention of an Exclusion Order by Government served on her on April 4, 1926.

Sergt J. Ferguson (Belfast) gave evidence of having served the Exclusion Order mentioned on defendant in the Belfast Detective office in April 1926.

Mr Austin, RM asked Mr Collins if he was appearing professionally for Mrs Skeffington.

'I am here,' said Mr Collins, 'as a public representative of the people, and as a friend of Mrs Skeffington. She does not require my services professionally.'

Head-Constable Reid said he served the usual notice of trial on Mrs Sheehy Skeffington on January 21.

Cross-examined by defendant, witness said he understood she had already been detained nine days without trial.

Mr Austin – You are quite right to ask any questions you wish, Mrs Skeffington. Mrs Skeffington – I am very overjoyed to learn that a prisoner has some rights.

District-Inspector Coote gave evidence of finding the defendant in County Armagh on January 15, and he arrested her. She made no statement.

Defendant – How did I pass the serried ranks of Tuscany?

Witness – I believe you came in a bus from Dublin that morning.

Defendant – Why didn't the massed assembly arrest me?

Witness – We expected you at another place and you did not turn up.

Asked if she wished to say anything in reply to the charge, Mrs Sheehy Skeffington said that obviously it was fully proved.

'I make no denial or apology for having been in Co. Armagh or any part of the thirty-two counties,' she continued.

'I recognise no partition. I recognise it as no crime to be in my own country. I would be ashamed of my own name and my murdered husband's name if I did. I believe the time will come when partition will be as dead as Queen Anne. I am satisfied that I, personally, can be a pointer, through this action of the authorities, in helping to bring about the death-knell of partition, which another part of Ireland is bringing about today.

'It is a police hold-up,' she went on, 'and practically kidnapping. I have been held from the 15th to the 23rd, until whatever gentlemen are in control made up their minds as to what was to be done.'

'I can only say in the words of Tom Kettle, "Ulster is ours – not theirs."[7] That is all I have to say. You can proceed as you think fit.'

Mr Austin asked if, at the time the Exclusion Order was served, any civil offence had been committed.

Mrs Sheehy Skeffington – I think a civil offence had been committed. I did come to Belfast to see a relative now dead. I think that makes a civil or uncivil offence. I was held up in the same way and brought to the jail in Belfast.

Mr Austin said the law had been broken and the decision of the Court was that Mrs Skeffington must enter into bond on her own surety of £50 to keep the peace for 12 months or, in default, go to jail for one month.

Rising to her feet, Mrs Sheehy Skeffington said:

Of course I will give no bond, I have been guilty of no crime, and I will enter into no obligation. No doubt you gentlemen are carrying out whatever instructions you have received from Belfast. Long live the Republic!

In response to District-Inspector McNeill, Major McCallum said the sentence would date from that day.

Mrs Sheehy Skeffington – Go ahead, what does it matter – the farce is over.

Mrs Sheehy Skeffington was then conveyed to the Armagh women's jail by private car.

She was loudly cheered as she left the courthouse.

Subsequently Mr J. H. Collins, MP, protested to the police that the prosecuting officer had omitted the County of Down when he read the exclusion order.

'Behind the bars: experiences of a political prisoner in Armagh Jail'
An Phoblacht, 18 March 1933

The following was the statement which was to serve as a warning: 'All persons committed to prison are informed that they will not be able by willful injury to their bodily health caused by refusal of food, or in any other way to procure their release before their dismissal is due in course of law.' The English of the above is terrible but it was intended to warn off hunger-strikers.

Whether Sir Dawson Bates[8] has really the power to prevent death arriving to cut the striker's sentence short was not tested. Neither a fight for clothes nor for political status had to be staged. Later that evening word came officially (Belfast apparently having been communicated with) that I could retain my clothes and no one said another word about 'suitable tasks'. All of which illustrates the oft-repeated experience that prison is a continual fight for politicals and that one never knows when it may have to begin all over again. Eternal vigilance is the price you must pay even in jail for whatever restricted 'liberty' you may attain.

Two days later a visiting justice, Mr Cope, came to Armagh Prison to sign the order permitting me to wear my own clothes! If ever you are in jail – as well you may, reader of *An Phoblacht*, whatever else your jailers may take away from you, do not let them deprive you of your sense of humour. For you will be sure to need it in jail more than anywhere else. I was always glad to have kept mine – in Armagh, in Mountjoy, in Holloway and in various bridewells, barracks and police stations.

My Third Jail
Armagh was my third jail experience. (Arrests and detentions in bridewells and police stations do not count.) Already I had spent terms in Mountjoy and in Holloway; the Six-Counties completed the freedom of the so-called British

Isles – Britain, with her Western pieces. Jails have a certain sameness, with local differences. It is amazing how little do they change! Now there are salt-cellars of brown pottery instead of the unhygienic wooden containers of old, but the horn spoon that serves for entire table cutlery survives even the Great War. Its characteristic is that when you are stirring your tea there lingers a flavour of cabbage soup and vice versa. I got a knife and fork, but prisoners still are unprovided with these, lest they commit suicide. Persevering indeed would be the captive that would have attempted felo-de-se with mine! Also against suicide is a stretched trapeze-like net (rope in Armagh, wire, I think, in Mountjoy) that spans the top storey of the jail's inner court, round which the cells are built in a long oblong. I was located in A wing, having the top ring of it entirely to myself. Below were the 'stars' (i.e. first offenders), lifers, convicts and remands. In B wing were the rest. A and B exercised separately each morning and, as I was alone, I had perforce to take the air in the afternoon for an hour and a half in solitary state, of course with accompanying wardress. After the first days, as already narrated, my abode was the condemned cell, built to accommodate two wardresses, plus prisoner, for they must perforce spend the interval between the death sentence and its consummation, or reprieve, with the condemned person. Not very long ago a woman found guilty of infanticide had gone through the gamut of suffering and suspense in this spot. (She was reprieved and, later, her sentence in part remitted, she was released.) Several men had at various times been hanged within the walls of Armagh Prison – Fee was the last to suffer death here. Whether he and others (it was then a mixed prison) reposed in this or another cell I know not. But poor Fee's grave is in the garden where we walked, a nameless, unmarked one, the usual unconsecrated resting-place of executioner's victims. The condemned cell had a grate and it was welcome; its windows opened like small French casements and one could, with the aid of table and stool, a rickety structure, see the skyline and the silhouette of Patrick's old cathedral.

A City of Chimes

Armagh is a city of chimes – market clocks and curfew bell as well as two cathedrals – and on Sunday one heard the bells rendering 'There is a green hill far away' and other appropriate airs. Unlike Mountjoy, where pigeons reign supreme, Armagh has only crows, daws and starlings. These the prisoners fed, for birds are welcome visitors here, and already early in February nesting operations were afoot, even amid the snow. The chattering and squabbling of the starlings, the grating of the reluctant bolts, the rattle of endless keys, the clang of the prison bells – they start at 6.30 – and the slow, measured strike of quarter, half-hour, three-quarter and hour from various clocks – never was time so long drawn out to listening ears, counting in the dark – such are permanent impressions of Armagh. The only commodity that prisoners possess in unstinting abundance is time – and it is the one thing one would most gladly barter for anything else under the sun. Having so much of it on one's hands was like having a hoard of gold sovereigns on a desert island.

Jail Comparisons

Armagh is the humanist jail I have known. It surpasses far both Mountjoy and Holloway in the treatment of prisoners. That does not, of course, mean that, like all prisons, it is not full of barbarism – I wonder when will decent folk wake up to the iniquity of the whole system? – but certainly it had certain ameliorations and to this I gladly testify in the fond hope that some day some Minister of Justice here may copy. Association in cells, at work room and laundry and even at exercise for prisoners (who are allowed to walk and talk in twos in these infernal rings) is a great mitigation of the prisoner's lot and has had, I understand, since its introduction a good effect upon general conduct and discipline. It was a relief to see the prisoners talking together as they took exercise. The rigid silence rule, enforced in Mountjoy and Holloway, no longer holds. This accounts, too, I think, for the fact that there seem to be fewer outbreaks of 'nerves' among prisoners than take place in jails where kindly human speech is well-nigh eliminated. The general tone, too, as between jailers and jailed, is certainly more humane in Armagh. Women prisoners no longer wear the silly caps that Mountjoy insisted upon, they possess pockets and their handkerchiefs are not strung to their sides. These seem small affairs, but they bulk large to prisoners. Most of the prisoners had bobbed hair, I noticed, so do fashions spread. They are allowed, after a certain period and in certain classes, the weekly papers. This, too, is a happy innovation, though the prison library itself left, as usual, much to be desired. Plank beds still prevail for the majority, but they are going. Female prisoners do garden work and greatly enjoy it – in mixed prisons this is reserved for men and women's health suffers accordingly. Tea in the evening replaces cocoa – a happy suggestion of one of the women visitors.

Prison Blindness

Formerly, as one sees still in spots, Armagh had its cells and corridors coloured green. Now these are white, partly for economy, partly for that drab uniformity that jailers' souls so hanker after. The result is terrible to the eyes, as all prisoners will testify. After six weeks I felt as if my eyes had sand under them – what must the year-long prisoner endure? I have heard that Mr de Valera's eye-strain which caused him serious trouble of late, arose out of the year he spent in a Free State jail and the long months preceding it in other prisons, in England and in 'Northern' Ireland. A simple reform, one would fancy, to get a coloured wash, but these little things require imagination and those responsible – the higher powers that is – for prisons rarely possess this quality.

LOOKING BACKWARDS: WAR, ELECTION AND THE FINAL YEARS

INTRODUCTION

The last decade of Hanna's life saw no diminution of activity. Lacking a pension, she continued to teach languages in two technical colleges, but found German classes cancelled during the war, either a casualty of anti-German feeling or because travel to Germany was impossible. Journalism was therefore an important source of additional income, and she wrote light articles for a variety of publications on subjects like 'East coast seaside resorts', 'Brittany: the country most like Ireland', and 'Ireland from the air'. The latter demonstrated that she retained her spirit of adventure, writing in the *Irish Press* (25 October 1940) of her first plane journey, a treat she had promised herself when prices became 'reasonable'. Once they became 'well, reasonably reasonable, I took the plunge, or rather the flight', taking the last trip of the season to the west of Ireland with Aer Lingus and revelling in the landscape unfolding beneath.

She mourned the death of a number of close friends and associates, all part of an ageing generation of activists. The obituaries she wrote for old friends involved in political struggle were full of vivid detail, evidence of the vast amounts of material she had retained and used continually to inform her writing. When recalling the life of Sarah Harrison she remarked 'Looking over old files (is there anything sadder than glancing through cemeteries of dead hopes?)'. It was obvious that many memories were stirred up. Frank was mentioned more than once in these accounts of past lives, an indication that he remained a tangible presence in her life.

Ireland, as a neutral country, did not have first-hand experience of the horrors of the Second World War, but Hanna followed events closely and kept in touch with old friends. Her daughter-in-law Andrée belonged to a new generation of feminists, one of the young married women who now found themselves confined to the home, victims of the marriage bar. The role of campaigning consumer, working to improve the quality of life for poor families through campaigning for a fair distribution of food during the 'Emergency' as the war was described in Ireland, led to the formation of the Irish Housewives Association in May 1942. Hanna did not approve of the name, with its connotations that women were tied to the home, but supported their efforts to make links with working-class women. The Irish Housewives Association was one of the groups that lent support to the decision by the Women's Social and Progressive League to run candidates in the 1943 election to the Dáil. It was a response to the fact that since the Civil War the Dáil had never had more than three women at any one time and it was what Hanna had been arguing for since women's fight against the Constitution. Four women were chosen to stand as independents and Hanna was one of them, standing for South Dublin, a constituency she had represented as a councillor almost 20 years previously. The lack of funds and personnel for her campaign is evident in her letter to the electors, explaining her difficulties in not being able to canvass adequately. The *Irish Times* described her as an 'uncompromising politician' who was 'one of the most colourful candidates' (18 June 1943), but her republican feminist platform did not appeal to the electorate and she received only 917 first preference votes, losing out to James Larkin junior in the radical stakes. Her article in the *Bell* on 'Women in Politics' reflects her frustration regarding the lack of political representation of women. The situation in Britain at the end of the war, when Labour triumphed over the Conservatives, resulted in the election of a number of women, and Hanna, characteristically, not only welcomed the result but provided information on key personalities and the promises regarding women that had been made in the Labour Party manifesto. That her article appeared in the journal of the Fabians indicates that she remained a person of note to sections of the British left. However, by early 1946 she had lost her optimism regarding the ability of British Labour to fulfil its election promises and told the writer Ethel Mannin that she was 'more and more' inclined towards Ethel's anarchist point of view.

In May 1945 Hanna's health began to deteriorate and she was confined to bed for four months. Knowing she was ill, she reminded her son Owen that she was 'an unrepentant pagan' and did not want a priest at her deathbed. She was interviewed about her life for RTÉ radio in November and still attempted to teach classes, needing the money. Her friends hoped she would be able to continue with her life history, but as ill-health began to limit her capabilities, she instead devoted her energies to the re-publication of her pamphlet dealing with Frank's murder. Friends organised a testimonial on her behalf, in recognition of her long service 'to the cause of justice and freedom', hoping this financial support would enable her to rest and convalesce. She was still busy with her typewriter, promising an article for the first issue of the journal of the Irish Housewives Association. Hanna died on 20 April 1946, aged 69, and the article was published posthumously. Its content was as usual informed by her wide reading. She retained her robust and direct style, laced with characteristic humour, to the end.

'George Lansbury: a tribute'
Irish Press, 11 May 1940

I first met George Lansbury when he paid a hurried visit to Dublin after the 1913 lock-out. Constance Markievicz was just starting her 'kitchen' in Liberty Hall, where she served out hot soup and stew all day to the families and children of the locked-out victims. George Lansbury came with offers of help, with him came too, Dora Montefiore[1] and others in England. Mrs Pethick Lawrence and Mary Neale helped by putting up some children in her cottage. Others again collected food and ran a laden 'Peace Ship' into the quays and the workers came down to the dock to cheer, while it was unloaded. There was a great burst of real brotherliness amongst the workers in both islands. It was natural that George Lansbury should be the representative.

When most of male mankind (especially MPs) railed against Suffragettes, he was with them, resigning his seat (he was a member for Bow and Bromley) as a test, and standing again on that one issue; he was a valiant friend of Ireland and stood for complete independence when separatists were few in England; he was an ardent and absolute pacifist and held that faith unshaken through two great wars, pleading for peace to his last breath. He stood the test of office too, a fierce one. When he held a Ministerial post in the Labour cabinet he helped to secure release for Irish Republican Prisoners; he threw open London's parks for the poor; he lived among his people and kept the 'common touch'. He was never afraid of championing lost, desperate or unpopular causes. His personality triumphed and he has died one of the most beloved and popular of men.

When he threw down the gauntlet in the House of Commons, going forth to refight his seat in Bow and Bromley in 1912, Frank Sheehy Skeffington went over to help in the whirlwind suffrage campaign – the friendship between him and Lansbury, kindled in 1913, had continued undiminished, for they shared a common belief and ideals. He was beaten by but 751 votes (the only example of a candidate risking his all for the voteless). Later he went back again, with re-inforced strength. Once, during the militant suffrage campaign he was arrested (on what occasion now I do not recall, on some 'protest' arising from the campaign). He hunger-struck and was released, his health impaired.

Sylvia Pankhurst, in her book on the women's movement, *The Home Front*, has much on Lansbury and his family – he flung them all into his causes – Mrs Lansbury, his wife; Edgar and Willie, his sons; Jessie and Minnie, his daughters-in-law; Violet, his daughter. (His son-in-law, Raymond Postgate,

has written the finest and most understanding *Life of Robert Emmet* that I know.)
He, Keir Hardie, Olive Schreiner, Henry W. Nevinson and Sylvia Pankhurst,
were the storm centre of many a fight for freedom before and during the last
War. While Lansbury and others were in Dublin in 1913 the difference of
meaning of words, as used in Dublin and in London was illustrated. One
night a horrified woman journalist (British) rushed into Liberty Hall to
Madame Markievicz, stating that a girl, a blackleg, had just been set upon by
the other girls and 'murdered' – she had heard them actually boasting of it
with her own ears! 'What did they say?' asked Constance, a twinkle in her eye,
'Oh' she replied, passionately, 'they said, "we are after *murdering* one of them
scabs, a girl from (naming the factory)"'. Madame explained that 'murder' in
Dublinese means merely a 'beating-up' – at least, in such a context.

In July 1916, writing in Skeffington's paper the *Irish Citizen*, George
Lansbury pays a tribute to him and to the Easter Week men who fell. Of him he
has said 'He stood for the kind of nationalism that knows neither creed nor sect,
race nor colour, but stands out for humanity.' Of Ireland he writes: 'She has lost
some of her noblest and best. There are many in England with the Irish people
in spirit in their struggle. Long years ago when it was written I heard "God Save
Ireland" sung in the East End of London. Later on I heard it in Newry, Dundalk,
Draperstown and Belfast. These occasions were in the coercion days of Balfour.
I have never forgotten the fervour and enthusiasm with which it was sung.' A
faithful friend of Ireland has passed away in George Lansbury.

'Obituary of Emma Goldman: pioneer (1869–1940)'
The Distributive Worker, August 1940

When I read the other day of the death, in a Toronto hospital, of Emma
Goldman my thoughts went back to December, 1916, when I first met her on
my arrival (by the underground route) in New York. She had previously met
Frank S. Skeffington when he was in USA in 1915, with an unexpired sentence
hanging over him, cat and mouse fashion, after a hunger strike. We as rebels
spoke the same language, though sometimes with a different idiom, for Emma
despised nationalism, though she revered its Irish and other martyrs. I have
beside me a book she inscribed for me (her essays) with this challenge: 'To
Hanna Sheehy Skeffington, I give this volume in the hope that it may help
you to see beyond nationalism and woman suffrage, adding a rebel tribute to
bravery.'

Her Tribute to 1916

In her autobiography, she pays tribute to the spirit and the men of 1916; like
Lenin, she understood the revolutionary Irish background. Outwardly Emma
looked little of the rebel – that is, according to the common acceptance of the

word, suggesting wildness, extravagant attire, and all manner of eccentricity. Of course your gentle Anarchist or Socialist (or whatever rebel kind you will) often surprises in this way: the mildest-mannered folk I have known – Connolly, Skeffington, Pearse – were of that ilk, while the most truculent, I need not name any! are strictly law and order. Emma looked like a busy 'hausfrau' (she was of Germano-Russian race and Jewish stock), stood peasant-like in build, sturdy and direct, her fine eye and brow revealing the leader. At her home I met too, Alexander Berkman, her close associate of many years. Both ex-prisoners, of course, bearing many scars in the class-conflict. Emma was an editor – her paper, *Mother Earth*, was soon to be banned when the US went into the war – a fine lecturer, an almighty publicist. Her life story would make a great background to a romance full of colour and adventure. I confine myself here to personal impressions and contacts.

Meaning of Bolshevik

In 1917, the Russian revolution broke and the Russian rebels and refugees – a big colony – went mad with joy as the news came over. I remember being at a packed meeting in Madison Square Gardens; it reminded one of Wordsworth's lines on the French revolution: –

> Bliss was it in that dawn to be alive,
> But to be young was very Heaven.

Emma had packed meetings. I was only able to go into one in New York on my Press ticket for the *Irish Citizen*, but it worked. It was from Emma Goldman that I first heard the literal meaning of the word 'Bolshevik', as much maligned and twisted, as Sinn Féin was, by hostile propaganda. Emma explained that it meant 'majority' or 'majority party', as contrasted with minority, i.e., Menshevik. She was the heroine of the hour – she told me with a twinkle in her blue-grey eyes that she wasn't used to the role of popular heroine. Well, it didn't last. The war waves submerged her and her party and ere long she, Berkman and other Russians were deported to the Soviet Union, and crowds came to see them off. Hopes were high, but Emma and Alexander were destined – I don't think they were surprised, for Anarchism and communism do not mix – to a bitter fate, full of disillusionment. And they were to see another expulsion, this time from Russia. They were too strongly individualistic to fit into the new regime, though Emma Goldman to the end held the Russian strain predominant and always wished for the triumph of its earlier ideals, hating imperialism and capitalism relentlessly. When last we met, in London a few years ago, she was working with her party for Spain, where there had always been, especially in Catalonia, a strong anarchist movement. At her flat she was phoning Paul Robeson, the great coloured artist, and enlisting his help for Republican Spain. The Spanish episode, too, was to end tragically – though perhaps it is not the end. Emma returned to America, where she primarily belonged, and where she said her most effective work was done. But the US only allowed its exportee six weeks at a time in the country so she alternated USA with Canada and here, a few weeks ago, she died, in double exile, from her adopted land and from the country of her fathers. She died in harness, at 71, as she would have wished to, her faith in humanity's future unshaken through many vicissitudes. A great woman, to whom time and history will bring its proper perspective when she takes her place among world pioneers.

Women and Smoking
Iconoclastic in small things, as in big, I remember a characteristic remark of hers when, at one of our last meetings, a friend offered her in the lounge of a big hotel in Montreal a cigarette. 'Once,' she said, 'I was expelled from this very hotel for smoking in public, then not permitted to "ladies". (We smoked but in bedroom privacy or out the window of the bathroom!) Now it's no fun anymore. All the bourgeois ladies smoke – it's now "peculiar" not to – so I don't.'

That was Emma – non-conformist to the last. And her little book of essays – it has taught me much. I quote the following characteristic avowal: 'I know the malady of the oppressed and disinherited only too well, but I refuse to subscribe to ridiculous palliatives which allow the patient neither to die nor to recover. My lack of faith in the majority (she deals with all this in her essay Minorities versus Majorities, in a way that is strikingly topical, though it was published away back in time before the two world wars) is dictated by my faith in the potentialities of the individual. Only when the latter becomes free to choose his associates for a common purpose can we hope for order and harmony in this world of chaos and inequality.'

Message to Women
Not a believer in the ballot as a liberator, Emma Goldman was none the less in her own way a feminist – she went farther, deeper than many suffragists. Of woman, she writes, 'Her freedom, her independence, must come from and through herself . . . refusing to be a servant to the State, society, husband, family . . . making her life simpler, deeper, richer . . . freeing herself from the fear of public opinion and public condemnation . . . a form hitherto unknown in the world, or real love, peace, harmony; a creator of free men and free women.'

'Jennie Wyse Power'
Irish Press, 11 January 1941

In this remarkable, gifted and truly valiant woman is epitomized a life-time of service of many great causes: Irish nationalism, the emancipation of women, the revival of the Irish language and the kindred movements for Irish industries and culture. A friend, while yet in her girlhood, of Anna and Fanny Parnell, she joined the militant Ladies' Land League, being one of the youngest and most active of its organizers. She ministered to many political prisoners and their dependants in her time, covering not only the Kilmainham suspects, catered for by the Ladies' Land League in the eighties, but also the families of the Invincibles, later the militant Irish suffragettes, whose meals, when political status was won, were supplied by her from her famous café in Henry Street, rendezvous of all the rebels, a pendant in its way to Tom Clarke's shop in Great Britain Street. Again, after 1916 (when her shop and home had been burnt out) she helped in the National Aid organization for Republican prisoners. She was a follower of Arthur Griffith and a close friend and colleague of Constance Markievicz. Shortly after 1916, while yet the ashes of the ruins of the GPO smouldered, she was to stand by the graveside of her brilliant daughter, Maire – as she put it later, 'I have died many times,' for in her long life she saw many tragedies and buried some cherished hopes.

Her social work engaged her actively: she was one of the first women to serve as Poor Law Guardian in North Dublin Union when women were made eligible to serve. When Sinn Féin put up women on the PR panel for the City Council in Dublin, Mrs Wye Power was one of the five elected – Mrs McGarry, one of these, died in 1940, so now only three remain, one being the Lord Mayor.[2] Mrs Wyse Power's great executive ability showed in her service for many years on the Council, she being Chairman of the Finance and General Purposes Committee until the Corporation was dissolved by order of the Cosgrave Government. She was also for many years on the Executive of Sinn Féin. I remember her first act on the Corporation, the signing of her name in Irish on the Roll of Councillors. This was disallowed by the then Town Clerk, Mr Henry Campbell, but she fought and won her point. Mrs Wyse Power was one of the women who accepted the Treaty, a decision, doubtless, affected by her friendship for and years-long close association with Arthur Griffith, but one that, nevertheless, severed many old ties and cost some friendships. Independent, however, in many ways, she refused to vote for the Flogging Clause in the Cosgrave Coercion Act. Later, she supported the Fianna Fáil Party. With Mrs Stopford Green and Mrs Costello she was chosen by Mr Cosgrave to the first Senate he nominated, which contained three women. In the struggle for Woman Suffrage she also played a considerable and courageous part: at one time she and Constance Markievicz broke with Arthur Griffith on the question of admissibility of women into the Senate under a proposed Constitution he worked out.

She was on the Executive of the Constitutional Suffrage – the Irish Women's Citizen's Association, led by Anna and Thomas Haslam, but later threw in her lot with the militant Irish section, being one of the founders of the Irish Women's Franchise League in 1908. She acted on its executive for many years and contributed at times to the *Irish Citizen*, the organ of the women's movement, edited by F. Sheehy Skeffington. She attended with her daughter, Dr N. Wyse Power, one of the famous international congresses held in Berlin by the International Suffrage Alliance – in the days when Germany had several women deputies and notable leaders in various walks of life.

Her judicial mind and sterling honesty of purpose were specially valuable in her work as Justice of the Republican Courts which she continued from 1920 until they were superseded. These justices served on panels in rotation and were elected, not nominated, to the office. The courts met in all kinds of places (sometimes in a schoolhouse, sometimes on the premises of a laundry, sometimes in a public hall) and their work in the height of the Tan war was strenuous and dangerous at times.

Mrs Wyse Power had actually passed her 80th year before her death and remained keen and active in her interest in public affairs right to the end, though increasing deafness had cut her off from direct participation in public life. Her character stands out for singleness of purpose, strong commonsense and a keen feeling for progress, both for men and women; an epitome of good citizenship. One of the last times that we met, she said, referring to the handicap of her deafness, 'There is nothing for me now to do but write my reminiscences.' I doubt if she ever got down to the task: many of her important papers and relics were destroyed when her house in Henry Street was burnt, but much treasure trove remains – one would like to see someone tackle the task of recording the work of the Ladies' Land League and other kindred groups of women who helped in the fight for freedom: they have not had justice done to them so far. In this record the name of Jeannie O'Toole, Mrs Wyse Power, will have an honoured place.

'Sarah Harrison'
Irish Press, 5 August 1941

Nearly forty years ago Sara Cecilia Harrison came to Dublin and made it her home ever since, identifying herself more closely than most of its citizens with the cultural and public life of the capital with a selfless and single-minded devotion that was unique, even in Dublin. She was born in Holywood,

Co. Down. Her family had links with '98; she was the great grand-niece of Henry Joy McCracken and was proud of her rebel ancestry. Mary McCracken is preserved in the well-known picture, *Cup Tosser*, where she and the young niece of Teeling are re-presented – Mary, the fortune-teller, cup in hand, reading the tea-leaves for her eager young friend. Miss Harrison often referred with pride to her great grand-aunt's picture. Another link was through her brother Henry; he was Parnell's youngest colleague and later his biographer. Miss Harrison remained all her life a strong and staunch nationalist; she had a keen political mind, but never associated herself with party politics, being essentially an individualist.

Her art training was at the Slade School, London, where she studied under Alphonse Le Cros; she was also influenced by Watts. She is known best as a portrait painter. Her portraits of well-known figures in Irish life include those of Hugh Lane, George Moore, Dr Best, Monsignor Laverty, Dr Esposito, Michael Collins, Francis Sheehy Skeffington, Anna and Thomas Haslam. The last-named is generally accounted her best: it illustrates her careful and conscientious study of her subjects. Into it especially, through a long series of sittings, she put her very best. It was a labour of love, for she was associated with the veteran pioneers in the woman suffrage movement for many years. Miss Harrison was an ardent feminist; she served for many years on the constitutional committee of the women's suffrage and local government association, spoke for them, wrote and worked for them, giving to the cause her characteristic passionate championship. Of militant methods she did not approve, but she remained friendly to those who deemed them necessary. Hers was essentially a generous and free spirit and when she deemed it essential she, too, had little respect for obstructive regulations that seemed to block progress: she could, and did, cut through red tape in slashing fashion when championing the poor or the oppressed. She was a bonny fighter.

The only painting of her extant is the one in the Gallery – a youthful self-portrait, very characteristic. Harcourt Street became a dangerous spot in the Anglo-Irish War. I remember during the 'Tan period how our Libraries Committee had to take down the sign in Irish outside the gallery lest it attract undue attention and get the building sacked.

The other public causes, women suffrage and the poor, were welded in her candidature for the Dublin Corporation, into which the United Women's Societies flung themselves. She was returned for the South City ward (the Irish Women's Franchise League had its premises in the heart of it in Westmoreland Street), and she was the first woman member of the Council. The women's societies presented her with an Irish poplin gown of office. In the Council she was the means of forcing two Government sworn inquiries into certain matters connected with the then Distress Committee and into the affairs of the South Dublin Union. In her efforts to throw the searchlight of publicity into dark places she was helped by Sinn Féin and labour members, both, of course, in a minority. She conducted her own case with great ability, and did succeed eventually in achieving certain reforms, though much blocked by vested interests. To her the granting of unemployment relief to single men is due; also the establishment of a labour yard and the initiation of the plot-holders movement. Any poor man or woman with a grievance had the entrée into her office in her Stephen's Green Studio and received a patient hearing. On her sideboard was food for them, always ready, a cold joint for the cutting. 'Lady Harrison' the poor called her – they have their own nobility. Friends lamented (probably with reason) of her overflowing charity, which the un-deserving poor may have preyed upon – it was the very quixotry in her nature that often impoverished her, to which there was no gainsay. She reaped, after all, a harvest in the love of the poor. Her charity was like that of Dean Swift, with his pockets of pennies when he was abroad, as Constance Markievicz who gathered the children of the slums into her little car and took them to her cottage in the mountains.

At the end of her one term of office (1912–1915) she was not re-elected: Big Business put its nominee against her and he was successful. Too much dust had been raised. For years until 'PR' and 1918 – no woman member was returned to the Corporation and then the Sinn Féin Party had five elected, the highest number since then.

Miss Harrison, as Secretary, promoted the first Dublin monument to a woman – the memorial set to Anna and Thomas Haslam in St Stephen's Green. She designed it as well as raised the funds: it was unveiled shortly after the Civil War and again she was instrumental in combining women of all groups and parties assembled to honour the pioneers. International peace also claimed her support – though she lived to see two World Wars – perhaps because of this she remained a convinced pacifist.

Looking over old files (is there anything sadder than glancing through cemeteries of dead hopes?) I came across, in the *Irish Citizen*, January 1915, Miss Harrison's election address in which she boldly set out her programme to the Dublin voters. It embodies questions essentially of interest to women – public health, housing of the poor, extension of school meals for children, safeguarding of food supplies during war, right of free access of the public to Corporation debates. Some of these reforms have been slowly and partially achieved: others yet await realisation. The 39 Lane pictures have never been returned to Dublin.

With all the name of Sara Cecilia Harrison will be associated.

A restless, restless race!
A beloved race in all. I

Mourn and yet exult –
Pioneers, O Pioneers!

'Looking backwards'
The Distributive Worker, **December 1941**

Looking down the vistas of the years, one is conscious of the continuity of Irish history. We Sheehys are – happily or unhappily – a long-lived family. One of my earliest recollections is meeting, about the age of three, my great-grandmother (then well over the century), a tall, straight, old lady with bright eyes. She in her youth knew Lord Edward, who used to come for holidays with her brothers in Kerry; remembering him as a gay, dashing lad – 'the boyo' she used to call him. (This, of course, I gleaned later.) My grandfather (who had turned 95 when he died) recalled as *his* first memory the excitement in Co. Limerick over Waterloo – he was about three at the time. My father's earliest recollection was seeing the 'Levellers' coming into his native village of Drumcollogher in the days of wholesale clearances by landlords. My earliest memory politically is of the 'Suspects' in Kilmainham, where I visited my uncle, Father Eugene Sheehy, gate-crashing into the place when the Ladies' Land League contingent came into the big hall to serve the mid-day dinners. So Lord Edward, Waterloo, the Levellers, the Suspects, Davitt and Parnell are linked. I like to think I looked into those bright old eyes that had once beheld Lord Edward, that later I again met that 'Suspect' uncle in the GPO in 1916, ministering to his old friend, T. Clarke, at the dawn of another era.

History does not begin at 1916 as some to-day would have it: there were many fights before it. Early years count a lot, and, as one gets older, they loom larger. Mine were spent in an old mill in Loughmore, Co. Tipperary; the sound of the mill-wheel and of the waters of the Suir, the smell of fresh bread from the adjoining bakery are forever linked in childhood's memories in the way that smells and sounds have of evoking the past. Ours was a rebel household – father had been out in '67. When the Fenians took up methods of militant Parliamentarianism, he joined the newly-formed Irish Party of Parnell. When he started a long exile, he gaily promised us Home Rule with the next Xmas turkey! (Many Xmas turkeys came and went but no Home Rule; in 1917 he did not stand.) We played Boycott and Evictions as children now play war games. We sang and recited rebel ballads, topical ones such as 'The Peeler and the Goat', 'Harvey Duff', the 'Land League Upheld' or 'Fanny Parnell's Hold the Harvest'.

My first visit to Dublin I recall vividly. Standing on O'Connell Bridge I was thrilled with the beauty of the view, a beauty I have never ceased to admire, at all hours and seasons every time I pass. My aunt held my hand, looking down at me, and asked me what I thought of it. A horrible thought flashed on me – you know the best adults, however trusted, sometimes let one down. Was this a *trap*? My geography was weak. 'Is this *Ireland*?' I queried anxiously. I had the country-bred distrust of the foreignness of the town – perhaps unawares we had wandered outside our boundaries? When the answer came – an amused, puzzled, reassuring, 'Yes' – I drew a sigh of content. I could admire to the full 'my own, my native land' without paying unwitting tribute to any strange capital. Another childish illusion from green Érin and all that was that the grass in *no other* country was green. I was much disappointed to find it green in Holyhead. Great Britain was *red* on the map. I expected its grass to conform.

When my family moved permanently to Dublin, I began my studies at a large school on the north side. That is one thing, by the way, that somehow has never changed with the changing years – the difference in outlook between north and south in Dublin. The gap was wider then, distances being greater, with only horse-trams, and fewer of these.

Irish

Grandfather was a native Irish speaker and used to tell how he got a stroke of the cane duly from his teacher at the end of each day for each word of Irish spoken. Father knew some Irish, and wished, when I was being prepared for the Intermediate to have me taught Irish – Celtic, as it was called. It was not a 'marks' draw, and had less than German or French or Latin. He was told that, as I would be the only pupil, it would not be possible to form a class for me alone. Now that same school has a section wholly devoted to teaching through the medium of Irish, and, to bring the wheel full circle, a young niece of mine, going recently to Ring, told of two students sent home for having been found speaking English. After three generations, Irish had come into its own again.

The bicycle did much to emancipate women. In the early days of the century a woman was mobbed for riding a cycle on the quays in Dublin, and narrowly escaped ducking in the Liffey. A girl was expelled from our school for being caught smoking a cigarette. No unmarried woman went unescorted to the theatre; fathers were stern in their vetoes, and from these there was no appeal. So when, some years later (1912), women broke windows in Dublin Castle, the Custom House, the GPO and other Government strongholds as a protest against votes being denied Irish women in the then Home Rule Bill, there was much commotion. Yet, when we graduated by way of jail, we got a good deal of popular sympathy. Six out of the seven 1916 signatories were our supporters. I have Connolly's word for it about a week before the Easter Rising that there was only one dissentient (and he did not persist) to the full citizenship clause for women in the 1916 Proclamation. That was an achievement.

Electoral Address³

1943

I am standing in South City, where many of you will remember me, as I represented this area for seven stormy years (1919–25) in the Dublin Corporation.

I appeal to the electors, men and women, for a clear mandate to represent their joint interests in the Dáil by giving me their number 1 vote. If elected I shall be a representative not tied or gagged by any party, but free to vote on progressive lines on all issues requiring independence. I am not a member of ANY POLITICAL PARTY, nor have I been since 1927, when I resigned from Fianna Fáil.

I have been actively associated both with the National Movement and the fight for women's rights – both causes still claim my wholehearted allegiance. There can be no true democracy where there is not complete economic and political freedom for the entire nation, both men and women. Nor can there be effective administration where the political machine is entirely controlled by one sex only. James Connolly said: – 'The worker is the slave of capitalist society: the female worker the slave of that slave. In Ireland that female worker has hitherto exhibited in her martyrdom an almost damnable patience.' This is as true today as when Connolly wrote it.

Nationally I stand for complete independence of Ireland and for the abolition of partition which has dismembered our country. My attitude towards Ireland's right to unfettered nationhood is unchanged and unchangeable. Irishwomen have always been active in our national struggles. Their help is as readily received as it is readily forgotten. Today their aid is more than ever needed. Under the 1916 Proclamation, Irishwomen were given equal citizenship, equal rights and equal opportunities. Subsequent constitutions have filched these, or smothered them in mere 'empty formulae'. While the general position has grown steadily worse for both men and women, women have everywhere been the greater sufferers, directly or indirectly, as wage earners, nurses, civil servants, wives, mothers, widows. They have endured hardships that press harder on them even than upon the men. Young Irishwomen have been forced to emigrate in great numbers. We have the lowest marriage rate in Europe.

I appeal, therefore, to the women voters – and to the men with progressive ideas, for how can they progress without the active co-operation of women? MY PROGRAMME includes such fundamentals as equal work, equal opportunities for women, the removal of the marriage ban on teachers, doctors and other skilled women, the restoration of Jury rights, the abolition of the means test, proper pensions for the aged, widows and the blind (the present allowances are a national disgrace), nurse's pensions, adequate meals and free books for school children, family allowances, a clean milk supply, an effective anti-TB campaign, and civilized treatment for our unemployed – in short a community whose FIRST concern will be for the welfare of its people.

Any progressive or humane legislation will have my support in the Dáil. Women are responsible for the feeding, the clothing, and the nursing of the sick, the tending of the aged, the running of the home. They will play an immense part in the rebuilding of the world in the present chaotic condition. Our own country needs desperately the experience and help of its women in the National HOUSE-KEEPING. My candidature has been endorsed by five leading non-political women's societies: the Women Graduates' Association, the Irish Countrywomen's Association, the Irish Housewives' Committee, the Women Citizens' Association and the Women's Social and Political League.

ELECT AN INDEPENDENT WOMAN TO REPRESENT YOUR INTERESTS AND THOSE OF YOUR FAMILY.

'1943 election', letter
Evening News, 16 June 1943
As I earn my living as a technical school teacher, and as some of my classes go on as late as 5 pm, it has not been possible for me in this election to carry out as wide a personal canvass as I would have liked. I hope my friends in Dublin South City will understand the circumstances, therefore, if I have not been able to call on them personally. And I should like to ask them to help me not only on election day with their vote but before it, by speaking on my behalf to those whom, most reluctantly, I have been prevented from visiting in person.
(Mrs) Hanna Sheehy Skeffington

'Women in politics'
The Bell, 7 November 1943
Is the Dáil a fit place for Women? The answer of the electorate would appear to be No. *The Bell* in a recent issue expressed strongly the view that more women – independent of party – are badly needed to play their part in national housekeeping; other organs of opinion, including *Dublin Opinion*, expressed the same view, backed by many individuals of various (and of no) party politics; so did several women's societies, led by the Women's Social and Progressive League, which launched a campaign.

Four women stood at the recent General Election as Independents, pledged to a programme mainly, though not exclusively, addressed to women-voters, standing for a freedom from party affiliation. Their platform stressed the need for greater representation of women in the councils of the nation and their slogans included 'Equal Pay for Equal Work', 'Equal Opportunities for Women', the removal of the many disabilities economic, social and domestic that still restrict women; their election literature stated – 'there can be no true democracy when the voice of half the community is silent in Parliament'. That women should be elected to play their part in 'Leinster Housekeeping' was their plea as housewives to whom education, the care of the young, the old, the sick, are largely entrusted. Two women, Miss Corbett and Miss Phillips, stood in Tipperary (one of our largest counties, with two Ridings and two Councils, yet forming only one constituency). Both were active members of the Irish Country Women's Association, with experience on local bodies: they conducted a joint, lightning campaign over their big area. Miss Margaret Ashe stood for Galway, where she has for several years been Chairman of the Council and is an able administratrix. The writer of this article stood for South Dublin, choosing that area because she had represented it for two terms of office in the then Sinn Féin party (which had 5 women councillors between 1918 and 1925). Thus for the first time in both city and country districts independent women stood for the Dáil: a possible nucleus of a Women's Party. (In Great Britain there are now 14 women MPs. With one exception, Miss Rathbone, who represents the Universities and is an Independent, all belong to parties and are selected and run by the party machines – not, of course, under the PR, but under the single-member scheme which should make the selection of a woman much harder. They are, one Liberal, four Labour and eight Conservatives: one from Wales, two from Scotland, and the rest from English constituencies. All are trained women who are especially articulate and effective on questions affecting women.)

Our experiment, a bold enough challenge to masculine monopoly, failed. We were all beaten. Only one, Miss Ashe, retained her £100 deposit. The various parties, all but Fianna Fáil, which is the most conservative where women are concerned, put up new candidates. Labour put up one, Miss Crowley, in Cork; Fine Gael one in Dublin County, Miss Ennis; and the Farmer's Party Miss Bobbett, the organizer of the Party. In this constituency the two women divided votes, unfortunately, while in Cork the women had no chance, as the constituency could not even carry the sitting TD. Parties have a way of running two women in the same constituency in the hope of dividing votes, in others of running a woman as an 'extra' where she has not an earthly hope of winning.

The net result therefore was that the same three women previously elected – Mrs Rice, Mrs Redmond and Miss Reynolds, called often 'the three R's', also 'the Silent Sisters', were returned. All are widows of former TDs. The first is Fianna Fáil, the other two Fine Gael. They are obedient party women and have never shown any interest in questions affecting women. Thus, in a total of 138, the eleventh Dáil has still but three women TDs. The first had six, one a Cabinet Minister, Countess Markievicz, Minister for Labour in the

Republican Dáil; the first woman elected in 1918 to the House of Commons at the first election after women received the vote – it was limited then to women over 30. (No British woman was then returned, and, ironically, the only woman MP, then under a life-sentence in Holloway Jail, did not sit. Ireland led then as to female representation: now it has fallen back. It is also interesting to note that all the Republican women deputies voted against the Treaty: since then there appears to be a slump, after the other side won out.)

There are certain areas – though our country has a majority of males – where there are more women-voters on the register than men. This year, furthermore, a large number of men-voters, particularly in the cities, were absent in Britain, no means being afforded them to register their vote legitimately: though there is little doubt that many 'voted' nevertheless. The following facts refer to the constituency, Dublin South City, in which I stood. There are seven seats and over 82,000 names are on the register. Of these 42,000 are women. As the Government sprang the election, giving only the briefest possible notice – many experts believed up to the last moment, for the secret was well kept, that there would be no General Election – all organizations, save Fianna Fáil, had a difficult task, the Women Independents an almost insuperable one. In Dublin our venue was chosen in South City partly because of my previous connection therewith municipally, partly because its seven seats seemed to afford a better chance for an Independent, and partly because Mr Lemass, Minister for Supplies, was standing, whose ministry was under fire for many reasons owing to potato shortage, bread queues, coupon crises and the like. South Dublin is mainly a working-class area, and the voters could, if agreed, have returned the majority of the seven TDs. Voting was over 60 per cent of those on the register; the voters had 19 candidates on the panel to choose from, representing a wide choice, Fianna Fáil, Fine Gael, Labour, Córas na Poblachta (a new group) and Independents – of whom the man, Mr Rice, was the typical Business-Conservative.

I built up my platform on James Connolly's Republic, which included feminism, for Connolly did not restrict freedom to one sex. He said (I quoted it in my election address): – 'The woman worker is the slave of a slave.' South City therefore seemed for all these reasons favourable ground.

Under PR if voters cast their votes in order of personal preference rather than party – they do not, as it happens – there should have been enough First Preferences for the woman to stay the course until she got sufficient second votes from elimination to be returned. This did not happen, however, though eleven of the men walked the plank, eight losing deposits. Mr Lemass topped the poll with the big figure (larger than his chief's, Mr de Valera's) of 16,000 first preferences, and surplus enough to carry in three more of his party with him. Fine Gael had enough of the Big Business element in the area to secure two seats, and Labour (in this predominately Labour area) got just one seat. Ironically this Minister, who has often boldly declared himself an opponent of woman suffrage, holding that women are sufficiently 'represented' by their nearest male relatives, owes his return apparently to the votes of women.

So what? Will women not vote for a woman? They did in that first Dáil and still do in municipal elections. Do voters dislike Independents? Possibly. Were the dice loaded in favour of Fianna Fáil? All these factors counted. Women, the average and sub-average, still have that inferiority complex, just as there were negro-slaves who were opposed to emancipation. Yet they did vote for women in the areas where the three previously-elected women TDs stood! The party machine (true this of all the parties) is still male and still allergic to women, most of all, naturally, to Independents. (The Independent man too is disliked, because he is not amenable to the party whip.) Other factors are the increased cost of elections. Where £300 would formerly be enough running expenses, £1,000 would now be needed. Shortness of time was another handicap, for many experts declined to the last to believe that any election would take place: when it did, an appeal was successfully made to Panic – the 'Don't-swap-horses-crossing-a-stream', and 'Dev-will-keep-you-out-of-the-war' arguments. The women suffered a press boycott, that paper wall Griffith used to talk of as round Ireland, wrapped them round: and though posters did speak, they were not enough.

Another factor that acts as a deterrent and handicap to the Independent is that £100 deposit, frozen until after the election and passing into the Government's maw if a sufficient quota is not obtained. The only excuse given for this relic of the British regime is that it prevents freak candidates: it prevents, however, only those to whom £100 is a definite loss. The wealthy freak is not hampered. There are other ways of eliminating the 'freak', a larger number of nominators, for instance; say one hundred nominations in the area by responsible citizens. But here again the Big Parties do not worry: for them the fewer the candidates the better. That the three Independent women should have to pay £300 to swell the Government's coffers savours of the cruelty condemned in the Bible of seething the kid in its mother's milk. It punishes the citizen who has the spirit to stand against the Big Battalions.

If women in Ireland are not yet sufficiently educated politically to vote for women the blame rests largely with the various political machines that disregard them save as mere voting conveniences. Certain blame, too, of course, attaches to the women themselves, those smug ones especially, who declare that they have 'no interest in politics'. There are still great possibilities in PR if properly applied. Should the nation's woman-power be mobilized to full strength – as it is in the Soviet Union, for instance – it could be made possible to include women on each panel, from each party, so that each elector could be given the opportunity of voting for a woman. (In setting up the National University Senate this principle was adopted to ensure that the Senate would not be entirely male.) A slower process would be the other alternative of peaceful penetration by women into the party-machines, and of educating public opinion by training women to take more than a silent part in politics. Yes-women and yes-men are in the long run mere dead weight, though parties like them. (Some one has suggested flippantly that if the statue of Queen Victoria were placed inside the Dáil it might replace inexpensively one of the robots now sitting there.)

The challenge to the party-system has at least been made by the Independent women; their election campaign has set the public thinking. It took a while before the slogans 'Equal Pay' and 'A Square Deal for Women' on Dublin's hoardings were superseded by the device 'Bisurated Magnesia'. When next an election comes the seed sown should be ready to germinate – the seed beneath the snow as Silone calls it, speaking of those seeds of new growth that lie for a while submerged, but living.

Tributes to the Memory of Dorothy Evans 1889–1944[4]
From Mrs Hannah Sheehy Skeffington, Chairman, Irish Women's Social and Progressive League

I first met Dorothy Evans[5] when she came to Dublin to interview me regarding organization in Ulster; she had letters of introduction from Christabel Pankhurst. It was about 1912. (The Irish Women's Franchise League – Irish militant group – had been founded in the autumn of 1908.)

For obvious reasons we had taken our own line, pressing mainly (and vainly!) for the inclusion of votes for women in the Home Rule Bill as a protest against the non-inclusion of votes for Irishwomen in that measure. We had made a militant protest with the usual result – prison – in 1912. The North had militants who sometimes joined us; many were WSPU or WFL members also.

Dorothy at once understood our position and special problems, and in organizing the North (chiefly Belfast) she did splendid work, understanding the psychology of the people. Her work there is well known and still remembered with enthusiasm and affection.

When war came she remained faithful to suffrage principles and continued the campaign, linking her lot more as time went on with the Women's Freedom League when other societies gave up. For suffrage had still not been granted.

Her later work in Britain and in Geneva for the Six Point Group[6] is well known; in the latter city she worked closely with Alice Paul, the American suffrage leader.

Dorothy Evans was one of the best and most whole-hearted feminists I have ever known; her friendship endured the many upheavals of later days, true to feminist principles as the needle to the Pole. In international feminist gatherings her clear brain, her logical outlook, her humour and personal kindliness and tolerance marked her out. She was a born leader.

What a gap she leaves, cut off in her prime; a victim to her abounding energy which overtaxed a frame weakened by earlier prison hardships. May her great work survive and thrive – that would be her best monument.

Tom Mooney: Three Visits[7]

c. 1945

There came to my meeting in San Francisco, April 1917, a little old woman who stood in the hand-shaking file that is part of the ritual – practically the entire audience comes up to shake the speaker's hand. 'Will you go to see my son Tom in jail?' Her voice (she was a native Irish speaker) recalled Mayo. Her son was then in prison in the city under sentence of death. I had attended the trial of Rena Mooney, Tom's wife.[8] (She, too, had been accused of being an accessory in the famous 'Preparedness Day' Bomb 1916.) Bourke-Cockran, the great Irish-American pleader, had defended Tom, and Frank P. Walsh, champion of the Irish republic, took up the case; the *Irish World*, then edited by Robert Ford, championed Mooney from the first – but all in vain. Now the world knows that Mooney was the victim of a frame-up. The bombs were planted.

I saw Tom Mooney a few days later: the first and only time I had any influence with a Prison Warden (Governor) was with Pete Kelly, his jailer. Ireland and 1916 moved him to give me an interview in a special room 'for as long as you like to stay'. 'God loves the Irish!' said Mooney when the door opened to admit him. Ordinary visits had to be taken in the 'cage'. He was then a stocky, sturdily-built man in the prime of life, thirty-three years old, full of vitality, a quiet humour which never deserted him in his dark eyes. Waiting for death?

When the Russian revolution burst out, all US was roused by the news that the revolutionaries had stormed the doors of the American Embassy in Moscow, clamouring for the release of one 'Muni'. President Wilson was moved to intervene with the Governor of California – Mooney was not hanged. He firmly declined to plead for 'pardon', stating that, as he was innocent, only unconditional release, not an act of grace, would satisfy him. Bit by bit the case against him crumbled, even Judge Griffen, who had tried him, joining with several of the jury in a demand for a reversal of the judgment, but the years rolled on, and still he was held, the modern Bonivard[9] in remote San Quentin in a lonely sea-locked prison-fortress, some 20 miles from San Francisco. It was there in 1923 on my next visit to the West that I was again to see him, now bowed, prematurely aged, his hair snow-white, 'rusted with a vile repose . . . for he had been a dungeon's spoil'. Yet even there, he was a personality, a force even with the prison authorities. Tom had a way with him. His union – the Moulders – still kept up the fight, he had a huge mail from all over the world and he still kept hope. His mother later toured Europe for his release. She died before he won his freedom – her coffin was carried past the prison gate, and paused there as if to salute him.

The last time I saw him, he was still in San Quentin, still waiting, grimmer, yet hopeful, for at last there was a prospect of release. Other politicals – the Macnamaras, lifers – had died meanwhile. Shortly after, Mooney was summoned to Sacramento, here to testify before a Commission set up by the California state to go into his case; he received an ovation from the legislators, who were deeply impressed by his statement and replies. The Governor granted his release accordingly. At last, after over 20 years the creaking doors opened: Mooney was free, but prison was to take its toll; he was a sick man. He lived but three years to taste the long-deferred freedom. Meanwhile the world had moved on; the second world war occupied the stage; new problems, new alignments made emergence into a changed world difficult. The curtain fell at last silently upon that long drama. Mooney's name will be remembered as one of that long Roll of Honour – eternal spirit of the changeless minds.[10]

Post 2nd World War reflections[11]
17 September 1945

Dear Alice,[12]

I sent you a parcel, mixed, as usual today. I haven't written you lately, as I was ordered to give up almost everything, typing included. Only reading and writing in bed. Now I am better, but easily tired, on a diet, light, having to rest whole chunks of the day, go early to bed, up late and so on. However I'm past the worst. I wouldn't mind dying, but I would (hate) being a helpless invalid. I agree with Mrs Gilman. And what a world this is! How glad we saw things while we could, you more than I. I got equal rights, but I am not clear how far they (are) won yet. US and Britain the opposers, and all the tosh about Democracy. Thanks for your card and for the papers you and Mrs Gartz sent. She is great to keep on. How does Gloria[13] do? Brilliant, but spoiled. Was disappointed in Upton – he <u>always</u> falls for War. I would surely have loved to be with you all in SF. Notice how they keep out women from their conference. The horror of the Atomic Bomb is just ghastly & there's a scramble for it for the next War. Was glad to note that there was a Peace group in US & in Britain, but countries get swept in, whatever the peace-lovers do, Kellogg Pact

& all that. It's great to have an end to the carnage, the censor and all that. US seems to have suffered least of the combatants, but the common people do everywhere. Had a PC from Mrs Gatty. She is on way home.

The Brit. Lab. Govt was a protest against Churchill & Co., but they are not likely to do much in foreign affairs & are very tame. My grandson, Francis, is thriving, children are being born in great numbers here, in Gt Brit., France. I guess Nature's filling up gaps, but one wonders for what? Anyhow Owen & Andrée are very happy & the babe is bonny, more French, I think, than Irish, as sons favour mothers. Interesting to watch, just four months old today!

This is just to keep in touch. Let me hear from you.

Love, HANNA

'Women MPs in Britain'
Fabian Quarterly, October 1945
No publicity has been given so far in Irish newspapers to the fact that the number of women M.P.s in Britain has increased from fourteen at the General Election to twenty-four in the New Parliament – still too small as against 600, but a notable gain. Eighty-seven women candidates offered themselves, many stood for constituencies where they had not the ghost of a chance, some ran as Independents and those too plough a lone furrow. Of those elected 21 are Labour, one Liberal (Lloyd George's daughter, Lady Megan Lloyd George; her father fought against votes for women all he could and she herself is not strongly feminist). Another is a Conservative, Viscountess Davidson – like Lady Astor she succeeded her husband when he moved up to the House of Lords. Only one Independent was returned, Eleanor Rathbone; she is MP for the combined Universities. Her name is associated with the Family Allowance scheme, her life's work. She is rather conservative in outlook, as University MPs are apt to be.

Of the newly-elected Labour women some are already well-known. Ellen Wilkinson, now Minister for Education, was one of the Labour delegates who visited Ireland to inquire into the Black and Tan atrocities, her then constituency having a large Irish electorate. She was in the recent Coalition Government and very orthodox. Jennie Lee[14] is well-known as a progressive Leftist. Mrs Ayrton Gould (journalist)[15] is one of the few Suffrage veterans; it is curious though quite comprehensible and regrettable that no 'votes for women' stalwarts got into the House of Commons. Partly, of course, because they did not make good party members, parties being scared of them, partly because (see our own history) rebels do not make parliamentarians. Lady Noel-Buxton[16] is specially interested in child welfare. She was a member of the Peace with Ireland Council which did much valuable work in exposing

Black and Tan brigandage during the Anglo-Irish War; she is a pacifist by conviction.

Outstanding in the Labour group is Dr Edith Summerskill, now Parliamentary Secretary to the Ministry for Food, a strong feminist and a forceful personality. She is President of the Married Women's Association, and Vice-President of the Socialist Medical Association. She will probably lead the women MPs group in matters affecting women.

As to their professions the majority of the new women MPs are (or were) school teachers, a good sign; next some journalists and trade union officials, one is a barrister and a member of London County Council (Mrs F. Corbet). Most have good records of public service on boards and councils and are therefore good parliamentary timber. Some have stood already in previous elections and so won their spurs. Lady Astor who retired was the first woman MP to take her seat in Parliament, though Countess Markievicz was the first to be elected but did not take her seat. Lady Astor is now replaced by Mrs Middleton, one of the earlier Labour pioneers, a former Organising Secretary to the party. Labour, like other parties in Britain as well as here, has a tendency to run the widows of former Labour officials.

Two stories are told of the first woman elected. Countess Markievicz, a prisoner undergoing a life sentence after 1916, when summoned to take her seat replied from Holloway Jail that she was already His Majesty's guest there and declined to attend. Lady Astor, a good feminist, though in other respects a supporter of the privileged classes, narrates in her memoirs that no male MP spoke to her for two years so shocked was the House, that hitherto exclusively male club, at women's sacrilegious entry! The only trace of Constance Markievicz in the House of Commons was the appearance of a peg to hang her hat on!

Now for the casualties. In the landslide the women MPs suffered the loss of their best leaders who had successfully fought for women's equality (for instance, for equal compensation for loss of life and limb in war time, originally a woman being rated in value at one-third of a man). Mrs Tate,[17] Miss Irene Ward, Mrs Cazalet-Keir[18] and Miss Horsbrugh[19] were whole-hearted champions of women throughout the war period and earlier, disregarding party ties in so doing. They were also capable parliamentarians, mistresses of tactics. (It will be recalled that Churchill himself had a fall on the equal pay vote and had to retrieve himself by falling back on a vote of confidence.) These women belonged to the defeated parties – Conservative and Liberal.

It is up to Labour now to look to its laurels and to prove that the new team does not disappoint them. The women's programme is thus expressed: the rate for the job, no bar to the employment of women on equal terms with men in all spheres of industry, no marriage bar, entrance to the Diplomatic service (still in Britain a male preserve), the right of women to retain their nationality on marriage. In fact the application by the government of the principles of democracy to women as to men.

'Random reflections on housewives: their ways and works'
The Irish Housewife, 1946

I dislike the word, described in the dictionary as 'female domestic manager' or, alternatively, 'a small case for articles for female work'. The Irish *Bean a Tighe* (woman of the house, or Herself) and the French *ménagère* are better, they at least fit the idea. I believe wife is still described in legal documents as of 'no occupation' just as an unmarried woman has to be called a spinster even if she's an architect or Chief Executive and never saw a spinning wheel unless in a museum. These clumsy man-made words remind us how little free we really are, so 'housewife' is accepted more or less meekly by most women as we accept men's names in marriage and live in their inconveniently-constructed houses. There is no masculine form of the word – house-man, the nearest, being a superior servant. Well, let it pass.

During World War I, the organization comparing most nearly to the Irish Housewives' Association, started in the USA and was called the Consumers' League, not a good name either. It set about fighting exorbitant prices, chiefly the racket of the middleman and the profiteer; it did excellent work on co-operative lines, chiefly in the Middle West and West, by bringing down prices with a bang, picketing and so forth, getting excellent publicity (our press is very coy about any publicity, except belittling or comic, about the 'Fair Sex'). In US they are lavish, always eager for a story and realising that the public, after all, is largely feminine. In a recent number of *The Women's Bulletin*, organ of the Women's Freedom League, England, occurs this paragraph, entitled the 'Average Housewife's Working Day'. Some male research workers have been investigating it at the request of the British Board of Trade. Here it is: 'The following jobs take up the most time, Cooking 30 per cent, Cleaning 30 per cent, Washing up 13 per cent, Clothes-washing takes up less time than any of these, but it is the most arduous and unpopular of all.' (We verified this during the laundresses' strike, when men had to go about in limp or soiled collars if they had no female belongings to do them up.) This schedule certainly leaves little time to play or invite one's soul, unless, of course, the daily shopping hunt with basket and string-bag comes under the heading, Morning Constitutional. Nowadays the housewife's marketing round, comparing prices, searching for the unattainable and taking most of her purchases home would absorb another large block of her time. Then what about sewing, darning, those odd jobs and household emergencies? Lenin called domestic work the 'tyranny of the Pots and Pans' – is it any wonder that most women fled from it to war-work as a pleasant diversion from the daily round, the common task?

When, some years ago, a band of energetic and determined women started this organization in Dublin, thoughts like the above overwhelmed me. My conscience exacted a subscription now and then, I applauded heartily their victories from the fence. Like the lilies I dust not, neither do I darn, and wash-up only in acute domestic crisis, when I have worked through all the ware in the pantry and piled it perilously in the kitchen sink without a housewifely qualm. All through War Emergency and the present phoney Peace the Association went valiantly ahead at its appointed task – its adversaries being the price-ring, the Black market, rocketing prices, and the Under-the-Counter Brigade. With the proverbial patience, acquired by women through the ages, it kept after ministers, forcibly feeding them with statistics, exposed ruthlessly individual cases of flagrant overcharging, carefully compiled and compared costs as among shops, wrote letters to the Press so often that at last some actually were printed and, lo, a week or two before Christmas, when the oranges came to town from Spain and Brazil the Government controlled prices (it had been hoped that the fruit would sell in a 'free' market at 1/– each as apples are selling, but alas, 7d per pound was the allotted sum). Wholesalers, middlemen, Moore Street basket-women were all by the ears, the public revelled in its oranges and within a week of Christmas they vanished overnight into thin air – better let them rot than submit to the tyranny of controlled prices. The Housewives won the first round, though I doubt if they got credit for it; in the second one the traders seemed to win, but it was a Pyrrhic victory; they had been (and are) severely shaken.

So I bow my thanks to the valiant band, the Irish Housewives' Association, shamelessly benefiting by their labours and paying conscience money ever and anon.

What of the large mass of indifferent women who even now fail to realize that Politics control our lives, who shrug and say with coy femininity, 'I don't take any part in Politics, I leave all that to the men.' The example of the Housewives has shown that women *too* must organize, must educate themselves in citizenship, must become vocal, if need be, clamorous. The Association needs more members, additional subscribers, investigators, workers, politically-minded women – much work remains to be done in '46. Go to it, housewives!

(Editorial Comment: It is with deep gratitude for the work she has done for women and a keen sense of loss in her passing, that we publish the above article by Hanna Sheehy Skeffington, written for this handbook shortly before her death.)

16

BOOK AND THEATRE REVIEWS

INTRODUCTION

Hanna and Frank were both voracious readers. Their house was described as 'one mass of books and papers all over the ground floor' with 'another room full upstairs'.[1] The *Irish Citizen* carried reviews of books and plays of interest to feminists, with reviewers often using only initials or pseudonyms, and Hanna often used her family pet name of 'Joan'. In later years a wide variety of publications carried reviews written by her; they were not always directly political, but they always contained a feminist or Irish nationalist message. In the late 1920s and early 1930s her frequent attendance at meetings of the Minerva Club, the off-shoot of the Women's Freedom League, gave her a new outlet for her writing as she published articles on the state of feminism in Ireland and wrote a number of book reviews for their journal *The Vote*. Not all are included here, for example, *The Life of the Duke of Flamborough* by Laurence Housman was significant mainly because of the author, rather than the subject. What she demonstrates, as ever, is a robust good sense, a modern attitude towards life and impatience with those who will not face up to such evils as sex trafficking, prostitution and venereal disease.

Elsewhere she used her facility with German and French to good effect, for example discussing 'sex bias in language' in the *Irish Citizen* (September 1919) or writing about 'Goethe: through Irish (and other) eyes' for *The Distributive Worker* (December 1937) and reviewing a biography of the life of Marie Curie, written in French by Curie's daughter, beginning with the firm declaration 'I liked this book' (July 1938). For the *Irish Library Bulletin* (May–June 1942) she considered a range of books on women in Irish sagas – Maeve, Granuaile, Gormflaith amongst them – commenting on how many of the women retained their maiden names, 'partly because it was a sensible Irish custom and partly because they were outstanding personalities'.

In the 1930s Hanna earned some income by writing for the *Irish Press*, but only as second review editor. Her relationship with its editor Frank Gallagher was difficult, although their lives had often intertwined: both had been correspondents for the *Irish World* (although Hanna was dropped when she resigned from Fianna Fáil) and he and his wife had for a time been tenants of her top floor. In early 1935 their relationship came to an end as Hanna wrote to sever her connection after a review of hers had been suppressed. She and Gallagher had a tempestuous meeting and she complained about being treated as if she was 'an illiterate', but, characteristically, also apologised later for how she had behaved:

> I wish to express regret for a personal remark made by me at the end of our conversation tonight. The extraordinary tone adopted by you provoked me, but the retort was none the less unworthy.[2]

At the start of 1940, however, she was again writing for the *Irish Press*, not only with a range of obituaries of key political figures she had worked with over the decades, but also more populist articles.

Below is a selection of book and play reviews written by Hanna from the earliest period of the *Irish Citizen*, to her later years as a journalist and polemicist with feminist and republican journals. She was a reader with a wide knowledge of history and a playgoer who did not hesitate from blunt criticism when necessary, but who also delighted in many of the productions emanating from the Abbey theatre. Her writings have the consistency of a life-long commitment to feminism; her analysis of issues such as prostitution, human trafficking and the role of the housewife remain equally pertinent today.

Women and Prisons, by Helen Blagg and Charlotte Wilson. Fabian Tract. No. 163. Price 2d.
Irish Citizen, 28 December 1912

The above tract no suffragist should be without: into 27 pages it compresses a brief, clear history of the development of prisons, a detailed account of the working of British prisons and their classification, followed by analysis of criminals and crime, with a glance at the 'paths of change' along which the reformer of the future will move. At the end of the little volume is a valuable bibliography of criminology. There is much valuable information on the dark places of prison-life illuminated by large-hearted, practical humanity. It is shown that women suffer more keenly and in more diverse ways under the present administration of criminal law than men – that for them the way of reform is made harder by social ostracism, that prostitution lies at the root of most female delinquency. Since Elizabeth Fry, that noble pioneer of prison reform, described Newgate as 'hell above ground' few women have been actively associated with prison reform, while the world of prison still awaits the regenerating influence of a Florence Nightingale to show by example that 'work in prisons is of equal importance with the tending of the sick or the care of the mentally afflicted'. Though Davitt, Oscar Wilde, Kropotkin, Stead and other men prisoners have recorded their personal experiences in jail, no woman prisoner dealt with hers until suffragists invaded Holloway in 1907. One result of their wholesome criticism has been the establishment of a woman inspector of prisons, who has introduced many valuable reforms in women's prisons, including a more hygienic and less hideous prison dress. The experiences of suffragists in Holloway are quoted extensively to show the terrible defects of our prison system, – the horrors of solitary confinement, the want of ventilation, the brutalising effect of prison 'discipline', the absence of 'love and beauty', the deadening and crushing of every kindly human impulse. Small wonder then that women-criminals are rarely reformed by prison. With regard to the class of crime, women are shown to offend more largely against property than the person, while very few indeed are among the skilled professionals of crime – probably the men's trade unions frown on their competition.

In dealing with the causes of crime, the writers state that 83 per cent of the convictions in England are for misconduct that cannot be correctly termed crime at all – such as begging, obstruction, vagrancy and the like. 'The question will some day arise whether it is really necessary to maintain 56 local prisons, with all their elaborate paraphernalia, to maintain discipline in daily life.' It is instructive of our delightful social order to learn that 'we have nearly always some men and women in our prisons who are there for zeal in social reform or individual experiment distasteful to custom or to the powers that be'. Doubtless, as Voltaire observed, 'pour encourager les autres'.

The pamphlet contains some illuminating suggestions as to the need of special training for prison officials, which all suffragist victims of prison will gladly welcome. 'At present only the medical officers are required to have any scientific training at all, and it is quite possible that they have never studied criminal psychology.' Women doctors for women prisons, more women inspectors, women governors, and women as 'moral and spiritual advisors' are deemed eminently desirable. We are told of a local prison in the Rhone Valley where a woman governor is in charge of both men and women – 'Why not at Holloway', or we might add, Mountjoy? The necessity of having at least one of the Prison Commissioners a woman, of a women's auxiliary to the police force (as in Germany), of women magistrates and women jurors is demonstrated in the interests of society. 'There is no path of change along which women are more particularly concerned to press forward than that which leads them to an official share in judicial procedure and in the administration of the penal system.'

Prostitution: Its Nature and Cure. **Penal Reform League Pamphlet. No. 9.**
Price 2d.
Irish Citizen, 22 February 1913
This pamphlet is issued by the Penal Reform League, whose sensible remarks
on forcible feeding, embodied in its Annual Report, have already been quoted
in our columns. It begins with some valuable suggestions on the White Slave
Traffic Bill, such as condemnation of the principle of flogging (unhappily not
acted upon by the framers of the Bill), and a recommendation of a special court
for the trial and protection of women, with women police, probation officers,
magistrates, etc. Such suggestions savour of Utopia, and will doubtless continue
to do so – till women get the vote. The whole outlook of the tract is sane and
practical, and agreeably free from that maudlin sentimentalism that usually
stains such treatises. It recognises, for instance, that prostitutes are recruited
as well from among the 'high-spirited, adventurous and ambitious', as from
the feeble-minded, the lazy and the vicious, and such recognition must accompany any attempt at cutting off this hideous supply. Its attitude to the white
slave trafficker is also healthy and helpful, for are we not at present a little in
danger of losing our heads over this ghastly business and becoming panicky on
the subject? 'By all means let us do what we can to frustrate the designs of the
procurer . . . but let us not forget that the community itself is the chief "bully".
So long as the present injustice continues, we are all white slave traders.' And,
as such, need at least spiritual flagellation. 'We are all bartering to one another,
either what we should freely give, the means of life; or what we should never
give, fraudulent or mischievous products; or what we should never part with,
our own individuality.' Practical suggestions follow as to special courts for
dealing with unprotected women, the prey of these harpies, so that the community be safeguarded (both men and women) from what is at present its
greatest danger, this unchecked traffic in women's bodies openly conducted in
its midst under the eyes of the law.

   The various remedial measures for diverting women from this career of
ruin are dealt with. They do not, as is usual in this country, begin and end with
the wash-tub as the basis of sainthood for the Magdalen. In fact, the potency
of the wash-tub is completely ignored. Homes, friendship and its safeguards,
industrial settlements of a voluntary character, suitable employment, a living
wage, and rehabilitation are the valuable counter-attractions offered. Even the
procurer and procuress, it is suggested, may not be always irreclaimable, no
more than is the burglar or swindler.

   If some of the suggestions are necessarily vague and over idealistic in our
present state, the right note is struck throughout: let the community look to it,
for the traffic threatens its existence.

'The *Citizen*'s bookshelf'
Where Are You Going To . . . ?, by Elizabeth Robins. Heinemann. Price 6s.
Irish Citizen, 15 March 1913

As Votes for Women has its literature, so the White Slave Traffic is beginning to have its also. Already there is Zola's *Nana*, a ponderously documented treatise in guise of a novel as is Zola's way, there is Matilda Böhme's *Tagebuch einer Verlorenen* from the German point of view, and from the American Kaufmann's study, *The Daughters of Ishmael. Where Are You Going To . . . ?* is typically English in outlook and atmosphere. It is Elizabeth Robins' second contribution to the feminist movement – her *Convert* was her first frankly propagandist work, and was the direct outcome of her own conversion to militancy – in her earlier novels, especially the rather crude *George Mandeville's Husband*, there is much evidence of an anti-feminist bias. There is a general family resemblance between *The Convert* and *Where Are You Going To . . . ?* apart from the propagandist tendency. There is a shadow of tragedy over both, accentuated in the latter: there is the trace of Elizabeth Robins' worship of the 'strong man' – usually a bit of a brute of the Rochester-Heathcliff type, so loved by the Victorians. No more unlikely material for the white slaver could be well imagined than Bettina and her sister, who at the last moment makes good her escape and lives to tell the story of Bettina, the petted radiant darling, 'all white except her green shoes and hair of sunset gold', into whose sheltered life this blighting desolation comes. We have a carefully drawn picture of a devoted widowed mother, watching over the lives of her two daughters with almost feverish solitude. All intercourse with the outer world is carefully checked, even charitable incursions into the lives of the poorer neighbourhoods are taboo – the selfishness of the exclusively maternal type of woman who guards her young at the expense of her duty to other motherless ones less befriended is well brought out, and its commonness does not redeem it. A little kindly maid-servant who 'goes under' is instantly banished from the sheltered cosy home into outer darkness. Interesting side-lights are thrown on the tender if rather trivial preoccupations of the little household in the chapter where the heroine is found planting thyme: 'Why must you have wild thyme there?' he grumbled. 'So as not to disappoint the blue butterflies,' I said gravely. 'They "know a bank", and this is it. They've an understanding with my mother about it for years. If they don't find thyme here, they're annoyed. They go on dying out. My mother says a world without blue butterflies would be a poor sort of place.'

It is no wonder that the elder sister of this home is looked on with horror when she proposes to study medicine in order to relieve the family exchequer. Seeing that her mother – that genteel widow of a cavalry officer, with all the genteel vices of her class – does not permit her children to use the public telephone for fear of microbes from the common mouthpiece, it is not likely that she will be permitted to get at grips with disease and festering ugliness. Then there comes an invitation for the girls from a wealthy neighbour, who gives sage advice on marrying-off daughters, and whose wisdom is summed-up in this epigram on balls: 'After all, very little is done at balls! . . . As a rule, only boys and ineligibles care about dancing. The thing for people in Rosamund's position to do . . . was to spend August in London . . . all the other women leave. The field is clear. There are always men in London when the town is supposed to be empty.' The British matron's ghoulish chase after eligible men makes one feel that there is something to be said for the French system. So the story wanders on pleasantly, a trifle dull, as people so divorced from life cannot help being. The 'strong man', Eric Annan sums up his life philosophy thus: 'A revolution might have swept England. I should have gone attenuating serums and inoculating guinea-pigs.' Then suddenly the fear that haunts the book is upon us: the mother, feeling her end upon her, with her darlings unprovided for, negotiates with an unknown aunt, who has hitherto neglected them, an invitation comes for the coronation festivity, and there are 'prospects' from the eccentric relative in Lowndes Square. A little French dressmaker is introduced to furbish up the girls' scant wardrobes. Madame Aurore is a procuress in disguise. There is the rapturous journey to London, the girlish enthusiasm over the wealth and magnificence of their supposed stranger-aunt, whose role is played by the keeper of 'one of the most infamous houses in Europe' – then gradually there comes to these country-bred girls, in this strange house, with barred windows and foreign, stealthy-footed servants, the sense of nameless horror, in spite of the lights and the glitter of diamonds, through the laughter, the flowers and the champagne. The elder sister – I think we never get her name – is at last initiated into the dreadful truth by one of the guests (or clients) of the brothel, who pities her, Bettina playing and dancing the while for the other guests. Here is her first contact with reality: 'Take India – I've been there. I knew an official who had charge of the chaklas. You don't know what chaklas are? Your father knew. If you'd gone riding around any one of the cantonments you'd have seen. Little groups of tents. A hospital not far off. Women in the tents . . . they are called "government women". The women are needed by the army . . . Even Governments . . . had to recognise human nature and shape their policies accordingly. I was too young to remember . . . about the mysterious movements of British battleships in the Mediterranean. Instead of hanging about Malta, the ships had gone cruising about the Irish coast. Why? The officials said for good and sufficient reasons. The "reasons" were known to those who had to know. Not enough women at Malta. The British fleet spent some time about the Irish coasts.' Pleasant for the natives of those Irish coasts, that visit of the Fleet!

So while Bettina sings 'Where are you going to?' to the thrilled roués and the young guardsman soon about to enter Parliament, her sister gets away – and, in spite of all her frantic search, she never lays eyes on that little sister left behind those iron bars in that army of bullies and obscene traffickers in maidenhood. Her frenzied chase after elusive clues, her weary round of the police stations, where her case is reported by the 'blunt lead pencils' of slow officials – we know those inspectors and superintendents and their 'vigorous pursuit' of clues of which one never hears any more! – all end in nothing. Usually, the police tell her, these 'cases' are of poor girls – there is the tragedy. Possibly if the daughters of a few retired generals or the nieces or cousins of Cabinet Ministers were trapped into slavery, we should have an end of it. Elizabeth Robins has set herself the task of awakening the lethargic middle-class English to the peril of their sheltered daughters by showing them how vitally this business is meant for their bosoms. Her novel is a tract for the times: being such, it has many improbabilities; the story is forced too often for the sake of the moral. Bettina, for all her kittenish, dainty ways, is rather a minx; it is indeed a question whether the theme itself is not too ghastly-crude for firm artistic handling, for certainly the charged atmosphere at times seems overcharged. It is Josephine Butler's *Queen's Daughters* in the guise of a modern six-shilling novel. And like the original, it makes the heart burn within one.

Joan

'The *Citizen* at the play'
Irish Citizen, 27 September 1913
Marriage, a translation of Dr Douglas Hyde's *An Pósadh* was produced at the Abbey last Thursday by the second company. The play is of the slightest, a glorification of the blind poet, Raftery, whose spirit materialises after death to make, by a rather crude strategy, two lovers happy – or rather to make them rich. There is no drama in the little sketch, and though the actors did their best to enliven the dialogue, they could not succeed in relieving its monotony. Mr Conniffe's portrayal of the blind poet shows that he has possibilities, outside mere comic acting, but Raftery's improvised verses did not strike one as justifying his reputation as the 'greatest poet in Connaught'. Charles Power made a pleasant boy-husband adding another to his many successes, and Nell Byrne, as his young bride, played with winning grace. The piece aimed at showing the awe, not unmixed with terror, inspired in simple peasant folk by the wonder-working magic of the 'maker'.

The Country Dressmaker illustrates the tendency of Abbey plays to verbiage, as revealed on this occasion by the romantic caprices of the love-sick, novelette-reading little dressmaker, well sustained by Nell Byrne. The intriguing Clohesys, who plan to rob her of her former lover, the returned Yank, are over exuberantly

acted, and the family byplay sometimes degenerates into mere clowning. Una
O'Connor as the hoydenish 'slip of a girl', Minn Dillane, was wonderfully
fresh and natural, though her brogue does not ring true. Helena Molony,[3] as
usual, plays to the life, with delightful, effortless simplicity, the old peasant
mother. One misses the earlier manner of the Abbey plays, when the heroic
side of life was not neglected, as it seems of late to be. The 'eternal peasant'
and his money-grubbing intriguing, huckster-soul, is becoming a fetish – an
exclusive diet of him is as soul sickening as the unvarying 'girl' series in musical
comedy. Is 'romantic Ireland dead and gone' even in counterfeit presentment?

Joan

The King's Threshold, by W. B. Yeats
Irish Citizen, 25 October 1913

The King's Threshold, which Mr Yeats describes as his 'least compromising
play', is to suffragists as to poets an undiluted joy. It is a glowing and radiant
glorification of the Hunger-Strike, all the more convincing because it is not
propaganda; but eternal in its nature and appeal as is poetry. 'There is a
custom . . . that if a man be wronged . . . and starve upon another's threshold
till he die, the common people, for all time to come, will raise a heavy cry
against that threshold, even though it be the King's.' So Seanchan, refused his
place at the king's table by the intrigues of 'Bishops, Soldiers, and Makers of
the Law', refuses food and drink until the ancient right of the poet be restored.
The King sends to him his pupils, his sweetheart, his townsfolk, offers him, as
is the way of the authorities, bribes of various sorts, presents the daintiest
food, as is the way of jailers, to tempt his appetite – in vain. And in the end it
is the King who yields – lesser than Cat and Mouse McKenna, yet much
greater – for 'while he is lying there, perishing, my good name in the world is
perishing also'. The plea for poetry might be the plea for outlawed womanhood, or for anything oppressed and defiant unto death. The play is a vindica-
tion of the 'fragile almighty things of God', the human spirit against the forces
of the world. In Gordon Craig setting, with Donovan as the starving poet,
Sinclair as King, and Kerrigan as mayor of Kinvara, *The King's Threshold*
enraptures: everything conspires to make this flower of Yeats' genius perfect.

Women as World Builders, by Floyd Dell. Studies in Modern Feminism.
Chicago: Forbes and Co. Price 75 cents
Irish Citizen, 20 June 1914

The range of these studies is designedly wide. They include women of various
nationalities, various ideals and achievements. They range from Mrs Pankhurst,
the leader of advanced militancy, to Isadora Duncan, the dancer, and the
variety serves to emphasise a lesson which even modern women (and almost

all men) need to be reminded of from time to time, namely, that women when free to develop will vary as much from type as men do. If now they fall more readily into classes, the tendency is due, not to any permanent feminine characteristic as some scientists would have it, but rather to lack of opportunity and real freedom of choice. Olive Schreiner, Jane Addams, Beatrice Webb, Ellen Key, to name some of the women who are subjects for these studies, reveal the eternal feminine working out its salvation in very different spheres of activity; all are pioneer women, all have contributed to the advancement of womanhood. Some, too, like Dora Marsden (the Freewoman), Emma Goldman (the Anarchist), and Charlotte Perkins Gilman (who has done so much to explode the 'Angel of the Hearth' theory of women), are frank and jubilant iconoclasts. Those who are best acquainted with Mrs Gilman's prose (her fame in her native town is so great that they have named a street after her), will find a rare treat awaiting them in the discovery of her verse. She wars in especial against base and trammelling domesticity, as in her poem on 'Wedded Bliss', a parable of the Eagle and the Hen. Mrs Gilman wars on complacent and enervating 'Hendom', and in her poems makes us see this harem ideal of wifehood in all its naked ugliness. They are excellent antidotes to the maundering of Coventry Patmore and the false gospel of Ruskin's Sesame and the Lilies, which deserve to be burnt by the common hangman as false and cruel libels on womanhood.

The studies do not aim at comprehensive or complete analysis of the possibilities of modern womanhood. They give illuminating glimpses of new vistas that may lead far. They indicate that while 'women have a surer instinct than men for the preservation of the truest human values', they will nevertheless come into their own only after having scrapped many of the ideals that man holds dear.

Joan

'The *Citizen* at the Abbey'
Irish Citizen, 10 October 1914
Last week *The Prodigal*, a play in four acts by Walter Riddall,[4] was produced for the first time at the Abbey Theatre by Mr A. P. Wilson, and the production was in every way worthy of the play. *The Prodigal* is admirable in every respect – in dialogue, in dramatic fitness, in keen and accurate observation of Northern human nature in all its phases. The cast was well chosen, and every part, down to the smallest, was well filled, the whole play running with that perfect smoothness in every detail that only efficient staging can give. The author (now, unhappily, no longer living) chose an entirely new environment, that of upper-middle Belfast religion, both Church of Ireland and Evangelical, and finds both wanting. The Walker family are a creation not unworthy of Ibsen: the father, a wily man of business, who exploits even his own son; the

daughter Helen, bent on hooking a curate and finding some little difficulty in landing her fish; the cynical George, the 'good son'; and the wayward Stanley, the 'prodigal'; the sweet care-worn mother trying, as is the lot of woman, to propitiate and appease the eternally warring males; the shrewd old family servant – all these divergent types constitute a 'family' atmosphere electric with life, furnishing a scathing indictment of Belfast commercialism, whose god is Mammon. Stanley's vices are objected to because of the danger to 'business', and he is to be shipped to Canada as an incubus to be got rid of in 'our Colonies', so that his vagaries may not be a stumbling-block to the family's prosperity. When he startles everyone by being suddenly 'converted' and taking religion in its most virulent form of street-preaching, the family horror is but intensified: for does he not proceed to denounce smugness and expose hypocrisy? Finally, poor Stanley is twice shipwrecked, finding evangelicalism equally a failure in coping with human needs.

Thus, in outline, *The Prodigal*: but so dramatic in essence, so full of striking situations and telling juxtapositions, that no summary can do it justice. As an exposure of 'cant', it is not to be surpassed by anything the Abbey yet produced. Its production adds another to the long roll of Abbey masterpieces, and shows that the theatre that produced *Riders to the Sea*, *Patriots*, *The Land*, *Kathleen ni Houlihan*, is full of new possibilities and promises of fresh growth. *The Dark Hour*, another Northern study, was also produced. The Abbey Company is gaining a freedom and a familiarity in dealing with Northern plays that augurs well. After all, the Boyne may first be bridged at the Abbey.

Joan

Woman Suffrage in Practice. The International Woman Suffrage Alliance. Price 1s. 6d.
Irish Citizen, 5 December 1914

'What would women do if they got the Vote?' is a question that frequently meets the suffragist speaker and propagandist. To that question this book gives the fullest reply: it examines each country where women vote, and gives a record of legislation since the enfranchisement of women in each particular country. If women in those States where they are voters reveal a definite interest in temperance, in protection of child life, in certain educational reforms, the record of what they have effected in Australia, in New Zealand, in Finland, in the suffragist area (now spreading like a flame) of the United States may be cited a fair example, almost amounting to prophecy, of what women in Ireland or Great Britain would lay their reforming hands on first. The fact that New Zealand, for example, has been a pioneer in social legislation is largely attributed to the stimulating influence of the woman's vote. The list of measures passed since 1893 is instructive reading: at a glance one sees how wise in their generation are the anti-suffragist vested interests – drinks, debauchery, exploitation – in refusing women citizenship. They are frightened by the terrible example of suffragist States! The New Zealand Parliament has time to deal with food alteration, to prohibit the sale of opium, to provide for the training of midwives, to pass a Deceased Husband's Brother Marriage Act, to provide equal pay for equal work in the case of teachers, to deal with legitimation – to name but a few of the measures passed. It is not obsessed with the exclusively male concerns, with voting millions for purely destructive purposes, and giving male legislators long holidays (on full pay) in time of war in order to avoid 'contentious' issues.

This work further deals with the progress (or lack of progress) of suffrage in non-suffrage countries, giving an exhaustive account of the various petty franchises enjoyed by women throughout the world. This complete survey is a most valuable study in comparisons, and helps one to realise the universality of the woman's movement and its far-reaching aims, the progressive countries reacting on the more backward with powerful driving force. The history of suffrage in Finland is peculiarly suggestive for Irish women. The following might be a plea for Votes under a Home Rule Parliament:

> **A small country has urgent need of the help of every one of its citizens** in carrying out its political and social work. It is not with us merely a question of abstract justice or of a wise and proper concession to the growing claims of women, but it is a question of pure expediency, of concern for the well-being of the nation. **Now we have the whole Finnish people acting together**.

This valuable work of reference is indispensable to every suffragist, and should find a place in every library. It has been most thoroughly and capably edited; the arrangement of the matter is well systemised, and the price brings it within reach of all. There is also added a valuable bibliography of suffrage in various countries. In addition *Woman Suffrage in Practice* is eminently readable.
Joan

Human Merchandise: A Study of the International Traffic in Women, by H. Wilson Harris. Benn. Price 6s.
The Vote, 11 May 1928
This work, appropriately dedicated to Josephine Butler in her Centenary year, presents in popular form the gist of the League of Nations Report on the Traffic in Women and Children, published in March, 1927. It is the first time that this question has been tackled internationally and made the subject of expert investigation, aided by Government. Whatever may be said about the effectiveness of the League as an anti-war machine, there is no doubt as to its

usefulness in dealing with problems of this kind. Much good has already been done by the investigation and the Report. This volume gives the facts elicited by the inquiry a still wider currency, 'letting in more light on evils that batten on darkness', as the author, Mr Wilson Harris, sets out in his Preface. No feminist can fail to welcome such publicity. There is no pandering to sensationalism in the setting forth of the facts – even the nomenclature is changed, the term, 'White Slave Traffic', being dropped as inaccurate, inasmuch as the traffic includes not only white, but black, yellow, and brown. Two women – Miss Grace Abbott and Dame Rachel Crowdy – are closely associated with the investigation, the former as head of the Child Welfare Bureau, Washington, being the first to suggest such inquiry, the latter having acted as Secretary to the Body of Experts that carried it out. Questionnaires were sent to the various Governments, 112 cities were visited in 28 different countries, and 6,500 persons were interviewed, of whom 5,000 were engaged in the traffic. Thus the traffickers actually helped the inquiry unknowingly, mistaking the investigators for members of the ring, and supplying them with letters of introduction and other facilities. In this way, the inquirers were able to check the Government reports, comparing these with actual conditions in the underworld. For Governments and police have everywhere a childish faith in the panacea of regulations, of passports, visas, and licences not borne out by the actual conditions. One fact that emerges in this work is the utter futility of all these in preventing the free circulation of the traffickers from one country to another. There is a thriving forged passport industry, the profits of the trade justifying the risk and expense of getting round the regulations. Wealthy patrons can pay their agents lavishly – the *souteneur*, the madame, and their kind – to run risks and suffer vicarious punishment, if need be; in this, as in so many other cases, the worst criminals are often immune. A case for international action has been established, no country being able to deal adequately with a problem that transcends all frontiers. A chapter dealing with *The Public's Part* is appropriately added to the findings. In many countries already the ventilation of the question through inquiry has had a good result. Several have already abolished that plague, the licensed house, which it was Josephine Butler's mission to wage war upon.

It is clear, however that, notwithstanding all the Conventions signed, there is still a world-wide traffic in women. Russia is not included in the Report, the Soviet Republics not coming within the scope of the inquiry – one would like to know how far the claim made by the Soviets, that they had abolished prostitution, has been maintained.

'If the "third party" who organises the traffic for gain could be eliminated, the traffic would wither up within a twelvemonth', is the conclusion reached by the author. Upon the prostitute preys a still fouler parasite – the man who lives and grows rich upon her earnings. Man's inhumanity to woman has its darkest depths in the sad story of prostitution as told here. The father violating his young daughter before launching her upon the vice market, the lover 'breaking in' his girl victim at home, previous to shipping her to a foreign country for profit, the procurer who purveys his merchandise of human flesh to suit the whim of organised lust and its devotees: all these are part of the chain forged by man for the enslavement of women. The exploited women have not the initiative to organise the traffic themselves, part of which entails the transport of girls under 14 to the ends of the earth. It is explained that in foreign countries these girls can be more readily exploited and debased; hence women are driven across the frontiers from Germany to South America, from France to Algiers, from Britain and Europe to Egypt ('in Egypt you can do what you like,' says a *souteneur*), from Roumania to Mexico, and from China to California.

Conditions prevailing in various countries investigated are detailed and compared. The United States appears to be at one end of the line – where the traffic flourishes least – while South America is at the other. London, Liverpool, and Southampton are visited in Britain; Scotland, Ireland, and Wales being apparently 'lumped in'. Canada and the United States are similarly classed under the entirely misleading heading, 'Anglo-Saxon America'. These defects would seem to be, however, in the original report.

The conclusions arrived at are specially interesting to women. The outstanding fact would appear to be that the causes of prostitution are largely economic. The raising of the age of consent and the age of marriage are urged, both being still too low in every country. In but four is the age of consent 16 (in the United States, in parts, it is 18), while in most it is 13 or 14, and, in some, such as Florida and Esthonia, it is but 10! The age of marriage in Britain is still scandalously low, being but 12 for girls, a curious anomaly in a country which condemns child-marriages in India. The need for more policewomen is also stressed, most countries still employing none, and all of them having still far too few.

It is clear also, from the report and this summary, that there is a close connection between prostitution and the traffic on the one hand, and the economic and social condition of women on the other. Those countries that are the worst breeding-places for sexual commercialised vice are those where women are least free. France, where women are still voteless, still clings to State regulation and the licensed house while Hungary, Portugal and Japan insist upon maintaining it, the last-named naively alleging that 'its origin is rooted in centuries-old tradition, and its abolition would, therefore, have serious social reactions, for it would be practically equivalent to the complete suppression of prostitution'. Germany, on the other hand, has just abolished the licensed house, and other countries, where women have won freedom, are gradually banning it. Another result of women's emancipation is that, notably in the USA, increasing emphasis is being given to the part played by man in prostitution. In 12 of the United States the man no longer belongs to the 'protected sex', and is punished equally with the woman with whom he has immoral relations, being by legal definition also classed as a prostitute. This excellent summary is well indexed. It is commended warmly to every feminist and to every social reformer.

Mary Anne Disraeli, by James Sykes. Ernest Benn. 10s. 6d.
The Vote, 5 October 1928
This is the first life of that curious and remarkable woman, Viscountess Beaconsfield, created by Queen Victoria, at Disraeli's own request, a peeress in her own right. Mr Sykes' penetrating and sympathetic study removes many myths that had sprung up around her, and shows the triumph of personality over social inequality, disparity in age, physical unattractiveness, lack of culture and breeding. He succeeds where more pretentious biographers of Disraeli have failed in making husband and wife more human and real to us; in itself, by the way, quite an achievement, for hitherto the sphinx-like, showy Oriental has been most manifest in portraits of 'Dizzy' and in those of his wife, the grotesque and vulgar old woman. Disraeli's tributes to his Mary Anne, like John Stuart Mill's to his Harriet, have been represented as exaggerated by the male biographer, who dubs such manifestations as mere 'uxoriousness'. Oh, for a woman artist in words to give us the pendant some day to fit a wife's undue devotion, a term lacking to our vocabulary! Those 'twelve years older than her husband' loom so large in Disraeli's biographies that it is invariably hinted that her money was her chief, if not her only, attraction. The present biographer does not, however, fall into such error; he faithfully strives, by delving into contemporary anecdotage, to give a true and sympathetic portrait, devoting an interesting chapter, by way of introduction, to the wives of Victorian Prime Ministers, an almost unexplored field and another evidence that women, even Victorians, are at last coming into their own. In his foreword to the volume, A. G. Gardiner thus sums up this strange couple: 'He was a poseur to the world, but he wanted a refuge from the pose, and he found it in the good-natured, volatile little lady who worshipped him, kept his housekeeping accounts in order, trimmed, and, it was suspected, dyed his hyacinthine locks, plastered down his famous curl, pulled the strings of his shower-bath, and saw that he came home to a well-lit room and an abundant table, no matter at what hour.'

This compendium of the whole duty of wives of great men is only redeemed from absurdity by the pendant picture of Disraeli's knightly devotion.

At her graveside – made Viscountess at 76, she died at 80 – he is depicted as the living embodiment of woe, 'regardless of the heavy rain, standing for full ten minutes in the sodden grass, the cold wind playing with his suspiciously black hair, turning up streaks of white in unexpected places. "He'll have no one to dye his hair for him now," somebody said.' And there is another picture of this 'little woman's' pluck that stamps her as truly great in her passion of devotion: 'Once, driving with her husband to the House, her hand was caught in the carriage door by a careless footman. The pain was excruciating, but no sound escaped her lips, lest his equanimity be disturbed on the eve of one of his great speeches.' No wonder Disraeli described her as 'the soul of his home'. One lays it down, loving, like Disraeli, his Mary Anne, and feeling a little nearer to the great man himself. For Disraeli owed much to women, and acknowledged his debt. And one likes human nature a little better, too, after one has read this singular and romantic love story, as here told by Mr Sykes.

Halcyon, or the Future of Monogamy, by Vera Brittain. Kegan Paul. Price 2s. 6d.
The Vote, 25 October 1929
In this volume, in the stimulating and versatile 'Today and Tomorrow Series', the author, a well-known feminist, deals with marriage, and by means of a dream-fantasy, cleverly and tellingly worked out, shows how, after many vicissitudes, the institution monogamy will eventually triumph. But first she arraigns marriage as we know it, finding it guilty of much of our resent misery and muddle. Within the convenient framework of a dream, Vera Brittain manages to work off many daring and original suggestions – much is permitted as long as one shifts one's ground some centuries ahead.

Victorian and Georgian pruderies, taboos, inhibitions, shibboleths, come in for deserved satire – our silly euphemisms, our indirect 'polite' terminology – how funny they are made to seem to this Professor Minerva Huxterwin of the 21st century. How many words are still avoided by cumbrous circumlocutions, even in this 20th century. I recall a personal experience when first women were appointed on Dublin's City Council – a colleague, not daring to refer, even indirectly, to venereal disease (though a grant to a city hospital for treatment was on our agenda) found a way out by asking us to turn our downcast eyes to the 'fourth word of the second-last line on page 21'.

The instruction of the young in sex-knowledge, companionate marriages, censorship in Dublin, Tennessee, and Westminster are among the topics touched upon, while the ban upon married women working at their professions is rightly censured as a factor tending to discredit marriage. The victory of monogamy finally came when all such restrictions went. The period 1930–1975 is covered in Chapter II, which deals with various sexual reforms. The servility of assuming a man's name and nationality automatically with his marriage-ring, 'with full panoply of veil and vegetable decorations', the archaic imposition of the word 'obey' in the marriage service, and the general failure of 19th and 20th century marriage to live up to its monogamistic professions – all these points are touched upon. Television, easy travel, broadcasting, and the 'talkies' are represented as strengthening monogamy because they help to break into the monotony of the home.

It is impossible to summarise adequately this little volume packed with explosives as it is. It is challenging, and provocative, and essentially sane and sound. And, as it is all a dream, no one can really feel offended, for who can control dream-vagaries? The next time I have something startling to say, I think I'll dream it. Meanwhile, I shall seek out everything Vera Brittain publishes, and I advise all feminists to do the same.

Susan B. Anthony: The Woman Who Changed the Mind of a Nation, by Rheta Childe Dorr. New York: Frederick Stokes. Price 5 dollars.
The Vote, 14 February 1930

There have been several fully documented and painstaking lives of this great American feminist pioneer. Valuable as these works are, however, the present one stands out alone, giving us not only Susan B. Anthony, as she lived, but making the reader also realize the background from which she emerged and the well-nigh insuperable obstacles and difficulties that she and the other brave women-pioneers had to face and to overcome. It is a book that does one's soul good to read, recording as it does the victories of the indomitable woman spirit, making one's heart warm towards these women who blazed the trail and making one glad to think that, however incomplete, even to-day, woman's emancipation is, she never again will have to face the bitter prejudices, the soul-numbing taboos of seventy years ago.

It is a pleasant sign of the times that there are so many biographies of great women, written by women, for women. Yet, as the author points out, when Susan B. Anthony died at the ripe age of 86, in 1906, the final goal of complete political enfranchisement for women, had, after fifty years' activity, not yet been reached. Then only four Western States and Finland had the vote. Though much else such as higher education, the opening up of various avenues of industry, the lifting of various male bans, had been accomplished, men had not yet dared to give women citizenship. Judged by ordinary standards her life had been 'a study in failure' – yet what a blossoming-time was coming. By the time the century of her birth had rounded, November, 1920, the women of America were voting and in a few more years most of the countries that had hung back or, like Great Britain, gave only partial citizenship with a silly age-limit, had swung into line. This impetus is largely due to the spirit of Susan B. Anthony, for she was the first among the leaders of her time to aim at carrying the United States, not piecemeal, state by state, but by federal amendment. The later militants of the USA, headed by Alice Paul (herself a disciple of the militants in England), pinned their faith upon the Susan B. Anthony amendment and won.

Susan B. Anthony was neither a writer nor a great orator. Nor was she a statesman nor a politician. What she possessed was a genius for leadership and organization. She was, in fact, a great, a supreme general. As far back as the Civil War she declared that the charter of woman's liberties must be written into the constitution itself. Complete victory, not armistice or shambling compromise, was her objective.

She was brought up in a Quaker environment, a child of unusual parents. Her mother, Lucy Read, gave up her beautiful voice on the altar of matrimony, this being one of the gravest crimes urged against her by the elders. Except for cradle tunes she was never to raise her voice in song again. Susan had a struggle to learn long division, which the male pundits of the time considered unwomanly! Some writer ought one day to tabulate and check up all these curious male taboos, religious, social, political, economic, sartorial. They would make an illuminating contribution to the history of the male. Lucy Anthony's 'protected' wifehood included such tasks as baking, cooking, washing, spinning, weaving, and sewing, in addition to the production of a large family, and the care of eleven boarders! Susan, in spite of many difficulties, set out to be a teacher, and to equip herself accordingly. In those days only one obscure college admitted women students. No woman, unaccompanied by a man, was admitted into a restaurant or hotel. If you travelled your men-folk brought you sandwiches after they had dined, and real tragedy was, according to her biographer, to turn Susan's mind definitely from marriage. 'Her dearly-loved cousin, Margaret, gave birth to a fourth child and after lingering several weeks in suffering, meekly died. Lingering over her sick bed, Susan witnessed an incident which shocked her. Margaret's husband, supposed to be a very good example indeed, complained to his dying wife that he had a bad headache. "I have had one for days," ventured Margaret. "Oh, yes," said Joseph, "but I mean that I have a real headache, yours is just a *natural consequence!*"'

The first Women's Rights Convention was held in Seneca Falls, New York, in 1848, and was the direct outcome of the protest movement launched by American women against their status. Here the women drew up their Declaration of Independence. Sixty-eight women and thirty-two men signed the resolutions, eleven in number, laying down such principles (then revolutionary, now obvious), as equality of education, the opening of professions and industry to women, free speech and participation of women in public affairs. The only resolution not adopted unanimously was one which called for the franchise – that was too revolutionary even for such an assembly. Of the women who voted for it only one lived to record her vote, over seventy years after! The first reaction, however, was immediate, when many of the signatories hastily withdrew their names, unable to bear the storm of vituperation and ridicule poured upon them. 'They had expected disapproval, but atheists and hermaphrodites they were not prepared to be branded.' We later suffragettes had much worse, and infinitely more varied terms thrown at us. However, in 1848, as later, the leaders remained undisturbed by the commotion.

Interesting developments followed as the movement grew. It is instructive to see how other reforms, such as the abolition of slavery and the emancipation of the negro, the temperance crusade, the struggle for educational equality, that sprang from the co-operation of women, got through on their backs, as it were, still keeping suffrage back. Time and again men (and some women) urged their special reform, pleading 'not just yet' to the appeal of women urging that their emancipation be taken up next. Here is the story that I like best about Susan B. Anthony. The incident occurred when Wendell Phillips asked the Equal Rights Association, built up by Susan B. Anthony, Cady Stanton and others, after how much toil and sacrifice, to forego all plans for woman suffrage, and work only for the negro and the 14th amendment. It was 'The negro's hour', and his claim was paramount. Therefore, it was women's patriotic duty to petition for the removal of the word 'white' in the constitution, leaving the word 'male' as it stood. And next time – perhaps in 20 years, perhaps not so long – the woman's turn would come.

'Susan's gaze turned to Mrs Stanton, but she, as if hypnotised . . . sat smiling and apparently acquiescent. Walking closer to the group, Susan thrust out her arm at full length. "Look at this, all of you," she said. "And hear me swear that I will cut off this right arm of mine before I will ever work for or demand the ballot for the negro and not the woman."' Her timely protest at least rallied the outstanding women leaders to her to continue the fight undaunted by the defection of the men.

The author claims that Susan B. Anthony, not her disciple Emmeline Pankhurst, invented militant suffragism. 'Susan was always militant. To a group of reformers who adopted prayer as one of their chief weapons against vice, Susan said, "Frederick Douglass used to tell me that when he was a Maryland slave and a good Methodist, he would go into the farthest corner of the tobacco field and pray God to bring him liberty; but God never answered his prayers until he prayed with his heels."'

Susan B. Anthony, Elizabeth Cady Stanton and Lucretia Mott have their sculptured monument today in the Capitol at Washington. These women have written their names eternally upon the history of their times, and this volume is a fine record of the greatest of the three, Susan B. Anthony.

'*An Phoblacht* at the Abbey'
An Phoblacht, 8 March 1930

Last week saw a revival of a classic, W. B. Yeats' poetic drama, *The Countess Cathleen*, dedicated to Maud Gonne, who also inspired his *Kathleen ni Houlihan*. It is a pity that the present generation of playgoers has so few opportunities of seeing the heroic plays of Yeats and other early Abbey dramatists – *Deirdre*, *The Hour-Glass*, *On Baile's Strand* would well repay revival, while some of Lady Gregory's historical pieces would also more than justify themselves. *Countess Cathleen* is a play on an Irish 'Faust' *motif*: it seems hard to understand now why rival bands of University students (pro and con) demonstrated with passion over it. Some called it pagan to barter one's soul for one's starving people; others glorified the sacrifice. But, as in Faust's case, heaven did not, apparently, disapprove, for Cathleen, too, is saved, for

> The Light of Lights
> Looks on the motive, not the deed,
> The Shadow of Shadows on the deed alone.

The 'demons, disguised as merchants', were well played by Mr McCormick and Mr Dolan, though the former was hardly devil enough; Eileen Crowe made a lovely and appealing, but not a heroic, Cathleen; Mary Craig, as Mary, wife of the starving peasant, Seamus Rua, was altogether satisfying. The scene where the auction of souls takes place culminating in Cathleen's death gives the poet at his best and is full of poignant beauty:

> The people starve . . .
> I hear a cry from them
> And it is in my ears by night and day.

And again –

> A sad resolve wakes in me. I have heard
> A sound of wailing, in unnumbered moods,
> And I must go down, down – I know not where –
> Pray for all men and women mad with famine,

pleads Cathleen, striking her bargain. The play would send those who see it back to the heroic text, re-reading it, and back to the heroic mood of its creation.

The Shadow of a Gunman, played after it, seemed a sad anti-climax, accompanied as it was by the yahoo shrieks that mark the reaction of the audience to O'Casey.

'When Shaw went up to Mountjoy Prison: a fragment of history'
Doctors' Delusions Crude Criminology and Sham Education, by George Bernard Shaw. Constable & Co. Price 7s. 6d.
An Phoblacht, 12 November 1932

This volume of the standard edition of Shaw's works is full of the usual Shavian doctrines or heresies, expressed with his usual force and vigour. The second section is particularly interesting, containing a forceful indictment of the whole prison system in all its dreadfulness. Here Shaw tells how he came to visit 'the Joy': –

> When I was a boy in my teens in Dublin I was asked by an acquaintance of mine who was clerk to a Crown Solicitor and had business in prisons, whether I would like to go through Mountjoy Prison, much as he would have asked me whether I would like to go through the Mint or the cellars at the docks. I accepted the invitation with my head full of dungeons and chains and straw pallets and stage gaolers: in short, of the last acts of *Il Travatore* and Gounod's *Faust* and of the Town of London in *Richard III*. I expected the warders to look like murderers, and the murderers like heroes . . . What struck me most was that the place was as bright and clean as whitewash and scrubbing could make it, with all the warders looking thoroughly respectable.

Such is the introduction to his thesis that the best prisons are really the worst, because the whole system is iniquitous. Shaw states that, though he has never himself been to prison – what opportunities he has lost! – he was frequently brought into contact with men of character who were prison victims, guilty of 'treason, sedition, obstruction, blasphemy, offences against press laws and so forth'. He quotes Karl Marx as declaring that British prisons were the cruellest in the world and Prince Kropotkin, who had experience of the worst convict prisons of Siberia and the 'best' model prison in France, saying that the difference between the worst and the best was so slight as to be negligible. Shaw concludes, 'What with European "politicals" and amnestied Irish Fenians – and he knew both kinds – none could feel easy in their conscience about the present penal system.' Reference is also made to conscientious objectors and to suffragettes, and to the searchlight which both these types of prisoners fling into the dark places of medieval torture known as prisons. Within Shaw's memory the hanging, drawing and quartering of felons was on the British statute books.

Shaw holds and, as usual, assigns much plausible ground for his belief, that public executions – 'blood sports' as he calls these entertainments – are really less cruel than solitary confinement in antiseptic and hygienic cells. The better a prison seems to be the worse in its effects for public conscience, instead of being roused to a fury against it, is deadened and doped. He considers the problems of deterrence, of vindictive punishment, of society's retribution or reprisal, the ethics of capital punishment, of the lethal chamber.

'Stone dead hath no fellow' was a handy formula for Cromwell's troops in dealing with the Irish, still that precedent is not very reassuring. Shaw is full of such wisdom packed into epigram and paradox: there is not a page that does not afford matter for quotation in a rebel's anthology and the worst of attempting to deal with a work of Shaw's is the temptation offered for unlimited quotation.

He naturally finds the prison system a relic of barbarism on the whole penal code anachronism today. On the whole he finds that prison manufactures criminals, his conclusion being that 'imprisonment cannot be fully understood by those who do not understand freedom'.

Sham Education

Shaw next castigates the evils of the British public school system (and these apply in a certain degree to our own, for much Irish education is still but a reflexion of the British system). There are times when one is reminded of Pearse's Murder Machine, for that great educator thought on similar lines, revolting also against the system that turns schools into prisons for the young. Among things discussed are corporal punishment 'ragging' (a peculiarly English form of 'education', which accounts for the playing fields of Eton and Harrow producing the Anglo-Indian administrator, examinations, on all of which themes Shaw has much to say that is worth considering. In a contribution to the Education Year Book of 1918 (the date is significant) on Schools and School Masters, reprinted in the present volume, he mentions among modern educational experiments on professional lines 'President Pearse's Sgoil Eanna'.

In the third part (the first in chronological order) Shaw repeats, reiterates and develops anew his theories (already well-known through his Plays and Prefaces) on Doctors and their Delusions. He carefully distinguishes between a reasonable belief in doctors and an unreasoning fetish-worship, repeating his not in reply to the query in an English periodical's symposium on 'Have we Lost Faith?' Certainly not: but we have transferred it from God to the General Medical Council. Shaw is one of the pillars of the anti-vaccination and anti-vivisectionist movement (he calls the former the Lister superstition). He backs up the opposition in Ireland to forcible vaccination and has wholesome advice to offer the new Irish Medical Council, urging it forward to throw off the 'despised and self-disgraced trade union, the British Medical Council'. Here is his remedy. 'Let the new body be accessible to practising doctors in the capacity of consultants only and consist exclusively of representatives of disinterested scientific culture and of the laity . . . If that condition is complied with (this was written in 1925) an Irish degree will soon stand higher than an English one and the nonsense talked about Irish students deserting our schools for foreign ones will be succeeded by complaints of our being crowded out by English youths in search of Irish qualifications.'

Whether one agrees or disagrees with Shavian theories one will find, unless one possesses the fatal disability, a closed mind, much in this volume and in *Essays in Fabian Socialism* to stimulate, exercise and divert. And few writers manage to do all this nowadays, still fewer to keep on being iconoclasts into the seventies and to thrive on it, as does G. B. S.

Women of the French Revolution, **by R. McNair Wilson. London: Hutchinson and Co. Price 18s.**
Irish Press, 2 June 1935
The author in this volume tells in historical sequence the story of the outstanding women who lived in the period immediately before, during and after the French Revolution, grouping them around that great event. Not only does he treat the women who helped on the Revolution – and these are numerous and important – but also those who opposed it and suffered for their intransigence. Queens and royal mistresses, Marie Antoinette, Madame De Barry, Madame Pompadour, patrons of art and literature, Madame de Staël, Madame Roland, empresses, Josephine and her supplanter, Marie Louise, are dealt with, a varied and colourful gallery. Only two great male personages, Napoleon and Robespierre, remain uninfluenced politically by women, driving them out of the political arena, though not from the guillotine: in both cases women played no small part in the downfall of both dictators.

Napoleon wrote at the beginning of the revolution, 'the men are in love with Liberty: they are no longer interested in women.' There were women too in love with that intoxicating goddess, as the writer shows, of many types, 'Sibyls, Egerias, feminists, soothsayers . . . vampires'. He has a bias – one is safe, I think, in assuming the masculine pronoun against the Amazon type, holding that the great mass of Frenchwomen of the time were opposed to revolution, as if it were not the active minority, of both men and women alike, who always make revolutions, though they do not always survive them.

Beauties and Blood-Suckers
The book is divided into three sections: the Beauties, reigning by the heart; the Bluestockings, by the head, and the blood-suckers, preying on the vitals of

men; it is an arbitrary and artificial classification. A pet theory of the author is also forced, namely, that the Revolution was merely a battle between the monarchy and the Money Power; according to him, from Louis XIV onwards, the kings of France were protectors of their people against money lords; in England likewise he sees Charles I losing his head, a martyr to his struggle against the inventors of the gold corner, while William of Orange was its champion. So the women are also grouped, the author being at great pains to make his case, with the same energy and ingenuity that some writers have brought to proving that Bacon is responsible for Shakespeare, and with as much success.

If one forgets the fantastic thesis and reads just for entertainment the book will be found not lacking in such material, with its court intrigues and backstairs gossip of the *valet de chamber* type. As the battle is waged, not between the people and their kings, but rather 'between the daughter of the Caesars and Madame Necker, the daughter of a moneylender', so Marie Antoinette becomes one of its martyrs, while Charlotte Corday is 'the angel of the assassination'. Madame Roland's stature on the other hand is lessened: she becomes merely a narrow Puritan. Passing on to the Napoleonic era, Josephine and Letizia, the emperor's flighty first wife and his grim peasant mother loom large. To Marie Louise the author gives the last word, 'the means of supporting the plan for drawing gold out of London'. Sixteen portraits illustrate the text.

'The "Big House"'
An Irishman and His Family, by Maud Wynne. London: John Murray. Price 10s. 6d.
Irish Press, 27 April 1937
This book, written by his daughter, is the chatty chronicle of a famous and gifted Irish peer, Lord Chief Justice of Ireland in the eighties and later Lord of Appeal in London. A Catholic, a dyed-in-the-wool Conservative, Irish withal in his very marrow and a clannish Galwegian at that, 'Himself' as he is fondly called, as painted by a loving but by no means uncritical daughter, is a delightful character, an odd amalgam of diverse qualities and a tragic figure because (on account of his origin and outlook) neither firmly rooted in his native soil, nor really belonging at heart to the Imperial world of London. There is a moral in the tale, though not one that the author herself would point perhaps: the missed opportunities of the Irish gentry, their frustrations because of their divided allegiance. The book is full of good stories; we glimpse high personages from the transient English chief secretaries and English visitors to Ireland (paying flying visits with political notions) whose complacency and ignorance are pilloried, to figures like Lecky, Oscar Wilde, Emily Lawless, the witty raconteur Father Healy of Bray; the Gore-Booths. By an odd irony

of life Constance Gore-Booth, afterwards Countess Markievicz, was brides-
maid to the writer, with Lady Rachel Wyndham Quin, both cousins of the
bridegroom – 'they were dressed in a soft pinky, silky stuff with tunics of
Carrickmacross lace, Shamrock pattern, white hats and pink roses.' As it was
a mixed marriage there was neither music nor flowers, she adds. Later she gives
a quaint (but very biased) picture of a visit to Sligo town with Lady Gore-
Booth in 1922–23: they were stopped by Free Staters as well as Republicans
and had to get a permit from each side before proceeding.

The Anglo-Irish War

On the Anglo-Irish war period the writer has also a good store of racy
anecdotes and shrewd observations. But her prejudices emerge often as in her
tribute to the bravery of the Black and Tans 'who carried their lives on their
finger-tips'. She tells of meeting one at Sligo station. 'He had a pistol in his
hand, strapped to his wrist, which he constantly kept clicking and another
strapped to his leg, he had a dagger sort of knife in his breast pocket and
bombs in each side pocket, that was his active service equipment. He was a
nice little man, debonair, who bore no grudges, ready to take life or death as
they came. His eyes were ceaselessly on the alert, his finger on the trigger. He
warned me not to come too close and pointing out a couple of children who
had edged near us he said in a quiet voice, "They are spies."' We are not told
how these 'spies' were armed.

The Big House at Spiddal (the author records proudly how she and her
husband entertained the Bedfordshires with tennis parties at her place in
Sligo) eventually went the way of other Big Houses. One is conscious of how
she and her family loved it – she tells bitterly why she does not want to see
Ireland again. In spite of all this (a congenital defect for which one can no
more blame those afflicted than one could for physical short-sight) the book
is interesting for its graphic pictures of a day that is dead and a race that has
vanished, a race not without its qualities, like the Czar's nobility or the pre-
revolution French aristocrats. And I like 'Himself' best of all.

H.S. S.

17

OBITUARIES OF HANNA SHEEHY SKEFFINGTON

'Hanna Sheehy Skeffington'
Bakery Trades Journal, April–June 1946
Desmond Ryan

HANNA SHEEHY SKEFFINGTON belonged to that rare class, small in any age, whose contemporaries take for granted not only that they cannot but that they should not die like the rest of us. And when they do, then surprise and resentment possess us. It is characteristic of Mrs Sheehy Skeffington that she was correcting the proofs of her last pamphlet within a month of her death, and that in one of the last articles she wrote she jested about the excessively musical character so often given to heaven. For music, she had not the enthusiasm she had for books, and in this article she expressed the hope that in the other world there were libraries as well as orchestras, adding with that flash of wit she could bring into the most serious discussion, 'after all, we are told that there are many mansions'.

During the last year, Mrs Skeffington undertook at last the task that probably no other living person could do better: to write her life-story. Fortunately, she succeeded in finishing more than a third of these memoirs, while over the years she had written and told to many audiences the more important phases of her remarkable and militant life. Her last pamphlet, which is published by the *Kerryman* at sixpence, *British Militarism As I Have Known It*, is the story of Francis Sheehy Skeffington, the pacifist whose murder, after he restrained the looters in the insurrection of 1916 and fell into the clutches of the notorious Bowen Colthurst (whether told in the pamphlet or in the hardly more restrained language of the Simon Report) must still move every reader to horror even in a generation well hardened to organised sadism and neurosis in uniform obscured or glorified by subtle propaganda.

To be sure, Portobello Barracks in 1916, even with a Colthurst so domi-nating his dithering subordinates and superiors that a London journal of the time tartly said it was a mercy that he had not ordered them all to shoot themselves as they certainly would have obeyed him, was more a panic-ridden garrison than a Belsen. Moreover, in Portobello there was what he himself termed the 'fortunate accident' of Sir Francis Vane, who, at the cost of his own career, unmasked the Skeffington murder and turned the fierce light of publicity on Dublin Castle methods. A letter of Vane's here printed for the first time has, as Mrs Skeffington noted, 'some strangely topical illusions'.

Pending the publication of her memoirs, there is much in this small booklet which will recall the writer to her friends. Her retort, for instance, when a certain officer regretted that they had not shot her, too: 'It would have saved them (and me) much trouble if they had.' It also recalls her power of ironic description in this flash of Asquith tactfully trying to shelve an inquiry with an offer of 'adequate even generous compensation'. Here is the picture: 'Mr Asquith now putting this point ever so delicately (it was clearly his object in sending for me) tapping his fingers on the green baize table – he sat with his secretary in the middle, and my friend and I at the end – and glancing sideways at me, for he never looked me straight in the face throughout the interview. He is mellow and hale with rosy, chubby face and silver hair, a Father Christmas air about him.'

A record of militant agitation in the women's suffrage struggle Mrs Skeffington and her husband already possessed. From then onwards, she carried on in two continents her campaign for Irish freedom, which to her was nothing more or less than that defined in Connolly's Worker's Republic. Of the power of that propaganda this pamphlet is eloquent as it flashes out in such phrases as this:

> I knew the Irish Republican leaders, and am proud to call Connolly, Pearse, MacDonagh, Plunkett, O'Rahilly and others, friends – proud to have known them and had their friendship . . . They were filled with idealism . . . Their proclamation gave equal citizenship to women, beating all records, except that of the Russian Revolutionists, and their Revolution came later. It is the dreamers and the visionaries that keep hope alive and feed enthusiasm. Sometimes it is harder to live for a cause than to die for it. It would be a poor tribute to my husband if grief were to break my spirit. It shall not do so. I am not here to harrow your hearts by a passing thrill, to feed you on horrors for sensation's sake . . . At the end of the war we hope to see a 'United Europe' on the model of your own United States, where each state is free and independent, yet all part of a great federation. We want Ireland to belong to this united Europe, and not to be a vassal of Great Britain, governed without consent.

Thirty years later, after experiences of struggle, imprisonment, the passage of wars in Ireland and abroad, Mrs Skeffington stubbornly hoped on. She had battled valiantly for the just against the unjust, with pertinacity, with wit and more intellect than any Irishwoman of her time. One thing will die out with the memories of those who knew her unless she has left it for other times in her memoirs, a gracious, unbending, humorous personality who loved a garden and a book as much as she loved a battle in any good cause at all. Uncompromising as she was in those innumerable battles, yet she was never vindictive, bitter, petty. Indeed, she perplexed some of her jailors by her urbanity. To her delight once, she was housed in a condemned cell with the apology that it was the most cosy spot in that Northern prison. Politics even never obsessed her to the exclusion of a good laugh. Of certain politicians with whom she worked somewhat uneasily she said gaily: 'They suspect me. I should suspect myself if they didn't!' Such was Hanna Sheehy Skeffington, a woman whose like we shall not see soon again. Some of the immortal part of her is happily preserved in the memories of her friends, and in this little book.

'Hanna Sheehy Skeffington'
Irish Times, 23 April 1946
Cathal O'Shannon

HANNA SHEEHY SKEFFINGTON, I would say, was the ablest of the women we have had in public life in the Ireland of the last 30 or 40 years. Among them, she stood apart, and in some respects she had a place of her own even among those of her political class and calibre in America and Great Britain. That distinction impressed many who observed her at gatherings of leading women from different countries.

For one thing, she seemed to have more of a masculine mind than any of her sex in Irish politics. She would not thank me for saying so, but that is how she always struck me. Now that does not at all mean that there was anything commonly called 'mannish' about her actions, or her interests, or her demean-our, or her appearance. And it does not mean that she aped in any way her opposite sex or fashioned herself that way. It was her approach to affairs that created that feeling. She spoke and acted and shaped her course as a person endowed with more sheer intellect, and making fuller use of it, than any of the women who were her contemporaries. That and the rare gift of very definite logic and reasoning power gave her outlook and her expression of it, an air of coldness and hardness which the inner reality did not really altogether justify. The truth is that she had schooled herself to exercise her reasoning powers and intellectual qualities in the coolest and calmest manner, and the smooth, equable, excellently ordered and modulated speech in which she spoke her mind was the natural product of that process of discipline.

Fires under Control
To think that what she said or did sprang from any lack of emotion or any iciness of heart or nature would be to misjudge her badly. Fires burned deep

within her – indeed, some burned into her from outside, like the murder of her husband – but unlike many Irish public speakers, men as well as women, she had them under her own sure control. Sunburstry and rhetoric of the all too familiar brand, and loose, slovenly thinking, were not, as too frequently with others, the general stock in trade with Hanna Skeffington. That was one of her qualities I appreciated most even when I was most in disagreement with what she was saying or supporting. In that she could not rightfully be classed among 'wild women', although in another way she was a more dangerous adversary than some who would fall within that category.

She was not of the effusive, romantic type of some of her friends. I do not think that type is either to be despised or to be derided, and neither did she. It has its place and its work but these were not hers. She was deliberate in everything – calculating, if any prefer that word – determined in everything, ruthless in much – unscrupulous at times, to my way of thinking – but the most determined and most self-willed woman in any of the movements she took up. All that was the result of her step by step and point by point approach to problems until, she had, by real process of thought, reached conclusions that satisfied her.

Clever Speaker

As a public speaker she was in a class by herself, and in irony, humour, quickness of wit and sharp, penetrating thrust a real delight. In private conversation, to these were added a warmth and a kindness sometimes held back in public. Her oratory was mostly critical, often destructive, always analytical, never dull, never boring, never empty. She was a grand fighter with pen and tongue. She had all the arts and the tricks of the great conversationalist, knew how and when to use this one, and how and when that one, and, if sometimes she hit below the belt, she hit with grace and dexterity that compelled admiration, sometimes even from her unfortunate victim.

If I were asked what her politics were I would have to admit that I could not give myself a satisfactory answer, although I knew her from 1912 or 1913 onwards, and often campaigned with her. First and foremost, and above all, and maybe last as well as first, she was a feminist. And as a feminist, she was an internationalist and a libertarian in things of the mind and the spirit as in all else. I doubt if she was quite the Tolstoyan pacifist Francis Sheehy Skeffington was, and yet, perhaps, but for his death, and the terrible circumstances of his death, and the turn affairs took in Ireland, she might have been our companion with him in that, too.

Advanced Feminist

As a feminist she had something of an air of superiority to men in politics and in literature, and in everything she was devastatingly outspoken. But in much she was far ahead of some feminists I could name. To a degree, she was militant, but I do not think a militant to the point of violence, although I confess I often enough asked how she found herself in the same galley with the most violent of comrades. Was it that, unlike her husband, she was no pacifist? Her resoluteness, her hunger-strikes and her sacrifices are no clue, for in them her husband was her peer.

She was nationalist and separatist and republican. And she was these on principle, just as she was anti-imperialist on principle, and against censorship of thought, although, like her husband, she could be a protesting party at an Abbey Theatre play. She was all these because she was opposed to oppression and dominance as much of a State or a class or a system as of a sex. But the restrictions and shackles of a party she could not abide; she was too independent and individualist for that.

Before 1916 she was not of Sinn Féin, nor before or after it, I think, of Cumann na mBan, and when she was in Sinn Féin in a later phase, neither she nor Sinn Féin could have been very happy about it. I believe that in 1918 she could have had a constituency if she had accepted it. Maybe she felt rightly that that was not the proper choice for her.

No, in politics, as in nearly everything, Hanna Sheehy Skeffington was herself and a free-lance of freedom and liberty. But what a great freelance she was!

'Late Mrs Hanna Sheehy Skeffington'
Workers Review (Dublin), May 1946
Editorial Board

It is with feelings of profound regret that we record the death at her home in Dublin, on April 20th, after a short illness, of Mrs Hanna Sheehy Skeffington.

As a young woman she entered public life alongside her husband, Francis Sheehy Skeffington, and was soon a foremost figure in the campaign of thirty odd years ago for Women's Suffrage. With sincerity, courage and tenacity, that were to be characteristic of her support of every cause throughout her life, she braved the bitter opposition of the ruling classes and the deliberately-fostered prejudices of large sections of the people against the recognition of women's rights. The women of Ireland and Britain, to-day enjoy the right to vote, to be elected to parliament and public bodies and to qualify for most public positions, thanks to the tenacious struggle of women like Mrs Skeffington, and the active support of the Socialist leaders of the time and the more intelligent Labour leaders. James Connolly was always a forcible advocate of women's rights.

Mrs Skeffington, who was an able public speaker and a prolific writer never tired in both her speeches and writings to express her admiration for James Connolly and not only for his progressive views on women's rights but for his Socialist teachings. James Connolly, along with Michael Davitt were two men she held in special esteem and just before illness overtook her she was endeavouring to interest publishers to reprint her husband's forthright biography of Michael Davitt.

During the 1913 Dublin workers' strike Mrs Skeffington and her husband were ardent champions of the workers' cause.

In the week of the Easter Uprising, 1916, her husband, who held pronounced pacifist views and was a vigorous supporter of republican and socialist principles, embarked on the formation of a citizen's committee to prevent looting and wanton destruction of property by elements entirely unconnected with the Uprising. He was seized, taken to Portobello barracks, put against a wall and shot. In a face-saving attempt the British Government put forward the plea that the officer responsible for the murder of Francis Skeffington was insane. Mrs Skeffington contemptuously refused an offer of compensation; she was refused permission to travel to America because she would not give an undertaking that she would not inform the American public of the facts of her husband's death and about Irish affairs generally; she succeeded, however, in beating the British Government's ban, reached America and there, to the great annoyance of the British rulers, addressed hundreds of meetings and wrote articles for many papers. The widespread support that was accorded by the Irish population in the US and Americans generally for the War of Independence (1916–21) was in no small measure due to the energies of Mrs Skeffington during her speaking tour in that country.

Back in Ireland in 1918, she was arrested and lodged in Holloway Prison. This was not her first prison experience, as she served a sentence in Mountjoy in 1912 in connection with the fight for women's suffrage. She opposed the Treaty settlement of 1921 and was a prominent figure at most meetings held in protest against the wholesale arrests and executions under the Cosgrave Government.

She visited the Soviet Union in 1929 and was very much impressed with the social developments in that country. She related her impressions of the Soviet Union at meetings held under the auspices of the Irish Friends of the Soviet Union and other auspices.

In 1933 she defied the Six-County Government's ban on her entering into that territory, spoke at a meeting in Newry and was arrested. Refusing to give an undertaking, she served a month's imprisonment in Armagh jail.

We especially remember Mrs Skeffington's outspoken defence of the Communists in Dublin, when they were being attacked by clerical and fascist-blueshirt inspired mobs. When their offices (Connolly House) were being attacked, she was, along with another grand old fighter, Mrs Connery, assailed by a section of the mob. The police on that occasion did not busy themselves to prevent the scandalous scene of an angry mob attacking two women.

In 1936 when the fascist-supported generals of Spain launched war on the Spanish Republic, Mrs Skeffington immediately revealed on which side she stood. By correspondence to the papers, at public meetings and as President of the Irish Friends of the Spanish Republic, she put the case for Republican Spain and along with Father O'Flanagan and many others she was an untiring worker in the organisation of support for Republican Spain and the International Brigade. Anti-fascists in Ireland and throughout the world will mourn the passing of this truly great woman.

From the beginning she was a keen supporter of our journal and in the October, 1945, number she contributed an article entitled 'Women MPs in Britain'.

In her, the cause of Irish freedom had no better champion, though every cause that sought to uplift people, no matter where, received her full support. She intensely hated imperialism because she realised that so long as that system holds sway there can never be national and social freedom for the people.

With her passing Ireland has lost a really outstanding woman, and the working class a genuine friend.

'Hanna Sheehy Skeffington: an appreciation'
Irish Press, 27 April 1946
Anna Kelly
Hanna Sheehy Skeffington's great heart stopped too soon. She was young for her age; there were many more years left to her mind and intellect, to her frame, too, but the heart, the engine on which everything depends, was worn out.

It was worn out in the pursuit of many causes, none of them lost causes, though some of them are not fully gained yet.

To people who did not know her personally she was but a name in the newspapers. She made a great noise in her time, always in full action at the centre of memorable events.

People sometimes get a wrong impression, especially when it is a woman, of a personality so strong in public life. And especially of a woman who fought for women.

The Suffragettes
Some of that might be attributed to the old vulgar notions about the Suffragettes, who suffered more from the world's coarse thumb than did any other pioneers for freedom. These women of every class faced death and

imprisonment; manhandling by police, the torture of hunger striking and forcible feeding. Timid and retiring women steeled themselves to lead processions and create 'scenes'.

It is not so long since the echoes of the laughter died away since 'Votes for Women' ceased to be a side-splitting joke.

Some of the old notions may have stuck. There may be people who still think that Hanna Sheehy Skeffington was a nervous hectic type, one of the so-called 'wild women'.

Cool Intellect

Far from it. She was essentially a quiet woman, serene and poised. She had not the dash and romantic appeal of Madame de Markievicz, for instance, but she had more intellect and more understanding.

It was a very cool intellect, sharp as a sword, and it was the only sword she believed in. In debate she showed great logic and reasoning power. She had an absolute grasp of first principles and never twisted or turned. She never lost her temper. She never played on her sex as many women do. This used to infuriate her men opponents who, to their astonishment, found themselves baffled on their own ground. She hated humbug and codology. She hated injustice in all forms, from the injustice of war to injustice to animals. Spirit, courage and character she had to a high degree.

Warm-Hearted

With all that she was very human and warm-hearted. The photograph I have selected is the one I like best of my beloved 'Skeffy'. You can see the twinkle in her eye. She had great wit and humour. She liked clothes and dressed well, always wore becoming hats. She got great fun out of the minor pleasures of life, gardens, flowers, going to the theatre, and the pictures. She'd go off by herself with her modest shilling and sit in the back seats of the theatre. She would meet her sisters, Mrs Kettle and Mrs Casey to go to the pictures as happy as larks. She was no hard-boiled highbrow.

Neither was she a 'frustrated female'. Another opinion held by the unenlightened is that whenever women agitate for something more serious than new hats they must be either old maids with nothing better to do or women whose private life holds so much unhappiness that they must escape from it. Wrong again in this case. Hanna Sheehy Skeffington was a happy woman in her private life.

Her marriage was one of those rare unions which combine intellectual comradeship and love. Her 'Frank', dead this thirty years, never died in her mind. She would bring his name into conversation as if they had been together but a moment before. The tragic pity of that. With what wonderful courage she had sublimated her bitter loss.

Her son adored her, she had the joy of being a grandmother. Seldom are sisters of a family so united in affectionate friendship as were the four Sheehy sisters when they were all alive.

I give these little family touches to show that her life as a woman was fully rounded and fulfilled.

Father Sheehy

It was her uncle, Father Eugene Sheehy of Bruree, a Fenian priest, who loved her, spoiled her and taught her rebellion and fine literature.

She was born in Kanturk, but spent most of the first nine years of her life at Loughmore, Co. Tipperary. Her father, the Fenian David Sheehy, had a mill there and she remembered the mill wheel and the mill race as part of her childhood setting. She loved the mill, the village and the people. She had a great affection for Tipperary and Limerick. Her first schooling was at the old national school there and although the Sheehy family left for Dublin in 1886 some of the old people still remember them. Old Mrs Bourke remembered Hanna sitting on the school benches of Loughmore.

Feminist

Her dominant passion was feminism. She was out to raise the status of women. A girl said to me once, 'I like Mrs Skeffington, but she's too much out for women.' You might as well say that Éamon de Valera was 'too much out' for Ireland or Jim Larkin for the working man. She was a leader and a leader has to be a propagandist, hammering home the one idea all the time.

Proclamation

'Just before the Rising,' says R. M. Fox in his book, *Rebel Irishwomen*, Connolly came to Mrs Skeffington and said: 'You will be glad to know that in the Proclamation of the Irish Rebellion we are including equal citizenship for women.'

'I know who is responsible for that,' she replied.

'We were practically unanimous,' said Connolly. 'Only one questioned it.'

'Actually,' Fox goes on to say, 'the Skeffingtons were more responsible than anyone else, for their ceaseless agitation had kept the question to the front. It is probably their initial work which has resulted in equal suffrage being part of the Constitution in Ireland to-day.'

Irishwomen can crown this enduring monument to her memory by carrying on the work she began, but did not live to finish.

'In memoriam: Hanna Sheehy Skeffington'
Women's Bulletin, 10 May 1946
M. Reaves
It is with great sorrow that we record the death, during the Easter weekend of our loved friend and colleague Mrs Sheehy Skeffington.

Until the war Mrs Skeffington was a frequent visitor to London, where her ready wit, her great ability as a speaker, and her warm personal affection for her English friends – however divergent their political outlook – made her popular and welcome in any gathering.

Mrs Skeffington was a keen suffragist and went to prison during the militant movement. For many years she has kept us in touch with the Women's movement in Ireland.

She leaves with us a fragrant memory of loyalty and devotion to those causes in which she believed, and the women's movement everywhere is the poorer for her passing.

Our sympathy goes to her many friends in Ireland, particularly to her son, and to her sister, Mrs Kettle.

Notes

1   This was to be the start of 'Hanna's House', a project that continued even after it became clear that the physical house was not appropriate for this.

1   MS 41,190, Sheehy Skeffington Papers, NLI, Dublin.

2   Peadar O'Donnell, left-wing republican, editor of *An Phoblacht*, and later first editor of *The Bell*.

3   Hanna did not add a name to this.

4   Hanna is incorrect, the date was May 1882.

5   W. T. Stead, campaigning journalist, feminist, supporter of Esperanto (which was popularised in the journal), published the *Review of Reviews* from 1890–3. Many of his causes would have been supported by the Sheehy Skeffingtons. He drowned in the sinking of the *Titanic* in 1912.

6   Hanna circled the word 'free' and added a question mark but did not elaborate.

7   Space left in manuscript but no poem added.

8   This is a handwritten manuscript.

9   Nora Connolly, daughter of James Connolly, an activist with Belfast Cumann na mBan, who visited her father in Dublin Castle shortly before his execution. Margaret Skinnider had been badly wounded while participating in the Rising and subsequently hospitalised, thereby escaping imprisonment. Her autobiography *Doing My Bit for Ireland* was published in America in 1917.

10   Hanna had stayed there in December 1915, having travelled to Liverpool to greet Frank on his return from America where he had gone following his release under the 'Cat and Mouse Act' after imprisonment for anti-recruiting activities. Sean McDermott had also been prosecuted.

11   Defence of the Realm Act, passed in August 1914, enabling the government to imprison without trial.

12   This is a handwritten manuscript.

13   Hanna included (* footnote) at this point, undoubtedly intending to give details of Frank's murder on the orders of Bowen-Colthurst.

14   Margaret Culhane née Sheehy had been widowed in March 1916, left with four young children.

15   Hanna and Frank had rejected religion. In later years Hanna described herself as a 'pagan'.

16 Charlotte Despard née French was a founder of the Women's Freedom League and a member of the British Labour Party. She was a pacifist and highly critical of her brother, John French, commander of the British forces and later lord lieutenant of Ireland. Charlotte settled in Ireland after the war, supporting the republican cause, sharing her home Roebuck House with Maud Gonne MacBride. The Minerva Club in London, set up by the WFL, organised meetings and had a hostel for activists. In the inter-war years Hanna was a frequent speaker at its meetings.

17 Mary Kettle née Sheehy was the third of the four Sheehy sisters and a life-long feminist and activist. Tom Kettle was killed at the Somme in 1916.

18 Edward Shortt was a Liberal Party politician and chief secretary for Ireland 1916–19.

19 A subtle dig by Hanna, revealing her sense of betrayal, recalling Shakespeare and Julius Caesar's comment as he is assassinated, with Brutus last to make a stab, 'Et tu, Brute?'

20 This is a handwritten manuscript.

21 William O'Brien and Cathal O'Shannon.

22 The question mark is Hanna's query. She is correct. The other four women were Jennie Wyse Power, Kathleen Clarke, Margaret McGarry and Anne Ashton. In Rathmines six out of 21 women were councillors, including Mary Kettle, Kathleen Lynn, Áine Ceannt and Madeleine ffrench-Mullen.

23 Hanna's query again. It was January 1920.

24 Unfortunately Hanna did not return to this in order to include details.

3

WOMEN, THE NATIONAL MOVEMENT AND SINN FÉIN

1 MS 22,266, Sheehy Skeffington Papers, NLI, Dublin.

2 The Kensington Society was formed in 1865; in 1897 the 17 suffrage groups then in existence in England formed the National Union of Women's Suffrage Societies, led by Millicent Fawcett from 1900. The Dublin Women's Suffrage Association formed in 1876 by Anna and Thomas Haslam had close links with this moderate reforming group.

3 Women who contributed to the *Nation* (1842–8), journal of the Young Ireland movement, included Jane Elgee, mother of Oscar Wilde, who wrote as 'Speranza', and Ellen Dempsey and Mary Kelly.

4 Negotiated by Parnell and Gladstone in May 1882, the government promised to enable tenants to negotiate rent arrears and to release Land League prisoners, under the condition that the land agitation was brought to an end. This included the disbandment of the Ladies' Land League.

5 The writing pseudonym adopted by Sydney Gifford (who wanted to sound like a Wexford farmer), one of six Gifford sisters, whose sisters Grace, Muriel and Nellie were also active in nationalist, feminist and labour movements.

6 Helena Molony.

7 On 12 May 1910 the lord mayor of Dublin travelled to London to lay the views of Dublin Corporation, supporting women's suffrage, before parliament, in accordance with a long-standing privilege.

4

VOTES FOR WOMEN

1   James and Margaret Cousins, *We Two Together* (Madras, 1950), p. 85.

2   Published in Andrée Sheehy Skeffington and Rosemary Owens, eds, *Votes for Women: Irish Women's Struggle for the Vote* (Dublin, 1975).

3   Hanna has misremembered. She and her three colleagues were fined 40s. with the alternative of one month imprisonment and 10s. bail for good behaviour or another month in default. They chose to go to prison. Suffragette Files, Box 1, Chief Secretary's Office, National Archives, Dublin.

4   Jennie Wyse Power, former member of the Ladies' Land League, Inghinidhe na hÉireann, vice-president of Sinn Féin and, in 1914, founding member of Cumann na mBan, and also a member of the IWSLGA.

5   There were in fact three members of the WSPU in Ireland. The third, Jessie Baines, with a lighter sentence, was released from prison before the other two, which was possibly why Hanna forgot her existence.

6   Home Secretary McKenna introduced the Prisoners' Temporary Discharge for Ill-Health Act in March 1913. It was soon dubbed the 'Cat and Mouse Act' by suffragettes as women refused to comply with its terms, particularly that stating that they should present themselves for re-arrest when they had recovered their health.

7   From October 1912 the authorities decided to send suffrage prisoners to Tullamore Prison, approximately 60 miles from Dublin, in order to isolate them from other prisoners and from their supporters. This was unsuccessful as they acquired a new set of supporters in Tullamore.

8   Gwynn was one of the few Irish Party MPs to support women's suffrage. In 1915 his wife May was a co-founder, with Professor Mary Hayden, of the Catholic Women's Suffrage Association.

9   Henrietta Jacob from Waterford, of Quaker background, mother of Rosamond Jacob, suffragist and republican, who was to become a close friend of Hanna's in later years.

10   Margaret (Meg) Connery, vice-chairwoman of IWFL and a close friend of Hanna's, remaining active on women's and prisoners' issues during the 1918 election, in the War of Independence and in the 1930s.

11   Reginald McKenna, MP, Home Secretary.

12   Margaret McCoubrey, originally from Scotland but married to a trade unionist and living in Belfast.

13   Sylvia Pankhurst had broken away from her mother and sister in the WSPU and in 1914 set up an explicitly socialist group, the East London Federation of Suffragettes.

14   Henry Nevinson, a British radical journalist, a founder of the Men's League for Women's Suffrage and friend of Frank and Hanna Sheehy Skeffington.

15   Dora Mellone, from Warrenpoint, born in England and daughter of a clergyman.

16   Suffragettes set up a 'Watching the Courts' Committee in 1914 to observe and report on court cases of domestic violence and sexual assault and to highlight the impact of the all-male nature of the court system.

5

WAR AND PACIFISM

1   Lecturer in Irish at University College Dublin, colleague of Mary Hayden and activist in the Gaelic League.

2   R. M. Fox, *Rebel Irishwomen* (Dublin, 1935), p. 76.

3   In 1913 Dawson Bates, secretary of the Ulster Unionist Council, wrote to state that the provisional government franchise would be on the basis of the local government register, and therefore women would have the vote. For a brief time Ulster unionists were being congratulated for this stance. However, in spring 1914 Carson, an anti-suffragist, declared he had no intention of giving women the vote. This led to the WSPU declaration of war on the Ulster unionists and months of intense militancy in the north.

4   A Latin phrase – 'Go Back to Satan!'

5   The *British Journal of Nursing* 53 (19 December 1914) contained an editorial on 'Emotional nursing'. It argued against the British Red Cross sending 'inadequately trained but socially influential ladies to serve as nurses near front lines'. Hanna's impassioned article reflected the mood of the time and indeed, was ahead of many.

6   A nurse in *Martin Chuzzlewit* by Charles Dickens, who comes to stand for a stereotype of the untrained, drunken nurse.

7   Tom Kettle, married to Hanna's sister Mary. He would be killed in September 1916 at the Somme.

8   Joe Devlin, leader of the Belfast nationalists.

9   Louie Bennett of the non-militant Irishwomen's Suffrage Federation.

10   Chrystal Macmillan and Emily Hobhouse. Emmeline Pethick-Lawrence (formerly WSPU) of the United Suffragists attended but travelled from America with the US delegates.

11   MS 24,134, Sheehy Skeffington Papers, NLI, Dublin.

12   The WSPU renamed its paper from the *Suffragette* to *Britannia* and received funding from government to encourage women to enlist in the war effort.

6

DEATH OF A PACIFIST

1   T. M. Healy, *Letters and Leaders of My Day*, vol. 2 (London, 1928), p. 575.

2   Mary Sheehy.

3   Margaret Sheehy.

4   A member of the Women's Freedom League, Matters had chained herself to the grille in the Ladies' Gallery in the House of Commons and in 1909, at the opening of parliament, went up in a balloon to throw out 'Votes for Women' leaflets. She was anti-war and worked with Sylvia Pankhurst in the East End of London.

5   AE (George Russell), 'To the Memory of Some I Knew Who Are Dead and Loved Ireland' (1917) was a favourite poem of Hanna's, one she would often quote from. He did not approve of the Rising, but mourned the loss of many friends. It includes lines to the imprisoned Constance Markievicz.

6   Rooney was a close friend of Arthur Griffith, with whom he founded the Celtic Literary Society and Cumann na nGaedheal, forerunner of Sinn Féin. He died of TB in 1901, aged 37.

7
AFTER THE RISING: IN AMERICA

1   Sir John Randolph Leslie was an Irish-born diplomat and first cousin to Winston Churchill. He preferred to use the Irish name Shane and was a supporter of Home Rule. He was in Washington to help the British ambassador there to enlist US support for England.
2   Mary Colum née Maguire was an organiser for Cumann na mBan on its inception in 1914. She also taught in Pearse's school. She and her husband moved to America in late 1914, staying there for eight years.
3   Margaret Skinnider took an active part in the Rising and was badly wounded leading a raiding party from the College of Surgeons.
4   Lawrence Ginnell was an independent MP, joining Sinn Féin after the Rising. His wife Alice was a member of the League of Women Delegates, comprising feminists from a number of different groups who joined together in 1917–19 to ensure women received an equality of representation within the nationalist movement.
5   During the land agitation of the late 1880s Balfour, as chief secretary of Ireland, introduced tough coercion laws, mass evictions, and encouraged firing upon protestors. Three people were killed in Mitchelstown, prompting his infamous nickname.
6   Irish Nationalist MP, representing the Irish community in Liverpool.
7   Mooney's death sentence was commuted to life imprisonment as even the president doubted the validity of his conviction. However, he was not freed from jail until 1939, on the eve of the Second World War.
8   This is an error in the original uncorrected proof as Hanna spoke in Madison Square Garden in New York.
9   This was a British government initiative, sitting in Dublin from July 1917 to March 1918 to consider the revival of Home Rule as a solution to the Irish question. It failed to agree on the issue of partition and its collapse signalled the collapse of the Irish Party and the ending of the political career of John Redmond.
10   The Nineteenth Amendment was passed by Congress on 4 June 1919 and ratified on 18 August 1920. American women finally gained the right to vote.
11   Hanna is quoting from Verdi's *Rigoletto*, 'unstable like the feather in the wind', no doubt ironically, as Verdi is referring to women.
12   Lord French was commander-in-chief of the British Home Forces and lord lieutenant of Ireland 1918–21. He was the brother of feminist Charlotte Despard.
13   Edward Shortt.
14   Reproduced in William O'Brien and Desmond Ryan, eds, *Devoy's Post Bag*, vol. 2 (Dublin, 1953).
15   Case File Number 9848–10204, Department of Justice, National Archives Record Group No. 60, US National Archives, Washington DC.
16   MS 17,638, Joseph McGarrity Papers, NLI, Dublin.

8

THE WAR OF INDEPENDENCE AND THE TREATY

1   Edited by Alice Paul and Lucy Burns and linked to the National Woman's Party in America.
2   MS 22,697, Sheehy Skeffington Papers, NLI, Dublin.
3   MacArthur was a trade unionist and suffragist. All women were anti-war activists, which adversely affected their support.
4   She studied medicine in Edinburgh and Berne, but actually qualified to practise medicine through the College of Physicians in Dublin.
5   The first line of AE's poem in memory of those involved in 1916.
6   Paper of the Women's Freedom League, then edited by Charlotte Despard.
7   Paper of the National Union of Women Suffrage Societies. Its first editor was Helena Swanwick. Maude Royden resigned as editor in 1915 over the decision of NUWSS not to support the Women's Peace Congress at The Hague.
8   MS 48,066/12, Erskine Childers Papers, NLI, Dublin. With thanks to Dr Marie Coleman, QUB, for bringing this document to my attention.
9   McGrane was also a Cumann na mBan activist and organiser, joining the organisation while a student in UCD in 1915.
10   MS 33,621 (vi), Sheehy Skeffington Papers, NLI, Dublin.
11   Alice Park Collection, Hoover Institution Archives, Stanford CA.
12   Copy of one handbill, ibid.
13   A New York publication.
14   'On his own impulse' – a phrase taken to describe a document issued on their own initiative by a pope or monarch.
15   A Latin phrase meaning an unsupported, dogmatic assertion.

9

OPPOSING THE FREE STATE

1   Helena Swanwick, *I Have Been Young* (London, 1935), p. 450.
2   Sinn Féin headquarters were in Harcourt Street.
3   P. J. Ruttledge was acting in place of the imprisoned Éamon de Valera.
4   Hanna wrote this article in December 1923, but it was not published until January 1924.
5   Originally conceived before the Civil War as a platform for sporting and cultural events, it was organised by the Free State 1924–32 as a way of showcasing the new state.
6   Thomas Johnson, leader of the Labour Party.
7   Better known as the writer Francis Stuart, he had recently married Iseult Gonne, daughter of Maud Gonne MacBride.
8   Sister of Kevin Barry, the 18-year-old student hanged by the British in 1920.
9   The Sinn Féin Ard Fheis narrowly defeated de Valera's proposal to enter the Free State Oireachtas if the Oath of Allegiance was removed. Fr O'Flangan sided with the majority and de Valera resigned from Sinn Féin in order to found a new political party, Fianna Fáil. Hanna, Constance Markievicz, Kathleen Clarke and Margaret Pearse were amongst the women to follow de Valera.

10 They were arrested while campaigning against the treatment of prisoners in Maryborough Jail.

11 Jack Keogh, a prominent member of the IRA had been transferred from prison to Grangegorman Mental Asylum. He escaped when the IRA used a bread van to smuggle him out.

12 Home of Maud Gonne MacBride and Charlotte Despard.

13 Sigerson (1886–1918) was an Irish poet and sculptor who wrote under the name Dora Sigerson Shorter.

14 Frank Sheehy Skeffington was the 'one who died for Peace'.

15 Typed MS, Alice Park Collection, Hoover Institution Archives, Stanford CA.

16 The historian Alice Stopford Green was an influential figure in nationalist circles, a close friend of Roger Casement.

17 Mary MacSwiney was the sister and Muriel MacSwiney the wife of Terence MacSwiney, the lord mayor of Cork, arrested on a charge of sedition, who died in October 1920 after 74 days on hunger strike.

18 Formerly Mary Kate Ryan, one of a number of activists from the Ryan family of Wexford.

19 Albinia Broderick Gaelicised her name to Gobnait ni Bhruadair, joined Cumann na mBan and Sinn Féin and was a close friend of Mary MacSwiney. She was imprisoned by the Free State during the Civil War.

20 Lemass was kidnapped by Free State troops in Dublin and his mutilated body was found in October 1923, three months later, in the Dublin hills.

21 Peadar O'Donnell.

22 Frank Ryan.

23 T. M. Healy, politician and barrister, had been counsel for Hanna during the inquiry into the murder of Frank Sheehy Skeffington. He was now governor-general of the Irish Free State.

24 Gilmore was a Protestant member of the IRA, and part of the socialist group that included Peadar O'Donnell, Frank Ryan and Hanna. He had organised the escape of 19 IRA prisoners from Mountjoy Jail in October 1925, which earned him the particular enmity of the Free State.

25 Eoin O'Duffy later became leader of the Army Comrades Association, the Irish fascist organisation known as the 'Blueshirts'.

26 Kevin O'Higgins was Minister for Justice in the Irish Free State. During the Civil War he signed the execution orders of 77 prisoners, including that of Rory O'Connor, who had been best man at his wedding, and Liam Mellows, who Hanna had known well.

27 The 1924 Juries Act, following feminist opposition, retained women on the jurors' list, but allowed women to opt out of jury service. The 1927 Act exempted women totally from service, although they could opt in if they chose. In practice, however, women found that they were passed over when they did present themselves.

28 De Valera led his Fianna Fáil deputies to the Dáil, but they were prevented from entering because they did not sign the Oath of Allegiance. Two weeks later, on 10 July, O'Higgins was assassinated and the government passed a fourth Public Safety Act which included an Electoral Amendment Act which in effect forced Fianna Fáil to take their seats. On 11 August they ended the policy of abstention by accepting the oath and taking their seats rather than forfeit them.

29 Handwritten letter, MS 33,609 (ii), Sheehy Skeffington Papers, NLI, Dublin.

30 Records of the Fianna Fáil Party, UCD Archives, Dublin.

31 John Jinks, a member of the National League, failed to appear in parliament when the opposition had a chance of defeating the government by one vote, so the Cumann na nGaedheal government survived.

32   Larkin refused to pay a libel award when he lost a case and so was an undischarged bankrupt. His son did not take up the seat.

33   A Committee on Evil Literature had been established in 1926. The Censorship of Publications Act of 1929 followed and established the Censorship of Publications Board, with the power to ban books and newspapers considered indecent or obscene.

34   Eithne Coyle, president of Cumann na mBan.

35   Cumann na mBan had instigated a juror campaign, exhorting juries not to convict republicans. The leaflets were issued under the heading 'Ghosts'.

10
HANNA AND SEÁN O'CASEY

1   Lily and Nora Connolly went to visit Hanna after Connolly's execution, to pay their condolences regarding Frank's death and to tell Hanna of Connolly's response to the tragic news. (For the transcript of their letter, left at the house as Hanna was out, I am indebted to the staff of the Department of Manuscripts, NLI.)

2   Sean Connolly was a noted Abbey actor; he was also the head of the Irish Citizen Army group that occupied City Hall at the start of the Rising. He was the first insurgent to be killed.

3   A deliberate quotation from W. B. Yeats's and Lady Gregory's iconic play *Kathleen ni Houlihan*, which had inspired a generation of nationalists.

11
TRAVELS IN EUROPE

1   Women from Northern Ireland, England, Scotland and Wales between the ages of 21 and 30 only gained the extension of the franchise in 1928. In the 26 counties women over the age of 21 were granted the franchise by Article 3 in the Constitution of the Irish Free State, 1922. A promise extracted after the acrimonious debate over the Treaty.

2   Russell was a socialist and campaigning journalist, one of the founders of the National Association for the Advancement of Coloured People (the suffragist Jane Addams was another founder).

3   Hoda Shaarawi (1879–1947) founded the Egyptian Feminist Union in 1923 and was a founder of the Arab Feminist Union in 1945. After returning from the Paris Congress she removed her veil in front of a crowd at Cairo train station, a key moment in the movement for women's equality. Pacha was the surname of her husband, who died in 1923.

4   'A Long Way to Tipperary' was a British music hall song which was adopted as a First World War marching song.

5   Wilkinson was a British Labour Party politician and a former Manchester suffragist and anti-war activist.

6   MS 24,163 (i), Sheehy Skeffington Papers, NLI, Dublin.

7   MS 24,163 (iii), ibid.

12
MEMORIES OF COUNTESS MARKIEVICZ

1   Chapter 8.

2   MS 24,189, Sheehy Skeffington Papers, NLI, Dublin.

3   *Eleanor's Enterprise* was not produced until December 1911 so it is more likely that Hanna actually first saw Markievicz playing in *The Memory of the Dead*, which was performed in the summer of 1910.

4   MS 21,816, Eva Gore-Booth Papers, NLI, Dublin.

5   Robert Barton was a wealthy Protestant land owner and Minister for Economic Affairs. He became one of the Irish delegates for the Treaty negotiations. He supported the Treaty.

6   Sydney Gifford.

7   Michael Collins.

8   Jan Smuts, prime minister of South Africa 1919–24.

9   MS 21,816, Eva Gore-Booth Papers, NLI, Dublin.

10   Jennie Wyse Power.

11   Hanna makes the point that although Ireland was still governed by the British in 1915, they had not prevented full honours being accorded to the Fenian O'Donovan Rossa, in distinction to the Free State refusal of official buildings for the funeral of Markievicz. Hanna had been present at the funeral of O'Donovan Rossa despite at the time engaging in heated debate with nationalist women over their failure to support the suffrage movement and their acquiescence within Cumann na mBan as a subordinate group to the male Irish Volunteers.

12   William Partridge.

13   Maud Gonne MacBride and Charlotte Despard lived together in Roebuck House, which had become a centre of resistance to the Free State. They set up small-scale enterprises making jam and shell ornaments to provide some work for republican women unable to find employment.

14   Éamon de Valera was commandant of the Boland's Mill outpost.

15   MS 33,609 (ii), Sheehy Skeffington Papers, NLI, Dublin.

16   MS 24,134, ibid.

17   Eva Gore-Booth had established the Barmaids' Political Defence League to fight against the curtailment of their employment rights. At a by-election Churchill, a member of the Liberal Party at this time, stood against the Conservative Johnson-Hicks. It was an historic event as the campaigners attacked the government candidate and Churchill lost the by-election. The barmaid campaign was successful, a victory that would not have been possible without the initiative of Gore-Booth.

18   See Hanna's letter to Lady Aberdeen in Chapter 14.

13
THE 1930S: FEMINIST REFLECTIONS AND FEMINIST FIGHTBACK

1   Kathleen Clarke was a senator from 1928–36.

2   The historian Alice Stopford Green, senator from 1922–9.

3   Kathleen Browne, Cumann na nGaedheal.

4   Jennie Wyse Power, who left Cumann na mBan because she supported the Treaty. However, although a government nominee in the senate, she remained an outspoken champion of women and she and Kathleen Clarke joined forces to speak against the curtailment of women's employment rights.

5   Eleanor Rathbone, an independent MP, suffragist and anti-war activist, who was best known for her campaign for family allowances.

6   David Sheehy was imprisoned six times for his part in the Land War. He became an MP in 1885.

7   Microfilm torn so legibility regarding MacDonagh and Connolly slightly affected.

8   A prominent member of the WSPU and close friend of Emmeline Pankhurst, Smyth composed the suffragette anthem 'The March of the Women'.

9   Founded in New York in 1912, its members included Elizabeth Gurley Flynn, Charlotte Perkins Gilman and Crystal Eastman. They were radical feminists, many of whom were lesbian or bisexual, and outspoken campaigners on many issues, including birth control and women's rights at work.

10   Kathleen Clarke in 1920.

11   The Kellogg-Briand Pact of 1928 was intended to resolve international disputes by peaceful means through signatory states promising not to use war to solve disagreements.

12   MS 41,192/12, Sheehy Skeffington Papers, NLI, Dublin.

13   Kathleen Browne, a republican activist who took the pro-Treaty side and was elected to the Irish senate in 1929.

14   Anthony Comstock (1844–1915) was an American postal inspector and politician, founder of the New York Society for the Suppression of Vice, thereby giving rise to the term 'comstockery' for those promoting censorship.

15   This was the term given to the coming together of the Fenian and parliamentary traditions (exemplified by Michael Davitt and Charles Stewart Parnell) to work for land reform.

16   Hanna was surprised to encounter her uncle in the GPO when she reported there to offer her help.

14
PRISON EXPERIENCES

1   See Hanna's memoirs in this volume, Chapter 1, pp 24–6.

2   Irish Women's Suffrage Society (Belfast).

3   Irish Women's Reform League.

4   Independent Labour Party of Ireland.

5   MSS 1/5 Mixed Letters 1906–15, Papers of Lady Ishbel Aberdeen, Haddo House Estate. With thanks to Dr Catherine Morris for bringing this letter to my attention.

6   MS 24,103, Sheehy Skeffington Papers, NLI, Dublin.

7   From Tom Kettle, 'Ulster (A Reply to Rudyard Kipling)' (1920), '"Ulster" is ours, not yours, / Is ours to have and hold.' This was a reply to a pro-union poem by Rudyard Kipling.

8   Minister of Home Affairs in the Northern Ireland government.

15

LOOKING BACKWARDS, WAR, ELECTION AND THE FINAL YEARS

1   Montefiore was a socialist-feminist who instigated the 'Kiddies' Scheme' during the Lock Out of 1913, to take Dublin children suffering from starvation to the homes of sympathisers in England for the duration of the labour conflict. The Catholic Church accused the organisers of trying to proselytise and they were charged with kidnapping, so the scheme had to be abandoned. Frank Sheehy Skeffington had been an enthusiastic supporter.

2   Kathleen Clarke was the first woman mayor of Dublin.

3   MS 41,201/12, Sheehy Skeffington Papers, NLI, Dublin. The Women's Social and Progressive League sponsored four candidates in the 1943 election. Hanna stood as a candidate in Dublin South. None of the women were successful. Hanna received 917 votes.

4   From *Dorothy Evans and the Six Point Group*, published by the Six Point Group (*c.*1945), the Fawcett Library. I am grateful to Catriona Beaumont for this reference.

5   Dorothy Evans, an English suffragette, was sent by Christabel Pankhurst as organiser for the WSPU Ulster Centre in Belfast. She was a leading militant in the north, undergoing numerous arrests and hunger and thirst strikes in the first half of 1914 as the WSPU waged war against the Ulster unionists.

6   The Six Point Group was a British feminist campaigning group, active in the inter-war years and the post-war period. *Time and Tide* was the highly regarded journal of the group.

7   MS 41,193/14, unpublished typescript, Sheehy Skeffington Papers, NLI, Dublin. Hanna mentions the framing of Tom Mooney and the mood of the times in *Impressions of Sinn Féin in America*, see Chapter 8 in this volume.

8   Rena Mooney née Hermann, also a member of the Socialist Party of America, was found not guilty but kept in prison until 30 March 1918. After 22 years of campaigning she welcomed her husband on his release from San Quentin.

9   François Bonivard (1493–1570), imprisoned from 1519–21 as a Geneva patriot against the French. He inspired Lord Byron's poem *The Prisoner of Chillon* (1861).

10   Byron describes the 'Eternal Spirit of the chainless Mind!' a reference to how it cannot be imprisoned even if the body is shackled.

11   Alice Park Collection, Hoover Institution Archives, Stanford CA.

12   Alice Park, a socialist, feminist and pacifist, lived in Palo Alto, California. She was a founder of the Women's International League for Peace and Freedom and attended the International Women's Suffrage Alliance in Budapest, 1913, visiting Dublin on her return home, where she met the Sheehy Skeffingtons and began her long-lasting friendship with Hanna. She supported Hanna in Washington in 1917 as she was at that time working for a Californian congressman. Park and Hanna both attended the Tenth Congress of the International Women's Suffrage Alliance in Paris in May 1926. Hanna sent her all her published articles, which were widely disseminated in radical circles in America.

13   Gloria Gartz from Pasadena, California was a wealthy supporter of women's suffrage and the American Civil Liberties Union.

14   Scottish Labour Party activist.

15   Barbara Ayrton Gould had been a member of the WSPU and the United Suffragists. She was honorary secretary of the Women's International League for Peace and Freedom and a Labour Party activist.

16   Originally Lucy Burn, she married Lord Noel-Buxton in 1914 and returned to parliament when she succeeded her husband as MP for Norfolk North in 1930.

17   Mavis Tate was a Conservative who campaigned for equal pay for women during the war and reported on Nazi atrocities. She was re-elected in 1950.

18   Thelma Cazalet was a feminist and Conservative who married David Keir in 1939 and amalgamated their names out of feminist principle. She became president of the Fawcett Society in 1964.

19   Florence Horsbrugh had been Scottish Unionist Party MP for Dundee 1931–45. She was re-elected to a Manchester seat as a Conservative in 1950.

16
BOOK AND THEATRE REVIEWS

1   Andrée Sheehy Skeffington and Rosemary Owens, eds, *Votes for Women: Irish Women's Struggle for the Vote* (Dublin, 1975), p. 13.

2   MS 33,609/2, Sheehy Skeffington Papers, NLI, Dublin.

3   Inghinidhe na hÉireann member and ICA activist, she was also an actor of merit. Molony was a member of the Abbey Theatre and despite her political commitments continued to act sporadically until finally retiring in 1927. See Nell Regan, *Helena Molony: A Radical Life, 1883– 1967* (Dublin, 2017).

4   This was the only play by Walter Riddall (1874 –1914). He was an Irish artist and writer who died from TB shortly before the opening of his play.

Selected Reading

BOOKS AND ARTICLES ON HANNA SHEEHY SKEFFINGTON AND HER TIMES

Beaumont, Catriona, 'Women, citizenship and Catholicism in the Irish Free State, 1922–1948', *Women's History Review* 6:4 (1997).

Bradley, Anthony and Maryann Gialanella Valiulis, eds, *Gender and Sexuality in Modern Ireland* (Amherst, 1997).

Breathnach, Eibhlin, 'Charting new waters: women's experience in higher education, 1879–1908', in Cullen, ed., *Girls Don't Do Honours*, pp 55–78.

Clarke, Kathleen, *Revolutionary Woman, Kathleen Clarke, 1878–1972: An Autobiography*, Helen Litton, ed. (Dublin, 1991).

Cousins, James and Margaret, *We Two Together* (Madras, 1950).

Cullen, Mary, ed., *Girls Don't Do Honours: Irish Women in Education in the 19th and 20th Centuries* (Dublin, 1987).

Cullen, Mary and Maria Luddy, eds, *Female Activists: Irish Women and Change 1900–1960* (Dublin, 2001).

Cullen Owens, Rosemary, *Smashing Times: A History of the Irish Women's Suffrage Movement 1889–1922* (Dublin, 1984).

___, *Louie Bennett* (Cork, 2001).

___, *A Social History of Women in Ireland 1870–1970* (Dublin, 2005).

Ferriter, Diarmaid, *A Nation and Not a Rabble: The Irish Revolution 1913–1923* (London, 2015).

Foster, R. F., *Vivid Faces: The Revolutionary Generation in Ireland 1890–1923* (London, 2014).

Fox, R. M., *Rebel Irishwomen* (Dublin, 1935).

Harford, Judith, *The Opening of University Education to Women in Ireland* (Dublin, 2008).

Hearne, Dana, 'The *Irish Citizen* 1914–1916: nationalism, feminism and militarism', *The Canadian Journal of Irish Studies* 18:1 (July 1992).

Levenson, Leah, *With Wooden Sword: A Portrait of Francis Sheehy Skeffington, Militant Pacifist* (Syracuse, 1983).

Levenson, Leah and Jerry H. Natterstad, *Hanna Sheehy Skeffington: Irish Feminist* (Syracuse, 1986).

Luddy, Maria, *Hanna Sheehy Skeffington* (Dundalk, 1995).

Markievicz, Constance de, *The Prison Letters of Countess Markievicz* (London, 1987).

McCoole, Sinéad, *No Ordinary Women: Activists in the Revolutionary Years, 1900–1923* (Dublin, 2003).

Mooney Eichacker, Joanne, *Irish Republican Women in America: Lecture Tours, 1916–1925* (Dublin, 2003).

Murphy, Cliona, *The Women's Suffrage Movement and Irish Society in the Early Twentieth Century* (Hemel Hempstead, 1989).

Murphy, William, 'Suffragettes and the transformation of political imprisonment in Ireland', in Louise Ryan and Margaret Ward, eds, *Irish Women and the Vote: Becoming Citizens* (Dublin, 2007), pp 114–35.

Pašeta, Senia, *Nationalist Women in Ireland, 1900–1918* (Cambridge, 2013).

Regan, Nell, *Helena Molony: A Radical Life, 1883–1967* (Dublin, 2017).

Ryan, Louise, *Irish Feminism and the Vote: An Anthology of the* Irish Citizen *Newspaper 1912–1920* (Dublin, 1996).

___, *Gender Identity and the Irish Press, 1922–1937: Embodying the Nation* (New York, 2002).

Sheehy Skeffington, Andrée, *Skeff: A Life of Owen Sheehy Skeffington, 1909–1970* (Dublin, 1991).

Sheehy Skeffington, Andrée and Rosemary Owens, eds, *Votes for Women: Irish Women's Struggle for the Vote* (Dublin, 1975).

Swanwick, Helena, *I Have Been Young* (London, 1935).

Tiernan, Sonja, *Eva Gore-Booth: An Image of Such Politics* (Manchester, 2012).

___, ed., *The Political Writings of Eva Gore-Booth* (Manchester, 2015).

Valiulis, Maryann Gialanella, 'Defining their role in the new state: Irishwomen's protest against the Juries Act of 1927', *Canadian Journal of Irish Studies* 18:1 (July 1992).

___, 'Power, gender and identity in the Irish Free State', *Journal of Women's History* 6:4 and 7:1 (1995).

Vane, Sir Francis Fletcher, *Agin the Government: Memories and Adventures* (London, 1929).

Ward, Margaret, *Unmanageable Revolutionaries: Women and Irish Nationalism* (Dingle, 1983).

___, *Hanna Sheehy Skeffington, a Life* (Cork, 1997).

___, 'Nationalism, pacifism, internationalism: Louie Bennett, Hanna Sheehy Skeffington and the problems of "defining feminism"', in Bradley and Valiulis, eds, *Gender and Sexuality*, pp 60–84.

___, 'Hanna Sheehy Skeffington, 1877–1946', in Cullen and Luddy, eds, *Female Activists*, pp 89–112.

KEY WORKS BY HANNA SHEEHY SKEFFINGTON

PAMPHLETS

British Militarism as I Have Known It (New York, 1917).

Impressions of Sinn Féin in America (Dublin, 1919).

Reminiscences of an Irish Suffragette, in Andrée Sheehy Skeffington and Rosemary Owens, eds, *Votes for Women: Irish Women's Struggle for the Vote* (Dublin, 1975), pp 12–26.

JOURNAL ARTICLES

'Women and the university question', *New Ireland Review* 17 (March–August 1902), pp 148 –51.

(with Mary Hayden) 'Women in university: a reply', *Irish Educational Review*, 1908, pp 410 –18.

'Women and the national movement', *Irish Nation*, 6, 13, 20 March 1909.

'Sinn Féin and Irishwomen', *Bean na hÉireann* 13 (November 1909), pp 5–6.

'A reply to some critics', *Bean na hÉireann* 16 (February 1910), pp 3–4.

'The women's movement: Ireland', *Irish Review*, July 1912, pp 225–7.

'Irish secondary teachers', *Irish Review*, October 1912, pp 393–8.

'Memories of the suffrage campaign in Ireland', *The Vote*, 30 August 1929, p. 277.

'Irishwomen's place in the sun', *The Vote*, 15 August 1930, pp 257–8.

'Women in the Free State: a stocktaking', *The New English Weekly*, 19 March 1936, pp 452–3.

'Women in politics', *The Bell* 7:2 (November 1943), pp 143–8.

'Random reflections on housewives: their ways and works', *Irish Housewife*, 1946, pp 20–2.

CHAPTERS IN BOOKS

'An Irish pacifist', in Julian Bell, ed., *We Did Not Fight* (London, 1935), pp 339–53.

'A pacifist dies', in Roger McHugh, ed., *Dublin 1916* (London, 1966), pp 276–88.

Index

...rmally about the
...about group [? Br...
...up with them b...
...ing S.F. & did not
...S.F. was in the
fighting front. Le...
...with Alo T. Kell...
its Executive t...
it [i.e up to 1925
...for Dublin Co...
that body till it
...Cosgrave a cu...
...enter publi...
...I was co-op...